IN THE LIGHT OF CHRIST

LUCY BECKETT

IN THE LIGHT
OF
CHRIST

Writings in the
Western Tradition

IGNATIUS PRESS   SAN FRANCISCO

Cover art: © Royalty Free / Corbis

Cover design by Riz Boncan Marsella

© 2006 Ignatius Press, San Francisco
All rights reserved
ISBN 978-1-58617-107-0
ISBN 1-58617-107-0
Library of Congress Control Number 2006923029
Printed in the United States of America ∞

To
Christoph

Deambulat autem in nobis praesentia maiestatis,
si latitudinem invenerit caritas.

Yet the presence of his glory walks among us,
if love finds room.

—Saint Augustine: Sermon 163

AUTHOR'S NOTE

For support, criticism and encouragement, in general and in particular, I am grateful to those who taught me and whom I taught at Ampleforth Abbey and College over twenty years, to Michael Black, to my children and above all to my husband, John Warrack.

—Lucy Beckett

CONTENTS

INTRODUCTION

The Order of Love

This is a book about value, specifically the value to us now, in the twenty-first century, of some great texts written in relation to the truth of orthodox Christianity, or, in the case of pre-Christian texts, understood in the light of that truth. These texts, many of which have long found places in familiar versions of the Western canon, belong or are in various ways close to the Catholic, specifically the Augustinian Catholic, tradition, and it is the thesis of this book that their value—that is to say, their truthfulness, beauty and goodness—rests in their relation to the absolute truth, beauty and goodness that are one in God and that are definitively revealed to the world in Christ.

That the value of these texts is real, and that it is relative—but not relative to nothing—are both now highly contentious and in some academic circles even ridiculous statements. In the intellectual climate of the liberal West in our time, the very words "truth", "beauty" and "goodness" cannot be used without embarrassment except in relation not to God but to the individual, who, a biological accident in a random universe, chooses what seems, for the moment, to be true or good or beautiful to himself. That individual may defend such choices, but on personal, subjective grounds only; the one remaining moral imperative commanding general assent is that the choices of others must have equal status to one's own and should not be regarded as bad unless they do harm to others, measurable in a utilitarian fashion. Anyone may try to persuade others that his view, his perspective, is "better" than theirs, but this effort will be no more than a game, a power game, played in emptiness. Nietzsche, who presides over the contemporary academy, toward the end of the nineteenth century called "perspective" the basic condition of all life and the "will to power" the basic drive of the human world. "Truth", Richard Rorty, a strong philosophical voice on both sides of the Atlantic, has said, "is what your contemporaries will let you get away with." [1] In what the English philosopher Simon Blackburn has called "the *après*-truth salon", [2] temporary persuasion of more people than someone else can persuade is, while it counts, all that counts. The only intellectual consensus is that there is no consensus.

That there would one day be agreement on, for example, the rational basis for morality or the rational basis for aesthetic judgement—truth upon which judgements of the good or the beautiful might be founded—was the hope of the Enlightenment. It rested on the assumptions that reason is universal and that its proofs are bound to be accepted by everyone sufficiently educated to follow its arguments. It was assumed, in other words, that there is a common, neutral ground from which all traditions, all claims to truth, including the Christian, can be rationally assessed. As time went by, the ground shrank, eventually leaving only facts, only what is empirically verifiable, as that upon which we may properly stand, while "all those large dreams by which men long live well"[3] evaporated into mere personal opinion. The hope of the Enlightenment turned out to be forlorn, its assumptions baseless. In an acute analysis of the resulting disappointment, and the resulting consensus that there is no consensus, Alasdair MacIntyre in *Whose Justice? Which Rationality?* wrote:

> The most cogent reasons that we have for believing that the hope of a tradition-independent rational universality is an illusion derive from the history of that project. For in the course of that history liberalism, which began as an appeal to alleged principles of shared rationality against what was felt to be the tyranny of tradition, has itself been transformed into a tradition whose continuities are partly defined by the interminability of the debate over such principles.[4]

He goes on to concede that the failure of liberalism to "provide a neutral tradition-independent ground" does not prove that there is no such ground. However:

> Liberalism is by far the strongest claimant to provide such a ground which has so far appeared in human history or which is likely to appear in the foreseeable future. That liberalism fails in this respect, therefore provides the strongest reason that we can actually have for asserting that there is no such neutral ground.[5]

If there is no such ground, we are left with two possible ways in which to think of ourselves and our lives. One is to trust nothing but empirically verifiable facts. These, because they work, all of us trust every day, though few of us have ourselves been through the process of verification. We believe that the earth goes around the sun although it still looks to us as if the sun goes around the earth; we believe those who tell us of the dangers of bacteria or radiation that we cannot see. The very effectiveness of science and technology, the ever-increasing power of the human race over nature which is the result of the discovery and use of verifiable facts, incline us, however, to trust nothing else beyond the personal mix of objectives that we arrange as we choose to achieve a (self-) fulfilled life. In a neat formulation by the philosopher John Rawls, which MacIntyre quotes twice, "Human good is heterogeneous because the aims of the self are heterogeneous. Although to subordinate all our aims to one end does not strictly speaking violate the principles of rational choice, ... it still strikes us as irrational, or more likely as mad."[6] And so, beyond our selection of various aims and our confidence in science done by other people, we are educated to remain, in the words with which Pascal at the dawn of the Enlightenment described the sceptics of the 1650s, "neutral, indifferent, suspending judgment on everything, not excepting ourselves".[7]

But there is an alternative, a different choice, as MacIntyre convincingly argues. The alternative is to choose to trust a tradition in which to think, to judge, to live, because we discover that a tradition does exist, a collaborative achievement of coherent intellectual effort with a long history still accessible, that confirms our own experience of what we have found—using, quietly, words we cannot do without—to be good, beautiful and true. What we may then discover is that the tradition we have come upon makes more and more sense to us, makes more and more sense of our own lives, which begin to take on the very unity the liberal consensus regards as "irrational, or more likely as mad", a unity that turns out to be real and full of infinitely explorable meaning. If we choose a Christian tradition—MacIntyre distinguishes the Augustinian from the Thomist—we will discover that this unity is in God.

It is the contention of this book that for someone who is drawn to texts written in relation to Christian truth—who already loves at least some of them for the nourishment of the soul that they provide—an encounter with the central, the Augustinian, Catholic tradition, broader and less philosophically exacting than the Thomist, may turn out to be what MacIntyre calls "an occasion for self-recognition and self-knowledge.... *This* is not only, so such a person may say, what I now take to be true but in some measure what I have always taken to be true."[8]

The educated person who experiences such an encounter, unless he is already an adult Christian who is also open-minded and brave, is likely to find that his discovery brings with it feelings of isolation, exposure, confusion and perhaps even panic, made worse by other people's association of Christianity with the abandonment of the intelligence, with sentimental nostalgia for the past or with various kinds of oppression—and probably with all three. But as Henri de Lubac wrote fifty years ago, "To reject God because man has corrupted the idea of God, and religion because of the abuse of it, is the effect of a sort of clear-sightedness which is yet blind." [9] His friend Hans Urs von Balthasar, the most widely learned Catholic theologian of the twentieth century, was never unaware of the difficulties bound to be met by the modern person who believes Christianity to be true. In *The Moment of Christian Witness*, a little book written in 1966 in the theological melee that followed the Second Vatican Council, he described these difficulties succinctly. The temptation, he says (and many Christians have given in to it), is

> to pay the tribute demanded by the rise of the secular spirit. . . . There is the purely practical problem of how [the Christian] as a man with a message, is to speak to and find common ground with his fellow man, who is already dyed in the wool of the [secular] system. Then there is the more serious problem of how far he should go in the course of solidarity with his fellow man in adopting the perspectives of the system. The most serious problem of all is one that concerns his conscience. As a "modern" man, how can he be a Christian? Or should he refuse to be modern and up to date, for the sake of Christ? If he does the latter, he runs the risk of being ignored by everyone and falling prey to a kind of schizophrenia by trying to live in two different centuries at once. [10]

What, in other words, he will quickly discover is that the statement at the heart of Christian belief, that "God so loved the world that he gave his only Son so that those who believe in him should not perish but have eternal life", not being empirically verifiable, is regarded by most educated people as no more than what is now called a "truth-claim", and a particularly bizarre one at that. Such claims, thrown by one group or another, one person or another, into the void, are relegated to a past well left behind in the childhood of the human race. Christianity's "truth-claim" is commonly abandoned to the simplistic naïveté of fundamentalists whose minds are closed to the complexities of the world of Western thought. This is now a world in which stories compete—the grand narratives of science, and a plethora of "little stories" in Lyotard's phrase, told in pursuit of power of various kinds. The grand narrative of Christianity has become no more than one among many stories purporting falsely, or at best in fictive terms, to give a true account of how things are, what things mean. A Christian would be less than intelligent not to agree that there is much in this world of thought that is both interesting and fruitful. In the area of written texts, for example, the area with which this book is concerned, it is clearly the case that any text, even a great masterpiece, is partial and patchy, is relative to the whole truth, because it was written by a fallible human being approaching in story, argument and image the reality that lies beyond all stories, arguments and images. But for the Christian, that reality exists. And for a Christian, the gap between the words, the languages, the narratives of fallen humanity and the truth that is in God was closed, once, in Christ.

Among Western intellectuals, however—there are, of course, exceptions, but not many—God has been dead for at least two centuries, or pushed so far from mankind and its concerns that he has vanished into vacuity. It took some time for the consequences of this disappearance to become evident. Here are a few. If God is dead, he can never, by definition, have been alive. To console ourselves in a universe without meaning, we invented him and all the stories about him, including the story that he sent his Son as a man to rescue human life from the consequences of disobedience to him. There is no connexion between even the noblest of lives, the best and most beautiful human achievements and any transcendent reality, because there is no transcendent reality. All self-sacrifice, unless helpful to other people in a measurable utilitarian sense, becomes pointless: the countless victims of tyranny who in the twentieth century died anonymous deaths because they would not yield to lies imposed on them by force would have done better to save their skins, since their skins were all they had. With the disappearance of God, the soul, what there is in us that the grace of God may touch, must also disappear. So must our confidence in the kind of truth that is for all of us closest to home, the truth in which we trust when we are entirely alone with our conscience, and the truth of our own lives, the story that each of us is, from birth to death, fitful in our own memory, unreliably judged by ourselves, largely unknown to anyone else. For to believe in the reality of one's own story—or the reality of the story of the human race—as whole and true and as containing much evil and ugliness as well as much goodness and beauty, and to know both that one does not know more than patches and parts of it and that the final judgement of it is not one's own, is to believe in God. Czesław Miłosz asks in a poem: "Where is the truth of unremembered things?" [11] The root meaning of *aletheia*, the Greek word for "truth", is "the unforgotten", or, as Balthasar put it in his most philosophical work, "Truth is the unconcealment of being, while ...

the someone to whom being is unconcealed is God." [12] Without belief in God, without belief that the truth is real, is in him, all our attempts to "tell the truth" become no more than stories told for human purposes—to persuade, to comfort, to stake claims, to build power—but none of them means anything, or, more accurately, means anything else. Behind the images and metaphors of paintings and poems, behind the patterns, broken and mended, of music and verse, behind the imagined characters of plays and novels, there is no mysterious depth of meaning, there is nothing. Yet a child of four knows what a lie is and knows what a story is and knows that they are not the same.

In the second half of the nineteenth century, which was late in the day, Nietzsche understood with clarity, and with a charged mixture of exhilaration and terror, the inevitable consequences of the death of God. For him, as he wrote more and more feverishly before the final loss of his mind in 1889, the solitary existence, unanchored in any meaning guaranteed by transcendence, of the individual in a world of savage competition where the only motive is the will to power, was both to be celebrated as liberation from the delusions of the past and to be greatly feared. He saw that, in the jungle of every man for himself, "human, all-too-human" notions of goodness and beauty have nothing to do with truth and that the pretence that, in the absence of God, they have a connexion either with each other or with truth is intellectually incoherent. In a desperate note, he wrote: "For a philosopher to say 'the good and the beautiful are one' is infamy; if he goes on to add, 'also the true', one ought to thrash him. Truth is ugly." To save something he loved from the wreckage of the past, he added, "We possess *art* lest we *perish of the truth*." [13] Art, in his view, was the enlivening expression of joy in the face of despair. This expression gives pleasure; that is to say, it is aesthetic. But the aesthetic is now necessarily severed both from the ethical and from the ugly and frightening truth.

> The greatest suspicion of a "truth" should arise when feelings of pleasure enter the discussion of the question "What is true?" The proof of "pleasure" is a proof of "pleasure"—nothing else: how in all the world could it be established that true judgements should give greater delight than false ones? [14]

The answer to this question, as Nietzsche knew well, is "only in God". Meanwhile, what we have made, fabricated or invented may give us pleasure, but all of it is no more than the result of human ingenuity, of the games we play in the dark:

All the beauty and sublimity we have lent to both real and imaginary things, I claim on man's behalf as his property and manufacture. This is his finest *apologia*. For man is a poet, a thinker, a god, love, power! O the kingly generosity by which he has endowed all things, so that he himself feels *poor and wretched*! This was hitherto his greatest self-forgetfulness: he wondered and worshipped, concealing from himself the fact that he had created the very object of his wonder.[15]

Little read in his lifetime, Nietzsche became for later generations the most powerful intellectual influence of all. Both before and after Nietzsche there have been some who, one way or another, have tried to show that, in the absence of God, "poetry can save us." Later in this book the brave attempts of Matthew Arnold, F. R. Leavis and George Steiner will be examined. Nietzsche himself nursed no such illusion.

Nor did he suppose—as many, without thinking clearly, have hoped—that Christian morality, which Nietzsche despised as "slave-morality", is sustainable without Christian belief. In a diatribe against English Victorian moralists, in particular George Eliot, he wrote:

> When one gives up Christian belief one thereby deprives oneself of the *right* to Christian morality. For the latter is absolutely *not* self-evident: one must make this point clear again and again, in spite of English shallowpates. Christianity is a system, a consistently thought out and *complete* view of things. If one breaks out of it a fundamental idea, the belief in God, one thereby breaks the whole thing to pieces: one has nothing of any consequence left in one's hands. Christianity presupposes that man does not know, *cannot* know what is good for him and what evil: he believes in God, who alone knows. Christian morality is a command: its origin is transcendental; ... it possesses truth only if God is truth—it stands or falls with the belief in God.[16]

It is "absolutely *not* self-evident", for example, that all human beings are of equal value, a moral principle claimed in the twentieth century as an achievement of the Enlightenment, but a notion that runs counter to every rational perception and judgement of the value of other people. Only in the sight of God are all human beings of equal value; most certainly in the sight of Nietzsche they were not. He, who aspired, for himself and very few others, to the self-induced "transcendence" over everyone else of the *Übermensch*, would have had only contempt

7

for what has been described by Balthasar as "Christianity's constant outpouring of light into the world, where it is renamed and regarded as humanism." [17]

"The importance of Nietzsche", as Erich Heller's perceptive book on him is called, is that Nietzsche never underestimated the scale of the consequences of the loss of belief in God. Fear and celebration at an equally high pitch ringingly clash in his most famous passage on the death of God:

> Have you not heard of that madman who lit a lantern in the bright morning hours, ran to the market-place and cried incessantly: "I am looking for God! I am looking for God!"—As many of those who did not believe in God were standing together there, he excited considerable laughter. Have you lost him then? said one. Did he lose his way like a child? said another. Or is he hiding? Is he afraid of us? Has he gone on a voyage? Or emigrated?—thus they shouted and laughed. The madman sprang into their midst and pierced them with his glances. "Where has God gone?" he cried. "I shall tell you. *We have killed him*— you and I. We are all his murderers. But how have we done this? How were we able to drink up the sea? Who gave us the sponge to wipe away the entire horizon? ... Are we not straying as through an infinite nothing? Do we not feel the breath of empty space? Has it not become colder? Is more and more night not coming on all the time? ... Is not the greatness of this deed too great for us? Must we not ourselves become gods simply to seem worthy of it? There has never been a greater deed— and whoever shall be born after us, for the sake of this deed he shall be part of a higher history than all history hitherto.[18]

If God does not exist, if the transcendent has been wiped away, there is no longer a vertical axis for the human soul, but only a horizontal, that is, a historical, axis for the human mind. More particularly, the vertical never crossed the horizontal in the Incarnation. Toward the end, Nietzsche with good reason called himself "the Antichrist". And it is not surprising that Nietzsche's perception of the probable consequences of the death of God was shared most fully by Christians, by Fyodor Dostoyevsky, for example, in his accurate prophecy of the Russian future in *The Devils*, and in particular by Catholic thinkers of the twentieth century who had watched Nietzsche's direst premonitions become reality. "Must we not ourselves become gods?" as Stalin and Hitler, crushing underfoot what was Christian in the past and present of their people, became. Writers such as de Lubac and Balthasar understood exactly why the most highly organized and most dreadful cruelties of "might is right" in the whole of history had been perpetrated in what had for many centuries been Christendom, where, in Balthasar's words, "the vertical axis (insofar as it is revelation *from* above) [was] claimed by Christianity as its own." Once the claim is rejected,

> man's openness *to* the upper realm becomes a purely anthropological fact that belongs henceforth to the immanence of horizontal world history. When this happens, in short, man's "upward" openness, which is the organ of ultimate meaning, is obliged to look for meaning at the horizontal level; hence people's tendency to attribute absolute significance to relative fragments of meaning in history and to commit themselves utterly to such constructions. Thus, in the post-Christian period, we find the development of various philosophies of history—"ideologies" in the strict sense. In this way, certain finite (and hence only partially true) ideas are foisted onto man's spirit, which has an inherent yearning for the absolute.... However, none of the passing moments of the world of time can encapsulate that desired absolute meaning—not even that moment, projected into an ever-receding future, when "positive humanism" will have been attained.[19]

Balthasar, already an old man (he was born in 1905 and died in 1988), wrote this in 1980, before the collapse of Soviet Communism. What he said in this passage is plainly true of the totalitarian ideologies of Marxism and Nazism. That it is no less true of optimistic liberalism, and also no less true of global domination by capitalist America, is concealed from many by the cloaking of both with a patchwork Christian morality and of the second also with the appropriation of God's approval. They belong equally, however, to "the passing moments of the world of time" wrongly taken to "encapsulate ... absolute meaning", even if liberalism takes "absolute meaning" as its absolute absence, and even if capitalist democracy affords its citizens freedoms denied to the citizens of totalitarian states. It should be added here that the long history of the Church has been scarred by her own failure at various periods to distinguish "absolute significance" from "relative fragments of meaning in history". The corruption of the Church as a human institution by her triumphalist assumption of worldly power was perhaps the worst of such failures. In 1965 Balthasar wrote of the old perils of the Church in relation to power and of her new peril in relation to the secular utopianism of human omnicompetence:

This anxious flight of the Church and of Christians from the Cross was always, and is once again today, the flight into ideologies of world domination: the Constantinian, Carolingian, Ottonian, Hapsburg, Bourbon, and Napoleonic domination of the world in the past; and today, since the external forms of power are no longer within reach [of the Church], the flight into intellectual forms of familiarity, of the desire to be there, too, when the world is worldly, when the world is rising upward, when the world is taking possession of itself, as if it were possible to bestow Christian sweetness on the whole affair by tossing a saccharin tablet into this raging ocean.[20]

But the truth of God disclosed in Christ is itself and not another thing.

*   *   *

The first "ideology of world domination" to tempt the Church into the "anxious flight" of identification with it was that of the Roman Empire, into which Christ was born. The identification could not be conceived until the fourth century, when the emperor Constantine became a Christian and persecution of Christians ended. Less than a hundred years later, in a disintegrating empire whose plight was blamed by both Christians and pagans on the God of Christianity, who was failing to hold it together, Augustine understood and explained what Balthasar, with Augustine in his bones, understood and explained in both the above passages sixteen centuries later. The idea of Rome, the *pax Romana*, *Roma aeterna*, had provided all its people knew of security and stability, and in the upper levels of society also prosperity, scope for ambition, comfort and freedom, for hundreds of years. It had long been, precisely, a "finite idea foisted onto man's spirit, which has an inherent yearning for the absolute." That the emperor was now a Christian, and the fact that most cities and towns in the empire now had churches and bishops seemed to have given to the idea of imperial Rome God's specific blessing. How could it decay, crumble into "relative fragments of meaning in history"? "The emperor has become a Christian," Augustine replied to this question, "but the devil has not."[21]

Augustine knew that the "inherent yearning for the absolute" in the soul of man—he called it *desiderium*, "longing"—finds its only rest, its only true home, in God. He knew that "relative fragments of meaning in history", "finite (and hence only partially true) ideas"—and not only those of world domination—can very easily be mistaken for the absolute for which the soul longs. He also knew, no less clearly than Nietzsche knew, that "without God we ourselves become gods", that love of God leads to contempt for the self and that love of the self leads to contempt for God. He also knew that the drive, the motive of human life without God is what he called the *libido dominandi*, precisely Nietzsche's will to power.

Augustine's carefully elaborated distinction between the *civitas Dei*, the city of God, and the *civitas terrena*, the worldly city, and between the true Christian's unconditional, absolute love for the first and his loyalty, relative and conditional, to the second is one of the foundations he laid for the tradition that is the subject of this book. Another foundation of this tradition is his acknowledgement of the real value of our love of each other and of the beauty of the created earth, and of the human gifts—from God—of intelligence and imagination that deliver poetry and music, science and technological progress: "What have we", Augustine asked (changing Saint Paul's "you" to "we"), "that we have not received?"[22] These loves and gifts and what they produce, all of which are in constant danger of vitiation by the will to power, he places and judges, that is to say, criticises, always in relation to the love of God, his for us and ours for him. These elements in Augustine's thought are not separable. Each is an aspect of the greatest achievement of his reflection on Scripture, on everything else he had read and on his own experience: the clarification, for the whole subsequent life of the Church, of what is absolute and what is relative. As we shall see, a further consequence of this achievement is his perception of the Church herself as both the perfect Body of Christ, as she will be in the eschatological future, and as an imperfect body of imperfect human beings, a *corpus permixtum* to be sorted out only in the judgement of God. The Church, that is to say, is an institution both divine and human, both to be believed in with faith and to be loved and amended, with clarity and compassion, as she is.

Of most importance for the story—and it is a story, patchy and partial as all human stories are—that this book attempts to tell is Augustine's understanding, in the context sketched above, of the value, but the relative value, of writing itself. He had been educated to write and to persuade in a culture of words that for centuries had been regarded as an indispensable means to fame and fortune in the *civitas terrena*, the only city there was. In the pre-Christian Roman world, religion was relegated to practices performed in the interests of public order, to the superstitions of the illiterate and of an array of sects, and to the contentious arguments of a few philosophers. Edward Gibbon, in the eighteenth century, with the hope (fulfilled, as it eventually turned out) of restoring some such situation, wrote of the Antonine Rome he so much admired: "The various modes of worship, which prevailed in the Roman world, were all considered by the people, as equally true; by the philosopher, as equally false; and by the magistrate, as equally useful." [23] When Augustine, trained for fame and fortune, and having been himself a superstitious sectarian (a Manichee) and then a sceptical philosopher, became a Christian, he used his extraordinary literary gifts in the service of Christian truth. He read the Scriptures with an attention and depth that have seldom been equalled. He wrote for forty years, long books and short, his writing at its best the most beautiful Latin prose we have. Using the rhetorical skills learned in his youth, he preached sermons, taken down in shorthand as he spoke, the quality of which ensured that more than five hundred of them have survived. He never cut his attachment to the writers of the Roman past, Cicero and Virgil in particular, on whose work his memory and his critical sense had been formed, but the value of literary culture became for him as firmly relative as the value of anything else made by human beings. It was, however, this placing of the literary, the expressive and persuasive uses of words, in relation to truth that enabled him to think more profoundly and more interestingly than anyone else in the ancient world about what is involved in reading, about words and imagery, and about language itself, the signs by which we partially and patchily communicate with each other. Even the words of Scripture, he said, are signs that in the eschatological presence of God we shall no longer need. Meanwhile, we may listen as we read—and not only as we read Scripture—for what Stephen Prickett has called "whispers of divinity within the machine of language". [24] No human being can grasp, encompass or comprehend God: "If you have understood", Augustine said, "then this is not God." [25] Words are always provisional, fluid and temporal, infected with the transience of everything human. Augustine also said: "Whoever thinks that in this mortal life a man may so disperse the mists of bodily and carnal imaginings as to possess the unclouded light of unchangeable Truth ... understands neither what he seeks nor who he is that seeks it." [26] Balthasar wrote of literature and music, another human language: "*Art*, great art, has a special, reserved place among human endeavors. It is close to that side of the absolute that we call 'grace', free gift. Nonetheless it is always the fruit of the highest human effort too.... Ultimately, however, it is all a writing in the sand." [27]

There is always a gap between the words, the stories, of fallen humanity and the truth that is God, between the Creator and his creation. But because Christ came into mortality and history as "the image of the unseen God", the absolute made visible, the Word made flesh, the gap was in him closed. Aidan Nichols explains how it is that the definitive identity of Word and truth in Christ guarantees the meaning of the imperfect words and images we use every day, but also in great writing:

> The Word incarnate renders the absent God present; in Christ the signifier *par excellence*, God the signified (equally *par excellence*) is perfectly expressed. Such a supremely successful act of the sensuous "presencing" of an absence, an act duly represented in the language of the New Testament [and daily re-presented in the sacraments of the Church, especially the Eucharist], furnishes the final validation of a logorhythmic world where the patterns of language give access to nature in its actual order and course.[28]

It is, in the end, on account of the Incarnation that there is validity, value upon which we can rely, in our efforts to find or make (the Latin verb *invenire* carries the force of both), in the infinitely open and variable "patterns of language", what is true. We do not decide, but are given to discover and love, what is true; we do not measure God: he measures us. In Augustine's words, "See how God is true, not by participation in truth, but by making truth."[29] "The soul is to seek that good over which it will not preside as judge but to which it will cleave in love."[30]

It is in Augustine's spirit that this book is written, and with the twentieth-century example and encouragement, as has already been evident, of Balthasar. His seven-volume work *The Glory of the Lord*, itself the first part of his immense trilogy on the beauty, the goodness and the truth of God, reunites the aesthetic to the ethical and the philosophical in our approach to Christian truth. We are drawn, attracted, to truth and to goodness because they are beautiful: our response is a response of love, as our response to God is a response of love to his love for us. "The Christian knows", wrote Balthasar, "what the philosopher does not, that God is love."[31] Pascal wrote, in a note that is clearly a memo to himself (the Pléiade edition makes it the first of all his *Pensées*), "People have contempt for religion; they hate it, and fear it may be true. To cure this, it is necessary to ... show that it is attractive, lovable (*aimable*), so as to make the good wish that it were true; and then to show that it is true."[32] In another *Pensée* he wrote, in about 1660, "truth is so obscured in our time, and lies are so established, that unless we love truth we will not know how to recognise it."[33]

The texts discussed in this book are of different kinds. There are poems; plays; novels; books and essays of theology, criticism, history and autobiography; a monastic rule (Saint Benedict's); a collection of short prose passages (Pascal's) never ordered by their author; and a few of the hundreds of letters and thousands of notebook entries written over decades by Coleridge. These writings have been chosen both for their quality and for their closeness to an Augustinian understanding of absolute and relative value. Where and when these writers were at varying degrees of distance from the Catholic tradition, particularly in their conceptions of the nature of the Church, as in Orthodox Russia, Protestant England, and America, I have attempted some explanation of the historical accidents or choices responsible for the distance. A few writers appear in the book for their instructively negative relation to the tradition: in quite different ways, the negative clarity of Nietzsche has considerable bearing on, for example, Wordsworth, Schopenhauer, Tolstoy, Arnold and D. H. Lawrence.

All the texts discussed, however, belong, positively or negatively, to Christian culture, a culture shared by many who do not share Christian faith. Many more, of course, across the world and across the centuries shared and do share Christian faith with little or no knowledge of Christian culture. No one who reads the sermons of Augustine the bishop should forget that they were preached, Sunday after Sunday, to a congregation of illiterate dockers and farmhands in an African port. There is no need for a Christian to have any idea of the work of Dante or Dostoyevsky. But there is surely a need for those who are drawn to Dante or Dostoyevsky to have some idea of Christianity.

Those who love at least some of these texts—and some are among the greatest masterpieces ever written—and are certain that God is dead and therefore has been an illusion always, are liable to divinize great writing, or art of any kind, to make it into their god, the supreme good to which they devote the best efforts of their lives. This is because writing that reflects much goodness, truth and beauty really does bring us close to God (the same could be said of the music of Bach or Mozart or the painting of Michelangelo or Rembrandt) and is therefore more properly justifiable and less disappointing than the more common divinization of other things made or hoped for by fallible human beings: a secular utopia, a perfect relationship, the irresponsible freedom of the individual, wealth, fame, enough power over nature to deliver exactly what we want when we want it, and the postponement of age and death as if they were evil (and the only evil). Augustine, who accurately understood the constant human impulse to divinize anything other than God, prayed for the ordering of love and wrote that "the great achievement is to break the idols we keep within us."[34] Unless our loves are ordered in relation to God, any of them can and will become an idol. Nietzsche, surveying in the nineteenth century the desolation in store for the twentieth, knew this well, foreseeing intoxication taking the place of faith:

"intoxication with music, with cruelty, with hero-worship, or with hatred ... Art for Art's sake, Truth for Truth's sake, as a narcotic against self-disgust".[35] Or the intoxication, his own, of the self-divinized into godless sublimity. With Nietzsche in mind, de Lubac wrote:

> One must "reject the gods," a certain writer says, "all the gods." That is precisely what the disciples of Jesus taught us to do from the beginning.... They denied everything that the men around them took for the divine—everything that man, at every epoch, tends to deify in order to adore himself and tyrannize over himself, in and through his gods.
> The Gospel is the only "twilight of the gods."[36]

*　*　*

And so, in its proper place, which is in relation to Christian truth, and to be appropriately loved, which may be very much but not in the place of God, the writing of the Christian tradition awaits the reading, the remembering and the understanding of anyone with a fresh and open mind. It may be as a course of study that it first strikes a reader. But it is not, or not primarily, material to be stored as "known". Augustine often in his work uses the distinction between knowledge and wisdom, but never to denigrate the Christian's use of his own intelligence. A characteristic sentence runs: "The mind's understanding of eternal things leads to wisdom, rational understanding of temporal things only to knowledge."[37] In the nineteenth century, Schopenhauer, who, as we shall see, was very close to but also very far from Augustine, memorably described the difference:

> For the man who studies to gain *insight*, books and studies are merely rungs of the ladder on which he climbs.... On the other hand, the many who study in order to fill their memories do not use the rungs of the ladder for climbing, but take them off and load themselves with them to take away, rejoicing at the increasing weight of the burden. They remain below for ever since they are carrying what ought to have carried them.[38]

Knowledge increases generation by generation; wisdom does not. "The great minds that have spoken about God", de Lubac wrote, "are all our contemporaries."[39] "Wise men", Schopenhauer said just before the above passage, "can live in any age, and those of antiquity remain so for all the generations to come." Schopen-hauer's example is Plato. Ours, in this book, is Augustine, who recognised Pla-to's wisdom although Plato lived and wrote long before Christ. Both of them belong—as, to a greater or lesser degree, do all the writers discussed in this book—to what Pascal called "the order of love":

> The heart has its order. The mind has its own order, which is estab-lished through principle and demonstration. But the heart has another order.... Jesus Christ, St Paul, have the order of love, because they wanted to warm, not to instruct. St Augustine the same.[40]

1. Quoted in Simon Blackburn, "Richard Rorty", *Prospect*, April 2003, p. 58.
2. Ibid.
3. William Empson, "This Last Pain", line 21.
4. Alasdair MacIntyre, *Whose Justice? Which Rationality?* (London, 1988), p. 335.
5. Ibid., p. 346.
6. Ibid., pp. 165, 337.
7. Blaise Pascal, *Pensée* 438; numbered according to *Oeuvres complètes*, ed. Jacques Chevalier, Bib-liothèque de la Pléiade 34 (Paris, 1954), p. 1206; my translation.
8. MacIntyre, *Whose Justice?* p. 394.
9. Henri de Lubac, *The Discovery of God*, trans. Alexander Dru (Edinburgh, 1996), p. 154. Orig-inally published as *Sur les chemins de Dieu* (1956).
10. Hans Urs von Balthasar, *The Moment of Christian Witness*, trans. Richard Beckley (San Fran-cisco, 1994), pp. 73–74. Originally published as *Cordula oder der Ernstfall* (1966).
11. Czesław Miłosz, "The Separate Notebooks", *New and Collected Poems 1931–2001* (London, 2001), p. 383.
12. Hans Urs von Balthasar, *Theo-Logic*, vol. 1, trans. Adrian J. Walker (San Francisco, 2000), p. 12.
13. Friedrich Nietzsche, *The Will to Power*, quoted by Erich Heller, *In the Age of Prose* (Cambridge, 1984), p. 45.
14. Friedrich Nietzsche, *The Antichrist*, 50, in *The Portable Nietzsche*, ed. and trans. Walter Kauf-mann (London, 1971), pp. 631–32.
15. Nietzsche, *Will to Power*, quoted by Hans Urs von Balthasar, *Theo-Drama*, vol. 4, trans. Graham Harrison (San Francisco, 1994), p. 158.
16. Friedrich Nietzsche, *Twilight of the Idols*, trans. R.J. Hollingdale (London, 1968), pp. 69–70.
17. Balthasar, *Theo-Drama*, trans. Graham Harrison, vol. 4 (San Francisco, 1994), p. 467.
18. Friedrich Nietzsche, *The Gay Science*, 125, in *A Nietzsche Reader*, ed. and trans. R.J. Hollingdale (London, 1977), pp. 202–3.
19. Balthasar, *Theo-Drama* 4:72–73.
20. Hans Urs von Balthasar, "Tragedy and Christian Faith", in *Creator Spirit*, trans. Brian McNeil, Explorations in Theology, vol. 3 (San Francisco, 1993), pp. 409–10.
21. Augustine, *Enarrationes in Psalmos* 93.19.
22. Augustine, *On Christian Teaching*, preface 8; 1 Cor 4:7.
23. Edward Gibbon, *Decline and Fall of the Roman Empire* (1787; London, 1910), 1:29.
24. Stephen Prickett, *Narrative, Religion and Science* (Cambridge, 2002), p. 170.
25. Augustine, sermon 52.
26. Augustine, *De consensu Evangelistarum* 4.10.20.
27. Balthasar, *Theo-Drama* 4:109.
28. Aidan Nichols, *Christendom Awake* (Edinburgh, 1999), p. 60.

29. Augustine, *In Johannis evangelium* 39.8.
30. Augustine, *De Trinitate* 8.4.
31. Hans Urs von Balthasar, *La Foi du Christ* (Paris, 1968), p. 110.
32. Pascal, *Pensée* 1, *OC* 1089.
33. Ibid., *Pensée* 793, *OC* 1331.
34. Augustine, *Enarrationes in Psalmos* 80.14.
35. Quoted by Erich Heller, *The Importance of Nietzsche* (Chicago and London, 1988), p. 13.
36. De Lubac, *Discovery of God*, pp. 179–80.
37. Augustine, *De Trinitate* 12.15.
38. Arthur Schopenhauer, *The World as Will and Representation*, trans. E. F. J. Payne (New York, 1966), 2:80.
39. De Lubac, *Discovery of God*, p. 61.
40. Pascal, *Pensée* 72, *OC*, 1102.

CHAPTER TWO

AESCHYLUS AND SOPHOCLES

A eschylus lived from 525 to 456 B.C., Sophocles from 496 to 406 B.C. Both of them took part as soldiers, citizens and poets in the extraordinary rise to military, political and artistic preeminence of the city of Athens. Aeschylus, who had fought at the battle of Marathon, died just as this rise achieved its brief peak. Sophocles died after Athens had overreached itself, seen its brand-new, fragile democracy founder, and lay at the mercy of invaders. Aeschylus wrote about eighty plays, Sophocles about a hundred. Of these, seven by each poet, through the frailest and chanciest descent of manuscripts down the centuries, survive.

It may seem strange to begin this book altogether outside the Augustinian, the Latin Christian, tradition, with a handful of archaic texts written in one pagan city far from Israel, four hundred years and more before Christ was born. These beautiful, frightening, profoundly moving plays were unknown to Augustine himself. They were, indeed, unknown to the Christian West for so many centuries that by the time they began to be familiar to more people than a few scholars, the intellectual world was already losing touch with Christian truth. One Athenian tragedy, Sophocles's *Antigone*, was remade as a Christian play by a French poet, Robert Garnier, in the late sixteenth century. Otherwise, it was Greek tragedy's very distance from the Latin Christian tradition that gave it much of its appeal to Europe in the eighteenth, nineteenth and twentieth centuries, when Europe was more and more priding itself on having left Christianity behind. Nietzsche, understanding accurately the connexion between Plato and Christianity, regarded the eclipse of Athenian tragedy by Athenian philosophy as a disaster to be surmounted by a leap backward over the whole God-infected tradition to an understanding of the truly Greek spirit, which he saw expressed in the tragic plays as a joyful celebration of cruel fatalism. This, as we shall see, has been a strongly influential view for the last hundred years.

It is nevertheless the case that the anger, the justice and the love of God, all that we mean by his glory, can be glimpsed in these ancient plays, and the awe that they inspire has a meaning for the Christian that is deeper and richer than the meaning found in them by those for whom "God" is an empty word.

When Saint Paul preached to the curious, mocking Athenians in the early 50s of the first century, he was speaking in a provincial city of the Roman Empire that was nevertheless regarded as the intellectual capital of the world. In fact, for almost a thousand years—from, say, the death of Socrates in 399 B.C. to Justinian's closing of the schools of Athens in A.D. 529—the fame of Athens as a university never faded. This was the place where, because it was the city of Plato and Aristotle, people had learned, and continued to learn, to think philosophically. Most of the Greek Fathers of the Church collected at least some of their education in Athens, and when, in the seventh century, Saint Theodore of Tarsus, the only Greek archbishop of Canterbury, came to England with the African Saint Adrian to begin the proper organisation of the English Church, everyone in the Latin world assumed he had been educated in Athens, which he probably never even visited.

The actual work of the schools of Athens had become shallow and derivative long before Paul's visit. But the great and deserved reputation of Athenian philosophy was, as Nietzsche rightly saw, however bizarre his judgement of it, one of the reasons for the disappearance from view of the Athenian tragedies of Aeschylus and Sophocles by the time Christianity was being preached in the eastern Mediterranean, and for many centuries thereafter. There were two other important reasons for this almost complete disappearance.

One of these was the lasting influence of Euripides. The third and youngest of the great Athenian tragic poets (he lived from 484 to 407 B.C.), he was, in the reckoning of the judges who awarded the prizes for plays at the city's festival of the god Dionysus, considerably less successful in his lifetime than either Aeschylus or Sophocles. But after his death, his effect on the future of tragic writing was far stronger than theirs. Nineteen of his plays survive. Compared to those of Aeschylus or Sophocles, Euripides's plays have a brittle, ironic, secular atmosphere. In them the glory of divine power, regarded with reverence in Aeschylus and Sophocles, has faded in the equivocal representation of gods as frightening manipulators, with mixed human qualities. These plays seem late, though Euripides died before Sophocles wrote his last play. They have always seemed modern. When literary Romans, educated in Greek and keen to copy in Latin its different kinds of poetry, turned to tragedy, they looked mostly to Euripides, as, sixteen centuries later, did the neoclassical French. Seneca in the first century A.D. wrote stiff, bloodthirsty imitations of Euripidean models, displays of extravagant rhetoric rather than performable plays; his were the only classical tragedies known to Shakespeare.

The third reason for the long disappearance of Aeschylus and Sophocles from the furniture of the civilised mind was the understandable revulsion of the Church of the late Roman Empire against the theatre. The gladiatorial tradition of spectacular competitive violence, often including actual killing, was old before its victims included Christian martyrs, and the theatrical performances Augustine was ashamed of having enjoyed in the Carthage of his youth were coarse, frivolous popular entertainment, more like pantomimes than serious plays. The disapproving distance Augustine in particular put between the Church and the theatre outlasted the Latin empire by many centuries.

For all these reasons Aeschylus and Sophocles were not where most people were looking even when the study of classical Greek texts revived in the Renaissance, first in Italy and then in France, England and Germany. Renaissance scholars, like the Alexandrian and Byzantine editors and lexicographers on whose work they built, were more interested in philosophy and history than in poetry, and more interested in Homer than in tragedy. The one or two manuscripts of Aeschylus and Sophocles that had reached the Vatican and Medici libraries were not edited until the sixteenth century. Only *Antigone* was translated into Italian and then into Latin and French before 1600, and Melanchthon is the only sixteenth-century professor of Greek known to have lectured, in Luther's Wittenberg, on Sophocles. There was no English translation of any Aeschylus play until the nineteenth century.

It was, indeed, the heavily Romantic classicists of the nineteenth century, predominantly German, predominantly grateful that Greek tragedy was written long before Christianity, who opened the main path by which the plays of fifth-century-B.C. Athens have reached us. On their way they lost much. Not until Balthasar in our own time has a serious Catholic mind been applied to the extraordinary religious force of these ancient texts.

We have only the texts of what, because against the odds they survived, we may assume to be the masterpieces of Aeschylus and Sophocles. The texts are short. Sophocles's three plays on the Oedipus story, *Oedipus the King*, *Oedipus at Colonus* and *Antigone*, not written in this order, are, taken all together, shorter than *King Lear*. Aeschylus's trilogy on the doomed house of Atreus, *Agamemnon*, *The Choephori* and *The Eumenides*, is shorter still. Otherwise we have the remains of the great stone theatres of various Greek cities, all of them, even the one at Athens on the site of the fifth-century theatre, later than the texts. We have some idea of what a play's two or three actors, above and behind the chorus, looked like. They had masks and distinctive clothes. The king, Agamemnon or Oedipus, for example, would have been recognisable from far away, as the celebrant at Mass is recognisable by his vestments from the far end of a vast cathedral. We have no music. We have no certain information about movement or dance, about exactly how the choral odes that punctuate the dialogue of these plays would have been sung, choreographed or otherwise conveyed to their enormous audience of citizens. Our impression of the plays must be constructed from fallen stones and difficult words, as the impression of a feast-day High Mass at Cluny in the eleventh century might be built by someone with a knowledge of Latin from an imperfect text of the liturgy and acquaintance with the ruins of a few twelfth-century Cistercian churches.

*   *   *

Aeschylus is the father of all tragedy, taking what seems to have been an annual ritual of sung and danced celebration of the gods and the city and turning it, in strong, supple verse of great metaphorical power, into what we can recognise as performable drama. Pericles himself paid for and organised, in 472 B.C., the production of Aeschylus's first surviving play, *The Persians*. A couple of years before Aeschylus died, at about age seventy, his masterpiece and only surviving trilogy, the three plays about Agamemnon, Clytemnestra and their children, were performed in an Athens just reaching its noble moment of civic glory. The story the plays tell is a terrifying one, of sin and retribution, pride and its punishment, in a cycle of revenge that it seems, until the last scene of the last play, will never end, will never be healed in reconciliation and peace. Bits in the background of the story strike notes that are familiar to a Jew or a Christian. The original sin of the devastated descendants of Atreus is the abduction of Helen by Paris, prince of Troy. Her beauty and his weakness, their disobedience, their sin against the immemorial laws of marriage and trust, have destroyed the golden order of the world. There is even an apple in the story, and, still further back in the mythological mists, an ancestor who sacrificed his son to the gods and found him restored to life.

Agamemnon, leading the Greeks in a war of vengeance against Troy for the stealing of his wife's sister, Helen, sacrifices his daughter for a favourable wind, like Jephthah in the Book of Judges. Ten years later Agamemnon returns victorious, claiming for himself the glory that always belongs properly to the gods, and is murdered by his wife, Clytemnestra, in revenge for their daughter's death. Their son, Orestes, in his turn, must kill his mother in revenge, and does. Is he now guilty of murder, of deep family sin, as his mother was before him and as his father was before her, and therefore also to be punished? Will the linked chain of killings never end? The extraordinary answer to these questions, given at the end of the last play, is that vengeance and justice are not the same, that the gods can reconcile, can restore peace to the human family through words instead of violence, through the agreed order of the human city. The Eumenides, who are the pursuing Furies—the title of the last play—track down the guilty Orestes. They will always be there in human life. But they can be tamed, brought into the fabric of the life of the city, so that through persuasion rather than murder, peace can prevail, and he who carries the sin of the family can be released from the cycle of revenge. At the end of the play, Athena, the goddess of her chosen people, her chosen city, leads the now-friendly Furies, divine anger tamed, in a great procession into the city, which must have pulled the thousands of citizens watching the play into a united movement of reconciliation, hope and resolve, which it is accurate to describe as liturgical.

Aeschylus's search, through the human suffering, cruelty and bitterness of these plays, whose characters die under the hammerblows of divine anger, is for a justice that can come only from above, from outside the human mess. The blessing given to the city is given from heaven to the place "where gods and mortals meet", and Aeschylus's piety is in his fear and respect for the holiness of divine power and in his hope for the just and peaceful future of Athens, pulled by divine words from the darkness of the old order into the light of the new. Pallas Athena's intervention, in a court of justice that has replaced the bloodlust of vengeance, saves Orestes. And Athena's words convert the Furies into protectors of the city. At the end of the *Eumenides* they sing:

> Rejoice, Athena's people—
> poised by the side of Zeus,
> loved by the loving virgin girl,
> achieve humanity at last,
> nestling under Pallas' wings
> and blessed with the Father's love.[1]

Balthasar wrote of the conclusion of the *Eumenides*:

> This transformation of the goddesses of revenge into the well-meaning Eumenides ... has no parallel in world literature, if for the time we leave out of the reckoning the great biblical arch between the Old and the New Covenant. It is the greatest endeavour of the myth forcefully to unify the most extreme tensions of the world through a personal, divine act which, as grace,—Orestes after all has grace bestowed upon him—establishes a form of justice which is human and divine. The

world order is neither given at the beginning, nor attained at the end by philosophical syntheses; everything is orientated to the glory of the divine event, all is dependent on the unforeseeable revelation.[2]

It is only Athens that the tamed Furies will inhabit in the grace brought by Athena, daughter of Zeus. We are not in Jerusalem. We are not in the light of Christ's revelation of the love and mercy and justice of God himself for all mankind. We are in a single Greek city, at a unique moment of achievement and promise. Soon the promise faded, as all human glory always fades, overtaken by pride, ambition and the bullying politics of growth and greed. Aeschylus lived and wrote, for the greatest religious festival of his city, in a still-pagan world. His name for the goodness of heaven that comes to bring reconciliation instead of vengeance has to be Athena, the goddess of his city, and behind her, her father, Zeus, king of the gods, guaranteeing her just order, because Aeschylus does not know the name of God. Near the beginning of *Agamemnon*, the sky darkening with the horrors that are to come, the chorus of old men of Argos, awaiting Agamemnon's return, struggle with, precisely, the name of God:

> Zeus, great nameless all in all,
> if that name will gain his favour,
> I will call him Zeus.
> I have no words to do him justice,
> weighing all in the balance,
> all I have is Zeus, Zeus. . . .[3]

A few lines later the chorus finds words for the mystery of wisdom learned through suffering, through the recognition of the truth of sin and for the divine love hidden in this suffering, or passion (which is the same word). This mystery is at the heart of all great tragedy:

> Zeus has led us on to know,
> the Helmsman lays it down as law
> that we must suffer, suffer into truth.
> We cannot sleep, and drop by drop at the heart
> the pain of pain remembered comes again,
> and we resist, but ripeness comes as well.
> From the gods enthroned on the awesome rowing-bench
> there comes a violent love.[4]

Aeschylus could not know that God's love for us, opened to us in the sacrifice of the Cross, would draw into itself the truth, and forgiveness, that we learn through suffering. But the light that Aeschylus caught, gleaming through his darkness, because it is the light of healing in the darkness of sin, is the light of God. It is, though still fitfully perceived, the light of truth that a later, complacent, no longer religious Athens will laugh at when Paul preaches the judgement of God in Christ on the hill of Ares, the hill of the god of war where Orestes is tried for murder at the end of the *Eumenides* and pardoned.

There is one other late play by Aeschylus, *Prometheus Bound*, that no Christian can read without astonishing moments of recognition. The play is the first of a trilogy of which the two subsequent plays have not survived. Prometheus, whose name means "providence" or "forethought", even "wisdom", is, at the beginning of the play, nailed to a rock, crucified (the word is suggested by what the text makes clear is happening on the stage) by Strength and Violence, who mock him as the nails are driven in. Until he is alone he says nothing. Then he cries out to the firmament of heaven; to earth, his own mother and the mother of all; and to the all-seeing sun:

> See what things I, a god, suffer from the gods.[5]

This word *pascho*, "I suffer", strangely so close to the word *pascha* (the Greek version of the Hebrew word for Passover), will echo through the play. So will the prayer *to be seen*: tragedy is, above all (in every sense of "above all"), the spectacle of suffering, the one who suffers, who carries his own sin and often the sin of others, held up so that heaven and the watching people can *see him*. "Do you think God sees me?" cries the suffering Estragon to his friend Vladimir as they "do the tree" in a visual echo of the Crucifixion, two and a half millennia away from Aeschylus in Samuel Beckett's *Waiting for Godot*.[6]

Prometheus, one of the old gods of Greece ousted from power by Zeus and his Olympian gods, is being punished by Zeus. For what offence? For his love of mankind. He has stolen fire from heaven and given it to men, teaching them the skills from which civilisation will develop. More mysteriously, he has given them hope. Impatient with the wretched human race, Zeus had resolved to annihilate it. Prometheus explains:

> This purpose there was no one to oppose but I.
> I dared. I saved the human race from being ground
> To dust, from total death.

> For that I am subjected to this bitter pain—
> Agony to endure, heart-rending to behold.
> I pitied mortal men; but being myself not thought
> To merit pity, am thus cruelly disciplined—
> A sight to fix dishonour on the name of Zeus.
> . . . .
> I caused men no longer to foresee their death.
> . . . .
> I planted firmly in their hearts blind hopefulness.[7]

There is a faint promise in the play that one day Prometheus, separated from Zeus as he now is, although he is also in some ways Zeus's own wisdom, Zeus's own care for men, will be reconciled to Zeus. There is also the suggestion that one day the power of Zeus will disappear into a whole new divine order. Because the other plays of the trilogy are lost, we have no idea how Aeschylus dealt with the rest of the story. But this figure from so long ago, so far away, everlastingly nailed to his rock for his love of helpless mankind, "a sight to fix dishonour on the name of Zeus", most strikingly foreshadows the crucified figure of Calvary.

When, in the middle of the play, Io, herself persecuted by Zeus, visits Prometheus on his rock, she says to him:

> Patient [suffering, battered] Prometheus, who brought to light
> a common benefit [blessing] for all mankind,
> for what justice do you suffer?[8]

The question of this last line, containing both the words *dike* (justice) and *pascho*, is always the central tragic question. Both words recur, as does *koinos*, the strong Greek word for "common, universal", at the end of the play in Prometheus's last cry:

> O my most holy mother,
> O firmament turning
> the common light of all,
> look at the judgement I suffer.[9]

So *pascho* is the very last word of the play, while the word that precedes it, *ekdika*, can mean either "judgement" or "injustice" or, of course, both.

*   *   *

Sophocles's masterpieces, the three plays about Oedipus and his children, were not written together to be performed on one occasion as Aeschylus's trilogies were. Like the Agamemnon-Orestes plays, they tell a terrifying story of family sin and its appalling consequences. But in Sophocles's plays, no god appears to set things right, to contain the dark forces of a primeval past within a new order of light. On the contrary, in each play human beings struggle through the suffering of sin, their own and that of others, toward knowledge, and penitent acceptance, of the truth. The first play to be written, *Antigone*, tells the last part of the story. Antigone, doomed child of the dreadful marriage of King Oedipus and his mother, symbolically buries her dead brother, enemy of the city, against the command of the king, Creon, whose priority is the unity and civic order celebrated at the end of Aeschylus's last play, but now in Creon's godless power. Against the human daylight of the city, Antigone chooses the ancient duty to the dead, to her brother and to the gods, and for her clear and lonely choice the king has her put to death. She has perceived, as Sophocles had in the fallibility of his own city, that human law (*nomos*) may contravene divine law (*dike*), the ancient, absolute requirements of divine justice. When it does, it is to be disobeyed. The collision between Antigone and Creon is a premonition in pagan myth of the often-repeated collision that Augustinian Christianity will understand as that between the earthly city and the city of God, the *civitas terrena* and the *civitas Dei*.

The famous second choral ode of *Antigone*, "Mysteries are many and there is nothing more mysterious than man", concludes with a warning:

> With his wisdom and his devices
> that surpass all dreams, man edges now
> toward good, now toward evil.
> If he honours the laws of earth and the justice held in heaven,
> his city stands high; citiless is he
> who lives an evil life in reckless daring.[10]

The audience at this point sees Antigone brought to the king in disgrace. But it is he rather than she who is breaking the bond between justice and the law. She argues with the king, who has decreed that her brother's body is to be left unburied, to be eaten by the dogs and vultures:

> It wasn't Zeus, not in the least,
> who made this proclamation—not to me.
> Nor did that Justice, dwelling with the gods
> beneath the earth, ordain such laws for men.
> Nor did I think your edict had such force
> that you, a mere mortal, could override the gods,
> the great unwritten, unshakeable traditions.
> They are alive, not just today or yesterday:
> they live forever, from the first of time,
> and no one knows when they first saw the light.[11]

Virginal, childless, she goes to her marriage with death, her entombment in stone, a sacrificial victim to an eternal law of love that the city's king refuses to acknowledge. By the end of the play, Creon himself has lost both his son and his wife to death occasioned by the love he has turned his face against. Alive, alone, stricken, he is left with the truth of his guilt. In Balthasar's (Augustinian) words on Greek tragedy: "The agent (or patient), driven by intramundane, second-order motives, is finally surrounded like a hunted deer: he becomes the focus of an absolute light and, for the first time, becomes aware of it."[12] The chorus concludes the play with these words:

> Wisdom is by far the greatest part of joy,
> and reverence towards the gods must be safeguarded.
> The mighty words of the proud are paid in full
> with mighty blows of fate, and at long last
> those blows will teach us wisdom.[13]

In *Oedipus the King*, the best known of all the Greek tragedies, written in the middle of Sophocles's long life, Oedipus resolutely and agonisingly brings himself to the knowledge of the shattering sin that he, unknowingly, committed. Brought up by others from babyhood, he, heroic king of Thebes though he is, has murdered his father and married his mother. Simultaneously innocent and horrifyingly guilty, he blinds himself at the moment of complete sight of what he has done and goes out into the wilderness carrying alone the punishment his sin has brought upon his city.

Sophocles's last play, *Oedipus at Colonus*, is also the last Greek tragedy that has survived, written after the death of Euripides and performed after the death of the ninety-year-old Sophocles himself. In it the old, banished king, blind and visionary, powerless and full of the power of wisdom, deeply guilty and deeply penitent, dies at last, a cursed figure peacefully bringing blessing to the land— now the land of Sophocles's Athens, not the land of Oedipus's own city of Thebes. But between the old age of Aeschylus, full of the hope of his last play, and the old age of Sophocles, the pride of Athens had met its fall. When Sophocles was writing *Oedipus at Colonus*, invading Spartans were laying waste the countryside around Athens. When the play was performed in 402, Sparta had conquered the city, which never again recovered its brief worldly glory.

In this play the promise of blessing is otherworldly. The burden of sin that Oedipus bears to and beyond the grave has in it a hope of healing and peace that is beyond human explanation. When the chorus question him about his past, they start a sentence: "What you have suffered—". Oedipus interrupts: "Suffered, unforgivable, unforgettable. . . ." But the dialogue goes on:

CHORUS.　What you have done!
OEDIPUS.　　　　　　　　　No, not done—
CHORUS.　　　　　　　　　　　　　What, then?
OEDIPUS.　　　　　　　　　　　　　　　　Received,
　　　　Received as a gift, a prize to break the heart—[14]

This exchange has in its mysteriousness the secret blessing of the victim who is also, somewhere beyond our sight, the victor. A few moments later, Theseus, king of Athens, asks the ragged, blind old man why he has come. Oedipus replies:

OEDIPUS.　I come with a gift for you,
　　　　my own shattered body, no feast for the eyes,
　　　　but the gains it holds are greater than great beauty. . . .
THESEUS.　And when will the gifts you offer come to light?
OEDIPUS.　When I am dead and you have put my body in the grave.[15]

When Oedipus, leading the daughters who for years have had to lead him, leaves the stage to die, the chorus, themselves old men, pray:

　　　　Not in pain, not by a doom
　　　　that breaks the heart with mourning,
　　　　let our friend go down to the world below
　　　　the all-enshrouding infinite fields of the dead
　　　　the dark house of Death. Numberless agonies

blind and senseless, came his way in life—
now let some power
some justice grant him glory![16]

(Or "Let a just God grant him glory!" which is closer to the Greek.) The messenger who soon brings news of Oedipus's death describes the fallen king's last moment, seeing with his blind eyes some blaze of divine light, invisible to the bystanders, at which he could not bear to look. Of all the Greek tragedies, *Oedipus at Colonus* demonstrates most clearly the intuition, the conviction, that meaning lies beyond suffering, beyond death, in the transcendence of divine justice, truth and beauty, which can be perceived by sinful man with sureness, but only through suffering and death. Balthasar wrote of this play:

> Here is the essence of Sophoclean glory: not for one moment, amid the night he is depicting, does he doubt that it is God's night and therefore "God's lightless light". His figure, his construction, remains intact only by virtue of this mighty affirmation, namely, that reality is good and, on God's side, eternally just, and that in man's very powerlessness the power of being reveals itself, so inconceivably raising him up amid all his humiliation. . . . In this ecce peccatum! and its terrible exposure there is nevertheless an ecce gratia! of reconciliation.[17]

The figure of Oedipus, crushed by suffering, loss and the knowledge of his own sin, a curse and a blessing for his people, his beloved son his enemy, has much in common with the heartbroken figure of the old King David in the Second Book of Samuel. Sophocles is caught, as is the author of 2 Samuel, in his time, the time before God's Word became flesh; and like Aeschylus, he is also caught outside God's covenant with Israel and has to articulate his hope in mortal terms, in the terms of the city of Athens. If Theseus, its noble king, keeps secret forever the place of Oedipus's grave, that burial place will bring peace to the city and blessing to its people. Meanwhile, Antigone has promised burial to her doomed brother, and we know what the price of that burial is to be.

In Sophocles's works, Antigone, Creon and Oedipus are solitary figures, lit by suffering, knowledge and courage against a dark sky, hated and loved by the gods, by God himself, in the singular, as Sophocles's grammar occasionally allows. The light these characters catch gleams and fades and had faded from Athens long before Saint Paul came to preach to the city the light that does not fade. But it is the light, nevertheless, of the sacrificial victim who carries the sin of the royal, the conspicuous, family into the night of death and guilt for the good of the city, the people. The spring festival of which the original performances of these plays were part was held in honour of the god Dionysus the deliverer, the wildest and darkest of the Greek gods, whose exuberant life, extinguished by death, was always restored and whose epiphanic appearances were no less mysterious. The festival had as its centre and climax the sacrifice of a male animal, a goat or a lamb; sacrifice, followed by a feast of unity and thanksgiving, was the central religious act of ancient Greece.

* * *

There are two ways of seeing these plays—the conventional way of the eighteenth, nineteenth and twentieth centuries, which is the modern, secular way, and the Jewish or Christian way. From the secular point of view, the evident coincidences and echoes back and forth between Athenian tragedy and Christianity suggest influence or shared historical derivation, adding substance to the commonsense assumption that much in Christian theology and liturgy has roots in Greek as well as in Jewish tradition, for together they were the seedbed of the Church. Further, from this point of view, the parallels between scriptural episodes and manifestations of the divine, on the one hand, and episodes in Greek mythology, focussed to particular characters, images and words in the burning-glass of Athenian tragedy, on the other hand, simply go to show how much old mythologies have in common. The parallels serve to confirm the secular conclusion that Christianity is merely another mythological construct, that it has no more properly ascertainable or testable truth in its narratives than have the stories of the houses of Atreus, Prometheus or Oedipus. If there is not, and never has been, God, if divine justice and divine transcendence, giving meaning to the most profound suffering of man, has never been more than an illusion produced by the anguish of the human psyche, then Athenian (and Shakespearean) tragedy, and Jewish and Christian liturgy, are reduced to dramatic performances referring to nothing outside themselves.

George Steiner's *The Death of Tragedy* (1961) is a well-known exploration of this secular view. In a key passage, he says:

> Until the advent of rational empiricism the controlling habits of the western mind were symbolic and allegoric. Available evidence regarding the natural world, the course of history, and the varieties of human action were translated into imaginative designs or mythologies. Classic

mythology and Christianity are such architectures of the imagination.... [After the seventeenth century] concepts such as grace, damnation, purgation, blasphemy, or the chain of being, which are everywhere
implicit in classic and Shakespearean tragedy, lose their vitality. They
become philosophic abstractions of a private and problematic relevance, or mere catchwords in religious customs which had in them a
diminishing part of active belief.[18]

Once the knowledge of, the obedience to, transcendent truth, God in his eternity, has been lost, the symbol loses the life, the fire struck by the throwing
together of two realities—which is what the word "symbol" means. As Coleridge, already a late Christian among unbelieving English Romantics, wrote in
1816: "A symbol is characterised ... above all by the translucence of the Eternal
through and in the Temporal. It always partakes of the Reality which it renders
intelligible, and while it enunciates the whole, abides itself as a living part in that
Unity, of which it is the representative."[19] This, of course, is not an idea that a
secular critic can seriously entertain.

The Death of Tragedy was written in 1961. In Steiner's Antigones (1984), a discussion of Sophocles's play and its many modern reworkings, Steiner's secularism
shows occasional cracks: he does point out that aspects of the play are striking
"prefigurations of Christian truths".[20] But in general he insists, with Nietzsche,
that Antigone is closer to us in the modern or postmodern world than Christianity can any longer be. "The transcendent absolutes to which Antigone appeals
in her debate with Creon, are, in a radical sense, secular."[21] What, in the climate of radical empiricism, a secular absolute might be is not explained, nor is
it much clarified by an earlier pronouncement in which Augustine would be
astonished to find himself: "[Antigone's] justification is also secular or, more exactly,
'humanistic' in a very precise sense inherited from Cicero via St Augustine."[22]

The real upshot of a consistently secular view of Aeschylus and Sophocles has
to be that tragedy, being about suffering and death, conveys despair. According to
Nietzsche, it may deliver beauty, or even joy, in the face of despair; according
to Steiner, in a 1990 essay called "Absolute Tragedy", it can express only despair.
"Strictly defined, absolute tragedy is the performative mode of despair."[23] Among
the powerfully prevailing secular assumptions of our time, this has inevitably
become the standard view of what tragedy is. If there is no meaning, no love, no
eternity, no God beyond death, tragedy is necessarily emptied of hope and becomes
a howl of misery whose value to us can be accounted for as no more than
paradoxically exhilarating Schadenfreude. "Greek and Shakespearean tragedy revel

in exploding the solidity of explanations, in discomposing and scattering the agencies of consolation, public and political, private and psychological. These agencies would have us believe that man's state is single, solid and central. Tragedy affirms with savage jubilation that man's state is diverse, fluid and unfounded." This passage is on the second page of Adrian Poole's *Tragedy* (1987),[24] a Nietzschean book of considerable acuteness flawed by the same inconsistencies that weaken Steiner's work on tragedy. (The proper place for discussion of these inconsistencies will be in relation to Shakespeare.)

Poole ends with three sentences that may be taken as representative of the late twentieth century's intellectual confusion: "Tragedy embodies our most paradoxical feelings and thoughts and beliefs. It gives them flesh and blood, emotional and intellectual and spiritual substance. Through tragedy we recognise and refeel our sense of both the value and the futility of human life, of both its purposes and its emptiness."[25] Well, which? And does it matter? That having it both ways is rationally impossible does not seem to strike such writers. Either everything means something, or nothing means anything. But the first requires belief in God, while the second is perhaps too frightening to be faced by those (and that is almost everyone) without Nietzsche's desperate courage.

The secular view of the Athenian tragedies is rarely consistent because the power of the plays themselves often pushes its way into the soul of the reader against his secular principles. A clear example is the fine essay "The Serpent and the Eagle"[26] on Aeschylus's trilogy, written by the trilogy's best translator of recent times, Robert Fagles. Most of the time, with infectious enthusiasm, Fagles regards the affirmative ending of *The Eumenides* as a celebration of human progress and of the new order of the city of man, which has to be sustained by constant effort to keep the Furies friendly. "The birth of tragedy and the birth of democracy" were simultaneous. But he knows also, and is not sure how or where to anchor his knowledge, that Aeschylus is a poet of the divine guarantee of human meaning, of divine intervention in human life. "At the end of the *Oresteia*," he says, "when the joy of the people blends with the Escorts' song of praise to the gods, Aeschylus might say with the Psalmist, 'Not unto us, O Lord, not unto us, but unto thy name give glory.'"[27] But a little earlier in the essay, perhaps because his own tradition is Jewish rather than Christian—he echoes Psalm 126—he misses an even closer parallel:

Conflict remains the medium of our destiny in the *Oresteia*. Here it is always anxious spring, yet always harvest too. Sown in tears and reaped in joy, Dionysus is continuously dismembered and reborn. How could the trilogy embody so much grief and so much joy at once? Perhaps it arose at a time, never again recovered, when tragedy was so inspired by Dionysus it could re-enact his death and resurrection in one dramatic span.[28]

The strong answer to the question asked here is that the profound meaning of the tragedies as analogy would not become evident until God's revelation of himself in Christ made the dramatic span of the Triduum—Holy Thursday, Good Friday, Holy Saturday, Easter Sunday—an embodiment of both grief and joy that was, that once, not a metaphor (though always an image) and not a play.

Analogy: this is the key to the alternative, the Christian, view of the great tragic plays of Aeschylus and Sophocles. In the introductory chapter to *The Realm of Metaphysics in Antiquity*, which forms the fourth volume of *The Glory of the Lord*, Balthasar writes:

> If a concept that is fundamental to the Bible [the glory of God] had no kind of analogy in the general intellectual sphere, and awoke no familiar echo in the heart of man, it would remain absolutely incomprehensible and thereby a matter of indifference. It is only when there is an analogy ... between the human sense of the divine and divine revelation that the height, the difference and the distance of that which the revelation discloses may be measured in God's grace. When the farthest-reaching systems of human thought (and these are to be found perhaps more in the myth and mythical art than in philosophy) are presented to man then he will be inwardly convinced that it was not he himself who discovered the system which God set out.[29]

The account Balthasar gives of Athenian tragedy in *The Glory of the Lord* rests on this firm foundation. It is an account that has a clarity and a consistency that no other post-Nietzschean discussion of the subject even approaches. This is because it restores the lost connexion between the partial and relative truth, goodness and beauty of the plays to their intelligible place beside, or within, the truth, goodness and beauty of God. If the only glory is the glory of God, then the degree of contingent glory in what has been made by men, in this case the ancient, imperfect texts of plays whose complete, performed impact we can never regain, returns to the coherently describable.

The figures of Orestes, the driven killer of his mother rescued from the cycle of vengeance; of Prometheus crucified for his love of mankind; of Antigone sent to her death for obedience to justice rather than the law; of Oedipus, horribly guilty yet both redeemed and redeeming, are newly illuminated in analogical thinking that sees them as both foreshadowing mysteriously the figure of Christ on the Cross and as representing, in their particular characters and destinies, the special fate, the special suffering and possible redemption, of each of us. In one of Balthasar's summarising paragraphs, he puts this perception with characteristic force:

> In tragedy, man acts against the background of the god and man only reveals himself, emerging into the light of his own truth, because of the appearance of the god, even in wrath and concealment. There is no trace of an aesthetic effect on this stage, it is concerned solely with bloody truth and justice, which ... [are] revealed simultaneously in the god and in man, in that communion which they enjoy and yet which divides them. . . . The situation in which this truth emerges is now that of suffering, and preferably a most horrendous form of suffering which lays man bare in his vulnerability, forcibly exposing and humiliating him. Only a great and majestic human being is equal to this; he alone can bear such a burden, and only from him, when he is finally and necessarily broken apart, can there rise, like a fragrance, the pure essence of human kind, indeed, of being as such. What is unprecedented here is that the suffering is neither denied (declared to be only apparent and philosophically reduced), nor is it shunned for the sake of an attainable *euclaimonia* [happiness], but rather the way of man to god and the revelation of the deep truth of existence passes directly through the most extreme form of suffering. That is the valour of the unshielded heart, which philosophy will lack, and which stands in a direct relation to Christ.[30]

It is obvious that the Christian view of Greek tragedy is in important respects antithetical to the secular view. In the first place, the parallels between the tragic and the Christian sense of divine justice or of the redeeming recognition of dependence on God reached through suffering, or between tragedy as the sacrificial drama at the heart of a whole city's annual festival and the liturgy of Easter, now become, not confirmation that Christianity is one more myth, but confirmation that myth, both barbarous and glorious, prefigured the truth of Christianity. In the second place, the sense, powerfully conveyed by Sophocles in particular, that death—the death of Antigone, the death of Oedipus—does

not conclude the significance of an individual human life, but that the significance of an individual life is held in the eternity of God, is recovered from
embarrassed intuition and becomes secure conviction. In the third place, more
simply, our awe at the ancient splendour of these searing plays becomes something we can understand and discuss in a context familiar to millions of people
beyond the ranks of classical scholars or literary critics.

That grace comes through truthful recognition of our own sin; that human
judgement can never do more than fitfully approach the justice of God; that our
suffering has a meaning, and a healing, bestowed on it by the Passion, death and
Resurrection of Christ, whose shadowy precursors were the heroic mediators
between God and man in Greek and other mythologies: all this, in a Christian
view of tragedy, returns to the sayable, the comprehensible. In his five-volume
Theo-Drama, Balthasar immeasurably broadens the discussion of the theatre begun
in *The Glory of the Lord*. There is an undaunted (and undaunting) theological
simplicity at the core of this huge and complex work. Here is one example from
the third volume:

> Religion has always presupposed the existence of a stage on which God
> and the world can interact. Since the world comes from God, God is
> involved in it and somehow accessible to it. Thus man can hope: he has
> the prospect of attaining fulfillment, in spite of his finitude, in the realm
> of the divine. In the religions, this mediating locus is rendered con-
> crete in a wealth of mediator-figures, whose multiplicity yields a kind
> of *negative* and *inchoate Christology*.... The step from negative or incho-
> ate Christology to a fully developed Christology can only be taken on
> the basis of an acceptance of the biblical testimony. No religious or
> philosophical speculation can do it. The real Jesus Christ cannot be
> invented by men.[31]

This is the context in which the Christian may read or, better, watch the
tragedies of Aeschylus and Sophocles, recognising their place in the story of our
civilisation's patchy awareness of God before the birth of Christ and disregarding
the post-Christian appropriation of the plays that is bound, to say the least, to
do the works less than justice. The Christian will see in the plays anguished
evidence that the terrifying glory of God, who tests his chosen ones to and
beyond the limits of ordinary human patience, or passion, and courage, was
perceived outside Israel and before the coming of Christ. The perception was
clothed, as it was bound to be, in myths, myths of great violence but also of the

love of goodness, of the piety, which had long identified the Athenians to themselves. Without the name of God, given then to Israel alone, the poets used the names of passing generations of gods, and these very names were to vanish, not long after Sophocles's death, in Plato's perception of absolute goodness and of the love for its beauty that draws us to recognition of its existence. But the search through the depths of human suffering and sacrifice for the justice that could be only the justice of God is evident in tragedy and would find its objective, its real and eternal meaning and resting place, in the Easter mystery, on Calvary and on Easter morning, and in every Mass.

No believing Christian has lost the tragic sense, the knowledge that justice leads us through suffering into truth. Nor, outside the intellectual world, has the spectacle that is tragedy on the stage of the world ceased to move millions in the West. In Britain in 1997, the death of Diana, Princess of Wales, evoked in the mass of ordinary people a response of collective grief, collective guilt and collective turning toward often long-neglected Christian consolation that shocked only those entirely resistant to God. The royal, the conspicuous, family, whose sins and suffering affect a whole people; the pursuit by the Furies that the city tries to harness as the friendly ones; the hurtle toward violent death of those in the hands of Dionysus: the impulse to respond to this event with prayer would not have surprised the tragic poets, who, to put it at its very simplest, feared God. The story of the Kennedy family, protracted over three generations, has had a similar, if less concentrated, impact in the United States. And in film, the art form of our time that pulls in huge audiences of citizens as once the Athenian plays did, an acknowledged masterpiece of the late twentieth century is the *Godfather* trilogy. Here, against a background of ancestral Christianity that becomes real only in the agonised contrition of the central character, three generations of a proud, successful family are watched through an appalling narrative of blood and revenge until the tragic hero, Michael Corleone, guilty and penitent as the self-blinded Oedipus, the murderous Creon, is left at the end, alive after so much death, with no one and nothing but his knowledge of the truth. As the *Agamemnon* chorus sings:

> Justice tips the scale so that those
> who suffer should learn understanding.[32]

For us still, as for Aeschylus and Sophocles and the Athenian people long ago, the fear of God is the beginning of wisdom.

1. Aeschylus, *Eumenides* 998–1005, in *The Oresteia*, trans. Robert Fagles (London, 1979), p. 275.
2. Hans Urs von Balthasar, *The Glory of the Lord: A Theological Aesthetics*, vol. 4, trans. Brian McNeil et al. (San Francisco and Edinburgh, 1989), p. 120.
3. Aeschylus, *Agamemnon* 160–65, in *Oresteia*, p. 109.
4. Ibid., 174–81, p. 109.
5. Aeschylus, *Prometheus Bound* 92; my translation.
6. Samuel Beckett, *Waiting for Godot* (London, 1965), p. 76.
7. Aeschylus, *Prometheus Bound* 236–43, 250, 252, trans. Philip Vellacott (London, 1961), pp. 27–28.
8. Ibid., 613–14; my translation.
9. Ibid., 1090–94; my translation.
10. Sophocles, *Antigone* 365–72; my translation.
11. Ibid., 350–59, in *The Three Theban Plays*, trans. Robert Fagles (London, 1984), p. 82.
12. Hans Urs von Balthasar, *Theo-Drama*, trans. Graham Harrison, vol. 4 (San Francisco, 1994), p. 111.
13. Sophocles, *Antigone* 1349–53, in *Three Theban Plays*, p. 128.
14. Sophocles, *Oedipus at Colonus* 538–40, in *Three Theban Plays*, p. 316.
15. Ibid., 537–39, p. 319.
16. Ibid., 1561–68, p. 377.
17. Balthasar, *Glory of the Lord* 4:129.
18. George Steiner, *The Death of Tragedy* (London, 1961), pp. 196–97.
19. S. T. Coleridge, *Lay Sermons*, ed. R. J. White (Princeton and London, 1972), p. 30.
20. George Steiner, *Antigones* (Oxford, 1984), p. 140.
21. Ibid., p. 271.
22. Ibid., p. 140.
23. George Steiner, *No Passion Spent* (London, 1996), p. 140.
24. Adrian Poole, *Tragedy: Shakespeare and the Greek Example* (Oxford, 1987), p. 2.
25. Ibid., p. 239.
26. Robert Fagles, "The Serpent and the Eagle", in *Oresteia*, pp. 13–97.
27. Ibid., p. 96.
28. Ibid., p. 94.
29. Balthasar, *Glory of the Lord* 4:14.
30. Ibid., pp. 102–3.
31. Balthasar, *Theo-Drama*, vol. 3 (San Francisco, 1992), p. 42.
32. Aeschylus, *Agamemnon*, lines 250–51; my translation.

CHAPTER THREE

PLATO

Augustine, unlike some of his richer contemporaries in the Latin West of the late Roman Empire, never learned to read Greek fluently: his parents could not afford to keep a Greek tutor in the house, and their clever son, by his own account, was a rebellious and easily bored schoolboy. He knew nothing of the plays of Aeschylus and Sophocles. They had never been translated into Latin and had long disappeared into a few libraries in the Greek East. Of the writing of Plato, whom Augustine all his life revered as the greatest of Greek philosophers, he knew much less than the average modern student of the classics. Only one complete text by Plato, the *Timaeus*, translated into Latin by Cicero, was readily available to him. Otherwise, his knowledge of Plato's writing was limited to still-famous passages—from the *Republic*, *Phaedo* and *Phaedrus* in particular—in anthologies and encyclopaedias and to what of Plato's own work could be distinguished from the grand philosophical systems of the pagan Neoplatonists, Plotinus and Porphyry, teaching in Rome but writing in Greek, much nearer to Augustine's own time. Their books had been translated into Latin, and Augustine read them with passionate enthusiasm not long before he became a committed, adult Christian. Of the essentials of Plato's thought, however—and above all, of the closeness to Christian truth to which that thought, and the grace of God, had led him—Augustine was keenly aware. In his maturity, engaged in the huge work of discrimination in the light of Christianity that was the *City of God*, he placed Plato and his followers "above the rest of the philosophers" because "coming to a knowledge of God, [they] have found the cause of the organized universe, the light by which truth is perceived, and the spring which offers the drink of felicity." [1]

Plato in the fourth century B.C. could not, and Plotinus and Porphyry in the third century A.D. did not, see in Christ the visibility of the invisible God, not only for the few capable of living a philosopher's life in the love of wisdom, but for everyone. Augustine knew that they were wrong about many things. But Plato's acknowledgement of God and of the unity in God of truth, goodness and beauty, fitfully intelligible but not yet visible in the Word made flesh, gives to his writing a value unique in the pre-Christian world. Augustine, for whom all truth was of God, revered Plato because Plato had been given the grace to know that "God himself ... is the light of the mind." [2]

* * *

In book 2 of Plato's *Republic*, written in Athens in about 380 B.C., there is a discussion about the true value of justice. Socrates, the narrator of the story and the leader of its lengthy conversations, has been arguing that justice, the doing of what is right, is in all circumstances better, leads to more real happiness, than injustice or the doing of what is wrong. In order to get Socrates to define his terms more clearly and defend his case more convincingly, Glaucon, another of those present, paints a compelling picture of the unjust man.

The unjust man will cleverly assemble wealth and friends, using his wealth to secure the loyalty of his friends; he will always get away with his wrongdoing, which he will be expert at concealing; he will preserve in all circumstances an unblemished reputation; he will make magnificent sacrifices to the gods, whose approval of his actions will be shown by their successful outcome. "If he makes a mistake he must be able to retrieve it, and, if any of his wrong-doing comes to light, be ready with a convincing defence, or when force is needed be prepared to use force, relying on his own courage and energy or making use of his friends or his wealth." [3] He will, in sum, know how to get hold of power and how to keep it. He has learned the secret of success, which is not to be, but to appear to be, just.

This description of worldly success and how to achieve it has never lost its resonance, its piercing accuracy, because the obtaining and retention of power has never lost its connexion with the studied maintenance of the semblance of virtue. Its bearing on contemporary Western society will not be lost on a modern reader.

Glaucon goes on to describe, in a contrasting portrait, the perfectly just man:

> Beside our picture of the unjust man let us set one of the just man, the man of true simplicity of character who, as Aeschylus says, wants "to be, and not to seem, good". We must, indeed, not allow him to seem good, for if he does he will have all the rewards and honours paid to the man who has a reputation for justice, and we shall not be able to tell whether his motive is love of justice or love of the rewards and honours. No, we must strip him of everything except his justice, and

our picture of him must be drawn in the opposite way to our picture of the unjust man; for our just man must have the worst of reputations even though he has done no wrong. So we shall be able to test his justice and see if it can stand up to unpopularity and all that goes with it; we shall give him an undeserved and lifelong reputation for wickedness, and make him stick to his chosen course until death.... The just man, then, as we have pictured him, will be scourged, tortured, and imprisoned, his eyes will be put out, and after enduring every humiliation he will be crucified, and learn at last that in the world as it is we should want not to be, but to seem, just.[4]

This portrait will strike a Christian reader with hardly less prophetic force than the familiar passage from Isaiah always read before the Passion narrative on Good Friday: "Without beauty, without majesty we saw him, no looks to attract our eyes; a thing despised and rejected by men, a man of sorrows and familiar with suffering, a man to make people screen their faces; he was despised and we took no account of him." [5]

Glaucon's contrast has been drawn over and over again down the almost two and a half millennia since the *Republic* was written. Its essence is there in Augustine's contrast between the man who belongs to the city of God and loves God to the contempt of himself, and the man who belongs only to the earthly city and loves himself to the contempt of God. It is there in Niccolò Machiavelli's prescription for worldly success in *The Prince*, written in the early sixteenth century as the Christian moral consensus began its slow, crumbling collapse. Neither Augustine nor Machiavelli is likely to have read this passage in the *Republic*. Nietzsche in the nineteenth century, the professor of Greek who knew Plato's work well, dispensed with the hypocrisy Glaucon and Machiavelli thought necessary for the success of the unjust man and raised him to the dizzy heights of master-morality, the will to power stripped of any pretended "goodness". Driven as he was by his own need to put beyond further question the death of God, Nietzsche, as we noticed in relation to his view of Greek tragedy, regarded Plato as the most destructive philosopher in history and, in particular, the wrecker of all that was properly "Greek".

Ultimately my mistrust of Plato extends to the very bottom of him: I find him deviated so far from all the fundamental instincts of the Hellenes, so morally infected, so much an antecedent Christian—he already has the concept "good" as the supreme concept—that I should prefer to describe the entire phenomenon "Plato" by the harsh term "higher swindle".[6]

As so often, Nietzsche here is profoundly right in his analysis and at the same time profoundly wrong in his judgement. "In the end to be 'righteous' is simply not to have enough power to be the opposite."[7] This sentence, Balthasar's summary of the above passage in the *Republic*, could have been written by Nietzsche, but his intention would have been precisely the contrary of Balthasar's.

The discussion has indeed taken us into a world of thought very different from that of the tragic poets in manner, but in substance not as different as Nietzsche wanted it to be. The depth of meaning, for example, in Plato's use of the word always translated as "just" he shares with Sophocles, his older contemporary. The word is *dikaios*, from the great noun *Dike*, what is right, the rightness of God, with which, as we saw in *Antigone*, human laws and human deeds may be consonant or not. The word Plato uses for the justice attainable by man, relative rather than absolute goodness, is not *Dike* but *dikaiosune*, translatable perhaps as "justness" or "righteousness".

It was, however, no play, no mythological story brought to life by a poet in a theatre, but a real death imposed, acted and suffered in his own city that inspired not only the portrait of the just man that Glaucon paints in the *Republic*, but the whole of Plato's thinking and writing life.

* * *

When Sophocles's *Oedipus at Colonus* was performed in a defeated and demoralised Athens in the year 402 B.C., Plato was almost certainly in the audience. He was then about thirty years old, a deeply serious young man and a devoted disciple of the great teacher Socrates. He had been much affected by the pain inflicted by, and inflicted on, Athenians during the shambles of the war Athens had lost and by the savagery of Athenian politics since the city's defeat by Sparta. A shaky democracy had just been restored in the city after an unpleasant couple of years in which the brief rule of the so-called Thirty Tyrants, a brutal regime sponsored by Sparta, had been overturned in a violent coup. Two of Plato's uncles were among the Thirty Tyrants. One of these uncles, Critias, also an admirer of Socrates, was killed in 403 in the battle that brought the regime to an end. Although there was an amnesty, to include everyone except the Thirty themselves, the atmosphere of political distrust and defamation in the city was probably responsible for the much more traumatic event, for Plato, of the year 399, the trial and condemnation to death of Socrates.

Plato left Athens. He returned to his city, in quieter and better times, about ten years later and lived there, except for various visits to other Greek cities, as a teacher—the founder, indeed, of the first university of the world, the Academy—until the end of his long life, in 347, when he was nearly eighty. During these forty years of his maturity, he taught the young to think. One of his pupils was Aristotle. And he wrote books that, ever since, have taught his readers to think.

In one of his books, Plato says that he does not rate writing very highly when compared to talking. The trouble with writing, he says, toward the end of the *Phaedrus*, which is itself a soaring flight of the poet-philosopher's imagination, is that people can read what is written without understanding it and then reckon they know what the writing says. A living teacher, questioning, talking, arguing, would not let this happen. Written words cannot explain themselves. "If you ask them what they mean they simply return the same answer over and over again.... Besides," he goes on, "once a thing is committed to writing it circulates equally among those who understand the subject and those who have no business with it; writing cannot distinguish between suitable and unsuitable readers." [8]

Plato, however, wrote nearly thirty separate books that have survived. He was one of the most skilful writers there has ever been, of attractive, vivid, always readable, if sometimes demanding prose. He wrote so well that the spirit of enquiry in his writing, his own excitement in thinking as he wrote, is contagious. This is a rare quality (Augustine has it), different from the systematic exposition of ideas already organised in the writer's mind. Partly through his use of the dialogue form, Plato not only persuades you to think as he does, at least for the time being; he also persuades you to think for yourself as you read. For this very reason it is important to grasp the point of Plato's misgivings about the written as opposed to the spoken word. He would have been, one suspects, depressed by the shelves of commentary on his books that have been produced in the last three hundred years, and, perhaps more, by the complete systems of thought extrapolated from his books by the Neoplatonists whose work was familiar to Augustine.

Plato knew, because Socrates, who wrote nothing, had taught him, that listening, doubting, questioning and understanding mistakes and leaving them on one side is the only way to learn to think. Plato's books do not add up to a system, to a comprehensive explanation of everything; inconclusive, though helpful, arguments over the order in which he wrote them, and anxious tracking of inconsistencies that bother lesser but tidier minds, only show that this is so. He wrote about what interested him most, which was for him and is for us the most profound question there is: how to live. And he wrote out of his own experience of what had impressed and moved and saddened him most: the life and talk and death of Socrates, killed on the city of Athens's charge of corrupting with impiety the minds of the young men of whom Plato himself was one.

A generation earlier, Plato, who could have written anything, might well have written tragedies. He is known to have considered doing so. But, for two reasons that are easy to deduce from what we know, he wrote philosophy instead.

One reason is the change in the Athenian atmosphere that had overtaken everything since the middle of the fifth century B.C., when Aeschylus was old and Sophocles was in his prime. Confidence had seeped from the city, while cleverness—in talk, in government, in the courts, in education and in rhetoric—had climbed to a pitch of wordy conceit, in every sense, that was like nothing seen again until seventeenth-century London and Versailles. The Olympian gods had been sophisticated out of serious consideration by anyone regarding himself as educated: "sophisticated" is the right word, since the fashionable teachers of the time were called "Sophists". Their educational priority was the acquisition of rhetorical skills; this was still the priority of the public world, the *civitas terrena*, eight centuries later, when Augustine was a student in Carthage and a teacher in Rome and Milan. Adeimantus, like Glaucon a Sophist taking part in the discussion in the *Republic* we have looked at above, adds to Glaucon's description of the successful unjust man an elegantly sceptical dismissal of the reality of injustice in relation to the gods:

> If there are no gods or if they care nothing for human affairs, why should we bother to deceive them? And if there are gods and they do care, our only knowledge of them is derived from tradition and the poets ... and they tell us that they can be persuaded to change their minds by sacrifices. . . . If we believe them then the thing to do is to sin first and sacrifice afterwards from the proceeds.[9]

This strikes a note often heard in the modern world and no less familiar to Augustine among the intellectual sceptics of his time. In Plato's Athens, as in the late Roman Empire and in modern Europe, however, observance of the old rites was thought necessary for good order in the city; hence the accusation that Socrates, by his persistent questioning of lazy assumptions, was destroying the piety of the young.

"A man is the measure of all things—of the things that are, that they are; of the things that are not, that they are not",[10] said, according to Plato, Protagoras, the most successful Sophist of Socrates's generation. Socrates, and Plato, could see the terrifying arrogance in this view. It meant in ethics, as it still does, "every man for himself"; in aesthetics, "beauty is in the eye of the beholder" and nowhere else; and in philosophy in general, that there is no objective truth. Plato, on the contrary, devoted years of patient enquiry to the effort to establish that nothing imperfect is the measure of anything and, eventually, that God is the measure of all things. Plato's quest was to find, out of the not knowing that had been Socrates's own faithfully kept position and out of cautious thought checked for error and pride at every point, a reliable truth, a reliable goodness and beauty that could not only be understood but shared in, with which to counter and defeat the brittle relativism that had overtaken Athenian intellectual life.

The second reason that deflected Plato from tragedy into philosophy was the real disaster, the real misery for himself and his friends, and the real mistake, or sin, committed by his city, of Socrates's death. The very priorities that had impelled Sophocles's Creon to have Antigone put to death for her fidelity to the gods had, in the everyday reality of his own shiftless Athens, killed Socrates. Plato, who had loved Socrates and learned from his teaching and from the manner of his death that goodness could be lived, could be shown, could be talked about in words that anyone with a bit of patience could understand, and could be died for, was not going to let his master fade into oblivion with the lives of those who had known him. There was something here that, for the good of people one by one, and for the good of any city prepared to make a serious attempt to improve the quality, the real moral worth, of its citizens' lives, had to be written down. What was it?

As has already been suggested, it was no neat, comprehensive conclusion. Nor was it anything at which Socrates himself had definitively arrived. His method of argument had cleared the way for the asking of large questions but had not, he insisted, answered them. In almost all Plato's books, Socrates himself talks, mostly, but not always, at the centre of the reader's attention. It is obvious that as time passed, the Socrates Plato had known and loved faded into the character he had brought to life over and over again in his own words. The gap between the two has been endlessly and fruitlessly discussed. No reader of Plato needs to worry about what the historical Socrates did or did not say. Socrates was only a human being, if a very remarkable one. Plato tells us who Socrates was for those who learned from him. He tells us how he died and why he did not escape his death when he could have. He gives us, without ever going so far as to describe them, Socrates's goodness and his brilliant intelligence, his wisdom, his sense of humour and his ability (touchingly referred to in the *Theaetetus*)[11] to deliver the unborn thoughts of others. These qualities have survived from that day to this in Plato's words, and whether Socrates actually said most or only a few of the things Plato put into his mouth matters not in the least.

Socrates died because he recognised, and had taught his pupils to recognise, that behind the less and less convincing multitude of gods, often in conflict with each other as they are in tragedy, and especially in Homer, on whose poems every educated Greek was brought up, must lie a single, superior goodness, absolute goodness, by which even the behaviour of the gods may be measured and judged. We recognise this goodness by the shining of its beauty. Once we have seen the beauty in which the good shines, we will love it, and its pursuit will become more important than the pursuit of wealth, reputation or power, the ordinary goals of the educated young men of Athens. Accused by the city of impiety, Socrates's defence at his trial, given us by Plato in the *Apology*, rests on his unshakable piety, his fidelity to this single, absolute good that, often in the dialogues, has to be translated as God. The words he uses in his speech to the court are simple and clear:

> Neither [of my accusers] can do me any harm at all; they would not have the power, because I do not believe that the law of God permits a better man to be harmed by a worse. . . . I suggest, gentlemen, that the difficulty is not so much to escape death; the real difficulty is to escape from wickedness, which is far more fleet of foot. In this present instance I, the slow old man, have been overtaken by the slower of the two, but my accusers, who are clever and quick, have been overtaken by the faster: by iniquity. . . . You too, gentlemen of the jury, must look forward to death with confidence, and fix your minds on this one belief, which is certain; that nothing can harm a good man either in life or after death, and his fortunes are not a matter of indifference to the gods.[12]

The implications of these words were evident to Plato, and if Socrates did indeed speak them at his trial, it could be said that all the rest of Plato's life was devoted to their working out.

Several times in the dialogues that tell the story of Socrates's trial and death, Socrates talks of his own divine sign or protective voice. The untranslatable Greek word is *daimonion*. We can get some idea of what Socrates meant by the word from his insistence that his *daimonion* never tells him to do things, but occasionally tells him only *not* to do things. It is a kind of warning from God, a signal from his conscience, we might say, that prevents him from committing a sin. Accepting his death sentence from the city's court, Socrates says that during his imprisonment and trial his conscience has been quiet, his *daimonion* has not told him to alter his defence or to find a way out of his punishment. If he were offered acquittal on condition that he keep quiet, stop teaching, in the future, he would, he says, reply:

> I am your very grateful and devoted servant, but I owe a greater obedience to God than to you, and so long as I draw breath and have my faculties, I shall never stop practising philosophy. . . . I shall go on saying, in my usual way, ". . . Are you not ashamed that you give your attention to acquiring as much money as possible, and similarly with reputation and honour, and give no attention or thought to truth and understanding and the perfection of your soul?" [13]

The demand that is being made of Socrates, by the pressure of a sense of goodness that he knows is for the good of the whole city, is one that he has to meet.

So Socrates, in the *Apology* and the *Crito*, goes contentedly toward death. For interesting reasons, he refuses the chance to escape. To escape, he says, would be to evade the laws of the city, to which he has long consented, even though in this instance they have been used unjustly against him. He would, by escaping, be returning injustice for injustice, and his soul, concerned with doing what is just, matters more than his body, which will die in any case before very long. Plato wants to astonish us with this, and he does.

In the *Phaedo*, which gives us Socrates's last conversation and quiet death, the value of the soul is explained, as it has to be, by its immortality. Suicide is never the right course, because we do not possess our souls; they belong to God and after death will join the good, those close to God, with him. The soul is from God and returns to him, if we face in the right direction, if we face the light rather than the darkness, while we are alive:

> True philosophers make dying their profession, and to them of all men death is least alarming. Would they not naturally be glad to set out for the place where there is a prospect of attaining the object of their life-long desire, which is wisdom? Surely there are many who have been happy to follow those they have loved to the next world, in the hope

of seeing and meeting there the persons whom they loved. If this is so, will a true lover of wisdom who has firmly grasped this same conviction—that he will never attain to wisdom worthy of the name elsewhere than in the next world—will he be grieved at dying? Will he not be glad to make that journey? We must suppose so, my friend; that is, if he is a genuine lover of wisdom; because then he will be of the firm belief that he will never find wisdom in all its purity in any other place. . . .

The soul, the invisible part, goes away to a place that is, like itself, glorious, pure and invisible—the true Hades or unseen world—into the presence of the good and wise God, where, if God so wills, my soul must shortly go. . . .

If the soul is immortal, it demands our care not only for that part of time which we call life, but for all time; and indeed it would seem now that it will be extremely dangerous to neglect it. If death were a release from everything, it would be a boon for the wicked, because by dying they would be released not only from the body but also from their own wickedness together with the soul; but as it is, since the soul has emerged as something immortal, it can have no escape or security from evil except by becoming as good and wise as it possibly can.[14]

The immortality of the soul, the whole truth of its goodness or evil known in the eternity of God, is the answer, of course, and the only sufficient answer, to the worldly scepticism of Socrates's opponents both in the *Republic* discussion and in real life. These pages of the *Phaedo*, the tentative sketch of what we would call heaven (reversing the negative sense of "Hades" ordinary in the Greek world), the calm and humour—not unlike Sir Thomas More's—with which Socrates dies, unjustly killed among his grieving friends, are a golden moment in Greek classical writing. They cannot fail, to this day, to move and amaze a Christian.

Nor can a quite different passage, this one written by Plato the poet, the image-finder. In the parable of the cave in book 7 of the *Republic*, a famous passage known to Augustine, people are imprisoned in a cave with their backs to a fire, watching shadows on the wall, taking them for reality. (We think the physical, material world of time and change is all the reality there is.) Plato imagines that someone is taken outside, past the fire, into the light. Gradually, as his eyes become accustomed to the brightness, he can see more and more, first reflections in water, then objects themselves, then the moon and stars and at last the sun itself. Then he will understand that it is the sun that gives all life and light, and therefore all sight, even to the prisoners among the shadows in the cave. A few minutes earlier in the conversation, Socrates has explained to Glaucon how he is using the sun as an analogy for ultimate good, for God, for the truth itself:

"The sun, I think you will agree, not only makes the things we see visible, but causes the processes of generation, growth and nourishment, without itself being such a process."

"True."

"The Good therefore may be said to be the source not only of the intelligibility of the objects of knowledge, but also of their existence and reality; yet it is not itself identical with reality, but is beyond reality, and superior to it in dignity and power." [15]

So the sun in the parable of the cave is the Good; the sight it makes possible is the perception of the truth and is also love. Augustine, criticising materialist philosophers, who look only at the reflections in the cave, wrote: "I always wonder what bodily senses they use to see that beauty which they say is found only in the wise. With what physical eyes have they beheld the beauty and grace of wisdom?" [16] But Socrates ends his lesson:

"What do you think would happen if [the man who has learned to see] went back to sit in his old seat in the cave? Wouldn't his eyes be blinded by the darkness, because he had come in suddenly out of the daylight?"

"Certainly."

"And if he had to discriminate between the shadows, in competition with the other prisoners, wouldn't he be likely to make a fool of himself? And they would say that his visit to the upper world had ruined his sight, and that the ascent was not worth even attempting. And if he tried to release them and lead them up, they would kill him if they could lay hands on him." [17]

They would take him for a fool and, perhaps, a criminal. And then they would kill him—as they had killed Socrates. As, four centuries after Plato wrote this parable, they killed Jesus.

* * *

The imagery of light and dark, of the seeing, in the light of the good, of truth, things as they really are, recurs often in Plato. After much talking in dialogue after dialogue, many attempts tested, failed and left behind at the definition of goodness, justice and beauty, Plato comes back over and over again to the absolute goodness that is never to be possessed but is, at last, to be seen. "Seeing" is more than a metaphor, and we are used to it. When someone explains something difficult to us and at last we understand, "I *see*", we say. It is at the heart of Plato—and "heart" is the right word—that to see the good is to know it, and to know it is to desire it, to want to come closer and closer to it in the course of a virtuous life. Through much lucid discussion and many parables and examples taken from the life he knew and also, when plain prose fails him, from the myths and stories of Greece, this is Plato's answer to the questions Socrates had asked. How should we live? And *why* is this how we should live? If we transpose Plato's answers into words we know well, we find that they tell us we should live in the love of God, so as to live at last in the sight of God, *in conspectu Dei*, with the full force of the double meaning of the words: "in God's sight of us; in our sight of God". It could be said that it is Plato's discovery of answers to Socrates's questions that took him to his conviction that absolute beauty, truth and goodness are not only intelligible, as Socrates had taught, but really exist, in the being, in the unity, of God.

The *Symposium* is the book in which Plato comes closest to writing of the love of God, in particular of how we may find our way from our experience of human love to a love of God's goodness, beauty and truth in which human love is not cancelled but taken up into a greater reality. This is a short and compellingly readable account of a dinner party at which the guests speak in turn on the given subject of love. The people at the party are real historical figures; its date, in the year before the disastrous Athenian expedition to Sicily, is too early for Plato himself to have been present but gives the occasion a glow of cheerfulness that Plato's readers would have recognised as doomed. This is particularly true of the glamorous Alcibiades, hubristic leader of the Sicilian expedition, here a young man of dazzling talent and shameless charm.

The relaxed atmosphere of the evening, and the cumulative effect of half a dozen speeches on love that vary in quality and length, are presented by Plato with such skill that the most engaging speech before that of Socrates does not immediately precede his but is allowed to make a memorable impact of its own. Aristophanes, the comic dramatist, gives his audience a fable, both funny and poignant, which accounts for love as a universal human drive by supposing an original state of wholeness, severed by a resentful Zeus, so that all human beings are no more than halves, each searching, usually in vain, for his or her only other half. The effect of this fable is to remind those present, and every reader, of the neediness, the pain, and the always-possible fulfilment, of their own experience of love. This prepares us for the climax of the book, Socrates's speech, which is the longest and, of course, much the most profound.

Socrates gives the party the story of a lesson on love he himself received from a wise woman, Diotima, clearly invented by Plato for this purpose. To account for his intermediary character, for love is between the human and the divine, Love himself is given a mythical birth as the child of Poverty, his mother, and Resourcefulness, his father. He is poor, like his mother, homeless and lives in need. But he is "wise and fertile in expedients" like his father, and the ultimate object of his efforts is always wisdom. "Wisdom is one of the most beautiful things, and Love is love of beauty, so it follows that Love must be a lover of wisdom, and consequently in a state half-way between wisdom and ignorance."[18] "Love is love of beauty": this turns out to be the key to what follows, a description of love gradually increasing in depth and intensity until it reaches the love of God.

We ordinarily speak of love, says Socrates, as if it meant only sexual love. But, though our experience of love is bound to start with love for "one particular beautiful person", we are capable of rising by steps, through love of the goodness of others (beauty of soul), of the beauty of ideas, and of knowledge, to our "final goal", the love of beauty itself, "which neither comes into being nor passes away". The lover who has reached this goal will see beauty "as absolute, existing alone with itself, unique, eternal, and all other beautiful things partaking of it, yet in such a manner that, while they come into being and pass away, it neither undergoes any increase or diminution nor suffers any change."[19] A Christian reader will be most of all impressed by the consequences of this vision, which are consequences for the soul in the life of God, affirmed by Socrates in the conclusion to his account of Diotima's lesson:

> Do you not see that in that region alone where he sees beauty with the faculty capable of seeing it, will he be able to bring forth not mere reflected images of goodness but true goodness, because he will be in contact not with a reflection but with the truth? And having brought forth and nurtured true goodness he will have the privilege of being beloved of God, and becoming, if ever a man can, immortal himself.[20]

Socrates's speech in the *Symposium* is perhaps the high point of what has often been called Plato's natural theology, the ascent through contemplation of what is beautiful, true and good toward belief in the existence of God. It is the perception of the whole speech that the quality, the goodness, of love is given it by that to which it is directed. Knowledge becomes goodness only if it is knowledge of God. Plato's thought here and in the other passages we have looked at is flawed, for a Christian, only by his unsurprising separation of the soul from the body, a dualism that with his conviction that the soul is immortal he had no way of avoiding. His belief in God awaits its completion in the light of the Incarnation and Resurrection of Christ and of the revelation of the Holy Trinity.

*   *   *

Two hundred fifty years nearer to Plato in time than Augustine was, and much better acquainted with Plato's books, Saint Justin, a Greek convert to Christianity, was martyred in Rome during the persecution of the emperor Marcus Aurelius in 165. In direct homage to Plato, and to Socrates, whose death Justin regarded as a martyrdom in the cause of God's truth, he wrote two *Apologies* (borrowing the title from Plato) making the case for Christianity to the emperor himself. Justin saw no reason not to welcome truth as truth wherever it was to be found. "Whatever has been spoken aright by any man", he wrote, "belongs to us Christians; for we worship and love, next to God, the Logos which is from the unbegotten and ineffable God ... [and] those writers were able, through the seed of the Logos implanted in them, to see reality darkly." [21] He by no means adjusts Christian truth to fit what was by then the mould of late, academic Platonism. Rather, he uses Christian truth to sort out what was consonant with it, in what Plato had actually written, from what was not. One of the strongest points in the case he makes is that Christianity, unlike the philosophy of Plato, can be understood and lived at any level, by the illiterate or by slaves as well as by the privileged or the philosophically educated. He was also confident, as Pascal and Coleridge in the far future would be, that once Christianity has been properly explained, and Christian life faithfully lived has been observed with an open mind, conversion is sure to follow.

This engaging and hopeful freshness marks Justin's whole approach to the harmonies between Plato and Christian truth. He perceived, with awe, that Plato, by the use of reason (at its highest always one with Christ, the reason, or Logos, of God) had come very near to much truth, though making, as he was bound to, mistakes now evident in the light of revelation. On his way to a fully orthodox understanding of God as three-in-one—though the use of the word "Trinity" was still fifty years in the future at his death—Justin was particularly impressed by the hints of such an understanding that he found in Plato's *Timaeus*.

The *Timaeus* has an exceptional place in the history of Plato's works in the West. We have seen that Cicero translated it into Latin, so that Augustine read it properly. Chalcidius in the fourth century translated it again; his version was read in the monasteries and schools of Latin Christendom during all the centuries in which the rest of Plato was unknown in the West. The *Timaeus* is a remarkable text, even by Plato's always remarkable standards. It is a narrative of creation that ascribes the creation of the universe, as a work of art with a purpose, to the will of God put into effect by a *demiourgos*, or maker, who "fixed his gaze on the eternal". This is a wholly original notion in Greek philosophy. It has enough in common with the account of creation in Genesis for many down the ages (including Augustine and, more surprisingly, Nietzsche) to have deduced, certainly wrongly, that Plato had some contact with ancient Israel. It is the case, however, that there is some influence the other way around: the Jewish translators of the Hebrew Scriptures into Greek in third-century B.C. Alexandria (the Septuagint) used, in their version of Genesis, some of the important words in the *Timaeus*—for example, *arche* (beginning), *genesis* (creation) and *kosmos* (order)—with the same freight of meaning as Plato. It was difficult to reconcile the Creator God of Genesis with the *demiourgos* of the *Timaeus* until the revelation of God in his Son made it possible for early Christian writers, Saint John above all, to identify the maker of all things with the Logos, the Word, of God, before long to be recognised as the second Person of the Trinity.

The part played by Plato in this process is more definite even than the influence of the *Timaeus* on the Greek translation of Genesis. The Book of Wisdom, written in Greek by a Jewish sage in the first century B.C. and always included in the Catholic, though not the Protestant, Bible, has in it not only much of Plato's vocabulary but also some of his most penetrating thought:

> The godless say to themselves ... "Let our strength be the yardstick of virtue, since weakness argues its own futility. Let us lie in wait for the virtuous man, since he annoys us and opposes our way of life, reproaches us for our breaches of the law and accuses us of playing false to our upbringing. He claims to have knowledge of God, and calls himself a son of the Lord. Before us he stands, a reproof to our way of thinking, the very sight of him weighs our spirits down; his way of life is not like other men's, the paths he treads are unfamiliar. In his opinion we are

counterfeit; he holds aloof from our doings as though from filth; he proclaims the final end of the virtuous as happy and boasts of having God as his father. Let us see if what he says is true, let us observe what kind of end he himself will have. If the virtuous man is God's son, God will take his part and rescue him from the clutches of his enemies. Let us test him with cruelty and with torture, and thus explore this gentleness of his and put his endurance to the proof. Let us condemn him to a shameful death since he will be looked after—we have his word for it."

This is the way they reason, but they are misled, their malice makes them blind. They do not know the hidden things of God, they have no hope that holiness will be rewarded, they can see no reward for blameless souls.... But the souls of the virtuous are in the hands of God, no torment shall ever touch them.[22]

We are poised here between Socrates and Christ. Saint John, Saint Paul and the writer of the Letter to the Hebrews made constructive use of the Book of Wisdom in their finding of words for the coming, which they knew had changed everything, of the Word of God as a man among men. It is not the case that Plato's philosophy makes sense of the revelation of God in Christ, but that the revelation of God in Christ, the Incarnation and Resurrection that healed Plato's soul–body dualism, makes sense of Plato's philosophy, the sense that Plato himself could not make. "Man", in Balthasar's words, "is not able to anticipate the synthesis of the *Verbum-caro*; it is the only solution and yet could never be arrived at by guesswork."[23] Plato came very close. In the fable of the chariot of the soul in the *Phaedrus*, where, in the fallen world of mortality, Love, the charioteer, may or may not regain lost control of the fighting horses he has to drive, Plato wrote:

There is not a single sound reason for positing the existence of a [human] being who is immortal, but because we have never seen or formed an adequate idea of a god, we picture him to ourselves as a being of the same kind as ourselves but immortal, a combination of soul and body indissolubly joined for ever. The existence of such beings and the use of such language about them we must leave to the will of God.[24]

In the *Timaeus*, he wrote: "To discover the maker and father of the universe is indeed a hard task, and having found him it would be impossible to tell everyone about him."[25] Origen in the third century made the exactly appropriate comment on this sentence:

But consider whether there is not more regard for the needs of mankind when the divine word introduces the divine Logos, who was in the beginning with God, as becoming flesh, so that the Logos, of whom Plato says that after finding him it is impossible to declare him to all men, might be able to reach anybody.[26]

* * *

And what of Plato now? Like the tragedies of Aeschylus and Sophocles, Plato's books, as whole texts, were, except for the *Timaeus*, unknown in the West until well into the Renaissance. Meanwhile, all the surviving works of Aristotle had arrived by the twelfth century; Aristotle, for the philosophical theologians of the Scholastic period, was "the philosopher", as Plato had been for Augustine. Aristotle took Plato's exemplary use of reason forward in all sorts of ways but had nothing himself to say about the love of God. So the Plato that is in Scholastic theology, and much is, is coloured by the late and partial understanding of him in Augustine's work and then tidied by the orderliness of Aristotelian method and terminology. When Plato himself became properly known—there were no translations of Plato into English, for example, until the seventeenth century—it was too late for the truth in Plato to be received as simply vindicated by the fuller truth of Christianity. All theological discussion had become muddied by the upheaval of the Reformation, and theology and philosophy, as we shall see later in this book, had long since definitively parted company. While Plato in the eighteenth and nineteenth centuries was regarded by most philosophers with respect, as the founder of disciplined, rational enquiry into the nature of thought, of the soul and of man, he was also generally regarded, by thinkers slipping rapidly and easily from theism to atheism, as wrong, wrong above all in his inescapable emphasis on transcendent truth, goodness and beauty as real and as one. At the end of the nineteenth century, Nietzsche, as we have seen, despised him as a harbinger of Christianity and prime denier of the ugliness of the truth.

Contemporary thinkers in Nietzsche's shadow who respond to the beauty, the attractiveness, of Plato's central ideas are likely to find themselves faced with a serious difficulty. If intellectual honesty compels us to recognise "man as the measure of all things" in the meaningless universe we inhabit, then any concession to Plato's sense of transcendent meaning must be intellectually dishonest. And yet the *Symposium* in particular, the subject of which appeals to everyone always, pulls its reader powerfully in the direction of the God who is supposed to be dead. Two Jewish intellectuals of our own time provide instructive examples of this dilemma.

George Steiner has written with anguished warmth about, in particular, the *Phaedo* and the *Symposium*, comparing the deaths of Socrates and Jesus in a manner familiar since Saint Justin. Steiner has an understandable fear of the possible reality of the transcendent evident to Plato and more evident to Jews and Christians in the God who, in Balthasar's words, "[*turned*] *toward* a lost world, in Jesus Christ and, earlier, in the election of Israel".[27] This fear arises from Steiner's horror of Christian anti-Semitism, a dreadful evil and an indelible stain on the history of the Church, though no part, as Pope John Paul II repeatedly insisted, of true Christian belief. Because of it, Steiner slides away from the real demand for consent that even Plato makes. He does this by asking immense questions— "What would happen if we had to pay our debts towards theology and the metaphysics of presence? What if the loans of belief in transcendence, made to us since Plato and Augustine in reference to signifying form, were called in?"[28]— and then by refusing to answer them. And also by denying, in true Nietzschean style, that truth is anchored in the eternal truth that gave, for Plato, its meaning to Socrates's death and gives, in Christian plenitude, its meaning to the Cross. In an essay on the *Phaedo* and the death of Jesus, Steiner finds it necessary to say, in accordance with the spirit of the age: "The language-games of the sacred may well be more widely sovereign, more poignant and unsettling, than are others played (i.e. spoken and written) by men. But they remain language-games whose only validation must be internal."[29] But he ends the essay with a tentative "And yet ..." This essay was written in 1993. The "and yet" allows one to hope that he has moved a little from the Nietzschean contempt of a 1981 essay in the same book: "Ninety-nine per cent of humanity conducts lives either of severe deprivation—physical, emotional, cerebral—or contributes nothing to the sum of insight, of beauty, of moral trial in our civil condition. It is a Socrates, a Mozart, a Gauss or a Galileo who, in some degree, compensate for man",[30] a sadly revealing couple of sentences. (It is, incidentally, typical of Steiner to make the ordinary literate reader hurry to a reference book for news of Gauss. He was a nineteenth-century mathematician.)

Allan Bloom, by contrast, in a fine chapter of more than a hundred pages on the *Symposium* in his posthumously published book *Love and Friendship*, fully acknowledges that at the top of the ladder of love described in Socrates's speech there is God. Physical love gives place to intellectual love, which in turn gives place to spiritual love. "This last segment", says Bloom,

> contains the most mysterious and mystical pronouncements of his teaching, and access to them is certainly beyond me.... It is a description of

the rewards in store for the one who undertakes the philosophical life, which are parallel to the rewards promised to the person who undertakes the Christian life. Of course, this description is much less admissible by a philosopher, who is by definition a doubter, than by a Christian, who is by definition a believer.[31]

A little later he even says, of one of his intellectual heroes: "It is not so clear that Nietzsche is as right as most scholars today believe."[32] But, as a doubting philosopher, he has, or believes he has, no alternative to his conclusion: "It is true that the objects of the philosopher's contemplation are immortal, but Diotima wishes to make us forget that the philosopher is not."[33]

This, as Plato knew very well, is the nub. He could not connect his belief in the immortality of the soul to the eternal trinitarian life of God, which had not yet been revealed. But it is permissible to suppose that he would have consented at least to the strength of a single sentence of Balthasar: "[Christianity] solves the unbearable contradiction that runs right through the very form of man: that he, knowing and touching what is immortal, yet dies; if it does not solve this then it solves nothing at all."[34]

What Plato knew of the love of God was to be immeasurably deepened in the light of revelation by the Fathers of the Church and especially by Augustine, but what he knew was already true. "For God", wrote Clement of Alexandria in about A.D. 200,

is the source of all good, either directly, as in the Old and New Testaments, or indirectly, as in the case of philosophy. But it may even be that philosophy was given to the Greeks directly; for it was "a schoolmaster", to bring Hellenism to Christ, as the Law was for the Hebrews.[35]

1. Augustine, *City of God* 8.10, trans. Henry Bettenson (London, 1972), p. 313.
2. Ibid., 8.7, p. 309.
3. Plato, *Republic* 361, trans. H.D.P. Lee (London, 1955), p. 92.
4. Ibid.
5. Is 53:2–3.
6. Friedrich Nietzsche, *Twilight of the Idols*, trans. R.J. Hollingdale (London, 1968), p. 106.
7. Hans Urs von Balthasar, *The Glory of the Lord: A Theological Aesthetics*, vol. 4, trans. Brian McNeil et al. (San Francisco and Edinburgh, 1989), p. 170.
8. Plato, *Phaedrus*, trans. Walter Hamilton (London, 1995), p. 77.
9. Plato, *Republic* 365, p. 97.
10. Plato, *Theaetetus* 152a, trans. Robin A.H. Waterfield (London, 1987), p. 30.
11. Ibid., 148e–151d, pp. 25–29.

12. Plato, *Apology* 30d, 39a–b, 41c–d, in *The Last Days of Socrates*, trans. Hugh Tredennick and Harold Tarrant (London, 1993), pp. 54, 64, 66–67.
13. Ibid., 29d, p. 53.
14. Plato, *Phaedo* 67e–68a, 80d, 107c–d, in *Last Days of Socrates*, pp. 121, 139, 174.
15. Plato, *Republic* 509, p. 273.
16. Augustine, *City of God* 8.7, p. 309.
17. Plato, *Republic* 516–17, p. 281.
18. Plato, *Symposium* 204b, trans. W. Hamilton (London, 1951), p. 83.
19. Ibid., 211b, p. 94.
20. Ibid., 212a, p. 95.
21. Justin, *Apologia II* 13, in *The Early Christian Fathers*, ed. and trans. Henry Bettenson (Oxford, 1956), pp. 63–64.
22. Wis 2:11–22; 3:1.
23. Hans Urs von Balthasar, *Theo-Drama*, trans. Graham Harrison, vol. 4 (San Francisco, 1994), p. 104.
24. Plato, *Phaedrus*, p. 30.
25. Plato, *Timaeus* 29, trans. H. D. P. Lee (London, 1965), pp. 40–41.
26. Origen, *Contra Celsum* 7.42–43, quoted in Jaroslav Pelikan, *What Has Athens to Do with Jerusalem?* (Ann Arbor, 1997), p. 95.
27. Balthasar, *Theo-Drama* 4:76.
28. George Steiner, *Real Presences* (London, 1989), p. 134.
29. George Steiner, "Two Cocks", in *No Passion Spent* (London, 1996), p. 388.
30. George Steiner, "The Archives of Eden", in *No Passion Spent*, pp. 274–75.
31. Allan Bloom, *Love and Friendship* (New York, 1993), pp. 517–18.
32. Ibid., p. 521.
33. Ibid., p. 523.
34. Hans Urs von Balthasar, *The Glory of the Lord: A Theological Aesthetics*, vol. 7, trans. Brian McNeil (San Francisco and Edinburgh, 1989), p. 83.
35. Clement of Alexandria, in *Early Christian Fathers*, p. 168.

CHAPTER FOUR

ROME

Cicero and Virgil

Cicero and Virgil, the greatest Latin writers of the last century B.C., were those on whose work Augustine, four hundred years later, was brought up. It was an education in reading and writing, though for him in his native language, that he shared with every well-educated person in Western Christendom until the second half of the twentieth century. Cicero and Virgil lived in the period of protracted and bloody power struggle that destroyed the old Roman republic. The eventual result of the struggle was the Augustan peace, sole rule over the Roman world by Octavius Caesar Augustus, Julius Caesar's great-nephew and adopted son, who became the first Roman emperor. Cicero, orator, statesman and writer of prose so supple and compelling that it became the model for Western writers thinking in prose for many centuries, was killed in 43 B.C., before the convulsions of the civil wars were over. Virgil the poet, a generation younger, lived to celebrate, with the favour of Augustus, the new order of the empire and died in 19 B.C. Between them, these two, Cicero consciously, Virgil on account of the particular weight of his work, were responsible for the literary and historical emphasis of Roman education after their time, and of, ever since, "the humanities". This label Cicero, who wrote, "not to know what happened before you were born is to remain always a child",[1] would have thoroughly approved.

Late in the imperial day, Augustine, a small boy at school in Thagaste, the North African Roman town where he was born, hated learning multiplication tables and lists of Greek words but loved the stories in Virgil's *Aeneid*. Virgil's poems never left his memory and his imagination; they were as distant from him in time as Shakespeare is from us and as inwardly familiar as Shakespeare is to a literate English speaker anywhere. Cicero's example, for Augustine as for hundreds of other gifted boys in the Roman world, was a matter of public life and of success in it as well as a matter of the mind. The way to fame and fortune for those without senatorial rank or military talent, in Cicero's late republic as in

Augustine's late empire, was the art of persuasive speaking and writing. It was the path that Cicero, born in 106 B.C. to an ambitious, rich, but not senatorial father, had followed with conspicuous success. It was still the path out of obscurity for Augustine, born in A.D. 354 to a minor local official with little land or money but one or two useful connexions. At grammar school in Madauros, twenty miles from home, the thirteen- or fourteen-year-old Augustine read more Virgil with more attention and began, no doubt from the famous speeches and textbooks of Cicero, to learn the art of oratory. As an eighteen-year-old student of rhetoric in Carthage, the metropolis and university city of Roman Africa, he came across the *Hortensius*, a dialogue, now largely lost, in which Cicero recommended a life of philosophy, or the pursuit of wisdom, in a world of suffering and distraction. Augustine was supposed to be reading this work for its "refining effect on my style and literary expression". However, he found himself reading it for what it said, and the effect on him was indelible. Twenty-five years later in the *Confessions*, his autobiography, he wrote, with hindsight lit by faith, "The book changed my feelings. It altered my prayers, Lord, to be towards yourself." [2]

Both Cicero and Virgil came, as we shall see, in the course of Augustine's long career as a Christian writer and thinker, to be placed by him in appropriate, and in many ways distant, relation to Christian truth. But because of the particular qualities of what they wrote, and because what they wrote had a lasting influence on the writing of the Christian tradition, each of them deserves a brief discussion in the story this book is attempting to tell.

* * *

Cicero was educated as well as it was possible for a young Roman of his generation to be, and very much better than Augustine. He spent two lengthy periods in Athens studying philosophy, history and rhetoric from the texts that remained from the city's golden age and in the schools that had inherited the traditions of Plato and Aristotle and of the later Stoics and Epicureans whose founders, Zeno and Epicurus, had also lived and taught there. As well as being a public servant and a politician mired in the grisly realities of the late republic, Cicero always thought of himself as a "philosopher" and, until Augustine himself, came closer to being one than anyone else whose first language was Latin. He was an eclectic popularizer of Greek thought in all its conflicting variety, a serious reader, moved by ideas, and a serious writer on the large questions of life and death, but not a coherent independent thinker. He never departed from the convictions that truth is to be sought and respected, that there is a real difference between right and wrong, and that a great man will always choose to do what is right, but he was never sure of the grounds for these convictions, and at the deepest level he remained undecided, a civilised and liberal sceptic. Of Plato he said, according to Plutarch, who wrote Cicero's biography a century after his death, that "if it were in the nature of God to converse in human words, this would be how he would do it." [3] But Plutarch quotes this only as a clever remark, and on the subject of God, or the good to be aspired to for its own sake whatever the consequences in the world, Cicero never abandoned the conditional "if". "He lives", Balthasar wrote of him, "entirely on a knife-edge in this respect",[4] as Plato had not. Cicero is sharply critical of the proto-Nietzschean materialism and self-sufficiency of the Epicureans, who reckoned it was possible "to live like a god among men: it is meaningless to demand from the gods what human beings can do for themselves." [5] On the other hand, his own proto-Nietzschean perspectivism—"let each man defend what he believes: judgement is free"[6]— made him hesitant about, for example, the immortality of the soul. His late, wise and heartfelt dialogue *On Old Age* ends with the cautious hope that there is "a better world" beyond the grave, but also with the thoroughly perspectivist rider—what one believes will be what happens—that since the Epicureans do not believe in the immortal soul, "at least I need not fear that after their own deaths they will be able to mock my conviction." [7]

The half-serious, half-playful tone of this is characteristic of Cicero's philosophical writing, as is the less attractive confusion, in this same concluding section of *On Old Age*, between immortality and fame. "Somehow my soul seemed to understand that its true life would only begin after my death: alertly, unceasingly, it fastened its gaze upon the generations to come. The souls of our finest men engage in this pursuit of immortal fame—and they would not feel this urge unless immortality were really in store for them." [8] He would have been delighted to find himself still famous more than two millennia after his death. His most renowned short piece, *The Dream of Scipio*, attached to the end of his *On the State*, most of which was lost for centuries, was popular all over Christendom throughout the Middle Ages. It gives a cosmological sketch of heaven, compared to which the lives of human beings are small and transient, but this heaven is nevertheless only for heroes, great public figures who have been good and wise in the service of the state.

The times Cicero lived in were so dreadful, so racked by the consequences of unchecked *libido dominandi*—his phrase, adopted by Augustine—that his own integrity, when he held positions of authority in Sicily and Cilicia and when he attacked, in speeches that have resounded down the ages, the most disreputable

Romans of his day, did shine against a dark background just as he would have wished. As consul in 63 B.C. he bravely, but unconstitutionally, saw off the conspiracy of the criminal Catiline. He lived through and loathed the dictatorships of Sulla and Julius Caesar. He chose to back Pompey against Julius Caesar, and later Octavius Caesar against Mark Antony, but neither Pompey nor Octavius was any less driven by the lust for power than his opponents, nor could either rise to the magnanimity with which Julius Caesar treated Cicero, his enemy. The brutal first triumvirate (the rule of three, which included Pompey and Julius Caesar) Cicero saw disintegrate into new civil war. The second triumvirate murdered Cicero when one powerful member of it, Octavius, whom Cicero had supported against another, Mark Antony, failed to deny Antony his revenge for Cicero's fierce verbal attacks on him. All Cicero's life, he observed a political world, in his own words, of "theft, forgery, poisoning, assassination, the spoliation of fellow citizens and allies, a thirst for ascendancy—*libido dominandi*—over free men."⁹

He never failed to plead, in speeches and in books, for honesty, trustworthiness, fair dealing and justice in public life, even in the treatment of foreigners and slaves. He pleaded for these qualities because they were right and good, but above all because he was sure that only these qualities could bring to an end the corruption, violence and terror that prevailed in Roman government. His objective was always a return to what he saw as the virtuous republic of the past. In a speech, he listed the "foundations" of that republic. His list included "executive authority, senatorial influence, statute and customary law, imperial prestige, military and financial strength", but it began with "the official religion of worship and divination".¹⁰ The senior figures who conducted this religion were public servants appointed by the state; Cicero himself served as an augur, responsible for magic divination, in which he certainly did not believe. "It is part of wisdom", he wrote, meaning useful for the keeping of order in the state, "to preserve the institutions of our ancestors by retaining their sacred rites and ceremonies."¹¹ "Religion" in this Roman sense had nothing to do with philosophy, but philosophy, for Cicero, had much to do with morality, and morality was no less a civic affair than was religion. The virtues he recommends are virtues, but his principal reason for recommending them is that they work. In his most read book, *De officiis* (*On Duties*), he recognises that the civic virtues that are his subject belong to a "second-class kind of goodness", possible for anyone and not "the exclusive possession of the hypothetical man of ideal wisdom".¹² At the same time he insists that to do what is right brings happiness and that what is right and what is advantageous never conflict. It could be said that the eventual stability restored by Octavius Caesar as the emperor Augustus proved his case: comparatively benevolent and orderly government improved life for the citizens over whom the emperor ruled. But it was by no means true of Octavius that what was right was the same as what was advantageous. Octavius's behaviour up to his final defeat of Mark Antony in 31 B.C. had been more treacherous and cruel than that of Julius Caesar, of whom Cicero had written:

> If we follow the standards of public opinion, no greater advantage can be imagined than to be an absolute ruler. But when we apply the standard of truth instead, the man who has achieved this position by wrongful means proves to have acted entirely at variance with his own interests. Agonies of anxiety, terrors day and night, a life of incessant plots and dangers, cannot possibly bring any advantage.

This description, sure to have been familiar to Shakespeare, could be of Macbeth, a Christian sinner with a tortured conscience. But Cicero typically swerves from "the standard of truth" to the standard of reputation when he ends this passage: "How can anyone derive benefit from his own life, if unheard-of popularity and glory can be won by its destruction?" [13] Elsewhere in *On Duties*, he actually contrasts the evil of *libido dominandi* with the good, not of a clear conscience—much though he approves of a clear conscience—but with *appetitio principatus*, the desire for preeminence or glory. In *On Christian Teaching*, a textbook for preachers and readers of Scripture written in conscious apposition to Cicero, Augustine made a Christian distinction between what we should love or enjoy—the truth and goodness and beauty of God—and what we should use because it brings us closer to what we love. By this exacting standard, it is hard to avoid the conclusion that Cicero was inclined to regard a good and truthful life as useful because it brings a person closer to an unblemished reputation. In one of his own rhetorical manuals, used, though with caution, by Augustine because for him Cicero and eloquence were the same thing, Cicero says that it is *honestas*, honour or reputation, "that draws us by its power and entices us by its *dignitas*", which means that for which we are respected. [14]

Locked, as he was bound to be, into the *civitas terrena*, Cicero thought philosophy without value unless it was useful for the achievement of a happy life and in the development of a just society. He deduced from the mixed views of the philosophers he had read, however, that all human beings have in them a spark of reason given them by reason itself, which created the universe. "Since there is nothing better than reason," he wrote, "and since it exists both in man and God, the first common possession of man and God is reason." [15] Reason tells us that all our fellow men should be treated justly. "True law is reason, right and natural, commanding people to fulfil their obligations and prohibiting and deterring them from doing wrong." [16] Since reason is universal, people can be taught to understand the value to themselves and to the earthly city of integrity, honesty, respect and care for others. The morality that results from this view is readily compatible with Christianity, but the optimism is not. From Augustine to the "humanists"—a Ciceronian label—of the Renaissance, learned in classical literature and devout Christians, Cicero's ethics were absorbed without friction into Christian teaching: the cardinal virtues, for example—prudence, justice, temperance and fortitude—which he took from Plato and Aristotle, were, when supported by the theological virtues of faith, hope and love, sound Christian principles of behaviour. But when belief in trinitarian Christianity ceased to support Christian morality in the Enlightenment, as deism melted away to atheism, both Cicero's confidence in reason and his worldly priorities returned to favour along with his optimism. He was much admired by Voltaire. Coleridge early in the nineteenth century regarded "humanism" as the final stage of a descent from belief in Christ as the Word made flesh through admiration of him as a wise but merely human being to atheist disregard for him: "humanism" already meant what it means today, though "humane" and "humanitarian" are still words with some Ciceronian weight attached to them.

Cicero's own optimism, his confidence in reason and in education—he shared with all classical thinkers the assumption that once virtue was understood, virtuous action would follow—was constantly battered by the realities of the world in which he was living. The ugliness of how things were in the first century B.C. made him a conservative as well as a liberal, not unlike Matthew Arnold in the second half of the nineteenth century hoping to improve the moral quality of his time by getting people to understand "the best that has been said and thought" in the past. Cicero in despair—"The real Rome is gone for ever"—had to look back to great men of the previous century to find examples of virtuous lives for his contemporaries to remember and copy. The characters who speak in his dialogues are Cato the Censor, Laelius, Scipio Aemilianus and Scaevola, heroes of the old republic; if their nobility were to reappear, the virtuous republic would perhaps after all reappear with it and because of it. The picture he paints of them has more than charm. His warm and perceptive dialogue *On Friendship*, for example, much loved in the Middle Ages, makes of the friendship between Laelius and Scipio an ideal placed in relation to real goodness that allowed it to become a model for Christian friendship for Augustine and his successors. The dialogue ends: "No one can be a friend unless he is a good man. But next to goodness, I entreat you to regard friendship as the finest thing in all the world." [17]

Cicero is at his best in *On Friendship*, *On Old Age* and *On Duties*, his books most read in Christian times. They were all written in the year 44 B.C. while he stayed at a distance from Rome, hoping, in vain as it turned out, that the republic would recover its sanity after the dictatorship and then the assassination, to Cicero very welcome, of Julius Caesar. In the same year, Cicero wrote *On Glory*, a lost essay on fame, that for which, according to Brutus, the doomed hero of the assassination, Cicero would put up even with servitude.[18] Nevertheless, in the writing of this year, and also in his resounding attacks on tyranny in the most powerful of his speeches, he distilled, with great intelligence and a lawyer's common sense so steady as to be almost itself nobility, much that he had learned from Greek thought for a Latin future that would be for centuries almost without Greek.

Cicero not only taught Augustine a good deal of what Augustine ever knew of Greek philosophy before Plotinus; he also taught him how to write and speak persuasively in the cause of the truth that Cicero could not know. In *On Christian Teaching*, which Augustine began in 397 at the time he wrote the *Confessions* (then perhaps forgot about, and finished thirty years later as an old man), Cicero's three requirements of oratory—that it should teach, please and move its audience—are given a firm objective: the preacher's hearer, or the writer's reader, should understand, be delighted by and obey what is true, beautiful and good and is reaching him through the mere words of a human being. By demonstrating in this book that Cicero's skills are a permanent and effective means by which truth can be conveyed and that they are present in the writing of the Bible and of the Fathers of the Church, Augustine provided a solid argument for not neglecting classical writing where and when it too conveys the truth. It is here that Augustine says:

> Now although God alone is thought of as the god of gods, he is also thought of by those who imagine, invoke, and worship other gods, whether in heaven or on earth, in so far as their thinking strives to reach a being than which there is nothing better or more exalted.[19]

And in his preface to the book, surely added (scholars disagree about this) when he completed the work in old age, he wrote that God could have made the whole truth clear to everyone by means of an angel but chose not to. We need books, we need teachers, we need human words:

> The human condition would be wretched indeed if God appeared unwilling to minister his word to human beings through human agency. . . . There would be no way for love, which ties people together in the bonds of unity, to make souls overflow and as it were intermingle with each other, if human beings learnt nothing from each other.[20]

It is a thought from which Cicero would not have wished, and does not deserve, to be excluded.

Cicero's *Hortensius* was never excluded from Augustine's memory or from his library. Late in Augustine's life, arguing strongly with the Pelagians, who thought man by himself capable of attaining virtue, Augustine, in defence of the grace of God without which we can do nothing good, quoted Cicero's anguished description of the suffering of humanity, the evil and wretchedness we bring upon ourselves through the lust for power. In his theological masterpiece *On the Trinity*, completed equally late in his life, Augustine, discussing death and judgement, quotes Cicero in the *Hortensius* recommending the life of philosophy either because, if the soul dies with the body, "our extinction will not then be an offence to us but rather a repose from living", or, "if, on the other hand, as the greatest and most famous of ancient philosophers have believed, our souls are eternal and divine, then we may fairly suppose that the more constant a soul has been" in the life of rational enquiry, "by so much the easier will be its ascent and return to its heavenly country". The equivocation, the failure to choose between Plato and Epicurus, is wholly characteristic of Cicero and earns him a brisk ticking-off from Augustine for this "scepticism on even the most manifest of truths". Why could not Cicero simply accept "the tradition which came to him from those philosophers who on his own admission were the greatest and most famous"? Augustine's reply is Christian and forgiving: "But the course that is set in the love of truth . . . is not enough for men unhappy as all must be whose mortality is supported by reason alone, without faith in the Mediator."[21]

* * *

Virgil was seven when Cicero was consul, twenty-seven when Cicero was killed by the second triumvirate. The competition for absolute power that destroyed the Roman republic continued for another twelve years. Rome had already conquered most of the known world, from Gibraltar to the Euphrates and from the German North Sea coast to the Sahara, but for two generations Romans had been killing Romans, in far-flung land and sea battles, in massacres on the fields of Italy, in government-authorised "disappearances" from the streets of Rome. Nor was it evident to contemporaries for several years that Actium, the final battle of the civil war, was indeed its end or that Actium's victor, Octavius, would become the initiator of a new Roman order, which would in due course summon Joseph and Mary, obscure subjects of a distant but efficient government, to Bethlehem for the census.

In the century of Cicero and Virgil, Latin became for the first time a language not only of the city that ruled the empire, of the army and of the higher reaches of the administration, but also a language in which it was possible to speak and write with the subtlety, the intellectual finesse, the beauty that had belonged for centuries to Greek. Cicero himself did much of the work that made this possible, finding Latin equivalents for Greek philosophical terms and writing prose of a grace and strength new to his native language. What happened to Latin in this period was both a conscious effort and a moral crusade. A hundred years earlier, Cato the Censor had said that Greek culture would be the ruin of the Roman state, though he learned Greek in old age and taught grammar and rhetoric to his son. Virgil, in the sixth book of the *Aeneid*, acknowledges without rancour a familiar Roman self-definition when he has the ghost of Aeneas's father tell his son to leave art and science to the Greeks and get on with the task of equitable Roman government:

"Others will beat more gently breathing forms from bronze
(I know they will), and coax from marble living faces;
they will make better speeches, track with their measurements
the wanderings of the heavens and say when stars will rise;
you, Roman, are to mind your power, rule over nations
(these will be your skills), to impose the habit of peace,
to spare those you have conquered and bring down in war the proud." [22]

It is a noble project, and it is fraught with moral danger, now as then.

Cato was among the first writers of Latin prose. He was also the arbiter of Roman austerity and the driver forward of Roman ambition who, at the end of every speech he made in the senate, repeated his slogan "Carthage must be destroyed", the African city that for generations had contended with Rome for control of the western Mediterranean. Cato's great-grandson, a friend of Cicero, killed himself in 44 B.C. to avoid accepting Julius Caesar's pardon for the just stand he had taken against Caesar's tyranny; he was reading, the night before his death, the *Phaedo*, Plato's account of the death of Socrates. This Cato, after another thirteen centuries, was the only pagan admitted by Dante into the finite pain of Purgatory. Meanwhile, the connexion in the Roman mind between decadent, dangerous Greece and decadent, dangerous Carthage was to find its apotheosis in the figure of Cleopatra, Queen of Egypt, a country and a queen both African and Greek.

When peace did come at last to the Roman world in 31 B.C., with Octavius's victory over Mark Antony and the disastrously seductive Cleopatra at Actium, Latin poetry, recent and sophisticated, had reached only a small audience in scurrilous Roman high society or the more serious few who could understand Lucretius's *De rerum natura* (*On the Nature of Things*), a long poem that presents in measured verse the bleak materialist philosophy of Epicurus. Gifted younger poets were taken up and honoured with support, as long as they remained loyal to the regime, at the court of the new ruler of the empire. The work of Horace, Ovid, Propertius and Tibullus would in any case have made Augustus's reign the golden age of Latin poetry. But the poems of their friend and contemporary, Virgil, for a number of reasons, entered the bloodstream of what would become the Christian West in a quite different way.

When Octavius returned to Rome in 29 B.C., with all his rivals dead, he was presented with Virgil's second masterpiece. There were three in total.

The first, a set of ten shortish poems—the longest just over one hundred lines—was the *Bucolics*, or *Eclogues*. Virgil wrote these poems in the years following Julius Caesar's murder, during the very worst of the civil war. As with both his other works, the *Eclogues* were written with close attention to Greek models, here particularly the pastoral poems, the *Idylls*, of the third-century-B.C. Sicilian poet Theocritus. It would have been inconceivable for any serious Latin poet to have struck out entirely on his own: the first ambition of a Roman poet was to compel his clumsy, intractable language to something near Greek flexibility and polish, as he wrote the kinds of poetry that already existed in Greek.

Virgil's nymphs and shepherds, happy or lovelorn, much affected by death, much given to singing as they absentmindedly watch their flocks, live in an Arcadia he shifts from southern Greece to various places in Italy and Sicily until it becomes a place of the imagination, to be found on no map. Their lives are framed by a landscape of hills and streams, trees and flowers, which Virgil made into a country of the heart for the whole of the rest of European poetry. Into these lives break the harsh realities of Virgil's own time: the expropriation of peasant farms for greedy troops by the same Octavius who has not yet won the civil war and the icy northern frontiers or the searing desert sun where conscript soldiers had to live and die. The flight to a gentle landscape; the gritty facts from which there is no escape: Virgil brings home the contrast, establishes the ironic gap between the two, so well that all later pastoral harks back to his example. Shakespeare's *As You Like It*, Milton's *Lycidas* and Keats's *Ode to a Nightingale* are only the most familiar of the many pieces of writing in English that make use of this contrast, this gap.

But this is not all that Virgil does in the *Eclogues*. There is here and there in them, particularly in the fifth poem, which frames rival elegies for a dead shepherd, and in the tenth, a lament for a lost love, poignantly sung on behalf of someone else whose heart is broken, a yearning for rescue from sadness, even from death, in eternity. This yearning—which Augustine called *desiderium* and christened as the longing for God—can be expressed by Virgil only in pagan terms. But the fourth poem takes the yearning for redemption and gives it words familiar to every reader of the prophecies of Isaiah. A new age is about to begin. A child, the first born of the new age, is on his way from heaven. His father's power will bring peace to the world. The ox will no longer fear the lion. No snake will lurk near the child's cradle. All labour will cease. Everything rejoices in the age that is to come, and it is very near:

> Now there comes the last of the ages the Sybil foretold;
> a great series of centuries is born from the whole of time,
> now a virgin returns, the golden age returns;
> now its firstborn is sent to us, down from the height of heaven.
> Look kindly, goddess of childbirth, on the birth of this boy;
> for in him shall the people of iron fail, and a people of gold
> arise in all the world. . . .
> . . . .
> Come soon (for the hour is at hand) to the greatness of your glory,
> dear offspring of the gods, great child of Jove himself!
> Look how the round world bends in its weight,
> the lands, the tracts of the sea and the deep sky;
> look how all things rejoice in the coming time![23]

Even before Virgil died, two or three all-too-human characters claimed to be, or were flattered as, the prophesied child of the Fourth Eclogue. Classical scholars have long argued the merits of various children, born and not yet born in 40 B.C., or never to be born, to Octavius, to Mark Antony, to the consul to whom the poem is addressed. The most likely child to have carried such high hopes was the son who might have been born to Mark Antony and Octavius's virtuous sister, Octavia, who were married in 40 B.C. to seal, in vain as it turned out, a reconciliation between the two most powerful men in the world. The marriage, destroyed by Antony's passion for Cleopatra, produced only two daughters.

Some scholars allow it to be possible for Virgil to have read Isaiah in the Alexandrian Greek of the Septuagint or to have seen somewhere some version of Old Testament prophecy. However it happened, the vision of an imminent new dispensation for the whole world reached Virgil's imagination and became Virgil's resounding lines. The poem has inevitably been read by Christians as a prophecy of the birth of Christ. This is how it was taken in the early Church by many who saw the providence of God in the Roman peace into which Christ was born, a peace still ten years away when the poem was written. Constantine, the first Christian emperor, read the Fourth Eclogue in 325 to the bishops, almost all of whom were Greek, when he opened the Council of Nicaea, probably hoping they would hear in the poem a foretelling of his own Christian reign as well as a prophecy of the birth of Christ. Augustine, whose literary sense, trained on Virgil, never deserted him, wrote of the poem with cautious exactness in the *City of God*: "The most renowned of poets also spoke of Christ, in a poetical manner certainly, for Christ is represented by an imagined portrait of another person, but with complete truth, if the picture is referred to Christ."[24]

Virgil was writing his second poem, the *Georgics*, during Octavius's last campaign against Mark Antony. Though the new ruler of the world is awarded passages of somewhat uneasy panegyric in the *Georgics*, and the last thirteen years of bloodshed are laid at the door of the murderers of Julius Caesar, Virgil also reminds his readers of the far-from-exemplary behaviour of Octavius himself during the civil wars. The hope for the future in this poem is not at all Messianic. It is a quiet faith in the continuing goodness and fruitfulness of the earth, looked after by the hard, grateful work of people blessedly able to ignore the greed and cruelty of those competing for power. Far away from wars and the crowd-pulling ostentation of the wealthy live humble countrymen:

> Peace that is safe from harm and a life that knows no deceit,
> the wealth of a range of skills, and the freedom of open land,
> . . . .
> young men patient at work and used to a simple life,
> to sacred respect for God and their fathers; among these people
> Justice, going from the earth, left her last footprints.[25]

The scale of the *Georgics* is larger than that of the *Eclogues*: four books of about five hundred lines each, organised with the skilful variations of tone, texture and pace with which a great composer puts a symphony together. The subject and manner are derived from Hesiod, the archaic Greek poet who wrote about the land, farming, the weather and the stars. A number of later Greek texts, now lost, are thought to have provided further models for some of the kinds of writing in the poem, and Varro's contemporary agricultural manual, in Latin, contributed a good deal of the practical advice. Virgil's four books take as their themes the earth itself, trees and fruit, herds and flocks, and lastly the miraculous airy world of bees, hard-working, intelligent, co-operative, productive of sweetness but (it was then thought) sexless. The poem is much more than an inspiring text for city-dwelling Romans nostalgic about the countryside and its timeless demands. Deeper notes sound often in its course: the whole work is like a piece of music in which both melody and harmony are inventively composed. Discords and noble cadences are carefully placed; there are several modulations into a surprising new key.

A famous passage[26] in the first book is a Virgilian version of the story of the Fall of Man, in "the time of Jupiter", from a golden age of plenty like that prophesied in the Fourth Eclogue to a familiar world of property, rivalry, inventiveness and hard labour. But the toil made necessary by the challenges of an imperfect world is much celebrated in the poem. The Italian countryside; its kind seasons; the tended land producing oil and wine, corn and apples and honey, olives and cold water; harvest rejoicing after the work of ploughing and sowing and pruning; the return of spring as if to the lost paradise: many passages are reminiscent of the celebration of God's earth and its goodness in the Psalms. Virgil's "almighty father" in book 2 is close, in feeling if not in theology, to the Spirit of God moving on the face of the waters at the very beginning of the book of Genesis:

> Then the almighty father, the spirit, in fecund showers
> comes down to the lap of the earth, his rejoicing spouse,
> his greatness mixing with hers to bring forth offspring of theirs.
> . . . .
> None other than this was the growing world from its first beginning,
> one may well believe, when the days became light and an even course
> was set; then it was spring indeed, great spring impelled the earth,
> and the east winds did not blow with their wintry breath,
> when the first cattle drank up the light, and man,

sprung from the earth, raised his head from the stony fields,
and wild beasts appeared in the woods, and stars in the sky.[27]

A new note in the *Georgics*, something that will not return in European art for centuries, is delight in landscape itself, with people as tiny figures to give scale, or often no people at all. The effect on the reader is like the surprise delivered by the first painters, Albrecht Dürer and one or two sixteenth-century Italians, to paint landscape without figures, landscape for its own sake, as if to say to the spectator, Look, look better, at the world God made. As with many landscape painters, the works of man, his cultivation of the land, his building of towns and villages, are part of what is celebrated, part of the beauty of the real, presented to move us and to encourage us in its praise.

A discordant sound, as in the *Eclogues*, is the jarring clamour of warfare, of the violence and injustice that human beings inflict on each other, ruining the peacefulness of the right relation between mankind and nature. A remarkable passage in book 3, full of savage vigour and sharply observed detail, describes the havoc wrought among normally docile animals, and people, by the raging of the sexual instinct:

> All kinds of creature on earth—men and the beasts of land
> and water, cattle and bright birds—rush to this fire and fury;
> love is the same for them all.[28]

Not until Schopenhauer in the nineteenth century does a writer give such a vivid and frightening account of sex as the cutting edge of the competitive will to life. But this passage has in it also a powerful bass note of celebration and is without the puritanical disdain of the clinically reductive passage (about human sexuality only) in Lucretius's *De rerum natura*,[29] to which it is an evident reply.

The deepest chord struck by the *Georgics* is more mysterious, more complex and sadder, and it is the chord on which the whole poem ends. Afflicted with the loss of all his bees, a legendary character, Aristaeus, is told that he must sacrifice to Orpheus for his bees to return to life, because Orpheus's beloved wife was killed running away from a bee. There follows the telling of the Orpheus story, his rescue of Eurydice from the land of the dead only to lose her again, forever, in her death and his, because he disobeyed the injunction not to look back when leading her up to the light. Aristaeus finds new bees, in the carcases of oxen sacrificed to Orpheus, as Samson finds honey in the carcase of his slain lion. But Orpheus has been torn to pieces and nothing remains of him but the echo of his voice grieving for Eurydice. As Balthasar says in his essay on Virgil in *The Glory of the Lord*:

> All Vergil's skill can be seen here in this reticence and refusal of reso-lution; the two conflicting myths are only loosely plaited together . . . , like fingertips resting against each other. The legend that deals with death, the legend that deals with eternal life: but this suffices to let that radiant glow that lies over the entire work suffuse the end of the poem, a glow that arises from the poet's Yes to life in all its dimensions, the harsh and the beautiful. That Yes, however, can only be consciously uttered when it is a response to an intimate, barely audible Yes on the part of being itself.[30]

The collision of the two legends in the closing pages of the *Georgics*, the contrast between the successful, though cruel, regeneration of the bees, which are already established as a model of ordered and selfless, but also loveless, society, and the yearning desolation of Orpheus's love must have had an extra resonance for Vir-gil's contemporaries. Virgil finished writing this poem in 30 or 29 B.C. The battle of Actium and the suicides of Antony and Cleopatra took place in 31 and 30. It is impossible not to suppose that Virgil, particularly if somewhere in the background of the Fourth Eclogue had been high hopes for Antony's possible son, was much affected by these events. Perhaps the triumph of the cruelly suc-cessful Octavius and the love and death of Antony and Cleopatra, the three of them the most public figures in the world and Virgil's exact contemporaries, found their way, transformed in the crucible of metaphor that is a poet's imag-ination, into the fourth book of the *Georgics*. After—indeed, because of—loss and death comes, in the poem, regeneration; out of the slain carcases of cattle come new swarms of bees; out of the funerals in Alexandria came Octavius's mastery of the world and the restoration of order to Roman society. The same collision is even clearer in the *Aeneid*, where the necessarily cruel but successful founding of Rome will be the context for the love, abandonment and death of Dido, and Aeneas will have to choose, in pain that is both his and Dido's, to foreshadow Octavius rather than Mark Antony.

* * *

To write his last, longest and greatest poem, Virgil turned to epic, to the most beloved and most distant Greek poetic model, Homer. Octavius was now established as sole ruler of Rome, an equivocal figure marked for worldly glory only by success. Soon he was to be called Augustus Caesar, his family name to become synonymous with "emperor" for the rest of Roman history, and as "Kaiser" and "Tsar" long after it. A few years of peace demonstrated that he was indeed fulfilling the hopes placed in him, that a new stability was developing in the empire, that people could breathe again, reflect again, be pleased again to be Romans. The emperor Augustus outlived Virgil by thirty-three years, and when Augustus died, Jesus was a boy of fourteen or so (the dating of Jesus's birth has never been exact).

The *Iliad* and the *Odyssey* celebrated the Trojan War, a story of heroes, of their courage, fury, death, inventiveness and endurance, set in a past already legendary when the poems were written. In Homer, or the bards who put together for listening audiences the poems Homer wrote down, an even, dispassionate light plays over the battlefields of Troy and the hazardous sea Odysseus must cross on his long travels from Troy back to his home. The poetry is on no one's side, and on the side of all the victims and survivors of the wilfulness and jealousy of the gods. Virgil's case was different and easier to identify with. He wrote the *Aeneid* alone at his desk, with Homer's poems in front of him, under the double pressure of immediate events, some of them horrifying, and of immediate imperial requirements. Augustus expected—Rome expected—of this now-famous poet a national epic in praise of Rome, the most powerful state recorded history had ever seen, in praise in particular of Augustus, his rise to preeminence, his victories, his wise government of the world.

What they got was an epic indeed, taking its Trojan hero, Aeneas, from the ruins of Troy and bringing him to Italy in the far past to be the father of Rome, the ancestor of Augustus, the patriarch of the empire. Virgil chose one from the penumbra of legends accounting for Rome's beginning, rather as Milton chose one of various biblical hints to elaborate as his story of the coming of evil into paradise. But what the Romans, and the future, also got from Virgil was the poet's own profoundly mixed response to the human power and glory celebrated in the epic. Virgil produced, in the first half of his poem, the perilous adventures of a journey to the predestined home, with a spell in the underworld, as in Homer's *Odyssey*, and, as in Homer's *Iliad*, in the second half of his poem, battles, deaths and anguish over slaughtered sons. But although only seven or eight centuries separate Virgil from Homer, and twenty separate Virgil from us, he seems our contemporary in a way that Homer never does. For Virgil is beset with moral complexities thoroughly familiar to us, particularly the problems of conscience raised by the whole issue of however well-intentioned an empire.

The constant qualification of his praise for Rome's past, and hopes for Rome's future, brings us, and brought Augustine—who knew more than Virgil could know of Rome's history—very close to his solitary figure.

In the *Aeneid* the Homeric bloom has gone from the epic world, and Aeneas is a different kind of hero from Achilles, Hector or Odysseus. Aeneas, compared to them, is a colourless, dutiful character. He does what he has to do, at terrible cost, particularly to others. He is obedient to his destiny, given him in the providence of Jupiter, whose supreme power and ultimate rightness, at least in historical terms, make it unavoidable for his providence to strike the reader as the providence of God. In burning Troy, Aeneas is forbidden to fight the conquering Greeks or to look for his lost wife Creusa, because he must found Rome. In Carthage, where he loves and is loved by the widowed queen, he has to abandon her to heartbroken suicide, because he must found Rome. Here he is resisting the pull of his love for Dido and his longing to yield to the pleas of the queen and her sister that he should stay in Carthage:

> But he is not moved by tears,
> nor does he bend to the tug of their pleading words;
> fate blocks his way; God blocked his gentle ears.
> As when north winds of the Alps, roaring this way and that,
> struggle among themselves to uproot a mighty oak,
> strong with the age of years; in the whistling gale
> high leafy branches fall to the earth and the trunk is shaken;
> but the tree stands fast on its rock, for as tall as it grows to the sky
> and the air, so deep do its roots reach down to the bowels of the earth:
> in just the same way the hero is battered this way and that
> with tireless pleas, and feels their grief to the depths of his heart;
> his mind remains made up; the tears roll down in vain.[31]

Lacrimae volvuntur inanes: her tears, but also his, falling like leaves from the tree. Dido is both Carthage, the long-destroyed enemy of early Rome, and Cleopatra, who had wrecked Mark Antony's Roman resolve, leaving the way open for Augustus's triumph. Aeneas in these lines stands firm against the storm of both Dido's love and his own because the height of his courage is sustained by the depth of his fidelity to his destiny. The gale-battered oak is a typical Virgilian image, holding for the reader the dense emotional complexity of a single human moment. There are dozens of such images in the *Aeneid*.

In Italy, because he must found Rome, Aeneas has to make war on harmless peasants, spreading death and destruction among people who have much of the ancient virtue and simplicity celebrated in the *Georgics*. It is the set-upon Latins, not Aeneas's attacking Trojans, who are compared, in another of Virgil's heavily charged images, to a panic-stricken community of bees, harried out of their rock home by a shepherd's acrid, blinding smoke.[32] The end, both the objective and the conclusion, of this war, Aeneas promises, will be not conquest but unity: *aeterna in foedera* (Let both peoples submit to equal laws in an everlasting league).[33] Later, the goddess Juno, the enemy of Troy and Aeneas throughout the poem, begs Jupiter to confirm this promise of unity, which he does. The Trojans will disappear into the Latin race, mixing their customs, their traditions and their blood, and becoming, together, the new Roman people: *Sit Romana potens Italia virtute propago* (Let the powerful shoot be Roman in the strength [or "on the stock"] of Italy).[34] The language of this new people will be Latin, Jupiter proclaims,[35] and the reconciliation prophesied in these passages may well be an expression of Virgil's hope for the inclusive future of imperial Rome, a hope not wholly misplaced.

But the *Aeneid* does not end on this optimistic note. In the last seventy desperate lines of the poem, Aeneas finally has to fight Turnus, the brave, impetuous leader of the Latins. Aeneas fells Turnus to his knees with a dreadful wound. Then Aeneas wavers at Turnus's noble plea for his life to be spared. And it is the sight of a trophy Turnus is wearing, stripped from the body of Pallas, a beloved prince Aeneas has failed to protect, that goads him to deliver the fatal sword-thrust on which the poem ends. The effect on the reader is even more ambivalent, even more emotionally searing, than the effect of the closing passage of the *Georgics*. No wonder Virgil has Aeneas say sorrowfully to his son Ascanius, earlier in book 12, as he leaves the boy for the last battle:

> Learn courage from me, my son, and true toil;
> good fortune learn from others.[36]

It is clear throughout the poem, to Aeneas and to the reader, that he himself will not found Rome: the real glory is still in someone else's future when the poem ends. His burdened sense of what will be is perceptively described by Balthasar:

> The one point at which the father of the race [Aeneas] has a direct visionary encounter with the future is in Hades, whither his departed

father Anchises has summoned him for the sake of this confrontation with his descendants, as yet unbegotten but already existing as souls. In theological terms, this is the mystical privilege of a founding father, comparable to the visions of Adam in Christian legend, Abraham's vision of his people in the stars of the sky, ... the experiences of John on Patmos, of Benedict, Ignatius and Teresa. It is the vision that turns hope into certainty by its light, without destroying its nature as hope, a "commissioning" vision that is given more for the sake of the children still in the loins than for the father himself. This perspective of hope releases Vergil from the obligation to depict the Augustan present as an unsurpassable eschaton and so to narrow down the vista opened up in the [*Eclogues* and the *Georgics*].[37]

This last point was evident also to Augustine. Meanwhile, Aeneas is a responsible figure, answerable both for his little band of Trojans and for the fulfilment of his destiny, answerable to God for his part in the story of Rome, which is itself clouded by the misery of those who must be conquered so that it should be great. Aeneas is the servant of providence. He must shoulder the past: he carries his old father from Troy on his back. Then, when his father is dead, he must shoulder the future his father's ghost has described to him: he puts on the shield that has engraved on it, not the beautiful world that was pictured on the shield of Achilles in the *Iliad*, but the long, violent history of Rome, right up to the battle of Actium at its centre, a tableau representing a vision, of the right-minded West conquering the sinister East, which has haunted the imagination, with sometimes terrible consequences, of Europe and America ever since.

The poem celebrated the greatness of Rome and of Augustus, as was expected, but, as was probably not expected, at the same time qualified its celebration with sorrow for the past and warning for the future. It is impossible (as with the *Eclogues* and the *Georgics*, only more so) to separate the strands of the poem, to take apart the notes of its harmonies. So the sorrow and the warning entered the consciousness of the poem's readers with its lasting popularity and in many ways have been more important, ever since, than the celebration. Much of what has always been meant by *romanitas*, "Roman-ness", at its civic best—perseverance in the task undertaken, a self-effacing sense of duty, care for justice and for the weak, a suspicion of all extremes, unspectacular responsibility for fair administration and for long, patient years guarding usually quiet frontiers—is given its definitive expression by Virgil in this poem. Aeneas's virtues are evidently Cicero's recommended prudence, temperance, fortitude and justice. Before Christianity absorbed them into the ethics of conformity of the human will with the will of God, Cicero and Virgil between them had given these virtues a Latin weight, which was later reinforced for the West in the very different sixth-century texts of the Rule of Saint Benedict, the daily guide of all monks, and the emperor Justinian's great codification of Roman law, written in Latin although achieved by committees of lawyers in Greek-speaking Constantinople. The dutiful orderliness and fair dealing recommended in all this Latin writing much affected the whole future of those parts of Europe converted to Christianity from Rome.

But Aeneas is not only a civic hero. The burden of responsibility he shoulders, as he shoulders his old father and his new shield, is of course the future of Rome, "so heavy a load", Virgil says very early in the poem, "to found the Roman people".[38] But it is also a personal, private thing, the weight of his duty to what has been given him to do, ultimately his duty to God. He is a hero not of the mind but of the will, good because of what he does, despite the suffering he endures and causes, in persevering obedience. "Cede deo", he says in the poem. "'Yield to God.' He spoke and with his voice dissolved the conflict."[39] Augustine recognised in Virgil one who shared with him a sense of what Augustine called *pondus amoris*, the weight of love that pulls a person toward God or, alternatively, toward his own interests: "a material body is borne along by its weight in a particular direction, as a soul is by its love."[40] In the *Eclogues*, Virgil had described the rage of the will to life that pulls human beings, no less than animals, toward their own pleasure:

> The savage lioness pursues the wolf, the wolf the goat;
> The greedy goat seeks out the flowering clover;
> And I seek you, Alexas; our own delight pulls each of us.[41]

Trahit sua quemque voluptas. Aeneas has to abandon both his beloved wife and his beloved Dido for the greater pull of his fidelity to his duty. No wonder Augustine, who deceived and left his grieving mother on the African shore to go to Italy without her and later, though for purely worldly reasons, had to send away forever the heartbroken woman with whom he had faithfully lived for fourteen years and who had borne him his son, saw in the sorrowful pilgrimage of Aeneas a pattern of his own. There is also in Aeneas's *pietas*, his obedience to God, the "fear of the Lord" that, in one of Augustine's favourite quotations from the Old Testament, the Book of Job calls "wisdom";[42] and in Virgil's anguish over the struggle, *labores*, mankind cannot avoid,[43] and the *verus labor*, the "true toil" or "true distress" Aeneas asks his son to learn from him, there is the Book of Job's anguish for "man born to trouble" (homo nascitur ad laborem).[44] In other words, there is a sense of the inevitable sadness of a fallen world in Virgil—"There are tears in how things are, and mortality touches the soul"[45]—as there is not in Cicero, and to it Augustine owed something of his certainty of the sinfulness into which we are all born.

Augustine was haunted, in particular, by a passage in book 6 of the *Aeneid* where the ghost of Anchises in the underworld explains to Aeneas a theory of the soul that Virgil learned from Plato but that, in its moral implications, is even closer to Christianity:

> "A fiery energy sprung from its origin in heaven
> sows life, so long as the poisons, the sins of our physical bodies
> do not slow, drag down, our souls to mortal earth.
> In the body, our souls feel fear, love, joy and grief, shut up
> in the blinded dark of their prison, they no longer see the heavens.
> Indeed when life abandons the last of the light, not even
> then does every evil, every trace of corruption
> utterly leave poor souls, for it has to be that in them
> their many sins, mysteriously, have long ingrown and fused.
> Therefore they will be schooled with punishments, and pay
> the penalty for old faults
> . . . .
> until the long day of time, its destined round complete,
> has worn our sin away, and left the spirit cleansed,
> its heavenly perception simple fiery light."[46]

In the *City of God*, Augustine carefully refutes the dualism of this passage in the light of Christianity, explaining that it is possible for Christians "in the pilgrimage of this present life, to feel fear, desire, grief and joy" in conformity with Christian truth: "because their love is right, all these feelings are right in them."[47] Emotion, a matter of body and soul as one, is not in itself either good or bad. But Virgil's suggestion of the purgation of sins after death, a finite cleansing of the polluted soul, Augustine quotes later in his book with qualified approval, allowing that "some will receive forgiveness in the world to come for what is not forgiven in this, so that they may not be punished with the eternal chastisement of the world to come."[48] The judgement is not for us to make: it belongs to the inscrutable justice of God. But that there is a purging of the soul after death, a possibility that eventually developed into the Latin, the Catholic, belief in Purgatory, unshared by the Orthodox tradition, is an idea that has Augustine's reading of Virgil in its background. For this reason among many, it was altogether appropriate that Dante, the supreme poet of Catholic Christianity, in the *Divine Comedy* chose Virgil as his guide through hell and almost to the top of the mountain of Purgatory, where Virgil has to leave him: "You have come to a place where I of myself can discern nothing further." [49]

Early in the *Aeneid*, Jupiter guarantees an everlasting Rome to Aeneas and his band of Trojans: "I set for them no bounds of space or time: I have given them an empire without end." [50] In a sermon of the year 410, after the traumatic sacking of the city by Alaric and his Goths, Augustine contrasted these lines with Christ's promise: "Heaven and earth will pass away, but my words will never pass away." [51] And Augustine's whole argument for the city of God as in God's eternity, while the earthly city is limited and transient, can be said to turn on his alteration of Virgil's lines in the *City of God* so that they prophesy "the heavenly country, where you will find no Vestal hearth, no Capitoline stone, but the one true God, who 'sets for you no bounds of space or time: I will give you an empire without end.'" [52]

* * *

It is not only because of Augustine's and, nine centuries later, Dante's love for Virgil that Virgil has a unique place in the story of writing in the Christian tradition. Virgil's knowledge of the soul and of the conscience, his apparent prophecy of the birth of Christ in the Fourth Eclogue, and the noble beauty of his poetry all contributed to the sense that, in the Roman world but not quite of it, he was an instinctive inhabitant, before it could be described, of the city of God. It was this that made him the classical poet most read and most familiar in the Christian West for many generations. The earliest life of Saint Patrick, written in Ireland in the sixth century, quoted Virgil. Saint Adamnan, abbot of Iona in the seventh century, quoted the *Aeneid* in his Life of Saint Columba and wrote a commentary on the *Georgics*. At Charlemagne's court in the ninth century, the monk Alcuin from York explained to a no doubt bemused audience that the way "to construct a good and lucid poem" was to follow the shape of the *Aeneid*. [53] In the eleventh century, Odilo, one of the abbots of Cluny, then the greatest monastery in the West, wrote a long poem in Virgilian hexameters and consoled his exhausted monks, after a freezing journey, with a few lines appropriately altered from Aeneas's praise of his shipwrecked Trojans on the African coast. [54] It was partly as a precursor and a component of the tradition of the

"Middle Ages", not so called, disparagingly, until the late eighteenth century, that Virgil was neglected in favour of Homer by the Enlightenment. There are several references to Homer in Gibbon's *Decline and Fall of the Roman Empire*, but not one to Virgil. John Lemprière, although a clergyman in the Church of England, in his *Classical Dictionary* of 1788 regards Lucretius as the greater poet. Romantic and post-Romantic advocates of the notion that poetry should be some kind of replacement for God—Percy Bysshe Shelley, Matthew Arnold and Nietzsche, for example—leave Virgil out of their lists of the indispensable poets of the past but always include Homer. Coleridge reported that his rigorous school-master at Christ's Hospital in the 1780s taught him to prefer Homer to Virgil;[55] later in his life, his deepening Christian conviction and his discovery of Dante brought him closer to Virgil, with whose poetry he was intimately familiar. John Henry Newman in the 1850s, writing in countercultural fashion on the Bene-dictine educational tradition, which he regarded as the model for an ideal uni-versity, described accurately the "congeniality" with the spirit of Virgil of "what may be called the Benedictine idea".[56] T. S. Eliot, after his conversion to Christ-ianity, wrote with keen appreciation of Virgil and of his relation to Christian truth and judged him to be "at the centre of European civilization, in a position which no other poet can share or usurp".[57] Balthasar's chapter on Virgil in *The Glory of the Lord* defines with sympathy and care his unique place in the light Virgil could not fully know.

It could be said that the combination of knowledge and lack of knowledge of God is the key to Virgil's poetry, and in particular to its sadness. Peering through the shadows of a paganism that had already faded as belief, although its public rituals retained a Ciceronian utility for centuries to come, he both understood unselfish obedience to divine command and felt keenly the sorrow of love lost in death. The deaths mourned in the *Eclogues*, the deaths of Orpheus and Eury-dice in the *Georgics*, the deaths in burning Troy, the loss of Creusa, the death of Dido, the prophesied death of Augustus's nephew and heir, Marcellus, the deaths of Pallas and Turnus: these are the passages in Virgil's poems that their readers never forget. Christian truth, in which the meanings of both obedience and death are taken up and resolved in the revealed, trinitarian love of God, is closed to Virgil. But his melancholy is pierced from time to time in all his poems by shafts of a hope that he can only turn toward and by an affirmation of existence, his "Yes to life in all its dimensions", which made Christian commentators down the ages see in him *anima naturaliter Christiana* (a soul naturally Christian). It is certainly the case that, in the time and circumstances in which he lived, he made one of the most engaged of all responses to the beauty of the world God created and to the moral demands God makes of all men. "Nothing more clearly characterises *pius Aeneas*", Balthasar wrote in his chapter on Virgil, "than the mysterious expansion in him of a childlike willingness to please the father, the authority that is also the object of love, in an attitude of reconciled acceptance before all of reality: *cede Deo*, 'yield to God', becomes the basic postulate of all human virtue." [58] And, in the conclusion to his previous chapter:

> The question cannot be avoided of *why* exactly Rome turned to the Christian faith, if it was indeed, as Augustine depicted it, the counter-image of the heavenly city. How did it come about that Rome, harsh, warlike and calculating, immediately recognized Vergil as its own particular genius, the tender, utopian Vergil, preoccupied with nothing but peace, and celebrated him as only emperors had hitherto been celebrated? In Vergil, the subterranean stream flowing from myth into revelation becomes visible for a brief instant. [59]

1. Cicero, *Orator* 120, quoted in Owen Chadwick, *The Secularization of the European Mind in the Nineteenth Century* (Cambridge, 1975), p. 189; my translation.
2. Augustine, *Confessions* 3.4.7, trans. Henry Chadwick (Oxford, 1991).
3. Plutarch, *Fall of the Roman Republic*, trans. Rex Warner (London, 1958), p. 297.
4. Hans Urs von Balthasar, *The Glory of the Lord: A Theological Aesthetics*, vol. 4, trans. Brian McNeil et al. (San Francisco and Edinburgh, 1989), p. 229.
5. Quoted in ibid., p. 230.
6. Quoted by Michael Grant in his introduction to Cicero, *Selected Works*, trans. Michael Grant (London, 1960), p. 14.
7. Cicero, *On Old Age* 8, in ibid., pp. 246–47.
8. Ibid., p. 246.
9. Cicero, *On Duties* 1.20.
10. Cicero, *Pro Sestio* 97.
11. Cicero, *De divinatione* 2.72, quoted in Balthasar, *Glory of the Lord* 4:217.
12. Cicero, *On Duties* 3.2, in *Selected Works*, p. 164.
13. Ibid., 3.8, p. 191.
14. Cicero, *De inventione rhetorica* 2.157, quoted in Balthasar, *Glory of the Lord* 4:387.
15. Cicero, *On Laws* 1.7.22, quoted by Michael Grant in his introduction to *Cicero: On the Good Life*, trans. Michael Grant (London, 1971), p. 9.
16. Cicero, *On the State* 3.22.33, quoted by Michael Grant, ibid., p. 11.
17. Cicero, *On Friendship* 27.102, ibid., p. 227.
18. Quoted in Ronald Syme, *The Roman Revolution* (Oxford, 1960), p. 136.
19. Augustine, *On Christian Teaching* 1.6.7, trans. R. P. H. Green (Oxford, 1997).
20. Ibid., preface, 6.
21. Augustine, *On the Trinity* 14.25.19, in *Augustine: Later Works*, ed. and trans. John Burnaby (Philadelphia and London, 1955), pp. 124–25.
22. Virgil, *Aeneid* 6.848–53. Translations from Virgil are my own.
23. Virgil, *Eclogue* 4.4–10; 48–52.
24. Augustine, *City of God* 10.27, trans. Henry Bettenson (London, 1972).
25. Virgil, *Georgics* 2.467–68; 472–74.

26. Ibid., 1.121–35.
27. Ibid., 2.325–27; 336–42.
28. Ibid., 3.242–44. See whole passage: 3.211–83.
29. Lucretius, *De rerum natura* 4.1037ff.
30. Balthasar, *Glory of the Lord* 4:261.
31. Virgil, *Aeneid* 4.438–49.
32. Ibid., 12.587–92.
33. Ibid., 190–91.
34. Ibid., 827.
35. Ibid., 837.
36. Ibid., 435–36.
37. Balthasar, *Glory of the Lord* 4:265–66.
38. Virgil, *Aeneid* 1.33.
39. Ibid., 5.467.
40. Augustine, *City of God* 11.28.
41. Virgil, *Eclogue* 2.63–65.
42. Job 28:28.
43. Virgil, *Aeneid* 10.759.
44. Job 5:7.
45. Virgil, *Aeneid* 1.462.
46. Ibid., 6.730–40, 745–47.
47. Augustine, *City of God* 14.8–9.
48. Ibid., 21.13.
49. Dante, *La divina commedia: Purgatorio* 27.127–28.
50. Virgil, *Aeneid* 1.278.
51. Augustine, sermon 105.7; Lk 21:33.
52. Augustine, *City of God* 2.29.
53. R. R. Bolgar, *The Classical Heritage and Its Beneficiaries* (Cambridge, 1954), p. 115.
54. R. W. Southern, *The Making of the Middle Ages* (London, 1953), pp. 172–73.
55. S. T. Coleridge, *Biographia Literaria*, ed. James Engell and W. Jackson Bate (Princeton and London, 1983), p. 8.
56. J. H. Newman: *Rise and Progress of Universities and Benedictine Essays*, ed. M. K. Tillman (Notre Dame, 2001), p. 453.
57. T. S. Eliot, "What Is a Classic?" (1944), in *Selected Prose of T. S. Eliot*, ed. Frank Kermode (London, 1975), pp. 128–29; see also "Virgil and Destiny", in *Selected Prose*, ed. John Hayward (London, 1953), pp. 96–99.
58. Balthasar, *Glory of the Lord* 4:255.
59. Ibid., p. 248.

CHAPTER FIVE

AUGUSTINE I

Confessions

Augustine's *Confessions* is a book without precedent in the ancient world and, in the blaze of its self-understanding in the light of God, without a successor either in the Christian or in the post-Christian world. It is an autobiography addressed throughout to God, written in middle life—Augustine was probably forty-three when he began it—by a man who had been a baptized Christian for only ten years. It is the story of a soul that has been drawn by God through childhood, adolescence, young manhood and an adult career as a professional rhetorician toward conversion to a constantly deepening faith in Christian revelation. All the events, the experiments in thought and belief and the turbulent feelings of this life are now placed by the writer in relation to Christian truth. Much is not wholly, or not yet, understood, and the book has no sense of finality or completeness.

There is always rest for the soul in God. In his first paragraph, Augustine says, in much-quoted words, "You have made us for yourself, and our heart is restless until it rests in you." [1] But we shall reach eternal rest in God only after death, and this is the book of a man who is very much alive, a man of quite exceptional gifts of mind, heart and spirit. He has reached the end of nothing—not of living his own life, not of reflection and certainly not of increasing his love for God and, therefore, his understanding of God. In the very last sentences of the book, he returns to the rest that is in God alone and for which we may hope after this life is over. To understand this, even a little, he says to God, "[O]nly you can be asked, only you can be begged, only on your door can we knock. Yes indeed, that is how it is received, how it is found, how the door is opened." [2] The whole of the *Confessions*, in other words, is a prayer, the prayer of a man who still has much life, much thought, much need and increasing capacity for the love of God in him and perhaps ahead of him. As it turned out, more than thirty years of life, thought and love, tirelessly undertaken and received followed the writing of this interim report on his stormy passage toward his home in God.

Roman Africa, where Augustine was born in 354, had been for more than four hundred years a wealthy imperial province. Carthage, its capital city, was a great metropolis, second only to Rome in the western half of the empire. There were many smaller cities and towns. When Augustine became bishop of Hippo, itself an ancient port and a large city, there were more than six hundred bishops in Roman Africa; the average diocese was therefore a modest town and its surrounding countryside. The cities and most of the towns were Roman in layout and atmosphere, each with its forum, its theatre, its baths, its pagan temples, its schools, and many with not one but two large churches, one Catholic and one Donatist. The Donatists were a schismatic sect peculiar to Africa: orthodox in belief, they identified themselves by the purity of their forebears's response to Roman persecution in the past. They were scornful of what they regarded as Catholic compromises under persecution; sectarian violence between Donatists and Catholics was common. Local officials of the empire, such as Augustine's father, and merchants, craftsmen and slaves lived in these towns, speaking mostly Latin, some Greek and Punic, the old North African language of the Berber population. The rich, in the towns and on their prosperous estates, lived in comfortable villas, with fountains and mosaic floors and marble copies of Greek statues. Punic-speaking peasants and slaves worked their land, growing vines, olives and corn for the towns and for the fleets of ships that carried African produce regularly to Rome.

Thagaste, Augustine's hometown in what is now Algeria, was two hundred miles from the sea and nearly as far from Carthage. Augustine at the age of ten, according to his own account, was an unruly boy, highly intelligent, mulish and often beaten at school. The *Aeneid* he loved with the passion for noble words of a clever, emotionally tempestuous child who finds in poetry more colour and feeling than everyday life seems to offer. In the *Confessions* he is rueful about his early delight in "the vain spectacle of the wooden horse full of armed soldiers and the burning of Troy and the very ghost of Creusa" and puzzled by the tears he shed for Dido, saying that, "had I been forbidden to read this story, I would have been sad that I could not read what made me sad." [3] He was all his life unaware of Aristotle's sophisticated explanation of the cathartic effect of the tragic, instinctively caught in this sentence. Augustine's father, who died when Augustine was seventeen, was irascible, restless but kindhearted; his mother, Monica, made the best of a difficult marriage. She was loyal, earnest, loving. She was also possessive and demanding of her favourite child. Her Christian faith, not in the least intellectual, won over her pagan husband before his death; it was a constant pressure in her son's life, to be reacted against for many years, but to give great joy to both mother and son when his own conversion eventually took place.

* * *

In the year 430 the age-old security of Roman Africa is over. Eighty thousand barbarian invaders, Vandals from north and east of the Rhine, have poured into the province in the last few months. They are Christians, but Arian heretics, and they are after the wealth of the province, for which they are killing and humiliating the rich and the priests, burning and looting towns, churches and villas, starving the people out of fortified cities. In the besieged port of Hippo, the streets are crowded with ragged refugees from smaller towns and the countryside, the landowners now indistinguishable from their peasants and slaves. The Vandal forces are at the gates, and the city officials hope, with decreasing conviction, that a Roman army will appear from the east to raise the siege. In the Catholic bishop's house, where a number of priests and students live in a usually quiet community, Augustine, now seventy-six and bishop of the city for the last thirty-five years, is alone in his room, as he has asked to be. He is close to death. There are many books in his room, and little else. Ninety-three of these books, in 232 codices, or large bound volumes, not counting hundreds of letters and sermons, are his own, written by him throughout his long and extremely busy life. Each of his books has been checked by him in the last four years for errors, omissions, misleading emphases, even tedious passages, to warn against which he has written another book, the *Retractationes* (*Revisions* is a better translation of this title than *Retractions*). "Cicero, the prince of Roman orators," Augustine wrote to a friend in 412, "says of someone that 'He never uttered a word which he would wish to recall'. High praise indeed!—but more applicable to a complete ass than to a genuinely wise man." [4] That there will be many future readers of his books perhaps Augustine realises. He knows that the future is dark, that Roman power in the West is fast losing its hold on the old provinces of the empire, that a way of life that has preserved civilisation for half a millennium is collapsing around him. He also knows that copies of his books are already prized by bishops and priests and some early Western monks, wherever Latin is read, and especially wherever Greek is not also read.

On 28 August 430 Augustine died. Hippo fell to the Vandals, apparently without much violence, the following year. Augustine's works, carefully catalogued after his death by his friend Possidius, seem to have reached Rome by the middle of the century "under conditions and by means", a recent biographer writes, "which remain mysterious, if not miraculous". [5] Odd letters and sermons, lost for centuries, are occasionally discovered even now. Augustine's is by far the largest surviving body of work by any ancient author, and for at least a thousand years after his death, he taught the Latin Christian world, his books read more carefully and cited more times than any other author's works, outside Scripture itself.

He wrote in one of his commentaries on the Book of Genesis, and the resonance of the observation is typical of him, that "the tree is hidden in the seed, but such is the principle of its being that there is no seed from seed without the intervention of a tree." [6] The tree that intervened between the rebellious schoolboy and the old bishop in his library, surrounded by the books from which a great forest was to grow, was his life. We know much more about this life than about that of anyone else in antiquity, and, although it was lived long ago, among the pressures of a time and a world that might seem irrecoverably alien to us at the beginning of the twenty-first century, there is, in fact, little in all that Augustine had to contend with that is not astonishingly familiar.

* * *

Augustine was born less than thirty years after the emperor Constantine's Council of Nicaea had, in the interests of orthodoxy and unity, produced the first version of the "Nicene" Creed, used ever since in all churches of the Orthodox and Catholic traditions. When Augustine was seven years old, the pagan emperor Julian had done his best, in too short a time to succeed, to pull the whole empire back from its as yet only patchy official Christianity to full pagan belief and ritual. It was then still the case, as for more than a century it has again been the case, that Christian intellectuals, certainly in the Latin West, were almost all converts, less often from weak public paganism than from various schools of Greek philosophy, abstract, exclusive and difficult to understand, contemptuous of the apparent naïvetés of Christian belief. Augustine was, among such converts, more unusual then than he would be now in having had an elementary education in the faith that for many years he found impossible to connect to the problems and questions of adult life.

He was a brilliant boy. The structure of late Roman society was rigid, but not too rigid for a young man of real talent, with patronage and help from the right people, to break out of an obscure provincial background and rise to fame and fortune at the centre of the Western world, Rome itself, and then Milan, by this time the effective capital of the Western empire. Ambitious parents, financial uncertainty—Augustine at sixteen spent an unhappy year at home because funds had temporarily dried up—and a sharp, competitive academic atmosphere in Carthage, where he went for his university education: all this is easy to match in contemporary Western experience. So is the high-pitched frivolity of off-

campus life in student Carthage: parties; clubs; girls; and violent, sensational entertainment, the enjoyment of which Augustine later bitterly regretted. Like almost
everyone young—but especially in the rootless, religionless freedom of a big city
far from home—he found sex the most difficult area of his life to deal with. His
solution to its problems was, for his class and time, with a "suitable" arranged
marriage lying far ahead in what was supposed to be his dazzling public future,
the most respectable available: he set up house with a simple Carthage girl and
lived with her faithfully for the next fourteen years. They had a son, born when
Augustine was eighteen, whom he loved and admired, thinking him cleverer
than himself. The boy, called Adeodatus, "given by God", died at seventeen, his
father's grief tempered by confidence in the goodness of his son, who had two
years earlier been baptized beside his father. At the very end of his life, Augustine wrote: "Surely what Cicero says comes straight from the heart of all fathers,
when he wrote: 'You are the only man of all men whom I would wish to surpass
me in all things.' " [7]

To correct the cliché that describes Augustine as a great sinner who became
a great saint ("Lord, make me chaste, but not yet" is, sadly, the only quotation
from the *Confessions* that many people know), one or two things should be said
about the relationship with the woman who was, in effect, his wife. He tells us
very little about her. He lived with her from when he was seventeen to when he
was thirty-one. Then she was sent home to Africa from Italy, because it was
time for him, now in an important post at the imperial court, to become engaged
to a rich girl whose family would advance his career. The pressure came from
his mother. The planned marriage never took place because Augustine's conversion to Christianity and lasting commitment to celibacy intervened. But the
parting cut him to the quick, and he never forgot his grief. "My heart which
was deeply attached was cut and wounded, and left a trail of blood." [8] Marriage
to this Carthage woman, either in the public, legal form by which Roman society understood marriage, or in the vows of the Christian sacrament by which
the Church understood it, was, in his circumstances at the time, impossible. He
was too young; she was too poor; he was not yet a Christian. His life with her
may have been mostly a means of coping with his ordinary youthful sexuality,
but this is not an objective to be despised, and if she was never an intellectual
companion for him, he at least learned both from what was there and what was
not there in this long domestic relationship what marriage at its best, its most
complete, could be like. Selective quotation, and lack of knowledge and understanding of the range of his mind and work, have made of him the villain of the
story of the Church and sex down the centuries, the despiser of the body, the

oppressor of women. The *Confessions* indeed records the anguish of his struggle with both his feelings and his body. But his later writing on sexuality and marriage, of which there is a good deal, has a candid realism, a compassionate acceptance of the difficulties of this whole side of life for both men and women, and a positive appreciation of how these difficulties can be managed with love and unselfishness, qualities that are rare indeed among the great theologians. Regarding natural functions as simply natural, he disagreed with the view that women should not receive Communion while menstruating. He defended the African martyrs Felicity and Perpetua as deserving an honoured place among the saints (which, in the Roman canon of the Mass, they have to this day), though the first was a pregnant slave girl and the second imprisoned with her baby. And against the local custom, which had women walking behind their husbands, he recommended Christian couples walk side by side. The woman he sent away after fourteen years, and whom he could not bear to name in the *Confessions*, should not be regarded only with pity.

Years before her loss, while he was back from Carthage as a teacher in Thagaste, Augustine suffered the loss of an exact contemporary who had become a close friend. This young man Augustine had influenced away from the Christian faith in which both of them had been brought up. Desperately ill, the friend was baptized while unconscious; when he regained consciousness, Augustine laughed at the baptism; his friend "was horrified at me as if I were an enemy".[9] They were not reconciled, and a few days later, in Augustine's absence, his friend died. Augustine does not give his name, as he does not give the name of Adeodatus's mother. His pages describing the misery of this loss and his own remorse are characteristically truthful, warm and complex. Unselfconsciously and in passing, he echoes a passage in Cicero's *On Friendship* and quotes Horace's poem on the death of Virgil, "half my soul",[10] but now, in the *Confessions*, he understands, as he could not at the time, both the friendship, indeed all close friendship, and his friend's death, in relation to the love of God.

Meanwhile, his intellectual life tacked from aspiring rationalism to superstitious belief and eventually back to rationalism. When he was nineteen his encounter with the urbane philosophical high-mindedness he discovered in Cicero's *Hortensius* caused what he afterward understood as his first conversion, to the search for wisdom as the supreme priority of life. Cicero hit home with a passage, which Augustine never forgot, on the disastrous distraction of sexual love: "What man in the grip of this, the strongest of emotions, can bend his mind to thought, regain his reason, or, indeed, concentrate on anything?"[11] Augustine was at least now peacefully living with the Carthage woman, and his domestic life certainly did not prevent his sudden realisation of the obligations of his own giftedness and the waste of time that most of his life had so far been. His brain was there to be used; he must use it in the pursuit of truth, the quest for calm wisdom that he admired in Cicero. He did not yet know that this was a search for God. He remembered that his mother had always told him that the truth is to be found in Christianity if only he would look. So he began to read the Bible, in the rough African Latin of second-century missionary translations (Saint Jerome, Augustine's exact contemporary, had not yet begun the Vulgate). Augustine, brought up on Virgil and inspired by Cicero, was appalled at the clumsy language, the brutal stories in the Old Testament, the inconsistent genealogies given for Jesus by Matthew and Luke. He left the Bible to one side of his life for years and joined the followers of Mani, a charismatic heretic from the east, a hundred years dead but still a guru—"his followers thought themselves to be going after not a mere man but your Holy Spirit" [12]—for many of those in search of enlightenment in the eclectic religious fog (also familiar to us now) of the late empire. Mani's teaching instilled a heavily mythical and dualistic set of beliefs. Only the most severe asceticism could release the good spirit in man from a physical world irredeemably evil. An elite few, of whom Augustine was never one, were expected to live a "perfect" life; other members of the sect were called "hearers".

It is surprising that the brightly coloured fables—comprehensive, extreme and bold, yet shallow—of the Manichaean creed could have held someone as intelligent as Augustine for as long as nine years, although Manichaean circles first in Rome and then in Milan provided company and support for the African making his professional way in Italy. In fact, Augustine's life during these years was an uneasy period of conflicting aims, superficial success, suppressed guilt and the gradual realisation of the sect's failure to deliver the promised light in the darkness of human confusion. As he freed himself from the Manichees with the relief that many an intellectual has felt on abandoning a closed and simplistic version of Christianity that he has taken for Christianity itself, Augustine returned to the consoling agnosticism of philosophers who could not agree with each other. Truth is somewhere, no doubt, but since the physical world is all that is real, the only thing to be done about truth is to suspend judgement. Thinkers now seemed attractive who "taught that everything is a matter of doubt, and that an understanding of the truth lies beyond human capacity. . . . I did not think anything existed which is not material." "I had no hope that truth could be found in your Church, Lord of heaven and earth, maker of all things visible and invisible. The Manichees had turned me away from that." The Incarnation, in particular, was evidently impossible, a "shameful" idea.[13] Describing this period in the *Confessions*, he uses the image of Plato's cave, unknown to him at the time:

> I had by myself read and understood all the books I could get hold of
> on the arts which they call liberal.... I enjoyed reading them, though
> I did not know the source of what was true and certain in them. I had
> my back to the light and my face towards the things which are illu-
> minated. So my face, by which I was enabled to see the things lit up,
> was not itself illuminated.[14]

He could not look at the light, because he did not know where it came from. As he read and explained with ease material that his colleagues and students found difficult, he discovered how quick and acute his own intelligence was: that it was a gift to be used in the service of the giver he had no idea.

By 385, in Milan as professor of rhetoric and orator, or minister of propaganda, to the emperor, writing complimentary speeches to welcome visiting generals and teaching rich, bored students, he began to feel that perhaps he should give some proper attention to the Christianity that had framed his childhood. His mother, who had joined him in Milan, became a friend and disciple of the bishop. Ambrose of Milan was the most striking figure in late fourth-century Italy. A Roman patrician, governor of the city and its province before he became a Christian and its bishop, steady in opposition to imperial encroachment on his Church and people, he was calm, wise, well-read and a celebrated preacher. A deep-dyed Ciceronian, Ambrose wrote *On the Duties of Ministers* as a Christian version of Cicero's *On Duties*. Ambrose's book, which sets Cicero's civic morality in a context of obedience to God and the Christian's need for grace, was a standard textbook in the training of priests for centuries. As an expert critic of rhetorical method, Augustine went to hear Ambrose preach. Describing this carefully to God, as always in the *Confessions*, he wrote:

> I was not interested in learning what he was talking about. My ears
> were only for his rhetorical technique; this empty concern was all that
> remained with me after I had lost any hope that a way to you might lie
> open for man. Nevertheless together with the words which I was enjoy-
> ing, the subject matter, in which I was unconcerned, came to make an
> entry into my mind. I could not separate them. While I opened my
> heart in noting the eloquence with which he spoke, there also entered
> no less the truth which he affirmed, though only gradually.[15]

The experience recorded here, a deeper version of his experience with Cicero's *Hortensius*, is not unlike that of a modern student reading Dante or George Herbert or Gerard Manley Hopkins or Eliot's *Four Quartets* and beginning to wonder if some challenge beyond that to his literary judgement is being made to his heart. Might this text, these words, suggest that a way to God does, after all, lie open for man? Augustine's first response was only to take refuge in the paralysis of a busy life:

> Here I was already thirty, and still mucking about in the same mire in a state of indecision, avid to enjoy present fugitive delights which were dispersing my concentration, while I was saying: "Tomorrow I shall find it; see, it will become perfectly clear, and I shall have no more doubts.... Let me fix my feet on that step where as a boy I was placed by my parents, until clear truth is found. But where may it be sought? Where can it be sought? Ambrose has no time. There is no time for reading. Where should we look for the books we need? ... Great hope has been aroused. The Catholic faith does not teach what we thought, and we were mistaken in criticizing it.... Why do we hesitate to knock at the door which opens the way to all the rest? Our pupils occupy our mornings; what should we do with the remaining hours? Why do we not investigate our problem? But then when should we go to pay our respects to our more influential friends, whose patronage we need? When are we to prepare what our students are paying for?[16]

So he dithered. And before he found his hesitant way to the Church he had blundered past for so long, he was bowled over by the intellectual excitement of the great Neoplatonist philosophers of the previous century. Plotinus and Porphyry were neither of them Christian, and Porphyry, an acute thinker, was scornful of the evident absurdity of Christian doctrine. Augustine learned much from their books. In particular he learned more of Plato than he could have collected from Cicero. From Plotinus's work he discovered how close Plato had come to an understanding of the being of God. (That some of Augustine's thinking is nearer to Plato, whom he had not read, than to the Neoplatonists, whom he had read, is an indication of how close Plato did come to an idea of God compatible with Christian truth.) With Christian hindsight, Augustine in the *Confessions* says that, "to these philosophers, who were without Christ's saving name, I altogether refused to entrust the healing of my soul's sickness."[17] But some of the Milanese Neoplatonists were Christian. It was well known that Marius Victorinus, a famous teacher of rhetoric in Rome a generation earlier and the translator into Latin of both Plotinus and Porphyry, had startled the theosophist intelligentsia of Rome by being baptized and had died a faithful Christian. An old priest in Milan, Simplicianus, had known Marius Victorinus: his telling of the story of the philosopher's conversion and of his courage, as a Christian, in defying the pagan emperor Julian made a deep impression on Augustine. One way or another, Augustine now found himself, for the first time in his life, in the company of highly educated Christians who could hold their own in argument with sophisticated sceptics, Stoics or pagan Neoplatonists. Perhaps it was possible after all for someone of Augustine's intelligence and education to take seriously the extraordinary claims that Christianity makes.

When at last real conversion came, it was, as Christian conversion must always be, to Christ himself, to Christ as the way to God, to Christ as truth, to Christ as a life to be lived. Augustine describes in the *Confessions* how he arrived at the gulf that separates Plato and his followers from Christian revelation. In the books of the Platonists, he read of the Word of God as "the true light which illuminates every man coming into the world".

> Further, "he was in this world, and the world was made by him, and the world did not know him." But that "he came to his own and his own did not receive him; but as many as received him, to them he gave the power to become sons of God by believing in his name", that I did not read there.... That "the word was made flesh and dwelt among us" I did not read there.[18]

In Balthasar's last retrospective talk, delivered in Madrid in the month before his death, he said:

> St. Paul would say to the philosophers that God created man so that he would *seek* the Divine, try to attain the Divine. That is why all pre-Christian philosophy is theological at its summit. But, in fact, the true response to philosophy could only be given by Being himself, revealing himself from himself.[19]

The scale of the difference that God's revelation of himself in Christ made to man's search for the truth never left Balthasar's mind, as it never left Augustine's. "I had broken the most hateful bonds", Augustine wrote to a friend, "the despair of finding truth, truth which is the nourishing food of the soul."[20] For the rest of his life Augustine never forgot that truth in Christ is a gift of God, not our own but his, a gift from transcendence to and for humanity. "Of itself," he wrote much later, "the human heart is devoid of light; of itself, devoid of strength. All that is beautiful—virtue and wisdom—has its residence in the heart. Yet it is not wise of itself nor strong of itself; it is neither its own light nor its own strength." [21]

Until the fullness of Christian revelation became that to which he was able to respond from his heart, Augustine—and this has been for more than a century a common opinion among many who call themselves Christians—"thought of Christ my Lord only as a man of excellent wisdom which none could equal." Then, he says, he was sure of the conception of God current among the Platonists, but "to enjoy you I was too weak. I prattled on as if I were expert (*peritus*), but unless I had sought your way in Christ our Saviour, I would have been not expert but expunged (*periturus*).... Where was the love which builds on the foundation of humility which is Christ Jesus? When would the Platonist books have taught me that?" [22] He thanks God, nevertheless, for having led him to the philosophers before leading him to Christ. What he had learned from the Platonists was valuable because it gave him the wherewithal to distinguish, as a Christian, "the difference between presumption and confession, between those who see what the goal is but not how to get there and those who see the way which leads to the home of bliss, not merely as an end to be perceived but as a realm to live in." [23] To grasp this distinction is essential for an understanding not only of Augustine but also of what genuine conversion to Christianity always is. An intellectual conclusion, "an end perceived", it is not; a way of being, a commitment of a life into the hands of God, "a realm to live in", it is.

Christ as the way haunts these pages of the *Confessions* until, in a flurry of scriptural quotation, at last Augustine says: "I sought a way to obtain strength enough to enjoy you, but I did not find it until I embraced 'the mediator between God and man, the man Christ Jesus', 'who is above all things, God blessed for ever'. He called and said, 'I am the way, the truth and the life.'" And the paragraph ends: "I did not know what his weakness was meant to teach." [24] The contrast between strength sought and weakness discovered in this passage is beautifully caught in a single Latin verb elsewhere in Augustine: "Repuerescat Deo" (Let [the believer] become a child again for God). [25] In Jesus's words: "Whoever does not receive the Kingdom of God like a child will not enter into it." [26] Balthasar's very last book, written when he was eighty-three, the manuscript lying finished on his desk when he died, was called *Unless You Become Like This Child*.

So Augustine became a Christian, and Ambrose baptized him in the basilica of Milan at the Easter Vigil of the year 387.

In the months between his conversion and his baptism, with his mother, his son and a group of friends, he lived in retirement at Cassiciacum in the north Italian countryside, thinking and writing in the civilised peace of ancient classical tradition. The short books he wrote here, including the *Soliloquies* (a word he invented), he criticised in detail in the *Retractationes* when he looked back to them at the end of his life. They show how narrowly he had escaped the temptation of Neoplatonist philosophy as enough to engage his mind for the rest of his life. That phrase—"engage his mind"—is one key to his rescue into the truth of Christian revelation. Manichaean dualism, disgusted contempt for the body and the whole material world, and then Neoplatonist abstraction each suited, for a time, a young man anguished above all by the temptations of the flesh. The philosophers of the day—like the philosophers of our own day—regarded the specific, physical reality of Christianity, of the Incarnation and death and Resurrection of Christ at a particular point in history, and of the sacraments, most of all the Eucharist, as scandalously material in relation to the meaning claimed for it, fit for the belief only of women, children and slaves. In a sermon only recently discovered, Augustine recorded this lofty attitude: "Me! Become a Christian, be what my doorkeeper is, and not what Plato was or what Pythagoras was!" [27] That the Word was made flesh was to the Manichees a repulsive notion because all flesh was evil. To the trained philosophical mind, it was simply beyond credibility. A vital discovery that Augustine made in Milan was that while Christianity required him to abandon his Manichaean horror of the physical, it did not require him to abandon or blunt his trained mind, his critical sense, the use of the intelligence that he now recognised as a gift and a responsibility. The grace of God that had pulled him over the chasm that separated Plato from Christ was not an end but a beginning. His task for the rest of his life was to learn: he says in the *Soliloquies* that his only occupation is "to learn God and the soul, nothing more".[28]

In 390, now back in Thagaste after his mother's death in Italy but still with a group of friends, he wrote *Of True Religion*, his last work before he was ordained priest. Here, in an elegant reconciliation of the Platonism to which he owed so much with the Christianity that had superseded it, he imagines Plato imagining Christ. Only a man who is himself the wisdom of God would be able to "despise all that wicked men desire, to suffer all that they dread, to do all that they marvel at, and so with the greatest love and authority to convert the human race" to faith in God. Such a mediator is as necessary to the philosophers who have come close to a true idea of God as he is "to persuade the peoples that such things were to be at least believed if they could not grasp them with the mind." [29]

That in apparently scandalous Christianity the philosophers too must believe before they could understand, Augustine already knew. One of his favourite phrases became the priority of faith over understanding: "unless you believe, you will not understand", or more exactly, because the Latin uses the common grammatical form of a verb in the future-perfect followed by one in the future tense—"nisi credideritis, non intellegetis" (unless you have believed, you will not understand). The phrase is an alteration of Augustine's to the phrase in Isaiah: "unless you believe, you will not stand firm" (nisi credideritis, non permanebitis).[30] In both phrases, faith is the gift offered, the response made; understanding and perseverance are the open future. In a sermon of the year 418, now in the present tense of long experience, Augustine says to his people: "If you can't understand, believe in order to understand; faith comes first, understanding follows."[31]

His writings before he became a priest were early steps on the road toward the great theological works of Augustine's maturity, a road on which the Confessions, begun seven years later, was itself only a staging-post. Augustine saw his life, any Christian life, as a pilgrimage through "the land of unlikeness" (a phrase he borrowed from Plato) that is the fallen world and in it our own fallenness. The writer of the Confessions addresses God with much joy and gratitude and praise, but he is still in the grip of his complicated past, still restless, sometimes unhappy, divided against himself. He knows, keenly, how often failure and sin have to be recognised, repented of, forgiven and learned from; with how much pain the love God teaches has to be accepted, answered and practised, because the process is not a gentle one; how insecure our response to the goodness of God always is. As an old man, a bishop of constantly increasing influence and fame for more than thirty years, he wrote: "No one is known to another so intimately as he is known to himself, and yet no one is so well known even to himself that he can be sure as to his conduct on the morrow."[32]

* * *

The Confessions, the whole of which is not dauntingly long to read, is divided into thirteen books. The autobiography stops at the end of book 9 with the death of Augustine's mother. This took place in Ostia, near Rome, a few months after Augustine's baptism. Much had happened to him since; he had made and accepted important changes in his way of life. He had returned from Italy to Africa, lived quietly for a while at Thagaste (where Adeodatus died), moved with his household to Hippo, been ordained priest in 391, and in 396 been persuaded to accept consecration as bishop. He does not bother to describe any of this in the Confessions, as if—and any reader of the book will understand this—his baptism and the death of the mother whose passionate Christianity and exigent love for him had always been a mixed blessing had together brought him (a far from simple) relief.

The *Confessions*, together with much in the books, sermons and letters that Augustine wrote in the subsequent decades of his life, give us an exemplary record of interior truthfulness in the terrifying but also consoling sight of God. The historical detail is compelling: Augustine lived in and closely observed a time of critical importance for the future of the Church and of the world. More compelling, and timeless in its value, is his clear-eyed self-observation, surprise, regret, fear and resolve, his penetrating honesty about himself in the light shed by God into the mysteriousness of his own being. His self-awareness chimes over and over again with the self-awareness, unmitigated by disguise or pride, that all of us, if only at our best, are capable of. Augustine in the *Confessions* presents his reader with the texture and feel of his unique experience, reminding the reader that all human life is no more than life lived by one person at a time. In book 10 of the *Confessions*, a long meditation in the present tense, he explores the workings of his own memory in relation to his senses, to pleasure and pain, to truth of different kinds, to his conscience, to God, and even to his unconscious mind, something of which no one before him, and no one after him for many centuries, took any account. The book is, and is intended to be, a lesson in introspection, a lesson in learning more of God from the depths of the self. "Summa magistra veritas intus docens",[33] Augustine says elsewhere: "Truth, the supreme master, teaching within."

He begins book 10 with the hope that his confession in both senses, confession of his own sinfulness and confession of belief in the truth of God—neither of which God needs because "you hear nothing true from my lips which you have not first told me"[34]—will help his readers to know themselves better. "The human race is inquisitive about other people's lives, but negligent to correct their own. Why do they demand to hear from me what I am when they refuse to hear from you what they are?"[35] There follows an astonishing exploration of the inner life of a person, Augustine himself. His knowledge is given him by God. His knowledge will not, this side of death, be complete. "Let me confess what I know of myself. Let me confess too what I do not know of myself. For what I know of myself I know because you grant me light, and what I do not know of myself, I do not know until such time as my darkness becomes 'like noonday' before your face."[36] The true story of each of us is only in God.

What he feels for the beauty of the created world, apprehended through his senses, he uses, as an analogy that is also a means, to describe his love for God. In these two paragraphs,[37] beautiful in themselves, is a complete theory of aesthetics grounded in the being of God. He asked the sea, the air, living creatures, sun, moon and stars: "'Tell me of my God who you are not, tell me something about him.' And with a great voice they cried out: 'He made us'. My question was the attention I gave to them, and their response was their beauty." Exploring further his soul, which gives to the evidence of his senses this meaning, which is beyond the scope of the animals who share our senses, he turns to his memory, a bottomless mystery in its workings that is also his own, ungraspable, self. How is it that one can see a remembered picture, its forms and colours, in the darkness of one's mind or hear remembered music in its silence? What is it that sees and hears when the ears and eyes are closed? If he had known that *Paradise Lost* would be seen and dictated from Milton's blindness or known the last quartets heard and written from Beethoven's deafness, his awe at the capacity given to the mind by God would have been only confirmed.

As for our ability to think and to communicate in abstractions, including the abstractions of simple mathematics, which everyone can recognise—where does this come from? How does it relate to the power of memory? And what about emotion? How is it that we can remember, and talk about, feelings of different kinds without feeling them? "What is going on when, in gladly remembering past sadness, my mind is glad and my memory sad?"[38] What is forgetfulness? What is going on in the mind when we search it for something we have forgotten? "If something other than what we want is offered us, we reject it until the thing we are looking for turns up. And when it comes, we say 'That is it.' . . . But if we have completely forgotten, we cannot even search for what has been lost."[39]

In an exhilarating rush of thought, these questions take him on to the further question of how everyone knows, without having learned it from experience and therefore remembered it, that happiness is what he seeks. This question, like all those preceding it, does not lead to an answer, and certainly not to Plato's theory that since we know things we have never been taught, we must have learned them in former lives. The question leads to God and to a further question: Since real happiness is to be found only in God, and since everyone agrees that happiness is what he wants, why do so many people fail in their search because they choose other kinds of happiness that do not make them happy? His observation as keen as ever, he declares:

> If I put the question to anyone whether he prefers to find joy in the truth or in falsehood, he does not hesitate to say that he prefers the truth, just as he does not hesitate to say he wants to be happy. The happy life is joy based on the truth. This joy is grounded in you, O God,

who are the truth. This happy life everyone desires; joy in the truth everyone wants. I have met with many people who wished to deceive, none who wished to be deceived.[40]

So the answer to the question of wrong choices lies, not in what we are able to recognise, but in the weakness of the will and in the weakness with which, in many lives, the light, "their tenuous consciousness of the truth", manages to shine. The truth, indeed, engenders hatred in those who have chosen something other than God to love:

> Their love for truth takes the form that they love something else and want this object of their love to be the truth; and because they do not wish to be deceived, they do not wish to be persuaded that they are mistaken. And so they hate the truth for the sake of the object which they love instead of the truth.[41]

Augustine had written several years earlier, in *Of True Religion*—and the perception is fundamental to the whole later development of his thought: "Whether he will or no, a man is necessarily a slave to the things by means of which he seeks to be happy. He follows them wherever they lead, and fears anyone who seems to have the power to rob him of them."[42] To confirm the pull of God as the object of a properly directed quest for happiness, the discussion returns to the beauty with which it began, in the famous paragraph that starts: "Late have I loved you, beauty so old and so new: late have I loved you. And see, you were within and I was in the external world and sought you there."[43]

The key issue of what people choose to love, and why, will be richly amplified in Augustine's later and much longer book, the *City of God*. Meanwhile, he continues book 10 of the *Confessions* with a probing examination of his own conscience, realistic as he always is in the awareness that "anyone who could change from the worse to the better can also change from the better to the worse."[44] With candour and not without humour, he describes how easily distracted he is, how beset with the dangers of respect and praise that a position of successfully exercised authority brings ("the enemy of our true happiness is constant in attack, everywhere laying traps with 'Well done, well done'"[45]); how alarming are the impulses of the subconscious, "which your eyes know but mine do not";[46] how easy it is to be proud of resisting the temptations of pride.

Book 10 ends with a return to the truth, the whole and only truth of God in revelation, in the Incarnation of the Word as Christ the true mediator, as God and man, between man and God, who in his sacrificial death and in his Resurrection has opened the way to God for us all. "We might have thought", with the philosophers, "your Word was far removed from being united to mankind and have despaired of our lot unless he had become flesh and dwelt among us." [47] But it is now possible for us to recognise the love of God for us in the life, death and Resurrection of Christ. A concluding paragraph of scriptural quotation from all over the Bible ends with a simple line from a psalm: "And they shall praise the Lord who seek him." [48]

This single book of the *Confessions* is remarkable in at least three ways. In the first place, the book is a complex meditation before God on the "things invisible" that the Nicene Creed had declared that God created, as he created "things visible". The beauty of things invisible is intelligible rather than perceptible through the senses: the pregnant phrase "intelligible beauty" was used by Augustine as early as the *Soliloquies*.[49] In the second place, many of the questions Augustine asks himself about the nature of consciousness and of what lies impenetrably beneath it, of the workings of the mind and the memory and of the unreliability of the will are still unanswered sixteen centuries and a great deal of modern science later. To present them to God as he does, in a spirit of wonder and gratitude at the depths of reflection and possibility in each of us, is, now as then, simply the best thing to do with them, not so that answers may be arrived at, but so that the mystery of the human soul may come, humbly but consciously, closer to the mystery of the God who made it. In the third place, nothing in the *Confessions*, and very little anywhere in Augustine's writings, is difficult to understand if approached with no more than an open, intelligent mind prepared to follow him into the always much greater openness and intelligence of his own mind.

The last three books of the *Confessions* form the third of five commentaries (the last, *De Genesi ad litteram*, being one of the long works of his maturity) that he wrote on the creation story at the beginning of Genesis. Book 11 mostly consists of a thrilling investigation into the nature of time, prompted by the first words of the Bible, "In the beginning". With the uncluttered bafflement of a bright child—"What then is time? Provided that no one asks me, I know" [50]— Augustine dissolves the past (which no longer exists), the future (which does not yet exist) and the present (which is of such immeasurably short duration that it cannot exist). Constantly asking for God's help in his enquiry, he travels swiftly to the realisation that somehow, somewhere, all time must be present. "Stand firm, my mind, concentrate with resolution. God is our help, he has made us and not we ourselves." [51] After a dozen pages of irresistibly fresh thinking, though a number of earlier philosophers, absorbed rather than quoted, lurk in the background, he arrives at the eternity that is only God's. In God's eternity the incoherence, the distractions, of time disappear, and there God is (has been? will be?) known, in whom we also are known. In the excitement of following the tremendous sweep of Augustine's exploration of time as God's creation out of his eternity, it is easy to miss a single sentence that affirms what, at last, a person is, in God: "Then shall I find stability and solidity in you, in your truth which imparts form to me."[52] This is one of the most powerful statements in the whole of the *Confessions*, illuminating, for example, the "stability and solidity" in God of the person we see, in time, impaired or apparently destroyed by illness or old age, and then see no longer, inevitably gone from us in death.

Augustine ends the book with a musical analogy: "A person singing or listening to a song he knows well suffers a distension or stretching in feeling and in sense-perception from the expectation of future sounds and the memory of past sound."[53] Time, in other words, is essential to our sense of form in music, as to our sense of our own life or anyone's life. "With you," Augustine says, abandoning the analogy and giving up his spirited attempt to fathom the mystery of God's eternity, "it is otherwise. You are unchangeably eternal, that is the truly eternal Creator of minds.... Let the person who understands this make confession to you. Let him who fails to understand it make confession to you."[54] It is wholly characteristic of Augustine to leave, in this fashion, nobody beyond the reach of what he is saying.

The concluding two books of the *Confessions* struggle against Neoplatonist conceptions of time and matter to establish a Christian account of God's creation of the universe that will also help both Augustine and his reader to realise more deeply the mysteries of the Trinity and the Church. The argument is a firework display of metaphor and scriptural quotation, brilliant against a darkness that Augustine acknowledges still surrounds his efforts to understand the ways of God. Toward the end of book 13, in an analogy that, again, owes a good deal to Plato's cave, he distinguishes the moon and the stars of knowledge shining in the night, which are all the light "the natural man" can cope with in "the darkness of those who are infants but not without hope",[55] from the sun of wisdom, which is the shining of God himself. "Join the society of those among whom he speaks wisdom, for he knows what belongs to the day and what to the night; then you too may know that. For you lights in the firmament are created. This will not happen unless your heart is in it, and that will not occur unless your treasure is there."[56] Faith and love, in other words, and only faith and love, will take you toward, though always only toward, the whole truth that is God.

Looking back to the *Confessions* after thirty years in his *Retractationes*, Augustine said very little. The praise of God in the *Confessions* still moved him, and he was glad that the book had pleased and moved many people. Generation after generation, the book has astonished its readers, drawing them into the drama of Augustine's journey toward the truth, understood by him in the light of that truth. Augustine with a pen in his hand, always but most of all in the *Confessions*, is not writing as a professional philosopher, an academic communicating his conclusions to other academics. His knowledge of himself, and even more his knowledge of God, are not static, not possessions to be handed over to his readers. He writes to discover what he thinks, as a companion, persuading his reader to try to live, as he is trying to live, in and for the truth, in which understanding will constantly grow but never in this world reach its end—in one of his most celebrated phrases, "Deus semper maior" (God [is] always greater).[57] It is, indeed, that the *Confessions* is a conversation with God, who is always greater than even the greatest, cleverest and most thoughtful of his children, that gives the book its particular quality. In 1956 Karl Rahner, in a few sentences not specifically about the *Confessions*, exactly defined this quality:

> Man is a mystery. He is so in his very essence, in his nature. Not because the infinite fullness of the mystery which touches him is actually in himself, for it is strictly inexhaustible, but because he is fundamentally a *pour-soi* purely in reference to that fullness. When we have said everything the mind can take in, everything definable that is to be said about ourselves, we have as yet said nothing, unless we have included in every statement the fact of our reference to the incomprehensible God; and that reference, and therefore our nature itself in the most fundamental sense, is not really understood at all unless we freely allow ourselves to be caught up by that incomprehensible God.[58]

If we allow ourselves to be caught up, for the time being, by God, Augustine will take us by the hand and lead us some way along his own path of understanding and of love. In the simpler words of Henri de Lubac, writing about conversion: "We are shown a new country, a home we had originally ignored, and as soon as we perceive it we recognize it as older and truer than anything we had known and with claims upon our heart."[59] "We have no fear", Augustine concluded book 4 of the *Confessions*, "that there is no home to which we may return because we fell from it. During our absence our house suffers no ruin; it is your eternity."[60]

1. Augustine, *Confessions* 1.1.1, trans. Henry Chadwick (Oxford, 1991).
2. Ibid., 13.38.53.
3. Ibid., 1.13.22, 21.
4. Augustine, *Epistulae* 143.2, quoted in Peter Brown, *Augustine of Hippo* (London, 1967), p. 353.
5. Serge Lancel, *Saint Augustine*, trans. Antonia Nevill (London, 2002), p. 476.
6. Augustine, *De Genesi ad litteram* 5.23.
7. Quoted in Brown, *Augustine of Hippo*, p. 135.
8. Augustine, *Confessions* 6.15.25.
9. Ibid., 4.4.8.
10. Horace, *Odes* 1.3.8, quoted in ibid., 4.6.11.
11. Quoted in Brown, *Augustine of Hippo*, p. 50.
12. Augustine, *Confessions* 5.5.9.
13. Ibid., 5.10.19.
14. Ibid., 4.16.30.
15. Ibid., 5.14.24.
16. Ibid., 6.2.18.
17. Ibid., 5.14.25.
18. Ibid., 7.9.13–14.
19. Hans Urs von Balthasar, *My Work in Retrospect*, trans. Brian McNeil et al. (San Francisco, 1983), p. 113.
20. Augustine, *Ep.* 1.3, quoted in Brown, *Augustine of Hippo*, p. 110.
21. Augustine, *Enarrationes in Psalmos* 58.18.
22. Augustine, *Confessions* 7.20.26.
23. Ibid.
24. Ibid., 7.18.24.
25. Augustine, *De qualitate animae* 55, quoted in Hans Urs von Balthasar, *The Glory of the Lord*, vol. 2, trans. Andrew Louth et al. (Edinburgh, 1984), p. 106.
26. Mk 10:15.
27. Quoted in Lancel, *Saint Augustine*, p. 316.
28. Augustine, *Soliloquies* 2.7, in *Augustine: Earlier Writings*, ed. and trans. John H. S. Burleigh (Philadelphia and London, 1953), p. 26.
29. Augustine, *Of True Religion* 3.3, in *Augustine: Earlier Writings*, p. 227.
30. Is 7:9.
31. Augustine, sermon 118.1, quoted in Lancel, *Saint Augustine*, pp. 154 and 496; my translation.
32. Augustine, *Ep.* 130.2.4, quoted in Brown, *Augustine of Hippo*, p. 405.
33. Augustine, *De libero arbitrio* 2.4, quoted in Balthasar, *Glory of the Lord* 2:111, n. 93.
34. Augustine, *Confessions* 10.2.2.
35. Ibid., 10.13.3.
36. Ibid., 10.5.7.
37. Ibid., 10.6.8–9.
38. Ibid., 10.14.21.
39. Ibid., 10.19.28.
40. Ibid., 10.23.33.
41. Ibid., 10.23.34.
42. Augustine, *Of True Religion* 38.69, in *Augustine: Earlier Writings*, p. 260.
43. Augustine, *Confessions* 10.27.38.
44. Ibid., 10.32.48.
45. Ibid., 10.36.59.
46. Ibid., 10.37.60.
47. Ibid., 10.43.69.
48. Ps 21:27.
49. Augustine, *Soliloquies* 5.11, in *Augustine: Earlier Writings*, p. 30.
50. Augustine, *Confessions* 11.14.17.

51. Ibid., 11.27.34.
52. Ibid., 11.30.40.
53. Ibid., 11.31.41.
54. Ibid.
55. Ibid., 13.19.25.
56. Ibid., 13.19.24.
57. Augustine, *Enarrationes in Psalmos* 62.16.
58. Karl Rahner, *Schriften zur Theologie* (1956), p. 47, quoted in Henri de Lubac, *The Mystery of the Supernatural*, trans. Rosemary Sheed (London, 1967), p. 275.
59. Henri de Lubac, *The Discovery of God*, trans. Alexander Dru (Edinburgh, 1996), p. 159.
60. Augustine, *Confessions* 4.16.31.

CHAPTER SIX

AUGUSTINE II

City of God

The *Confessions* has always been a much-loved book, at least in part because of the reader's impression that in it Augustine represents not only each of us in our own struggle to recognise the light of God that shines in our lives, but also all of fallen mankind, into whose night, lit only by philosophical stars, the sun had broken in Christ. In the story of his own life, but much more in his understanding of it, we see and feel, with a clarity to be found nowhere else, the impact of the Christian revelation on the human world both as it was at the time of Christ's coming into the Roman Mediterranean and as it always and everywhere is. Balthasar describes this impact as

> the self-disclosure of infinite freedom [that] has lit up human history like a lightning flash. . . . Now that infinite freedom has become accessible to finite freedom, the latter has the opportunity—for the first time—to fulfill itself. Who could "have treasure in heaven" while heaven was unattainable by the creature? In concrete terms, infinite freedom appears on stage in the form of Jesus Christ's "lowliness" and "obedience unto death". Thus he can call to himself the "weary and heavy-laden" and summon even the clumsy and hesitant to be his disciples.[1]

The context of this passage is a discussion of the relationship between the infinite freedom of God and our finite freedom to respond, or not, to the grace of God. In even the few sentences just quoted, Balthasar glances at several major Augustinian themes, visible in the *Confessions* but developed with more weight in Augustine's later writing, particularly in the *City of God*.

The *City of God* was begun as Augustine's response to the crisis in the Western Roman world, a crisis of confidence and of long-held assumptions, caused by decades of barbarian invasion across inadequately defended frontiers and sharpened by the Goths' sack of Rome itself in 410. He started work on it in 412, planning it from the outset in twenty-two books. He finished it in 426 at the age of seventy-two. During these years he was also writing *On the Trinity* and his commentaries on Saint John and on the Psalms.

The *City of God* was written both for educated pagans and for educated Christians, who were watching, with different kinds of grievance and bafflement, Latin civilisation apparently coming to an end. Considerable numbers of both had arrived in Africa as refugees from Rome. Pagans were blaming Christianity for the weakening of *romanitas*, traditional civic and military morale that should have been preserving the Western empire from collapse. Christians, misled by the propaganda of Constantine's church and court a century earlier that the kingdom of God had become, or would become, earthly reality as a Christian empire, were relying on God to protect Rome from its terrifying, though awed, destroyers. Both sets of assumptions, despite Augustine's exposure of their flaws and despite the respect in which the *City of God* was held for many centuries, had a long, if discontinuous, future. The view of the nostalgic pagans received, in the eighteenth century, a ringing endorsement from Gibbon, whose huge work of scholarship, *The Decline and Fall of the Roman Empire*, chimes with the intellectual consensus of his time in regarding the Christian millennium in the West (from, say, 500 to 1500) as an unfortunate aberration now happily outgrown. In the two hundred years since Gibbon's death, that consensus has much strengthened, the accelerating achievements of modern science seeming only to confirm its evident correctness. Meanwhile, Constantinople's identification of the kingdom of God with a Christian empire haunted the Middle Ages, driving, if also judging, centuries of conflict between empire (and kingdoms) and the papacy, Church and state. In direct descent from Constantinople, it inspired tsarist Russia. In indirect descent from a Christian utopianism that Augustine carefully dismantled, it combined with the secular idealism of the founding fathers (Gibbon's exact contemporaries, born in the "Augustan" age and educated by the Enlightenment) to inspire the prosperous and recently aggressive self-righteousness of America.

The *City of God* is a very long, very complex and densely specific work, written in the maturity and old age of a constantly busy man. With a range and power for which there was no model, it delivers a Christian judgement on the thought, history, ideals and priorities of the classical world as that world was falling to pieces. The achievement of Greece, particularly in philosophy, and the achievement of Rome, particularly in government, are reviewed and placed in relation to Christian truth. Both are subjected to detailed criticism; neither is deprived of value. But the value of each, and of much else that men prize, is shown, now, to be relative.

The texts of classical Greek philosophy were, as we have seen, only scantily available to Augustine. Nevertheless, he manages a fair survey of the pre-Socratic enquirers into the nature of the universe, a warm tribute to the intellectual penetration, the moral example and the charm of Socrates, and a good discussion of Plato's closeness to Christian truth, most evident in the startling parallels between the account of the creation in Genesis and some passages in the *Timaeus*. Augustine suggests various explanations for these parallels. Although modern scholars know much more than he did of the history of the texts,[2] there is still some truth in his tentative: "It may be that with the intuition of genius Plato observed 'the invisible realities of God' presented to the mind by means of his creation."[3] He disposes at length of the pagan gods believed in by some philosophers and of the hierarchies of spirits populating, in Neoplatonism, the space between mankind and God: we need no other mediator but Christ. Using, as he often does in the *City of God*, the juxtaposition of false and true to arrive at the clearest possible definition of the true, he compares Neoplatonist angels, the miracles supposed to be produced by magic and the sacrifices of superstition with the angels and miracles of God attested by Scripture and with the one true sacrifice of Christ on the Cross and in the Eucharist, where "the Church, being the body of which he is the head, learns to offer itself through him."[4]

The most acute, and the most enthralling, section of this confrontation with the philosophy known to Augustine is his argument with Porphyry in the last six chapters of book 10. Porphyry was Plotinus's most impressive disciple and died in Rome fifty years before Augustine was born. Augustine confronts him as a representative of all those educated people in the Roman world who, secure in the rationality of their own positions, regarded Christian teaching as ridiculous. Happy to consign "the vast majority [who] have no taste for philosophy" to the darkness of superstition, they pride themselves on their intellectual superiority, regarding it as unassailable wisdom. Quoting Virgil's Fourth Eclogue, and Isaiah and Saint Paul on the folly of God destroying the wisdom of the wise, Augustine puts his finger on precisely why the philosophers resist the revelation of truth in Christ: contemptuous self-sufficiency blinds them to the humility of Christ in his Incarnation, in his death, in his bodily Resurrection. "Grace ... heals the weakness of those who do not proudly boast of their delusive happiness, but instead make a humble admission of their genuine misery [need]. ... Humility was the necessary condition for submission to this truth; and it is no easy task to persuade the proud necks of you philosophers to accept this yoke."[5] It is in this physical life that we are, that we sin, that we suffer and inflict suffering; it is to redeem this life that Christ entered it. But the philosophers reckon themselves to have redeemed themselves from suffering, from the constraints of the physical, by thinking. This is "the difference between presumption and confession"[6] that Augustine had already described in the *Confessions*.

Augustine does not leave Porphyry here. In the last chapter of book 10, he handsomely concedes that a powerful reason for Porphyry's rejection of Christianity was that he did not recognise it, persecuted and apparently fragile as it was at the time, as "a universal way of liberation for the soul", something Porphyry consciously sought. "That such a way exists is not doubted by a man so exceptionally talented as Porphyry", but that Christianity is, precisely, this way did not "come to his notice". The philosophers sought one way of liberation, their own, through the intellect; they left other ways, "spiritual" or "for the body", to the rest of the human race. They could not see that "it was to avoid such quests that ... the all-powerful Saviour took upon himself man in his entirety."[7] It was for everyone that Christ came, foretold as he was by the prophets "where they could find a hearing, among men who enjoyed the favour of God, and in particular among the Hebrew people". In the penultimate paragraph of book 10 Augustine lists all the essential tenets of Christian faith, as prophesied in the Old Testament and as fulfilled and amplified in the New, and concludes: "This is the right road which leads to the vision of God and to eternal union with him; it is proclaimed and asserted in the truth of the holy Scriptures. And all those who do not believe in it, and therefore fail to understand it, may attack it; they cannot overthrow it."[8] That "therefore" is not only Augustine's last shot, for the moment, at the proud philosophers; it is another instance of his own confidence, resting on his own experience, that faith leads to understanding, rather than the reverse.

Much later in the *City of God*, Augustine describes with his usual penetration the endless, literally endless because without conclusion, disagreements of philosophers with each other, with their predecessors, with their own pupils. Philosophers ask the right questions. "They do not seem to have had any other aim in their laborious pursuits than to discover how we should regulate our lives towards the attainment of happiness."[9] Why is there this chaos of opinion among the rational, when philosophers suppose reason to be irrefutable common ground, the only certain basis for any truth? "Must it not be because they sought the answers to these questions as men relying on human senses and human powers of reasoning?"[10] And, one might add, must it not be because each of them relied on his own use of his own reason? In the *Confessions*, Augustine had already noticed that God's truth is never the private discovery of a philosopher: "Your truth", he says to God, "does not belong to me nor to anyone else, but to us all whom you call to share it." [11] Unity is to be found through faith in the truth of God's revelation in Christ and evidently not in the use of reason, however free, however sophisticated. "Some of these philosophers, it is true, were able to perceive a certain amount of truth.... And yet they were ignorant of the end to which all these [fragments of truth] were to be referred and the standard by which they were to be assessed." [12] There is a striking parallel between this chapter of the *City of God* and Alasdair MacIntyre's critique in *Whose Justice? Which Rationality?* of liberal philosophers' pursuit of "alleged principles of shared rationality" and of the transformation of this project "into a tradition whose continuities are partly defined by the interminability of the debate over such principles". [13] Philosophy, in other words, has returned to the very condition it had reached in the classical world four centuries after the birth of Christ. Nor is its return recent. Pascal in one of his exasperated little notes said that for the philosophers of seventeenth-century France, there were 280 kinds of sovereign good.

Augustine, meanwhile, in the course of his confrontation with Porphyry, returns to the gulf between philosophy and Christianity, the gulf that he himself had eventually managed to cross. "Christ is humble, and you are proud. No doubt it seems disgraceful for learned men to desert their master Plato to become disciples of Christ, who by his Spirit taught a fisherman wisdom", [14] he says, of the inspiration that made possible the writing of the opening of Saint John's Gospel. Augustine's celebration, in these chapters of the *City of God* and elsewhere, of the universality of Christian truth, disclosed by God to anyone, anywhere, at any time, who hears it and turns toward it not to close but to open the mind as well as the heart, is central to his whole life as a teacher. He knew a great deal, from his own experience both outside and inside the Church, about the perils of exclusiveness. The Roman Empire itself, shutting out from the privileges of citizenship women, children, slaves, and many others living under its authority, was a state organised on the principle of exclusiveness. The Manichees focussed all the efforts of the sect on the preservation of the ascetic purity of "the elect". Neoplatonist salvation through philosophical ascent to truth was naturally confined to the few who were educated to follow complex trains of thought. The Donatist church in Africa, like many churches since, regarded itself as institutionally pure, to be sustained in self-righteous separation from the universal (Catholic) Church, which in this instance the Donatists despised as corrupted by compromises with secular authority during the period of Roman persecution. Later in Augustine's life, his passionately argued case against Pelagius and Julian of Eclanum would rest on his belief in the grace of God, freely given to anyone and finally fulfilled only in God's eschatological judgement, as against their conviction that man can attain his own virtue, his own salvation, by his own efforts, which human judgement is perfectly capable of assessing. Accustomed as he was to preaching in Hippo Sunday after Sunday to a congregation very few of whom had even an elementary education, the old Augustine wrote briskly to a correspondent about the difficulty of his own book on the Trinity, "If Christ had died only for those who could with certainty apprehend these matters, we are virtually wasting our time in the Church." [15]

This golden thread in Augustine's life and work, spun from his own unfading gratitude for the grace which had brought him home to live in the truth, gleams throughout the *City of God*. Upon it, indeed, is strung the massive and varied discussion of the distinction for which the work is chiefly famous, that between the city of God and the earthly city, in both of which the true Christian lives, but in the earthly city, however it happens to be governed, as a *peregrinus*, a foreigner, a pilgrim not sharing within himself its love for earthly glory as the purpose of human life. Had Augustine identified, as, alas, he has often through the centuries been assumed to have identified, the city of God with the Church, he himself, of course, would be open to the charge of a different, a Christian, exclusiveness. But this he does not do. It is essential for a proper understanding of his two cities to grasp that, both inside and outside the Church, they are always intermingled, and that the judgement of who belongs to the *civitas Dei*, the kingdom of God that will be fully realised in eternity, is God's alone. It is in the judgement of God that the Church as the Body of Christ will at last be revealed. Her beauty we can believe in and dimly apprehend in this life; in eternity her completed beauty will no longer be sullied by the wrongly directed lives of those of her members who are not, in the eyes of God, pilgrims travelling to his City.

The distinction between the cities is made, first of all, to place the achievement of Rome, an achievement of conquest and government six centuries old in Augustine's time and now under threat, in proper relation to the promise of the kingdom of God revealed in Christ. Pride in the earthly city, fear for its future, the conviction among pagan intellectuals that the pagan gods had made Rome great and the God of the Christians had destroyed its ancient glory: these are the targets for Augustine's sustained attack, which is also, again, an attack on exclusiveness. Human power and fame, belonging to only a few, to emperors, generals and governors; and the orderly, or terrified, lives of those whose security depends on the effectiveness of the great who hold the empire in place: all this is the earthly city, all this is made by men, all this will pass, as human glory and human institutions always pass, though Augustine never denies that some political systems are better, more just, more peaceful, less cruel and arbitrary, than others.

The Roman past, of conquest and then of government, was an extraordinary human achievement, but the overriding motive of even the noblest of those who put it together was human glory. In the first five books of the *City of God*, Augustine surveys Roman history, making respectful and intelligent use of the Latin historians. He gives full credit to their heroes, the exemplary figures of the early republic whose moral qualities were unimpeachable:

> They took no account of their own material interests compared with the common good, that is the commonwealth and the public purse; they resisted the temptations of avarice; they acted for their country's well-being with disinterested concern; they were guilty of no offence against the law; they succumbed to no sensual indulgence. By such immaculate conduct they laboured towards honours, power and glory, by what they took to be the true way.[16]

In the terms of the earthly city for which they laboured, they were successful. "They were honoured in almost all nations; they imposed their laws on many peoples; and today they enjoy renown in the history and literature of nearly all races. They have no reason to complain of the justice of God, the supreme and true. 'They have received their reward in full.' "[17] The ironic reference, here, to the Sermon on the Mount, to Jesus's warning against the parading of virtue to win admiration, seems at first sight harsh. But Augustine is in the course of distinguishing worldly glory from the glory of the city of God, and he is not insensitive to the pathos of those born too soon and outside Israel, to whom knowledge of the city of God was not disclosed. "What else was there for them to love save glory?" he asks, understanding that, not knowing anything of the eternal glory of God, "through glory, they desired to have a kind of life after death on the lips of those who praised them."[18] And, acknowledging the sound moral judgement of the pagan historians who praised the early heroes and also condemned the profligate evils of the later republic, he says of them sadly that "they have not another City which is a truer one than theirs, one whose citizens are to be chosen for eternity."[19] They praised what was praiseworthy in Rome, but, having no other city in which to place their love, they took Roman virtues, civic virtues, real but relative, to be the absolute standard that they cannot, for a Christian, ever be. These chapters of the *City of God* are, among many other things, Augustine's definitive confrontation with Cicero and the exemplary republican heroes of Cicero's dialogues.

An obvious danger in the crisis of the early fifth century in which Augustine was writing was that leading pagans, looking back to the long-distant days of the republic, would infect Christians with their condemnation of Christianity as the prime cause of current Roman collapse. "Our opponents hold Christ to blame for these present ills, which may turn the minds of the weaker and more foolish away from that City in which alone there can be a life of eternal happiness." [20] Equally dangerous, in Augustine's judgement, was the almost contrary view of many influential Christian contemporaries that the conversion of Constantine, whose vision of the Cross had promised him before a victory, "In this sign you will conquer", had been providentially ordained by God to guarantee the continuing integrity and prosperity of the Christian empire. The divine mission claimed for the Christian emperor should surely result in success. If the empire was collapsing, some Christians would suppose that God was failing to look after his own and need no longer be believed in. If the pagan gods had done better for Rome, what was the point of faith in Christ?

Augustine set himself in the *City of God* to face squarely both these dangers, both these, as he saw them, very serious errors, by asking his readers to follow him in a forceful process of discrimination, a cumulative critical analysis of both ends and means. He brought to the task a profound knowledge of the whole Bible, wide reading in the Roman historians, poets and moralists—Cicero and Virgil are most frequently quoted—and the distanced view of a provincial. The capitulation of Rome to the Goths seemed to Jerome, educated and baptized in the city where he later lived, taught and acquired lifelong friends, like the end of the world. "Where is salvation", he wrote, "if Rome perishes?" [21] Augustine was unimpressed by his brief stay in Rome, where he was lonely, unhappy and cheated by his students. [22] Surviving the disgrace of the city seemed to him not only possible but a constructive and even hopeful necessity.

Augustine insisted that Christianity, long preceded by the collapse of unselfish, public-spirited morality in the higher reaches of the empire, was not responsible for "these present ills". Nor would Christianity preserve the Roman world from their consequences. Empires rise and fall, and will while history lasts. The Roman empire had been the most successful yet known, but it was no more than a human arrangement, flawed in the very pride and lust for domination— *libido dominandi*—that established it and temporary as all human arrangements always are. At its best, it had given countless people peace and security, within which, in recent times, it had been possible to worship God without fear of oppression and for the knowledge of God to spread. But peace and security, the highest achievements of the *civitas terrena*, the earthly city, while always valuable in themselves, were not necessarily the result of imperial greatness. Much of Roman history had been marred by faction, civil war, dreadful cruelty and bloodshed. How were the subject territories of the empire acquired? With aggression, fuelled by greed. In a famous passage, Augustine compares the might-is-right story of Roman expansion to mere brigandage:

> A gang is a group of men under the command of a leader, bound by a compact of association, in which the plunder is divided according to an agreed convention. If this villainy wins so many recruits from the ranks of the demoralised that it acquires territory, establishes a base, captures cities and subdues peoples, it then openly arrogates to itself the title of kingdom, which is conferred on it in the eyes of the world, not by the renouncing of aggression but by the attainment of impunity. For it was a witty and a truthful rejoinder which was given by a captured pirate to Alexander the Great. The king asked the fellow, "What is your idea, in infesting the sea?" And the pirate answered, "The same as yours, in infesting the earth! but because I do it with a tiny craft, I'm called a pirate; because you have a mighty army, you're called an emperor." [23]

Augustine goes so far as to suggest that just as a man of moderate means, living at peace with his neighbours, is happier than a rich man constantly worrying about his wealth, so it may be better that small kingdoms should live side by side without aggression "as there are multitudes of homes in our cities", rather than that one great political structure should strive for an imperial grandeur that it will always be in danger of losing. [24]

Of the hubris of empire, the pride that goes before a fall, Augustine was keenly aware. Even more deplorable in his view than the gaining of the empire was the society that its wealth and its arrogance delivered. Drawing on the outrage of Cicero and Cicero's political enemy Sallust, who both described the moral squalor of the late republic, Augustine, in a splendid diatribe, castigates the values and priorities of the Roman rich, and not only the rich, in his own time. They say of the Roman state: "'So long as it lasts, so long as it enjoys material prosperity, and the glory of victorious war, or, better, the security of peace, why should we worry? What concerns us is that we should get richer all the time, to have enough for extravagant spending every day.'" Meanwhile, the mass of the people look to their rulers "as controllers of material things and providers of material satisfactions". Luxury and excess of every kind are reckoned to be good; so is "the din of dancing everywhere, and theatres full of fevered shouts of degenerate pleasure and of every kind of cruel and degraded indulgence. Anyone who disapproves of this kind of happiness should rank as a public enemy; anyone who attempts to change it or get rid of it should be hustled out of hearing by the freedom-loving majority." [25] It is not only philosophy that has come full circle, after sixteen centuries, in the rich and powerful West.

But the *City of God* is by no means a despairing book. All its negative criticism, all its careful placing of what is relatively good as well as what is bad in the earthly city, is there to make clearer and clearer what Augustine means by the city of God. Early in the book, he makes sure that the reader understands that the city of God is not the same thing as, is not coterminous with, the Church. Just as among the present enemies of the city of God are some who will one day be her citizens, so there are some within the Church "united with her in participation in the sacraments, who will not join with her in the eternal destiny of the saints. Some of these are hidden; some are well known, for they do not hesitate to murmur against God, whose sacramental sign they bear, even in the company of his acknowledged enemies." [26] Years later, toward the end of the whole work, Augustine grieves over the many Christians who give Christianity a bad name: "There are always some inside [the Church], indeed there are many, who by their unprincipled behaviour torment the feelings of those who live devout lives. For such people cause the name of 'Christian' and 'Catholic' to be defamed." [27] Augustine the bishop—whose belief in the Church as one, as good, beautiful and true, never weakened—was familiar for decades with the failings of some other bishops, some priests, some Christian laymen. "Some of these are hidden": the public disloyalty of the baptized is one thing; the secret attitude or intentions of those whose disloyalty to the city of God is known only to God is another. Everyone knows who belongs to the Church; who belongs to God is known only to God. "In truth, these two cities are interwoven and intermixed in this era [the time between the coming of Christ and the end of the world], and await separation at the last judgement." [28] This is a perception of sanity, humility and generosity that Catholics have often forgotten. Balthasar, in this as in many other respects a true Augustinian, restated it in 1980: "The Church will remain mixed until the end of time; ... there are members of the Church outside her and enemies of the Church within her." [29]

It is also one important key for the unlocking of what is central to Augustine's whole presentation of the city of God. Whether or not we—who have to live in the earthly city and may or may not also live in the city of God—ultimately are of the city of God rather than of the earthly city depends, not on anything visible to human observation or susceptible to human judgement, but on the direction, visible only to God, and susceptible only to his judgement, in which our love takes us. "Let us pine", Augustine wrote, "for the City where we are citizens. . . . By pining, we are already there; we have already cast our hope, like an anchor, on that coast. I sing of somewhere else, not of here: for I sing with my heart, not my flesh. The citizens of Babylon hear the sound of the flesh, the Founder of Jerusalem hears the tune of our heart." [30]

* * *

The twelve books of the longer second part of the *City of God* tell the story not any longer of Rome, but of the human race from its creation to its fallenness, from its fallenness to its redemption in Christ, and from its continuing fallenness, lit now with the truth of its redemption, to the end of time, which will one day come. The city of God has existed since the time of Abel, because *desiderium*, the yearning for God, has always existed, in the philosophers as in the saints of the Old Testament. "In order to show", Balthasar wrote, "that genuine yearning is always directed toward a divinely planned and divinely willed encounter with God's free grace in the world, Augustine stresses that the saints of all ages, even before Christ, yearned for the advent of the Son in the flesh." [31] The coming of Christ was the coming into our sight of the object of this yearning. Now, living in fallenness, but living also in the truth of redemption in Christ, we are no less free to choose than man has always been, since first he could hear and choose to disobey the voice of God. We are free above all to choose what to love. Long before writing the *City of God*, Augustine had arrived at this conviction. "Whether he will or no, a man is necessarily a slave to the things by means of which he seeks to be happy", [32] he wrote when he had recently become a Christian. Virgil's Aeneas, as we have seen, is one of Augustine's models for the idea that our love is the weight that carries us in the direction we have chosen. Augustine used this image in the *Confessions*: "My weight is my love. Wherever I am carried, my love is carrying me." [33] He uses it again in the *City of God*: "The specific gravity of a body is, in a manner, its love; whether a body tends downwards by reason of its heaviness or strives upwards because of its lightness." [34] As he grew older, Augustine became increasingly sure that heaven is where we will receive what we have loved if what we have loved is God. And hell is also where we will receive what we have loved. In the *City of God*, it is this profound and also terrifying thought that is given expression in the central image of the whole work:

> The two cities were created by two kinds of love: the earthly city was created by self-love reaching the point of contempt for God, the Heavenly City by the love of God carried as far as contempt of self. In fact, the earthly city glories in itself, the Heavenly City glories in the Lord. The former looks for glory from men, the latter finds its highest glory in God.... The one city loves its own strength shown in its powerful leaders; the other says to its God, "I will love you, my Lord, my strength." [35]

The difference is the difference, familiar from much of Augustine's writing, between pride, which turns us away from God, and humility, which turns us toward him. We turn toward, we follow, we pursue what we love. Augustine says, simply, in the following book, "A brief and true definition of virtue is 'rightly ordered love'." [36] In the *Confessions*, he had written: "He loves you less who together with you loves something which he does not love for your sake."

No classical thinker would have recognised the truth in these two sentences, although the Plato of the *Symposium*, for whom, as for Augustine, beauty, truth and goodness are one in God, came close. But to Plato most of the time, to Aristotle, and to the Stoics and the Neoplatonists, Augustine's definition of virtue would have been incomprehensible, as would the central place that he gives, in much of what he has to say about our freedom and the possibility of our goodness, to the will, more precisely to the flawed will, a concept unknown to classical ethics. It had always seemed to philosophers self-evident that once goodness was intellectually grasped, right action would inevitably follow. Augustine, with a deeper psychological understanding of man than any thinker before him, was sure that what we choose to love is a matter of the will. The emotions, he says in the *City of God*—love, fear, joy and grief—are not to be despised as produced in us only by the flesh. We have seen him deal with this contempt for the flesh as he found it in a passage in the *Aeneid*. Emotions, Augustine knew, are also of the soul and are good or bad according to the choices made by the will. "If the will is wrongly directed, the emotions will be wrong; if the will is right, the emotions will be not only blameless, but praiseworthy." [37] Rightly ordered love is the direction of the will toward God, the opening of the heart to the beauty of Christ, to the *attractiveness* of truth, of goodness, that anyone can turn toward if he allows himself to respond to the Word of God, spoken to him.

As Augustine said more simply in a sermon preached in Carthage in 418: "Everyone loves. The question is, what does he love? Consequently we are not told not to love, but to choose what to love. But how can we choose, unless we are first chosen? God offers himself to us; there is no need to offer us more." [38]

Augustine knew, too, that the will, even when turned toward God and away from less-worthy objects, is still in itself unreliable, always fallible, always dependent on the grace of God. "Free will is sufficient for evil, but is too little for good." [39] In old age Augustine prayed for the grace of perseverance. In an early work he remarked, in a few sentences of what Balthasar described as "astounding profundity", [40] that our turning our backs on God, our refusal of his grace, is a turning toward—nothing:

> We cannot doubt that this movement of the will, this turning away from God, is sin; but surely we cannot say that God is the author of sin? God, then, will not be the cause of this movement; but what will be its cause? If you ask this, and I answer that I do not know, probably you will be saddened. And yet that would be a true answer. That which is nothing cannot be known. Only hold fast to your faithful belief that no good thing can happen to you, to your senses or to your intelligence or to your thought, which does not come from God. [41]

Honest self-exploration and sharp observation strengthened in Augustine the sense that original sin, his own phrase, [42] which we all inherit from the fallenness of Adam, makes it impossible for us to be sure, this side of the grave, this side of the final judgement of God, of the lastingness of our own goodness, or indeed that we are good at all. Augustine is the first writer to notice in tiny babies, with amusement as well as compassion, the signs of original sin, competitiveness, jealousy and the furious assertiveness that is familiar to all mothers. [43] He knew from his own experience the sulky idleness and daredevil sins of children—the pears he stole as a boy, when he did not even like eating pears—and the wild confusion of unresisted adolescent temptations. It is in Augustine's lifelong exploration of human motivation, of what moves what in us to live as we live, what moves us to sin, what moves us to tears, what moves us to pray, that he made discoveries about people one by one that have lost none of their force or their relevance to each of our actual lives. As we have seen, Augustine never forgot what had moved him, gradually through the muddled years of his youth, toward his final conversion to Christianity: God's love for him, which had awakened and nourished in him his love for God. As we have also seen, he understood that in the Godless past of Rome noble men had been moved to live just lives, without lust for gain or personal domination, but by their love of the earthly city and their hope for lasting fame. He knew that people are often moved by bad intentions—by pride (which is self-love) or by another love leading away from God—to good actions.

He knew also, for nowhere in all his writings does he take leave of his common sense, that to live in the city of God is not to abandon the loyalties and loves of the earthly city. The good things of everyday life are good; only if they are regarded as absolute, as the ultimate good, will they become hindrances to a life lived for God. In a short passage of exact discrimination, Augustine describes the priorities of a Christian family:

> A household of human beings whose life is not based on faith is in pursuit of an earthly peace based on the things belonging to this temporal life, and on its advantages, whereas a household of human beings whose life is based on faith looks forward to the blessings which are promised as eternal in the future, making use of earthly and temporal things like a pilgrim in a foreign land, who does not let himself be taken in by them or distracted from his course towards God, but rather treats them as supports which help him more easily to bear the burdens of "the corruptible body which weighs heavy on the soul"; they must on no account be allowed to increase the load.[44]

In the last few words the point is made with characteristic acuteness.

In the same chapter of the *City of God*, Augustine also describes the real goodness and, again, the proper valuation of sound political arrangements to show how the two cities may live in harmony with one another if the earthly city is run well and itself makes no absolute claims. "The earthly city, whose life is not based on faith, aims at an earthly peace, and it limits the harmonious agreement of citizens concerning the giving and obeying of orders to the establishment of a kind of compromise between human wills about the things relevant to mortal life."[45] This single sentence fairly represents the whole of Augustine's positive contribution, a moderate and reasonable one, to political thought. The peace and stability of a sensibly organised earthly city is, after all, the analogy Augustine chooses to explain the much deeper, and eternal, peace of the city of God, for, as this chapter ends, "the life of a city is inevitably a social life." But the city of God transcends the boundaries of all earthly societies or states. In Greece the *polis*, in Rome the *res publica* and then the empire, had frontiers beyond which lay barbarism, danger, the "citiless" outcast of Sophocles's chorus about human achievement in *Antigone*, or just others who did not belong. In contrast to this "civilised" exclusiveness, the city of God

> calls out citizens from all nations and so collects a society of aliens, speaking all languages. She takes no account of any difference in customs, laws or institutions, by which earthly peace is achieved and preserved ... provided that no hindrance is presented thereby to the religion which teaches that the one supreme and true God is to be worshipped.[46]

This relativization of the earthly city and all that may be good in it is the radical achievement of the whole of Augustine's book. Once it has been understood that the supreme, the absolute, good in human life is God and that therefore the soul's direction should be toward him in Christ, Augustine's many illustrations of this principle in application can be easily grasped. Usually, to take one important example, we should obey the laws of whichever earthly city we happen to live in, because they are generally conducive to peace and order. "What does it matter under whose rule a man lives, being so soon to die, provided that the rulers do not force him to impious and wicked acts?"[47] If, however, a law is made that is contrary to the justice of God, requiring of us impious and wicked acts, we are right to disobey it. "Whosoever refuses to obey the laws of the emperors which are enacted against the truth of God, wins for himself a great reward."[48] The horrors inflicted on their subjects by twentieth-century totalitarian regimes have shown that anyone able to make this judgement rightly, and brave enough to follow it through, is indeed close to the city of God. In Augustine's own life, to take a quite different example, he greatly valued his friends, learning early the dangers of friends who drew him away from God and later the strengthening support of friends who shared his faith in God. But friendship, like other pulls on the will that may be chosen or resisted, must find its proper place in the ordering of love. In the city of God, even though known only in part, as it always must be in mortal life, the death of a friend will cause us less sorrow than his fall from faith or into serious sin.[49] The upshot of both these instances is that, in the light of God's truth, the perpetrators of evil are always more to be worried about than their victims, even if their victims are killed, a clear illustration of the clarity of the distinction Augustine, resting his whole case always on Scripture, throughout confirms between the values of the city of God and the values of the earthly city.

Toward the end of the very last book of the *City of God*, he allows himself a chapter celebrating the astonishing beauty and possibilities of God's created world. That by means of natural reproduction, not biologically different from that of the animals, God continues to create human beings who, even in fallenness, are capable of knowing, loving, learning God is the first gift. In every person "there is still the spark" of the image of God in which we are made, still the mind and heart "ready for the perception of truth, and able to love the good".[50] Then, as well as the virtues in which we may grow toward God, "given solely by the grace of God in Christ", there is all the creative capacity of every kind of artist and scientist, every maker and discoverer and inventor; it is impossible not to admire the skill of even those who invent new weapons of destruction or attempt to undermine truth: "The brilliant wit shown by philosophers and heretics in defending their very errors and falsehoods is something which beggars imagination!"[51] The human body is a marvel in itself and will become more marvellous as more is discovered about how it works. The whole physical world is rich, various and beautiful in its generosity to the human race, in ways that Augustine can only begin to describe. And all these blessings are for everyone, even for those who have, as yet, no idea of "how complete, how lovely, how certain will be the knowledge of all things, a knowledge without error, entailing no toil"[52] in the life of the resurrection that is promised to the citizens of God.

In this catalogue of wonders (which anyone who thinks of Augustine as a repressive puritan afraid of the body, or afraid of free intellectual enquiry, should read), the use of language is, not surprisingly, given a special place. "Consider the multitudinous variety of the means [*media*] of information and persuasion, among which the spoken and written word has the first place; [and] the enjoyment afforded to the mind by the trappings of eloquence and the rich diversity of poetry."[53] We are here, of course, in the realm of only relative goods, blessings available to all of fallen humanity. If Augustine had not been educated, and well educated in spite of his long-remembered resentment of schoolmasters, not in philosophy, which he explored for himself as an adult, but in literature, he would not have been able to write as he did for the Christian West. On the one hand, he was well aware that a classical education was by no means necessary to a good Christian life. "Many holy people", he said in his *Retractationes*, "are ignorant of philosophy and the liberal arts, and many who know them are not holy",[54] and to an ambitious student he wrote in a letter of 410 that "eternal salvation does not require a knowledge of the dialogues of Cicero."[55] On the other hand, he was no less well aware of how much, as a writer and preacher, he himself owed to his training in literature and rhetoric. With typical judgement and balance, he said to God in the *Confessions* that "none other than you is teacher of the truth":

> I learnt from you that nothing is true merely because it is eloquently said, nor false because the signs coming from the lips make sounds deficient in a sense of style. Again, a statement is not true because it is enunciated in an unpolished idiom, nor false because the words are splendid. Wisdom and foolishness are like food that is nourishing or useless. Whether or not the words are ornate does not decide the issue. Food of either kind can be served in either town or country ware.[56]

(QED, the reader of this paragraph is inclined to think. Among so very much else that he is, Augustine is often a writer's writer.)

We have seen that it was "the trappings of eloquence" that drew Augustine to the seriousness of Cicero and then to the Christian truth of Ambrose's preaching, and also that "the rich diversity of poetry", Virgil's in particular, was something he valued always. In a letter, he identified the almost sacramental force of imagery, which carries the soul from what Shakespeare, sketching the poet's imagination, called "a local habitation and a name", to "the forms of things unknown", or known as propositions:[57]

> The presentation of truth through signs has great power to feed and fan that ardent love, by which, as under some law of gravitation, we flicker upwards, or inwards, to our place of rest. Things presented in this way move and kindle our affection far more than if they were set forth in bald statements.... When the soul is brought to material signs of spiritual realities, and moves from them to the things they represent, it gathers strength just by this very act of passing from the one to the other, like the flame of a torch, that burns all the more brightly as it moves.[58]

Here, it is clear, Augustine was writing about the Bible. His literary education had trained him to read great texts with a keen awareness of the weight and relationship of words, with an understanding that always included feeling, with an aesthetic sense that became, when the powerful beam of his attention was focussed on Scripture, more and more a love for the beauty of God's truth. He quoted the Bible constantly, with the easy familiarity of someone entirely at home in the texts. Knowing scarcely any Hebrew and only a little Greek, he was never a biblical scholar, properly speaking, as was Origen or Jerome. But he had an accurate sense of the different kinds of writing in the Bible, and the differentiation of his response to the creation story in Genesis, to the Sermon on the Mount, to the poetry of the Psalms, to the tough arguments of Saint Paul, to the luminous weight of Saint John, adds much to the quality of that response. His constant purpose in the reading and quoting of the Bible was to grow in the love of God and to treasure the understanding that this growth will always deepen. "Look into Scripture, the eyes of your heart on its heart." [59] The Scriptures must be read, as the Christian life must be lived, with a decision, a choice of the will, for love of the truth, love of God. Love will deliver increased understanding; understanding will increase love. This is why Augustine wrote to someone who thought the mind and Christianity had nothing to do with each other, "Intellectum valde ama",[60] which does not mean "greatly love the intellect", but "greatly love understanding".

Our understanding of God in this life will never be complete. If we think our understanding is complete, it will not be right, for love, God's for us and ours for him, has its end only in his eternity: "You know what God is? You know what God is like? Whatever you have made of him, he is not; whatever you have understood by thinking, he is not. But so that you may receive something of him by tasting, God is love; the love by which we love." [61]

During the years in which he was writing his theological masterpiece *On the Trinity*, Augustine developed his always imperfect but gradually increasing understanding of what God is largely through his use of analogy, through long reflection on "what God is like". If we are made in the image of God, then what we are may help us to understand what he is like. We may, for example, separate for the sake of clarity in thinking about ourselves, and then restore to wholeness for the sake of truth, memory (or being), understanding (or knowledge) and love (or the will). This is the most fruitful of several analogies that unfold and then come together in *On the Trinity*, as there is a brief unfolding of each Person of the Trinity and then a coming together in our acknowledgement of God as one in Saint Paul's single verse: "For of him, and through him, and in him are all things; to whom be glory for ever", taken apart and reconnected by Augustine in the first book.[62] The whole work is a profound and demanding process, for both writer and reader, of thought and prayer on the fundamental Christian mystery of the threeness and oneness of God and, as a consequence of the use of analogy, on the mystery of the nature of man: he had written years before that "my occupation is to learn God and the soul." [63] He was aware of the groundbreaking exploration of the mystery of the Trinity done in Greek, the language of philosophy as Latin was not, by the great theologians

who preceded him, but his firsthand knowledge of their writings was not exten-
sive, and in many respects he started all over again. He is here, as in all his books,
in a sense encouraging for his reader, an amateur (the word does mean "lover"),
using his mind and his experience to explore with his usual freshness and immediacy the revelation in Christ of what God is. At least since the *Confessions*, he had
recognised in the life of the soul which is, in Balthasar's words, "an image of the
trinitarian light and so capable of seeing God",[64] an analogy for the life of the Trinity. The *Confessions* is the account of his own life—his own being, understanding
and love—up to the time of his conversion and in the time at which he was writing. *On the Trinity*, a work of wider and deeper intellectual range, a work of maturity, is no less tentatively presented to God as a patchy and partial human enterprise.
Concluding a short summary, Rowan Williams has written: "The genius of *On the
Trinity* is its fusion of speculation and prayer, its presentation of trinitarian theology as, ultimately, nothing other than a teasing out of what it is to be converted
and to come to live in Christ."[65] Augustine ends the labour of the whole work
with this prayer: "O Lord, one God, God the Trinity, whatsoever I have said in
these books that comes of your prompting, may your people acknowledge it: for
what I have said that comes only of myself, I ask of you and of your people pardon."[66]

Among much else, *On the Trinity* develops, beyond its use in analogy, the
Christian concept of the *person*, the unique, intelligible being that each of us is,
made, body and soul, in the image of God, a creature of inalienable value whose
fallen brokenness can be mended by the grace of God. The *City of God*, completed later but written during some of the same years as *On the Trinity*, is, also
among much else, an account of the being, understanding and love—the right
way of living, the right judgement of things, the right direction of the will—in
any set of historical circumstances, for any Christian *person*. Augustine believed
that the Incarnation and Resurrection of Christ had healed forever the philosophers' separation of the possibly noble soul from the despised body. The *City
of God* ends with an account of the resurrection of the body, which will at the
end of time allow the senses a share in the sight of God, which will allow God's
faithful people "restored by him and perfected by his greater grace [to] be still
and at leisure for eternity, seeing that he is God, and being filled by him when
he will be all in all."[67] It could be said that the whole of the *City of God* is a vast
elaboration of a single sentence in the Sermon on the Mount: "Blessed are the
pure in heart, for they shall see God."[68]

It was because Augustine was sure that the meaning of our lives, whether we
belong to the city of God or not, lies not in what we do but in what we love
(from which what we do will follow) that he spent so much effort and energy

toward the end of his life in arguing against what he saw to be the serious heresy of Pelagius and his followers. That all goodness is of God, that all human goodness is the gift of God in his grace, Augustine knew so profoundly that he regarded the Pelagian insistence that we can do much good of and by ourselves—an unexceptionable assumption, now as then, of the earthly city—as *not Christian*. "Some men", he wrote, early in the controversy, "try hard to discover in our will what good is particularly our own, owing nothing to God; how they can find this out, I just do not know." [69] All good done in disinterested love of goodness (not, for example, in pride or for love of fame) is done with the grace of God, whether or not the person knows it. It is the scale of the difference that the revelation of God in Christ has made that underlies this long dispute: Augustine's Christian understanding of the human soul in relation to God has simply dissolved in him the sense of human merit, always only a single step from human pride. Redemption from sin in Christ Augustine knew for certain to be a gift we do not deserve. As the Augustinian scholar Étienne Gilson wrote: "Pelagianism was the radical negation of Augustine's personal experience—or, if you will, Augustine's personal experience was ... the very negation of Pelagianism." [70]

Julian of Eclanum, Augustine's most formidable Pelagian opponent, a philosopher trained on Aristotle, regarded the notion of original sin as a Manichaean neurosis of Augustine's. To Augustine, as to many people who look dispassionately at the mess man always makes of even the noblest projects, original sin was self-evident. We can be rescued from it only by the grace of God in Christ. Augustine's understanding of grace, together with his understanding of all time as present to the knowledge of God in the eternity of God, led him to the doctrine of predestination, which seemed to the Pelagians to deprive us of free will. But as Augustine wrote: "The teaching of predestination hampers and ruins only one thing: the pernicious error which would have it that the gift of grace depends on our merits." [71] The idea of predestination seems repugnant only if we do not, as Augustine did, halt in awe before the paradox that we can do nothing good without God's grace and are nevertheless free to choose to respond, or not, to him. He was aware of the problem. "When free will is defended, the grace of God seems to be denied; when the grace of God is asserted, free will is thought to have been abolished." [72] But as de Lubac wrote in this connexion, only "rationality, believing that it can get to the bottom of everything, because it makes itself the yardstick, and thinks that its own limits are the limits of being itself" thinks "that what is incomprehensible must therefore be unintelligible." [73] Before the mystery of God, human reason, as Augustine always acknowledged, must humbly admit defeat. In the words of Jaroslav Pelikan, "disclosing a mystery was not the same as dispelling it." [74] Preaching to people to whom the word "predestination" would have meant nothing, Augustine said:

> Someone will say to me: "So we are directed and do not direct; we are acted on and do not act." My reply is: You both direct and are directed; you act and are acted on; and you direct your life well when you are directed by that which is good.... When Jesus was speaking about good works he did not say: "Without me you can do such and such but with me you can do it more easily"; he did not say "Without me you can bear your fruit, but with me you can bear it more plentifully." That is not what he said. Read what he said. It is not Augustine who says it; it is the Lord who says it. What does the Lord say? "Without me you can do nothing." [75]

Or, in a short sentence that blows apart many of the recommendations of our own earthly city: "If we try to build ourselves up, we build a ruin." [76]

What Pelagianism would have built up was an excluding meritocracy, the survival of the ethically fittest, those able to earn salvation. Augustine's deepest objection to the Pelagians was rooted in his by-now-instinctive, and wholly Christian, resistance to exclusion from the Church, from the city of God, from grace. He detected in the Pelagians the old pride of the classical philosophers, including Plato, in human capacity to act rightly having thought rightly. Accustomed as he was to explaining to ordinary people leading untidy lives in a sinful world who were incapable of much thought, that the grace of God was also for them, he knew that the gift of grace in Christ was the adequate reply, as no reply given by philosophers or Pelagian moral heroes could be, to the suffering of humanity. As Balthasar put it:

> No philosophy can ever do justice to the groans of a man hidden away in some ancient, medieval or present-day torture chamber.... Such attempts [as Plato's] play down the ultimately hopeless situation of finite existence in the face of a transcendence that does not automatically disclose itself, or, put more concretely, in the face of the as yet hidden world plan whereby God becomes man. [77]

In Augustine's view, Pelagian optimism about human nature made Christianity unnecessary. If we are able to earn grace, Christ becomes no more than the ethical model, the good man to be copied, that Augustine himself had once taken him to be. But it was because God had become man that it was possible to write of the city of God as commanding the ultimate love and loyalty of those who find themselves, as we all do, alive in the fallenness of the earthly city.

* * *

At the very end of the *City of God*, the old Augustine wrote: "This huge work may be too much for some, too little for others. Of both these groups I ask forgiveness. But of those for whom it is enough I make this request: that they do not thank me, but join with me in rendering thanks to God. Amen. Amen."[78] The "huge work" became a central book of the Christian tradition, not because it is in every detail right or even consistent, but because it so thoroughly achieves its objective, the placing of the human endeavours of any earthly city at any time in history in their proper place in relation to the eschatological city of those who love God above all else. The book has been more revered than it has been taken to heart. That it systematically undermines any utopian, and in particular any imperial, project was probably not grasped by Charlemagne at the start of the ninth century, who was reviving the empire of the West as he listened to the *City of God*, his favourite book, daily read aloud in his court. The book is about grace in the soul, not about victory in the world. The triumphalist popes of the late Middle Ages, mired in the power struggles of the earthly city, had much to learn from it and learned nothing. In the first five years of the printing of classical texts, 1465–1469, with Cicero the printers' favourite author, the *City of God* was the only Christian, and much the longest, classical work to be printed. The young Thomas More gave a course of lectures on it in 1501. In 1522 the Spanish classicist Luis Vives published a scholarly edition dedicated, in vain, to Henry VIII. By the end of the same century, the monarchs of England, France and Spain had in different ways seized control of the Church in their realms in a spirit diametrically opposed to the lessons of the *City of God*, with damaging consequences, not yet over, for Christianity in each of their countries. At the start of the twenty-first century, those in control of the new righteous empire would do well to listen to those lessons, summarised by Balthasar in 1980 when influence in the earthly city was still divided between a worse and a better superpower:

> As it arises on the foundation of nature, power is primarily self-affirmation, whether it be the affirmation of an individual, a group or a people; and it involves the overpowering and subjugation of others.... Where it

prevails by means of oppression, thinking that it alone is right—whether on the basis of the theory that "might is right" or of the ideology that says that a race or class must assert itself with all available means, because it represents some peerless good, some quasi-absolute in the sphere of the relative—it has become demonic.[79]

The work Augustine did, all through his life and with no sense of completion—"I would not want people to adopt all my views, but only those where it can be clearly seen that I have not been mistaken",[80] he wrote at the end of his life—has never been lost, nor has his voice ever been silenced. Jerome wrote to him: "Catholics acknowledge and revere you as the second founder of the ancient faith."[81] "The great luminary of the western world", Newman wrote in 1864, "is, as we know, St Augustine; he, no infallible teacher, has formed the intellect of Christian Europe."[82] And not only the intellect. Jaroslav Pelikan in 1986 went further: "There has, quite literally, been no century of the sixteen centuries since the conversion of Augustine in which he has not been a major intellectual, spiritual, and cultural force."[83]

For eight centuries after his death, Augustine, after the Bible itself, was the most respected, the most read, the most quoted authority in the monasteries and schools of Latin Christendom. The minds of the monks and bishops who thought and wrote in the constantly changing circumstances of those centuries were formed by Augustine. Saint Benedict, Saint Gregory the Great, Saint Bede, Saint Anselm, Saint Bernard and Saint Aelred were in various ways his direct heirs. When Aristotle (and not yet Plato) was rediscovered by Latin intellectuals in the twelfth century and became in the thirteenth "the philosopher", a critical change overtook the mind of the now almost wholly Christian West. Saint Thomas Aquinas's great ordering of Christian thought in his *Summae* is difficult, professional theology-as-philosophy, of a kind that Augustine did not and was not equipped to write. It is therefore both hard for the untrained reader even to approach and dangerously susceptible, as Augustine is not, to dry textbook summary. More importantly, Thomas, while frequently quoting Augustine as an authority, actually abandons Augustine's distinction between the relative values (natural) of the earthly city and the absolute value (given as revealed truth) of the city of God in favour of a unifying conception of a hierarchical society divinely ordained for the good of all. The change was great enough to make the Augustinian and the Thomist traditions, at least in this important respect, irreconcilable thereafter. If we believe with Augustine that all systems of government, some of course being better than others, are transient human arrangements inspired by the familiar mixed motives of fallen mankind and that all people, one by one, may turn in their own lives toward God and away from the absolute claims of the earthly city, we cannot also believe, with Thomas, that everyone in human society has his proper place, sanctioned by God, and that all human authority exercised by Christians—there was no other authority in Thomas's world—is divinely guaranteed.

The Augustinian tradition, as we shall see, has never died. Dante and Petrarch, Shakespeare and Pascal, Coleridge and Newman, and Balthasar and Miłosz in our own time are Augustine's heirs, taking forward, as Augustine's heirs have always been able to do, his tradition into new historical circumstances. A characteristic passage, not mentioning Augustine at all, in the last volume of Balthasar's *The Glory of the Lord* is both of our time and profoundly Augustinian:

> The qualitative immanent expectation of the Church remains a matter of a decision about values: "Seek first the kingdom of God" (Mt 6.33). The eye looks first to the *eschaton*, to the Lord of the Church, and it is within this perspective that the inner-worldly tasks find their place. Because the Lord, who always stands already at the end of history, is also "with you all days, until the end of the world" and thus is immanent with the Church in history, her act of looking ahead to the end does not need to be hostile to the world and history, taking flight eschatologically from the world; it can be just as much a look *through* the worldly tasks to the *eschaton*. And if the heart proleptically dwells with its definitive treasure in heaven, the things of earth can be lit up for it in the light of its definitive love.[84]

At Balthasar's funeral in 1988, Joseph Cardinal Ratzinger (elected as Pope Benedict XVI in 2005) said in his homily: "What von Balthasar wanted can be well encapsulated in a single phrase of St. Augustine: 'Our entire task in this life, dear brothers, consists in healing the eyes of the heart so that they may be able to see God.' "[85]

If Augustine, summing up in his own life the complicated transition from classical to Christian priorities, from the never-possible perfection of the earthly city to the always-promised perfection of the city of God, is for all time, he is surely and most evidently for our own time, more like his in a multitude of ways than any other time has been in the centuries that have elapsed since his death. We live in another secular world, and Christianity is again folly to the wise. "God has humbled himself—and still man is proud."[86]

1. Hans Urs von Balthasar, *Theo-Drama*, trans. Graham Harrison, vol. 2 (San Francisco, 1990), p. 250.
2. See especially Jaroslav Pelikan, *What Has Athens to Do with Jerusalem?* (Ann Arbor, 1997).
3. Augustine, *City of God* 11.21, trans. Henry Bettenson (London, 1972).
4. Ibid., 10.20.
5. Ibid., 10.28, 29.
6. Augustine, *Confessions* 7.20.26, trans. Henry Chadwick (Oxford, 1991).
7. Augustine, *City of God* 10.32.
8. Ibid.
9. Ibid., 18.41.
10. Ibid.
11. Augustine, *Confessions* 12.25.34.
12. Augustine, *City of God* 18.41.
13. Alasdair MacIntyre, *Whose Justice? Which Rationality?* (London, 1988), p. 335.
14. Augustine, *City of God* 10.29.
15. Augustine, *Ep.* 169.4, quoted in Peter Brown, *Augustine of Hippo* (London, 1967), p. 354.
16. Augustine, *City of God* 5.15.
17. Ibid.
18. Ibid., 5.14.
19. Ibid., 3.17.
20. Ibid.
21. Jerome, *Ep.* 123.16, quoted in Serge Lancel, *Saint Augustine*, trans. Antonia Nevill (London, 2002), p. 393.
22. Augustine, *Confessions* 5.12.22.
23. Augustine, *City of God* 4.4.
24. Ibid., 4.3, 15.
25. Ibid., 2.20.
26. Ibid., 1.35.
27. Ibid., 18.51.
28. Ibid.
29. Balthasar, *Theo-Drama*, vol. 4 (San Francisco, 1994), p. 467.
30. Augustine, *Enarrationes in Psalmos* 64.3, quoted in Brown, *Augustine of Hippo*, p. 315.
31. Balthasar, *Theo-Drama* 4:372.
32. Augustine, *Of True Religion* 38.69, in *Augustine: Earlier Writings*, ed. and trans. J. H. S. Burleigh (Philadelphia and London, 1953), p. 260.
33. Augustine, *Confessions* 13.9.10.
34. Augustine, *City of God* 11.28.
35. Ibid., 14.28.
36. Ibid., 15.22.
37. Ibid., 14.6.
38. Augustine, sermon 34.
39. Augustine, *De correptione et gratia* 11.31, quoted in Jaroslav Pelikan, *The Mystery of Continuity* (Charlottesville, Va., 1986), p. 86.
40. Hans Urs von Balthasar, *The Glory of the Lord: A Theological Aesthetics*, vol. 2, trans. Andrew Louth et al. (San Francisco and Edinburgh, 1984), p. 105.
41. Augustine, *On Free Will* 2.20.54, in *Augustine: Earlier Writings*, pp. 168–69.
42. E.g., Augustine, *Confessions* 5.9.16.
43. Ibid., 1.7.11.
44. Augustine, *City of God* 19.17; the reference is to Wisdom 9:15.
45. Ibid.
46. Ibid.
47. Ibid., 5.17.
48. Augustine, *Ep.* 185.2.8, quoted in Pelikan, *Mystery of Continuity*, p. 122.

49. Augustine, *City of God* 19.8.
50. Ibid., 22.24.
51. Ibid.
52. Ibid.
53. Ibid.
54. Augustine, *Retractationes* 1.3.2.
55. Augustine, *Ep.* 118.2.1.
56. Augustine, *Confessions* 5.6.10.
57. Shakespeare, *A Midsummer Night's Dream*, 5.1.
58. Augustine, *Ep.* 55.11.21, quoted in Brown, *Augustine of Hippo*, p. 263.
59. Augustine, *De doctrina Christiana* 4.5.
60. Augustine, *Ep.* 120.13, quoted in Brown, *Augustine of Hippo*, p. 277.
61. Augustine, *On the Trinity* 8.8, quoted (in Latin) in Henri de Lubac, *The Mystery of the Supernatural* (London, 1967), p. 297; my translation.
62. Rom 11:36; Augustine, *On the Trinity* 1.6.
63. Augustine, *Soliloquies* 2.7, in *Augustine: Earlier Writings*, p. 26.
64. Balthasar, *Glory of the Lord* 2:99.
65. Rowan Williams, "De Trinitate", in *Augustine through the Ages*, ed. Allan D. Fitzgerald (Grand Rapids and Cambridge, 1999), p. 850.
66. Augustine, *On the Trinity* 15.51, in *Augustine: Later Works*, ed. and trans. John Burnaby (Philadelphia and London, 1955).
67. Augustine, *City of God* 22.30.
68. Mt 5:8.
69. Augustine, *De peccatorum meritis et remissione* 2.18.28, quoted in Brown, *Augustine of Hippo*, p. 374.
70. Quoted in Lancel, *Saint Augustine*, p. 516, n. 16.
71. Augustine, *De dono perseverantiae* 42, quoted in ibid., p. 434.
72. Augustine, *De gratia Christi* 47.52.
73. De Lubac, *Mystery of the Supernatural*, p. 223.
74. Pelikan, *Mystery of Continuity*, p. 35.
75. Augustine, sermon 156.
76. Augustine, sermon 169.
77. Balthasar, *Theo-Drama* 4:74–75.
78. Augustine, *City of God* 22.30.
79. Balthasar, *Theo-Drama* 4:107–8.
80. Augustine, *De dono perseverantiae* 55, quoted in Lancel, *Saint Augustine*, p. 434.
81. Jerome *Ep.* 141, quoted in F. Van der Meer, *Augustine the Bishop*, trans. Brian Battershaw and G. R. Lamb (London, 1961), p. 593, n. 5; my translation.
82. J. H. Newman, *Apologia pro Vita Sua*, ed. Ian Ker (London, 1994), p. 236.
83. Pelikan, *Mystery of Continuity*, p. 140.
84. Hans Urs von Balthasar, *The Glory of the Lord: A Theological Aesthetics*, vol. 7, trans. Brian McNeil (San Francisco and Edinburgh, 1989), pp. 187–88.
85. *Hans Urs von Balthasar: His Life and Work*, ed. David L. Schindler (San Francisco, 1991), pp. 291–92. The reference is to Augustine, sermon 88.6.
86. Augustine, sermon 162.6.

CHAPTER SEVEN

THE BENEDICTINE CENTURIES I

Benedict, Boethius, Cassiodorus, Gregory and Bede

Augustine died in 430. Fifty years after his death, the untidy disintegration of the Roman Empire in the West was more or less complete. Ostrogoths, Visigoths, Vandals, Burgundians, Franks, Angles and Saxons had set up, or were fighting to set up, kingdoms in the old provinces of the empire; the unruled and unruly territory conquered by Attila the Hun stretched from the Rhine to the Caspian Sea and from the Baltic to the Black Sea. The last, powerless Western emperor, grandly called Romulus Augustulus, disappeared into retirement in 476. Two Gothic warlords fought for control of Italy, the victor, Theodoric, king of the Ostrogoths, becoming ruler of all Italy, with the remote blessing of the emperor in Constantinople, in 493. Theodoric was an illiterate barbarian and an Arian heretic. Nevertheless, impressed by what he had acquired, he ruled from Ravenna, the last imperial capital in the West, with the help of Roman officials a kingdom in which Latin remained the language of government, and there was no sectarian violence between his Arian Goths and his Catholic subjects. The Catholic Church, meanwhile, was governed from the city of Rome by her bishop, often at long-distance loggerheads with the emperor in Constantinople, variously effective in the new barbarian kingdoms according to the personal qualities of the successor of Saint Peter. In a period of weak institutions, strong men flourish, to build or to wreck. One pope, Leo the Great, who died in 461, had consolidated the bishop of Rome's authority over the Western Church, stiffened the Greek defence of orthodox Christianity at the Council of Chalcedon and personally confronted Attila the Hun and Gaiseric the Vandal, mitigating the ferocity of their assaults on Italy and Rome itself. He had also struck a note, ominous for the future, of papal arrogance, confusing the power of the *civitas terrena* with the organisational necessities of the Church. Addressing the people of Rome, he said:

> You are a holy people, an elect nation, a priestly and royal city, become, through the see of St Peter established here, the head of the world;

ruling more widely now through divine religion than it did by worldly dominion. Though enlarged by many victories, you have spread the authority of your rule over land and sea. What your warlike labours have obtained for you is less than what the Christian peace has brought you.[1]

In Theodoric's Italy, where he himself was the strong man of the earthly city, a different kind of strength, a different kind of building for the future, was achieved by three men who prayed, thought and wrote on the foundations laid by Augustine. One of them, Benedict, was a country boy from the Umbrian hills who became, long after his death, the father of all monks in the Latin Church. The other two, Boethius and Cassiodorus, were Roman patricians of ancient lineage who worked for Theodoric in public positions with titles familiar to Cicero half a millennium earlier. Benedict and Boethius were born in about 480; Cassiodorus was a few years younger and lived to be over ninety.

* * *

On the day of Augustine's conversion to Christianity, he was sitting in a state of emotional turmoil in a Milan garden with his friend Alypius when he heard the voice of a child chanting, as if in a game, "tolle, lege" (take up, read). So he picked up the copy of Saint Paul's Letter to the Romans, which he had left on a bench, and read a single verse that at last resolved all his hesitation, all his doubt, about committing himself forever to Christ.

What is less familiar than this story is the immediate reason for the emotional crisis of that afternoon. Earlier that day Augustine and Alypius had been visited, on some mundane business, by Ponticianus, an important Roman official who was also a baptized and practising Christian. He was surprised and pleased to find Augustine reading Saint Paul. During the conversation that then took place, Ponticianus told the two friends about Saint Antony of Egypt, always regarded as the first monk, who had left the *civitas terrena* for the desert and there lived a life of ascetic austerity and prayer, attracting many disciples to follow his example. Antony had died two years before Augustine was born, and his *Life*, written by Saint Athanasius, the great Greek bishop of Alexandria, had been translated into Latin only a few years before this providential Milanese morning. Augustine, who had never heard of Antony, was much impressed by the purity and boldness of his story and was even more impressed, and upset, when the official went on to describe the effect on two other imperial officials of reading Athanasius's *Life*.

Instantly, the very same day, they had abandoned their promising public careers and the women they were expected to marry and committed themselves to a monastic life of poverty, celibacy and prayer in a small community of like-minded men, leaving Ponticianus sad because he knew he was not capable of following their example. What was more, Ponticianus told Augustine and Alypius that there were now many such communities in the Christian world and even that "there was a monastery full of good brothers at Milan outside the city walls, fostered by Ambrose, and we had not known of it." [2]

This conversation threw Augustine into a state of acute anguish, a mixture of remorse, envy of the straightforward choice he was unable to make and indecision more agonising than any he had known. He said to Alypius: "What is wrong with us? What is this that you have heard? Uneducated people are rising up and capturing heaven, and we with our high culture without any heart—see where we roll in the mud of flesh and blood." [3]

Telling the story ten years later in the *Confessions*, Augustine here inserts before the blessed intervention of "tolle, lege" a few perceptive pages on indecision, on the puzzle of the divided will, on the struggle to escape from any hated, but loved, addiction:

> The mind commands the hand to move, and it is so easy that one hardly distinguishes the order from its execution. Yet mind is mind, and hand is body. The mind orders the mind to will. The recipient of the order is itself, yet it does not perform it. What causes this monstrosity and why does this happen? ... We are dealing with a morbid condition of the mind which, when it is lifted up by the truth, does not unreservedly rise to it but is weighed down by habit. [4]

He describes the whispering voices of habit that were still holding him back in this last hour from real, wholehearted response to the simple summons of Christ. These were the voices of ambition and of intellectual embarrassment before the simplicity of the Christian challenge, and also of the sexual activity—he was supposed soon to marry a suitable bride found for him by his mother—to which he was long accustomed. He knows that God will help him; he cannot risk asking for that help. "Why are you relying on yourself, only to find yourself unreliable? Cast yourself upon him, do not be afraid. He will not withdraw himself so that you fall. Make the leap without anxiety; he will catch you and heal you." [5] A tempest of tears and self-reproach overcame him in this last crisis of indecision. Then the child's voice reached him through the tempest and resolved the crisis.

This was the turning point of Augustine's life. He was too self-aware and too conscious always of the disorder of the human condition to think that the turn toward God had suddenly cured the unreliability of the will (or the sexual disobedience of the body, however unimpeachably celibate its Christian existence: into his old age Augustine regarded the involuntariness of the sexual response as the indelible mark of human fallenness). But that his submission on this day to the truth of God was final, was conclusively liberating and was a gift for which he was infinitely grateful and that made sense of the imperfect life that he lived both before and after it, he never doubted.

This whole passage of the *Confessions* is full of resonances that sound not only in the life of Augustine himself but in the life of all of Latin Christianity. At this moment in the year 386, as the passage shows, the monastic idea was flooding into the West from its sources in the Greek East. Athanasius, whose *Life of Saint Antony*, translated by Evagrius, was having such an impact so far from Egypt, and Basil the Great, whose writing on the monastic life was of much importance for its future in the West as well as in the East, had only recently died, in 373 and 379 respectively. Basil's Rule, a series of questions and answers, was being translated into Latin by Rufinus even as Augustine was hearing about monks for the first time. The irascible scholar Jerome, after living as a solitary ascetic in the East and then as a priest in Rome, settled in this very year, 386, into the monastic community in Bethlehem, where he lived and worked until his death in 420. He had translated into Latin the monastic regulations of Saint Pachomius, the first organiser, in the Egyptian desert, of large numbers of monks in stable communities. John Cassian, a year or two younger than Augustine, had already lived as a monk in Palestine and was in 386 studying the monastic life in Egypt. Wherever Cassian was born, probably in the Balkans, his perfect knowledge of both Greek and Latin made him a clear channel for the flow of monastic example from East to West. He spent the last twenty years of his life as a monk in Provence, where he died in 435, and his *Institutes* and *Conferences*, foundational monastic texts, were written in Latin.

Other early Western monks were wholly Latin. Honoratus, a little older than Augustine, was a Roman of consular family and a convert to Christianity. In 386 he was travelling in monastic Egypt and Syria. In 410 he founded the monastery of Lérins, which had an unbroken history until the eve of the French Revolution, off the Provençal coast, and ended his life as archbishop of Arles. Paulinus,

Augustine's exact contemporary, was a highly educated nobleman from old Roman Gaul who was baptized four years after Augustine, became a (married) priest and spent the last twenty years of his life living chastely with his wife and a scholarly monastic community at Nola in southern Italy, where he was bishop from 409. Paulinus and Augustine corresponded for twenty-five years. A quite different monk-bishop, Martin of Tours, born in Pannonia (Hungary) and once a Roman soldier, in 386 still had eleven years to live in his monastery on the Loire, which was also a mission centre for the conversion of the not-yet-Christian people of northern Gaul.

Only with the categories of inappropriate historical hindsight could it be said that Augustine himself was not a monk. After his mother's death and his return to Africa in 388, he never again lived outside a community of ascetic discipline; property owned in common; regular prayer, particularly of the Psalms; and uplifting reading at meals. His community was lay until he was ordained; after he became a bishop, it was mostly clerical. Always it contained both friends and students. Its life, orderly, celibate, but moderate in its austerity and sociable in its everyday companionship, was inspired by the short passage in the Acts of the Apostles[6] describing the warm unity of the very early Church, and this life in turn inspired Augustine's own recommendations—later regarded as a monastic Rule—for organising such a community for the benefit both of its members and of others.

In Augustine's account of the day of his conversion, particularly in his cry to Alypius about "our high culture without any heart", we can plainly see the procrastinating intellectual's painful admiration for the courage and decisiveness of men less complicated than himself. All early monasticism had this note of the heroic that so impressed Augustine. After Constantine's conversion, Christians were no longer persecuted by the government of Rome. Now not called perhaps to lay down his life for the truth of Christ, the wholehearted Christian could at least lay down his worldly ambition, desire for wealth and position and ordinary instinct for marriage, children and family life. For Augustine, as for many others in his time, there was precisely this note of the heroic in the very act of becoming a Christian. That the call to monastic self-sacrifice for God, reaching him in stories about people he knew nothing of, presented itself to Augustine as no different from, no more extreme than, the call to become a baptized Christian is characteristic of his time as well as, of course, characteristic of him. Later he came to see his conversion, any truly Christian conversion, as the turn from the earthly city toward the city of God and the monastic life as simply the best way to sustain the momentum of the journey toward the city of God while living, as all men must, in the city of the world.

* * *

About a hundred years after Augustine's death, and probably a few years after the death of Theodoric in 526, there was written, in the monastery of Monte Cassino eighty miles south of Rome, the Rule of Saint Benedict, a document some ten thousand words long, which was to have an effect unparalleled outside the Bible itself on many thousands of Christian lives in the centuries to come. Of Benedict, who wrote it, very little is known. The only evidence for the events of his life is in the *Dialogue* written some decades after his death by Gregory the Great, a Roman patrician, monk and founder of monasteries, and Pope at the end of the sixth century. Gregory's portrait is of an exemplary saint, a young man from Norcia who abandoned his studies in worldly Rome to become a hermit, lived for years in a cave at Subiaco, attracted followers, moved his community to Monte Cassino, governed it as a much-loved abbot, and was throughout his life protected and helped (there are a number of miracles in Gregory's story) by the grace of God. Gregory, perhaps unaware of the Rule's existence, does not mention the writing of it. But it is the Rule, brief and impersonal as it is, that is the text from which we can glean a little evidence of the inner life of its author. Benedict was a wise man, experienced in the management of others, keenly aware of the range and depth of human fallibility but not shocked by it, modest in his recommendation of his "very small rule for the unformed",[7] and above all experienced in what was destructive and what helpful in the sustaining of a community dedicated to life in Christ.

It used to be thought that Saint Benedict's Rule was remarkable for its originality as well as for its perceptiveness and practicality. Detailed scholarly investigation has now established that much of what it says can be found in the Greek or Greek-inspired writing on monasticism already current in the Latin world in the time of Augustine and also that Benedict followed a much longer Latin document of his own time, known as the Rule of the Master, so closely that this was for centuries regarded as a later expansion of Benedict's own work. That Benedict's Rule was mainly a recension of the available writing on what was by then two hundred years of monastic living is not at all surprising. Frail human nature being a constant, the life of a celibate community in which each member is dedicated to the service of God in prayer and work will deliver at any period and in any circumstances the same problems and the same ways of resolving them. By the time Benedict wrote his Rule, there was a broad consensus about monastic essentials and best practice that had been developed through experience, some of it bitter, all over the Christian world. "Consensus", after all, means "common sense", one of the qualities for which Benedict has always been celebrated.

Nevertheless, Benedict's Rule does remain remarkable and does remain his. It is his own in its brevity and therefore in the judgement with which he surveyed the material available to him and decided what to leave out. The longer the time that has elapsed since the early sixth century, the clearer the soundness of his judgement has become. The relevance of the Rule not only to monasteries but to many other forms of community life, from families to large businesses, is the result of the universal applicability of some of its key chapters. Naturally there is much in the Rule, notably the sections on the daily routine of prayer, work and sacred reading (*lectio divina*,[8] private, meditative reading of the Bible and other works) and the prohibition of personal possessions and of free travelling outside the monastery, that concerns only the lives of monks. But that, for example, the abbot (or the father of a family or the head of a school or the chief executive of a firm) should consult a small group of advisers over less important decisions but the whole community over major ones, and that then he should attend carefully to what even the most junior members have to say because "the Lord often reveals what is better to the younger", is a sensible recommendation in all sorts of circumstances. For what qualities the abbot should be chosen (exactly how he should be chosen is left vague); how he should listen to and encourage individuals, but also, with help from senior members of the community, how he should shape them into good monks; how profoundly he should regard himself as responsible to God for every member of his community always: all this, and perhaps especially how much in the management of his monks the Rule leaves to the intelligence and discretion of the abbot, has much to teach anyone at any time who finds himself in authority over others. The superior's power over his community is great, but so is the burden that he has to bear: he is there to carry each of those for whom he is answerable toward the city of God, fully realisable only after death. In its calm and level provision of both authority and support— the consultation the abbot must engage in, the respect for the views of the wiser members of the community that he must show—the Rule is a long way from being a charter for irresponsible absolutism and a longer way from the undisciplined enthusiasm that had sometimes turned into frightening mobs the followers of early Christian ascetics in the deserts of the East.

A good deal of what one might call the political wisdom of the Rule, as well as of the famous chapter on humility, which describes the selfless obedience with which the monk should respond to God and to the abbot's authority, comes, shortened and rearranged, from the Rule of the Master, which rests in turn on the monastic wisdom of Pachomius, Basil and Cassian. A careful comparison between the texts of Benedict and the Master shows, however, sometimes in apparently slight modifications and additions, a more flexible, a kinder and gentler, approach in Benedict, not only to the relationship between the abbot and those he rules but also to other relationships within the community and to its treatment of outsiders. Two main chapters in the Rule describe the abbot and his task. The first, chapter 2, "What an Abbot Ought to Be", has an atmosphere of weight, sternness and fairness, stressing the heavy responsibility of teaching and example that the abbot must take up. The second, chapter 64, "On the Choosing of an Abbot", is a more interior portrait of a good abbot, whose prudence, love for his monks and flexibility in his treatment of them will ensure that he pays proper attention to the personal capacity of each one of them, giving scope to the strong and encouragement to the weak. Much in this second description of the abbot is Benedict's own, as is the emphasis elsewhere in the Rule on the fraternal love and respect that should prevail throughout the community, between the healthy and the sick, between the young and the old, and between all monks and strangers, especially the poor.

This note of warmth is especially clear in the chapters at the end of Benedict's Rule, which owe least to the Rule of the Master, notably in chapter 72, on the good fervour that should bind monks together in love and obedience to each other and lead them to the unanimity that is truly of the city of God: "May they put nothing whatever before Christ, and may he lead us all as one to eternal life." [9] The same note sounds at the very beginning of the prologue, in the sentence that establishes for the remainder of the Rule that the point of monastic obedience is that it leads toward Christ:

> Listen, my son, to the master's words, and bend the ear of your heart;
> follow cheerfully and put into full effect the advice of a faithful father,
> so that through the effort of obedience you may return to him from
> whom through the idleness of disobedience you had gone far away. [10]

The note is Benedict's, but it is also Augustine's. The ear (or the eyes) of the heart is a phrase characteristic of his insistence that understanding comes only through love, while the journey toward God from the region of unlikeness is the story told in both the *Confessions* and the *City of God*. There is no sign in the Rule of the Master that its author had read Augustine. In the parts of the Rule that are Benedict's own, on the other hand, Augustine is an evident presence, in the open humaneness and psychological insight of Benedict's additions to the Master; in Benedict's stress on the brotherly unity of the monastery, an Augustinian emphasis that balances the Eastern tradition of the master-disciple relationship; in semiquotation from a number of Augustine's works, including what was already called Augustine's own Rule for monks; and also in the Augustinian freedom with which Benedict treats his many references to Scripture and all his monastic sources.

Conversion, the gift of God that is the turning away from disobedience and the turning toward God, is a constant theme of Augustine's. In the light of his gratefulness to God for his own conversion, he understood everything in his own life, in his own soul. That conversion should be sustained for the rest of his life he knew to be as dependent on God's grace as its initiation had been. In his case, as we have seen, conversion to Christianity was also conversion to a monastic way of living, and for several more centuries, in a post-Roman West that was not yet wholly Christian, the same would be true for many men and women. Benedict's Rule requires the monk who has successfully completed a year as a novice to promise before his fellow monks and in the presence of God and the saints not only obedience to his superior and stability in his community but also what Benedict calls *conversatio morum suorum*.[11] The phrase has given scholars and translators a great deal of trouble. It is usually given, nowadays, as "fidelity to monastic life", because *conversatio*, a word used nine times by Benedict and never in the Rule of the Master, is not quite the same as *conversio*, the ordinary Latin word for "conversion", and means more than the modern English "conversation". In classical Latin, *conversatio* has in it the idea of frequency or repetition, so that it seems likely that Benedict's phrase really means something like "continuing conversion of his ways of living", or even "of his soul", a meaning that Augustine, with his lack of confidence in the finality of any human commitment, would have understood and thoroughly approved.

* * *

While Benedict, far from cities, armies and kings, was acquiring the monastic experience that made possible the writing of his Rule, Boethius and Cassiodorus, each as consul and then *magister officiorum*, head of the civil service—Cassiodorus then as praetorian prefect of Italy—were serving Theodoric, like ghosts from the long centuries of Roman power, as best they could in the interests of peace and public order. Boethius was the last Roman we know for certain to have been thoroughly educated in the entire heritage of the classical world. He set himself to translate all of Plato and Aristotle into Latin for what he saw would be the Greekless future of the West. He had completed only some of Aristotle's technical logic books, with commentaries of his own, when in 523 he was imprisoned by the king and in the following year executed on a charge of senatorial conspiracy. The politics of the charge concerned the fraught relationship between Theodoric and Constantinople: the emperor had appointed Boethius's two sons consuls in 522; their father's loyalty to ancient tradition now alive only in the East cannot have made him popular in the Gothic court. Boethius also wrote a commentary on Porphyry's guide to Aristotle's logic and some textbooks on the liberal arts, of which one on arithmetic survives, with one on music that was used in schools and then in universities until the nineteenth century. By far his most important book was *The Consolation of Philosophy*, a November rose of the classical tradition, which he wrote in prison and which became a small window into the almost-lost world of pre-Christian Greek thought— Platonist, Aristotelian, Stoic and Neoplatonist—for the whole of the Middle Ages. *The Consolation of Philosophy* was loved by Dante, was known to almost everyone literate in Latin and was translated into English by Alfred the Great, Chaucer and Elizabeth I. The book, also containing a number of poems, is a dialogue in the tradition of Plato, Cicero and Augustine between Boethius himself, as a miserable prisoner awaiting death, and the female figure of Philosophy. In five short books she leads him from despair, and also from worldly ambition and intellectual pride, into a moving Augustinian hope in God, in whose eternal knowledge we are nevertheless free, to whose love, which made and holds the universe in being, we are given grace to return and in the light of whose glory we may learn his truth. Philosophy's hymn in book 3 ends:

> Grant, Father, that our minds thy august seat may scan,
> Grant us the sight of true good's source, and grant us light
> That we may fix on thee our mind's unblinded eye.
> Disperse the clouds of earthly matter's cloying weight;
> Shine out in all thy glory; for thou art rest and peace
> To those who worship thee; to see thee is our end,
> Who art our source and maker, lord and way and end.[12]

In spite of the near-trinitarian sense of the last line, there is in this hymn, and in the whole of the *Consolation*, more of Plato than of Augustine, particularly the

Plato of the *Timaeus* and of the parable of the cave in the *Republic*. There is a good deal of Augustine in the lucid discussion of the paradox of providence and freedom. Nowhere, however, in the *Consolation* is there a single reference to Christ. Boethius wrote some short theological works: one, *On the Holy Trinity*, begins with him hoping that "the seeds sown in my mind by Augustine's writing have borne fruit". But the particular quality of the *Consolation*, its clarity and calm reminiscent of Socrates's report of Diotima's philosophy of love toward dawn in the *Symposium*, suggests that, for all Boethius's conviction of the closeness, uncluttered by Neoplatonist intermediary spirits, of the loving soul to God, he had not been truly converted in and to Christ. His faith in God is evident. The *Consolation* ends:

> Hope is not placed in God in vain.... Lift up your mind to the right kind of hope, and put forth humble prayers on high. A great necessity is laid upon you, if you will be honest with yourself, a great necessity to be good, since you live in the sight of a judge who sees all things.[13]

But of hope in Christ he says nothing. Perhaps there is a clue to Boethius's apparent distance from the flesh and blood, the redeeming sacrifice, of the figure on the Cross and of the Eucharist, in his horror at "the incoherence and arrogance of participants in the discussion", some of which he witnessed, between bishops quarrelling over christological definitions.[14] If the raucousness and rhetorical incompetence of ecclesiastical disagreement kept this highly civilised man outside the Church—and there is no certainty either way—it was not the first or the last time that the inadequacies of those inside the Church blocked the communication, to those outside, of the truth with which they were entrusted.

Cassiodorus was related to Boethius and succeeded him as Theodoric's *magister officiorum* when Boethius was imprisoned in 523. Cassiodorus continued to serve the Goths as a high official until 538, through the years of increasingly chaotic competition for power that followed Theodoric's death. He then worked for the Pope, some of the time in Constantinople, until about 550, when already an old man, he retired from public life to a monastery called Vivarium that he had established on his estate in the remote south of Italy. By this time the country, no longer a country, was in a terrible, fractured condition. In 535 Justinian, the emperor in Constantinople, had sent armies to reconquer Africa and Italy from the barbarians so as to bring them under Byzantine control. This ill-advised campaign was successful at first: the Goths could not defend Naples or Rome and eventually, in 540, lost Ravenna to Justinian's general Belisarius. But the reconquest soon became a protracted failure, the desolation it brought being worsened by Goths fighting each other and by opportunistic raids into Italy of Franks and Burgundians from across the Alps. Within two decades, and while Cassiodorus was still alive, the Lombards, the most destructive of all invaders of Italy, arrived from the north. Savage warfare wrecked the towns and the countryside, massacres were followed by disease and hunger, and Rome itself was besieged five times.

Cassiodorus had always been a writer and an archivist. For Theodoric he had drafted official correspondence for many years; he had also written a book integrating the patchy story of Theodoric's clan into Roman history and collected twelve volumes of state papers, with commentary, to guide possible Italian governments of the future. Later in his career he had written a treatise *On the Soul* and a long commentary on the Psalms, both heavily dependent on Augustine. Now, in his peaceful monastery, he set himself and his community to collect and preserve as much of the classical writing of the past as could profitably be used in the education of Christians. His guide for his own monks, *Institutes of Divine and Secular Writings*, an account of books useful for the study of the Bible and the training of the mind, became a model for monastic libraries and schools for centuries, ensuring above all that everyone charged with the education of Christians in the West knew that the works of Augustine were the first requirement after the texts of Scripture itself. *Of Christian Teaching* was the basis of Cassiodorus's enterprise; the *Confessions*, the books on Genesis, the *City of God*, *On True Religion* and the *Retractationes* were also warmly recommended and much quoted in the *Institutes*. Cassiodorus gathered a group of translators to put into Latin some of the works of the Greek Fathers of the Church. Aware of the necessity of accurate manuscript reproduction of all texts, sacred and secular, the very old Cassiodorus wrote at the end of his life *On Orthography*, a guide for his own monks and many more, to help them to read and to copy carefully and to sustain clear Latin. "I have taught you", he wrote, "the importance of correct spelling and punctuation, universally acknowledged to be a precious thing." [15] Cassiodorus hoped and deserved to be called *Antiquarius Domini*, the librarian of the Lord. The eventual result of all this work was the addition to the literate but unscholarly life described in Benedict's Rule of a solid monastic tradition of study, learning and copying. The importance of this addition was immense in the centuries, unpropitious to learning, that were to come.

Neither Benedict's nor Cassiodorus's monastery much outlasted its founder. Monte Cassino was sacked by the Lombards less than forty years after Benedict's death. Cassiodorus's Vivarium disappeared from history soon after. But the books of both, especially the Rule and the *Institutes*, waited, like acorns in the frozen winter ground, for the warmth of spring.

The monastic idea survived the horrors of the later sixth century in a few monasteries in France, in the monastic missionary Church in Ireland, and also in Italy, as the career of Pope Saint Gregory the Great shows. He began his public life as prefect of Rome, an old senatorial office. He retired from the world to live in his own monastery in the centre of the city, but an ancient, indeed Ciceronian, sense of duty sent him to Constantinople for several years as a papal emissary. There he realised that the emperor in the East, still ratifying the election of each Pope and in theory sustaining a permanent oversight of Italy through his representative in Ravenna, was going to do nothing to preserve or protect the Church in the West. In 590 Gregory was recalled and compelled by the desperate need of the citizens of Rome, stricken by famine and plague and beleaguered by the Lombards, to accept responsibility for them as their bishop and therefore for the whole Latin Church as Pope. As Augustine had, Gregory continued, as a bishop, to live as a monk, and indeed his monastery, Saint Andrew's, serving the needs of the city, was, though grander than either, more like Augustine's household in Hippo than it was like the rural communities of Monte Cassino or Vivarium. Gregory's own books were second only to Augustine's, to which they were much indebted, as an authoritative source of scriptural commentary, teaching and Christian example for the Middle Ages. His *Pastoral Rule*, which describes the responsibilities and proper priorities of anyone charged with the care of souls, became for many generations in the Latin Church a handbook, particularly for bishops, both widely disseminated and much neglected. This book was, most unusually, translated into Greek in his lifetime, and much later, like the *Consolation of Philosophy*, it was translated into English by King Alfred. Conscious though he clearly was of the dangers of cluttering the way to the city of God with the concerns of the *civitas terrena*, the desperate circumstances of Gregory's time forced him to fill, from his papal office in Rome, the vacuum left by the total collapse of civil administration in Italy. A Roman official given authority, he had to do what he could to impose some order on chaos. With no help from Constantinople, he had to deal on his own with the Lombard threat. With no resources but the estates of the Church with which to feed and arm starving, defenceless people, he had to organise properly what became the papal states, the basis of the temporal power of the papacy that damagingly confused the objectives of Popes into the far future. Yet it was Gregory who, preaching in Constantinople before he became Pope, foresaw that one day, in the time of the Antichrist, the Church would become powerless, "naked and exposed, without a public role", but that nevertheless "the desire for God would bring the souls of the elect back to Paradise, even out of that terrible world of the future."[16] This was Augustine's vision of the city of God transcending the horrors of the earthly city but narrowed and sharpened by a more acutely threatening historical moment. On Gregory's tomb in Rome was inscribed the phrase *consul Dei* (God's consul), which caught in two words the two kinds of life that Gregory had united in himself. His own ascetic devotion to duty is more exactly caught, with less of the Roman pride of Leo the Great, in his self-description, adopted by later Popes and borrowed from Augustine's writing about his mother[17] and later about himself: *servus servorum Dei* (servant of the servants of God).

By Gregory's time—he died in 604—the monastic life that he, the first monk-pope, so much loved and so strongly supported had everywhere in the West taken on a colour and purpose of its own. In the fourth-century Greek world of Egypt, Palestine and Syria, the monastic enterprise, in its enthusiastic devotion to God in the solitude of the desert, had been a sign of contradiction, often a disorderly one, raised against the settled and sometimes complacent Church of the great cities. In the Western empire of Augustine's time, the monastic enterprise had been a simple, self-sacrificial sign of contradiction raised, sometimes in the centre of cities and sometimes in the country, but not in any actual desert, against a society in which wealth, power and public success were still the prevailing magnets of the will. In the late sixth and seventh centuries, the monastic enterprise was still a sign of contradiction but was now a precious demonstration of order and faith and also of Roman coherence and equanimity in the midst of chaos, instability and the random violence of warring clans. In pagan lands, either those that had once been part of the empire or those that never had been, it was a living statement of the truth of Christian revelation to those as ignorant of the God of the Bible as they were of the classical tradition. Here monks became missionaries, proof to the pagans in themselves and in their lives that Christianity made men peaceful, brave, selfless, truthful, good, and sometimes also scholarly. For, outside of a few Italian towns, it was only among monks and in their classrooms and libraries that what was left of classical civilisation in the West was, with laborious effort, being saved from oblivion.

It was now, in a handful of old and a handful of new monasteries that Benedict's Rule, the most Roman of all monastic documents, found the beginning of spring.

Gregory was devoted to the figure of Benedict, as his hagiographic *Dialogue* about Benedict's life shows. However, the monks Gregory sent to England to convert the Anglo-Saxons came from his own urban background, were priests as most of Benedict's monks had not been, and seem not to have taken Benedict's Rule with them. At much the same time as Gregory's mission, Irish monks arrived at Lindisfarne in Northumbria from Iona to begin the conversion of the Anglo-Saxons in the north of the country. Ireland had never been part of the empire and had no towns, let alone cities. Contact with the Gaul of Martin of Tours and Germanus of Auxerre, a contemporary of Augustine and an anti-Pelagian bishop, and also with the British Christians pushed westward by invading Anglo-Saxons, had won to Christianity the powerful figures in Irish tribal society. This conversion produced a richly endowed and notably monastic Church, Celtic monks leading a life of holiness, considerable Latin learning and strong missionary enterprise; they were often out on the rough roads, preaching and baptizing. In Ireland the abbot carried more weight than the bishop and sometimes was the bishop, as Martin had been. Benedict had not been heard of.

England, in contrast, had for more than three centuries, until 410, been part of the empire. Here and there under the Romans it had been Christian; now it was mostly pagan territory. Gregory's missionaries brought with them monastic training and customs, a habit of life in which a routine of shared prayer, celibacy and common ownership of minimal property held a group of men together, and a firm allegiance to the Pope. Northumbria, at the extreme northern edge of what had been Roman territory, always wild country but with reminders of imperial power in its frontier camps, its long roads to the south, and Hadrian's Wall, was where these two missionary efforts met and, in some details of Church order and custom, collided. It was through the teaching and example of Celtic monks of the Irish tradition that Northumbria was becoming Christian, but it was nevertheless from Northumbria that two Anglo-Saxons, of wealthy chieftain families, set out in 653 to travel to Rome. They set out because in Rome, where Saint Peter and Saint Paul had been martyred and buried, they wanted to make contact of their own with the whole history of the Church.

One of them, Wilfrid, already a monk of Lindisfarne, stayed for three years in Lyons on the way back to England. Here he became a Benedictine monk and also much admired the state kept and the power exercised by the archbishop. The other Northumbrian, named Biscop (he was never a bishop), returned to the Mediterranean on a second visit and became a monk, taking the name Benedict, in his case usually anglicised as Benet, in the already old monastery of Lérins in Provence, the school of many abbots and a community that by this time had adopted Benedict's Rule. Both these travellers eventually returned to Northumbria—Biscop by way of Canterbury, where he was for a couple of years abbot in the cathedral monastery—bringing with them a deep love of the

Romanness that the Celts could not teach them and books that included the Rule. Both of them travelled to Rome several more times in the course of long lives.

Wilfrid founded Benedictine monasteries at Ripon and Hexham, building stone churches in Roman fashion, the one at Hexham using dressed stone collected from Hadrian's Wall. Wilfrid's weight of argument carried the day for Roman custom, in particular the calculation of the date of Easter, at the Synod of Whitby in 664, where differences between the northern and southern Christian missionary efforts were more or less resolved. He himself, though always concerned for the welfare of monks and always a missionary, was in temperament and ambition not so much an abbot as a bishop, and a grand bishop at that, and never concentrated his efforts for long on the nurture of a single community. His later journeys to Rome were mostly in the cause of strengthening his own episcopal position. Benet Biscop, on the other hand, gave the acorns of both Benedict and Cassiodorus unusually fertile ground. In the two monasteries he founded a few miles apart at Wearmouth and Jarrow, on cold river meadows close to the North Sea, and both with large stone churches, life according to the Rule was established with a purity and strength that became exemplary in the West for half a millennium. Benet Biscop's later journeys to Rome were to collect relics and holy paintings to teach the Gospel to the illiterate who came to his churches; to recruit skilled people who could teach his monks to sing the Office properly and glaze his windows with coloured glass; and above all, to gather books. A generation later there were three hundred books in the library he founded. A few came from the scattered collection of Vivarium itself; Biscop deserves to be called the Cassiodorus of the north.

However impressive to contemporaries the Roman solidity of these distant monasteries may have been, they were soon destroyed, along with Iona, Lindisfarne, Whitby and eventually all monastic life in England, by the Viking invasions that began within a hundred years of the deaths of Benet Biscop and Wilfrid. Only the providential combination of Benet Biscop's work and the giftedness and application of a single man gave them their impact on the future. This man was Bede.

Bede was given by his parents to the care of Benet Biscop as a boy of seven. In the monastic community that brought him up and educated him he remained until his death fifty-five years later, travelling scarcely at all and never further than York. As a monk, a priest, a teacher, and above all as a writer, he responded wholeheartedly to the Christian truth that reached him through the Bible, through Benedict's Rule and the daily routine of prayer that he lived for his entire life, and through the books Biscop had brought back from his journeys to Rome. Bede was familiar with thirty-six of Augustine's works, including the *City of God*; *On the Trinity*; *Of Christian Teaching*; the books on Genesis, Saint John and the Psalms; and collections of letters and sermons. He knew and quoted from a sermon thereafter lost until the twentieth century.[18] Toward the end of his life, Bede completed his own most famous book, *A History of the English Church and People*. At its conclusion he listed thirty-five other books he had written. Most of them are books of scriptural commentary, written to help monks and others in the spiritual enterprise of *lectio divina*. In all these commentaries Augustine is his chief authority and source of help. One of them is a handbook to Saint Paul "in which I have carefully transcribed in order whatever I have found on the subject in the works of St Augustine".[19] Later, Bede would write a modest *Retractatio*. After this list, Bede ends his history in Augustinian fashion, with a prayer in which he too acknowledges the Word that is the source of all truth spoken or written:

> I pray you, noble Jesus, that as you have graciously granted me joyfully to imbibe the words of your knowledge, so you will also of your bounty grant me to come at length to yourself, the fount of all wisdom, and to dwell in your presence for ever.[20]

A great monk-historian of the twentieth century called Bede "the only teacher of the first rank whom the west knew between Gregory the Great and the eleventh century".[21] In his scholarship, in the fresh companionableness of his writing, in the productive use he made of all that he had at hand and could find out from his monastery at the far end of the world, in his love for the saints of the Celtic as of the Roman monastic tradition, but above all in the calm security of his life dedicated to God, Bede was a beneficiary of the inheritance left to a dark future by predecessors who could never have predicted the monastic achievement of seventh-century Northumbria. Particularly striking is the combined impetus of Benedict's Rule, which turned out to be perfectly suited to a community of Anglo-Saxons farming and fishing at the back of beyond, and Cassiodorus's example of meticulous study and writing within a monastery. Bede tells us that the dying Benet Biscop begged his monks to choose, according to the Rule, from among themselves a wise and holy abbot to succeed him (and not Biscop's own brother in accordance with Anglo-Saxon and Celtic tribal custom) and at the same time ordered them to keep intact his library of books "which were so necessary for improving the standard of education in this church".[22] They did both. Ceolfrith was an outstanding abbot of Wearmouth and Jarrow for twenty-seven years, doubled the size of the library and organised the production by his monks of three huge and beautiful Bibles, one for each monastery church and one for the Pope, in the "new", as Bede calls it, translation of Jerome, on the model of a Bible in the library prepared by Cassiodorus himself. When he retired, Ceolfrith set out for Rome to deliver the Pope's gift—Benedictine Northumbria making a fine return to the source of its monastic life—and died on the journey. The Bible for the Pope, now in the Medici Library in Florence, is the oldest surviving single-volume Bible in the world.

Bede's short book *Lives of the Abbots of Wearmouth and Jarrow* tells us all this and much more. It begins with a brief account of Benet Biscop that, on the very first page, quotes both Gregory on Benedict and the Rule itself. Echoes of both continue through the *Lives*, showing not only how firmly Bede believed that his own community, so far from Rome, was living within the tradition Biscop had brought home in himself and in books, but also how well Benedict's prescriptions from a vanished world worked in a new and different one. A young abbot called Eosterwine, the best man for the job though only thirty-two, was chosen for the monastery at Wearmouth when Biscop set off on one of his journeys to Rome. The young man was a thane and Biscop's cousin. However, Bede tells us:

> When he had turned his back once and for all on the life of the world and had ceased to be King Egfrid's thane by laying down his arms and girding himself for spiritual warfare, he kept himself so humble and identified himself so completely with his brethren that he took a positive delight in sharing their ordinary work. He took his share of the winnowing and threshing, the milking of the ewes and the cows; he laboured in bakehouse, garden and kitchen, taking part cheerfully and obediently in every monastery chore. He was no different when he attained to the rank and authority of abbot.... When necessary he would correct wrongdoers according to the letter of the Rule but he much preferred to follow his normal affectionate bent and diligently admonish them by word of mouth, so that no one would think of sinning, for then their abbot's bright smile would be clouded over by anxiety on their behalf.[23]

In this ideal but not idealised portrait of a Benedictine abbot, there is an emphasis, often found in Bede, on the lack of separation, startling in a society of kings, thanes and peasants, between the man in authority and his community. Abbots walked; they did not ride like the thanes most of them had once been. That there should be no distancing state kept, even by a monk-bishop (a figure not envisaged in Benedict's Rule), was a monastic principle Bede consistently advocated. He twice quotes a warning letter from Pope Gregory to his leader of the Canterbury mission, who was acting as both abbot and bishop: "You, brother, have been brought up in the monastic rule. Now that the faith has been brought to the English you must not start living apart from your clergy. Introduce that way of life practised by the fathers of the early church, none of whom claimed as his own anything that he possessed—for everything was held in common." [24] The recommendation is strongly Augustinian: this is how Augustine lived as bishop of Hippo, and this fraternal emphasis is, as we have seen, his most evident mark on Benedict's Rule as distinct from the Rule of the Master. But it is also Celtic. Bede quotes Gregory's letter in his *Life of Cuthbert*, in support of his description of the community at Lindisfarne, where according to Celtic custom, the abbot ruled a monastery in which both he and the bishop, when different men, lived with, and in exactly the same way as, all the other monks.

This is only one instance of the spirit—also Augustinian—in which Bede, though brought up at Wearmouth and Jarrow in a Roman atmosphere, was always able to give full credit to the nobility and virtue of the Celtic monastic tradition. Indeed, the single predecessor he most admired was not Biscop, and certainly not Wilfrid, whose public grandeur as bishop followed a very different Roman pattern, but Cuthbert, an Anglo-Saxon boy called by God to monastic life, a prior in two monasteries, later for eight years a hermit on "a tiny island known as Farne which lies in the ocean about nine miles from the [Lindisfarne] church", [25] and finally bishop of Lindisfarne. Cuthbert obeyed without fuss the Roman injunctions of the Synod of Whitby, but Bede's description of his life as monk, prior, hermit and bishop, preaching, teaching, training monks, healing (there are many miracles in Bede's account), advising and above all praying, shows Cuthbert as in all respects an exemplary Celtic monk. There are elements in his story, particularly the years of solitude and increasing holiness, with the wild creatures of sea and sky tamed to the saint's assistance and bidding, that recall the early desert monks, alone with the wild, both without and within. Jerome had his friendly lion, Cuthbert his friendly seals, otters and ravens; both also had the persevering devotion to God that tamed the savagery within their souls. Cuthbert much feared, and when the time came, stoutly resisted, the office of bishop, which had long been predicted for him. Bede tells us that he would say to his monks: "If I could live in a tiny dwelling on a rock in the ocean, surrounded by the swelling waves, cut off from the knowledge and the sight of all"—which he did for years—"I would still not be free from the cares of this fleeting world nor from the fear that somehow the love of money might snatch me away."[26] Cuthbert as prior and, eventually, as bishop, however, often away from his monastery—travelling from village to village, from farm to farm, taking food to the poor, encouraging new Christians and consoling them in times of war, plague and bad harvests—is also a model of pastoral care.

The life of the Church in Bede's England was not a complex one. In an illiterate population given to clan violence at the slightest provocation and to a rapid return to pagan superstition when things went badly, monks, priests and bishops were all most of the time missionaries, trying to hold primitive converts to the basics of Christian existence, preaching to inspire the unbaptized to join the Church. Compared to the highly sophisticated Romans, who abandoned worldly ambition for the monastic life in the time of Augustine, even Bede, with his books and his careful scholarship, was a simple soul. Like Augustine, Benedict and Cassiodorus, Bede at the end of his life was, rightly, anxious about the present and fearful for the future. He ends his great *History* with no confidence in the current king of Northumbria and grave doubts about the number of people joining monasteries for no better reason than to escape the readiness for warfare otherwise expected of them.

Bede died an exemplary, peaceful and holy death in 735, dictating in his last illness a translation of Saint John's Gospel into Anglo-Saxon. He could not have known how complete the destruction of English monastic life was to be in the one hundred fifty years after his death. But nor could he, working away in his cell on the Tyne at Jarrow, have guessed that his own writing was to be an indispensable link in the chain that connected the almost-lost world of Augustine, in which the weight of the classical heritage was confronted by the apparent folly of Christianity, with a future that was for centuries to learn of the first only through the mediation of the second. For this process, Bede's monastery, and Bede's history of the great figures of the early English Church, set a naïve but golden precedent. Saint Boniface, an English monk, bishop and martyr, a little younger than Bede and regarded in Germany as the greatest of all missionaries to that country, called Bede "the candle of the Church which the Holy Spirit has lit".[27] Meanwhile, Benedict's Rule contributed to the process a Roman firmness and a fraternal ideal that shaped the lives of countless monks. The works of Gregory, Cassiodorus and Boethius shone in dark centuries with further shafts of Roman light. But behind them all was the writing of Augustine, without whose capacious and supremely intelligent grasp of Christian truth in relation to the classical world in which he lived none of them would have understood as they did the particular challenges of the circumstances in which each of them found himself, and found his way toward the city of God.

1. Quoted in R. A. Markus, *The End of Ancient Christianity* (Cambridge, 1990), pp. 126–27.
2. Augustine, *Confessions* 8.6.14, trans. Henry Chadwick (Oxford, 1991).
3. Ibid., 8.8.19.
4. Ibid., 8.9.21.
5. Ibid., 8.11.27.
6. Acts 4:32–35.
7. *Regula Benedicti* 73.8; my translation.
8. Ibid., 49.1.
9. Ibid., 72.11.
10. Ibid., prologue, 1–2.
11. Ibid., 58.17.
12. Boethius, *The Consolation of Philosophy* 3.9, trans. V. E. Watts (London, 1969).
13. Ibid., 5.6.
14. Henry Chadwick, *The Church in Ancient Society* (Oxford, 2001), p. 608.
15. Quoted in Markus, *End of Ancient Christianity*, p. 220.
16. Quoted in Peter Brown, *The Rise of Western Christendom*, 2nd ed. (Oxford, 2003), p. 203.
17. Augustine, *Confessions* 9.9.22.
18. Serge Lancel, *Saint Augustine*, trans. Antonia Nevill (London, 2002), p. 195.
19. Bede, *A History of the English Church and People*, trans. Leo Sherley-Price (London, 1968), p. 337.
20. Ibid., p. 338.
21. David Knowles, *The Monastic Order in England* (Cambridge, 1963), p. 24.
22. Bede, *Lives of the Abbots of Wearmouth and Jarrow*, chap. 11, trans. D. H. Farmer, in *The Age of Bede* (London, 1988), p. 198.
23. Ibid., chap. 8, pp. 194–95.
24. Bede, *Life of Cuthbert*, chap. 16, trans. J. F. Webb, in *Age of Bede*, p. 65.
25. Bede, *History*, p. 259.
26. Bede, *Life of Cuthbert*, chap. 8, p. 56.
27. Quoted (in Latin) in Leo Sherley-Price, introduction to Bede, *History*, p. 21; my translation.

CHAPTER EIGHT

THE BENEDICTINE CENTURIES II

Anselm, Bernard and Aelred

Charlemagne, the illiterate Frankish warrior who in 800 was crowned by the Pope as the new emperor of the west, had deep respect for the long past of Rome—its learning, its buildings, its law, its documents. In his capital Aachen (Aix-la-Chapelle), not much bigger than a village, he built a valiant copy of San Vitale, Justinian's church in Ravenna. To found a school and assemble a library at his rough court of fighting men, Charlemagne sent to York for a teacher. Alcuin came, pupil of a pupil of Bede, with Scripture commentaries, grammars, instructions on how to scan Virgil, Bede's *History* and most of the works of Augustine. Alcuin died, after twenty years of labour among the Franks, as abbot of Tours on the Loire.

Keen that everything under his control should be properly organised in Roman fashion, Charlemagne sent to Monte Cassino for what was supposed to be Benedict's autograph copy of the Rule and declared that the Rule was to be the norm for all monasteries in his empire. After Charlemagne's death, the firm management of Benedict of Aniane, a rigorous monastic administrator and scholar, ensured that this more or less came to be the case. A difficult hundred years later—Charlemagne's empire turned out to be neither as stable nor as helpful to the Church as he had intended—the foundation in 909 of the abbey of Cluny in Burgundy, answerable to the Pope rather than to Charlemagne's unruly heirs or their warring vassals, reinforced this Benedictine pattern. Cluny, under a succession of holy and long-lived abbots, became the monastic wonder of the next two centuries, famous everywhere for the size and good order of its community, the elaborate splendour of its liturgy and the beauty of its great third church, built at the end of the eleventh century and then the largest church in the world. Meanwhile, in the whole of England at the time when Cluny was founded, there was not a single genuinely monastic community. The Viking invasions had destroyed every monastery in the eastern half of the country; in the south and west a few neglected collections of books remained in monastic buildings where there were groups of clergy, some with wives and children (not at all a scandal-ous state of affairs at the time), but no communities living according to a Rule. In Northumbria a little band of such clerics, harried from place to place, looked after the precious coffin and relics of Saint Cuthbert, which their forebears had saved from the sacked monastery of Lindisfarne. King Alfred in Wessex, having brought the wars with the Vikings almost to an end and having conceded half of England to their settlement, did his best to secure at the end of the ninth cen-tury a sound future for Christian life in his country. A pious and educated man himself, he collected a few scholars, some from abroad, and organised the trans-lation into Anglo-Saxon of one short book by Augustine (the *Soliloquies*) as well as Boethius's *Consolation of Philosophy* and Gregory's *Pastoral Rule* and *Dialogue* on Saint Benedict. But his efforts to restore one or two monasteries came to noth-ing. He died in 899.

In the middle of the tenth century, however, Englishmen did return, under the powerful guidance of Saint Dunstan, brought up near Glastonbury and familiar with the old books in its library, and his friends Saint Ethelwold and Saint Oswald, to properly disciplined monastic life. These three men, in the foundation or refoundation of a number of Benedictine abbeys, used the pat-tern and guidance of now-flourishing monasteries in the French and German lands into which Charlemagne's empire had split for good. They also used the Bede tradition of the exemplary monk-bishop, derived from Celtic precedent, from Gregory and his Roman mission that began in Canterbury and from Augustine's household at Hippo, to construct a uniquely English institution, the cathedral-monastery with, at its head, the bishop, who was also the com-munity's abbot. Dunstan, Ethelwold and Oswald were, respectively, archbishop of Canterbury, bishop of Winchester and bishop of Worcester; the monastery each ruled at his cathedral survived until the dissolution of all English monas-teries in the sixteenth century. Oswald was also archbishop of York, but there was no possibility of a cathedral-monastery in that now-Viking city. The cathedral-monastery was an institution that the Normans, conquering England in 1066 and strengthening their control of the country with Norman appointments to all powerful positions in the English church, found both congenial and useful.

The Normans were themselves Vikings. Having raided and then settled in a sizeable area of northwest France in the ninth century, they became, like their fellow Vikings in England, in two or three generations good Christians. By the time their duke became King William I of England, there were at least twenty-five Benedictine monasteries in Normandy, the most remarkable of which had been founded by an uneducated knight, Herluin, who had given up soldiering to become a monk when he was almost forty. His abbey at Bec began as a simple, poor, rustic community, as different, in the 1040s, as a Benedictine house could be from the liturgical splendour of Cluny or the already wealthy cathedral and other monasteries that Dunstan and his friends had established in England. Little might ever have been heard of Bec had not a most gifted man, an Italian scholar and lawyer, arrived shortly after its foundation to join the monastery when he, too, was nearly forty. Lanfranc of Pavia, soon prior of Bec, was an excellent and already-celebrated teacher. He attracted to the abbey, where he collected a fine library, some of the brightest and best young men of the time, to learn from him and in some cases to commit themselves for good to the serious, uncluttered life of the monastic community. One of these young men was Anselm, Italian and scholarly like his master. Holier and more of an intellectual than Lanfranc, much less adaptable to the demands of the world, he became an exemplary monk. He was also a writer of piercing brilliance, in certain respects the greatest writer of the Latin Christian tradition since Augustine.

Anselm was born in 1033, in the Alpine town of Aosta, geographically just in Italy but at the time in the very south of the kingdom of Burgundy. His father was a Lombard landowner, his mother a Burgundian whose family lived in the northern Rhône valley. Anselm, like Augustine, venerated his mother's memory always. At her death he quarrelled with his father, turned his back on the family estates and the secular education in law and administration of the Italian cities, and left Italy for the northwest, for Burgundy, for France, for what was, at the time, the moral and spiritual centre of gravity of the Latin Church. For several years he travelled, unable to make up his mind where or how to live for the best. There were three obvious possibilities open to such a young man in the 1050s. One was Cluny, approaching the peak of its Christendom-wide influence and grandeur; at Cluny the twenty-five-year-old Saint Hugh, whose wisdom was to affect the life of the whole Latin Church for six decades, had become abbot in 1049. Anselm seems to have considered joining the community at Cluny and decided against it because the weight of the liturgy left the monks almost no time for study. A second possibility was the life of learning in one of the new cathedral schools of northern France—Chartres or Laon, Rheims or Orléans—clerical but secular, and very much in and of the world. The intellectual future, as we shall see, lay with these schools. Anselm, however, chose a third possibility, one without the disadvantages, for him, of either Cluny or a cathedral school, but with the most attractive qualities of both. He chose Bec, a peaceful monastery, and Lanfranc, an inspiring teacher and a monk.

After a year as one of the secular, that is, non-monastic, students who were welcome in Lanfranc's school at Bec, Anselm asked Lanfranc to tell him whether he should go back to Aosta to run his estates, become a hermit or join the monastery. He was twenty-seven years old, a restless young man far from home, until this moment without clear direction. Lanfranc told him to join the monastery. So he did. This decision, which he had trusted Lanfranc to make for him, was the critical turning point of Anselm's life. The choice he then made, which he saw as one of obedience, he never regretted, becoming from that moment until his death nearly fifty years later a Benedictine monk of single-minded, wholehearted dedication. The decision was the equivalent in his life to Augustine's decision to become a Christian, and the difference in scale, though not in intensity, between these two decisions is an exact indication of the difference in scale, though again not in intensity, of their subsequent lives and, above all, of their writing. It is also an indication of the difference between the worlds in which they lived.

Anselm wrote nothing of consequence for more than fifteen years after he entered the monastery. He read a great deal, becoming deeply and widely familiar, in the same spirit as both Augustine and Benedict, with the Bible. Benedict's Rule, a chapter of which was read aloud daily at Bec as in all regular Benedictine communities (hence "chapter-house"), he must soon have known by heart. Augustine's works, which at Bec almost certainly included the *Confessions*, he read and reread with such profound attention and fellow feeling that it is no exaggeration to say that, if his life was shaped by Benedict, his mind and soul were formed by Augustine. Indeed, Richard Southern, the greatest modern authority on Anselm, has said: "If Anselm had had no other sources of inspiration than the Bible, the Rule of St Benedict, and Augustine's *De Trinitate, Confessions, De Civitate Dei*, and *Sermons on the Psalms*, he would have had all the inspiration he needed for everything of importance that he wrote." [1]

Anselm's quiet life at Bec soon included responsibility for others. After only three years, Lanfranc, in 1063, left Bec to become abbot of Duke William's monastery of Saint Stephen in his capital city, Caen, and Herluin appointed Anselm prior of Bec. He held this office for fifteen years. By 1078, when the aged Herluin died, Anselm's purity of monastic life and the exceptional quality of his mind as a teacher—students at the abbey were now all monks—and of his insight as a spiritual director had given Bec a glowing reputation for both piety and learning. The monks, not surprisingly, elected him abbot to succeed Herluin. He was not pleased: the work of an abbot was much in the wider feudal world and involved practical decisions of a kind that appealed to Anselm not at all. Since 1070, when William, now King of England, had sent for Lanfranc to be his archbishop of Canterbury, Bec monks had increasingly found themselves summoned across the sea to stiffen the monastic community at Canterbury and often to become the Norman abbots and bishops, who were the lynchpins of the new government of conquered England. Anselm was inevitably drawn into this magnetic field of power and politics, but he kept his monastic priorities clear and for five years was a firm, kind and much-loved abbot at Bec.

It was toward the end of his peaceful time as prior that Anselm wrote a handful of small masterpieces. His nineteen *Prayers*, too long and too dense with the thought and feeling of his uniquely compacted Latin for liturgical use, are meant for quiet, private devotional reading. Sending them to one of the pious lay people with whom he corresponded, Anselm says that "they should not be read cursorily or quickly, but little by little, with attention and deep meditation. It is not intended that the reader should feel impelled to read the whole, but only as much as will stir up the affections to prayer."[2] They are, in other words, for *lectio divina*, the kind of centred reading, open to the truth, beauty and goodness of God, open to grace, for which Benedict's Rule sets aside some time in every day of a monk's life. They explore the love of God, expressed in the life, love, death and Resurrection of Christ, for always-sinful, always-undeserving mankind. Those addressed to friends of Christ, to John the Baptist, Saint Peter, Saint Paul, and especially (two prayers) to Saint John the Evangelist, are driven by Anselm's longing to join in the love—Christ's for them, theirs for Christ—that steadied and held the saints. The three prayers addressed to Mary, the human being uniquely close to Christ, take further than anyone had yet gone an exploration, which is intellectual as well as devotional, of the truth that is the physical and emotional but sinless motherhood of God. The third and longest of these is Anselm's most famous prayer. A few lines from it will give some idea of how these prayers are written:

> Deus igitur est pater rerum creatarum,
> et Maria mater rerum recreatarum.
> Deus est pater constitutionis omnium,
> et Maria est mater restitutionis omnium.
> Deus enim genuit illum per quem omnia sunt facta,
> et Maria peperit illum per quem cuncta sunt salvata.
> Deus genuit illum sine quo penitus nihil est,
> et Maria peperit illum sine quo nihil omnino bene est.

> So God is the father of created things
> and Mary the mother of re-created things.
> God is the father of the ordering of all,
> and Mary is the mother of the restoring of all.
> For God fathered him through whom all things are made,
> and Mary bore him through whom everything is saved.
> God fathered him without whom there is absolutely nothing,
> and Mary bore him without whom nothing at all is good.[3]

The prayers are written in prose, not verse, but Anselm deploys simple, intense Latin with a resourcefulness, a precision and finish that belong to poetry. "Learn Latin properly", Anselm wrote to a young monk. "Pay particular attention to Virgil."[4] Anselm plumbs the relationships between Latin words with a concentration, in both senses, that makes rhyme the result rather than the objective of the process. Anselm is a writer alone with God, alone with revealed truth, struggling to put the right words in the right order so that others may be helped to pray their way a little deeper into mysteries to approach which we have only words, and silence. Some of the prayers were years in the writing.

In many of Anselm's prayers, there is a note of self-disgust and self-abasement, and sometimes almost despairing misery and terror: "Where can he hide himself, to whom can he show himself," he asks in the first prayer to Saint John, "this little man weighed down by the load of his sins which he is not able to shed?"[5] Rescue, safety, forgiveness in the mercy of God usually prevails in the prayers. But anguished self-reproach is characteristic of Anselm. He took literally and obeyed Benedict's injunction in chapter 7 of the Rule that "a monk should not only say with his tongue that he is worse, more vile, than all, but he should believe it with the deepest feeling of his heart."[6] Teaching his monks, Anselm recast Benedict's somewhat random "steps of humility" in a fierce descending scale that ends with the instruction "to rejoice when you are treated with contempt".[7] Anselm saw himself as a small, tangled knot of darkness against the blaze of the beauty and goodness of God, and his writing almost entirely lacks the confident celebration of all goodness, all beauty that is everywhere in Augustine.

But the celebration of truth it does not lack. In this same quiet, productive period at Bec, Anselm wrote two longer pieces of prose that are lit with his joy in the increasing discovery of truth that his faith had brought him. The first he originally called "An example of meditation on the meaning of faith". The phrase here translated as "on the meaning of faith" is *de ratione fidei*. *Ratio* is the nearest Latin equivalent to the Greek word *logos* in its strongest sense, so that Anselm's phrase could also be translated "on the rational necessity of faith" or "on the Word in which we believe". He called his meditation, in the end, simply *Monologion*. It is a meditation on belief in God and is plainly the fruit of his prayer, the prayer of any human being, "that God might reveal what earlier he concealed".[8] At the start, Anselm says that he is writing down "some thoughts on the divine essence and other related matters" in response to some of his fellow monks, who have asked him "that nothing should be put forward on the authority of Scripture" and "that whatever conclusion was reached in the course of each investigation should be expressed in plain language with intelligible arguments". "They also asked me not to leave any objections unanswered, however simple, or even foolish they might appear."[9]

This could be Plato representing Socrates's method of philosophical enquiry. More strikingly like Plato is the actual substance of the *Monologion*, which establishes the necessary qualities of God—absolute goodness, truth and justice—and also establishes that these qualities cannot be thought about at all unless, from the outset, the thinker is willing to believe in their reality. An act of faith, in other words, is necessary before the reason can be used in the seeking of understanding of what is believed. Or, more radically, an act of faith is necessary before thought can take place. Anselm knew no Plato, and no pagan Neoplatonism either. But his familiarity with Augustine and his own penetrating thought about God brought him closer to Plato than any other Latin writer of the Middle Ages came, and in the pure reasoning of his approach, closer even than Augustine himself. When he sent the *Monologion* to Lanfranc for his approval, Lanfranc objected that there were no authorities, no texts quoted in support of the argument, anywhere in the work: Lanfranc was unaware that Anselm had written exactly as his monks had asked him to. All other medieval writers on the things of God, including the most sophisticated theologians of the thirteenth century, quoted constantly from the Bible and from the Fathers of the Church. A contemporary of Anselm teaching in the cathedral school at Chartres described the scholars of his time as dwarfs standing on the shoulders of giants.[10] Anselm, an intellectual dwarf in nobody's company, replied to Lanfranc by saying that there was nothing in the *Monologion* that could not be found in Augustine. This is true in that there is nothing in the meditation, or in its more intense companion piece and distillation, the *Proslogion*, that is not derived from an entirely Augustinian sense of the greatness and incomprehensibility of God and does not rest on an Augustinian gratitude for the grace, given by God, of a little human understanding of him. But Anselm was an original thinker, nonetheless, and the discovery that he delivered with unmistakable excitement in one of the short pieces of reflection, interspersed with prayers, in the *Proslogion* was, as he realised, his very own.

"Understanding is the reward of faith" was Augustine's sentence; "faith seeking understanding" was Anselm's first title for the *Proslogion*. The meditation begins with a very Augustinian reflection on fallen humanity that is, acutely, Anselm's own lostness from God, the image of God in him "so darkened by the smoke of sin that it cannot do that for which it was made unless you [God] renew and refashion it".[11] (There are phrases here—"From our homeland into exile, from the vision of God into our own blindness.... Alas, I am indeed wretched, one of those wretched sons of Eve"[12]—which are so close to the words of the *Salve regina*, a prayer familiar to all Catholics and known to have been written at about this time, that it is tempting to guess that whoever wrote it knew the *Proslogion*. Perhaps Anselm wrote it.) But this first chapter is only a reminder of the place from which Anselm, from which each of us, starts. Having completed the *Monologion*, Anselm for some time had been searching for "one single argument, needing no other proof than itself, to prove that God really exists".[13] In the choir at Bec one night at Matins, he suddenly found it. This discovery is the subject of the second chapter, one paragraph not much more than three hundred words long, of the *Proslogion*, and the force and brilliance of its logic has dazzled and bemused philosophers ever since.

In eighteenth-century Germany, this paragraph was unluckily given the intimidating label "Anselm's ontological argument". But, though difficult, perhaps impossible, to refute—the atheist philosopher Bertrand Russell was horrified to find that he could not refute it—the argument is not at all difficult to understand. It says that because God is, by definition, that than which nothing greater can be thought, he must exist, since if he does not exist, he ceases to be that than which nothing greater can be thought. It is important to grasp that this paragraph was not meant to convince atheists of the existence of God; there were no atheists in Anselm's world. Rather, the argument was for Anselm a simple gift of God, a momentary perception of the inevitability of the reality of God, in which Anselm already believed, offered to him with the complete hardness of a cut diamond. He wrote it down because it delighted him and because "it seemed to me that this thing which had given me such joy to discover would, if it were written down, give pleasure to any who might read it."[14] We also should take it in the spirit in which Anselm received it. "I *see*", we might say, as Anselm, like Plato, said, on this and other occasions, some recorded for us in the chiselled words of his prayers. Later in the *Proslogion*, praying, as usual, as he thinks and writes, Anselm reflects on the light that is God:

Nothing can pierce through it to see you. I cannot look directly into it, it is too great for me. But whatever I see, I see because of it, like a weak eye that sees what it does by the light of the sun, though it cannot look at the sun itself. My understanding cannot take it in, it is too bright, I cannot receive it; the eye of my soul cannot bear to turn towards it for too long.[15]

We are outside Plato's cave in the light of reality, with Augustine, who said: "Whatever you have understood is not God"[16] and "See how God is true, not by sharing in, but by generating, truth."[17]

* * *

In 1093, at the age of sixty and after more than thirty years in the monastery, Anselm had to leave Bec. Lanfranc, one of the most effective of all archbishops of Canterbury, had died in 1089. Four years later, William the Conqueror's feckless son William II was at last frightened by a serious illness into appointing Anselm as Lanfranc's successor. To Anselm this was a terrible blow. For all the distinction of his private talents as a man, a monk and a writer, indeed perhaps because of them, Anselm was both unhappy and incompetent as a public figure. He was a bad administrator, vague about money and bored and impatient at meetings, and a worse politician, gullible, tactless and unbending; so clear about his own obedience and duty that he could not understand how unclear most other people were about theirs; and so single-minded in his uprightness that the very idea of compromise, of the more-or-less-acceptable half measures every statesman has to settle for, was abhorrent to him. He was unlucky to find himself the senior prelate of a whole country (he fought inflexibly, monastically, impractically, to establish, on the authority of Bede's account of the distant past, Canterbury's primacy over all of England) at a moment when Rome was issuing reform decrees that were more like aspirations toward ecclesiastical perfection than expectations likely to be put into effect anywhere. He failed to understand the difference and managed badly both William II and his brother and successor Henry I. The sixteen years of his archbishopric were a burden from which he several times begged the Pope to be relieved, and he was, during these years, contented and able to write only when in exile abroad or during brief peaceful periods at home with the Canterbury monks.

In the monastery at Canterbury, Anselm did what he knew best how to do: he was an exemplary abbot. He looked after his monks, talked to them, listened to them and united the Anglo-Saxon members of the community with their Norman brethren by respecting, as Lanfranc had not, the preconquest pieties of the house. His new cathedral, planned on the model of the church at Cluny, was to include noble shrines for Saint Dunstan and Saint Alphege, monk-archbishops of the past. As a bishop, however, reluctant to be involved in the affairs of the world, but necessarily involved in them and dealing with them badly, he was miserable. Talking to his monks one day, he compared himself to a mother owl, "glad when she is in her hole with her chicks, ... attacked and torn to pieces when she is among crows and rooks and other birds.... When I am separated from you, and my ways lie among men who are in the world, then I am torn this way and that by the onrush of disputes of many kinds and I am harassed by secular business which I hate." [18] Anselm was the last bishop of a cathedral-monastery to function as a real abbot; after him, bishops, even if monks, managed diocesan and, if necessary, political affairs, while priors ruled their monastic communities for them.

In 1097, despairing of William II, Anselm left England and was away for three years. He visited Cluny, stayed in Lyons and Rome, at the Council of Bari defended the Latin (mostly Augustinian) case for the inclusion of the *Filioque* in the Creed (a lasting bone of contention with the Greek Church) and spent six happy months in an Italian village near Capua, out of the world he so much disliked, finishing his last major work. This was an essay in theological thought, *Cur Deus homo?* (Why did God become man?). It addresses what is perhaps the deepest paradox of Christianity: How can it be that the humiliation of God in Christ's Passion and death does not diminish the glory of God but rather completes it in Christ's Atonement for the sinfulness of the human race? The topic was at issue among the new enquirers of the cathedral schools, stuck with the unsatisfactory answer given for centuries, that Satan was owed a ransom for man that only Christ could pay. The central question, of how the glory of God could not be lessened by the darkness of the Cross, was also being asked by learned Jews, the only serious opponents of Christianity in Anselm's world and at this period, before the horrors unleashed by the Crusades, being treated with measured respect by many in the Church. Anselm's answer is that the harmony and order of creation, its beauty—a word used here forcefully by Anselm for the first time, but often— spoiled by man's disobedience, had to be restored by an offering of obedience that neither sinful man nor God in his glory could make. Therefore it was necessary for God to become man and to offer the sacrifice of the Cross for the redemption of creation. This argument gave a decisive direction to thought about the Atonement. Like the *Proslogion*, though at much greater length, it is the working out, the rational demonstration, of what might be called the logic of a mystery in which Anselm, like all orthodox Christians, already believed. Augustine had, in a memorable image, touched the core of the paradox:

> By taking flesh, Christ took to himself, as it were, your ugliness to make himself like you and united to you, and to spur you to love inner beauty. Where do we find it said that Jesus was beautiful? "You are the fairest of the sons of men; grace is poured upon you for ever." Where do we find it said that he was ugly? Ask Isaiah: "And we looked at him, and he had no form, no beauty." They are like two flutes with different sounds, but the one spirit blows in both, the one fills both, and together they produce no discord.[19]

In a short meditation, *On Human Redemption*, written at the same time as *Cur Deus homo?* Anselm turns the argument of the longer work into a compressed few pages of intellectual perception combined with petition that could have been written only by him. The meditation ends with a prayer that his faithful search for knowledge (*fides quaerens intellectum*) may be answered, as it has been: "You who made me seek, make me receive; you who gave the seeking, give the finding; you who taught the knocking, open to my knock."[20] In its total dependence on the grace of God, this is very Augustinian. As Anselm wrote elsewhere: "Non video cur, nisi mihi ostendas"[21] (I do not see why, unless you show me), which would make an appropriate epigraph to *Cur Deus homo?*

Of Anselm, as of Augustine, it is pointless to ask whether he was a philosopher or a theologian. Like Augustine, he was a thinker and a writer, freed by his faith in the reality of God into love for revealed truth, which was rewarded by increasing security in that truth. Balthasar sees Anselm as writing and thinking toward God at a particularly favourable time (*kairos*), as the heir of Plato without the distractions of the alien world with which Augustine had to contend:

> The *monachos* [monk] (*i.e.*, a solitary and unified man, enfolding everything in himself and turned towards the One) brings the ancient *theoria* [contemplation; seeing] to perfection; he is therefore the philosopher in the Christian realm. The question whether Anselm is a philosopher or a theologian is therefore quite superfluous and fundamentally misconceived: the anti-pagan polemic of the Fathers is no longer relevant nor is the separation of disciplines which began in the period of high scholasticism yet acute: Anselm stands in the *kairos*, for the Bibilical

revelation can be understood simply as the transcendent consummation of ancient philosophy, which never was philosophy in the modern sense but was rather in its fundamental concerns theology: speech about God, about the eternal, about the being of the one who is.[22]

Anselm's time was indeed, after centuries of Benedictine practice, the time of the monk, and of all Latin monks Anselm stands by himself as an example of disciplined intelligence, understanding, *intellectus*, received from God and wholly dedicated to him. That both Anselm and his time had limitations unshared by Augustine, Anselm himself could have had no idea.

Eadmer, the Anglo-Saxon Canterbury monk who, against Anselm's express command, wrote his abbot's *Life*, reports a number of Anselm's discourses to his monks. These are very revealing. On one occasion Anselm, at supper, was talking to a visitor, a monk worried that the work he had been given took him out into the world and required him to be tough, political and grasping on his monastery's behalf. Anselm's reply divides people into three classes: those who live entirely in and for the world; those who pay occasional attention to God (each will receive what is due according to how he has lived); and monks, who may be given uncongenial work to do but can keep intact their obedience to their superior and to God. (With many years' experience as an abbot, Anselm adds a warning about permission given for worldly pursuits: "Permission is something which deceives many. Obedience and disobedience are contraries; permission lies between these extremes.")[23] We have already seen how badly Anselm managed the "secular business which I hate" that he was given to do as a bishop: he thought all worldly affairs unimportant unless they affected the honour of the Church, for which he contended without common sense and therefore without success. His many friends were monks or nuns, or potential monks or nuns. He believed, simply, that outside monastic life, real dedication to the love, the will, of God was impossible. In his sad farewell to the Canterbury monks as he set off for exile in 1097, he again contrasted the total submission of monks to God with the fitful piety of those in the world, "God's mercenary soldiers",[24] who turn away from God as soon as things go badly for them.

Anselm's inclination, in other words, was to regard a well-ordered monastery as a realised ideal. For him a miracle of God's grace had made him a monk; for Augustine a miracle of God's grace had made him a Christian. This difference narrowed decisively Anselm's view of human affairs. For all his familiarity with the *City of God*, Anselm remained blind to its central perception, that every human institution, the Church herself and every monastery, is mixed, a *corpus permixtum*, as Augustine called the Church, because people are mixed, the reality of their souls visible only to God. Personally, Anselm knew that the city of God may be reached only in eternity: this, for any Christian steeped in Augustine, is an article of faith. The *Proslogion* ends with an Augustinian prayer that includes this passage:

> My God, I pray that I may so know you and love you that I may rejoice in you. And if I may not do so fully in this life, let me go steadily on to the day when I come to that fullness. Let the knowledge of you increase in me here, and there let it come to its fullness. Let your love grow in me here, and there let it be fulfilled, so that here my joy may be in a great hope, and there in full reality.[25]

But meanwhile, only in monastic vows could a person live wholly for God. Anselm would never have understood Augustine's insistence that monks should always be willing to serve as priests and bishops because they are called, like every Christian, out of the pull of the *civitas terrena*, but not out of the Church. A hundred years after Anselm, the career of Saint Hugh of Lincoln, Carthusian monk and exemplary bishop of a huge diocese with a nonmonastic cathedral, showed exactly what Augustine meant.

* * *

When Anselm died in 1109, the Rule of Saint Benedict was about to deliver an astonishing renewal of Latin monastic life that no one at the time could have predicted. In Anselm's lifetime a number of monks and groups of monks had left conventional Benedictine abbeys for a simpler life, closer to the spirit of the Rule, or, like Herluin at Bec, founded new communities in that spirit. Many of these disappeared from history without a trace. One of them, a small enterprise at Cîteaux in the woods of Burgundy, received as new monks, three years after Anselm's death, a glamorous, forceful, twenty-two-year-old local nobleman, Bernard of Fontaines, and thirty of his friends and relations. What followed was quite extraordinary. Cîteaux itself grew rapidly: only three years after his arrival, Bernard was sent north to Clairvaux with twelve monks to found what was already Cîteaux's third daughter house. Meanwhile, Stephen Harding, Cîteaux's abbot, drafted a short document, the *Carta Caritatis*, which ordered familial, motherhouse to daughterhouse, lines of authority and responsibility that made the Cistercians the first, and for many others the model, religious order in the history of the Church. When Bernard died in 1153, there were over five hundred Cistercian abbeys in Latin Christendom, more than sixty of them direct descendants of Clairvaux, some of these already communities several hundred strong. Bernard himself, while accepting no position other than that of abbot of Clairvaux, had become the most famous man of his time, a figure of commanding influence in the affairs of Church and state everywhere, sorting out a papal schism more or less single-handedly, helping in the foundation or stabilization of several religious orders quite different from the Cistercian, preaching the (disastrous) Second Crusade, successfully defending the Jews of the Rhineland from a horrible bout of persecution, fearlessly lecturing and often reconciling quarrelling kings, princes, bishops and abbots, but always having time to reply to the humblest letter and never not attracting recruits from every level of society to Cistercian monastic life.

Bernard's was a career of constant travelling, long absences from his monastery, and wholesale interference in the affairs of the world that would have appalled Anselm. But his life was also profoundly monastic. It was not to follow his own example that Bernard, directly and indirectly, inspired so many souls, but to follow the Rule of Saint Benedict in a life cleared of the accretions of centuries, detached, so far as was possible, from the feudal world of rents and legal wrangles that had so depressed Anselm, and opened to far more people than ever before. The Cistercians founded their monasteries in wild places; did, at least at first, the building and farming themselves, returning to Benedict's injunction of daily manual labour for all; and accepted into their communities in their thousands the illiterate, from knights to peasants, whose life as lay brothers was simpler than that of the choir monks but no less wholeheartedly dedicated to God. It was a winningly attractive combination.

Bernard also wrote hundreds of letters, many sermons, a few short books and, during the last eighteen years of his exhausting life, his major work, the *Sermons on the Song of Songs*. Among his short books, *On Loving God* is a feat of condensed teaching on the approach of the soul to the truth of God revealed in Christ. Two consecutive sentences, the first a quotation from a psalm, illustrate the impact of Bernard's style: "How can I repay the Lord for his goodness to me? Through his first action he gave me myself, through his second action he gave me himself, and when he gave me himself he gave me back to myself." [26]

The *Sermons on the Song of Songs* are too densely written, too elaborately far from the text they are explaining (in eighty-six sermons he reached only the first verse of the second chapter of the Song of Songs) actually to have been preached in the form in which we have them. They are also too quiet. To be read and reflected on in the depths of the receptive heart, they are a literary achievement like Anselm's prayers, but very different in scale and also very different in the impersonal universality of their manner, which makes them surprisingly unrevealing of Bernard himself. Their subject is loving attention to God in prayer, what Simone Weil was to call *l'attente de Dieu*, waiting on God. The time scale is long: the soul must, through a whole life, learn the freedom of God, the alternation of his closeness and his distance, his just reproach for sin and the gift of his mercy, his speaking and his silence, his absence and his kiss. The initiative, the movement, is always God's; over years he moves the soul, moves it to love, moves it from the region of unlikeness (Augustine's phrase from Plato) toward the image of God in which it was made, which is also the image of each of us that God keeps in his love since the foundation of the world. The bride of Christ is the faithful soul within the Church as well as the Church herself. Through the finest passages of the Sermons, the spousal imagery of the Song of Songs, much developed by Bernard, sustains an incarnational and trinitarian presentation of the love of God: from prophecy to kenosis to passion, and on to death, resurrection and ascension, the story of God's love for the world is also the story of God's love for the soul. Both stories are about the completion of unity in love. Balthasar wrote:

> With Bernard ... , the Song of Songs becomes in a way the essence of the meaning of the world: here with the highest biblical authority human (and why not cosmic?) *erôs* is guaranteed and confirmed as the unmediated expression of all the mysteries of *caritas*, human passion as passionate feelings passes over without a break into the divine passion as the sufferings of Christ, enraptured love of beauty becomes the revelation of ultimate truth and wisdom.[27]

Because of the categorising and hence excluding modern use of the word "mystical" (is this or that person a "mystic"?) it is not helpful to describe Bernard's writing as "mystical". Bernard's writing about the love of God for the soul, the love of the soul for God, is just that. It is for anyone who can read. As Balthasar firmly said, the learning through love of the truth of God "is normal Christian spirituality, which for [Bernard] is wholly based on the principles of the First Epistle of John: God is love, and for this reason the possession of love is the presupposition for the knowledge of God. But only God is capable of giving love: it is the Holy Spirit's gift of grace."[28] Augustinian in his whole approach to God and to other people, Bernard, though so very much a monk, does not, as Anselm did, divide Christians into monks and the rest. He divides them, as Augustine did, into those who love God and those who love what is not God. In his long letter to Guy (Guigo I), the fifth prior of the Grande Chartreuse who with Bernard's help wrote the Carthusian constitutional documents that have ever since guided the order, Bernard says:

> There are those who praise the Lord because he is powerful, and these are slaves and fearful for themselves; there are those who praise him because he is good to them, and these are hirelings seeking their own good; and there are those who praise him because he is goodness itself, and these are sons. . . . The slave and the hireling also have a law, a law not from God, but which they make for themselves; the one by not loving God and the other by loving something more than God. They have, I say, a law, but a law of their own, not of God, yet a law which is, nevertheless, subject to the law of God. . . . It is the property of the eternal law of God that he who will not be ruled sweetly by him, shall be ruled as a punishment by himself; that he who, of his own will, throws off the sweet and light yoke of love shall unwillingly suffer the insupportable burden of his own self-will.[29]

In its ordered, rousing, rhetorical Latin, this whole letter is typical of Bernard's writing.

Bernard was only the most well known, his writing the most widely read, of a whole generation of monks, most of them his friends and not all of them Cistercians, who made the first half of the twelfth century a monastic golden period in the story of writing in the Christian tradition. Augustine, with the Bible itself, was the inspiration of all of them.

This was the period when Augustine's so-called Rule was adopted as a model for monastic life by many communities of priests, some in cities, some in the countryside; some enclosed, some engaged in pastoral work; and some far away in northeastern Europe, which was still mission territory. Augustine's "Rule" was put together from the simple principles of communal living in chastity and loving harmony that he had written down for his sister's convent, from another text about communal prayer, reading and silence, and from the example of his own apostolic household at Hippo, where all property was owned in common. All the different communities that lived by this Rule were called regular (as distinct from secular) canons. The Augustinian house that produced the best writing was the abbey of Saint-Victor in Paris, where Hugh, an exact contemporary of Bernard, and several of his younger brethren lived and wrote out of what Hugh described as a life of progress from reading (*lectio*) to thinking (*meditatio*) to prayer (*contemplatio*)—a life the very roots of which were deep in Augustine, Benedict and Cassiodorus.

Meanwhile, Bernard's correspondent the Carthusian prior Guy was presiding over the most austere of all the new kinds of monastic life that developed at this time in aversion to the involvement with the feudal *civitas terrena* of the long-established monasteries. Although the rhythm of their days was Benedictine in outline, Carthusian monks lived in silence and solitude, each in his own cell, meeting in the community's church only for the night office and Mass. Guy wrote a set of short, aphoristic *Meditations*, acutely observant and intelligent, the fruit of dedication to prayer and thought (not distinguished from each other in any of these writers). Guy's mind, like Bernard's, was steeped in Augustine:

> You should set truth at the centre of things, as something beautiful. Do not judge someone who abhors it, but have compassion on him. As far as you are concerned, though, if you desire to attain truth, why do you recoil from it when you are reproached for your vices?[30]

> People try to create true pleasure or happiness for themselves as if either there were no such thing, or it were possible to create it—whereas it alone really exists but cannot by any means be created. To create happiness and God for yourself is the same thing as to believe that happiness and God do not exist at all.[31]

> Either there is God, or there is nothing that can be known, considered, and said to be good.[32]

Naturally, most in sympathy with Bernard were his fellow Cistercian writers, particularly William of Saint-Thierry, older than Bernard and a more scholarly figure, acquainted with some of the writings of the Greek Fathers of the Church. William was educated in the cathedral school at Laon and then became a monk and soon the abbot of the important Benedictine monastery of Saint-Thierry in northern France. He admired and loved Bernard, who would not allow him to abandon his responsibilities to join the community at Clairvaux, but eventually, in 1135, he resigned his office nonetheless and spent the last years of his life in a remote Cistercian abbey in the Ardennes. His writings on love as the knowledge of God, particularly his early *On the Nature and Dignity of Love* and his later *Meditations*, are full of echoes of Augustine and so close to Bernard's that, although they are rather harder to read, they were thought for centuries to be Bernard's own.

Of all the writers of this monastic harvesttime, the most attractive, though neither the most learned nor the widest in scope, was an Englishman, a Yorkshire monk of old Anglo-Saxon stock, who began to write seriously because Bernard told him to. Aelred of Rievaulx was born in Hexham in 1110, the year after Anselm's death. Aelred's ancestors were among the group of priests who for generations had looked after the body of Saint Cuthbert on its travels through the north. Aelred's great-grandfather had guarded the saint in his new, and, as it turned out, final, resting place at Durham at the end of the tenth century and had raided the ruins of Jarrow for the bones of Bede to keep them safe with Cuthbert's relics. The tombs of both Cuthbert and Bede are still in the great church at Durham, which the Normans finished during Aelred's lifetime, having installed there a Benedictine cathedral-monastery and banished to Hexham the Anglo-Saxon married priests devoted to Cuthbert, one of whom was Aelred's father. After a childhood in the shadow of what was left of Wilfrid's stone church, Aelred at fourteen was taken into the pious and courtly household of the King of Scotland. Ten years later, discovering by chance the simple life and evident fervour of the monks who had only a couple of years before arrived in a wild Yorkshire dale from Clairvaux, he turned his back on a promising career and joined the monastery at Rievaulx. Echoing Augustine, but naturally, like Anselm, referring to his conversion as not to Christianity but to monastic life, Aelred wrote later that God "struck off the unbreakable shackles of bad habit. He rescued me from the world and welcomed me with kindness."[33] For the last twenty years of his life, 1147–1167, he was Rievaulx's third abbot, presiding over a community of several hundred monks and lay brothers. His biographer, Walter Daniel, a younger monk of Rievaulx, saw him as the fulfilment of Benedict's precise hopes for the abbot given in the Rule:

> He turned the house of Rievaulx into a stronghold for the sustaining
> of the weak, the nourishment of the strong and whole; it was the home
> of piety and peace, the abode of perfect love of God and neighbour....
> On feast days you might see the church crowded with the brethren like
> bees in a hive, clustered together and united as an angelic body.[34]

As a young monk Aelred was sent by his abbot on a mission to Rome. He called at Clairvaux on the way, and his meeting with Bernard led to Bernard's command that he should write a book on Cistercian life. Bernard at the time

needed someone to defend the apparent harshness of Cistercian life against resentful attack from old Benedictine monasteries. By this time an abbot of long experience, Bernard no doubt also saw in the earnest, fragile young man in front of
him someone who not only could, but needed to, write a book on the monastic
life as the school of love. The book was called *The Mirror of Charity*; with its
shorter and better-organised companion piece, the Ciceronian dialogue *Spiritual
Friendship*, written much later in Aelred's life, it made a modest but genuinely
new contribution to the tradition of Latin Christian writing.

Aelred was no scholar but had been well educated before he became a monk.
His reading, absorbed with intelligence and warm openness to the truth of God,
was the ordinary fare of any young monk of the time: the Bible, Benedict's
Rule, Bede (Aelred's debt to his Northumbrian childhood was paid in a number
of short history books he wrote in the manner of Bede), Augustine, Gregory
and Bernard himself. As a young man, driven more than most by the need to
love and be loved, he had been much impressed by Cicero's *On Friendship*, as
Augustine, the driven young intellectual, had been by Cicero's *Hortensius*. When
Aelred came to write of love, as a monk who had experienced the full rigour of
a Cistercian formation and later as an abbot of unusual dedication, compassion
and perception, he was able, with the help of what he had read, to recognise the
best that he had been given in his own ordinarily confused and struggling life as
a gift that had brought him always closer to God:

> A friend praying to Christ on behalf of his friend, and for his friend's
> sake desiring to be heard by Christ, directs his attention with love
> and longing to Christ; then it sometimes happens that quickly and
> imperceptibly the one love passes over into the other, and coming, as
> it were, into close contact with the sweetness of Christ himself, the
> friend begins to taste his sweetness and to experience his charm. Thus
> ascending from that holy love with which he embraces a friend to
> that with which he embraces Christ, he will joyfully partake in abun-
> dance of the spiritual fruit of friendship, awaiting the fullness of all
> things in the life to come ... [where] friendship, to which here we
> admit but few, will be outpoured upon all and by all outpoured upon
> God, and God shall be all in all.[35]

Aelred learned a good deal from Cicero, who was old and sad when he wrote
On Friendship but for whom friendship had been the sustaining consolation of
his disappointed life. Aelred learned more from Augustine, particularly from the

passage in the *Confessions* on the death of Augustine's Thagaste friend,[36] and from the discussion of the proper place of human love in relation to the love of God in *On Christian Teaching*. Here Augustine wrote, on the Gospel injunction to love God "with all your heart, all your soul and all your mind":[37]

> This leaves no part of our life free from this obligation, no part free as it were to back out and enjoy some other thing; any other object of love that enters the mind should be swept towards the same destination as that to which the whole flood of our love is directed. So ... loving [his friend] as he would himself, a person relates his love of himself and his friend entirely to the love of God, which allows not the slightest trickle to flow away from it and thereby diminish it.[38]

To Cicero Aelred added this Christian context and direction, making, particularly in *Spiritual Friendship*, of his own experience of virtuous friendship in shared growth toward the knowledge and love of God an attractive, honest account of the hazards and rewards of friendship. "Here we are," the dialogue begins, "you and I, and I hope a third, Christ, is between us."[39] Friendship, for Aelred, can by definition neither contain bad motives nor lead to bad consequences. If it does either, it is not friendship but self-seeking. The bond between friends is developed in stages—selection, probation, admission and perseverance— analogous to those of the monastic life. It is transparent always to the love of God and so becomes a sign, representative but partial (like all signs in Augustine's understanding of them) of the love that will be complete only in heaven. The other speakers in the dialogue are led by Aelred to a delicate and exact appreciation of what he means by friendship, and it is as a result of the tactful realism of his writing that, by the end of the book, his reader shares their acknowledgement that such a bond between people is not often to be found.

All his monastic life Aelred loved Augustine, "your Augustine", as his monks described Augustine to their abbot. He was never parted from his copy of the *Confessions*, "for it was this which had been his guide when he was converted from the world."[40] Recalling times of joy or distress—for example, his grief at the death of a friend when he was a young monk—Aelred uses phrases from the *Confessions* as we might use phrases from Shakespeare. On his deathbed, Aelred had beside him a psalter, the *Confessions* and, like Bede, Saint John's Gospel. In one important respect, Aelred is closer to Augustine than is any other writer of the Benedictine centuries. Much less brilliant than Anselm, less rhetorical and sweeping than Bernard, less of a poet than either, though he may have written the simple hymn *Jesu dulcis memoria*, he is easier than they are to know and love for himself because of the straightforward autobiographical honesty of his writing. The Augustine of the *Confessions* gave him the freedom and confidence to write, ruefully, of himself as a person rescued from the region of unlikeness by God. As a result he is the first Englishman, and the last for centuries, whose inner life it is possible to understand with some of the sureness, though by no means the breadth and the depth, with which one can understand Augustine's. And though his life and his audience were monastic, his experience and his advice are, like Augustine's, merely human and for all time.

* * *

The flowering of monastic writing in Latin Christendom during the hundred years from Anselm's maturity to the death of Aelred could not have taken place without the nourishment of the literary education all these monks shared. Brought up on Scripture and scriptural commentary; on the Rule that governed their daily lives; on a few classical writers, particularly Virgil and Cicero; and on the huge resource of Augustine's major works (and therefore, though they did not know this, on Plato), they inherited and developed a Latin tradition that was about to suffer a serious fracture. By the end of the twelfth century, the translation of all of Aristotle's works into Latin, and the awed enthusiasm for them as the key to all knowledge, had made Augustinian monastic writing old-fashioned. Aristotle rediscovered was the main cause of the fracture, but earlier cracks were visible to those with eyes to see.

One harbinger of the future was a sharp, belligerent teacher named Roscelin in the cathedral schools. Using only the elementary logic of Aristotle explained long ago by Boethius, and longer ago regarded by the twenty-year-old Augustine as easy but unhelpful,[41] Roscelin in 1089 announced that the traditional doctrine of the Trinity was logically unsustainable and that Anselm agreed with him. Anselm was shocked. He certainly did not agree with him but on logical grounds alone could not refute him. For almost the first time the impenetrable mystery of Christian truth had been challenged by pure rational procedure. In the next generation the formidable, tragic career of Roscelin's much cleverer pupil Abelard deepened the challenge so that it became a real division, the implications of which appalled Bernard, William of Saint-Thierry and the Augustinian canons at the Abbey of Saint-Victor.

Abelard was not a consistent thinker. His views changed constantly. Some, on the Trinity and particularly on the Atonement—he was unconvinced by the idea of original sin and saw the Crucifixion as not much more than an example of obedience for us to follow—were clearly not orthodox. He had a sharp philosopher's appreciation of the instability of language: "An easy solution to disagreements will often be found if we are able to show that the same words are used with different meanings by different authors."[42] He came close to a twentieth-century sense of the instability of meaning, and closer to a twentieth-century dissolution of objective morality: "All acts are in themselves indifferent and only become good or evil according to the intention of their author."[43] Most important, his whole approach presaged a future in which thinking about the things of God would be cut free from receiving truth, receiving God, as a gift of grace. He taught his students that it is not possible for anything to be believed unless it is first understood, a radical reversal of Anselm's *fides quaerens intellectum*, faith seeking understanding. He was liable, in the enjoyment of his own intellectual power and of logical method as display, to regard thought as an unaided human achievement and was therefore liable, though he would not have agreed with the formulation, to regard truth as also an unaided human achievement.

Bernard, eleven years younger and not yet famous, as Abelard was, responded with angry disapproval to what he saw as the grave danger posed by Abelard, particularly to the faith of the young who flocked in hundreds to listen to the most enthralling teacher of his time. "The faith of the simple is being held up to scorn, the secrets of God are being reft open, the most sacred matters are being recklessly discussed."[44] "He is a man who does not know his limitations, making void the power of the Cross by the cleverness of his words. Nothing in heaven or on earth is hidden from him except himself."[45] There is a Nietzschean ring to Abelard's "I began to think myself the only philosopher in the world, with nothing to fear from anyone."[46] No wonder Bernard was horrified. Abelard was redefining philosophy. One generation later, Aristotle, whose confidence in the scope of human reason undermined the Augustinian consensus on the absolute dependence of all of us on God's grace and mercy, had become "the Philosopher" for the whole Latin world.

Bernard won the battle. Abelard, summoned to a public confrontation with Bernard, refused to speak, referred his case to Rome and had his most eccentric formulations condemned. Afterward, it has to be said, he wrote: "I do not wish to be a philosopher if it means conflicting with Paul, nor to be an Aristotle if it cuts me off from Christ."[47] And he ended his chequered life, which had included the bitter drama of his love affair with Heloise, quietly and obediently at Cluny under the protection of its abbot, Peter the Venerable, another old adversary of Bernard's but by now his friend. When Bernard visited Cluny, he and Abelard met, talked and parted in mutual forgiveness. But Abelard, or the spirit of Abelard, won the war. Abelard's use of logic prepared the ground for the wholesale adoption of Aristotelian methods of thought, Aristotelian confidence in the intellect, when, in the century after Abelard's death, the rest of Aristotle was translated. Abelard liked to juxtapose apparently contradictory quotations from Scripture and the Fathers. His dialectical method, analytical reason used in pursuit of reconciliation of, or choice between, contradictory views, became the means by which the whole of Christian doctrine was to be sorted out and stabilized in the great *Summae* of the thirteenth century. Augustine, chopped into little bits as matter for dialectical investigation, became known to many of the educated as the author of quotations in textbooks rather than as the always approachable writer of his own books. This was how Abelard, with the help of Aristotle, invented "theology"—he was the first to use the term in its modern sense—as an academic discipline, not, of course, against, but separate from the leading of a Christian life. And Paris, largely because of Abelard, became the foremost theological university of Christendom for the next two hundred years.

A university exists to train minds. Its teachers are professionals. In the Middle Ages university teachers were lawyers and medical doctors; after Abelard, they were theologians, training more lawyers, doctors and theologians. A monastery, in Benedict's phrase, is "a school for the service of the Lord",[48] that is, a school for the whole man, not only for his mind. Monks join their communities for the rest of their lives, to learn, not how to "do theology", but how to live in the love of God. Like all faithful, fallible Christians, they are essentially amateurs, lovers. When the sheer difficulty of new, Aristotelian rational method—and its great usefulness to all the professions, and in due course to science—made knowledge of the truths of God an academic discipline, the continuum of Christian believers, from the illiterate to those capable of reading and learning from Augustine or Anselm, was broken for good. Without competent Latin and some training in dialectical method, it has always been hard even to understand what Aquinas is saying. Further, the arguments of what Aquinas calls "natural reason", assuming it to be universal, cannot be followed by most people because of the degree of intelligence and application they demand. Before the end of the Middle Ages, the line Aquinas drew between natural reason and revealed truth became a ceiling above which philosophers were not prepared to go, abandoning matters of faith to parts of their minds or lives not engaged in philosophical work and to those unable or unwilling to learn philosophical method.

So what Balthasar called the *kairos*, the favourable time, in which Anselm and the monastic writers of the twelfth century lived, faded out in "the separation of disciplines". "The question whether Anselm is a philosopher or a theologian is ... quite superfluous and fundamentally misconceived." [49] The same is true of Augustine and also of Plato. They were writers in and toward the truth. They were, in the largest sense of the word, poets. The commandeering of intellectual life by professional academics, some of whom "did" theology as others "did" medicine or law (or, much later, physics or chemistry or economics) had effects that have lasted ever since. A chasm opened between the professional and the amateur, the philosophically trained thinker and the mere writer, which deprived each of something essential. John of Salisbury, a pupil of Abelard, a friend of Thomas Becket and an intelligent and sympathetic observer of the intellectual scene in the middle of the twelfth century, wrote:

> Formerly everything the ancients had put well found favour. Today, novelties alone give pleasure.... He who studies the arts and the written texts is thought a poor debater, for an ally of the past cannot be a logician.... Aristotle is extolled, but there is nothing but scorn for Cicero and for all that vanquished Greece gave the Romans. Literature is becoming disgusting; only logic pleases. [50]

A little earlier Bernard wrote of poetry, or literature, particularly the Bible, as the soul's means of access to the truth of God:

> Let us model ourselves on Scripture which expresses the wisdom hidden in mystery in our own words: when Scripture portrays God for us it suggests him in terms of our own feelings. The invisible and hidden realities of God which are of such great price are rendered accessible to human minds, vessels, as it were, of little worth, by means of comparisons taken from the realities we know through our senses. Let us also adopt the usage of this chaste language. [51]

In this Augustinian case for the power of the image and the sign in literary writing to open to us "the invisible realities of God", it is fascinating to see Bernard regarding the sensuous, image-rich language of the Bible, and of his own work, as chaste and, by implication, the displays of fashionable logic as wanton self-indulgence. But there is a note of the anti-intellectual here that is a bad omen for the future. After this time, with the major exception of the great academic friars of the thirteenth century, holiness and the intensive use of the intellect became more and more separated in people's minds. Saint Francis forbade his brethren schools and universities, an injunction soon broken. Monks were inclined to forget Cassiodorus and return to the simplicities of Benedict. The very word "scholastic" divides academic writing from "spiritual writing", writing on prayer and the contemplative life, which remained monastic in provenance and character and blossomed again in the fourteenth and sixteenth centuries. This was often, but narrowly, Augustinian: neither the Carthusian author of *The Cloud of Unknowing* nor the Carmelite nun Saint Teresa of Avila, with her passionate autobiography and her passionate exploration of prayer, could have written as they did without him. But the unity of the intellect and the soul in Augustine's whole endeavour had come apart, with distant consequences that included Luther's rebellious return from the theology he was trained in to what he took to be the heart of Augustine and Saint Paul. But it was above all in literature, in the writing not of professionals but of amateurs, that Augustine's broad vision of God in Christ as the meaning and redemption of the human mess, the mess of any individual life, the mess of the *civitas terrena* in any set of historical circumstances, was sustained and developed.

In the Benedictine centuries it was possible sometimes to forget that the city of God belongs to eternity. "I saw a Paradise", a visitor wrote to Abbot Hugh of Cluny, "watered by the four streams of the Gospels, overflowing with spiritual virtues.... What else can I call the monastery of Cluny but a field of the Lord, where such a great company of monks living in charity stands like a harvest of heavenly corn?"[52] Bec when Anselm was prior, Rievaulx when Aelred was abbot: Were they not the city of God? They were not. Ordinary human failings, complacency, greed, laziness and restlessness, always present in any human endeavour, implicated Cluny, Bec, Rievaulx, the whole of Bernard's beloved Cistercian order, even at their best, in the *civitas terrena* and showed again that Augustine was right to insist that until after we are dead none of us safely or wholly belongs to the city of God. But Saint Anselm, Saint Bernard and Saint Aelred, in their lives as well as in their writing, showed that some in this life come very close. Balthasar, mourning the fracture that meant that after Saint Thomas Aquinas and Saint Bonaventure, theologians were no longer among the saints, wrote:

> The saints are not given to us to admire for their heroic powers, but that we should be enlightened by them on the inner reality of Christ, both for our better understanding of the faith and for our living thereby in charity.... The life common to Christ and the Church is the context of a living and realized theology, in the sense of actual life poised between perdition and redemption, sinfulness and sanctity.

The existence of sin within the field of force of grace, the impact, here and now, between despairing obduracy and crucified love, these, and not a colorless and static world of philosophy, are the matter of theology.[53]

It was in a literary work, in the imagined journey of an actual soul "poised between perdition and redemption", that the Christian tradition delivered, within fifty years of the deaths of Aquinas and Bonaventure, a new masterpiece, not even written in the Latin that for fourteen centuries had been the West's language of thought and poetry.

1. R. W. Southern, *Saint Anselm: A Portrait in a Landscape* (Cambridge, 1990), p. 58.
2. Anselm, *The Prayers and Meditations of Saint Anselm*, trans. Benedicta Ward (London, 1973), p. 90.
3. Anselm, from Oratio 7, quoted in Southern, *Saint Anselm*, p. 75; my translation.
4. Quoted in Jean Leclercq, *The Love of Learning and the Desire for God* (New York, 1962), p. 126.
5. Anselm, from Oratio 11; my translation. See Anselm, *Prayers and Meditations*, p. 159.
6. *Regula Benedicti* 7.51; my translation.
7. Southern, *Saint Anselm*, p. 450.
8. Quoted in Hans Urs von Balthasar, *The Glory of the Lord: A Theological Aesthetics*, vol. 2, trans. Andrew Louth et al. (San Francisco and Edinburgh, 1984), p. 216.
9. Quoted in Southern, *Saint Anselm*, p. 118.
10. Quoted in R. W. Southern, *The Making of the Middle Ages* (London, 1953), p. 211.
11. Anselm, *Proslogion*, chap. 1, in *Prayers and Meditations*, p. 244.
12. Ibid., pp. 241–42.
13. Ibid., preface, p. 238.
14. Ibid.
15. Ibid., chap. 16, p. 257.
16. Augustine, *On the Trinity* 8.8.12, quoted (in Latin) in Henri de Lubac, *The Mystery of the Supernatural* (London, 1967), p. 297; my translation.
17. Augustine, *In Ioannem* 39.8, quoted (in Latin) in Henri de Lubac, *Mystery of the Supernatural*, p. 303; my translation.
18. Eadmer, *The Life of St Anselm*, ed. and trans. R. W. Southern (London, 1962), p. 70.
19. Augustine, *In I Ioh.* 9.9, quoted in Balthasar, *Glory of the Lord* 2:136; Ps 45:2; Is 53:2.
20. Anselm, *Prayers and Meditations*, p. 237.
21. Anselm, *De casu diaboli* 3, quoted in Balthasar, *Glory of the Lord* 2:220.
22. Balthasar, *Glory of the Lord* 2:213–14.
23. Eadmer, *Life of St Anselm*, p. 77.
24. Ibid., p. 95.
25. Anselm, *Proslogion*, chap. 26, in *Prayers and Meditations*, pp. 266–27.
26. Ps 116:2; Bernard of Clairvaux, *"The Twelve Steps of Humility and Pride"* and *"On Loving God"*, trans. H. C. Backhouse (London, 1985), p. 97.
27. Hans Urs von Balthasar, *The Glory of the Lord: A Theological Aesthetics*, vol. 4, trans. Brian McNeil et al. (San Francisco and Edinburgh, 1989), p. 360.
28. Hans Urs von Balthasar, *The Glory of the Lord: A Theological Aesthetics*, vol. 1, trans. Erasmo Leiva-Merikakis (San Francisco and Edinburgh, 1982), p. 286.
29. Bernard of Clairvaux, letter 12, in *The Letters of St. Bernard of Clairvaux*, trans. B. Scott James (London, 1953), pp. 43–45.

30. *The Meditations of Guigo I*, trans. A. Gordon Mursell (Kalamazoo, Mich., 1995), no. 3.
31. Ibid., no. 267.
32. Ibid., no. 427.
33. Aelred of Rievaulx, *Treatises and Pastoral Prayer*, trans. several hands (Kalamazoo, Mich., 1971), p. 95.
34. Walter Daniel, *Life of Aelred of Rievaulx*, trans. F. M. Powicke (London, 1950), pp. 37–38.
35. Aelred of Rievaulx, *Spiritual Friendship*, trans. M. E. Laker (Kalamazoo, Mich., 1977), pp. 131–32.
36. Augustine, *Confessions* 4.4.7–9.14, trans. Henry Chadwick (Oxford, 1991).
37. Mt 22:37.
38. Augustine, *On Christian Teaching*, 1.22.21, trans. R. P. H. Green (Oxford, 1997).
39. Aelred, *Spiritual Friendship*, p. 51.
40. Daniel, *Life of Aelred*, p. 50.
41. Augustine, *Confessions* 4.16.28.
42. Quoted in Latin in R. R. Bolgar, *The Classical Heritage and Its Beneficiaries* (Cambridge, 1954), p. 159; my translation.
43. Quoted in Gordon Leff, *Medieval Thought* (London, 1958), p. 113.
44. Bernard of Clairvaux, letter 238, in *Letters*, p. 316.
45. Bernard of Clairvaux, letter 241, in *Letters*, p. 321.
46. Abelard, in "Historia calamitatum", in *The Letters of Abelard and Heloise*, trans. Betty Radice (London, 1974), p. 65.
47. Ibid., p. 270.
48. *Regula Benedicti*, prologue, 45.
49. Balthasar, *Glory of the Lord* 2:213–14.
50. Quoted in Leclercq, *Love of Learning*, p. 199.
51. Bernard of Clairvaux, *Sermons on the Song of Songs* 74; quoted in ibid.
52. Peter Damian, quoted in R. W. Southern: *Western Society and the Church in the Middle Ages* (London, 1970), p. 230.
53. Hans Urs von Balthasar, *The Word Made Flesh*, trans. A. V. Littledale and Alexander Dru, Explorations in Theology, vol. 1 (San Francisco, 1989), p. 204.

CHAPTER NINE

DANTE

Dante Alighieri, poet and lover of Beatrice and of God, was born in Florence in 1265. Less than a hundred years had gone by since the death of Aelred, far away in the north of Yorkshire. The monastic world to which Aelred belonged, its heart in the Burgundy of Cluny and Cîteaux, still existed: Benedictine, Cistercian, Carthusian and other monasteries were thickly scattered over the whole of Western Christendom. But the golden moment of monastic writing had passed. The writer as a companionable mediator of the mystery and light of God's love in Christ—and this description is as true of Benedict and Bede as it is of Anselm, Bernard and Aelred, all of them looking to Augustine as their example and guide—had been overtaken by the formidably trained theologians of the schools, the saints among them no less moved by the truth, but their writing of an altogether different kind.

Abelard's *Sic et Non* (Yes and No), which set out conflicting texts from the Bible and the Fathers on 158 issues, with no attempt at resolution of their differences, had begun a newly systematic enquiry into the topics of what soon became the university discipline of theology. In the later twelfth century and then in the thirteenth, with the help of translations into Latin of all of Aristotle's books and of learned Muslim commentaries on them, scholars laboured toward what was intended to be a complete, finished exposition of all that man could know of his place in God's world and of his moral obligations to his Creator and to his fellowman. By the middle of the twelfth century, Gratian, a Camaldolese monk, had collected thousands of juridical texts from the past of the Church and organised them into a coherent body of canon law, his *Decretals*. Also by the middle of the twelfth century, Peter Lombard, master of the schools and later bishop of Paris, had used the same method of collation and comparison to produce from the doctrinal writings of the Fathers, with his own commentary, his four *Books of Sentences*. These two works of systematic editing and arrangement, both using many quotations from Augustine as the leading authority among the Latin Fathers, were immeasurably useful to the Church for centuries thereafter. In the thirteenth century the new orders of friars, urban and itinerant in contrast to monks in their stable and mostly rural

communities, nursed in the universities, particularly Paris, the theological gifts of
the Franciscan Saint Bonaventure and the two Dominican philosopher-theologians
Saint Albert the Great and Saint Thomas Aquinas. Both Bonaventure and Albert
wrote important commentaries of their own on Peter Lombard's *Sentences*. None
of these books, put together from an increasingly vast array of sources, is literary,
that is, intended to be read straight through by one person at a time. The same can
be said of the immense works of Aquinas, who, with perhaps the most brilliant analytical mind in the whole teaching tradition of the Church, brought the organisation of theology to what is usually reckoned its highest, even perfect,
comprehensiveness in the *Summa theologica*.

There are three respects in which this moment of apparently achieved theological fulfilment has a bearing on Dante's *Divine Comedy*. The first is that the
intellectual effort of all these writers was paralleled and to some extent driven by
the long attempt, culminating in the career of Pope Innocent III, to establish the
papacy as the administrative and moral summit of a coherently organised Latin
Church, in which the emperor, kings and all other figures of authority in the
civitas terrena should, as lay Christians, be his obedient subjects.

The second is that, both intellectually and administratively, the movement
toward completion and fulfilment was nostalgically Roman. The universal order
of the empire presided over by Augustus Caesar in Rome, providentially granted
to the civilised world to be the earthly context for the birth of Christ, may have
been more a distant vision inspiring the efforts of its much-later inhabitants than
a properly known piece of history. But that it could be restored as, now, the
universal order presided over by the Pope in Rome seemed, after nine centuries
of recovery from the western empire's fall, at last a realisable project. For all the
Roman aspirations of seventh-century Northumbria, of Charlemagne's imperial
efforts, of the flowering of Benedictine life in eleventh- and twelfth-century
France and England, it had always been in Italy and in its cities that the real
connexions with classical Rome, with its learning and laws, were least unravelled
by the passage of time. And it was in Italy that the thirteenth century's consciously Roman drive to completeness was most strongly felt. Gratian and Peter
Lombard, both Italians, provided the legal and theological instruments for the
consistent government and teaching of the Roman Church, just as once law-
making, law-enforcing emperors—and in classrooms, Cicero and Virgil—had
provided for the government and sustained the morale of the Roman Empire.
Innocent III, Italian patrician and expert lawyer, called himself "the vicar of
Christ" but saw himself, in his "plenitude of power"—spiritual though he insisted
it was—as the evident heir to the Caesars.

The third is that, like every collective human achievement, however noble and permanent in intention, the whole enterprise of ordered universality was temporary, fallible and subject to change and decay. No Pope ever again was able to behave as much like an emperor as Innocent III had managed to. Popes who tried to imitate him, in the century after his death, more and more neglected their spiritual duty for their temporal ambitions. They attempted to control the *civitas terrena* from the summit of the Church on the shaky basis of Constantine's "Donation", a ninth-century forgery not exposed till the fifteenth, of Western imperial power to the Bishop of Rome; the greater their efforts, the worse for the Church as a spiritual institution. The probity of the Church as a bureaucracy was polluted, both long before and long after Innocent III's new efficiency, by the huge wealth that kept it running. And Aquinas's perfected theology, while surviving, of course, as one man's intellectual legacy, was not only attacked and misunderstood at the time but soon became, in its turn, material for textbooks assembled by lesser minds and the basis for a kind of philosophical writing that left the dealings of the living God with living men altogether elsewhere, a development that would have horrified Aquinas himself. It was from the embattled Rome of the late nineteenth century, in confrontation with the increasingly unbelieving modern world, that the thirteenth-century Church, in her universality, her order and her thought, looked to be, as the Augustan *pax romana* had looked from the thirteenth century, a recoverable ideal that had once been a reality. Like the Augustan *pax romana*, it was neither recoverable nor had ever been a reality.

Dante grew up, a clever, well-educated boy from a prosperous family, in a city, Florence, and a country, Italy, well acquainted with Roman—and Catholic—ideals of coherence and integrity and equally well acquainted with the gap between those ideals and their realisation in everyday life. Florence was a republican city-state, not yet ruled by a single despotic family but seething with personal ambition and competitiveness. Italy was suffering increasingly, throughout Dante's lifetime, from rival claims to power ruthlessly advanced by or on behalf of Popes and mostly absent emperors, each side in this long conflict split, in turn, into rival groups. Florence was a Guelf (papalist as opposed to imperialist) city, but often at war with neighbouring cities—Dante as a young man fought for Florence against both Arezzo and Pisa—and also with itself. Dante became involved in political in-fighting in his thirties, when the feuding factions of the Florentine Guelf party were swapping power, punishment and death with each other in a spiral of violence and conspiracy. In 1301, at the age of thirty-six, Dante, a celebrated poet and a married man with four children, found himself exiled in his absence, and without his family, from the city he both fiercely loved and fiercely scorned. A year later the faction in power in Florence condemned him to death. He never saw Florence again, but wandered Italy, finding lodging and the support of patrons in various cities until reaching a haven in the old imperial city of Ravenna, where he spent the last five years of his life, finished *The Divine Comedy* and died in 1321. In 1315 he was offered an amnesty by Florence on condition that he admitted his "guilt". A man whose pride and consciousness of his own rectitude are evident from his writing, he refused. By the time he died, the last hope that a German empire might bring peace to Italy in some kind of orderly partnership with the papacy had evaporated with the death of the emperor Henry VII, whose efforts had been foiled by, among others, the Pope. And the papacy itself—Pope, cardinals and bureaucracy—under the menacing domination of the king of France, had in 1309 left Rome for Avignon, where it was to remain for seventy years. No wonder an intelligent Christian's anguish at the gap between ideals and their realisation recurs constantly as grief and rage throughout *The Divine Comedy*.

The poem is like no other written before or since. It is set in the year 1300, when Dante, on the edge of the exile that colours the whole poem, was thirty-five, midway through the biblical lifespan of a man: "Halfway along the path that is our life",[1] as the first line says. The poem tells, in the first person, the story of Dante's descent to the depths of hell, his climb up the mountain of Purgatory to the earthly paradise, the garden of Eden, at its summit, and his ascent through the spheres of the eternal paradise of God to the empyrean that is both the circumference and the centre of everything. The organisation of the poem is grand in scale and firm in execution: an introductory canto to the journey to hell, but also to the whole poem, is followed by three sets of thirty-three cantos, one set for each afterworld through which Dante travels. Each canto has a slightly varying number of three-line stanzas (tercets) consisting of simple, relaxed, eleven-syllable lines, held together by a rhyme scheme Dante invented and consistently sustained but never allowed to become monotonous, requiring rhyming end-words for every three alternate lines. Dante's Italian is wonderfully economical and flexible, much easier to understand than to translate. The architectural clarity and lightness of his poem's structure, and his tone of voice—which, whether it is fearful, desolate, angry, amused, thoughtful or delighted, is personal and simple throughout—give it an atmosphere, a quality of immediacy and surprise, that is entirely its own.

The decision to write the poem in Italian rather than Latin, for all Dante's own Roman nostalgia, was the decision of a Florentine, a layman and a lover. "My mother tongue", he wrote, "took part in my begetting and is a contributory cause of my being."[2] Polished Italian love poetry was already being written by others in Florence for an audience that included well-born women, literate in Italian but not usually in Latin. Before embarking on his great venture—he often uses the image of a little boat for his writing of it—Dante himself had written a number of short poems in Italian and prose works in both Italian and Latin. In his first book, *La Vita nuova*, written in Italian, apparently informal but actually put together with exact, patterned balance, he connected thirty-one sonnets and longer poems with a commentary that is partly autobiographical and partly literary. The shape of the book owes a good deal to Boethius's *Consolation of Philosophy*, though its subject is quite different. From it we learn of Dante's distant love for Beatrice, a Florentine girl who was beautiful and good. He first saw her when they were both nine years old, and he never knew her more than slightly; she died when she was twenty-four and he had been married to another woman for several years. *La Vita nuova* is a book of sometimes dreamy, sometimes agonised self-revelation that strikes the reader as might a personal commentary written by Shakespeare himself on a series of his own sonnets. It not only gives us some beautiful poems lit by the glow of this always-idealised love and by the joy, grief, nightmares and contrition that it put him through. It also records his resolve, before Beatrice's death, to turn from the pain of loving her to the happiness of writing for her, and his hope, now that she is dead, to learn enough to write, one day, a new kind of poem for her. The book ends:

> I hope to compose concerning her what has never been written in rhyme of any woman. And then may it please him who is the Lord of grace that my soul may go to see the glory of my lady, that is of the blessed Beatrice, who now in glory beholds the face of him *qui est per omnia saecula benedictus* [who is through all ages blessed].[3]

The hope and the prayer were realised in the completion of *The Divine Comedy* more than a quarter of a century later. For Beatrice in heaven was more than the inspiration of the great poem. She is one of its three chief characters, and Dante's sight of the glory of God reflected in the eyes of Beatrice is the culmination of the arduous journey that the poem was and that it records. He had for years held in his heart his sense of her as "a thing come from heaven to earth to show a miracle",[4] as the finest of the *Vita nuova* sonnets says, and the *Comedy* is the story of his following her back to heaven.

*   *   *

The journey begins in the "dark wood"[5] of Dante's lostness on the path of his life. But the story, as the reader soon learns, begins where it is to end, in heaven. Taking pity on Dante in his plight, which Dante describes in the twelfth line of the poem as his abandonment of truth, a lady of grace and compassion in heaven (unnamed but clearly the Mother of God) has requested Saint Lucy to send Beatrice on a mission to hell, where she has asked Virgil to be Dante's guide on his pilgrimage:

> "My friend, who is not the friend of destiny,
> On a deserted shore of hindrances
> Has lost in fear the path he longs to find."[6]

Virgil undertakes to lead the poet as far as he, a pagan, is allowed to go up the mountain of Purgatory. Then he will consign him to the care of Beatrice herself, who will take him into heaven, where she lives with the blessed. Virgil has appeared as a figure of quiet consolation in the nightmare that is the first canto; in the second canto, he explains how he comes to be there. For almost two thirds of the poem, as he promises at the outset, he will be Dante's companion, keeping his courage up, explaining much of what they see as they descend the increasingly terrifying circles of hell, and then as they climb from ledge to dizzying ledge up the steeps of Purgatory.

It is a mistake to read Dante's Virgil, as it is to read Dante's Beatrice, as a symbolic figure. He does not "represent" human reason any more than she "represents" human love. For Dante, Beatrice is Beatrice, the woman he loved, and Virgil is Virgil, poet of the grandeur and cruelty of imperial Rome, of the dutiful pilgrim Aeneas and of the cost of faithfulness, of a mysterious intimation of Purgatory. Virgil was also a poet of the earthly paradise, known as already lost in the *Eclogues* and *Georgics*. Dante's very last connection with Virgil, at the top of the mountain of Purgatory, is his catching sight of a smile exchanged between Virgil and Statius, a slightly later Latin epic poet they have met, when a blessed spirit tells them that the ancient poets who sang of the Golden Age were "dreaming in Parnassus" of this very place, the garden of Eden.[7] And Statius has earlier said that he owed his Christian conversion (which Dante without evidence invented) to Virgil, whose apparent prophecy of the birth of Christ in the fourth *Eclogue* made Virgil

> "As one who travels in the night
> Holding his light behind him, not for his
> Own good but to make others wise."[8]

Virgil, poet of "the tears of things",[9] is moved in Dante's poem by the tears of Beatrice to come to Dante's rescue. Exploring in hell the consequences of unrepented sin and exploring in Purgatory the painful process of healing suffered

by penitent sinners, Dante wants Virgil beside him for the clarity of his imagination—
his sympathetic perception, that is, of how things are—and also for the clarity of
his judgement. And Virgil, in book 6 of the *Aeneid*, had already taken Aeneas to
the world of the dead and brought him safely back. Dante chose Virgil as his guide
because Virgil was the best poet Dante knew, and he loved him. It is a personal
thing, as is the whole of *The Divine Comedy* itself. "At the centre of Dante's work",
wrote Balthasar, "stands his personality—in extreme contrast to Thomas Aquinas,
with whom personality completely and intentionally disappears." [10]

Dante's sadness that the pagan Virgil must remain forever unredeemed pervades his presentation of him throughout. Early in their journey they meet—on
hell's still-gentle edge, called Limbo, to which Virgil will in due course return—
other virtuous but not Christian souls, the poets and philophers of Greece and
Rome and a mixed collection of figures from myth, from poetry and from classical and more-recent history. They include Orpheus, legendary poet of faithful
love; Hector and Aeneas, epic heroes; Socrates, Plato and Aristotle; Cicero and
Julius Caesar; Saladin, the chivalrous Muslim prince of crusading history; the
Arab philosophers Avicenna and Averroes, who had helped the West to understand Aristotle; and many more. The astonishing confidence with which Dante
puts this company of souls together in the shadows of outer hell shows us, very
early in the poem, the exiled poet alone, using his own imagination and his own
judgement to understand and place all that he has ever read and everything he
knows and cares about. It is for the pre-Christian writers who by using their
reason came nearest to the truth of God, their desire for it necessarily unfulfilled
because of when they lived, that he feels most deeply. Later, at the foot of Purgatory, as the scale of the climb ahead begins to become clear, Virgil, who shared
the philosophers' desire for the truth, explains to Dante their sadness:

> "Foolish is he who hopes that our reason
> Is able to travel the infinite way
> Held by one substance in three persons.
>
> Stay content, human race, with how it is;
> Had it been possible for you to see all things,
> There was no need for Mary to give birth.
>
> You saw the fruitless longing of their souls,
> Longing that otherwise would have been calmed,
> But is for ever given to them as sorrow:

> I speak of Aristotle and of Plato
> And many others." And he bowed his head
> And said no more, remaining in his grief.[11]

The gulf described in Virgil's words here is the gulf on the brink of which Augustine hesitated for so long, that between the Word dimly apprehended by the Platonists, the Word through whom all things were made, and the Word made flesh through the Holy Spirit, the revelation of the Trinity.

In this same region of Limbo used to dwell the souls of the just of Israel, and Virgil tells Dante, still in only the fourth canto of the poem, of how, when he himself had newly arrived there, he saw "a mighty one, crowned with the marks of victory" arrive to take away the souls of Adam, Abel, Noah, Moses, David, Abraham, Isaac, Jacob and Rachel, and "many more, and made them blessed".[12] The desolation of those left in Limbo after Christ—who is not named by Virgil— had come and gone, never to return, colours the melancholy in which he moves beside Dante until he has to go back. In canto 12 Virgil tells Dante that the precipitous landslide, which they must climb down to the terrifying seventh circle of the violent, crashed at the coming of Christ into Limbo: this is the poem's only other reference to the descent of Christ into hell.

In Limbo no punishment is undergone; the sorrow of its inhabitants is that of closeness to goodness, to truth, to beauty, which is nevertheless an unbridgeable distance from God as he is revealed in Christ. After Limbo the poets enter hell itself and begin their long descent through the circles of those whose punishment is to receive, according to Augustine's sense of the judgement of God, what in life they have loved. Even in the least dreadful circle, that of the lustful (canto 5), this is true. Countless lovers, among them figures from both poetry and history (Achilles, Paris, Helen, Dido, Tristan and Cleopatra) are blown about in eternal restlessness by a pitch-dark gale. Two recent lovers, Paolo and Francesca, murdered for their adultery during Dante's lifetime, are together in their misery, but no less storm-tossed than the rest. Francesca's account of their love makes Dante faint with pity for her (and is seductive enough to have robbed many readers of their judgement at this point in the poem), but Virgil's sternness reminds Dante, who is not yet being made to reflect on his own life, that there are no exceptions in this realm of final judgement on unrepented sin.

As the downward journey continues, sins and their correlative punishments become more and more horrifying, and Dante's description of the perpetrators of sin, now the victims of their own lives, becomes more and more vividly grotesque. In the thickening population of hell, devils and figures from legend or the distant past are joined by increasing numbers of Dante's contemporaries as his insistence on the wickedness of those who wreck the possible order and harmony of the real world deepens and darkens. In canto 19, three Popes—one, Nicholas III, dead by 1300, when the poem is set, and the other two with their places in hell awaiting them—are castigated by Dante for their abuse of their office. Boniface VIII, the reigning Pope in 1300, was Dante's personal enemy, Boniface's interference in Florentine politics having forced Dante into exile. His successor but one, Clement V, who died in 1314, was responsible for the removal of the papacy to Avignon. Their sin is the bribery and corrupt use of wealth and power that has dragged the Church into a mire of avarice and idolatry:

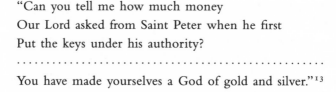

"Can you tell me how much money
Our Lord asked from Saint Peter when he first
Put the keys under his authority?
. . . .
You have made yourselves a God of gold and silver."[13]

Dante's rage at this particular gap between an ideal and its spoiled realization was nothing new. In 1145, writing to his own monk, just elected as Pope Eugenius III, Saint Bernard had said:

Who will grant me before I die to see the Church as she was in the days of old when the Apostles let down their nets to catch not gold and silver but the souls of men? How I hope that you will inherit the words as well as the office of him who said: "Silver and gold have I none." What words of thunder![14]

The last stages of the two poets' journey are horrifyingly macabre and bizarre. Giants and monsters, in a landscape changing with the unpredictable terror of nightmare, have among them in torture the souls of ever-more-appalling human villains. In the very depths of hell, together with Judas, Brutus and Cassius, those other traitors to their kind lords, Lucifer is frozen in everlasting ice. The reader's attention is held fast, particularly as the ordinary reactions—fear, tiredness, shock and mutual encouragement—of the two poets sustains a thread of realism through the nightmare. In these closing cantos of the *Inferno*, there is one passage of lyrical relief, when the flame that is the soul of Ulysses tells Dante of his last proud voyage, beyond the Pillars of Hercules across the unexplored Atlantic to the mountain where his ship was wrecked and he and all his sailors drowned.

Dante, who had not read Homer, knew Ulysses mainly from Virgil, where he is (only) the deceitful instigator of the plot that conquered Troy: hence his place so far down in hell. The story he tells here is nowhere in classical literature. Dante invented it, with perhaps some sense of identification with the foolhardy adventurer who leaves his city and his family because they could not

> "Conquer the burning fire in me
> To find myself experience of the world,
> And of the sins of men, and of their worth."[15]

That is a fair description of Dante's poem so far. Ulysses came to grief at the foot of the mountain that is Purgatory. Dante, no less ambitious, no less hungry for experience, will not, because he is able not only to commit and to understand sin, but also to repent. In the last seven lines of the *Inferno*, after the rigours of a descent that has lasted for thirty-three cantos, Dante and Virgil find a hidden path upward, climb it quickly and emerge from the darkness of hell "to see again the stars".[16] The word "stars" ends each of the three sections of *The Divine Comedy*.

*   *   *

There is, in the seventh line of the first canto of the *Purgatorio*, a note of resurrection: "But here let dead poetry rise again."[17] Dante's careful astronomy shows that we are now on Easter Sunday 1300, his descent into hell having taken place on Good Friday and Holy Saturday, although surprisingly little is made, anywhere in the poem, of these connexions with the supreme moment in God's dealings with the human race. The second stage in Dante's journey to God opens, not in Easter celebration, for much remains to be suffered and learned, but in an atmosphere of Virgilian peace, in which the renewed courage of Dante's "little boat"—his talent, his poem and his pilgrimage—is felt by the reader in implied contrast to the shipwrecked adventure of Ulysses's last voyage. The "deserted shore" at the mountain's foot has never yet seen anyone arrive who "afterward returned"[18] to the living world. Now it does.

A stern Roman figure, Cato the Just, appears to direct the two poets as he directs all souls recently arrived in Purgatory. Cato, Cicero's friend, who read Plato's account of the death of Socrates the night before his suicide, is here to help Christian souls as Virgil is here to guide Dante. A line in Virgil's description of the underworld pictured on Aeneas's new shield—"and in another place the dutiful, to whom Cato is giving laws" [19]—is probably the reason for his benign appearance at the foot of Purgatory immediately after the horrors of hell have been left behind. Following his instructions, Virgil girds the frightened Dante's waist with a reed to protect him on the journey to come, as he had protected his Aeneas with the golden bough on his entry to the realm of the dead. The starlit calm of this first canto does not last. In the second canto, Dante and Virgil and a crowd of other souls, rapt as they listen to a poem of Dante's own, which "used to quieten all my longing", [20] are startled out of this dream of mortal beauty and hurried on their way by Cato, whom we do not see again.

Poetry is no longer enough. After the desolation of hell, where live the souls of those whose unrepentant wills were set on their own ends in disobedient opposition to the will of God, Purgatory is the place where repentant souls struggle upward through the recognition of their sins, their sinfulness, toward the unity of their wills with the will of God. At the foot of the mountain are those who turned away from sin and toward God only at the very moment of death. Those who died unreconciled to the Church are at the very bottom; a little higher are those who through laziness or inattention left repentance until almost too late. They include the secular rulers too preoccupied with power and worldly security to remember God, emperors and kings of Dante's own lifetime from all over Western Christendom. All these souls must wait a certain time before they can even begin to climb the mountain, though the punishment they must suffer before they have learned anything may be shortened by God in response to the prayers of the living.

Dante asks Virgil to explain how it is that prayer can help those waiting for release into the process of purgation that the climb will be. His question is prompted by the Sybil's grim words to the restless spirit of Palinurus in Virgil's underworld: "Stop hoping that divine decisions may be altered by prayer." [21] Virgil's reply is one of the many moments in the poem when the reader sees how real a companion Virgil is to Dante: he now knows, as in life he did not, that "perhaps the fire of love may discharge in an instant" [22] the debts of a sinner. Beatrice, he adds, will explain this better than he can because she is "the light between truth and understanding", [23] a beautiful one-line description that reminds us that she herself is waiting, closer to God, for Dante to reach her. But the sinful world remains in Dante's mind. Later in this same canto, the pilgrims meet Sordello, a recently dead Provençal poet who was born, like Virgil, in Mantua. When the Mantuans greet each other warmly, Dante launches into a furious lament for Italy as she now is, abandoned by both emperor and Pope, perhaps abandoned by God, with Florence in the most deplorable condition of all its cities. But even before the climb has properly begun, the waiting of the negligent princes is softened by the singing of the *Salve regina*, with its reminder of "this our exile" that will end with the sight of Mary's Son, and then of the Compline hymn *Te lucis ante terminum*.

After the evening of longing and consolation suggested by these echoes from the world of regular prayer, Dante and Virgil, nine cantos into the *Purgatorio*, arrive in a fiery dawn at the gate to the mountain itself, where an angel inscribes with a sword seven letter Ps on Dante's forehead. These are for the seven deadly sins (*Peccata*) that he must acknowledge and shed on his way to the summit. The climb ahead is structured with the orderly articulation, sustaining a wide variety of incidents and characters, that holds the entire narrative of *The Divine Comedy* together. On ledges up the mountain are those being cleansed of the seven kinds of sin with which every honest human being knows he is one way or another sullied. All of them are the result of love deflected from its only proper object, which is God. As the mountain is climbed, the sins faced and suffered become decreasingly destructive of the love of God. Pride, then envy, then anger are sins of self-love, which produce harm to others; sloth is the failure to allow love of anything to direct the will; avarice, then greed, then, lastly, lust are sins of excessive love for things other than God. In canto 17, which is exactly in the centre of the *Purgatorio* and therefore exactly in the centre of the whole poem, Virgil lectures Dante, kindly and simply, on these categories of sinfulness, summing them up in the thoroughly Augustinian tercet:

> "So you may understand how it can be
> That love is the seed in you of every good,
> And of every act that deserves punishment."[24]

The lecture continues in the next canto with an exposition of the unity of the human person, body and soul, and an account of love, free will and grace that has the warmth of Augustine and at the same time the lucidity and balance of Aquinas. From the core of orthodox Christian doctrine on the relation of sinful man to God come these clear lines spoken by the pagan poet to his pupil. Virgil's teaching in these cantos anchors in faith and understanding the story of Dante's, as of anyone's, pilgrimage toward God.

As every ledge is climbed and the penance and sin of the souls being cleansed there are seen and understood, images appear of the countervailing virtue, one from the life of our Lady, one from classical history or myth. Then we are reminded of one familiar prayer or hymn of the Church; one P is removed from Dante's forehead by an angel; and he is blessed with the beatitude that best describes the virtue that has replaced the purged sin. Dante is no longer the observer that he was in hell. Having been taken to the depths of human depravity and the depths of divine judgement, he must now be part, with the souls he meets and passes among, of the experience of understanding, contrition and healing that is Purgatory. The pattern of the climb up the mountain can be briefly described; the variety and grandeur, compassion and peace, of its impact on Dante cannot.

In canto 27 Dante and Virgil together pass through the fire of the lustful—the last, and least, of the trials of Purgatory. They are directed by the angel of chastity singing (in Latin), "Blessed are the pure in heart", and they hear a voice out of mysterious light welcoming them, "Come, blessed of my Father." They sleep, and at dawn Virgil promises Dante that "today the sweet apple mortals, searching through so many boughs, long to find, will lay your hunger to rest."[25] He gives Dante, whose love can now be relied on because his will is sound, his own Augustinian blessing:

> "I brought you here with intuition and art:
> From now on take your own delight for guide.
> . . . .
> Free, righteous, healthy, has your will become:
> Fare forward in its soundness, and be safe."[26]

Neither Dante nor, perhaps, the reader, transfixed by the beauty and wonder of what follows in the next two cantos, grasps that this is Virgil's farewell.

In the garden of innocence restored we watch a magical procession pass by. Lights and figures move through the garden: they are the truth of Christian revelation, of the sacraments, the texts, the virtues and the saints of the Church. At the end of the procession, at last, her chariot drawn by a griffin that, in its double nature, is an allegorical figure of Christ, is Beatrice herself, veiled. Her appearance is greeted by a great choral shout of "Benedictus qui venis", which very oddly combines the familiar greeting to Christ on Palm Sunday with a greeting to Beatrice ("*you* who come"), and then, most touchingly, by the same voices singing a tribute (slightly misquoted) from the *Aeneid*: "O strew lilies with full hands!"[27] Profoundly shaken by the sight of his old love, Dante turns to Virgil for comfort. He has gone. Dante weeps. Beatrice calls him by his name, her first word and the only time Dante's name is used in the poem, and tells him not to weep yet, not yet because "at a different swordthrust it will be right to weep."[28] This stern admonition opens the scene that is the personal and emotional climax of Dante's pilgrimage.

He has travelled up the mountain through the sinfulness, and the consequences of sin, which are common to all who have repented enough for their
purgation at God's hands to be possible. Now he must face his own particular
failures, his unfaithfulness to Beatrice and to the truth, the waste of his talent,
his pursuit of false goods that he allowed to mislead his love, and his confusion
and despair from which he could be rescued only by the understanding of punishment and penance that his journey has brought him. In these two cantos (30
and 31), Beatrice, at first addressing, as in a court, her deliberate words of judgement to the attendant spirits, in effect confesses Dante. He is stricken with recognition of the justice of her words. A storm of shame and remorse breaks over
him—the physical effects on him are powerfully described—so that he sobs bitterly and finally faints. When he comes around, another blessed spirit dips his
head into the stream where all his sins are lost to memory, and angels sing the
Asperges me. So absolved, he is allowed at last to see Beatrice's eyes as she turns
from gazing at the wonderful griffin to look directly, with her face unveiled, at
Dante.

The sight of her eyes, ten years after her death (but he is writing this at a
distance of perhaps twenty-five years), for a while blinds him with joy. When he
recovers, he has to watch a horrifying distortion, representing the desecration of
the Church in human history, overcome the procession. But Beatrice, obscurely
prophesying even the Church's eventual cure, now allows him to remember all
his own goodness as he is immersed in a second sacred stream, and the *Purgatorio*
concludes quietly with this renewal of baptismal innocence in Dante, who is
"now pure and ready to rise to the stars." [29]

* * *

> The glory of the One who moves all things
> Penetrates the whole universe and shines
> In one part more and in another less.
> . . . .
> Our understanding, close to its desire,
> Travels so deep the memory cannot follow. [30]

Here, at the opening of the *Paradiso*, is an indication of the poetic difficulty
facing Dante, who now has to describe heaven, any experience of which, this
side of death, is momentary and wordless. Here also, however, in the line "in
one part more and in another less", is a hint of his solution to it. The nature of

the problem is obvious: any poet has, as his material for describing anything, only the transient fallen world in which we all live. Yet heaven is by definition perfect and changeless. It follows that any extended poetic treatment of heaven is likely to be dull, as Milton's is: Blake had an apparently unassailable point when he said: "The reason Milton wrote in fetters when he wrote of Angels & God, and at liberty when of Devils & Hell, is because he was a true Poet."[31] So how did Dante achieve something no other poet, certainly not Milton, ever attempted: the length, the constant interest and the very great beauty of his *Paradise*? The answer lies in movement, in light and, above all, in the population of heaven, the souls of those already among the blessed.

The reader follows Dante's own movement, with Beatrice as his guide, as he flies upward through the spheres of the Ptolemaic cosmos, and the reader also watches, with Dante, the ceremonious movement, in pattern and dance, of the souls who dwell there. Light of ever-increasing brilliance shines for Dante as he moves toward God, and this light is described in unpredictable patterns, in flames and sparks, in the light of eyes, and the reflected and then the unmediated light of glory. All through the spheres of heaven Dante uses to maximum effect, as he had in hell and then in Purgatory, the people he meets, now the communion of saints in ever more holy succession. As he and Beatrice travel upward and outward through the spheres of the moon, the planets, the fixed stars, the *primum mobile*, until at last they reach the empyrean, where everything turns inside out, so that God in his dazzling light is at the very centre of the cosmos, they meet in every sphere the souls who are, rightly and happily, where they are. "In his will is our peace",[32] perhaps the most famous line Dante wrote, is spoken by the soul of a lady in the lowly sphere of the moon. There is no discontent in heaven, where all the redeemed find the blessedness for which God created them. Augustine, at the end of the *City of God*, had written of heaven:

> What will be the steps of honour and glory here, appropriate to degrees of merit? Who is capable of imagining them, not to speak of describing them? But there will be such distinctions; of that there can be no doubt. And here also that blessed City will find in itself a great blessing, in that no inferior will feel envy of his superior.... No one will wish to be what it has not been granted him to be.[33]

Dante, accordingly, recommended by Beatrice to listen attentively to everything he is told, learns here, in the first or outermost sphere,

"that everywhere
In Heaven is Paradise, even if the grace
Of the Supreme Good He pours out differently."[34]

The spheres, and the increasing nearness to God of their inhabitants, give Dante his narrative and the reader rich variety of character and incident, even in heaven. Dante, against Augustine's expectation, turns out to be "capable of imagining them".

Beatrice's presence, her eyes, her smile, her encouraging teaching keep Dante's nerve steady as his learning of heaven and his love for her together increase. For this simultaneous growth in love and in knowledge he is more and more grateful, realising that they are not separable, that what Beatrice gives him comes through her from God because she is "beloved of love itself".[35] She tells him that he must not be surprised by the love he sees in her here in heaven, because in heaven perfect sight inspires the lover to move always closer to the good the soul sees, to God. The ascent to the good of Plato's *Symposium* here approaches ultimate fulfilment. "There shines", she says,

"In your understanding, the eternal light;
This sight alone makes love burn always more."[36]

And, she goes on, the will, so close to love, as in Augustine's terminology, is also always free to move, to be moved, toward God—or not. Here, and increasingly through the *Paradiso*, we realise the difference, for Dante, between Beatrice in heaven and Beatrice as she could ever have been as his love among the living. There comes, a few cantos later, a point at which Dante's love is so completely directed toward God that he, for a moment, forgets Beatrice.[37] Her delighted smile recalls his look to her.

He does not forget the world of conflict and hatred that he has temporarily left. In the sphere of Mercury, where dwell the souls of those whose pursuit of earthly fame distracted them from wholehearted love of God, Dante and Beatrice meet the emperor Justinian. Dante, in exile in Ravenna while he was writing the *Paradiso*, must have felt much for Justinian, whose mosaic portrait looks from the wall of his church of San Vitale and whose reuniting of the Roman Empire in the sixth century had lasted so short a time and resulted in such suffering. The disappointed emperor is given a whole canto to lament the failure of the ideals of ancient Rome, the collapse of his own and then of Charlemagne's efforts to build a new, a Catholic, empire, and the destructive strife of

Guelfs and Ghibellines in Dante's Italy. It will not be the last time that the disgraceful state of the contemporary world is mourned among the blessed. After listening to a simple explanation by Beatrice of the reasons for Christ's Incarnation and Crucifixion—a child's guide to Anselm's *Cur Deus homo?*—Dante meets, in the sphere of Venus, a number of reformed, re-formed, lovers. They include a twelfth-century troubadour-poet, Folquet of Marseilles, who became a Cistercian monk, abbot of Le Thoronet and bishop of Toulouse. He attacks the fourteenth-century Church for abandoning the Gospel and the great Fathers and instead turning to the study of decretals:

> "The Pope and Cardinals, intent on laws,
> No longer fly their thoughts to Nazareth,
> The place where Gabriel spread wide his wings."[38]

In the sphere of the sun, by no means at the height of paradise, Dante watches the philosophers and theologians moving in two dignified circles. Their cantos begin with a noble acknowledgement of the order of all things "seen and unseen"[39] created in the love between the Father and the Son and gradually understood down the ages by philosophers. Out of the shining dance of the learned, Aquinas speaks of his companions among the blessed. They include Boethius, Bede, Gratian, Peter Lombard and Albert the Great. Dante hears Aquinas, a Dominican friar, deliver a heartfelt tribute to Saint Francis, returned in the next canto by an exactly matching tribute to Saint Dominic from Bonaventure, a Franciscan friar. Unsurprisingly, by now, both angrily contrast the austere holiness of the founders with the greed and laziness of their present-day successors, Aquinas castigating his own Dominicans and Bonaventure his own Franciscans. With Bonaventure in the second circle of the wise are the more contemplative theologians, including Saint Anselm and Hugh of Saint-Victor.

After a vision of the Cross as vast rays of light, Dante, now in the sphere of Mars, meets, in the most personal encounter he has in paradise, his great-great-grandfather. Over three cantos, this Anchises of the twelfth century contrasts, in the same spirit as the great friars, the bloodthirsty rivalries of the present day with the virtuous, hard-working Florence—there is a note of the *Georgics* here—of his own time. He foretells the lonely exile in which Dante was living as he wrote and encourages his descendant to reveal without fear, on his return to the world of the living, the judgement on that world that he has learned on his journey. If he does,

"Then you will enfuture your own life
Way beyond their treacherous punishments."[40]

(He did; the made-up verb *infutura* has justified its oddness.) Lost in bittersweet thought at all this, Dante is recalled to where he is, and why, by Beatrice saying, with her usual directness:

"Think differently, think that I am
Close to the one who takes all injuries' weight",[41]

which is a gentle summary of how the blessed dead may help the living.

They are by now in the sphere of Jupiter, where the souls of just rulers move into the shape of the successive letters of the text (in Latin): "Love justice, you who judge the earth."[42] Gazing at them, Dante is driven to his own sarcastic attack on the greed and spiritual blackmail of the contemporary papacy. And Christian kings, too, may be so corrupt that the virtuous who have never heard of Christ may, in God's inscrutable justice, come closer to him than they do. As Dante puzzles over this mystery, which he is warned not to try to fathom, he sees, indeed, two pagans among the blessed, one, Ripheus, from the *Aeneid*, and one from history, the emperor Trajan, saved for heaven by the retrospective prayer of Gregory the Great. Higher than the just rulers, in the austere silence of the sphere of Saturn, are the (nonphilosophical) contemplatives. Here Dante talks to Saint Peter Damian, a monastic reformer of the eleventh century (and a son of Ravenna), and to Saint Benedict himself, though Benedict's place is not here but in the rose at the heart of paradise. These saints mourn, of course, the wealth and self-indulgence of those who profess to follow but actually have forsaken their example.

The pilgrimage through paradise reaches such a spectacular climax in the sphere of the fixed stars (canto 23), where Dante watches the blazing light of the triumph of Christ, whose power connected earth to heaven and cannot be resisted, that the reader wonders how ten more cantos can possibly add to the glory already made visible. The narrative of movement and flight does, indeed, pause here, for six whole cantos. Dante is cross-examined by the three apostles closest to Christ and present at the Transfiguration, Peter, James and John, on his knowledge, by now, of, respectively, faith, hope and love. The least philosophical and most attractive of these three catechism lessons is, not surprisingly, the third, in which the love of the good is simply explained as the love of God, and the rescue of Dante by the truth from false loves, the rescue of his will into the will

of God, is recorded. After Dante's satisfactory—and, to the reader, satisfying—
answers to the apostles, the sphere of Jupiter reddens in sinister eclipse, signifying
the desecrated condition of the Church, and the current Pope (Boniface VIII) is
furiously described by Saint Peter himself:

> "He who has usurped on earth my place,
> My place, my place which in the presence of
> The Son of God is now an emptied place,
>
> Has made out of my tomb a sewer of blood
> And stinking filth."[43]

Even this is not the last diatribe in the work on the disgrace (dis-grace) of Christendom in Dante's time. When he reaches, in canto 30, the miraculous rose where
the most blessed souls live in the sight of God, words for a time fail him. But they
do not fail Beatrice, whose last speech in the poem hopes, again, for a saviour emperor
for the Rome that, in both its meanings, has fallen into such dereliction and denounces
Boniface to the place in hell we know is waiting for him.

When Dante turns to Beatrice for help in understanding the wonder of the
rose, he finds beside him not Beatrice but Saint Bernard. This moment has none
of the sadness of Dante's loss of Virgil far below in the earthly paradise. He sees
Beatrice above him, in her place in the rose. At his thanks for her instruction,
her healing, her care of his soul, she smiles at him one more time and returns
her look to God.

Bernard, Dante's last guide, he chose, no doubt, as the exemplar both of the
pure monastic zeal and of the writing of the love of God that had lit the early
twelfth century, by 1300 a distant past. Bernard at once directs the pilgrim's gaze
to Mary, inspiration of his own spousal openness to God. Before Bernard's great
prayer to her, which puts the Incarnation at the summit of all the teaching of
the poem and asks for Mary's protection of Dante when he returns to the world,
Bernard shows him, in the rose of the most holy, the saints closest of all to God.
They include Adam, Eve and Moses, rescued from Limbo at the harrowing of
hell; some holy women of the Old Testament; Mary, of course; and John the
Baptist, Saint Peter and Saint John. From postapostolic times, there are mentioned by name only Saint Augustine, Saint Benedict and Saint Francis, greatest
of all lovers of God in Christ. Dante with difficulty finds words for the vision of
God that he has, after so much and so long, at last reached. Even here he remembers Virgil, in his contrast between the Sibyl's leaves of prophecy, scattered in

the wind—"write no poems"[44]—and the leaves of the universe bound with love in a single volume that he sees in the depths of the eternal light.[45] At the very end of his pilgrimage and of the poem that he has, after all, written, he sees the three circles of light of the Trinity, with the ungraspable image of Christ, "our image", within them. Failing to explain this ultimate mystery, he realises that this final incapacity of his imagination does not matter because, at last, his will and desire are moved by "the love that moves the sun and the other stars".[46]

*   *   *

Although most English-speaking readers will need a good translation with notes to identify the array of people who appear in the poem, to read *The Divine Comedy* from beginning to end is not difficult. It is an experience, aesthetic, intellectual and spiritual, like no other. Because of the poem's deeply personal quality, the experience of reading it has most in common with the experience of reading that other deeply personal record of a restless heart understood in the light of God's truth, Augustine's *Confessions*, "where", Dante himself said, "[Augustine] speaks of himself 'because his assessment of himself was a lesson for others and so of great benefit'." [47] However, the historical distance between us and the early fourteenth century has made it hard to read Dante's poem as, in Balthasar's phrase, "not a sum-total but an indivisible prime number".[48] There has been, for example, much distracting effort to "label" Dante in relation to large and vague sweeps of time or sets of ideas or both. If we pick "medieval" as the best label, we will be inclined to place Dante as the poet of the "high Middle Ages" whose work sums up a completed philosophy (Aquinas's) toward which the eleventh and twelfth centuries were finding their way. If, on the other hand, we pick "Renaissance" as the best label, we will be inclined to see Dante as a precursor of the individualism that marked, for the nineteenth century, the European mind finding its way out of the darkness of orthodox Christian belief. Both these perspectives drawn on Dante are teleological, though the second regards the *telos*, the achieved summit, of the first as not much more than the base from which real progress began.

But it is best to forget all labels. The lastingly valuable writing of the Christian tradition takes place between a writer and God, with more or less reference to and influence from the earlier books he happens to know—Dante knew Augustine and Aristotle but not Plato; Virgil, but neither Homer nor the Greek tragic poets— and with more or less weight contributed by the writer's own experience. To take *The Divine Comedy* as Thomist philosophy in verse is to miss not only the personal story and feeling, the fear, despair, pride, love and joy of the poem, but also its sustained criticism of the gap between noble theory and appalling practice that Dante saw in his world. To take the poem as the proto-Renaissance, or even proto-Romantic, self-revelation of a creative spirit making his own way through the constriction of medieval doctrine is to miss the height and depth of the orthodox Christian faith that sustains the whole enterprise. The poem is itself rich and strange in ways that can be appreciated only if all of it is read with an openness like his own to the truth that Dante, as we have seen, hoped he was humbly serving.

But the poem does raise three particular issues that deserve some comment. The first is Dante's often-repeated longing for the rescue of Italy from bloodthirsty chaos by a just and effective emperor. This longing rests on a combination of two different things. The first is nostalgia for Virgil's imperial Rome. The second is an Aristotelian (and Ciceronian and Thomist) confidence that once people, who all have to live in society, have understood how much happier virtue makes them than does vice, they will live virtuously, while those incapable of understanding can be made to live virtuously by good government. Dante chose Virgil's recently achieved *pax romana* over Augustine's disintegrating and in some respects well-lost empire. He chose Aquinas's calm reasonableness as to an intelligible and possible human order over Augustine's sharp awareness of the original sin that makes of every human society, even the Church, a *corpus permixtum*. For all his faith in the *civitas Dei* and the bitter clarity of his knowledge of the *civitas terrena*, Dante's choice of political ideals ignores the realism of the *City of God* and was doomed, of course, to disappointment.

The second issue, the role of Beatrice in the poem, has caused much misunderstanding, particularly among readers of Dante who are not Christians. At several important points in the narrative, Beatrice is so clearly in the image of Christ that she almost replaces him: she travels from heaven to hell to rescue Dante from desolation; when a hundred angels at the summit of Purgatory sing "*Benedictus qui venis*", it is she who appears; it is she who brings Dante to the contrition without which he cannot be absolved from his sins. But there is no danger, for a Christian reader, of confusion. Beatrice, at least in Dante's imagination (for we have no way of knowing whether, in life, she returned his love), is, in Saint Paul's phrase, an "ambassador for Christ". He explains that "it is as though God were appealing through us, and the appeal that we make in Christ's name is: Be reconciled to God. For our sake God made the sinless one into sin, so that in him we might become the goodness of God."[49] The Incarnation is for Dante the very heart of revealed truth, to which he refers again and again in the poem. Beatrice is only, but with wonderful emotional reality, the dead woman whose goodness and beauty have become the inspiration of a poet's journey back from the wasteland of misery to the truth of the love of God.

Balthasar says: "The love, which began on earth between two human beings, is not denied, is not bypassed in the journey to God; ... no, it is carried right up to the throne of God, however transformed and purified. This is utterly unprecedented in the history of Christian theology." [50] Whether Dante should be called a theologian is debatable, but in any case his carrying of his human love to the throne of God is, if unprecedented in a great poem, surely not even rare in the history of Christian people. The path in and through human love— where else do we learn what love is?—to the love of God, and the hope that the souls of those we have loved and lost to death will help us to live in truth and greet us when we reach the other side of death, are common in Christian experience. Aelred, as we have seen, knew both and wrote about them; it is more than a coincidence that Dante found, at Beatrice's death, consolation in Cicero's *De amicitia*. When the chastened Abelard, his intellectual arrogance and his tragic love affair long past, died in Cluny, Peter the Venerable wrote to Heloise, twenty years a faithful nun, "Him to whom after your union in the flesh you are joined by the better, and therefore stronger, bond of divine love, him under whose direction you have long served God; him, I say ... God cherishes in his bosom, and keeps him there to be restored to you through his grace." [51] And Abelard's beautiful Vespers hymn *O quanta qualia*, which celebrates the perfect fulfilment of all love in the eternal sabbath of heaven, is almost a summary of *The Divine Comedy*. Sublimation, however much exposed to reductive analysis by Freud and unvalued in our secular *civitas terrena*, has a full Christian meaning that was glimpsed by Plato, has been known by many and was given its most glorious expression in Dante's Beatrice.

The third and most difficult issue that needs some comment is Dante's treatment of hell. For many generations, at least in England, Dante was known as "the poet of hell". From Chaucer until the nineteenth century, when at last the whole *Divine Comedy* was translated into English, episodes only from the *Inferno* were translated, parodied, familiar to the literate. One reason for this neglect of the rest of the poem was, no doubt, Protestant resistance to the very idea of Purgatory and perhaps also to a heaven so thickly populated with Catholic saints. In the twentieth century, T. S. Eliot in *The Waste Land* finds himself, unsurprisingly, recalling the first circle of hell, where the undecided rush from idea to idea in vain, while Samuel Beckett, the most Dante-haunted of all modern writers, has, as we shall see, his characters wait, perhaps forever, in this same place, or at the foot of Purgatory with the lazy.

But for Balthasar, Dante's hell, about which Balthasar writes only at the end of his long chapter on Dante in *The Glory of the Lord*, poses a profound theological question:

> Dante's journey into Hell turns out to be a crucial test for that entire Christian theodicy derived from Antiquity. . . . This searing test of Christian existence, or more precisely, this searing test of Scholastic theology through Christian existence, is taken so seriously by Dante that he does not hesitate to transform its paradoxes into lived reality.[52]

What is shocking, of course, about Dante's hell is its finality. The famous inscription over its gate, "Abandon all hope, you who enter here",[53] strikes a chill into the reader that the rest of the journey to its frozen depths only confirms. Nothing here will ever change. Here there is no love for the loveless, no pity for the pitiless, no mercy for the eternally condemned—only the immutable punishment of divine *vendetta*, a word Dante uses often in the *Inferno*. Where, here, is the faintest glimmer of the light of Christ? Once, on Holy Saturday, he came to Limbo and released the blessed of the Old Testament. That is all. The problem is not only that Dante has imagined, and then peopled with terrifying specificity, the hell of the New Testament firmly accepted as existing by both Augustine and Aquinas. In a forceful chapter in the *City of God*,[54] Augustine, arguing against Origen's belief that all mankind will eventually be saved, is certain that many souls must suffer forever in hell. But in this chapter Augustine, himself quoting a good deal of Virgil, clearly distinguishes between the ancient underworld, the Sheol of the Old Testament, or Virgil's Hades, where all the dead dwelled, and the hell that is, in the New Testament, only for those who have set their will, without repentance, against the will of God, against the truth that is Christ. Dante, led, in all senses, by Virgil, does not make this distinction; had he done so, he could not have consigned Brutus and Cassius, for instance, dead before Christ was born, to hell. What is more, Dante ignores altogether—and this is the most powerful point made by Balthasar, in whose own theology Holy Saturday is central to the whole event of salvation—the redemptive scope of Christ's descent into hell, into, Balthasar insists here and elsewhere,[55] its very depths. Balthasar sees, no doubt rightly, Dante's absolute closing of hell to the mercy of Christ as connected to his almost Boethian neglect, throughout a poem full of acutely realised physical detail, of the reality of the Crucifixion: the Cross appears only in symbolic light, never as wood and nails, a man hanged, God in death. In Dante, Balthasar says, "There is no question, absolutely no question, of Hell in its innermost structure having been transformed by Good Friday and Holy Saturday." [56]

Augustine, responsible for the remorseless teaching on hell that pervaded Latin Christianity for centuries (and became even fiercer in Protestant doctrine because Purgatory was dispensed with), did in other texts recognize that Christ's descent into hell opens the possibility of salvation for souls even in its depths. "In view of plain evidence about Hell and its sufferings, no reason can be advanced for believing that the Saviour went there other than that he might thereby save from its sufferings. . . . That Christ was in Hell and conferred this favour upon persons subjected to these sufferings, I do not doubt." [57] Unless we are to go to the other, heretical, extreme and pronounce hell empty, a mystery must remain, as Balthasar fully acknowledges. The mystery is the inscrutable judgement of God, acknowledged by Dante himself elsewhere in his poem. As Augustine also wrote: "It is rightly believed that Christ came even to those places in which sinners are tortured, to release from their torments those whom he judged, in his justice hidden from us, should be released." [58] The real problem of Dante's hell is after all a simple one: by deciding who is in hell, and how far plunged in horrible torment they are, he has arrogated to himself knowledge of God's hidden justice that no one can possess. But if he had not, there would have been no narrative for his *Inferno*. Simone Weil observed that while imaginary evil is romantic and varied, real evil is gloomy and barren. Imaginary good, on the other hand, is monotonous, while real good is marvellous, intoxicating, always new. Dante's poem, with its real good and imaginary evil, magnificently proves the point.

Hell is eternal. Heaven is eternal. Purgatory, by contrast, is defined by time, for Purgatory is the realm, as life on this earth also is, of learning, of cleansing pain, of penitence and of forgiveness. Though Dante travels through hell with Virgil and through heaven with Beatrice, there is a sense in which he himself, throughout the poem, is always in Purgatory because he is always, being still alive, in time. Time is where we live. We may have occasional glimpses of heaven. We should count ourselves lucky if we have only occasional glimpses of hell, of the despair that underlies all grave sin. The deepest criticism of Dante's hell is that real experience of hell is solitary, the dark wood where the poem begins—and where, in Balthasar's words, paraphrasing Gregory the Great, the descent of Christ "is repeated each time that the Lord goes down into the depths of the despairing heart". [59]

By taking the uniquely bold imaginative leap of allowing his own love, Beatrice, to go down into his own despair, to find him Virgil and then herself to guide him all the way from the depths of lostness to the throne of God, Dante achieved the greatest of all single poems in the Christian tradition. And the pull of love toward the beauty of what is good and true, the thoroughly Augustinian pull of love from, to, for and in God, is the unbroken thread that runs through the whole *Divine Comedy*. Dante is indeed "the child of grace" [60] that Saint Bernard calls him at the height of paradise; he has both been chosen and chosen to belong to the city of God:

> For what has he which he has not received? Moreover, he is not only admonished to see you, who remain ever the same, but also healed to make it possible for him to hold on to you. So also the person who from a distance cannot yet see, nevertheless walks along the path by which he may come and see and hold fast to you. [61]

Or, as Augustine wrote elsewhere, "If you want to know the nature of a man's love, see where it leads." [62]

1. Dante, *Inferno* 1.1. All translations from *La divina commedia* are my own.
2. Dante, *Convivio* 1.13; quoted in Hans Urs von Balthasar, *The Glory of the Lord: A Theological Aesthetics*, vol. 3, trans. Andrew Louth et al. (San Francisco and Edinburgh, 1986), p. 15.
3. Dante, *La vita nuova*, trans. Barbara Reynolds (London, 1969), p. 99.
4. Dante, *La vita nuova*, sonnet in chap. 26, lines 7–8, my translation.
5. Dante, *Inferno* 1.2.
6. Ibid., 2.61–63.
7. Dante, *Purgatorio* 28.139–47.
8. Ibid., 22.67–68.
9. Virgil, *Aeneid* 1.462.
10. Balthasar, *Glory of the Lord* 3:24.
11. Dante, *Purgatorio* 3.34–45.
12. Dante, *Inferno* 4.52–61.
13. Ibid., 19.90–92, 112.
14. Bernard of Clairvaux, letter 205, in *The Letters of St. Bernard of Clairvaux*, trans. B. Scott James (London, 1963), p. 279.
15. Dante, *Inferno* 26.97–99.
16. Ibid., 34.139.
17. Dante, *Purgatorio* 1.7.
18. Ibid., 1.130–32.
19. Virgil, *Aeneid* 8.670.
20. Dante, *Purgatorio* 2.108.
21. Virgil, *Aeneid* 6.376.
22. Dante, *Purgatorio* 6.38.
23. Ibid., 6.45.
24. Ibid., 17.103–5.
25. Ibid., 27.115–18.
26. Ibid., 130–31, 140–41.
27. Ibid., 30.21; Virgil, *Aeneid* 6.883.
28. Dante, *Purgatorio* 30.57.

29. Ibid., 33.145.
30. Dante, *Paradiso* 1.1–3, 7–9.
31. William Blake, *The Marriage of Heaven and Hell*, note.
32. Dante, *Paradiso* 3.85.
33. Augustine, *City of God* 22.30, trans. Henry Bettenson (London, 1972).
34. Dante, *Paradiso* 3.88–90.
35. Ibid., 4.118.
36. Ibid., 5.7–9.
37. Ibid., 10.60.
38. Ibid., 9.136–38.
39. Ibid., 10.4.
40. Ibid., 17.98–99.
41. Ibid., 18.5–6.
42. Ibid., 92–93; Wis 1:1.
43. Dante, *Paradiso* 27.22–26.
44. Virgil, *Aeneid* 6.74–75.
45. Dante, *Paradiso* 33.65–66, 83–87.
46. Ibid., 33.145.
47. Quoted in Balthasar, *Glory of the Lord* 3:29.
48. Ibid., p. 13.
49. 2 Cor 5.20–21.
50. Balthasar, *Glory of the Lord* 3:31–32.
51. Peter the Venerable, Abbot of Cluny, letter, in *The Letters of Abelard and Heloise*, trans. B. Radice (London, 1974), pp. 283–84.
52. Balthasar, *Glory of the Lord* 3:85.
53. Dante, *Inferno* 3.9.
54. Augustine, *City of God*, chap. 21.
55. Cf. especially Hans Urs von Balthasar, *Mysterium Paschale*, trans. Aidan Nichols (Edinburgh, 1990), chap. 4.
56. Balthasar, *Glory of the Lord* 3:100.
57. Augustine, letter 164, to Evodius, quoted by Aquinas in his discussion of this issue, *Summa theologiae* 3a.52,8; my translation.
58. Augustine, *De Genesi ad litteram* 12.63, quoted (in Latin) in Balthasar, *Mysterium Paschale*, p. 162; my translation.
59. Balthasar, *Mysterium Paschale*, p. 176.
60. Dante, *Paradiso* 31.112.
61. Augustine, *Confessions*, 7.21.27, trans. Henry Chadwick (Oxford, 1991). Cf. 1 Cor 4:7.
62. Augustine, *Enarrationes in psalmos*, 122.1.

CHAPTER TEN

SHAKESPEARE I

Henry VI to Measure for Measure

It is usual to acknowledge Dante and Shakespeare as the two greatest writers of postclassical Europe: "Dante and Shakespeare divide the modern world between them; there is no third",[1] wrote T. S. Eliot. It is also usual to contrast them, in particular to contrast Dante, the self-revealer and the Christian, with Shakespeare, the unknowable poet concealed behind the opaque screen of all the characters in his plays, whose own beliefs are—mercifully, many contemporary commentators think—undiscoverable. The critical consensus nowadays, indeed, would probably be that Shakespeare has no place in this book. The very universality of his appeal is taken to demonstrate that the Christian tradition does not contain him but is, rather, that from which he triumphantly broke out. Shakespeare was Renaissance—or better, liberal—man leaving the constriction of Dante's medieval Christianity behind for the fresh air and freedom of beliefless modernity, where, in Allan Bloom's accurate summary of Nietzsche and his successors, "Man is a value-creating, not a good-discovering being."[2]

A recent and elaborate assumption of this kind underlies George Steiner's comparison of Dante and Shakespeare in *Grammars of Creation*. "The contrast", he says, "is compelling." He locates it above all in Dante's explicit Christian philosophy and in his self-consciousness as a poet, knowing and saying that he is creating in relation to God what must be true in relation to God's truth; neither is to be found in Shakespeare:

> Dante is a considerable figure in the history of western philosophic theology. . . . Was there ever a consciousness less seduced by theory and by abstraction than Shakespeare's? Was there ever a sensibility more receptive of the manifold disorders and instabilities of human existence, of the energies of unmastered being as they spill over the confines of doctrine or of reason? The abstention from any definable theology in Shakespeare, from any systemic [*sic*] philosophy, has often been observed.

It puts off a T. S. Eliot or a Wittgenstein. Every nerve in Dante comes alight when he grapples with a theological mystery.... These are impulses antithetical to Shakespeare's concrete universality, to his observant neutrality in the face of the extant.[3]

This is a late and sophisticated version of Samuel Johnson's view that Shakespeare was "above all writers, at least above all modern writers, the poet of nature; the poet that holds up to his readers a faithful mirrour of manners and of life", but

[h]e sacrifices virtue to convenience, and is so much more careful to please than to instruct, that he seems to write without any moral purpose.... He makes no just distribution of good or evil ... ; he carries his persons indifferently through right and wrong, and at the close dismisses them without further care, and leaves their examples to operate by chance.[4]

Had Johnson read Dante, whose "just distribution" of good and evil comes close to usurping God's, he would have seen between the two poets an even more compelling contrast than that drawn by Steiner.

Johnson writes out of an eighteenth-century piety that recognises in the plays "the real state of sublunary nature"[5] while regretting that Shakespeare does not more often reward the good and punish the wicked. William Hazlitt, another perceptive Shakespearean, only fifty years later rejoices, in the new libertarian atmosphere of 1817, at exactly what Johnson deplores: "In one sense, Shakespeare was no moralist at all; in another, he was the greatest of all moralists. He was a moralist in the same sense in which nature is one. He taught what he had learnt from her."[6] Both Johnson and Hazlitt would have consented to Steiner's summary phrase "observant neutrality". Among the major critics of Shakespeare, then and thereafter, the dissenting voice is Coleridge's. His observations on Shakespeare were mostly delivered in lectures, many of them attended by Hazlitt, of which only partial records survive. To some of what he said we shall return. He wrote, truthfully, in a note to himself in 1818:

In all the successive Courses, delivered by me, since my first attempt at the Royal Institution, it has been and it still remains my Object to prove that in all points from the most important to the most minute, the Judgement of Shakespear is commensurate with his Genius—nay, that his Genius reveals itself in his Judgement, as in its most exalted Form.[7]

Five years earlier he had said:

> The ... character belonging to Shakespeare as Shakespeare, was the
> *keeping at all times the high road of life* ... ; he never rendered that ami-
> able which religion and reason taught us to detest; he never clothed
> vice in the garb of virtue.[8]

Not "observant neutrality" but the constant judgement of "religion and reason".

Nevertheless, the consensus built. A major contemporary exponent of it is Harold Bloom, whose exhilarating, sometimes infuriating, commentary on all the plays, *Shakespeare: The Invention of the Human*, declares in its title what Bloom takes to be Shakespeare's radical originality in the creation of self-reflective personality, bringing us a "secular salvation",[9] a Nietzschean revaluing of our "inner selves" in his and our beliefless world. Shakespeare's "universalism", the book insists over and over again, has nothing to do with Christianity, nothing to do with religion, but everything to do with the creation of characters from supremely intelligent insight into human nature and supreme genius in the use of language.

It is the contention of these chapters that the consensus view rests on a non sequitur of profound significance. The consensus view is that Shakespeare is the greatest of all poets *because* he is bound, constrained, by no specific religious or ethical context or presupposition. He has been claimed, in other words, for precisely the "tradition-independent rational universality"[10] that Alastair MacIntyre describes as the goal of liberal thought in *Whose Justice? Which Rationality?* and shows, convincingly, to have been "an illusion". Thus untrammelled, the consensus holds, Shakespeare wrote of things as they are, and his "just representations of general nature"[11] (Johnson's phrase) will never lose their impact on human beings in times and places quite different from Shakespeare's own. These chapters will argue that, on the contrary, Shakespeare's incontrovertible hold on audiences and readers of here and everywhere, now and always, is not the result of his freedom *from* Christian belief but of his freedom *within* Christian belief, within the Augustinian tradition he inherited and to which he abundantly contributed. If, that is to say, our sense of Shakespeare's creative quality, his capacity to appeal to, to confirm, to refine our own sense of the truth of being, is secure, it is because it is secured in his sense of the truth of God and of the freedom and responsibility of the will, understood, if never explained, by a sensibility formed by the Christian, and specifically the Augustinian Catholic, tradition.

There are two levels here, to be distinguished for the sake of clarity. On the first level there is the formation of Shakespeare's mind and soul in the pre-Reformation Catholic Christianity that was more widespread in much of the England of his childhood and youth than were the doctrines of official Protestantism, held as belief by what was still only a minority. On the second level there is the rootedness in the truth of God that holds everything made by man that we perceive as true—and what Shakespeare gives us we perceive as overwhelmingly true—while we recognise also its human dependence, its human contingency. In Balthasar's words, not about Shakespeare, but containing a firm warning against what is now called "bardolatry":

> The creature, by God's liberality, acquires a share in God's truth, and God reveals his truth precisely by granting participation in this way. God thus equips the creature to be a relative center of truth, which is then able for its own part to know truth and to express something of itself.... A kind of plenitude ... can descend upon the creature, and, when it does, it gives the creature its greatest fascination. But it is so delicate, it requires such careful handling, that one has to have a completely ordered relation to God in order not to succumb to the temptation of divinizing the creature.[12]

To this second level, which is the level of our proper response to Shakespeare, I shall return. But let us begin with the first.

* * *

When Shakespeare was born in Stratford in 1564, Queen Elizabeth's Anglican settlement, not so called for several centuries, of the English church had been in place for five years. It was, most evidently, a compromise, and an accidental compromise at that, its founding documents produced at the point in Protestant reform that Thomas Cranmer had reached in 1553, at the end of the short reign of Edward VI. Its effects on people's lives were, however, clearer to everyone than the doctrine that justified them: the Mass itself, altars, crucifixes, images of the saints, vestments, candles, prayers for the dead—all restored to the churches and the people in the even shorter reign of the Catholic Queen Mary (1553–1558)—were again swept out, this time for good, though the fluid history of the Anglican church saw the patchy restoration of some of these Catholic trappings, but not of the Roman Mass, in some churches at some periods in subsequent centuries. No one in the early years of Elizabeth's reign could have known that her settlement of religion would last. At the time, after the radical switches in religious order under four monarchs in twenty years, the only thing that can have been certain was uncertainty. The queen was young, of child-bearing age; only after at least a decade did it become clear that she was resolved not to marry. Her heir, ten years younger, was the Catholic Mary Stuart, Queen of Scots, who by 1566 had married and produced a healthy son. A reversal in the country's religion, now organised by the government, that is to say, by the monarch through the legal instrument of Parliament, was possible at any time. Compliance with the new regulations was slow, enthusiastic in few places, resigned in many, mulish in others, and in some, far from London, less than even token. Many people were still alive, among them monks and nuns from the monasteries erased from the face of England by Elizabeth's father, as survivors who would carry their loyalty to the Catholic past unshaken to the grave. Some would follow them through the centuries of oppression to come.

Catholics were not persecuted in Shakespeare's childhood. In his young manhood, however, they had become "traitors". Those who were born early in the new reign had in due course to face a decision of which even the outlines were blurred until the 1580s. By then it had become clear that Englishmen must choose between obedience or disobedience to the religious requirements of the state and that there were degrees of both. Obedience could be wholehearted, informed, inspired perhaps by the Protestant conviction of those burned at the stake in the reign of Mary, often keen for the government to go further in reform; or it could be mere submission to the law of the land. Tudor citizens were, on the whole, docile by long habit and grateful to any firm government for keeping civil war at bay. Or it could be anywhere on the scale between these extremes. Similarly, disobedience could be silent, internal, a loyalty to the old faith kept in the heart, while outward submission, attendance at the nationally prescribed liturgy, was sustained, perhaps at a minimum level with the reception of communion avoided. Such was the disobedience of those eventually labelled "church Papists". At its other extreme, disobedience became, as the reign wore on, exceedingly dangerous. Catholic observance, particularly after Queen Elizabeth was excommunicated by the Pope in 1570, was identified with treason, partly because Mary Stuart, who, as the result of her own folly, had had to leave Scotland, her throne and her son and was imprisoned in England, became the focus of increasingly bizarre and foolhardy conspiracy against Elizabeth. Actual civil war, the dread of the Tudor century, realized in the next century under Charles I, threatened in 1569 when Elizabeth put down a Catholic rising in the north with the cruel firmness her father had meted out to the Pilgrimage of Grace in 1536. For the rest of Elizabeth's reign, and all through the seventeenth century, disguised priests and those who sheltered them were often betrayed to, then tortured and killed by, the government. The Elizabethan assumption that Catholicism and treason were always the same thing, because occasionally they were, pervaded English history for two hundred years and has never entirely disappeared from the mythological penumbra of English life.

This was the complicated and increasingly demanding religious atmosphere in which Shakespeare grew up. Stratford was a provincial town in the rural heart of traditional England, far from London and from the eastern trading ports in frequent touch with Protestant Europe. Members of Shakespeare's family were nuns at the nearby Wroxall Priory up to Henry VIII's dissolution of the house: the last subprioress, Joan Shakespeare, died in Stratford when Shakespeare was twelve. Shakespeare's parents were recusants, nonattenders at the established church, facing financial penalties that were steeply increased in 1581. In 1583, when there was a purge of Catholics in Stratford, Shakespeare's father hid in his attic a copy of Saint Charles Borromeo's "Testament of the Soul", a model Catholic will brought into England by Jesuits in 1580. Of the five schoolmasters at Stratford grammar school when Shakespeare was a boy, four were recusants; one of them later became a Jesuit; another was the brother of a martyred Catholic. These men had connexions with the recusant gentry families of Lancashire, the most Catholic region of England. It is probable that Shakespeare at sixteen, under the pseudonym Shakeshaft, was at Hoghton Tower in Lancashire with the Jesuit Saint Edmund Campion, who had set up a secret school for future priests. Campion was caught, tortured and executed in 1581, proclaiming to the end his loyalty to Elizabeth, which there is no reason to doubt. By 1582 Shakespeare was back in Stratford and, at only eighteen, married, by an old priest "unsound in religion" (i.e., a Catholic) to Anne Hathaway. He probably returned to Catholic Lancashire as a tutor—an early report says that "he had been in his younger years a schoolmaster in the country"[13]—during the "lost" period from 1585 to 1592, the year in which he surfaced in London as a playwright. If he did, he saw at first hand the resentment of the Catholic north, source of each revolt that shook the Tudors's hold on England. In February 1595 his distant relative Saint Robert Southwell, another Jesuit priest, was hanged, drawn and quartered in London after three years of imprisonment without trial and with repeated torture. His posthumously published poems were dedicated to "my worthy good cousin, Master W.S." A recent powerful case has been made[14] to establish that Shakespeare's magical poem "The Phoenix and the Turtle", always thought to be impenetrably mysterious, was a memorial, written in 1601, to a recusant couple, Roger and Ann Line; Roger died in exile in Flanders in 1594 or 1595, and Ann was executed for her faith at Tyburn on 27 February 1601. A note made by an Oxford cleric half a century after Shakespeare's death said, simply, "he died a papist".[15]

All this evidence for, at the very least, profound Catholic influence on Shakespeare's youth is patchy, as it was bound to be, given the atmosphere of terror in which Catholics lived after 1580. But it is powerful. Much of it has been known for centuries. It was ignored until the twentieth century and is still ignored by many. Just as now Shakespeare must be a beliefless neutral observer, so, in the past, he must have been a Protestant. England is a Protestant country; Shakespeare is England's national poet; Shakespeare cannot possibly have been a Catholic: so the reasoning went. The evidence from outside the plays supports the strong likelihood that Shakespeare's education and lasting sympathies were Catholic rather than Protestant. As a small-town parvenu, educated at neither Oxford nor Cambridge nor the Inns of Court, he had to make a public career as a playwright without incurring suspicion of loyalties that, if discovered, would have been regarded as seditious. If he was a Catholic, in other words, it is hardly surprising that we know so little about him.

What we know for sure, however, from evidence everywhere in his plays is his intimate responsiveness, intellectual, emotional and imaginative, to the tradition in which he was brought up, officially wrecked but persisting in secret corners of the country, and to the issues of sovereignty, power, responsibility and freedom, which the Tudor century had made the urgent topics of his England.

To Dante in the Italy of the early fourteenth century, the gulf, as we have seen, between Christendom as it should have been and Christendom as it was gave him cause for much rage and grief. Instead of a virtuous and orderly empire able to confine a virtuous papacy to spiritual authority only, a chaotic, strife-fractured empire was permanently at loggerheads with a papacy corrupted by greed and temporal power. Dante's poem was unknown to Shakespeare. So were the age-old, Christendom-wide issues of empire and papacy. But Shakespeare's political acuteness—his keen sense of how power is acquired, how it may be used and abused, how it is lost—was nourished by wide and intelligent reading as well as by his observation of the politics of his own country in his own time. In due course he delivered, from North's translation of Plutarch's *Lives of the Noble Grecians and Romans*, the three political masterpieces that were his Roman plays. Meanwhile, the English poet who most evidently connects Dante's Christendom to Shakespeare's England was Chaucer. In Chaucer's England, recovering with difficulty from the appalling losses of the Black Death, which killed between a quarter and a third of Europe's population in the 1340s, the gulf between Christian ideals and worldly reality was, if on a smaller scale, every bit as visible as it had been to Dante. A wave of anticlerical and antiaristocratic resentment followed the plague: many noblemen and many priests had fled from their people to save their own lives. Chaucer's criticism of lethargy and luxury in the old monasteries, irrecoverably depleted of monks, and of the uncontrolled proliferation of go-getting friars must have had targets recognisable to everyone. Meanwhile, the old harmony of life and thought in the Church, already a nostalgic memory to Dante, had further disintegrated. The distant spectacle of the papacy in the later fourteenth and fifteenth centuries was unedifying at best, scandalous at worst. In Oxford, William of Occam and John Wycliffe took into cutting intellectual abstraction and heresy the kind of speculation that Saint Bernard had long ago feared in the teaching of Abelard. Elsewhere in the English Church, however, a quiet, fervent, wholly orthodox piety was inspiring both lay patronage—six of the eight English Charterhouses were founded between 1340 and 1400—and the writers, in English, of some texts on prayer that would for the Protestant centuries to come form part of the hidden Catholic tradition of the country. Walter Hilton, Julian of Norwich and the almost certainly Carthusian author of *The Cloud of Unknowing* represent a strain of unworldly, unphilosophical, late medieval devotion that surfaced in the heroic martyrdoms of the Carthusian monks who resisted Henry VIII's break with Rome and in the early lives of Thomas More and Reginald Pole. These books were probably not known to Shakespeare, but the tradition of private holiness to which they belong certainly was.

When Shakespeare, in about 1590, began to write plays, he took as his subject the rackety and bloody upheavals, driven by baronial treachery, of the English fifteenth century. This was a thoroughly Tudor choice. The Tudor monarchs prided themselves, with reason, on having brought order and peace to a land sickened and exhausted by civil war. Both Henry VII and Henry VIII treated surviving Plantagenets, including Cardinal Pole's family, whose claim to the throne was better than the Tudor one, with ruthless cruelty. Henry VIII's momentous neurosis about fathering a male heir, Mary Tudor's phantom pregnancy, Elizabeth's fear of Mary Stuart and the ambitions of some of Mary's Catholic supporters: all were fuelled by memories of the dynastic shambles of the fifteenth century. So was the Tudor resurrection from the distant past of "the divinity", in Shakespeare's phrase, that "doth hedge a king".[16] The quasi-sacerdotal status of the king, conferred in the anointing of the coronation rite, was part of the social glue of the early, feudal Middle Ages: Saint Dunstan had devised, in 973, a rite for the coronation of the Anglo-Saxon king Edgar that was copied all over Latin Christendom. Almost unchanged, it was used at the coronation of Elizabeth II in 1953. But in the twelfth century, with a more confident Church and more businesslike clerical (in both senses) government in England and France, the sacred mystique surrounding the anointed king had swiftly evaporated. The king was a layman, and that was that. The French monarchy, in its long contention with the papacy, had revived the mystique in the fourteenth century. Tudor royal policy deliberately took up this revival to strengthen a hold on the throne achieved by conquest rather than descent and then to add weight to Henry VIII's self-proclamation as "supreme head of the church of England" when he threw off the spiritual authority of the Pope in 1534 and ruled through lay ministers, the first of whom, ironically, was the Catholic martyr Thomas More. By Shakespeare's time the sacred inviolability of the crowned head had become a powerful belief, to be tactlessly propagated as "the divine right of kings" by James I and then tested to destruction by his son Charles I.

* * *

Shakespeare's four apprentice works, the three parts of *Henry VI* and *Richard III*, written with increasing dramatic control of a mass of confused historical material, tell the story of a king, Henry VI, so manifestly feeble that his murderously competing cousins were able to disgrace the monarchy and the nation until both were rescued by an outsider, Henry VII, the first Tudor king. Henry VI inherited the crown as a baby; for years England was ruled for him. As an adult he was personally holy, even saintly, but unfit to rule. In all three plays Shakespeare shows us a guileless innocent, cast in a role he cannot play, others fighting, disastrously, for the power the king should gather to himself and use for the country's good order. Henry suffers because he understands his responsibility and can do nothing to halt the consequences of his inability to meet it. In a strange and beautiful scene in *Henry VI Part III*, Henry withdraws from yet another battle between the forces of his riven family and, with all the sorrow of Virgilian pastoral, mourns the fact that he is a king and not a simple shepherd with a mild and predictable rural routine to take him through his life:

> So minutes, hours, days, weeks, months, and years,
> Pass'd over to the end they were created,
> Would bring white hairs unto a quiet grave.[17]

As he reflects sadly on the contrast between a shepherd's peace and a king's anxieties, two figures, emblematic in their representativeness, stumble on to the stage as if from a mystery play. One is "a Son that hath kill'd his Father, with the body in his arms", the other "a Father that hath kill'd his Son, with the body in his arms". The dreadfulness of civil war could not be more graphically presented to an audience. Their grief, as each discovers what he has done, is taken on by the king as "ten times so much" as theirs because he is their king, the shepherd who has failed to care for them. "O that my death", he says, "would stay these ruthful deeds." [18] (It does not.)

The scene comes out of a long past. The mystery plays of late medieval towns, so proudly performed in the old Church calendar, so closely connected with lay piety, were gradually—the authorities knew how popular they were—suppressed in the first twenty years of Elizabeth's reign, the Catholic feast of Corpus Christi, with which they were most associated, having been abolished. Many remembered them in 1590, and Shakespeare as a child may have seen the last performances of the Coventry cycle. But the scene also has a long future. In play after play for the next twenty years, with increasing subtlety and much-increasing depth, Shakespeare explored the dilemmas of kingship, or any exercise of great power, and of the mismatch between men and the roles they must play, the healing qualities of human simplicity, the responsibility of the soul before God.

Laden with future dramatic scope is also the most successfully achieved character of these first plays, their villain, Richard Duke of York, later Richard III, the central figure in his own play, the last of this tetralogy. At the end of *Henry VI Part III*, Richard kills the king, who accepts death as a lamb accepts its slaughter, and an actor his part:

> So first the harmless sheep doth yield his fleece,
> And next his throat unto the butcher's knife.
> What scene of death hath Roscius now to act? [19]

After his needlessly repeated stabbing of the harmless king, Richard, in the first of many villains' soliloquies in Shakespeare's plays, attributes his cynical, merciless pursuit of his own interest to the deformities with which he was born. He plans to murder his own brother, the sin of Cain that "hath the primal, eldest curse upon it", [20] as Claudius says in *Hamlet*, to clear his way to the throne:

I have no brother; I am like no brother;
And this word "love", which greybeards call divine,
Be resident in men like one another,
And not in me: I am myself alone.
. . . .
Clarence, thy turn is next, and then the rest,
Counting myself but bad till I be best.[21]

This, as Richard bends to his own interest the real meanings of the words "bad" and "best", is the *libido dominandi* identified by Augustine as the motive force of the *civitas terrena*, "self-love reaching the point of contempt for God".[22] In Shakespeare's century the drive to achieve and sustain worldly power, a drive that to succeed must be crafty, single-minded and without scruple, had been described, even recommended, by Machiavelli in *The Prince*, and by the 1590s Shakespeare's audience would readily have recognised Richard, in his cruelty and in his cleverness, as a "Machiavel". Marlowe's play *The Jew of Malta*, exactly contemporary with *Henry VI Part III*, has Machiavelli himself as Prologue, saying:

I count religion but a childish toy,
And hold there is no greater sin than ignorance.[23]

Not many Englishmen had actually read Machiavelli. Cardinal Pole did. "I found that this book had been written", he wrote, "by an enemy of the human race."[24] He had had it recommended to him by Thomas Cromwell, Henry VIII's power-hungry right-hand man through the break with Rome and a disciple of Machiavelli if ever there was one. In general Machiavelli had become a symbol of a set of values that, as a new Europe of competitive nation-states replaced the old coherence, however flawed and fallible, of Christendom, struck traditional Catholic England, the "greybeards" of Richard's speech, as appallingly destructive. The solitary wicked man sketched in Richard III, out for his own ends at the expense of long-valued loyalties to family, to the legitimate king, to a master dependent on his sound advice, at the expense of the very order of society that such loyalties sustained, will recur in Shakespeare's plays as a destroyer of the good and of truth.

It is not far-fetched to see this figure, the "new man" at his most terrifying in the characters of Iago, Edmund and Macbeth, as representative of the new order of things in England in opposition to which Thomas More and the

Carthusians had been willing to die. The Scottish bishop John Leslie, a passionate supporter of Mary Stuart throughout the hopeless mess of her adult life, wrote in 1572 that England was now "a Machiavellian state". "And that is it", he explained, "that I call a Machiavellian state and regiment: where religion is put behind in the second and last place; where the civil policy, I mean, is preferred before it, and not limited by any rules of religion, but the religion framed to serve the time and place."[25] Thomas More, the most intelligent lawyer in England, had seen the full implications of what Henry VIII was doing in the 1530s. As a young man close to the London Carthusians, he had lectured on the *City of God*. As Lord Chancellor, he resigned his office because he understood that the king in Parliament was seizing ultimate authority over the souls of his subjects, by what More called at his trial "your statute", from God himself in his body on earth, "the common known Catholic Church". "Forasmuch", he said to the court,

> as this indictment is grounded upon an act of Parliament directly repugnant to the laws of God and His Holy Church, the supreme government of which or of any part whereof may no temporal prince presume by any law to take upon him, as rightfully belonging to the see of Rome, a spiritual preeminence by the mouth of our Saviour himself personally put upon earth, only to St Peter and his successors, bishops of the same See, by special prerogative granted; it is therefore in law amongst Christian men insufficient to charge any Christian man.

To which the presiding judge, More's successor as Lord Chancellor, could only reply: "If the act of Parliament be lawful, then the indictment is good enough."[26] In law-abiding, law-protected, law-bound England, the concept of a bad law, a law made by the king in Parliament that was unlawful according to the law of God, a law that should be disobeyed, was difficult to grasp. It had been familiar to Augustine in the half-Christian world of the late Roman Empire. A few others understood it as More did. Richard Reynolds, a Bridgettine priest at the exemplary Syon monastery, said to his interrogators in the Tower, who included Thomas Cromwell, that he would spend his blood in the Pope's cause and that, against the peers and prelates of the realm, he had on his side all Christendom and "the thousand thousand that be dead" and "all good men of the kingdom", too. Told to be silent, he replied: "If you do not wish me to speak further, proceed with the judgement according to *your law*."[27] Reynolds was martyred with three Carthusian priors two months before More's death in 1535.

The first four history plays launched Shakespeare on his career. *Richard III* in particular, with its luridly wicked central character, seems to have been at once the popular success it has remained. The mixed batch of half a dozen plays he wrote in the next three years included the gory Senecan tragedy *Titus Andronicus*, the very funny Roman *Comedy of Errors*, the exquisite *Love's Labour's Lost*, and one English history play, quite separate from the two sets of four history plays that preceded and followed it. This is *King John*. The dating of these early plays is uncertain, but it is impossible not to connect *King John*, set in the safely remote early thirteenth century, with Mary Stuart's execution after nineteen years of imprisonment in 1587 and with the defeat of the Spanish Armada in 1588. Elizabeth had agreed to the execution, which horrified Catholic Europe, only after heavy pressure from her Protestant advisers and increasing evidence of foolhardy Catholic conspiracy. The lucky defeat of the Armada in the following year seemed a vindication of the execution and quickly acquired almost mythical status as God's blessing on Protestant England.

King John is an awkward play, not often performed, conflating a few chronicled events of a long-ago reign into a tough, unevenly written drama out of which no adult comes well. The king has a weak claim to the throne; orders the death of the innocent boy Prince Arthur, who is the rightful heir to the kingdom; quarrels with Rome, provoking the excommunication of the realm; and faces a foreign (French) invasion, which is luckily dispelled by a storm at sea. The likelihood of the king's behaviour delivering the country into the horrors of civil war, so much feared throughout the Tudor century, haunts the play. King John is neither attractive nor competent; his illegitimate nephew Faulconbridge, in some respects a sketch for Edmund in *Lear*, is both, but is placed by Shakespeare at an odd tangent to the play. He is observant, satirical, brave and politically astute but not, or perhaps not yet—his take on his own future is equivocal—corrupted by power. He closes the play on a nobly patriotic note. His loyalty is to an England that has just escaped European entanglement and reached internal peace. It has also, the audience has seen, restored relations with Rome. The play has usually been regarded as a Protestant piece because John's defiance of the Pope echoes Henry VIII's arrogated title as "supreme head" (altered by Queen Elizabeth to "supreme governor") of the English church and summons the mystique of Tudor kingship to support his claim:

> What earthly name to interrogatories
> Can task the free breath of a sacred king?
> . . . .
> But as we under heaven[28] are supreme head,
> So, under him that great supremacy,
> Where we do reign we will alone uphold,
> Without th'assistance of a mortal hand,
> So tell the Pope, all reverence set apart
> To him and his usurp'd authority.[29]

But the king, a grasping bully about to order the murder of Arthur, is too unsympathetic a figure for either this speech or his command to Faulconbridge to loot the abbeys of England to strike the audience as admirable, let alone glorious. The Pope's ineffectual representative, Cardinal Pandulph, is taunted by the Dauphin, who no doubt reminded the audience of Philip II of Spain, with a premonition of Stalin's "How many battalions has the Pope?"

> What penny hath Rome borne,
> What men provided, what munition sent,
> To underprop this action?[30]

Faulconbridge's "Mad world! Mad kings!"[31] is an apt comment on the behaviour of the powerful in the world of this play, a world that the boy Arthur seems lucky to leave, jumping to his death as he tries to escape from prison. All ambivalence clears when a group of noblemen find his body and are horrified. Faulconbridge's lament cannot have failed to chime with the grief of those in the audience who understood and cared that Mary Stuart had been the last hope for the restoration of the old faith in England and remembered the ugly greed of those who manoeuvred for, and held on to, the old wealth of the monasteries:

> From forth this morsel of dead royalty
> The life, the right, the truth of all this realm
> Is fled to heaven; and England now is left
> To tug and scamble, and to part by th'teeth
> The unowed interest of proud-swelling state.[32]

Shakespeare's rapidly developing career was apparently not hindered by this: that loyalty to England and loyalty to the Catholic past could be combined in the same character, the same play, the same playwright; this was perhaps already, as it would be for centuries, thought impossible by Protestant complacency.

* * *

In the five years from 1595 to 1599, Shakespeare wrote eleven plays, among them *Romeo and Juliet*, *A Midsummer Night's Dream*, *Much Ado about Nothing*, *As You Like It* and *Julius Caesar*, and also among them his second set of English history plays, *Richard II*, the two parts of *Henry IV*, and *Henry V*. In this tetralogy, more various, more compelling, more dramatically confident in all sorts of ways than his first, he returned to more recent history, finding in the period before the reign of Henry VI the hubris of two kings, the nemesis that fell on both of them, and the shadowed heroism of the son of one.

Richard II is the first properly tragic character Shakespeare created. Romeo and Juliet, however poignant their love and their deaths, are no more than adolescent victims of the kind of Italian city feud that was well known to Dante: securely set in Catholic Verona, the play does not even hint at the religious split that was already dividing families in England. Richard III is too consistently evil to be a tragic hero. Our "pity and fear", in Aristotle's words, unknown to Shakespeare, "are not aroused by seeing an utterly worthless man falling from prosperity into misery" but by "undeserved misfortune, the misfortune of someone just like ourselves, whose fall is not due to vice and depravity but rather to some error".[33] Richard II in his folly, careless arrogance, mistaken (Tudor) confidence in divine protection of the anointed king, and most of all in his painfully acquired self-knowledge at the play's end, suffers a truly tragic fate against what Balthasar calls "God's horizon". He is in all these ways a youthful, shallower version of King Lear. Richard legitimately inherited his grandfather's throne at the age of ten; weighty uncles, particularly John of Gaunt, governed England for him for years. At the start of the play, we see a wilful, charming, spoiled young king enjoying his freedom to rule the lives of others, exercising his royal power with a frightening levity that makes a serious enemy of his cousin Henry Bolingbroke, Gaunt's son, carelessly sent into exile. Gaunt dies prophesying disaster for an England ruled by Richard. A petulant and resentful Richard confiscates Bolingbroke's inheritance, provoking Bolingbroke's angry, self-righteous return to claim not only what is due to him but the throne itself from so evidently frivolous a king.

The deposition of a legitimate king by a usurper, however much more competent to rule the country—and Bolingbroke in this play is a Machiavel, seizing his chances with the cynical ruthlessness of the man who efficiently plots his path to power—was, in Tudor England, a shocking spectacle. Shakespeare, in a compelling scene, shows us Richard attempting to make it all the more shocking by comparing himself to Christ and those who have turned against him to Judas. Bolingbroke's response is dignified, scornful silence. Shakespeare's ambivalence here is a sign of his new dramatic maturity. Bolingbroke's deposition of Richard is the original sin that will bring civil war to England, both in the short term and in the long. On the other hand, Richard's self-regarding sense of injury is of a piece with the childish decisions that have brought him to this lonely exposure; his self-dramatising flightiness is his own original sin. He has to learn the lesson that all Shakespeare's powerful men, and Cleopatra, too, with some good in them are brought to: that they are also, and in the end only, human beings. He tells his few remaining friends to

> throw away respect,
> Tradition, form, and ceremonious duty;
> For you have but mistook me all this while.

Then he adds:

> I live with bread like you, feel want,
> Taste grief, need friends. Subjected thus,
> How can you say to me I am a king? [34]

There is still a good deal of self-pity in this. But before his murder, even more shocking than his deposition, he goes far toward redemption in the audience's eyes by bravely facing his responsibility for what has happened. Alone in prison, no longer play-acting, he becomes a soul before God.

In the next two plays Bolingbroke, now King Henry IV, has to face the consequences of his own sin, or, in Aristotelian terms, error, in deposing the legitimate king. One consequence is external: a northern rebellion against the king, following the precedent recently set by the king himself and led by some of his then supporters. The other is internal: unabsolvable guilt, for Henry, like Claudius after him, will not lay aside the fruits of his sin. Adding to the grief and anxiety each of these causes him is the spectacle of his eldest son, Prince Hal, heir to his ill-gotten throne, apparently behaving as irresponsibly as Richard had, fooling about in taverns with the deplorable, but to the audience irresistible, Falstaff, and as much a contrast to the rebel hero Hotspur as the lightweight

Richard had once been to Bolingbroke. But a Machiavellian streak in Prince Hal is established very early in *Henry IV Part I*, when the prince, in soliloquy of course, reveals his calculation that his spell of dissolute life will do him nothing but good when he chooses to emerge from it, unexpectedly in command of himself and the kingdom. About the power of presentation in politics Shakespeare had nothing to learn from spin doctors.

Both *Henry IV* plays explore, among other things, the difficulties and anguish of the father-son relationship. The king longs for his son to be more like the dangerous Northumberland's son, Hotspur. The prince adopts, both for fun and for his long-term ends, Falstaff as a cheerful, doting father substitute. They play, Shakespeare again exploiting theatricality, a comic parody of the king's disapproval of his son, each taking first one part and then the other. This is hilarious until the last four words spoken by the prince playing his father strike a chill as they remind the audience of Hal's hidden plan:

> FALSTAFF. But for sweet Jack Falstaff, kind Jack Falstaff, true Jack Falstaff, valiant Jack Falstaff, and therefore more valiant, being, as he is, old Jack Falstaff, banish not him thy Harry's company, banish not him thy Harry's company. Banish plump Jack, and banish all the world.
>
> PRINCE. I do, I will.[35]

Very far from valiant Falstaff may be, indefensible in all sorts of ways, but we love him—more than the prince does—and his mockery of battlefields, reputation and honour has a bracing healthiness that is not far from goodness and truth. In *Henry IV Part II*, once the king, on his deathbed at last persuaded that Hal is fit to reign, has died, we see the new king adopt the sober, law-upholding Lord Chief Justice as his new father figure, while Falstaff, wildly imagining new scope for licence of every kind, has to be cast aside. Shakespeare's judgement here is complex; this never, in Shakespeare, means that he makes no judgement. The audience grieves for the discarded Falstaff but is convinced, nonetheless, that a king's duty to his people requires him not only to be competent but to be seen to be competent. In *Henry V* we watch Hal behave as a king of exemplary competence. There is no more question of civil war. Enemies at home are summarily disposed of; they plotted against the king (like some Catholics in Elizabeth's reign) with the national enemy, here France, which is defeated, against the odds, by brave Englishmen led by their king himself. The audience might well conclude that without a degree of Machiavellian calculation, a monarch is unlikely to be effective. Catholics among them would have to agree that Elizabeth had long demonstrated most impressive effectiveness. Civil war, when it reappeared in England forty-five years later, decades after Shakespeare's death, would be caused by the incompetence of a virtuous Christian king (behaving in some ways like Shakespeare's Henry VI, in others like his Richard II) signally lacking the Machiavellian streak.

But there is one further depth to all three of these *Henry* plays. War, civil in the first two plays, foreign in the third, bears hardest on simple people far below the level of chivalry and honour mocked by Falstaff. Shameless recruiter, with profit to himself, of the poorest, weakest soldiers he can find, Falstaff knows this well:

PRINCE.   Tell me, Jack, whose fellows are these that come after?
FALSTAFF. Mine, Hal, mine.
PRINCE.   I did never see such pitiful rascals.
FALSTAFF. Tut, tut, good enough to toss, food for powder, food for pow-
           der, they'll fill a pit as well as better; tush, man, mortal men,
           mortal men.[36]

After the battle, Falstaff, alone, says: "I have led my ragamuffins where they are peppered; there's not three of my hundred and fifty left alive, and they are for the town's end, to beg during life." [37] In the second play, the scene where Falstaff is recruiting Gloucestershire peasants has the audience poised, as only Shakespeare can manage, between laughter and tears as Falstaff allows the marginally better-off to buy themselves out. The plea of one lights for an instant a whole obscure existence: "And, good Master Corporal Captain, for my old dame's sake stand my friend. She has nobody to do anything about her when I am gone, and she is old and cannot help herself." [38] The weakest of all, whose name is Feeble, accepting the draft, foreshadows Hamlet in his courage: "By my troth I care not, a man can die but once, we owe God a death. I'll ne'er bear a base mind—and't be my destiny, so; and't be not, so." [39] All this undercuts, with swift economy, the envy of their poorest subjects expressed by kings, Henry IV among them in the scene immediately preceding this one.

On *Henry V* Shakespeare's developing complexity of judgement has led critics to diametrically opposed conclusions: the play is either a patriotic pageant or a lament for the horrors of war, either a paean of praise for a noble king or an attack on a Machiavellian reputation-burnisher. It is all these things. After Agincourt the French pointlessly slaughter the boys—one of whom the audience knows—guarding the baggage; this enrages Henry. But he himself has already ordered the equally pointless murder of all French prisoners. On the other hand, to set against his famous speeches of heroic bravado, the king in "a little touch of Harry in the night", as he wanders his camp incognito before the battle, reveals—though not to the soldiers, who do not recognize him—that he is as afraid as they are: "I think the King is but a man, as I am. . . . His ceremonies laid by, in his nakedness he appears but a man".[40] He has learned the lesson Shakespeare always wants the powerful to learn. Henry is appalled to find that the frightened soldiers regard the king as wholly responsible not only for the war itself, its justice or injustice being beyond their obedient ken, but for the judgement of God on them after their likely deaths. In limpid everyday prose Henry replies with a simple homily, complete with references to Scripture. Criminals cannot escape the truth of their lives in soldiering, for "they have no wings to fly from God". Each man's preparation of his soul for death is his own responsibility:

> Every subject's duty is the King's; but every subject's soul is his own. Therefore should every soldier in the wars do as every sick man in his bed, wash every mote out of his conscience; and dying so, death is to him advantage; or not dying, the time was blessedly lost wherein such preparation was gained.[41]

The soldiers are persuaded. But Henry, alone, nevertheless mourns the heavy load that must be carried by a king and reflects that only hollow "ceremony" distinguishes him from the poorest peasant who follows "the ever-running year / With profitable labour to his grave".[42] His envy of "such a wretch" is a less lyrical version of Henry VI's; his dissection of the "idol ceremony" shows that he has learned a good deal from Falstaff. Making his own peace with God, the king at the end of the scene prays for victory with keenly felt penitence for his father's deposition and murder of Richard II. Henry has done his best to wipe away this grave sin, reburying Richard, paying for the prayers of "five hundred poor" and founding "two chantries where the sad and solemn priests sing still for Richard's soul".[43] Some in Shakespeare's audience would have known that these were the Charterhouse at Sheen and the Bridgettine house at Syon, where priests no longer sang, though both had been among the very few monasteries revived by Queen Mary.

It is worth noting that deprived of its traditional Catholic assumptions, this scene would lose most of its meaning; it is also worth noting that Queen Elizabeth, like Harry in the night, had said she did not wish "to make windows into men's souls". This was why she was inflicting torture and barbarous death on Catholics as traitors, which most of them were not, rather than as heretics, which from the Protestant point of view they were. The policy was justifiable in terms only of power, of the *civitas terrena* that had become, in theory and in practice, all there was, now that the English church was no longer part of "the common, known Catholic Church". As one of Thomas Cromwell's propagandists had written in the 1530s:

A Commonwealth, as I think, is nothing else but a certain number of cities, towns, shires, that all agree upon one law and one head, united and knit together by the observation of the laws. These kept, they must necessarily flourish; these broken, they must needs perish.[44]

That efficient, obeyed government need not, but could, involve the crushing of the truth was an Augustinian perception shared by such as Thomas More and Edmund Campion. It was shared also by Shakespeare.

Shakespeare knew that power in the *civitas terrena* is a matter of the weight of the support on which a ruler, even an anointed king, can rely. Tudor monarchs had constantly to consolidate support from the weightiest—those, in turn, commanding most men—of their subjects. Queen Mary, to consolidate support, had been forced to leave the abbey lands in the hands of those who had acquired them from her father. The same support-commanding northern families who had threatened both Henry VIII and Elizabeth led the rebellions, put down with little mercy, in both parts of *Henry IV*. In *Richard II* the audience senses power shift decisively from the king to the usurper as weighty subjects move their loyalty and their troops from one to the other.

In *Julius Caesar*, Shakespeare's first Roman play, the audience actually sees this process take place. The assassination of the most powerful man in the world leaves a vacuum. Into it step two contenders. Each addresses the Roman mob, the weight that will tip the balance between them for control of Rome and all its territories. The first contender, Brutus, speaks well, simply, in prose. The mob is for him. The second, Mark Antony, speaks much better, in resounding rhetorical verse. The mob changes sides as we watch, worked up to such uncontrolled support of Antony that they lynch a harmless poet who happens to have the same name as one of Brutus's fellow-conspirators against Caesar. Shakespeare has shown us here not only power moving from one man to another before our eyes, but the triumph of a Machiavellian politician over an ingenuous idealist. Richard II was the ineffective play-actor to Bolingbroke's icy victor; Antony in the Forum is both a play-actor and icily effective. As soon as the lynch mob has left the stage, we see him disposing of his enemies: "These many then shall die; their names are prick'd." [45] Nor is the contrast between Brutus's goodness and Antony's competence the only collision of character in the play. Brutus and Cassius, leaders of the conspiracy and old friends, are, again, the virtuous innocent and the astute pursuer of power. Brutus's decisions are inept: he allows Antony to speak at Caesar's funeral; he insists on marching to Philippi rather than awaiting Antony's army. These mistakes lose the conspirators the struggle for power and then the battle. Each decision, each mistake, is made against the advice of Cassius—"He thinks too much; such men are dangerous",[46] in Caesar's words— whose superior grasp of political reality might have won both the struggle and the battle. Cassius's affection for Brutus undoes their cause, in ironic reversal of Brutus's early tribute to Caesar:

> I have not known when his affections sway'd
> More than his reason.[47]

In *Antony and Cleopatra* we shall see again and in a greater play the history of the world turn on the sway of affection and the shift of power from one man to another.

* * *

"Shakespeare's plays", wrote Dr. Johnson, "are not in the rigorous and critical sense either tragedies or comedies, but compositions of a distinct kind; exhibiting the real state of sublunary nature, which partakes of good and evil, joy and sorrow, mingled with endless variety of proportion and innumerable modes of combination." [48] Coleridge noticed with delight: "It is truly singular that Plato (whose philosophy & religion were but exotic at home & a mere opposition to the Finite in all things—a prophet and anticipator of the *Christian* era—) should in the Dialogue of the Banquet give a justification of our Shakespear." [49] The reference is to the end of the *Symposium*. Everyone else has gone home or is drunk or almost asleep when Socrates says that "the man who knew how to write a comedy could also write a tragedy" and that "a skilful tragic writer was capable of being also a comic writer." The text continues: "They were giving way to his arguments, which they didn't follow very well, and nodding." [50] No wonder, since Socrates's, or Plato's, intuition took nearly two thousand years to be vindicated in Shakespeare.

The history plays, particularly the two parts of *Henry IV*, demonstrate the truth of these observations. So do at least some of Shakespeare's other plays of this period, whether, appropriately but not exactly, classified as comedies or tragedies according to the happiness-in-resolution-and-weddings or sorrow-in-death of their endings. In several of these plays, one or more characters, for a single scene or for the duration of the whole piece, breaks out of the convention in which the play is written to transfix, and sometimes to challenge, an audience with the complexity of "the real state of sublunary nature". In *Romeo and Juliet* both Mercutio and the Nurse are characters from comedy whose moments of pathos, perhaps precisely because they are characters from comedy, may move us more than the confusions of plot that lead to the lovers' deaths. In the magic world of *A Midsummer Night's Dream*, the quarrel and reconciliation of Oberon and Titania have an adult grandeur against which the pairs of lovers strike the audience as muddling their way through the emotional uncertainties of mere adolescence, while Bottom, struggling in vain to articulate his fading "translation" as he wakes, for a moment gathers to himself all the enchantment of the play. In *The Merchant of Venice* the romance and bawdy of the last act, well within the conventions of comedy, cannot dispel the painfulness of the trial scene, in which Portia's noble speech about Christian mercy throws into harsh relief not only the understandably savage legalism of Shylock but also, and more upsettingly, the cruelty with which the victorious Christians break Shylock's spirit. In the golden *As You Like It*, Rosalind's realism, bracing and cheerful, and Jaques's, melancholy and sharp, transcend the airy unlikelihood of the plot, as does the loyal care shown for Orlando by the old servant Adam, and vice versa. In *Twelfth Night* Feste, acute and forlorn, and the wretched Malvolio, mocked victim of his own self-importance, darken the sunshine of a classical comedy of shipwreck, twins, disguises and the right coupling of young lovers at the end.

By now, about the year 1601, Shakespeare, thirty-seven years old, must have known that he could, in the theatre, do anything. What he did, in the next three years, was to write a group of plays that includes both his first great tragedy, *Hamlet*, and the generically unclassifiable *Troilus and Cressida* and *Measure for Measure*. All three of these plays, very different though each is from the others, and with *Hamlet* so obviously the most extraordinary achievement, present audiences with a dark world. The steady light of goodness and truth that shone over all the earlier plays, however often clouded by wickedness and folly, is not absent in *Hamlet*, though the hero has to struggle throughout the play to regain his sense of it. From the other two plays, it has disappeared almost completely. "Look,

Hector, how the sun begins to set",[51] says treacherous Achilles to the doomed Hector in *Troilus*, at one of the most chilling moments in all Shakespeare.

The four heroes of Shakespeare's great tragedies have, famously, almost nothing in common, but at least we watch Othello, Lear and Macbeth make errors, in true Aristotelian fashion, that bring down upon them the nemesis of their fates. Hamlet's only error is to be born into the common human condition, the tangle of sin and sinfulness where we all find ourselves: "Use every man after his desert and who shall 'scape whipping?"[52] The play has its original sinful error, but it is not Hamlet's. Claudius is his brother's murderer and the thief of his brother's wife; he is a successful Machiavellian achiever of power; but he is not "an utterly worthless man".[53] He acknowledges, in a soliloquy overheard by Hamlet, the truth of what he has done and knows that his remorse falls short of repentance because he will keep his crown and his queen. He has, in other words, the makings of a tragic hero. But he is not the hero of the play.

Hamlet, like Laertes and Ophelia, children of the other father in the play, is dragged into and eventually killed by the sinfulness of the older generation. The play demonstrates, shockingly, the spoiling of the innocence of youth by parental greed, lust and ambition: Polonius in his use of Ophelia is just as Machiavellian as Claudius. "The canker galls the infants of the spring", says Laertes to his sister, "Too oft before their buttons be disclos'd."[54] Hamlet's first soliloquy shows us a young man so disgusted by his mother's adulterous passion for Claudius that he is close to suicide. Once he realises that "the canker" that afflicts Denmark is the poison Claudius poured into old Hamlet's ear—that he has to deal with murder and not merely lust—he finds himself cast in a role his acute sensitivity and his intelligence make him quite unfitted to play. Not that he cannot *act*. His intelligence harnesses his hysteria: he *acts* madness while using his own behaviour to say much that he really means: teasing Rosencrantz and Guildenstern, he is also facing the possibility that man is indeed no more than "this quintessence of dust";[55] bullying Ophelia, more angry with his mother, with the eavesdroppers and with himself than with her, he also wants to save her from the corruption evident in his mother, which is the corruption of all mankind: "Get thee to a nunnery. Would'st thou be a breeder of sinners?";[56] crazily threatening Claudius after Polonius's death, he is also really threatening Claudius. That his "madness" is always, if only just, under his control is demonstrated to the audience by Ophelia's real madness, as if he had deflected to her the lightning of intolerable stress.

What Hamlet is unable to do is *act* as his role as avenger of his father's death requires, a role that gives Laertes no qualms. Considering suicide again, or perhaps the certain death that killing Claudius would bring, his "dread of some-thing after death",[57] that man is more than "this quintessence of dust", is real. It is also new: before he heard the truth from his father's ghost, he said to Horatio, his faithful friend:

> I do not set my life at a pin's fee,
> And for my soul, what can it do to that,
> Being a thing immortal as itself?[58]

He is now in a moral impasse: if he fails to kill Claudius, he fails his father; if he kills Claudius, he becomes himself a murderer. He defends, to himself, his inabil-ity to kill the praying Claudius with the horrible excuse that this would not be vengeance enough since his father was murdered unprepared for death. When he sees Fortinbras, another untroubled avenger of a father's death, leading twenty thousand equally untroubled soldiers perhaps to their graves, he descends to ordi-nary considerations of honour to galvanize himself to *action*.

We are no more convinced by this than he is. Trapped in a thicket of deceit, conspiracy and spies, Hamlet is rescued into brave resignation of his will to the will of God not by thought but by the instant use of his intelligence on the voyage to England. "Rashly", he tells Horatio on his return,

> And pris'd be rashness for it: let us know
> Our indiscretion sometimes serves us well
> When our deep plots do pall; and that should learn us
> There's a divinity that shapes our ends,
> Rough-hew them how we will.[59]

Thus he has sent Rosencrantz and Guildenstern to the death Claudius had designed for him, their own fault for allowing themselves to be involved in Claudius's "deep plot", and now, because of the proved threat to his own life, his con-science is clear as to Claudius's death:

> Is't not to be damn'd
> To let this canker of our nature come
> In further evil?[60]

So he is no longer afraid. He brushes aside his own misgiving before the rigged duel with Laertes that will deliver the carnage of the play's end, telling Horatio that he, and all of us, are both free and, as to the time of our deaths, in God's hands: "We defy augury. There is a special providence in the fall of a sparrow. If it be now, 'tis not to come; if it be not to come it will be now; if it be not now, yet it will come. The readiness is all." [61] (The sparrow is scriptural; the courage is that of Feeble in *Henry IV Part II.*) Hamlet is a hero, not of course sinless himself, enmeshed in the consequences of the much graver sins of others. In the course of the play, he kills Polonius by mistake, unwittingly contributing to Ophelia's madness and death, and sends two spies to a deserved death. But he rescues himself from despair and achieves rather than loses a nobility of soul that is a kind of recovery of innocence. Hamlet arrives at calm acceptance by himself, with Horatio, left alive to tell his story, as his only companion in the truth.

There is in the vile world in which Hamlet has to live and learn and die no radical uncertainty as to the reality of goodness and truth. Claudius and Gertrude recognise, when they have to face the truth, the evil they have done. The goodness of Horatio steadies Hamlet even at his most hysterical. Hamlet's own intelligent judgement, his sense of truth and of goodness, is never in doubt. But in neither *Troilus and Cressida* nor *Measure for Measure* is any security in the truth or in the reality of goodness established by or for any of the characters, except, briefly, Isabella in *Measure for Measure*, and, in a single speech, Hector in *Troilus*:

> But value dwells not in particular will;
> It holds his estimate and dignity
> As well wherein 'tis precious of itself
> As in the prizer.[62]

The cynicism that was wholesome in Falstaff and benign in Jaques, because its targets deserved some disbelief, has curdled in these plays to a despair of transcendental value that is close to nihilism. Whether a personal crisis in Shakespeare's life contributed to this darkness we shall never know, but it is unsurprising that the uncertainty and fear in England in these years affected both him and his public. Queen Elizabeth was old and had no English heir; in 1601 her rejected favourite, the traitor Earl of Essex, tried and failed to overthrow her. When she died in March 1603, she was succeeded by Mary Stuart's son, James VI of Scotland, clever, dissipated, foreign, cowardly, and Protestant. England was tense, nervous, afraid of the future, and English Catholics particularly so.

In *Troilus and Cressida* the only goodness suggested by the play is a distant horizon shared by the writer and his audience, and for that one moment

Hector, against which the nihilism of the play can be properly understood and judged. Although the play is set in the Trojan War and is much concerned with the wrath of Achilles, we are very far, here, from Homeric heroism. Deceit, treachery and contempt are the fruits of a pervasive and explicit moral relativism—Troilus's "What's aught but as 'tis valued?"[63] is the key question of the play—which has Machiavellian manoeuvring for "reputation" at others' expense and lust as its central motives. Ulysses' famous speech about "degree" is not the Thomist homily on order in society that it is often taken for, but a lecture on "degree" in the Greek army as an instrument for victory over the Trojans, an instrument now in disarray but to be restored by a trick played on Achilles. Ulysses' vision of the naked will to power that the fragile convention of consented-to superiority keeps at bay is Schopenhauerian in its pessimism, Nietzschean in its predictive weight:

> Take but degree away, untune that string,
> And hark what discord follows! Each thing melts
> In mere oppugnancy; the bounded waters
> Should lift their bosoms higher than the shores,
> And make a sop of all this solid globe;
> Strength should be lord of imbecility,
> And the rude son should strike his father dead;
> Force should be right; or, rather, right and wrong—
> Between whose endless jar justice resides—
> Should lose their names, and so should justice too.
> Then everything includes itself in power,
> Power into will, will into appetite;
> And appetite, an universal wolf,
> So doubly seconded with will and power
> Must make perforce an universal prey,
> And last eat up itself.[64]

To take this as "Shakespeare's view of life" is to miss the savage nihilistic thrust of this particular play. When the natural world and its "bounded waters" were upset in *A Midsummer Night's Dream*, the cause was lack of harmony, lack of love, between male and female in Oberon and Titania. When "the rude son" does "strike his father dead" in *King Lear*, the cause is not absence of degree but absence of love. *Troilus* is its own world, of opinion rather than truth, where "man is a value-creating, not a good-discovering being",[65] Thersites, appropriately, its bitingly contemptuous commentator. Between Troilus and Cressida, Cressida and Diomedes, there is lust but no love. Ulysses goads Achilles to action with a deeply cynical account of the vulnerability of reputation, reinforced only by "ceremony", all Achilles has, to "envious and calumniating Time".[66] Envy and calumny drive the play: here man is indeed no more than the quintessence of dust; in Ulysses' next line: "One touch of nature makes the whole world kin." One recalls the coldness of the young Prince Hal killing Hotspur to acquire Hotspur's reputation, and Hotspur regretting its loss more than his imminent death.[67] Troilus has no Falstaff, listening as he shams death, to prefer, with sensible cheerfulness, life to honour, perhaps to help the prince who will be Henry V discover that "ceremony" is an idol.

Less consistent than the sickening, brilliant Troilus, Measure for Measure is an even more disturbing play. Power and sex at their very nastiest are explored within the confines of a comedy plot ending in reconciliation and various weddings. The play was written in 1604, when James I had been on the throne for a year. To regard it, and in particular the character of the Duke, who manipulates everyone else in the play with really shocking cynicism, as a compliment to the new king is to underrate by a huge distance Shakespeare's critical intelligence. To increase his popularity, James was making great public play, in arbitrary punishments and sometimes cruelly protracted pardons, of his mercy in the exercise of justice. The Duke does the same. But to think that the Duke, and therefore James, has Shakespeare's approval is as insensitive to the atmosphere of the play as to think that King John, and therefore Henry VIII or Elizabeth, had Shakespeare's approval in taking defiant command of the English Church. The camouflage of a distant period in King John is achieved here in the camouflage of Vienna, a distant Catholic city.

The Duke in Measure for Measure is, throughout, a liar and a deceiver. He appears to echo the Gospel in his early advice to Angelo:

> Heaven doth with us as we with torches do,
> Not light them for themselves; for if our virtues
> Did not go forth of us, 'twere all alike
> As if we had them not.[68]

But it is only in a world of opinion that it is "all alike"; and the Duke's tone here is that of Ulysses in Troilus, cynically warning Achilles that he will lose his reputation unless he does something new:

No man is the lord of anything,
Though in and of him there be much consisting,
Till he communicate his parts to others:
Nor doth he of himself know them for aught
Till he behold them formed in th'applause
Where th'are extended.[69]

The note struck in both these scenes is thoroughly secular: the person's value exists not in the truth of the knowledge of God, but in fickle opinion, the affirmation, in current parlance, of others. And the Duke's Epicurean sermon on death[70] is as nihilist as Ulysses' speeches on degree and the ravages of time. The Duke's Vienna is, because of his own negligence, a city of licence and debauchery. Disguising himself as a Franciscan friar (giving himself licence fraudulently to hear confessions and plausibly to invent confessions he has not heard), he leaves his city under the authority of the repressed, puritanical Angelo, whose own arbitrary selection of a judicial victim echoes James I's behaviour. The victim's sister, Isabella, is a novice nun. The two scenes in which she pleads for her brother's life, and then discovers that Angelo's price for clemency is her body, are the dramatic high points of a play otherwise uncertain and often stilted in tone. These scenes are also as shot through with sadism as the blinding of Gloucester in *King Lear*. Angelo is revealed as a pitiless tyrant and a sexual predator. The Duke's comedy resolution of the mess he has created, while more successful in outcome than the similar machinations of the real Friar in *Romeo and Juliet*, reveals him, in his turn, to be as unfit a judge as Angelo, though for different reasons. He is a frivolous opportunist who play-acts not, as Hamlet play-acts, in self-protection, but to exercise total control over his variously deceived subjects, and in his pretence to Isabella that her brother is dead he is as cruel as Angelo. She does not reply to his proposal of marriage at the play's end, perhaps because Shakespeare intended her to turn away in disgust. Lucio, the scapegrace voice of occasional truth in the play, calls him "the old fantastical duke of dark corners",[71] and Isabella's scorching attack on Angelo is at least as applicable to him:

Man, proud man,
Dress'd in a little brief authority,
Most ignorant of what he's most assur'd—
His glassy essence—like an angry ape
Plays such fantastic tricks before high heaven
As makes the angels weep.[72]

The soul's reality before God, the "glassy essence" that it is easy for the powerful man (or woman) to conceal from himself with his own pride in the "little brief authority" that impresses or terrifies others, is of overwhelming Christian importance to Shakespeare. He will return to it in *King Lear*, in *Macbeth* and later. Meanwhile, those who think *Measure for Measure* a straightforward Christian parable, with the Duke representing an admirable combination of justice and mercy, have missed the sour taste of the whole play. Balthasar is among them, for once failing to catch the hollow ring of a text in what was to him a foreign language. Only Isabella, and Isabella only for a while, transcends this sourness. It is she who, pleading for her brother, says to Angelo:

> Why, all the souls that were, were forfeit once,
> And He that might the vantage best have took
> Found out the remedy. How would you be
> If He, which is the top of judgement, should
> But judge you as you are?[73]

But soon she, too, inexperienced and confused, particularly sexually, with as little self-knowledge as everyone else in the play except the sinister Duke, is pulled into the heartless deceptions of his plot.

Whatever darkness in his own life or in the world about him drew from Shakespeare the disgust evident in this group of plays, to which the weaker *All's Well That Ends Well* also belongs, he perhaps dealt with it by concentrating it, in his next play, in a single character.

---

1. T. S. Eliot, "Dante", in *Selected Essays* (London, 1932), p. 265.
2. Allan Bloom, *The Closing of the American Mind* (New York, 1987), p. 160.
3. George Steiner, *Grammars of Creation* (London, 2001), pp. 67–68.
4. Samuel Johnson, "Preface to Shakespeare", in *Prose and Poetry*, sel. Mona Wilson (London, 1950), pp. 491, 497.
5. Ibid., p. 494.
6. William Hazlitt, *Characters of Shakespear's Plays*, ed. FJS (London, 1906), p. 247.
7. S. T. Coleridge, *Lectures 1808–1819 on Literature*, ed. R. A. Foakes (Princeton, 1987), 2:263–64.
8. Ibid., 1:520.
9. Harold Bloom, *Shakespeare: The Invention of the Human* (London, 1999), p. 730.
10. Alasdair MacIntyre, *Whose Justice? Which Rationality?* (London, 1988), p. 335.
11. Johnson, "Preface to Shakespeare", p. 491.
12. Hans Urs von Balthasar, *Theo-Logic*, vol. 1, trans. Adrian J. Walker (San Francisco, 2000), pp. 232, 236.
13. S. Schoenbaum, *William Shakespeare: A Documentary Life* (Oxford, 1975), p. 88. See also Richard Wilson, article in *Times Literary Supplement*, 19 December 1997.
14. John Finnis and Patrick Martin, *Times Literary Supplement*, 18 April 2003.

15. Schoenbaum, *William Shakespeare*, p. 47.
16. *Hamlet*, 4.5.123. All references to Shakespeare's plays are to the Arden editions.
17. *Henry VI, Part III*, 2.5.38–40.
18. Ibid., 2.5.95, 112.
19. Ibid., 5.6.8–10.
20. *Hamlet*, 3.3.37.
21. *Henry VI, Part III*, 5.6.80–83, 90–91.
22. Augustine, *City of God* 14.28, trans. Henry Bettenson (London, 1972).
23. Christopher Marlowe, *The Jew of Malta*, Machiavel's prologue, lines 14–15.
24. Quoted in W. Schenk, *Reginald Pole, Cardinal of England* (London, 1950), p. 39.
25. Quoted in Peter Milward, *Shakespeare's Religious Background* (London, 1973), p. 190.
26. G.R. Elton, *The Tudor Constitution: Documents and Commentary* (Cambridge, 1960), pp. 238–39.
27. David Knowles, *The Religious Orders in England*, vol. 3 (Cambridge, 1959), p. 217.
28. Shakespeare probably wrote "God", not "heaven", in the third line; this change in printed texts was often made on account of James I's 1606 law against profanity in printed plays.
29. *King John*, 3.1.147–60.
30. Ibid., 5.2.97–99.
31. Ibid., 2.1.561.
32. Ibid., 4.3.143–47.
33. Aristotle, *Poetics*, chap. 14, in *Classical Literary Criticism*, trans. T.S. Dorsch (London, 1965), p. 48.
34. *Richard II*, 3.2.172–77.
35. *Henry IV, Part I*, 2.4.469–75.
36. Ibid., 4.2.61–67.
37. Ibid., 5.3.36–38.
38. *Henry IV, Part II*, 3.2.224–27.
39. Ibid., 3.2.229–31.
40. *Henry V*, 4.1.101–6.
41. Ibid., 4.1.174, 182–89.
42. Ibid., 4.1.282–83.
43. Ibid., 4.1.303–8.
44. Quoted in G.R. Elton, *Policy and Police: The Enforcement of the Reformation in the Age of Thomas Cromwell* (Cambridge, 1972), p. 202.
45. *Julius Caesar*, 4.1.1.
46. Ibid., 1.2.192.
47. Ibid., 2.1.20–21.
48. Johnson, "Preface to Shakespeare", p. 494.
49. Coleridge, *Lectures* 1:455.
50. Plato, *Symposium*, trans. W. Hamilton (London, 1951), pp. 113–14.
51. *Troilus and Cressida*, 5.8.5.
52. *Hamlet*, 2.2.524–25.
53. See Aristotle, *Poetics*, chap. 14.
54. *Hamlet*, 1.3.39–40.
55. Ibid., 2.2.308.
56. Ibid., 3.1.121–22.
57. Ibid., 3.1.78.
58. Ibid., 1.4.65–67.
59. Ibid., 5.2.6–11.
60. Ibid., 5.2.68–70.
61. Ibid., 5.2.215–18.
62. *Troilus and Cressida*, 2.2.53–56.
63. Ibid., 2.2.52.
64. Ibid., 1.3.109–24.

65. Bloom, *Closing of the American Mind*, p. 160.
66. *Troilus and Cressida*, 3.3.174.
67. *Henry IV, Part I*, 5.4.67–78.
68. *Measure for Measure*, 1.1.32–35.
69. *Troilus and Cressida*, 3.3.115–20.
70. *Measure for Measure*, 3.1.5–41.
71. Ibid., 4.3.156.
72. Ibid., 2.2.118–23.
73. Ibid., 2.2.73–77.

CHAPTER ELEVEN

SHAKESPEARE II

Othello to *Henry VIII*

As Hamlet dies, Horatio echoes the ancient Latin prayer at the end of the Mass for the Dead: *In paradisum deducant te angeli.... Chorus angelorum te suscipiat* (May the angels lead you into paradise.... May the choir of angels receive you). "Good night, sweet prince," Horatio says, "And flights of angels sing thee to thy rest." [1] Because of the inwardness through which Shakespeare presents Hamlet to us, at any performance faithful to the play the audience loves him as Horatio does, is with him in his bruised sensitivity, with him in his horror at what Gertrude and Claudius have done, and with him in the painful struggle of his intelligence toward an acceptance of the will of God that is not, in the end, won through intelligence but through the submission of his own will. The play pulls the audience into the suffering, and the learning through suffering, of a man exposed to the realities of sin, of justice and of grace; the tragedy has its origin in the failure of love, for husband, for brother, in Gertrude and in Claudius. Among the consequences of their failure is Hamlet's own failure in love for Ophelia.

In the three years, 1604–1606, that followed *Measure for Measure*, Shakespeare wrote the three further tragedies that stand with *Hamlet*, and then *Antony and Cleopatra*, the greatest of his history plays. *Othello*, *King Lear* and *Macbeth* are, as I have suggested, easier than *Hamlet* to fit into the tragic pattern set by Aeschylus and Sophocles and, after their deaths, described by Aristotle. Of the Greek model and Aristotle's description of it, Shakespeare almost certainly knew nothing; the influence of Seneca's grisly Latin tragedies and their English imitators Shakespeare left behind with *Titus Andronicus*. While Othello, Lear and Macbeth, unlike Hamlet, do, in Aristotle's phrase, "fall from prosperity into misery ... because of some great error" [2] of their own, each has to learn, as Hamlet does, truth that only suffering can teach, and each, as a character, differs from the others as much as all three differ from Hamlet. What they share, for all the particularities of their stories, is failure in love. "If you want to know the nature of a man's love," Augustine wrote, "see where it leads." [3]

For *Othello*, Shakespeare temporarily abandoned kings and dukes, those responsible for the worldly order of their own societies, and chose instead the story of an outsider. Othello is a grand outsider, a Moorish general hired by the wealthy, venerable republic of Venice, which always hired outsiders to fight its wars, in this case to protect its eastern Mediterranean empire against the Turks. So, although Othello is a mere employee, however much needed, in Venice, and is himself a convert, presumably from Islam, to Christianity, he is also a champion of Christian Europe, to which the Muslim Ottomans were a distant threat throughout Shakespeare's lifetime. We learn much about him very early in the play. He has ancestors, "men of royal siege",[4] of whom he is assertively proud; but he has been a soldier since boyhood and is a solitary, "an extravagant and wheeling stranger / Of here and everywhere",[5] in the words of an envious Venetian who despises him. As the play opens, he has his "unhoused free condition / Put into circumscription and confine",[6] his own words, by marrying, without her father's permission, Desdemona, the daughter of a haughty Venetian patrician who has treated him as an honoured guest.

This is the originating deed of the tragedy; it is important that it strike the audience as more an error than a sin. Daughters, everywhere in Shakespeare, should not marry without their fathers' blessing. As soon as they are married, however, their first loyalty is to their husbands. Desdemona, brought up according to these conventions, follows them exactly in her faithful love for Othello; as she dies, she says truthfully, "A guiltless death I die", and then, to Emilia's question, "Who hath done this deed?" she replies in loyalty to her husband who has killed her, and perhaps also in loyalty to her father, "Nobody. I myself."[7] The language of the play reminds us constantly that Othello, a mercenary soldier, an African, has stolen from Venice, city of treasure and gleaming white marble, a girl who is a jewel belonging to her father and to Venice. On the other hand, we see him, horrifyingly, fail to trust a trustworthy woman whom he has yet to learn to know. She was, he tells the Duke and Senators of the city, dazzled by his exotic glamour and by his thrilling account of his adventures:

> She loved me for the dangers I had passed
> And I loved her that she did pity them.[8]

His telling of this story is enough to mollify the authorities who need him to sail away to defend Cyprus, but not enough to calm the fury of Desdemona's father, who sees the couple off with the heavily laden line: "She has deceived her father, and may thee", to which Othello replies in five words: "My life upon her faith."[9] Though her faith, her fidelity to him, does not falter, his lack of trust, of faith, in her kills them both.

The exchange is overheard by Iago, who constructs from it at once the outline of his devilish—not too strong a word—plot that destroys Othello in the remaining four acts of the play, crucially piercing Othello's confidence in Desdemona with the deadly echo: "She did deceive her father, marrying you."[10] Iago is another solitary, another professional soldier, who has served Othello for years, but in his own selfish interests, and who has just been passed over for promotion in favour of Cassio, a young officer whom he intends also to destroy. A relativist, an opportunist, a merciless controller of others more gullible (Othello, Cassio) or more innocent (Desdemona) than himself, he is a moral nihilist— "Virtue? a fig! 'tis in ourselves that we are thus or thus"[11]—who loves nothing and no one but himself and who traduces a relationship, that between master and servant, which Shakespeare values almost as highly as a blood tie. It is painful to watch Iago using, in successful pursuit of purely destructive power, the vulnerabilities inherent in Othello's position, his awe of Venetian sophistication, his new pride in the conquest of a woman, his emotional inexperience. Even more painful to watch is Iago's manipulation of the best qualities of each of his victims, Desdemona's loving, guileless assumption of the role of a young wife, Cassio's courtesy and shame after Iago has got him drunk, and Othello's trust in his long-depended-on ensign, "honest, honest Iago". Cynical exploitation of emotional candour, of love, loyalty and truth, could not be more cleverly, or more cruelly, managed.

When chaos—"when I love thee not, chaos is come again"[12]—has overwhelmed Othello and he has nothing left, his soldier's life and his self-respect destroyed, his faithful Desdemona murdered by him in her bridal bed, he discovers Iago's "envy and calumny" and his own shattering error. He looks at his dead wife and sees the pair of them at the Last Judgement:

> When we shall meet at compt
> This look of thine will hurl my soul from heaven
> And fiends will snatch at it.[13]

In his final speech, his hand already on the hidden dagger with which he will kill himself—the bystanders have disarmed him twice—he puts together, for the report they will write to Venice, no less than the truth: his service to the republic, his rash love, his "wrought" jealousy and, at the heart of it all, the distance of the foreigner who never, in his shyness of her Venetian rarity, understood Desdemona's goodness and faithfulness: "Then must you speak", he says,

> of one whose hand,
> Like the base Indian, threw a pearl away
> Richer than all his tribe;

and he kills himself as

> in Aleppo once,
> Where a malignant and a turbanned Turk
> Beat a Venetian and traduced the state,
> I took by th' throat the circumcised dog
> And smote him—thus![14]

Although distinguished critics have tried to reduce his speech to mere self-justification, this is a noble death. It will strike the audience as noble, and Othello's fate will reach them as genuinely a tragic one, only if he has been played as the commanding soldier, experienced in war, inexperienced in love, that Shakespeare has written him to be and only if the full complexity with which Shakespeare has drawn his relation to Venice is grasped.

Venice needed but despised Shylock: money-lending was all a Jew was traditionally allowed to contribute to Christian society, but the service was vital to the merchant adventurers of a capitalist empire. Shakespeare understood, imagined (the words have the same force), Shylock's misery and hatred so thoroughly that he allows him, as we have seen, to break out of the conventions of romantic comedy that *The Merchant of Venice* mostly observes. It is easier to despise money, however much needed, than it is to despise military prowess. Othello is honoured in Venice until he marries Desdemona; even then only her father, his rage against the alien fuelled by Iago's reductive descriptions, just as Othello's jealousy will be, despises him as a primitive who must have magic powers. Iago, however, who drives the whole tragedy, despises Othello not because he is black but because he is good, openhearted, easily deceived. It should not need saying but, in the politically correct confusion of our time, does need saying that in both Shakespeare's Venetian plays the stance is wholly Christian. Shylock is who he is because he is treated with scorn. The play condemns the scorn by conveying to the audience's understanding, imagination, what it is like to be treated as Shylock is treated. Othello, in the much greater Venetian play, is destroyed by the scorn of

Iago, who, like Richard III and all Shakespeare's wicked characters, is a power-hungry individualist: that the will to power is a private intoxication Shakespeare understood exactly as Augustine had.

Power in human relationships is the contrary of love and redescribes "that you call love", in Iago's words, as "a lust of the blood and a permission of the will",[15] despising altogether the lasting obligations of love of every kind that bind human beings to one another. Power (self-affirmation, assertiveness and self-fulfilment) instead of love, "love" no more than the passing sexual impulse: all this has a familiar contemporary ring. Alasdair MacIntyre describes the shambles of late twentieth-century ethics in terms that fit Iago well:

> Each of us is taught to see himself or herself as an autonomous moral agent.... Seeking to protect the autonomy that we have learned to prize, we aspire ourselves *not* to be manipulated by others; seeking to incarnate our own principles and stand-point in the world of practice, we find no way open to us to do so except by directing towards others those very manipulative modes of relationship which each of us aspires to resist in our own way.[16]

To manipulate others, we must first despise them. Coleridge said: "Shakespeare never puts habitual scorn into the mouths of other than bad men."[17] The clash of contempt with love, trust, goodness and simplicity is deep in Shakespeare's work. Hamlet, casually firing off instructions to the players at Elsinore, famously says that "the purpose of playing" is "to hold as 'twere the mirror up to nature," and adds, "to show virtue her feature, *scorn* her own image"[18] (my italics). To think that the force of the first phrase neutralizes or cancels the force of the second is to misunderstand not only Hamlet but the whole of Shakespeare.

Immediately after *Othello*, he wrote *King Lear*, his greatest tragedy and a play in which the collision of power with love, of scorn with virtue, is worked through with new and profound complexity. Both *Hamlet* and *Othello* are set in explicitly Christian worlds. Hamlet lives in Protestant Denmark and is a student at Luther's own university, but an unabsolved soul comes from Purgatory to tell him what he must do. Othello's own Christianity makes his treatment at the hands of a fellow Christian all the more horrifying. *King Lear* is set (rather vaguely: there are earls in the cast, a King of France and a Duke of Burgundy, and Gloucester wears spectacles) in the mists of pre-Christian Britain. Much in *Lear* is developed from what Shakespeare had already written: a king who has to learn, but now from the depths of madness and grief, the familiar lesson that a king is no more than a man; the story, as in *Hamlet*, of two families, two sets of fathers and children; the murderous envy of one brother for another, which Augustine, on account of Cain and Abel, called "an archetype";[19] varieties of fidelity to the master-servant bond—all these borrow from and deepen elements in earlier plays. But *Lear*, like each of Shakespeare's plays, is its own world of character and language, and also ours. And *Lear's* setting in a distant pagan time does not remove it from Shakespeare's constant Christian context.

In this fallen world of darkness lit by grace, fathers and their children, masters and their servants, suffer and inflict suffering, reveal and are healed by loyalty and forgiveness, and recognise blindness in the light of understanding. All the misery in the play is caused by failure in love. Two old men fail at the outset in love for one of their children. Lear's failure is acute, a single fit of thwarted wilfulness. His carefully prepared display of generous resignation is spoiled because his youngest, most loved daughter will not lie to him as her elder sisters do. Enraged by Cordelia's Desdemona-like truth—"Sure I shall never marry like my sisters / To love my father all"[20]—he furiously casts her out, dowerless, to a foreign king who marries her for her truth rather than for her wealth. The original failure of love in the play's other father, Gloucester, is chronic: the audience observes, in a swift opening scene of thirty lines, the lasting humiliation and rejection of his illegitimate son. Edmund's response is the opposite to Cordelia's: instead of her faithfulness to the bond that holds her to her father, however badly he has treated her, Edmund sets himself to pursue power and wealth in a world he perceives, with the Machiavellian vision of the "new man", as a jungle of competitive self-interest. Without difficulty he persuades, with clever lies and Iago-like contempt for both his victims, his gullible father to turn against Edmund's innocent and equally gullible legitimate brother, Edgar, soon cast out with a price on his head. Later, Edmund devises the sadistic blinding of his father. Iago-like contempt for their father and sister also drives the bullying cruelty of Lear's elder daughters. We watch them reduce him to madness and drive him out into a night of storm and dereliction.

Nevertheless, in the very depths of loss, of brokenness from the ties of blood that should hold them in safety, Lear and Gloucester—the latter at a lesser depth of agony and of understanding—discover both truth and love. Lear, the old king long accustomed to power and "ceremony", now deprived even of shelter, prays to and for the poorest of the poor, neglected by him:

> Poor naked wretches, whereso'er you are,
> That bide the pelting of this pitiless storm,

> How shall your houseless heads and unfed sides,
> Your loop'd and window'd raggedness, defend you
> From seasons such as these? O! I have ta'en
> Too little care of this.[21]

Immediately he is confronted by Edgar, disguised as a mad beggar, and Lear's response, his wits now crazed, is to tear off his clothes, symbol in his mind and ours of the "little, brief authority" in which he has been "dressed":

> Unaccommodated man is no more but such a poor, bare, forked animal as thou art. Off, off, you lendings! Come, unbutton here.[22]

Later, the blinded Gloucester, with the sententiousness that always keeps him at a little distance from the anguish with which the audience suffers with Lear, echoes his perception:

> I stumbled when I saw. Full oft 'tis seen,
> Our means secure us, and our mere defects
> Prove our commodities....
> ....
>   Heavens, deal so still!
> Let the superfluous and lust-dieted man,
> That slaves your ordinance, that will not see
> Because he does not feel, feel your power quickly;
> So distribution should undo excess
> And each man have enough.[23]

The power of God to cleanse the eyes of the heart through suffering—the power that presides over all tragedy—is most evident in what many have thought to be the greatest scene in Shakespeare, the meeting of the two old men, one out of his "proper mind", the other blind, alone but for a single observer, Edgar, representing us all as the chorus does in a Greek tragedy. In a hundred lines, Lear, with a truthfulness and a soundness of judgement that are mad only in the flailing force of their expression, excoriates the lust that was Gloucester's sin in the careless begetting of Edmund and the injustice of carelessly exercised authority that was his own. The old men recognise each other; the warmth between them is their common suffering of the fallenness of a sinful world and of the consequences of their own sins: "Are you there with me?" Lear says to Gloucester. "A man may see how this world goes with no eyes." And later:

> If thou wilt weep my fortunes, take my eyes;
> I know thee well enough; thy name is Gloucester;
> Thou must be patient; we came crying hither.[24]

The darkness of the play—the cruelty with which both Lear and Gloucester are treated is almost unbearable to watch—is lit not only by truth but by goodness. Two loving children, Cordelia and Edgar, faithful to the ties their fathers have tried to sever, care for their fathers with unconditional forgiveness before they have seen in them any sign of penitence or self-knowledge. Edgar with a trick of stunning theatricality persuades Gloucester against suicide. Cordelia watches, gentle and reproachless, beside Lear as he wakes from madness. As Othello imagines Desdemona "at compt", Lear sees his wronged daughter:

> Thou art a soul in bliss; but I am bound
> Upon a wheel of fire, that mine own tears
> Do scald like molten lead.[25]

After the army of Edmund and Lear's cruel daughters has won the worldly, but not the transcendent, battle of the play, Lear, in the harmony of truth and goodness that is his mended love for Cordelia, is happy to go with her to prison, where "we'll live / And pray, and sing, and tell old tales, and laugh" at the competitiveness of the powerful,

> Who loses and who wins; who's in, who's out;
> And take upon's the mystery of things,
> As if we were God's spies.[26]

Editors print the apostrophe in "God's" after the *s* "since Shakespeare was writing of a pagan world".[27] Any audience anywhere will hear the noun as singular. Lear adds, with a definite plural:

> Upon such sacrifices, my Cordelia,
> The Gods themselves throw incense.

Editors disagree over the force of "sacrifices". There is a sentence in the *City of God* that may just possibly have lodged in Shakespeare's mind. He was in any case demonstrating its truth. "The true sacrifices are acts of compassion, whether towards ourselves or towards our neighbours, when they are directed towards God; and acts of compassion are intended to free us from misery and so to bring us to happiness." [28] The happiness, the lightheartedness of Lear on his way to prison with Cordelia was well described by Schopenhauer in typically combative form:

> The tragic heroes of the ancients show resolute and stoical subjection under the unavoidable blows of fate; Christian tragedy, on the other hand, shows the giving up of the whole will-to-live, cheerful (*freudiges*) abandonment of the world in the consciousness of its worthlessness and vanity. I am fully of the opinion that the tragedy of the moderns is at a higher level than that of the ancients. Shakespeare is much greater than Sophocles. [29]

These scenes are the first of several reconciliations between fathers and daughters in Shakespeare's later plays.

Interwoven in *Lear* with the faithful love of children for their fathers is the faithful love of servants for their masters. Lear's truth-telling Fool stays with him until the disturbance of the old king's mind begins to throw up its own truth; then the Fool vanishes from the play to be confused by Lear, at the very end, with the hanged Cordelia. Gloucester himself risks his life and loses his eyes by going out to help the cast-out Lear: "If I die for it, as no less is threatened me, the king, my old master, must be relieved." [30] The courage and loyalty of nameless servants recur in the play. One tries to save, from his own master, Gloucester's eyes and is killed for his pains. Others bandage Gloucester's bleeding sockets and bring, at great risk, clothes for the beggar Edgar. Above all, the Earl of Kent, banished by Lear at the outset for defending Cordelia, returns at once as an ordinary servant, enjoying the liberation of his disguise, to look after his old master. He is never recognised by Lear, but his goodness is a constant light in the play. Coleridge wrote of him: 'Kent is, perhaps, the nearest to perfect goodness in all Shakespeare's characters, and yet the most individualized. . . . [V]irtue itself seems to be in company with him." [31] Balthasar was not referring to Kent, or to this play in particular, when he wrote (and the bearing on *Lear* is obvious):

> [Shakespeare] knows the dimensions of the realm of evil. For he has an infallible grasp of what constitutes right action. It can be "ethical", or

can translate the ethical into a sphere where, behind the moral squalor, the good heart shines through.... The action never lacks orientation. In accordance with the Christian principle of forgiving mercy, the dramatist causes the Good to predominate without feeling it necessary to reduce the totality of world events to some all-embracing formula.... But all the time he is utterly certain that the highest good is to be found in forgiveness.[32]

Kent's resolution in telling Lear the truth, and then in not abandoning him, shines all the brighter for the contrast between him and Goneril's time-serving steward, of whom Kent says, in words that summarize the bond-breaking evil of the play:

> Such smiling rogues as these,
> Like rats, oft bite the holy cords a-twain
> Which are too intrince t'unloose.[33]

Among the many bitten cords in the play are the marriage ties of both of Lear's elder daughters, who fight to the death, like rats in a sack, in their lust for Edmund. Their deaths, and Edmund's, which is a little nobler, are no more than reported incidents in the long last scene of *Lear*, which takes the audience through an emotional switchback of pathos, fear, satisfaction, horror and sadness. It begins in the blessedness of Lear and Cordelia's departure for prison, contains Edgar's return as a champion of rectitude and his account of his father's death " 'twixt two extremes of passion, joy and grief"[34] at being told Edgar's story, and is interrupted by the shock of Lear's appearance carrying in his arms the dead Cordelia, hanged on Edmund's orders. Lear's own death, prefigured in the account of Gloucester's, ends the play. As Lear dies, Kent begs Edgar to let the old king go in peace:

> Vex not his ghost: O! let him pass; he hates him
> That would upon the rack of this tough world
> Stretch him out longer.[35]

Only if the play's "orientation", its Christian context of meaning and value, held in God's eternity, is felt as absent rather than present can the deaths of Cordelia and Lear be thought to cancel the goodness and truth won through suffering, the human love that manifests the love of God, that *Lear* has presented. As Balthasar wrote about the plays of Aeschylus and Sophocles:

> However great the tragedy, it takes place before the face of God. . . .
> The hero's ethos is "to bear well . . . what is laid upon him". In the
> tragedies the suffering man is lifted up like a monstrance and shown to
> the gods who, though invisible, are watching.[36]

The quotation is from *Oedipus at Colonus*, in which another old king, confused and made angry by suffering, is helped toward a blessed death by his devoted daughter. "Though invisible": the Olympian gods do not appear in the Oedipus plays; the people on the stage are particularized human beings just as Shakespeare's characters are. The Greek gods of course are often referred to, appear in the *Eumenides* and reflect to the characters and their audience the divine justice that sustains the dramas. But Oedipus and Antigone, Agamemnon, Clytemnestra and Orestes are in these plays no more "mythological" than Hamlet, Othello or Lear. As Balthasar says:

> In common with Christian drama [Greek tragedy] portrays the fate of
> individuals who fill the whole picture; no generalization is admitted.
> Neither Orestes nor Oedipus is a particular type of man; it would be
> simply a mistake to say that they stand for "man as such"; they are just
> themselves.[37]

Had Christian thinkers been aware of Athenian tragedy when the mythical gods of Olympus had vanished in the light of Christian revelation, they might have noticed the closeness to God's unmythological truth of some of the plays of Aeschylus and Sophocles. When the plays became known again, however, they were mostly read with post- or anti-Christian assumptions.

Many modern commentators, certain that God is dead and therefore has never been alive, respond to the evident power of great tragedy, both Greek and Shakespearean, with inevitable confusion. Highly intelligent books on these plays founder on the authors' conviction that death, in a world of mere time, merely human attempts at meaning, annuls goodness, love and truth. Adrian Poole in his *Tragedy*, for example, says of *Lear*:

> No cords are "too intrinse to unloose". . . . Tragedy affirms the ruthless
> truth that hearts must break, that the cords that bind people to each
> other and that hold the heart together must all in time fail.[38]

The book begins with the strong Nietzschean statement:

> Tragedy affirms with savage jubilation that man's state is diverse, fluid
> and unfounded. Tragedy diversifies man's universe, severing the cer-
> tainties that seem to bind human beings together, to make men and
> women at one with each other, with themselves, with their world.[39]

And this is Poole's conclusion, already quoted in relation to Greek tragedy:

> Tragedy embodies our most paradoxical feelings and thoughts and beliefs.
> It gives them flesh and blood, emotional and intellectual and spiritual
> substance. Through tragedy we recognise and refeel our sense of both
> the value and the futility of human life, of both its purposes and its
> emptiness.[40]

Read in relation to *Lear*, this is an admission that death cancels goodness, that
futility cancels loyalty and love and that emptiness engulfs all human purposes.

Nietzsche's religious despair, the result of his deep religious instincts combined with his rejection of Christianity, underlies much contemporary confusion
about tragedy. He knew tragedy to be connected to religion. Tragedy could not
be Christian on account of the falseness of Christianity. Therefore tragedy could
be only pre-Christian and could be religious only in Dionysiac abandon to passion and death. Therefore Shakespeare could not have written tragedy. This logic
persists with remarkable strength. It supports George Steiner's denial, in *The
Death of Tragedy*, that Christian tragedy can exist: Christianity is optimistic, its
promise of eternal meaning transcending death; tragedy is pessimistic because, in
it, death prevails; therefore Christian tragedy is impossible. "There has been no
specifically Christian mode of tragic drama. . . . Christianity is an anti-tragic vision
of the world."[41] Steiner knows that Shakespeare wrote tragedies. If they are
tragedies, they cannot, by definition, be Christian. *The Death of Tragedy* was
written decades ago, but Steiner has continued in book after book to worry the
issue. In 1984 he contrasts Greek tragedy, in which, because of its mythical relation to the Olympian gods, "the element of transcendence is of the essence",
with "the Shakespeare world", which

> is impartial, perhaps indifferent in regard to God. . . . Shakespeare . . .
> did not draw on myth. Some marvellous intuition kept him from doing
> so. His pluralism and liberality, his tragi-comic bias, his attention to the

child in man, refuse any unification of reality and with it the intolerant immensity of the mythical moment. The *Oresteia, Oedipus Rex, Antigone* ... lie outside Shakespeare's kaleidoscopic, *secular* humanity.[42]

This can be said only if Christian revelation is regarded as myth, another myth. If it is regarded as true, then it was no "marvellous intuition" that kept Shakespeare from drawing on myth, but the fact that Christian truth, without the need for myth, supplies in Shakespeare the context of transcendent meaning that dissolves the distinction between the sacred and the secular. Only if this distinction is insisted on can Shakespeare be said to give us no more than the "observant neutrality" [43] attributed to him in Steiner's recent book *Grammars of Creation*, in which he is in any case more interested, anachronistically, in what Shakespeare thought he was doing than in what he did.

If death does not annul goodness, truth and love, then the tragedy of *King Lear* returns to intelligibility. This is particularly the case at its ending, where the "unaccommodated" bareness of an old man's dying—"Cordelia, Cordelia! stay a little. Ha! ... Mine eyes are not o' th' best: I'll tell you straight.... Pray you, undo this button: thank you, Sir" [44]—keeps cutting across the aspirations to justice, to an "all-embracing formula", in Balthasar's phrase, of the onlookers. The bland Albany says,

> All friends shall taste
> The wages of their virtue, and all foes
> The cup of their deservings.[45]

But death deprives him, and all human beings, however well-intentioned, of the possibility of arranging such justice on earth. Justice belongs only to God, in a judgement beyond our knowledge but where the loving forgiveness between Cordelia and Lear, Kent and Lear, and Edgar and Gloucester has its eternal value. Shakespeare knew this. It was not necessary for him to have a character say it.

* * *

The central tragic relation is that between the hero's soul and God. The drama allows—compels—the audience to see this relation from, as it were, both sides, to watch the hero brought to a truth, a belonging to God, which the audience knows before the hero does. This is the case with Oedipus, Creon, Orestes,

Hamlet, Othello and Lear. It is again the case in the fourth of Shakespeare's great tragedies, *Macbeth*.

The play was written in the jittery year 1606, which followed the discovery of the Gunpowder Plot, a long-hatched Catholic conspiracy to blow up King James and his Parliament. Shakespeare may well have known some of the conspirators, several of whom were distantly related to his mother's recusant family. One can easily imagine the horror felt among law-abiding Catholics at the scale of the terrorist outrage planned by the plotters and at the likely consequences for Catholic life in England. Guy Fawkes, the representative villain of the Plot, has been burned in effigy on the anniversary of the plot's discovery in every town and village in England ever since. Harmless priests, when caught, were martyred in England for another eighty years, though less frequently than in Elizabeth's reign, and every English disaster was blamed on Catholics. The London monument to the Great Fire of 1666 bore until 1830 the baseless inscription, "begun and carried on by the treachery and malice of the popish faction". *Macbeth* puts the greatest possible distance between its author and any idea that treason might be acceptable. It flatters the king by its setting in pre-Reformation Christian Scotland, by presenting witches on stage—James I had written a book called *Demonologie* in 1597—and by contrasting a virtuous Scottish king, an unseen virtuous English king and a virtuous if legendary ancestor of the Stuarts (Banquo) with the traitor and murderer who is the play's tragic hero.

What is new in *Macbeth* is that we watch the hero's soul at war with itself before the play's original sin, the murder of King Duncan, is committed. In the earlier tragedies *Hamlet* and *Othello*, while sinfulness is already present, the actual error from which tragedy flows precedes the opening, and Lear's sin is the momentary impulse of an arrogant old man. In all three plays the audience is ahead of the hero in judgement, perceiving the journey of suffering toward knowledge that has to be undertaken from the injury of a youthful intellectual, from a fragile marriage, from elderly blind stubbornness. Macbeth, by contrast, is a fully competent moral agent, an ambitious man tempted by the devil (the witches' prophecy) to a deed his informed Christian conscience understands accurately while it is yet no more than a temptation. He knows exactly what treacherous murder is and decides, in the soliloquy that begins by connecting himself to Judas—"That thou doest, do quickly"[46] is echoed in his "If it were done, when 'tis done, then 'twere well / It were done quickly"[47]—not to commit it. His reasoning is at first Machiavellian: he would "jump the life to come",[48] but that murder will breed murder (as Bolingbroke's rebellion bred rebellion). He moves at once, however, into recognition of the bonds that hold him to Duncan, who is his king (master), his kinsman and his guest, and just such a king as Shake-speare has always held to be good, and the recognition takes him into full Christ-ian terror of the judgement of God, of, precisely, the consequences of the deed in truth, in eternity, in "the life to come":

> Besides, this Duncan
> Hath borne his faculties so meek, hath been
> So clear in his great office, that his virtues
> Will plead like angels, trumpet-tongu'd, against
> The deep damnation of his taking-off.[49]

His resolution—"We will proceed no further in this business" [50]—is swiftly dis-mantled by the taunting of his wife, the true Machiavel of the play, who has already, in a chilling villain's soliloquy, committed herself to evil in the interests of power, steeling herself against kindness, pity and also truth:

> That my keen knife see not the wound it makes,
> Nor Heaven peep through the blanket of the dark,
> To cry, "Hold, hold!" [51]

Macbeth kills Duncan and becomes king. Shakespeare compresses into three simple words, "the innocent sleep", both his old contrast between the peace of guiltless sleep and the guilty wakefulness of a king, and the goodness of Mac-beth's sleeping victim, Duncan:

> Methought I heard a voice cry, "Sleep no more!
> Macbeth does murder sleep"—the innocent sleep.[52]

Macbeth's suffering in the rest of the play, as he orders, now removed by power from actual killing, the murder of more and more people who threaten his power, is the suffering of the knowledge of the truth of what he has done, is doing and will do. Lady Macbeth resists this knowledge, with a prophecy that will come true only for her:

> These deeds must not be thought
> After these ways: so, it will make us mad.[53]

Macbeth does not go mad, but he arrives at a barren meaninglessness that is the hell he knows he has chosen. He knows it at once. Pretending to be surprised at the discovery of the slaughtered Duncan, he says, truthfully, with the agonised hindsight of one whose sin is irreparable:

> Had I but died an hour before this chance,
> I had liv'd a blessed time; for, from this instant,
> There's nothing serious in mortality.[54]

All the promises of the devil are hollow, "th' equivocation of the fiend";[55] he feels nothing at Lady Macbeth's suicide; only the return of his soldier's courage as he faces death at the hands of Macduff, whose entire family he has killed, is a ray of light in the darkness into which the audience has accompanied Macbeth throughout the play.

The moral bearings in *Macbeth* are absolutely secure and ordinarily Christian. "Nature" in this play is the nature of God's creation, beautiful and reassuring in the "temple-haunting martlet" with its "procreant cradle";[56] terrifyingly rejected in Lady Macbeth's stopping-up of the "compunctious visitings of Nature";[57] and terrifyingly upset in the chorus passage that records what happened in the natural world on the night of Duncan's murder. Nowhere in this play does anyone invoke, as Edmund does in *Lear*, the "new" nature of the competitive jungle, but the contrast between the two concepts of nature, one guaranteeing and requiring love, the other sanctioning remorseless pursuit of power, is nevertheless always present.

In the same year as *Macbeth*, Shakespeare, as if, like his murderous thane, he had "supp'd full with horrors",[58] returned to Plutarch's Rome, his source for *Julius Caesar* years before, and found himself a hero who loses the world but not his own soul. *Antony and Cleopatra* is a uniquely exhilarating play, its scope the widest Shakespeare ever encompassed, its freedom, vitality and richness unparalleled anywhere in his work. The sense of liberation from the smothering "blanket of the dark" that spread over Macbeth's mind, Macbeth's Scotland, is unmistakable. Antony and Cleopatra are free spirits on the grandest scale, and the play takes the audience through ten years of crowded history and across the map of the Mediterranean from Rome to Sicily to Syria, from Athens to Actium to Alexandria, with an unerring confidence and an attention to detail that even Shakespeare never matched.

Every educated person brought up on Virgil and in the Christian tradition knew in Shakespeare's time that the tremendous collision between Antony and

Octavius Caesar, the victors of Philippi after Julius Caesar's murder, was a turning point—even *the* turning point—in the history of civilisation. Octavius's triumph over Antony at Actium left Octavius undisputed master of the Roman world, inaugurated the empire on the ruins of the republic that had been wrecked in a century of civil war, and established the peace into which Christ was born thirty years later. The victory was not merely the overcoming of one ambitious man by another. It was the victory of Rome itself over the sinister decadence of Hellenism; the victory of law and justice and proper administration (the census that summoned Joseph and Mary to Bethlehem; the citizenship that made possible Saint Paul's appeal to Rome) over the arbitrary cruelties of oriental despotism; the eventual victory of Christian truth over magic, myth and ritual; and the victory of West over East. Most of these implications are there in Virgil's fifty-line description of Actium at the very centre of Aeneas's shield;[59] the rest were added in the Christian future. The dangerously complacent echoes of some of them have not yet faded.

All this was in Shakespeare's bones. Yet Octavius Caesar, who would become Augustus, Virgil's patron and therefore the unblemished hero of Virgil's fifty lines, the foretold consummation of all Aeneas's pain and effort, is no hero in Shakespeare's play. Caesar wins, of course. But he is a cold, a *scornful*, Machiavel on lines familiar from earlier plays who gathers to himself the weight of support necessary to succeed, not because he is a better soldier or a more attractive leader than Antony—he is neither—but because Antony's loss of grip on ambition and Caesar's rising "fortune" show enough people that Caesar will be the victor. The scales tip in his favour, as they tipped for Bolingbroke against Richard II, but in this play the whole world is in the balance. With swift economy Shakespeare touches in, throughout the play, the contrasting characters of his two contenders. In the riotous party on Sextus Pompey's galley, where the three masters of the world—Antony, Caesar and the soon to be disposed of Lepidus—have no idea that they have narrowly escaped death at Pompey's hands, Caesar alone remains primly sober. Heartless calculation marks his treatment of everyone from his sister Octavia to deserters from Antony's army, cruelly placed at the front of his own battle line "that Antony may seem to spend his fury / Upon himself".[60] From two lines of perfect simplicity after Antony's death, the audience realises that Caesar cannot distinguish Cleopatra from her women, nor she him from his entourage:

CAESAR.   Which is the queen of Egypt?
DOLABELLA.   It is the emperor, madam. (*Cleopatra kneels.*)[61]

Nobody ever fails to recognise Antony, who marries Octavia to hold the world together and abandons her to return to the irresistible Cleopatra but treats his gentle wife with kindness and courtesy. And when Enobarbus, his fellow soldier and servant of many years, after a struggle with his conscience deserts Antony for the rising man, his master sends his forgiveness and his treasure after him: Enobarbus dies of a broken heart. Enobarbus is to Antony as Kent is to Lear, the truth-telling right-hand man Othello takes Iago to be.

Shakespeare's old preoccupations, with power and how it shifts, with reputation and opinion, from one man to another, with personal priorities—"Everyone loves. The question is, what does he love?"[62]—as the motives of human life, with the master-servant bond, depended on or broken for good or ill, receive fresh, vivid treatment in this play. Enobarbus fearlessly gives his master sound advice that his master does not take. Enobarbus deserts for sensible (Machiavellian) reasons, but his love for Antony kills him, and the argument for loyalty that he makes and then fails to act on has a resonance that is, like so much in *Lear*, Christian in all but explicit reference:

> Mine honesty and I begin to square.
> The loyalty well held to fools does make
> Our faith mere folly: yet he that can endure
> To follow with allegiance a fallen lord
> Does conquer him that did his master conquer
> And earns a place in the story.[63]

"Honesty" here is its real self, the obverse of what Othello trusts in Iago, while the "I" with which it fights is the "I" of self-interest.

But the primary drive of the play is something Shakespeare gives us nowhere else: the passionate, reciprocated love of two grown-up people. That Antony, as an emperor, has gone to pieces over his love for Cleopatra is evident from the first words of the play:

> Nay, but this dotage of our general's
> O'erflows the measure.[64]

This is a Roman soldier's thoroughly Roman remark. In Cleopatra's Egypt, emotion, luxury, alcohol, the Nile and sexuality all "o'erflow", blur, melt and "discandy" the Roman austerity, control and efficiency that brought Antony military glory. Antony knows this perfectly well and to the end has "Roman" moments in which he pulls himself together and attempts to halt the slide of his life into dissolution and defeat. He fails, on account of Cleopatra's hold over him, which Enobarbus, whose description of her is the play's most famous passage, both rues and well understands. Antony's largeness of soul, the openhearted generosity with which he treats the meanest bringer of bad news, survives, in the audience's eyes, the collapse of his military judgement, his drunkenness on Pompey's boat, the undignified foolery he indulges in with Cleopatra, the ease with which he reduces his followers to tears, his botched suicide and the near-farce of his being hauled up to her monument to die. His self-understanding and self-deprecation develop movingly throughout the play. Only the sight of Cleopatra flirting with an ambassador sent by Caesar brings his behaviour down to her level: the rage with which he orders the ambassador flogged is shocking because it is out of character. And Cleopatra, who pulls a knife on the messenger telling her of Antony's marriage to Octavia, who deploys her wit, her intelligence, her capacity to play a part, her overwhelming sexuality, to sustain Antony's passion for her at the expense of his power over the whole world, the audience forgives as Antony does, forgiving at last even her sending him the false news of her death.

Shakespeare's imaginative understanding of power is equalled only by his imaginative understanding of sexuality. The joys and sorrows of adolescent love, its muddles, dreams and romantic suddenness, are everywhere in his comedies and in *Romeo and Juliet* and happily unconfused in the loves of Perdita and Miranda in his late plays. Adult use of sexuality in the pursuit of power is sickening in Claudius's hold over Gertrude, worse than sickening in Iago's corruption of Othello's passion for Desdemona, carelessly helpful to Edmund's ambition, and the means by which Lady Macbeth compels her husband to act against his conscience. In *The Winter's Tale* we watch the long security of a faithful marriage poisoned by a jealousy much less forgivable than Othello's. In *Antony and Cleopatra* the pursuit of power, Caesar's, is sexless, emotionless, pitiless and above all, successful, whereas reckless love brings "the old ruffian",[65] Caesar's contemptuous phrase for Antony, to the loss of the worldly battle, but has an otherworldly quality, evident most of all in Cleopatra's death, beside which power dwindles to mere politics—"who's in, who's out", in Lear's words. Shakespeare here, writing a real history play from a classical source, is presenting a pre-Christian moral world (as he certainly does not do in *Lear*). Adultery, for example, is not the Christian sin in Antony, married to Fulvia at the outset and married again to Octavia, as it is in every other play where it occurs. And yet as Cleopatra mourns Antony and then uses all her guile, for the last time, to discover Caesar's intention and outwit him in her suicide, there is a won humility, a recognition of

simple human truth, that is familiar in all his heroes, including Antony, who are
capable of learning through suffering:

> No more but e'en a woman, and commanded
> By such poor passion as the maid that milks,
> And does the meanest chares.[66]

The glory of her death has for her the transcendence only of her love for Antony, but for Shakespeare and his audience, familiar with the transcendence that
had not yet been revealed to Cleopatra's time, it takes its place with all human
love, in Cleopatra's case at last simple, truthful and good, in the glory of God.

After the marvels of *Antony and Cleopatra*, Shakespeare stayed with North's
translation of Plutarch's *Lives* for two more plays. *Timon of Athens* is a failed
experiment, combining elements of the old morality-play form with the legend
of the misanthropic ruler of Athens from Plutarch's life of Antony. Shakespeare
seems to have abandoned it unfinished, and the text as it stands is almost unperformable, its only memorable figure Timon himself, a character seen only from
the outside, who, in the second half of the play, is given a few powerful speeches
of bitter, sometimes grotesque, disgust uttered, in his exile in the woods, to
unwelcome visitors. It is as if a character left out of or left over from *Troilus and
Cressida* had survived for years in solitude and never found himself a play, and
Timon's vision of the world as unbridled will is even more savagely Schopenhauerian than that of Ulysses:

> The sun's a thief, and with his great attraction
> Robs the sea; the moon's an arrant thief,
> And her pale fire she snatches from the sun;
> The sea's a thief, whose liquid surge resolves
> The moon into salt tears; the earth's a thief,
> That feeds and breeds by a composture stol'n
> From gen'ral excrement—each thing's a thief.
> The laws, your curb and whip, in their rough power
> Has uncheck'd theft. Love not yourselves; away,
> Rob one another.[67]

Coriolanus, by contrast, is a fully achieved dramatic masterpiece, the most acute
and searching political play Shakespeare wrote, but chilling in its pre-Virgilian,
indeed almost counter-Virgilian, Romanness. In this early Italy of bloodthirsty

warlords, patrician Rome, incarnate in Coriolanus's mother Volumnia, must produce warrior heroes to fight off rival tribes (the Volsci in the play) so that the future should belong to Rome. It must also reach some kind of accommodation with the plebeians of the city so that the body politic—strongly described by Menenius, a canny old patrician, at the outset—should remain united. Coriolanus can do the first outstandingly well but refuses to do the second. His unyielding pride isolates him from everyone except the opposing Volscian general, to whom he is bound in a kind of blood brotherhood of enmity, then friendship and finally the convulsive fury that delivers Coriolanus's grisly death at the play's end.

As an analysis of power, the play has an incisiveness that is compelling in the theatre. Power gained by force, successfully directed violence, is what Coriolanus has been brought up by his mother to achieve. His little boy—his youth established in his single speech in the play: "I'll run away till I am bigger, but then I'll fight" [68]—is being raised in the same spirit: his grandmother rejoices in his tearing butterflies to bits. But power once gained has to be retained by policy, by presentation, dissimulation and currying favour with the people. All this Volumnia, the Machiavel of the play, understands, and all this Coriolanus disdains, not because of its untruthfulness—Volumnia urges him not to *be* mild and understanding with the citizens but to *pretend* mildness and understanding—but because of his contempt for those whose votes he needs. To be elected consul he "begs their voices" with such arrogant revulsion that they turn against their martial hero, but when they banish him he furiously reverses the rejection:

> You common cry of curs! whose breath I hate
> As reek o'th'rotten fens, whose loves I prize
> As the dead carcasses of unburied men
> That do corrupt my air: I banish you![69]

"He is himself alone":[70] the early description, echoing Richard III's "I am myself alone",[71] sounds through the play. "All alone"[72] he vanquished the Volsci; alone he storms out of Rome:

> I go alone,
> Like to a lonely dragon that his fen
> Makes fear'd and talk'd of more than seen;[73]

alone he returns at the head of the Volscian army to burn Rome; alone he resolves to resist the pleading of his mother, wife and child to save the city:

> But out, affection!
> All bond and privilege of nature break!
> . . . .
> I'll never
> Be such a gosling to obey instinct, but stand
> As if a man were author of himself
> And knew no other kin.[74]

The moment has deep Shakespearean roots: the bonds of nature are broken and mended everywhere in his plays, most evidently in *Lear*. Macbeth himself describes Duncan's murder as "a breach in nature for ruin's wasteful entrance". But so cold and manipulative is Volumnia's appeal for Rome that when, after an electric silence, Coriolanus gives in, we feel (as probably she would herself) his yielding to be weakness in the warrior rather than loyalty restored in the son, let alone the citizen. Taunted with this weakness—"Thou boy of tears!"—by the murderous, betrayed Volsci, he boasts, one last time:

> If you have writ your annals true, 'tis there,
> That like an eagle in a dovecote, I
> Flutter'd your Volscians in Corioles,
> Alone I did it. Boy![75]

Coriolanus, like the truncated *Timon* but unlike *Antony and Cleopatra*, has no properly tragic element in it. Coriolanus knows nothing of himself and learns nothing in the course of the play; the audience's judgement of him and of his world, a complex judgement that includes the recognition of the need for unity in any state, is not one that he is capable of catching up with. And neither he nor anyone else, except at one or two moments Menenius, in this bleakly loveless, for once really pagan, play strikes the audience as a soul in the hands of God.

* * *

In four years or so, Shakespeare had written *Othello, Lear, Macbeth, Antony and Cleopatra, Timon* and *Coriolanus*. In his comedies, his tragedies and his histories, he had achieved a matchless authority in the theatre, a mastery and a scope of which he must have been aware. Now, for reasons at which we can only guess, he tried a kind of play that was to him a fresh enterprise. We know that a new sophistication was about in London, that the court masque, with music, architectural sets and special effects of some complexity, was becoming fashionable. We also know that in 1609 Shakespeare's company acquired an indoor theatre, the candlelit panelled hall of the old Blackfriars priory across the Thames from the Globe. We may guess that Shakespeare needed a change, a lightening of atmosphere in his work, a new challenge. We may also guess, from evidence in the last five plays he wrote, or contributed to, that his feelings or his mood had softened in some way, perhaps particularly toward his elder daughter. Susanna Shakespeare was born in 1583, six months after her parents' marriage. Her father was only nineteen. Twins, a boy and a girl, followed in 1585; the boy died at the age of eleven. Shakespeare, busy in London, can have seen little of his children as they grew up in Stratford, or, for many years, of his wife. Of Susanna we know only that she was listed as a recusant in 1606, that shortly afterward she married a respected Protestant doctor and that she was Shakespeare's favourite daughter: he left her almost all his by then considerable property in Stratford. On her tombstone is engraved "Witty above her sexe", "Wise to salvation", and "Something of Shakespeare was in that".

To call Shakespeare's late plays "romances" is not merely to adopt a label attached to them by nineteenth-century critics defeated by the distinctive qualities that prevent their classification as either tragedies or comedies. The romances of the late Middle Ages, rambling prose or verse tales of chivalry, noble love, magic and many adventures, were familiar in Shakespeare's time to everyone who could read. Attempts to turn such tales into plays, a difficult project, had so far been feeble, and Shakespeare, in his first venture in this genre, *Pericles*, built three acts of his own, patchy in dramatic impact, on two weak acts written by someone else. The first scene of the last act, the long, slow recognition of his lost daughter Marina by the old king Pericles, rises far above the rest of the play in pace and feeling, almost as if Shakespeare had taken on the project in order to write this one scene.

The enchantment of a father's recovery of a child, and therefore a personal future, he has thought dead: this is the deep recurring note of Shakespeare's four romances. Cymbeline, in the second of these plays, is reunited in a final scene of almost absurdly efficient plot-unravelling with his lost daughter and his two lost sons. *Cymbeline*, though probably all Shakespeare's work, combines a disparate set of characters, periods, conspiracies and supernatural interventions: the result is more uncertain in tone than any other play he wrote. Its heroine, the old king's daughter Imogen, has a vitality and delightful (though not consistent) individuality that lift her, as if into a comedy from much earlier in Shakespeare's career, above the fairy-story flatness of her father, her dull, good husband and her brothers, and incongruously above the pantomime villainy of an Italian crook, a clodhopping stepbrother and a witch of a mother who is more like Mozart's Queen of the Night than she is like any other of Shakespeare's female characters.

Shakespeare cannot but have realized that neither *Pericles* nor *Cymbeline*, however knowingly put together as sophisticated entertainment, reaches the dramatic coherence that he had for many years been expertly delivering. From the imperfections of these two plays, three problems in particular in the transformation of romance tales into plays must have become clear to him: the problem of time: presenting, for ultimate recognition and reunion between fathers and children, or long-estranged friends, the story of two generations; the problem of motivation: something beyond accident or ludicrous wickedness must drive the disorder that needs resolution at the play's end; and the problem of control: if the playwright is the only author of coincidence, magic, the miraculous return to life of those apparently dead, the atmosphere cannot be other than that of fantasy untethered to the audience's reality.

With *The Winter's Tale* and *The Tempest*, Shakespeare returned to mastery, solving all three problems, differently but triumphantly. *The Winter's Tale* is boldly cut in half by a lapse of sixteen years, bridged for the audience by an explanatory chorus speech from Time himself. In the first half Leontes's unprovoked jealousy wrecks the harmony of his marriage and his friendship with a foreign king, causing the death of his son, the loss to shepherds in the foreign king's country of his infant daughter, and the apparent death of his faithful wife. These early scenes shock the audience with the realism of self-induced disgust and rage in Leontes, who is his own Iago, but they exert no tragic pull, for Shakespeare gives us no access to Leontes's soul. Meanwhile, Shakespeare allows Hermione, Leontes's wronged wife, the dignity and grace—a key word in the play—of an evidently truthful and uncowed defence of her fidelity, confirmed by an oracle (the period is vaguely classical). In the second half of the play, the abandoned daughter, a princess raised as a peasant, meets, in true romance fashion, the prince who is the foreign king's son: their match will restore harmony to their estranged fathers and rescue, for the old, the future that had seemed lost. More remarkably, Hermione turns out to be still alive, to be reunited with her penitent husband in a recognition scene of rapt simplicity. Shakespeare used an Elizabethan prose romance as his source, but, crucially, he invented the character, a splendid, spirited, forceful woman, who organises Hermione's preservation in seclusion, sustains Leontes's remorse, and presents his lost wife to him as, at first, a statue. *The Winter's Tale* draws fruitfully, in Perdita as well as in Paulina, on Shakespeare's old affection for intelligent, practical women (Portia, Beatrice, Rosalind, Viola) whose wholly unmagical charm can resolve confusion made and sustained by men.

The Tempest, Shakespeare's last masterpiece, derived from no one source and only distantly from several, solves the problems of the romance play even more successfully than *The Winter's Tale*, and more economically. The time problem disappears in the unique concentration of the action into real time, two hours within which the originating sins of the older generation are recounted and the guilt of those responsible for them is dealt with. Disorder is driven by familiar Shakespearean motives: usurping brothers with murderous intentions take, or attempt to take, in Machiavellian fashion, opportunities for seizing worldly power presented to them by the guilelessness of their brothers. Most remarkably, the organisation of the romance plot, the finding of the lost, the recognition of past failings and the securing of the reconciled future in the marriage of virtuous children is all in the control of a single, the central, character.

In a decisive shake of the romance kaleidoscope, Shakespeare in this play has the lost princess always with her father. Both were long ago cast by the dangerous sea (of *Pericles* and *The Winter's Tale*) on an island where Prospero's magic power, the art for which he neglected his dukedom, has been perfected to the point where he can, through the agency of Ariel, a captive spirit of the natural world, assemble his enemies after a harmless shipwreck to meet judgement and, in the case of the foreign king's temporarily lost son Ferdinand, to meet his Miranda. Not all of Prospero's enemies will accept the truth—"The devil speaks in him", says one; "No", says Prospero[76]—or the forgiveness with which Prospero deliberately accompanies it—"The rarer action is in virtue than in vengeance." [77] But harmony between estranged kingdoms is properly restored, and in the moment when Prospero reveals his daughter playing chess with her betrothed prince, the silent fury of Prospero's unrepentant brother serves to anchor the magic of the island to the reality to which they will all return.

So brief an account cannot begin to unpack the subtle complexity of this play, in which rapid contrasts illuminate in all sorts of ways the impact of the island and of Prospero's moral weight on different kinds of men. A triumph of Shakespeare's imaginative understanding is the wholly original Caliban, wild man and slave of the island, innocent but not innocuous, tamed but not civilised by Prospero's uncomprehending discipline, poignant in his naïve, often mistaken, responses. In respect to him alone, Shakespeare takes the audience further than Prospero in judgement, allowing us to feel that Caliban's simplicity has been betrayed, not only in his quick collapse into drunkenness at the hands of two comic clowns (unlike whom he is not distracted by the "trash" set by Prospero to confuse their clumsy plot), but also in Prospero's bitterness at Caliban's failure to meet unrealistic expectations of him.

Prospero's art, his learning, his magic, lost him his dukedom but lands his enemies on his island so that they and he may be released from the past. Before he leaves the island with everyone but Ariel (and possibly Caliban), to resume ordinary life in Milan, where "Every third thought shall be my grave",[78] he abjures his "rough magic",[79] freeing Ariel and his obedient spirits to the elements to which they belong. Magic was not yet clearly distinguished from science. Prospero's speech of renunciation has classical models, but in it there is perhaps also a premonitory sense of the powers latent in nature, "weak masters"[80] of magnetism, electricity and the possibilities of physical and chemical manipulation, which might better be left unexploited by learned men. Bacon's *Proficience and Advancement of Learning*, insisting that man's power over nature should and would be vastly increased by the proper application of empirical method, had been published six years before *The Tempest* was written. The future lay with Bacon's rationalist optimism, with magic become real science. *The Tempest* was already old-fashioned, or timeless. Caliban is by no means a noble savage; nobility in the play is in Prospero's, Alonso's, Ferdinand's and Gonzalo's submission to truth, responsibility and love in the "poor isle" where, Gonzalo says, Ferdinand has found his wife, Prospero his dukedom,

> and all of us ourselves,
> Where no man was his own.[81]

The Tempest, crowning with its lightness of touch and seriousness of intent the group of romance plays, of which it alone is set in Christian Europe, was almost certainly written in 1611. Its early audiences must have picked up, as we do, Shakespeare's own valedictory note in Prospero's rueful farewell to the "insubstantial pageant"[82] generated by his creative power: Prospero lays his art aside to return to everyday life and asks for the audience's deliverance, indulgence and prayers in a formal little epilogue. *The Tempest* was the author's last complete play, and it is, at least, more likely than not that Shakespeare at this point, prosperous enough to retire from the theatre, had decided to live mostly at home in Stratford, where his wife, his daughter Susanna and his three-year-old granddaughter all were.

One more project he certainly undertook, and certainly did not complete.

Henry VIII, for centuries a popular play on account of its opportunities for substantial pageantry on a crowded stage and its bland, upbeat ending celebrating Protestant England, is a muddled text that sets notorious critical problems. Some of it is evidently by Shakespeare; some of it is evidently not; some of it is most likely to be Shakespeare's writing softened by someone else. The consensus is that the second author is John Fletcher, who took over from Shakespeare as chief playwright to the company from which Shakespeare had retired. Two recent scholarly introductions to editions[83] of the play discuss many possible explanations for the oddness of the text, but not the one that seems, in relation to Shakespeare's times and constant preoccupations, the most obvious.

Asked by someone to write a play on Henry VIII, and in particular on the crisis of the reign, which wrenched England out of its Catholic past toward its Protestant future, Shakespeare felt positive enough about the task to take it on. One incentive was no doubt the historical location of the trial of Queen Katherine of Aragon's marriage in the very room in Blackfriars where the company was now performing. The evidence of the text, which is all we have, strongly suggests what then happened: Shakespeare found himself writing a Catholic play, its background source the quiet, dangerous tradition of loyalty to Katherine of Aragon and Thomas More, and abandoned it in alarm or in disgust at how the story had to be told or, under pressure, to be modified and completed by Fletcher, son of a Protestant bishop.

The sense of a world passing pervades the early scenes of the play. The villain is Wolsey, who organises the undeserved execution of Buckingham, fears Katherine's accurate perception of him and engineers her fall and, therefore—which he does not intend—the fall of Catholic England, by wounding the king's conscience as to the validity of his sonless marriage. Wolsey salves the wound in the delivery of Anne Boleyn, at a stage-managed party, as a distraction from Katherine's influence. These scenes demonstrate, at a speed which is almost history-play shorthand, Shakespeare's old expertise in the presentation of power and loyalty: how both are gained and lost; how the king's favour, and popular support, can be manipulated by a Machiavel; how nevertheless worldly pride goes before a worldly fall: Wolsey is allowed, in report, a humbled Christian end, to which Katherine pays forgiving tribute.

The king himself is an undeveloped character, unimpressive putty in Katherine's, then in Wolsey's, hands, impatient and stupid at Katherine's trial, autocratic and still susceptible above all to flattery (Cranmer's) once he has married Anne Boleyn and broken with Rome. A scene late in the play that is clearly Shakespeare's has Henry arbitrarily saving Cranmer, now archbishop, from a Catholic plot to unseat him as a heretic. Nothing could be less heroic than Cranmer's tearful, unprincipled weakness in this scene; Shakespeare's critical intelligence and Catholic bias are both surely at work in his depiction of the king's support of Cranmer, which is given not because he is a Protestant but because he is a pliable servant of Henry's self-will:

Stand up, good Canterbury.
Thy truth and thy integrity is rooted
In us, thy friend. Give me thy hand. Stand up.[84]

Contemplating his squabbling prelates, Henry a little later says: " 'Tis well there's one above 'em yet",[85] meaning not God but himself. By this time Fletcher has taken over, and Henry's resolution of the squabble in Cranmer's favour, by giving him a royal ring to flourish at his enemies, is not much more than preparation for the grand baptism of Elizabeth, the play's sycophantic finale, explicitly flattering to James I as Elizabeth's successor. (All this is wildly unhistorical—the plot against Cranmer took place in 1544, when Cromwell, present in the scene, and Anne Boleyn, the baby's mother, had been executed years before, and Elizabeth, no longer heir to the throne, was eleven years old.)

Libido dominandi, observed from the outside, is all the audience gathers of Henry, the central figure in the play, and of Wolsey, in a rather more inward portrait, until his disgrace. The moral centre of the play, the one soul truthful before God, is Katherine, whose trial, played, as it had been held, in Blackfriars hall, closely resembles Hermione's in *The Winter's Tale*. A chaste and virtuous queen and wife, daughter of a foreign king among enemies in a land not her own, she pleads her cause with courageous dignity. An oracle vindicated Hermione; nothing, no one, intervenes to authenticate Katherine's truth. Coleridge rightly placed her with the other heroines of Shakespeare's late plays, saying that "Miranda the maiden, Imogen the wife, Katherine the queen" share "blessed beauty" of character, arising "from the more exquisite harmony of all the parts of the moral being constituting one living total of head and heart" that "sees all things in and by the light of the affections, and errs, if it ever err, in love alone".[86] Hazlitt agreed with Coleridge's praise of Katherine's character, calling it "the most perfect delineation of matronly dignity, sweetness, and resignation that can be conceived".[87] The contrast between Katherine and Anne Boleyn—whose single spoken scene is a brilliant exercise of Shakespeare's craft, Anne's protestations of ambitionless pity for Katherine undermined by a cynical, knowing Old Lady of the court—is sharpened by pointed juxtapositions. Katherine's dying plea for the kind treatment of the daughter Henry has rejected, as Leontes rejected Perdita, immediately (and unhistorically) follows the spectacular celebration of Anne's coronation. Dr. Johnson thought Katherine's last scene "above any other part of Shakespeare's tragedies, and perhaps above any scene of any other poet, tender and patheatick".[88] Katherine's appeal to the king is heavy with irony: everyone knew that there had been no romance reconciliation with a penitent king for her or her daughter and of course no return to the obedience to Rome that such a reconciliation would have implied.

Katherine remained the heroine of the hidden Catholics of England; her daughter Mary turned out to have been the last—failed—hope for the restoration of the old Church. Shakespeare's presentation of the crisis of Henry's reign is neither unpatriotic nor uncritically papalist. Wolsey (who showed Henry and Cromwell how to rob the Church by dissolving monasteries) is thoroughly corrupt before Fletcher's intervention, and both cardinals come as badly as the king out of Katherine's trial. But Catholic it clearly is: no wonder he abandoned the play. And no wonder Thomas More is carefully kept out of it; he does not appear on stage, and the only reference to him, Wolsey's comment on More's appointment as Lord Chancellor, is, like the plea of the dying Katherine, loaded with historical irony:

> May he continue
> Long in his highness' favour, and do justice
> For truth's sake and his conscience, that his bones,
> When he has run his course and sleeps in blessings,
> May have a tomb of orphans' tears wept on him.[89]

It was no more permissible under the law in England in James's reign than it had been in Elizabeth's to stage explicit treatments of religious or political issues: censorship was fierce, if erratic, throughout Shakespeare's career. The sympathetic presentation of a foreign queen supplanted by Elizabeth's mother was one thing; presentation of the English statesman whose clarity of vision had led him to execution "for truth's sake and his conscience" and whose descendants were among the "orphans", the bereft Catholics, hunted priests and exiled nuns of James's reign, would have been another.

* * *

Shakespeare died in Stratford in 1616, leaving, in unpublished confusion, the only body of work in English that will always stand beside the work of Homer, the Greek tragic poets, Virgil and Dante. Once the performance of his plays had recovered from the efforts of the late seventeenth and early eighteenth centuries to tidy them up in the interests of neoclassical decorum, his commanding presence in the theatres and later on the screens and in the classrooms of the world became unassailable, particularly as English turned out, through the nineteenth and twentieth centuries, to be ever-increasingly the language, as Latin once was, of knowledge and power. It is a true good that Shakespeare's presentation of actual power is undercut by contrasting values more consistently and more definitely than Virgil's presentation of power. Non-English-speaking writers as different as Leopold von Ranke, Hugo von Hofmannsthal, Benedetto Croce and Romain Rolland, all concerned to preserve these values in a Europe succumbing to the desolation of nihilistic will to power, in theory and then in practice, fastened on Shakespeare, for his intelligence, judgement and compassion, as a beacon of hope.[90] Not all of them, and almost none of those writing about Shakespeare now, would agree that that hope burns, that Shakespeare's intelligence, judgement and compassion are as they are because all his writing is sustained by Christian faith in Christian truth, by the belief that the world is both fallen and redeemed and by a Christian understanding of love. "There is a very real sense, awesome to apprehension", writes George Steiner, seduced by Wittgenstein and seeing in the contemporary Church only oppressive fundamentalism, "in which Shakespeare does know and say everything; does he know and say anything *else*?"[91]

The common sense of Shakespeare's audiences always, of millions moved to pity and fear, laughter and tears, delight and gratitude by his plays, is that, in his celebration of being, there is also a celebration of goodness and truth recognisable by anyone. To say that this goodness and this truth reach us through a beauty from which they are not separable is to make a statement that, on one level, common sense would readily accept. On another level it is to restate the ancient Christian belief that goodness, truth and beauty are at one in the unity of God, the transcendentals dimly perceived by Plato and acknowledged and accepted by Christians as "the indelible presence ... at the heart of ... thinking".[92] The scale of the difference this belief, or its absence, makes cannot be overstated:

> The world as it concretely exists is one that is always already related either positively or negatively to the God of grace and supernatural revelation. There are no neutral points or surfaces in this relationship. The world, considered as an object of knowledge, is always already embedded in this supernatural sphere, and, in the same way, man's cognitive powers operate either under the positive sign of faith or under the negative sign of unbelief.[93]

In case this seems loftily remote from Shakespeare, let us take a simple example, as Balthasar does in this same book:

There may be people who, for some reason or other, have become used to doubting the existence of intrinsic goodness. On their view, what is called good or appears to be so in everyday life can be explained away in terms of mores, changing customs, unconfessed laziness and selfishness, a natural will to power concealed under various disguises. If, however, such people came face to face with the evidence of a selfless act that another, say a friend, performs for its own sake, and they realize by their own inward experience that the naked overcoming of self is a really attainable possibility, they forget for the moment their entire theory and bow before the simple fact of goodness. Their theory now has a breach in it; they may stop it up later, but for now they have stepped through it, naked and undisguised, into the presence of the Good.[94]

Kent's response to Lear's unjust punishment of him and Antony's response to Enobarbus's desertion will strike anyone in this way, as will the forgiveness of unrepented wrongs in the late plays, where "the atmosphere is inconceivable apart from the Christian background, but this background only diffuses an anonymous light over the miracles of earthly love." [95]

The denial of Shakespeare's judgement, or the denial that his judgement is Christian, is not attributable only to the victory of Nietzsche, of thinking "under the negative sign of unbelief", in the last hundred years. Also to blame are the misleading labels attached to periods and frames of mind by nineteenth-century historians. Shakespeare is undeniably an artist of the late Renaissance. Burckhardt, himself a Schopenhauerian pessimist of stoical fortitude, defined to lasting effect in 1860 *The Civilization of the Renaissance* as essentially unbelieving, though he acknowledged the Augustinian orthodoxy of, for example, the Florentine Platonist Pico della Mirandola. The secular connotations of the word "humanism" have now clouded its Renaissance meaning of fidelity to classical learning; its leading figures in England, Erasmus, Colet, Linacre, More (who translated Pico's *Life*) and Pole, were all faithful Catholics, though far from uncritical of the condition of the Church; all except More were priests. Another great historian pointed out in 1920:

The pagan element of the Renaissance has been extremely overestimated.... Petrarch and Boccaccio had wished to place antiquity completely in the service of the Christian faith. And among later figures as well there definitely was no dichotomy, such as one might assume on the face of things, between the passion for pagan antiquity and the Christian faith.[96]

Petrarch, in particular, was devoted to *Augustinus noster*. He bought the *City of God* when young and was later given a pocket copy of the *Confessions* from which, like Aelred, he was never parted. When, in 1347, he wrote *My Secret Book*, a dialogue owing much to Cicero and Boethius, in which he attempted to pull his will, assailed by melancholy and confusion, into accord with the will of God, he chose as his interlocutor Augustine himself, the teacher of his soul. Balthasar accurately wrote of the Renaissance:

> It splits clearly into two: there was a Christian movement, which wanted, through a revitalization of the ancient languages, to liberate the original spirit of the gospel from the rank undergrowth of late Scholasticism ... ; and there was a minority that cultivated a forced kind of paganism and adopted an explicitly anti-Christian stance.[97]

As for the history of the Counter-Reformation, failing in England under Mary Tudor before it had properly begun, and later, it has been assumed, inspiring in England only Jesuit conspiracy, it has never included Shakespeare.

To locate Shakespeare properly among the ideas and preoccupations of his time, we need only remember that he was English; that he had a good grammar school but no university education; that he was most likely brought up as a Catholic and influenced in his youth by Campion, the holiest of the English Jesuits and certainly not a plotting traitor; that he was a professional man of the theatre, his writing politically exposed in a dangerous period; and that he read, throughout his career, with enterprise and with critical judgement. That his religious loyalty should be to the long past and that he avoided specific avowal of it, except in "The Phoenix and the Turtle", for centuries impenetrably cryptic, is wholly unsurprising. The provincial Catholic gentry, almost all of whom were loyal to the monarchy that sporadically persecuted them, provided his immediate ambience and some of his London patrons. Beyond them it is reasonable to suppose in him some sense of the Catholic reform movement that predated the papal assertiveness of the later sessions of the Council of Trent (and Pius V's excommunication of Elizabeth). This had attempted to deal with personal and institutional corruption in the Church without destroying her unity but had failed to prevent the collapse of Christendom into permanent division. The Council's theology, while orthodox, was amateur rather than professional—its sense of the Church as a *corpus permixtum* in which there was much evil to be remedied and the awareness of the dangers of confusing spiritual with temporal authority were thoroughly Augustinian. "Before the tribunal of God's mercy," said Cardinal

Pole to the bishops of the Church, opening the second session of the Council of Trent:

> we, the shepherds, should acknowledge ourselves responsible for all the evils now burdening the flock of Christ. . . . It will be found that it is our ambition, our avarice, our cupidity which have wrought all these evils on the people of God, and that it is because of these sins that shepherds are being driven from their churches, and the churches starved of the Word of God, and the property of the church, which is the property of the poor, stolen, and the priesthood given to the unworthy. . . .
>
> I implore you that we should not be swayed in our deliberations by anger, hatred, or friendship. All classes of men are prone to this, and those especially who serve princes. They easily speak for love or for hate, according as they think their princes are affected, from whom they await reward. . . . [Bishops] must serve their princes as the servants of God and not as servants of men.[98]

By 1546 it was too late to save the unity of the Church for which More had died eleven years earlier. But Pole's acknowledgement that power and wealth in the Church, and competitive greed for both, had been at least partly to blame for her destruction has the great merit of truth. As Balthasar wrote in his essay of 1965, "Tragedy and Christian Faith":

> Where, finally, does the guilt lie for the appalling disaster of the Reformation? With those who ultimately carried it out and tore the fabric or with those who had prepared the way for centuries that led to this tragic act through scandals within the Church, perhaps making it truly unavoidable?[99]

The collision of values set out in Pole's speech is clearly presented in many of Shakespeare's plays. More, on the scaffold, said that he "died the King's good servant but God's first".[100] Wolsey in *Henry VIII* (again, the multiple irony obvious to the audience) says:

> Had I but served my God with half the zeal
> I served my king, he would not in mine age
> Have left me naked to mine enemies.[101]

As for "the property of the church", Shakespeare caught in a single line, "Bare ruined choirs where late the sweet birds sang",[102] the fate of the wrecked abbeys of England, brought down in what was for his parents living memory.

Frank Kermode has long suspected that Shakespeare drew, for Macbeth, on Augustine's account of the agony of indecision before his conversion.[103] That Shakespeare read the *Confessions*, a unique example, within his possible literary horizon, of the exploration of inwardness—Augustine invented the soliloquy as well as the word for it—is a fascinating possibility (not thought of by Harold Bloom, who describes Hamlet as "the first absolutely inner self").[104] Whether he did or not, he wrote his plays from the heart of the Augustinian tradition.

Moral failure everywhere in Shakespeare, that is to say, failure before God, is, as we have seen, failure in love, failure in the right direction of feeling by the will, which is free to respond—or not—to the good. Failure in Shakespeare is never failure of reason; indeed, reason—his wicked characters are, on the whole, much better reasoners than their victims—is usually employed as a means to self-advancement in deliberate blindness to the good. Augustine's meditation on love, death and eternity in book 4 of the *Confessions*, provoked by the memory of the death of his closest friend, is an apt commentary on the love that transcends death and worldly defeat in Shakespeare. As for power, *libido dominandi*, in Shakespeare as in Augustine, is the distinctive mark of the *civitas terrena*, precisely the opposite of love. "If we try to build ourselves up, we build a ruin."[105] Pride in oneself, Augustine says in the *City of God*, is always "the start of the evil will.... And what is pride but a perverse kind of exaltation? For it is a perverse kind of exaltation to abandon the basis on which the mind should be firmly fixed, and to become, as it were, based on oneself, and so remain."[106] What could better describe the motivation of Richard III, Iago, Edmund and Lady Macbeth?

If it is objected that this emphasis is merely Christian and not specifically Augustinian, it should be remembered that Aquinas's emphasis is more on sin as a corruption of reason than on sin as a corruption of love. Not that goodness in Augustine, or Shakespeare, is irrational, but, in Alasdair MacIntyre's exact summary of Augustine's ethics: "The rationality of right action ... is not its primary determinant, but a secondary consequence of right willing. Hence faith which initially moves and informs the will is prior to understanding."[107] MacIntyre refers to faith in the reality and eternity of the good, faith that disinterested goodness is "worth it". What is more, a close look at Shakespeare's view of politics will show that Shakespeare is demonstrably on Augustine's side of the divide that separates the *City of God* from Thomist confidence in worldly power as divinely sanctioned, a confidence that dominated the later Middle Ages.

Augustine regarded politics, the acquisition and use of power in the earthly city, as necessary for the maintenance of law and order, but of always relative value. Christians, travelling in this life toward the City of God, their home in eternity, belong also to the earthly city and should obey its laws so long as this obedience does not deflect them from their pilgrimage. But the state, concerned only with those things that can be regulated by its laws, has no absolute value: "As for this mortal life, what does it matter under whose rule a man lives, being so soon to die, provided that the rulers do not force him to impious and wicked acts?" [108] In the vulnerable late empire, Augustine was above all concerned to explain in the *City of God* why the Church, one, holy (though in practice a *corpus permixtum*) and Catholic, should not be tied to any transient institution of the earthly city. There is no doubt that he would have been appalled, as Dante was, by the spectacle of the warfaring secular state that the papacy had become in the later Middle Ages and also by Henry VIII's and Elizabeth's tying of the English church to the English monarchy. While the power of the state is a necessary but always regrettable element in fallen human life, the family, the married pair and their children but also their servants, has, if ruled by love rather than by feared power, a natural goodness that connects it to the goodness of God. In the household of a Christian paterfamilias, Augustine says, even slaves are treated with love, and "those who give orders are the servants of those whom they appear to command." [109] Orlando's fearless care for his father's old servant Adam in *As You Like It* is only one of many illustrations of what Shakespeare felt about the "constant service of the antique world". [110] He felt, we have seen, even more strongly about the natural bonds of the family, of marriage and blood relationships.

In Aquinas's vision, in contrast to Augustine's, all authority, very much including that of the state, is "natural", part of God's design, and every human being, like every animal and plant, has his proper place in the chain of being. A king, for example, is at the pinnacle of a divinely guaranteed social pyramid in which everyone has, and is to be treated according to, his natural level. Shakespeare's kings, their sense of their place reinforced by Tudor stress on the "divinity" that hedges them, must, if they are capable of it, unlearn this model, discover that their power belongs only to the earthly city, to the fallen condition of humanity, and that they are themselves no more than "unaccommodated man", their souls naked before God. Only if Ulysses' speech on degree in *Troilus and Cressida* is read without attention to its cynical, manipulative context can Shakespeare be thought to have given the state or the chain of being any absolute value, whatever the society he lived in may have aspired to. Aquinas's security in a commonly held faith, in the Church as coterminous with society, had already been lost to the factions of the Protestant Reformation and to Machiavelli and the small but significant Renaissance "minority that adopted a specifically anti-Christian stance". In Shakespeare's plays, goodness, truth, beauty and love confront an environment of greed, selfishness and the will to power—as, in fact if not in theory, they did in the thirteenth century, which was Dante's as well as Aquinas's. As they do now. As, Augustine would say, they always do.

"How with this rage", Shakespeare asked in a sonnet, "shall beauty hold a plea, / Whose action is no stronger than a flower?" [111] I have taken as read, in these two chapters, the beauty, the unequalled invention and grace, of Shakespeare's writing. The answer to his question, however, is that against the rage of mortality (the subject of the sonnet)—but also against the rage, which is not different, of meaninglessness—beauty at one with the goodness and truth of the God of Christian revelation may not only hold a plea but prevail. The alternative view remains that of Nietzsche in the desperate note, already quoted, that was printed in *The Will to Power*:

> For a philosopher to say "the good and the beautiful are one" is infamy; if he goes on to add, "also the true", one ought to thrash him. Truth is ugly. We possess art lest we perish of the truth. [112]

Shakespeare, in absolute contrast to this view, was not a "value-creating" but a "good-discovering" being, [113] and the truth of his work shares in the truth of God. "Your truth", Augustine says to God in the *Confessions*, "does not belong to me nor to anyone else, but to us all whom you call to share it as a public possession". [114] Balthasar makes the same point more grandly and with equal bearing on Shakespeare:

> Truth is the unconcealment of being, while the full notion of this unconcealment requires someone to whom it is unconcealed. This someone is God and can only be God, because not all worldly being can be revealed to every worldly subject. Because it is unveiled to God, it can also be unveiled to other subjects, without needing to be actually [115] unveiled to them. It has its objective truth thanks to its unconcealment before the eternal subject. [116]

---

1. *Hamlet*, 5.2.364–65. All references to Shakespeare's plays are to the Arden editions.
2. Aristotle, *Poetics*, chap. 14, in *Classical Literary Criticism*, trans. T. S. Dorsch (London, 1965), p. 48.

3. Augustine, *Enarrationes in Psalmos* 122.1.
4. *Othello*, 1.2.22.
5. Ibid., 1.1.134–35.
6. Ibid., 1.2.26–27.
7. Ibid., 5.2.121–22.
8. Ibid., 1.3.168–69.
9. Ibid., 1.3.294–95.
10. Ibid., 3.3.209.
11. Ibid., 1.3.320.
12. Ibid., 3.3.91–92.
13. Ibid., 5.2.271–73.
14. Ibid., 5.2.344–46, 350–54.
15. Ibid., 1.3.335–36.
16. Alasdair MacIntyre, *After Virtue* (London, 1981), p. 68.
17. S. T. Coleridge, *Lectures 1808–1819 on Literature*, ed. R. A. Foakes (Princeton, 1987), 2:272.
18. *Hamlet*, 3.2.21–23.
19. Augustine, *City of God* 15.5, trans. Henry Bettenson (London, 1972).
20. *King Lear*, 1.1.102–3.
21. Ibid., 3.4.28–33.
22. Ibid., 3.4.104–7.
23. Ibid., 4.1.19–21, 65–70.
24. Ibid., 4.6.143, 148–49, 174–76.
25. Ibid., 4.7.46–48.
26. Ibid., 5.3.10–12, 15–17.
27. Ibid., ed. Kenneth Muir (Arden, 2nd series), p. 188, n. 17.
28. Augustine, *City of God* 10.6.
29. Arthur Schopenhauer, *The World as Will and Representation*, trans. E. F. J. Payne (New York, 1966), 2:434.
30. *King Lear*, 3.3.17–19.
31. Coleridge, *Lectures* 2:329.
32. Hans Urs von Balthasar, *Theo-Drama*, trans. Graham Harrison, vol. 1 (San Francisco, 1988), p. 478.
33. *King Lear*, 2.2.70–72.
34. Ibid., 5.3.197.
35. Ibid., 5.3.312–14.
36. Balthasar, *Theo-Drama* 1:137.
37. Ibid., vol. 2 (San Francisco, 1990), p. 46.
38. Adrian Poole, *Tragedy: Shakespeare and the Greek Example* (Oxford, 1987), p. 230.
39. Ibid., p. 2.
40. Ibid., p. 239.
41. George Steiner, *The Death of Tragedy* (London, 1961), p. 331.
42. George Steiner, *Antigones* (Oxford, 1984), p. 303.
43. George Steiner, *Grammars of Creation* (London, 2001), pp. 67–68.
44. *King Lear*, 5.3.270, 278, 308.
45. Ibid., 5.3.301–3.
46. Jn 13:27.
47. *Macbeth*, 1.7.1.
48. Ibid., 1.7.7.
49. Ibid., 1.7.16–20.
50. Ibid., 1.7.31.
51. Ibid., 1.5.52–54.
52. Ibid., 2.2.34–35.
53. Ibid., 2.2.32–33.

54. Ibid., 2.3.89–91.
55. Ibid., 5.5.43.
56. Ibid., 1.6.4, 8.
57. Ibid., 1.5.45.
58. Ibid., 5.5.13.
59. Virgil, *Aeneid* 8.675–728.
60. *Antony and Cleopatra*, 4.6.10–11.
61. Ibid., 5.2.11–12.
62. Augustine, sermon 34.
63. *Antony and Cleopatra*, 3.13.41–46.
64. Ibid., 1.1.1–2.
65. Ibid., 4.1.4.
66. Ibid., 4.15.73–75.
67. *Timon of Athens*, 4.3.434–43.
68. *Coriolanus*, 5.3.128.
69. Ibid., 3.3.120–23.
70. Ibid., 1.4.51.
71. *Henry VI, Part III*, 5.6.83.
72. *Coriolanus*, 2.1.161.
73. Ibid., 4.1.29–31.
74. Ibid., 5.3.24–25, 34–37.
75. Ibid., 5.6.100, 113–16.
76. *The Tempest*, 5.1.129.
77. Ibid., 5.1.27–28.
78. Ibid., 5.1.311.
79. Ibid., 5.1.50.
80. Ibid., 5.1.41.
81. Ibid., 5.1.212–13.
82. Ibid., 4.1.155.
83. *Henry VIII*, ed. John Margeson, New Cambridge Shakespeare (Cambridge, 1990); *Henry VIII*, ed. Gordon McMullan, Arden 3rd series (London, 2000).
84. *Henry VIII*, 5.1.113–15.
85. Ibid., 5.2.26.
86. Coleridge, *Lectures* 2:270.
87. William Hazlitt, *Characters of Shakespear's Plays*, ed. FJS (London, 1906), p. 181.
88. Samuel Johnson, *Johnson on Shakespeare*, ed. Arthur Sherbo (New Haven, 1968), p. 653.
89. *Henry VIII*, 3.2.395–99.
90. See extracts in *Shakespeare in Europe*, ed. Oswald LeWinter (London, 1963).
91. George Steiner, *No Passion Spent* (London, 1996), p. 128.
92. Hans Urs von Balthasar, *Theo-Logic*, vol. 1, trans. Adrian J. Walker (San Francisco, 2000), p. 12.
93. Ibid., p. 11.
94. Ibid., p. 35.
95. Balthasar, *Theo-Drama* 1:384.
96. Johan Huizinga, *Men and Ideas: History, the Middle Ages, the Renaissance*, trans. James S. Holmes and Hans van Marle (New York, 1959), p. 273.
97. Balthasar, *Theo-Drama* 2:417.
98. Reginald Pole, "An Appeal to the Council of Trent", in *The Portable Renaissance Reader*, ed. James B. Ross and Mary M. McLaughlin (New York, 1968), pp. 665–72.
99. Balthasar, *Creator Spirit*, trans. Brian McNeil, Explorations in Theology, vol. 3 (San Francisco, 1993), p. 408.
100. R. W. Chambers, *Thomas More* (1935; London, 1976), p. 349.
101. *Henry VIII*, 2.2.455–57.

102. Sonnet 73.

103. Frank Kermode, *The Sense of an Ending* (New York, 1967), pp. 84–88; see also his *Shakespeare's Language* (London, 2000), p. 208.

104. Harold Bloom, *Shakespeare: The Invention of the Human* (London, 1999), p. 741.

105. Augustine, sermon 169.11.

106. Augustine, *City of God* 14.13.

107. Alasdair MacIntyre, *Whose Justice? Which Rationality?* (London, 1988), p. 158.

108. Augustine, *City of God* 5.17.

109. Ibid., 19.14.

110. *As You Like It*, 2.3.57.

111. Sonnet 65.

112. Quoted in Erich Heller, *The Importance of Nietzsche* (Chicago, 1988), p. 158.

113. Allan Bloom, *The Closing of the American Mind* (New York, 1987), p. 160.

114. Augustine, *Confessions* 12.34, trans. Henry Chadwick (Oxford, 1991).

115. I would suggest that *wirklich* here be translated as "completely" rather than as "actually".

116. Balthasar, *Theo-Logic* 1:269.

CHAPTER TWELVE

THE SEVENTEENTH CENTURY I

Donne, Herbert and Milton

The demands of the *civitas terrena*, particularly the demands of the state assert-
ing its identity with a national church, whether Catholic or Protestant,
have rarely been more confusingly imposed on writers whose real home was the
civitas Dei than they were in England and France in the seventeenth century.
Medieval Christendom finally vanished; modern Europe, secular, scientific and
colonial, trading all over the world, began to replace it. In the year after Caliban
was first seen by an audience, the East India Company's voyages were organised
on a joint stock basis for the profit of the whole company; less than eighty years
separated the death of Shakespeare from the birth of Voltaire. The "long" century began in England with the death of Queen Elizabeth in 1603 and ended in
1714 with the accession of George I; in France it began with Henry IV, once a
Huguenot, now a Catholic, signing the Edict of Nantes in 1598, and ended with
the death of Louis XIV in 1715. The unity of the Latin Church had been irrevo-
cably fractured in the sixteenth century. In the seventeenth, the period of the
Reformation's embittered aftermath, no writer, however far from the orthodox
heart of the Church, would have regarded himself, still less announced himself,
as an atheist. The cracks and chasms of disintegration, however, spread across the
whole Christian spectrum and helped to justify the fastidious deism, in effect
amounting to little more than atheism, of several important thinkers of the period,
notably Thomas Hobbes, René Descartes and John Locke. Meanwhile, confessional loyalties, rivalries and anxieties held even devoutly Christian writers in a
wide variety of relations to the wholeness of Catholic truth.

Conflict caused and driven by religious differences scarred the century. The
wars of religion in France, after nearly three decades, ended with the granting of
Protestant liberties by Henry IV, but a short generation later, first Cardinal Richelieu and then Louis XIV set themselves to rid France of all Huguenots. Meanwhile, as we shall see in our next chapter, a rift opened in the French Catholic
Church that disappeared only in the cataclysm of 1789. In Germany and central

Europe, the Catholic-Protestant Thirty Years' War of 1618 to 1648, in which France intervened first on one side, then on the other, and emerged the major victor, was the most savagely destructive conflict for noncombatants in European history before 1939. In England the civil wars of the 1640s swept away not only the monarchy and the aristocracy as essential to government but also the church of the Elizabethan settlement, the Book of Common Prayer and the bishops. None of these was, as it turned out, disposed of for long, though the rifts in English Protestantism that the civil war cut have never been healed, while the fear of Catholicism that all English Protestants shared at least contributed to the deposition of a legitimate king and the importation of a Dutchman in 1688 and of a German in 1714 to rule England and govern its church. Hobbes and John Milton and Locke, differing in many other respects, were united in recommending that all Christians except Catholics should be tolerated in England.

In the lives of the writers to be discussed in these two chapters, the problems of religious allegiance and identity were compounded with the demands of secular authority, the rigours of a nervous censorship and the memory or the menace of civil strife. This was no less the case in Catholic France than it was in Protestant England.

*   *   *

When Shakespeare died in April 1616, John Donne, aged forty-three, had written most of his poems. He had been a priest in the Church of England for only one year and would die fifteen years later. George Herbert, aged twenty-three, was a fellow of Trinity College, Cambridge. Eleven years later he abandoned a promising worldly career and in 1630 was himself ordained. He died at not quite age forty, after two and a half years of clerical life. The work of these two Christian writers, each in middle age becoming a priest in the national church, both dead several years before the outbreak of civil war, is marked in contrasting ways by the pressure of the times.

The late Elizabethan and Jacobean church, though in theory settled and united according to the Thirty-nine Articles and Cranmer's second (more Protestant) Book of Common Prayer, was in practice home to an increasingly wide variety of opinions and objectives, not excluding Puritan hopes for the abolition of bishops and the revision of the liturgy on a fully Calvinist model. King James, with his executed Catholic mother and his Presbyterian upbringing, was unpartisan on religious issues. In 1611 he appointed an archbishop of Canterbury, George Abbot, who was anti-Catholic, theologically pro-Calvinist but also pro-episcopal, hated in Scotland for the king's attempt to impose bishops on a Presbyterian church. This combination of opinions is typical of the times in its confusion: half the books published in England in the first forty years of the century were on religious topics, the great majority of them generating more heat than light.

When James died in 1625, Archbishop Abbot crowned King Charles I, though with considerable misgivings about the "divine right of kings" now explicitly claimed as the ultimate justification for royal control of the church. The most respected English bishop of the day was old Lancelot Andrewes, born in the reign of Mary Tudor and a bishop since 1605. Stoutly anti-Puritan and anti-Calvinist, Andrewes was liturgically and theologically of a Catholic cast of mind: he believed in the Real Presence of Christ in the Eucharist, which he defined as a sacrifice and celebrated, but only in his private chapel, with candles, incense and vestments. At the same time he was a stalwart defender of the supreme authority of the monarch in the church, writing firm replies to the case for Rome as the guarantee of unity and orthodoxy in the Church presented to James by Robert Cardinal Bellarmine. It was the consequence of the papal excommunication of Elizabeth, of the Jesuit presence in England and of the Gunpowder Plot that there was no hope of accommodation between Andrewes and Bellarmine, although they were two civilised and moderate men in substantial agreement on the central doctrines of Christianity. Had there been any such accommodation, the Church of England would, thus early in its life, have split in half, as it has several times threatened to since, and as it would have in the next reign if Archbishop Laud had accepted the cardinal's hat secretly offered him by Pope Urban VIII.

In this inconsistent, disunited ecclesiastical institution, a national Protestant church quasi-Catholic in parts and in most respects quite unreformed (feudal patronage, pluralism and absenteeism were still routine), the only universally held sentiment—the only glue holding the church together—was embattled dislike of Rome. A reasonable semblance of peaceful coexistence within the English church could be sustained by an intelligent monarch with no very strong religious views of his own. Evidently to favour and promote either the Puritan or the near-Catholic faction in the church would provoke outright opposition from the other. Elizabeth and James I understood this. Charles I, more serious in his own faith, more genuinely partial (to the near-Catholics) but much less astute than his father, did not. When Abbot died in 1633, Charles appointed William Laud to succeed him. Archbishop Laud had the same ecclesiastical views as the now-dead Andrewes but was tough, abrasive and domineering and enjoyed the king's full, tactless support. The Puritan ordering of churches was countermanded: altars replaced communion tables, were railed off at the east end of churches and became again the focus of the congregation's attention as the Puritans had made the pulpit. Music was encouraged; candles and vestments reappeared. Those who thought all this a betrayal of Elizabeth's Protestant settlement were, at least as far as the nontheological layman was concerned, correct. Nine years later Laud was in the Tower of London, where he was executed in 1645, and the king, not only on account of religion, was at war with a large minority of his subjects, led by his mostly Presbyterian House of Commons.

This was the religious background to the lives of Donne and Herbert, both of whom died before Laud brought to inescapable collision the ecclesiastical contradictions of the time.

Donne's childhood was devotedly, dangerously Catholic. His mother was the great-niece of Thomas More; no family in England was more faithful to the properly understood Catholic past than this one. Donne's uncle Jasper Heywood, his mother's brother, had been as a boy a protégé of Cardinal Pole and was the superior of the Jesuit mission in England in the terrifying 1580s. He was caught and condemned to death as a traitor in Westminster Hall. His five Jesuit companions were hanged, drawn and quartered; he himself was imprisoned for months in the Tower, where the twelve-year-old Donne visited him with his mother. He was then exiled to Italy, where he died. Another Heywood uncle was also a Jesuit priest. Donne's own elder brother Henry died of the plague in the squalor of Newgate prison, where Henry VIII had in 1537 starved ten Carthusian monks to death, their martyrdom vividly remembered among More's descendants. Henry Donne had harboured a priest in his house; for this, had he lived, he was likely to have been executed. Despite, or perhaps because of, this heroic family history, John Donne, a brilliantly gifted, ambitious, fiercely independent young man with no money, abandoned the Catholic faith toward the end of Elizabeth's reign when he was in his mid-twenties.[1]

Part of the reason for his change of allegiance was, no doubt, to open the kind of path to fame and fortune that in England was closed to a landless Catholic, however talented. He had a long, bruising time to wait, years of the humiliating toadying to the great that could not be circumvented by a place-seeking outsider in the corrupt small world of Jacobean influence. An improvident marriage set back his career in the service of the nobility and for years impoverished him further. Eventually, after much effort to assemble the right support in the right quarters, he was ordained in the national church, in which his uncle and brother had been condemned as traitors. Not long after, with the help of the scandalous Duke of Buckingham, an embarrassingly fawned-on favourite of the king, Donne became dean of Saint Paul's. He died the most celebrated preacher in England.

In the course of a hectic, worldly and in the end successful but mostly unhappy life, he wrote a good deal, in a wide variety of forms. In verse he ranged from fashionable Latinate satires and elegies in fluent, sometimes biting, couplets, to love poems in complicated stanzas invented as he wrote, to devotional sonnets of fire and force; in prose from brief, often perversely clever "Paradoxes and Problems", to a series of painful meditations written during an illness he took (wrongly) to be his last, to some of the most powerful and frightening sermons ever delivered. Two bravura pieces of prose, *Pseudo-Martyr* and *Ignatius His Conclave*, written in 1610 and 1611, several years before his ordination, are savage, clever, scurrilous attacks on the Catholic Church, the first in support of Bishop Andrewes and the king against Cardinal Bellarmine, the second a furious, mocking onslaught on the Jesuits. He wrote these pieces, no doubt, to strengthen his Protestant credentials and promote his notoriety as a sharp, employable propagandist. Perhaps he also wrote them to repress, or justify to himself, in an exhibition of the witty repulsiveness that went down well in James's court, his own treachery in the evasion of the demands made on his family by fidelity to Rome.

Fear of betrayal and acute consciousness of death mark his love poems, mostly written before his marriage. The best of them, in their bite and panache, are among the great love poems of the language. The unashamed, dazzlingly transmitted sexual charge they carry, the analytical range of the mind that shaped them, the sheer gusto of private exhilaration and bitterness they convey, suggest that in this period of his life Donne was reacting strongly against the beleaguered sacramental intensity of his Catholic upbringing. No doubt he was. But what gives his love poems their unmistakable quality is the habit of thinking clearly about the mysterious collision of the spiritual with the physical in sexual passion, a habit acquired, precisely, in the beleaguered sacramental intensity of thought about, and devotion to, the Incarnation, the Resurrection and the Mass.

Donne perceived everything, in other words, through the medium of a Catholic sensibility he could not lose simply by defecting from the hidden Church of his forebears. In his third Satire, probably written during the crisis—which the decision must have been for him—he tries to persuade the reader (or himself?) that to choose between different kinds of Christianity is a matter of strenuous pursuit of truth, not of listening to authority, whether royal (Philip of Spain, Harry of England), papal or Lutheran. Power, he says, has nothing to do with the problem, which is a question of unmediated closeness to God:

Fool and wretch, wilt thou let thy soul be tied
To man's laws, by which she shall not be tried
At the last day? Or will it then boot thee
To say a Philip, or a Gregory,
A Harry, or a Martin taught thee this?
. . . .

As streams are, power is; those blessed flowers that dwell
At the rough stream's calm head, thrive and prove well,
But having left their roots and themselves given
To the stream's tyrannous rage, alas are driven
Through mills, and rocks, and woods, and at last, almost
Consumed in going, in the sea are lost:
So perish souls, which more choose men's unjust
Power from God claimed, than God himself to trust.[2]

Milton himself, who became, as we shall see, churchless in the solitude of his independence, could not have improved on the Protestant purity of this aspiration. But for Donne, raised in the wholeness of Catholic tradition, churchlessness went against the very grain of his soul, as the ambivalence of this passage, the desolation of what happens to the flowers that have "left their roots", perhaps indicates. The same ambivalence is evident in the sonnet that begins "Show me dear Christ, thy spouse, so bright and clear", a prayer for a revelation of the true Church. The poem ends:

Dwells she with us, or like adventuring knights
First travail we to seek and then make love?
Betray kind husband thy spouse to our sights,
And let mine amorous soul court thy mild dove,
Who is most true, and pleasing to thee, then
When she is embraced and open to most men.[3]

Has he, like an adventuring knight, chosen, as was perhaps not too difficult at the time, the church of "most men", at least in his own country? At the cost of deserting her who "dwells with us"?

In any case, his religious poems (for example, *A Litany* and the sonnet sequence called *La Corona*) are crowded—the only word for the packed manner in which they are written—with doctrine and piety drawn from the tradition it is never his instinct to question, especially in reference to the Passion and Crucifixion of

Christ, and to our Lady, whose prayers are relied on in *A Litany* in most un-Protestant fashion. Paradox and puzzle fascinated Donne always, the simultaneity of opposites in particular. On 25 March 1608 Good Friday fell on the feast of the Annunciation. The poem he wrote for that day relishes a number of collisions that recur in his work: that "Death and conception in mankind is one"; that east and west, opposites on flat maps, become one on a globe; that in Christ it was "the same humility, / That he would be a man and leave to be"; that, as the Church's year records in time what took place in time but has its meaning in eternity, it is always true that "he shall come, he is gone." [4] The sonnet "At the round earth's imagined corners", on the Last Judgement, a topic to which he reverted again and again, ends with a startling double take that claps together two contrasting theological ideas—one more Catholic, the other more Protestant—though both present in the tradition, as if the truth were to resound from the collision:

> Here on this lowly ground,
> Teach me how to repent; for that's as good
> As if thou hadst sealed my pardon, with thy blood. [5]

There is no doubt that Donne's religious poems, most of them written in the period between his desertion of the Catholic Church and his ordination in the English church, would have been thought unacceptably Catholic by Protestants who had not included in their number some who agreed with Andrewes and Laud. Perhaps what his eventual acceptance as a Protestant clergyman shows most clearly is that, in some English church circles of the time, as in some to this day, rejection of the authority of the Pope was reckoned the only mark of Protestantism that mattered.

More Catholic in feeling even than his poems are his sermons. These were public; only three elegies, of all his poems, were printed in his lifetime. The sermons are extraordinary pieces of writing displaying with powerful dramatic effect high oratory, high passion, high showmanship, the Baroque combination of exuberant, almost surreal, expressionism with last-minute control usually associated with Counter-Reformation Rome, most of all with Jesuit churches. Here is Donne on Easter Day 1619, preaching to the House of Lords:

> The contemplation of God, and heaven, is a kind of burial, and sepulchre, and rest of the soul; and in this death of rapture, and ecstasy, in this death of the contemplation of my interest in my Saviour, I shall

find my self, and all my sins interred, and entombed in his wounds, and like a lily in paradise, out of red earth, I shall see my soul rise out of his blade, in a candour, and in an innocence, contracted there, acceptable in the sight of his Father.[6]

Death, judgement, the dereliction of the human condition without God and the mystery of redemption in the Passion, death and Resurrection of Christ are presented in sermon after sermon to what must have been rapt congregations stunned by the sermons' resounding rhetorical power.

Like Shakespeare, Donne knew well that scorn, especially the mockery of sophisticated London, was the most insidious contemporary enemy of Christian truth. In his funeral sermon for George Herbert's mother, an exemplary figure of the Protestant aristocracy, he contrasted her piety with the time in which she lived, a time of "scoffers and jesters in divine things.... For now, in these our days, excellency of wit lies in profaneness; he is the good spirit that dares abuse God; and he good company, that makes his company the worse, or keeps them from goodness."[7] What has become of the word "good" is sharply observed here. Much more than manners, however, is at stake. Truth is at stake. In a late sermon on the conversion of Saint Paul, Donne says:

Poor intricated soul! Riddling, perplexed, labyrinthical soul! Thou couldest not say that thou believest not in God, if there were no God; thou couldest not believe in God, if there were no God; if there were no God, thou couldest not speak, thou couldest not think, not a word, not a thought, no not against God; thou couldest not blaspheme the name of God, thou couldest not swear, if there were no God; for all thy faculties, however depraved, and perverted by thee, are from him; and except thou canst seriously believe that thou art nothing, thou canst not believe there is no God.[8]

This is intensely Augustinian in its sense of dependence—"What have we that we have not received?"—and in its consciousness of fallen sinfulness. Donne, who read a great deal in the period of his change of allegiance, held Augustine closer to his heart than he held any other writer on the things of God. In one of the *Devotions* composed during his illness in 1623 he wrote:

I would not make man worse than he is, nor his condition more miserable than it is. But could I though I would? ... What poor elements

are our happinesses made of, if Time, Time which we can scarce consider to be any thing, be an essential part of our happiness? ... How-
soever it may seem to have three stations, past, present, and future, yet
the first and last of these are not (one is not now, and the other is not
yet) and that which you call present is not now the same that it was
when you began to call it so.[9]

The first two sentences strike the reader with a real Augustinian shock; the last sentence is practically quoted from the *Confessions*, a book Donne knew intimately.

Donne's sense of the involvement, the sanctification, of the Christian's own
suffering and death in the Passion and death of Christ himself is his strongest
theme, for example in a Lent sermon of 1628:

He that will die with Christ upon Good Friday, must hear his own bell
toll all Lent. ... You would not go into a medicinal bath without some
preparatives; presume not upon that bath, the blood of Christ Jesus, in
the Sacrament then, without preparatives neither. Neither say to your
selves, we shall have preparatives enough, warnings enough, many more
sermons before it come to that, and so it is too soon yet; you are not
sure you shall have more. ... I will give God a cup, a cup of my blood. ...
No martyr ever lacked a grave in the wounds of his Saviour. ... [N]ot
only loss of life, but loss of that which we love in this life; not only the
suffering of death, but the suffering of crosses in our life, contracts the
name, and entitles us to the reward of martyrdom.[10]

Martyrdom, as we have seen, was no remote ideal to Donne. His mother, who
had lost a brother and a son to persecution and her greatly gifted second son to
Protestantism—which may have struck both mother and son as a martyrdom of
a different kind—died, in her eighties, in January 1631. A month later, dying
himself, Donne preached, before King Charles I in the palace of Whitehall, his
last sermon, a meditation he called "Death's Duel, or, a Consolation to the Soul,
against the Dying Life, and Living Death of the Body". According to Izaak
Walton, the congregation who "saw his tears, and heard his faint and hollow
voice" thought "that Dr Donne had preached his own funeral sermon".[11] The
self-dramatisation evident in much of Donne's writing could scarcely go further
than this text, this occasion.

The sermon is very long, full of references to Scripture, in Latin as well as in
English, to Augustine, and to the orthodox understanding of the Trinity, the

Incarnation and the Passion and death of Christ that is central to Catholic Christianity. In it the closeness of a dying man to Christ—we are again in Lent—finds its most elaborate, most intense expression in Donne's work, or perhaps anywhere in Christian writing. The extended climax of the sermon is a journey for preacher and listeners through Holy Week to the Cross, in the spirit of Saint Ignatius's *Spiritual Exercises*, with the pilgrim soul led to identify now with Christ and now with his persecutors and murderers. The whole passage is a tour de force of imaginative but profoundly theological writing: its concluding sentences at the Cross, the last words Donne uttered in public, are almost as stirring on the page as they must have been in the king's chapel on 25 February 1631:

> And then that Son of God, who was never from us, and yet had now come a new way unto us in assuming our nature, delivers that soul (which was never out of his Father's hands) by a new way, a voluntary emission of it into his Father's hands.... For ... as God breathed a soul into the first Adam, so this second Adam breathed his soul into God, into the hands of God. There we leave you in that blessed dependency, to hang upon him that hangs upon the Cross, there bathe in his tears, there suck at his wounds, and lie down in peace in his grave, till he vouchsafe you a resurrection, and an ascension into that Kingdom, which he hath purchased for you with the inestimable price of his incorruptible blood. Amen.[12]

Five weeks later, having had a portrait made of himself in his shroud, he died.

* * *

Although Donne was only eight years younger than Shakespeare, and although Donne certainly, and Shakespeare almost certainly, grew up as a Catholic in a time of persecution, there is a great and evident difference between the provincial playwright never out of emotional touch with the long past of Catholic England but careful to commit himself to no sectarian statement and the London courtier and Protestant cleric, educated for Catholic martyrdom and never out of emotional touch with the Counter-Reformation piety on which he had publicly and officially turned his back.

George Herbert, nobleman, poet and eventually country parson, had little in common with either. During Herbert's childhood, Donne, struggling to win influential friends, had engaged the attention of Herbert's rich, pious mother with poems and dedications. Later, he became her friend and, as we have seen, preached at her funeral. The life of her literary son was a contrast to Donne's in almost every respect. Privileged from birth, Herbert was related to the Pembrokes and the Sidneys, powerful Protestant families of the late Elizabethan court. Herbert had the best possible connexions and received the best possible education. An elegant, clever, delicate boy, he did everything his mother hoped for and at the age of twenty-seven was appointed to the prestigious position of public orator in the University of Cambridge, a job for which excellent Latin, quick wits and perfect manners were essential and which was usually a stepping stone to a government post at court. Herbert attracted the favourable attention of King James; of the weighty, disgraced but unpunished Francis Bacon, who dedicated his last, uncharacteristically pious book, a translation of the Psalms, to Herbert; and of old Bishop Andrewes. Everything promised well for a worldly career close to the king.

Donne the dashing love-poet and renegade Catholic had had to ingratiate his way into earning a meagre living and took the late decision to be ordained in the Church of England probably as a last resort in the advancement of his career. Herbert, by contrast, had to deal with the temptations of an easy life at court, for which his grand family had carefully brought him up. It is clear from the perceptive *Life* of him written much later by his friend and contemporary Izaak Walton, who outlived him by decades, that Herbert had to struggle long and hard in the opposite direction from Donne—that is to say, against the worldly success for which his birth, upbringing and gifts had so well prepared him. As a shy seventeen-year-old, recently arrived at Cambridge, Herbert wrote to his mother deploring the "vanity of those many love-poems that are daily writ and consecrated to Venus" and declared his own "resolution to be, that my poor abilities in poetry shall be all and ever consecrated to God's glory".[13] He kept his resolution and, in due course, consecrated not only his talent but his whole life to God. Pliable, obedient, irresolute by nature, he found it difficult not to do what was expected of him. He regarded with mixed feelings the calculating self-interest of those close to the king. "All rising to great place", wrote Bacon, who had every reason to know, "is by a winding stair; and if there be factions, it is good to side a man's self whilst he is in the rising; and to balance himself when he is placed."[14] On life at court Herbert later wrote: "I can now see plainly that it is made up of fraud, and titles, and flattery, and many other such empty, imaginary, painted pleasures."[15] But they had seemed real pleasures once. He always disliked what he called "the debates and fretting jealousies" of the Cambridge clergy, Andrewes's near-Catholic party quarrelling constantly with the Puritans:

Oliver Cromwell was a Puritan undergraduate at Sidney Sussex College when Herbert was a young fellow of Trinity. But in the university and on the edge of the court he remained, dutifully, unhappily, until his mother's death in 1627. He wrote later:

> I was entangled in the world of strife
> Before I had the power to change my life.[16]

At thirty-four, for once making up his own mind, he resigned as public orator and left Cambridge. More decisions needed to be made; characteristically, he left them to others. In 1629 he married an entirely appropriate wife he had met three days earlier, the match having been long planned by her father. In 1630, on the instructions of Bishop Laud (not yet archbishop of Canterbury), he accepted the modest living of Bemerton near Salisbury and five months later was ordained priest. Years earlier, he had written defensively to a courtier scornful of the clerical life: "It hath been formerly adjudged that the domestic servants of the King of Heaven, should be of the noblest families on earth: and though the iniquity of the late times have made clergymen meanly valued, and the sacred name of priest contemptible; yet I will labour to make it honourable."[17] Whereas the church gave Donne the fame and fortune he had always craved, Herbert abandoned fame and gave the wealth of his inheritance to a country parish, where he lived as an obscure parson for the remaining two and a half years of his frail, consumptive life. Preaching in Saint Paul's, to the House of Lords, before the king at Whitehall—none of this was for him. He cared for the villagers of Bemerton, instructing them in the meaning of the Gospel and the liturgy of the Book of Common Prayer, kindly and generously helping the poor and sick, sustaining regular communal prayer twice every day in his church until he was too weak to leave his house. He died a quiet, perfectly prepared, saintly death. There was in all this no element, no remote suggestion, of Donne-like display. Indeed, had Herbert not also been a writer, little thereafter would ever have been heard of him.

His single prose work, *A Priest to the Temple*, is a plainly expressed, careful and detailed handbook for the rural parish priest, an essential figure in the life of the Church, long neglected in training and esteem. Herbert's handbook did for the parish clergy of the Church of England what Gregory the Great's *Liber regulae pastoralis* had done for the medieval episcopate. Herbert finished the book in his second year at Bemerton, acknowledging in an introductory note how high he had pitched his "form and character of a true pastor ... since he shoots higher that threatens the moon, than he that aims at a tree."[18] The ideal he describes is that of the parson as example and teacher, responsible for the orderly Christian life and for the morals of his family, his household and all his parishioners. The Protestant emphasis is strong: the parson must carry a heavy load of responsibility, but the sacramental life of the Church, in the full Catholic sense, is scarcely present to support him in his work. Matins and Evensong, the said or sung services composed by Cranmer from elements in the age-old Office of the Church, are called by Herbert "the morning and evening sacrifice of the church liturgy", an odd use of the word "sacrifice" to a Catholic of any period. The first *Life* of Herbert, by Barnabas Oley, says that Herbert defended Matins and Evensong, as "gold from dross, the precious from the vile", from the charge of being "taken out of the Mass Book".[19] As for the Eucharist, he calls it, in ordinary Protestant fashion, "the Holy Communion" and expects the parson to celebrate it only "at least five or six times in the year",[20] and that frequency is, it seems, principally so that the churchwardens can have enough opportunities to make sure that the law imposing thrice-yearly reception of communion is being obeyed. With an anxious, near-Catholic glance backward to the Mass, he says that the service worries rather than consoles "the country parson", because "especially at Communion times he is in a great confusion, as being not only to receive God, but to break and administer him."[21] The difficulties of the middle way are exactly caught in his chapter "The Parson Blessing": "In the time of popery, the priest's *Benedicite* and his holy water were over highly valued; and now we are fallen to the clean contrary, even from superstition to coolness and Atheism. But the parson first values the gift in himself, and then teacheth his parish to value it."[22] It is clear from the book that the almost complete excision of the sacramental from the priest's life has left too heavy a demand on the character and strength of the man himself: an interfering bossiness has to be recommended in the place of sacraments, particularly the sacrament of penance, lost to the Christian life. "The country parson is in God's stead to his parish and dischargeth God what he can of his promises. Wherefore there is nothing done either well or ill, whereof he is not the rewarder, or punisher."[23]

A Priest to the Temple is a formative book written at a formative moment in the history of the Church of England. Its portrait of a diligent, faithful pastor is in some respects in accord with the reform of the parish clergy given urgent priority at the Council of Trent. The book reflects and expects, however, a superiority in the parson, a moral and educational but also a social—a class—gulf between him and most of his flock that at least contributed to the disintegration of the English church in the decades after Herbert's death and that has been a major problem for the Church of England ever since. A church that provides for the faithful a coherent sacramental structure gives dependable form to belief in Christ and survives incompetence and bad behaviour as well as outstanding personal quality in its clergy. A church that has lost, or only patchily retained, such a structure will have more difficulty.

On his deathbed, in his last deferral of an important decision to someone else, Herbert consigned to a visitor a manuscript containing more than 160 poems, none of which had ever been printed, asking for it to be given to Nicholas Ferrar:

> Tell him he shall find in it a picture of the many spiritual conflicts that have passed betwixt God and my soul, before I could subject mine to the will of Jesus my Master; in whose service I have now found perfect freedom; desire him to read it: and then, if he can think it may turn to the advantage of any dejected poor soul, let it be made public; if not, let him burn it; for I and it are less than the least of God's mercies.[24]

Ferrar published the book, and it is remarkable that the quiet and subtle poems it contained sold more than twenty thousand copies during the next forty years of contentious religious noise, and since the mid-nineteenth century have made Herbert probably the best-loved devotional poet in the language.

The poems are more various, and many of them are calmer and happier, than Herbert's self-deprecating description suggests. It is true that five of them carry the title "Affliction" and that Herbert's self-knowledge, his agonised consciousness of distance from God, marks many others, including some of his best. In "The Collar" a hectic series of questions and answers swiftly thrown in irregular rhymed lines from one side of his soul to the other ends simply:

> But as I raved and grew more fierce and wild
> At every word
> Methought I heard one calling, *Child*:
> And I replied, *My Lord*.[25]

The poems are like—indeed, are—beautifully crafted notes of a conversation with God conducted perhaps over many years. They are, in other words, prayers; some have long been used as hymns. For all the anguish of several of the poems, there is nothing extreme in Herbert's sense of God, no cries of terror from "cliffs of fall" as in Donne or Hopkins. It is not for himself but for England that he fears a future without faith; in his brief "Envoy", he prays to God:

> Let not sin devour thy fold,
> Bragging that thy blood is cold,
> That thy death is also dead,
> While his conquests daily spread.
> That thy flesh hath lost his food,
> And thy Cross is common wood.[26]

His own pain is the pain in the conscience of any Christian honestly listening to God in Christ and subject to the ups and downs of everyday emotion. He is familiar with the "tempering" of the soul in and through suffering. A poem called "Repentance" ends with the line "Fractures well cured make us more strong",[27] while a stanza in another, "Content", uses a different image to express the same thought, with the added note of obedience to his call to communicate his faith:

> Mark how the fire in flints doth quiet lie,
> Content and warm to itself alone;
> But when it would appear to others' eye,
> Without a knock it never shone.[28]

Of his own sinfulness he is acutely aware, as he is of the fallibility of all human life and effort, but his trust in God is nevertheless unwavering, thankful, serene. "The Flower" records a barren lostness but also his recovery into new confidence:

> Who would have thought my shrivel'd heart
> Could have recovered greenness? It was gone
> Quite under ground as flowers depart
> To see their mother-root, when they have blown;
> Where they together
> All the hard weather
> Dead to the world keep house unknown.[29]

"Our winter is the hiddenness of Christ", Augustine said in a sermon. "In wintertime the root lives on." [30] The secret life of the faithful soul in God, somewhere far below the level of conscious thought or feeling: this Herbert recognises in some of his greatest poems.

Many of his poems are written in the simple first person of a diary. In "Love Bade Me Welcome", deservedly the most loved of all his poems, Christ himself, unnamed, gently replies to the poet's first-person self-deprecation. Sometimes Herbert uses the first person with more distance, to tell the story of his whole life: "Redemption" is a sonnet of powerful resonance into which is compressed the narrative of God's love for the world in Christ's Incarnation and death and the poet's slow response to it. An equally skilful, quite different, sonnet is the famous "Prayer", which is no more than a list of phrases placed side by side without even a main verb.

In one poem only, "The Sacrifice", his masterpiece and the greatest poem on the Passion in English, he uses the first person differently. For sixty-three stanzas of sustained intensity, the speaker is Christ on the Cross. The poem begins with a loaded, arresting stanza, in a manner that persists and gains strength throughout the poem:

> Oh, all ye, who pass by, whose eyes and mind
> To worldly things are sharp, but to me blind;
> To me, who took eyes that I might you find:
> Was ever grief like mine? [31]

The echo of Lamentations, the presence of God, incarnate in the dying Christ, and the end-of-stanza question that tolls through the poem: all these set a high, sorrowful tone, held throughout with a powerful grip on the possibilities of meaning in single lines, single words in a difficult triple rhyme scheme, which Herbert never allows to subside. These stanzas come toward the end of the poem:

> O all ye who pass by, behold and see;
> Man stole the fruit, but I must climb the tree;
> The tree of life to all, but only me:
> > Was ever grief like mine?
> ....
> Now heal thy self, Physician; now come down.
> Alas! I did so, when I left my crown
> And father's smile for you, to feel his frown:
> > Was ever grief like mine?
> ....
> Betwixt two thieves I spend my utmost breath,
> As he that for some robbery suffereth,
> Alas! what have I stolen from you? death:
> > Was ever grief like mine? [32]

In 1930 the young William Empson, at the cutting edge of the new "practical criticism" and no Christian, was profoundly struck by "The Sacrifice": "Herbert deals in this poem, on the scale and by the methods necessary to it, with the most complicated and deeply-rooted notion of the human mind"[33]—with, that is, the truth that in all its simplicity and complexity is at the centre of Christian revelation, the self-emptying life, the love and death, of God.

Behind "The Sacrifice" lie the ancient liturgical questions of the Good Friday Reproaches: "My people, what have I done to you? Or in what have I offended you? Answer me." The Reproaches are not in the Book of Common Prayer, and the veneration of the Cross that they accompany had been banished from the Church of England as a superstitious papist practice. Yet in "The Sacrifice" the mild, conformist Protestant parson of *The Priest to the Temple* wrote of the Crucifixion with as much theological depth, as much traditional orthodox belief, as had the Donne of "Death's Duel". There is here an unresolved inconsistency: it is not surprising that Herbert's two poems called "The H. Communion" are awkward and argumentative, their eucharistic theology uncertain. His defence, in "The British Church", of an ecclesiastical middle way, uniquely protected by God's grace, between the Catholic and the Calvinist is assertive rather than confident. In the long, crudely antipapal "The Church Militant", he can find hope for the Christian future only in America. In "To all Angels and Saints", he apologises, forlornly, to the saints in heaven, particularly to Mary, for not being allowed to enlist their prayers on his behalf. To Mary, "Mother of my God", he says, remarkably:

> Chiefly to thee would I my soul unfold;
>
> But now (alas!) I dare not; for our King
> Whom we do all jointly adore and praise,
> > > Bids no such thing.[34]

By "our King" he means God: this is straightforward Protestant reliance on Scripture alone. But the king forbidding the faithful to ask the help of the Mother of God was actually, of course, the supreme governor of the English church, the king about to be fought, tried and executed—mercifully, for Herbert, after his own death—by the Parliament with which he was supposed to govern the souls of his people.

Herbert has often been taken as an exemplary figure representative of the Church of England at its very best, and at its best moment. But a reading of all his work, which includes a few poems deserving a high place in the story of writing in the

Christian tradition, leaves a Catholic reader with an overwhelming impression of confusion, of incompatible beliefs and obediences barely held together in a single, saintly life. Nicholas Ferrar's community at Little Gidding, where a quasi-Benedictine life of pooled resources, austere habits and much regular prayer was being led by a handful of married men and their families, inspired Herbert before his ordination; inspired Richard Crashaw, who later became a Catholic and a florid Counter-Reformation poet; and inspired Charles I, who visited Little Gidding on retreat. Ferrar translated the work of Juan de Valdés, a sixteenth-century reforming Catholic and friend of Cardinal Pole, and asked Herbert to contribute a preface and notes to the text. Herbert's preface expresses surprise "that God in the midst of popery should open the eyes of one to understand and express so clearly and excellently the intent of the Gospel, in the acceptation of Christ's righteousness".[35] The surprise is significant, and representative. Puritans could see that Ferrar was a Catholic in all but acknowledgement: after his death, he was attacked as a papist in a rabid Protestant pamphlet, and Little Gidding was razed to the ground by Cromwell's soldiers. Ferrar and Herbert believed that the central doctrines of Christian revelation were true, just as Valdés and Pole did, just as Donne did and just as Charles I did, who died for the belief in himself as the proper ruler of the national church. (Charles became a kind of Anglo-Catholic saint in some parts of the Church of England, but, as Augustine repeatedly said of murdered Donatists, "It is not the penalty that makes the martyr, but the cause."[36])

Of Herbert certainly it could be said, as Walter Daniel said, in Augustinian fashion, of Saint Aelred:

> The whole strength of his mind was poured out like a flood upon God and his Son; it was as though he had fastened to the crucified Christ a very long thread whose end he had taken back as far as the seat of God the Father. By this thread I mean the directed energy and concentration of his mind. He always remembered and strove after that which made us when we were not and, when we were evil, made us over again to be good.[37]

The same has no doubt been true of many Protestants in the English church and elsewhere before, during and after the seventeenth century. But a disaster, perhaps *the* disaster, of the Reformation, not yet overcome to this day, was the loss among Protestants of knowledge of Catholic tradition—the ignorance, in England reinforced by fear and prejudice, that blinded so many to truth profoundly shared. Those who saw most clearly that much in Charles I's Church of England was actually Catholic were the consistent Protestants, who abandoned it in disgust. Of these one of the most consistent, and one of the most disgusted, was John Milton, the greatest poet of the English seventeenth century after Shakespeare, but a breaker, not a builder, of the Christian tradition.

*   *   *

Born in 1608, Milton was the clever, indulged son of a prosperous middle-class Protestant Londoner. As a highly educated young man with little to do but read, write and travel, he decided at age twenty-five against a career in the Laudian church; he despised its unreformed place-seeking clergy, as *Lycidas* shows, and could not bring himself "to subscribe slave and take an oath withal" [38] to the Thirty-nine Articles. For the rest of his life, with increasing clarity and conviction, he regarded the divine right of the monarch to govern the church—Catholic or near-Catholic liturgy and belief—and bishops as not properly Christian, as "tyranny and idolatry" to be ended in England, in favour of "liberty", by whatever combination of bold exhortation, political manoeuvring and force might be necessary. For him, as for Presbyterians and "independents" among his contemporaries, the English Reformation, temporarily (they hoped) fixed in the Elizabethan settlement, had not gone nearly far enough. Rome had once been the oppressor, papal and hierarchical power reinforced by superstition. The replacing of the oppression of Rome with English oppression, royal and hierarchical power reinforced by superstition, had the sole advantage of not being foreign. Tyranny and idolatry still characterised the Church of England. But England, in Milton's view, was called to higher things than this prolongation of what he liked, according to a fanciful view of Anglo-Saxon independence of Rome, to describe as "the Norman yoke". The English were God's chosen people, on the analogy of the people of Israel in the Old Testament, and with a superhuman effort and the aid of God they should overthrow both monarchy and the episcopal church and free Christians into their own, individual, truly Protestant, relationship to God. This set of ideas, English, libertarian and Protestant, was of huge significance for the future. It not only inspired the left in English politics and the dissenting churches for at least two centuries after the restoration of the monarchy and the episcopal church in 1660, but conclusively guided the deliberations of the American Founding Fathers a hundred years after Milton's death. All of these ideas God's Englishmen managed to transform into temporary reality by 1649, defeating the king in battle, trying him for treason, executing him and setting up a free commonwealth, though on oligarchic-republican, certainly not democratic, principles. (A majority of Englishmen, if consulted, would have voted for the king in 1649, as they would have voted for the Pope in 1558.)

Milton was the leading propagandist for the English revolution. As Oliver Cromwell's Latin secretary, he defended the king's execution and the abolition of monarchy in a series of pamphlets, in English for home consumption and in Latin to mollify and convince a scandalized Europe. During the twenty years from his return from Italy to the restoration of Charles II as king in 1660, years of civil war in Scotland, England and Ireland and then years of constitutional experiment and muddle ending in the failure of the Commonwealth, Milton wrote almost no poetry, though this was the calling he always felt he himself had been given by God. He defended regicide and wrote against the restoration of the monarchy to the republic's bitter end: his *Ready and Easy Way to Establish a Free Commonwealth* was published less than three months before Charles II's triumphant return. In 1660 Milton was extremely lucky not to be executed: he owed his life to intervention from writers impressing his distinction on the king, to his blindness—he had entirely lost his sight eight years earlier—and, no doubt, to Charles II's canny reluctance to create famous martyrs in the republican cause. To the king's clemency, in any case, we owe the fact that *Paradise Lost, Paradise Regained* and *Samson Agonistes* were all finished and published in an England of "tyranny and idolatry", that is, monarchy, the House of Lords, bishops and the restored Church of England.

None of the ecclesiastical arrangements tried or recommended in the ruins of the national church satisfied Milton, who took to its logical conclusion of churchlessness the Protestant impulse to remove intermediaries between the soul and God. In stark contrast to Herbert, he thought that itinerant preachers, as far as he was prepared to go in the direction of ministry, should be artisans qualified only by not having received a university education. John Bunyan, of whom Milton probably knew nothing, was just such a preacher; he spent half of Charles II's reign in prison but there wrote *The Pilgrim's Progress*, a book of trust in salvation and faithful hope in the city of God. Bunyan never confused, as Milton always did, what is promised in the life to come with what is possible in the earthly city. None of the political arrangements made in the ruins of royal authority turned out to be more than frangible compromises between those jockeying for power. To Milton the Commonwealth was a profound disappointment: God's Englishmen failed again and again to live up to their own successes, to what Milton had called "the most heroic and exemplary achievements since the beginning of the world".[39] The Restoration was, from his point of view, much worse: not only a king returned but a cynical, frivolous, Frenchified king, far better at self-preservation than his naïvely virtuous father, subservient to the Catholic despot

Louis XIV of France, and suspected, rightly as it eventually turned out, of plotting to become a Catholic despot himself. And God? Cromwell himself had said in Parliament in 1655: "This cause is of God or of man. If it be of God, he will bear it up." [40] Was it not now clear that either the cause was bad or God was too weak to bear it up? Milton had enough sense of the distinction between the *civitas terrena* and the *civitas Dei* to condemn the restored state church he took to derive from Constantine, but not enough not to have expected God to be on his own, the revolutionary, side. In the 1660s, isolated, proud, stubborn and furious, convinced that God had abandoned England as a punishment for the mess it had made of its chance of freedom, he returned to his first vocation, which was to be England's Virgil.

Comus and *Lycidas*, written in Milton's prewar youth, are his *Eclogues*, sophisticated pastoral with a good deal of sharp contemporary commentary packed in among fashionable shepherds and enchanters. Now he set himself to complete *Paradise Lost* (his *Aeneid*); *Paradise Regained*, a much shorter, quieter epic, on the scale in fact of the *Georgics*; and, something never attempted by Virgil, a classical tragedy on strict Aeschylean lines. The intention of all three is declared at the end of the second sentence of *Paradise Lost* (so grand is the epic's opening that in two sentences we have reached lines 25 and 26). He is writing, he says, to recount and account for the Fall of Man, the loss of paradise, so that

> I may assert Eternal Providence,
> And justify the ways of God to men. [41]

By the time the Commonwealth had collapsed—and, it seemed to Milton, the dutiful effort of his whole life, the effort to further the providence of God by sweeping away all that impeded it, had been rewarded only by failure—the ways of God to himself and to others certainly needed justifying, to himself and to others. Milton's sense of history, of the teleological intention (of providence, of God), which man can either further or thwart, is proto-Marxist in flavour, and the twentieth-century critic who best understood him was the Marxist historian Christopher Hill.

Milton's relationship to God, and to Christianity, was the subject of fierce controversy for most of the twentieth century, partly because it was the subject of not nearly enough controversy through the eighteenth and nineteenth centuries. For the best part of 250 years, from 1688 until the attacks of T. S. Eliot and F. R. Leavis in the 1930s, Milton was almost universally regarded as England's Christian poet, and *Paradise Lost* was read along with *The Pilgrim's Progress* by almost everyone who could read, baffled as many must have been by Milton's intellectually unrelenting verse. Just as, if Shakespeare were the national dramatist, he must have been a sound Protestant, so, if Milton were the national epic poet—and there is as little competition in his case as there is in Shakespeare's—then he also must have been a sound Protestant, particularly as, unlike Shakespeare, he wrote all his major works on biblical subjects. The real eccentricity of Milton's beliefs was not known about until it was no longer of much interest to literary critics. In 1825, in a particularly flat period of English Christian history, an English translation of his recently discovered *De doctrina Christiana*, written during the same years as *Paradise Lost*, was published. The book shows that Milton was, by the 1660s—he died in 1674—scarcely a Christian at all, rejecting the Trinity and therefore the Incarnation; the orthodox significance of the Crucifixion and Resurrection of Christ; all the sacraments; and the survival of the soul after death. His views would have been regarded as heretical by any Lutheran or Calvinist, as of course by any Catholic. No wonder the book did not see the light of day in his lifetime. And no wonder these views, except by implication, do not appear in his poems: censorship, along with much else that Milton hated, had reappeared in 1660, after which date he was in no position to take risks.

Milton's sense of God was very strong. All his life he knew, as Donne knew, that if God is not goodness and truth, there is no sure goodness or truth in anything; and also that if God is not omnipotent, goodness will not in the end prevail over evil. In *Comus* in 1634 he wrote:

> But evil on itself shall back recoil
> And mix no more with goodness, when at last
> Gather'd like scum and settled to itself,
> It shall be in eternal restless change
> Self-fed and self-consumed: if this fail
> The pillar'd firmament is rottenness
> And earth's base built on stubble.[42]

The grisly reduction, in *Paradise Lost* book 10, of the glamorous figure of Satan to a hellish serpent who can only hiss and gorge and hiss eternally is an unforgettable dramatisation of this conviction. The moment is an unmediated intervention of the power of God (or the power of the poet); it has nothing to do with Christ's death on the Cross or with Christ's descent into hell on Holy Saturday. Milton always needs God simply to prevail; of the saving mediation of Christ as God and man he says little, and with little conviction, because he did not believe the central tenets of Christianity to be true. In *De doctrina Christiana* his need of God is plainly expressed: it is, he writes, intolerable and incredible that evil should be stronger than good, and should prove the true supreme power. Therefore God exists. Further evidence for the existence of God is provided by the phenomenon of conscience or right reason. This cannot be altogether asleep, even in the most evil men. If there were no God, there would be no dividing line between right and wrong.[43]

Satan in book 4 of *Paradise Lost* may say, "All good to me is lost; / Evil be thou my good",[44] but it is only in his confrontation with God, however unrepentant of rebellion he may be, that his words have meaning, that his reversal of their meaning makes sense.

Milton is as aware as his contemporary Hobbes, or as Nietzsche, that if God does not exist, there is for mankind nothing but "eternal restless change", a jungle of competitive wills in which evil, being in worldly terms stronger than good, will prevail, or, in other words, in which might becomes right. All three of Milton's major poems demonstrate in different ways his sometimes desperate hope (the oxymoron is like his own) that God will, on the contrary, cause good to prevail over evil—as if in the life and death and Resurrection of Christ, God had not already done so. It is at this profoundest level of disbelief that Milton is not a Christian poet.

Christ appears, of course, in both *Paradise Lost* and *Paradise Regained*. In neither poem is he ever called Christ. A chilling judge in Eden after the Fall, the Son is cruel enough to pretend not to know what Adam and Eve have done and cold enough to condemn Adam's (unfallen and nobly human) love of Eve that prompted him to join her in fallenness. In both poems Christ is presented, not as the second Person of the Trinity, bound in everlasting love to the Father and the Holy Spirit, but as someone—in *Paradise Lost* a kind of angelic deputy, in *Paradise Regained* a perfect man—who has *earned* his distinction from all other beings. God, addressing him in book 3 of *Paradise Lost*, says that he has

> though thron'd in highest bliss
> Equal to God, and equally enjoying
> God-like fruition, quitted all to save
> A world from utter loss, and hast been found
> By merit more than birthright Son of God.
> Found worthiest to be so by being good,
> Far more than great or high.[45]

Much later, in book 12, when the archangel Michael is telling Adam and Eve, banished from Eden, the future story of mankind, Milton describes redemption in Christ in correct Lutheran terms, but the lines are flat and the tone is legalistic, passionless and above all loveless, picking up a little warmth only for the foretold Second Coming, when

> the Earth
> Shall all be Paradise, far happier place
> Than this of Eden, and far happier days.[46]

Michael may conclude by telling Adam that if he believes correctly and behaves virtuously,

> then thou wilt not be loath
> To leave this Paradise, but shalt possess
> A Paradise within thee, happier far,[47]

but it is clear from Milton's fierce attack on the Catholic future and on the laziness and sinfulness of most people that those who decide rightly what to believe and how to behave will be a tiny minority of "the just" because

> the rest, far greater part,
> Will deem in outward rites and specious forms
> Religion satisfied. . . .
> . . . .
> so shall the world go on,
> To good malignant, to bad men benign,
> Under her own weight groaning, till the day
> Appear of respiration to the just,
> And vengeance to the wicked.[48]

The longed-for Day of Judgement was widely felt to be imminent as *Paradise Lost* was in the making. The republican moment in England was not only the free-for-all of the *libido dominandi* that Milton in book 2 bitterly contrasts with the unity of the fallen angels under Satan's command. It also released a seething ferment of ideas among which millenarian predictions of the imminent reappearance of Christ were common. A few preachers crossed the boundary of sanity and proclaimed themselves Christ returned. Milton wrote of "the shortly-expected King": when human replacements for the unsatisfactory human king had delivered no more impressive or just a government than his, the hope for the Second Coming to set all to rights can only have become stronger.

Certainly the account of Christ's first coming in *Paradise Regained* is very far indeed from the full Christian revelation of the New Testament. The only scene dealt with in the poem's four books is Satan's temptation of Jesus in the desert, where Jesus's overcoming of Satan makes him "By proof th'undoubted Son of God",[49] as if, before this, Jesus had been an ordinary child, an ordinary man. God confirms this, saying:

> I have chose
> This perfect man, by merit call'd my Son
> To earn salvation for the sons of men.[50]

This, in the poem, Jesus does by setting his obedience in the face of temptation against Adam's disobedience. "Now thou hast aveng'd", the angels say to him at the end of the poem:

> Supplanted Adam, and by vanquishing
> Temptation, hast regain'd lost Paradise.[51]

For whom? the reader asks. Not for many, as is always the case in Milton. No sense of the sacrificial love of God for sinful man colours the bleak righteousness of the Jesus of the poem. Indeed, his contempt for ordinary people ("And what the people but a herd confus'd / A miscellaneous rabble?"[52]); for Rome (in all its meanings) since the corruption of the mythically just republic; for "All monarchies besides throughout the world";[53] and for Athens and all of Greek philosophy suggests Shakespeare's Coriolanus rather than the Jesus of the Gospels:

> What wise and valiant man would seek to free
> These thus degenerate, by themselves enslav'd,
> Or could of inward slaves make outward free?[54]

Milton's sense of grievance, grievance against the people of England who wasted their chance of freedom, grievance against God who chose him to defend freedom and then let his side lose, are clearest of all in *Samson Agonistes*. The tragedy is stiff and awkward, as a play almost unperformable, but it is tense with passionate feeling:

> Why was my breeding order'd and prescrib'd
> As of a person separate to God
> Design'd for great exploits; if I must die
> Betray'd, captiv'd, and both my eyes put out?[55]

It was easy for Milton to identify with the blinded Samson, prisoner of the victorious Philistines, full of self-disgust and self-pity on account of his marriage to a treacherous daughter of the enemy (Milton had married a royalist wife; the marriage was a miserable failure), and grieving for God's disgrace in the contest with the Philistines' false God. Samson challenges the Philistine champion Harapha by combat to decide "whose God is strongest, thine or mine".[56] Harapha replies:

> Presume not on thy God, whate'er he be,
> Thee he regards not, owns not, hath cut off
> Quite from his people, and deliver'd up
> Into thy enemies' hand.[57]

"If it be of God, he will bear it up."[58] It is hard to avoid the sense that Milton regarded the ordinary defeat, in the *civitas terrena*, of his political cause as proof that God had failed to ensure the victory of those who had deserved to see the *civitas Dei* established, by them, on earth, the same profoundly foolish expectation that Hobbes in *Leviathan* had furiously attributed to "the Authors of all this Spiritual Darkness, the Pope, and Roman Clergy, and all those besides that endeavour to settle in the minds of men this erroneous Doctrine, that the Church now on Earth, is that Kingdom of God mentioned in the Old and New Testament."[59] Milton's understanding of power in relation to the kingdom of God is as far from Augustinian as it is possible to get.

Samson Agonistes ends in a horrible bloodbath, reported by a messenger because this is a classical tragedy. Samson, humiliated by performing for the Philistine lords, pulls the whole building down, killing himself and all the Philistine "choice nobility and flower".[60] Milton, the old revolutionary, celebrating this suicidal act of terror as the redeeming action of God, swerves from the biblical account to tell us, "The vulgar only scap'd who stood without",[61] a class exemption that makes the climax of the play even more like a successful version of the Gunpowder Plot than it is in the Book of Judges.

And yet, though Milton was a long way from orthodox Christianity always, and got further away as he aged, never believing that there was any need for such a concept as "orthodoxy", regarding "the Church", however understood, as misused power and idolatry, ending as a churchless rebel fighting for, perhaps just fighting, his God alone, there is more to be said. The greatness of *Paradise Lost* has to do with its evocation of the beauty of God's creation, not just in the garden but also in the innocent, blessedly consummated love of Adam and Eve before the Fall, and also with its evocation of sadness, sadness at the loss of paradise, which is Satan's loss of heaven through his own fault before it is Adam and Eve's loss of Eden through theirs. The sympathy no reader can help feeling for Satan, at least before his sinister corruption of Eve's obedience, is fellow feeling for one who has been cast out of the presence of God for his pride and has brought his loyal friends down with him to hell but is so responsive to the beauty of the earth and of Eve that he very nearly loses the impetus to spoil them. The fallen angel who has not yet lost all his brightness represents any human being darkened by sin but not yet without all trace of the image of God in which he was made. The upshot for the reader of the first two books of the poem is the pathos of attempts to construct in a Godless world (hell) an imitation of heaven that will dull the pain of its loss. That neither hard-working liberty nor the glamour of a material "paradise" will replace closeness to God the council in Pandaemonium clearly tells us, for all Satan's defiant assertion of his self-justified individualism in the face of a God who is only more powerful, not better, than he is:

> What matter where if I be still the same,
> And what I should be, all but less than he
> Whom thunder hath made greater?[62]

Of the nihilism, mere competition of self-interest and self-will, that was already on the distant European horizon Milton had a keener sense than any of his contemporaries in England except Hobbes, whose remedy for it was the absolute authority of an irresponsible totalitarian state, whether monarchist or republican, where "no law is unjust", a consummation of the enterprise on which Henry VIII had embarked with only More and a handful of others understanding the implications of what the king was doing.

Unlike Hobbes, Milton never let go of his idea of a God who is good, whose goodness will prevail, who is approachable by reason (rather than love), who should be obeyed. There is an unconsoled moral dutifulness in all this that strikes a modern reader as Kantian rather than Christian. At the same time, Milton's argumentative self-sufficiency in his relation to God, his pride in his own and England's chosenness, and his hope for the new world of the Messiah's reign on earth have a Jewish tone that is audible in more than one development of independent Protestantism in the seventeenth century. Certainly the Old Testament meant much more to Milton than the New; perhaps the cabbalistic studies of which his Cambridge college, Christ's, had been the English centre when he was an undergraduate had influenced him more than he realised. Passionate for liberty, in *Areopagitica* a resounding polemicist for freedom of the press, he would have censored only Catholics. The English (and traditional American) sense that Protestantism and liberty go together owes him as much as it owes Locke. Milton's Baconian hopes for reason and the progress of science were very high; he even thought that education of itself would "repair the ruins of our first parents".[63] It is not surprising that these expectations, together with his lifelong ambition to deliver people from the "tyranny and idolatry" of ecclesiastical Christianity, made him a hero of the Enlightenment: Voltaire, who regarded Shakespeare as a barbarian, wrote expertly and appreciatively of *Paradise Lost*. In England until the twentieth century, Milton was a hero of the nonconformist left; abroad, he was an example to both the American and the French Revolutions.

And yet the overwhelming sadness of the best passages in *Paradise Lost* suggests that, somewhere in this rugged forerunner of the Whig English future, there was a perhaps unrecognised sorrow for the lost security of a Christianity that had little to do with the power of kings or their replacements and within which strenuous, lonely efforts to justify the ways of God to men did not yet have to be made. The Catholic despotism that Milton and his contemporaries could see gaining ground in France, and rightly suspected to be the secret goal of Charles II, was another thing altogether. It was no more Augustinian as a version of the Church than the shaky anti-Roman nationalism of the Church of England and would bring no less grief to those whose sense of Christian truth it attempted to suppress.

1. See John Carey, *John Donne: Life, Mind and Art* (London, 1981), chap. 1.
2. John Donne, *The Complete English Poems*, ed. A.J. Smith (London, 1971), pp. 163–64.
3. Ibid., p. 316.
4. Ibid., pp. 328–29.
5. Ibid., p. 311.
6. John Donne, *Selected Prose*, ed. Neil Rhodes (London, 1987), pp. 149–50. (I have modernized the spelling.)
7. Ibid., p. 280.
8. Ibid., p. 300.
9. Ibid., p. 121.
10. Ibid., pp. 290–91.
11. Quoted in ibid., p. 351.
12. Ibid., p. 326.
13. Izaak Walton, *Life of George Herbert*, in George Herbert, *Works in Prose and Verse* (London, 1846), 1:21–22.
14. Francis Bacon, *Essays*, ed. John Pitcher (London, 1985), pp. 92–93.

15. Herbert, *Works in Prose and Verse* 1:51.
16. George Herbert, "Affliction (I)", lines 41–42, in *The English Poems of George Herbert*, ed. C. A. Patrides (London, 1974), p. 67.
17. Herbert, *Works in Prose and Verse* 1:35.
18. Ibid., p. 144.
19. Ibid., p. 121.
20. Ibid., p. 202.
21. Ibid., p. 199.
22. Ibid., p. 246.
23. Ibid., p. 193.
24. Ibid., pp. 84–85.
25. Herbert, *English Poems*, p. 162.
26. Ibid., p. 200.
27. Ibid., p. 69.
28. Ibid., p. 85.
29. Ibid., p. 172.
30. Augustine, sermon 36.4.
31. Herbert, *English Poems*, p. 48.
32. George Herbert, "The Sacrifice", lines 201–4, 221–24, 229–32, in ibid., pp. 54–55.
33. William Empson, *Seven Types of Ambiguity* (1930; London, 1961), p. 233.
34. Herbert, *English Poems*, p. 94.
35. Herbert, *Works in Prose and Verse* 1:254.
36. Quoted in Serge Lancel, *Saint Augustine*, trans. Antonia Nevill (London, 2002), p. 288 and note.
37. Walter Daniel, *The Life of Aelred of Rievaulx*, ed. and trans. F. M. Powicke (London, 1950), p. 19. (I have slightly altered the translation.)
38. Quoted in Christopher Hill, *Milton and the English Revolution* (London, 1977), p. 39.
39. John Milton, (Latin) *Second Defence of the People of England*, trans. C. Hill (1655), quoted in ibid., p. 182.
40. Quoted in Christopher Hill, *The Experience of Defeat* (London, 1984), p. 187.
41. John Milton, *Paradise Lost*, 1.25–26.
42. John Milton, *Comus*, 593–99.
43. Quoted in Hill, *The Experience of Defeat*, pp. 317–18. Translated from Milton's Latin by C. Hill.
44. Milton, *Paradise Lost*, 4.109–10.
45. Ibid., 3.305–11.
46. Ibid., 12.463–65.
47. Ibid., 12.585–87.
48. Ibid., 12.533–35, 537–41.
49. John Milton, *Paradise Regained*, 1.11.
50. Ibid., 1.165–67.
51. Ibid., 4.606–8.
52. Ibid., 3.49–50.
53. Ibid., 4.150.
54. Ibid., 4.143–45.
55. John Milton, *Samson Agonistes*, 30–33.
56. Ibid., 1155.
57. Ibid., 1156–59.
58. Quoted in Hill, *Experience of Defeat*, p. 187.
59. Thomas Hobbes, *Leviathan*, ed. C. B. Macpherson (London, 1968), p. 708.
60. Milton, *Samson Agonistes*, 1654.
61. Ibid., 1659.
62. Milton, *Paradise Lost*, 1.256–58.
63. Quoted in Hill, *Milton and the English Revolution*, p. 148.

CHAPTER THIRTEEN

THE SEVENTEENTH CENTURY II

Pascal

In seventeenth-century England it was not possible for writers in the Christian tradition to escape the pressures and deflections of competing versions of Protestantism and their implication in a confused struggle for political ascendancy. It might be thought that in contemporary France, a Catholic country under increasingly effective and centralized Catholic rule, a Catholic writer of genius might, in comparison with Donne or Milton, have encountered few problems. That this was not so reflects the fact that the England and France of the middle of the century shared in suffering the consequences of the Reformation, most inimical to life lived with and for the priorities of the *civitas Dei*. Thinkers and writers in both countries, with varying degrees of acceptance or pain, had to contend above all with the unleashed *libido dominandi* of the modern sovereign state and of the factions within it contending for influence.

In England, since the abrogation of papal authority in the reign of Henry VIII and its confirmation in the Elizabethan settlement of the English church, the secular government, whether royal or briefly republican, had regarded itself as charged with absolute control of religion in the country; even the libertarian Commonwealth had treated Catholics as beyond the national pale. In France, the monarchy had achieved this control before the Reformation had made any inroads into ordinary Catholic life. Fifteenth-century France had seen the consolidation of the all-justifying theory of the divine right of kings. In 1516 an agreement between an ambitious French king (Francis I) and a lazy Renaissance Pope (Leo X) had given the king the right to appoint all French bishops and other holders of high office in the French church. The decrees of the Council of Trent, for all the traditional conciliarism of the French bishops, were not promulgated in France for fear that their papalism would undermine the independence of the national church, at this period and for these purposes known as "Gallican" in defiance of Rome. Meanwhile, the feudal religious wars of the last third of the sixteenth century, fought between Catholic and Protestant nobles and their retainers, inflicted much misery on France. They ended, more or less, with the Edict of Nantes, in which Henry IV allowed parts of the country to exist under Calvinist, in France called Huguenot, local government. This was a different royal solution to the problem of Protestantism from the English attempt to include most shades of Christian opinion, barring loyalty to the Pope, in a single national church. To Henry IV's successors it was no more satisfactory than the English compromise turned out to be for Charles I. Civil war, though with religion a decreasing element in rebellious contention for power, threatened for decades and sporadically flared into open conflict. In the course of the seventeenth century, however, the rulers of France, culminating in the absolutist Louis XIV, set themselves to exclude the Huguenots altogether from a France of *un roi, une foi, une loi.* This was finally achieved in 1685 with Louis XIV's revocation of the Edict of Nantes, just as an openly Catholic king came briefly to power in England before his deposition and exile. Tens of thousands of Huguenots left France, many of them finding a new home in the now conclusively Protestant England.

Between the reign of Henry IV—assassinated in 1610 by a Jesuit-trained fanatic for whom the king was not Catholic enough—and Louis XIV's assumption of adult control of his country in 1661, firm government in France was sustained only by two cardinals. Richelieu, the pattern for as well as the enabler of Louis XIV's absolute rule, was one of the most effective practitioners of *Realpolitik* in European history. Machiavellian in his ruthless manoeuvring for the constant increase and strengthening of France's power, he played against each other, with a religious impartiality that shocked devout French Catholics, the forces involved in the Thirty Years' War to France's advantage and so as to weaken Habsburg Spain and Austria as much as possible. At home, he taxed France as it had never been taxed before, enriching a rapidly expanding bureaucracy but incurring the fury of jealous nobles—eliminated by execution or murder as soon as they became seriously dangerous—and the resentment of a regimented urban middle class with frustrated aspirations to liberty. Richelieu's grip on the French church was tight, and in it he would permit no rival influence. His whole career was like that of a successful Wolsey, combined with those of Queen Elizabeth's Lord Burghley and Charles I's Laud, Richelieu's exact contemporary. But Richelieu and his master, the pious, pliable, foolish Louis XIII, not unlike his brother-in-law Charles I in temperament, had no Parliament to contend with. Nor, in due course, did Louis XIV. The *États généraux*, the nearest institution in late medieval France to the English Parliament—not very near since the king had never depended on it for the granting of taxes—was not summoned between 1614 and 1789, when its assembly marked the start of the French Revolution. England owed its seventeenth-century revolutions and the survival of its tamed monarchy through the eighteenth, nineteenth and twentieth centuries to the precedents in the sixteenth for parliamentary restraint on, or necessary parliamentary collaboration with, the king or queen.

The church over which Richelieu presided as the king's chief minister from 1629 to 1643 had, on account of its Gallican separateness from the Tridentine programme, come late and patchily to the renewal of the Counter-Reformation. Individual reformers could achieve a good deal: Saint Francis de Sales, who died in 1622, had, a long way from Paris, converted many Huguenots and inspired many penitents to lead a more devoted Catholic life. Cardinal de Bérulle, personally resented by Richelieu, had overcome considerable opposition to bring to France the reformed Carmelite monasticism of sixteenth-century Spain and to found the French Oratory in Paris. Saint Vincent de Paul was, throughout Richelieu's ministry, working with considerable success for the raising of pastoral standards among the parish clergy and for the Christian relief of the poor, sick and victims of warfare. These were exceptional and saintly men. The French church in general, particularly at the top, was set in bad old ways, with entrenched nepotism, pluralism and absenteeism confining most of the senior positions to sons of the nobility unlikely to make much of their nominal responsibilities. Richelieu himself, then a soldier, had been consecrated as a bishop at the age of twenty-two in order to keep a lucrative benefice in the family. He did the job conscientiously for several years before his rise to "great place", but for him to have been, throughout his time as a constantly preoccupied minister, the Abbot-General of Cluny was all too characteristic of the period: the most prestigious monastic position in the country was held by a man who was not a monk and had little time to devote to the office's responsibilities. Meanwhile, the rapidly increasing presence of Jesuits at court, running schools for the rich, and much disliked by Richelieu, was bent less on reform than on the acquisition, through education and the confessional, of influence among the influential, power over the powerful.

In this complicated and contentious ecclesiastical world, at the centre of which were Paris and the all-powerful cardinal, another development was by the 1630s attracting much attention. In 1601 a ten-year-old girl, Angélique Arnauld, had become, in the unreformed fashion of old family privilege, abbess of the easy-going, upper-class convent of Port Royal, twenty miles from Paris. The homily of a passing Capuchin friar, preached to the nuns in 1608, precipitated Angélique into a personal conversion of lasting consequence for herself and her abbey, which she set about transforming, though she was only seventeen. Forty years later, Port Royal had long been an exemplary community, occupying both the old buildings in the country—now called Port Royal des Champs—and a new abbey, Port Royal de Paris, in the heart of the city. Recruits had flocked to join Port Royal, a good number of them belonging to Mère Angélique's own large family, her effect on which was not unlike that, long before, of Saint Bernard on his. The Rule of Saint Benedict, understood in accordance with the austere Cistercian foundation of the house, was now observed to the letter; the disciplines of silence, of enclosure, of absolute personal poverty had been restored; the community was renowned for its perpetual devotion to the Blessed Sacrament. In Paris the nuns were educating a number of girls consigned to them for an upbringing of high Christian tone and content. At Port Royal des Champs, a small group of celibate male scholars, not in monastic vows though some were priests, all committed to the interests of Mère Angélique's enterprise, were leading a life of prayer and work very like that of the exactly contemporary Little Gidding and would soon be educating a few boys, among them Jean Racine. They were known as *les solitaires* or *les messieurs des granges*, "the gentlemen of the barns".

Concerned, as all women superiors of any period have had to be, to find sound priestly direction for her nuns, Mère Angélique had asked Saint Francis de Sales shortly before his death to allow her community to join the new order of Visitandine nuns founded by him with his friend Saint Jane de Chantal. Unfortunately for the future of Port Royal, her request was refused, and in 1627 Port Royal became, by itself, the Order of the Blessed Sacrament, adding a scarlet cross to the nuns' white habits. In 1633 Mère Angélique invited a man she had known and admired for years, the most remarkable preacher and pastor of souls of the time, the Abbé de Saint-Cyran, to become the community's spiritual director. The choice was wholly understandable: Saint-Cyran had inspired many conversions from tepid to serious Catholic living and had fired with new dedication a considerable number of parish priests and religious. Nothing but the best was good enough for the formidable abbess that Mère Angélique had now been for many years. But in 1638 Richelieu had Saint-Cyran arrested and imprisoned on a charge of unorthodox teaching on the subject of contrition in the sacrament of penance. Saint-Cyran was unorthodox only in being more rigorous than was usual according to the conventions of lax formality then prevailing at court. His arrest shocked many, including Vincent de Paul, who held Saint-Cyran in high regard. But Richelieu, wanting a rival influence removed, particularly from proximity to the king, kept Saint-Cyran in prison. Richelieu died in 1642. Shortly after his release from prison in 1643, Saint-Cyran also died, but his association with Port Royal was the beginning of a theological controversy that burned its way through the lives of the nuns, innocent of theology though almost all of them were, until the community, decades later, was totally destroyed. It also ignited a theological firestorm in the French church from which it has not even yet entirely recovered.

Saint-Cyran had studied for years, in Paris and then in Bayonne, alongside an earnest theological scholar from the Low Countries, Cornelius Jansen, who became a close friend and a strong influence on him. Jansen was professor of theology at Louvain during the Thirty Years' War; he wrote a stinging attack on Richelieu for besieging the town and a year later became bishop of Ypres, a Habsburg appointment. Jansen's bold project as a writer was to rescue Catholic theology from the attenuated Scholasticism of the universities, to rescue the Counter-Reformation Church from the entanglement with the *civitas terrena* that he saw resulting from the deliberate policy of the Society of Jesus, and, above all, to rescue Saint Augustine from his appropriation by Protestantism and restore him to a central place in Catholic thought. Had the only consequence of this project been its effect on Saint-Cyran himself, infusing him with the Augustinian warmth and seriousness with which he preached the dependence of every soul on the freely bestowed grace of God, it would have been difficult for the enemies—of whom Richelieu was only the first—of such attractive, challenging teaching to find an excuse more substantial than Richelieu's for attacking Saint-Cyran and his pupils. But Jansen wrote an enormous, unappealing book, the *Augustinus*, which was published in 1640, two years after its author's death, and this book provided the necessary fuel for the fire that was eventually to smoke out the blameless nuns of Port Royal and all their supporters. The fire was called "Jansenism" by those who fanned its flames.

In 1643, the year of Saint-Cyran's death, Louis XIII also died, to be succeeded by his five-year-old son Louis XIV, for whom Richelieu's successor, Cardinal Mazarin, governed the country for the next eighteen years. A weaker character than Richelieu, on a weaker royal base, Mazarin, a clever, beguiling Italian with the close support of the Austrian queen mother and regent, nevertheless steered France safely through flurries of rebellion (the "Fronde") among the Parisian bourgeoisie and disaffected nobles during the minority of Louis XIV. Mazarin held the bishopric of Metz and a large number of abbacies: he died a very rich man. He had inherited from Richelieu, and sustained to hand on to the young king, the priorities of control and unity, in the French church as in the French state.

* * *

Blaise Pascal in 1643 was twenty. He was an exceptionally gifted mathematician who had already written a groundbreaking essay on conic sections and was working on a calculating machine that would add, subtract, multiply and divide eight-digit numbers. The project succeeded—he made fifty versions of the machine before he was satisfied with it—and the mathematical principles involved were used three hundred years later in the devising of early computer language. This brilliant young man and his family were living in Rouen. His father, Étienne, a prosperous tax official in Richelieu's bureaucracy, had narrowly escaped imprisonment for, once only, standing up to the great man on a policy issue. He had been widowed when Blaise was three, and he educated his son and two daughters himself in an atmosphere of hard work, books, intelligent encouragement for his children and conventional Catholic piety. Three years after Saint-Cyran's death, when Étienne Pascal's elder daughter had married and left home, a parish priest inspired by Saint-Cyran's teaching and example, and a couple of young men converted by the same teaching to a life of serious Christianity and good works, had a striking effect on the Pascal family. Blaise, then his younger sister Jacqueline, and then their father were drawn into a new and deeper commitment to the faith they had always practised. This is usually called Pascal's "first conversion", but the phrase is misleading in its suggestion of a sudden, surprising event. What happened to the Pascals in the mid-1640s was gradual and easy to imagine, a matter of impressive accidental encounters and the influence over several months of a fine priest. This family experience was not in the least academic and had nothing to do with books of theology; it was personal, private and of the spirit. Their everyday occupations did not change: Blaise Pascal at the time was busy with experimental research on atmospheric pressure and on the existence of the vacuum, denied by Aristotelian orthodoxy and by the pure reasoning of Descartes, still alive and a famous authority. Pascal defended his findings with the conviction of one who had seen the evidence.

When, in 1647, Blaise and Jacqueline moved to Paris, it was not surprising that they began regularly to attend Mass at Port Royal, where Père Singlin, a holy and wise disciple of Saint-Cyran, was now chaplain and where the young Pascals grew increasingly attached to the atmosphere and spirituality of the abbey. Nor was it surprising that, in due course, Jacqueline should become sure of her vocation to be a nun in Mère Angélique's community. The next few years were unsettled and unhappy. Étienne Pascal retired from his job in Rouen and joined his children in Paris but refused to allow Jacqueline to become a nun. In 1649 the family had to move out of Paris for more than a year to avoid the street violence of the Fronde, the feeble imitation of the English revolution that, early in that year, had achieved the trial and execution of Charles I. Soon after their return, Étienne Pascal died; now his son, always ill and perhaps afraid of living alone, tried to prevent Jacqueline from joining Port Royal. He failed. Temporarily estranged from his beloved sister, Pascal worked and travelled restlessly for nearly three years, advancing various mathematical and scientific projects, living much in the world and acquiring aristocratic friends and considerable fame. Then, suddenly, alone one evening in Paris, his relationship with Jacqueline and therefore his connexion with Port Royal restored, he had a profound experience of the living truth of Christ.

Only by chance do we know about the "night of fire", the critical event in Pascal's life, which took place on 23 November 1654. After Pascal's death in 1662, a servant, puzzled by a thick patch in the doublet Pascal always wore, cut it open and found a piece of paper wrapped in a piece of parchment. The writing on the parchment is a fair copy, slightly altered, of the rapidly written text on the small piece of paper. The document, known as the "Memorial", records, in twenty-four scribbled lines, not consecutive prose but separate statements of enraptured belief, the impact on Pascal of two hours of certainty and joy in the piercing presence of Christian truth.[1] The lines include three quotations from Saint John's Gospel, one from Saint Matthew, three from the Old Testament, and one from the priest's prayer just before receiving Communion: *a te nunquam separari permittas*, "let me never be separated from you." Three of the lines are quoted in Latin, including the words *Deum meum et Deum vestrum* in the accusative, from Saint John's account of Christ on Easter morning, "I am ascending to my God and your God"[2], but the quotation from the Mass is in French, suggesting that Pascal was in the habit of praying the words himself. In the parchment fair copy, he changed the line written on the paper as "Certainty, certainty, feeling (*sentiment*—perhaps 'love'), joy, peace" to "Certainty, joy, certainty, *sentiment, vue*". *Vue* means "sight" but also has the force of "understanding", as in the "sight", the "I see", the perception of "intelligible beauty" of Plato, Augustine and Anselm.

The text begins, after noting the date and the time, with the cry, as of a conclusive discovery: "God of Abraham, God of Isaac, God of Jacob, not of the Philosophers and scholars/scientists (*savants*)". The God of the Memorial is the God of Moses recognised in Christ: "God of Jesus Christ", declares the third line; "Jesus Christ" is repeated twice more; and the longest sentence in the text is quoted from Saint John's account of Jesus's prayer just before his arrest: "This is eternal life, that they may know you, the one true God, and him whom you have sent, Jesus Christ."[3] This registering of a moment of grace, of shining conviction that Pascal wished never to forget, may seem random in its references to Moses and Ruth, to Jeremiah and Psalm 119, to Jesus recognized by Mary Magdalen in the garden, to the Mass. But the upshot is a record of encounter with God in Christ, finding the words of scriptural encounters with God, of Christ's closeness to his Father, for a declaration of faith in the truth of Christian revelation and in the need of the contrite sinner to stay with Christ—"I have been separated from him. I have fled him, renounced him, crucified him"—for knowledge of God is in knowledge of Christ: "Father, the world has not known you, but I have known you." [4] What is more, the only sentence that appears twice, the second time slightly altered, is this: "He can be found [held onto] only through the ways taught in the Gospel." The coherence of the Memorial is here, in Pascal's defining, definitive obedience to the knowledge of God encountered in Christ, knowledge of a different order from the knowledge of God as a necessary being, rationally deduced from various kinds of data by philosophers and *savants*, of whom Descartes was an obvious contemporary example. "Descartes unhelpful and uncertain", [5] Pascal noted later.

The distinction between kinds of knowledge is the key to Pascal's writing, most of it now concerned with the things of God, in the less than eight years of life that remained to him. But while the exhilaration that certainty struck from him in the Memorial was new, the distinction between different orders of knowledge, of perception, was not. It is of capital importance in understanding what Pascal has to say about Christian belief, Christian truth, to realise that he arrived at the distinction between orders of knowledge from his training and experience as a rigorous experimental scientist, abreast of all the latest developments at a time of rapid scientific advance. As early as 1651, three years before the night of fire, he wrote, in the preface to a scientific treatise on the vacuum, the rest of which is lost or was perhaps never completed, of the distinction between what we can learn from experiments and what we can learn only from authority. The point of making this distinction here was to free his work on the vacuum from the weight of authority relied on by his opponents to refute results, contradicting the opinion of authority, that he had seen with his own eyes. That science makes progress is the implication of his argument: new facts may always be discovered, and in their discovery the antiquity of a scientific theory is likely to be a hindrance, not a help. With other kinds of information, on the other hand, such as

who was the first king of the French; where do geographers place the first meridian; which words were in use in a dead language ... only authority can enlighten us. But where authority has the greatest power is in theology, because there authority is inseparable from truth and except through authority we can learn nothing; to arrive at complete certainty on matters which are the most ungraspable by the reason, it

is enough for authority to make them visible in the sacred books ...
because the principles of theology are above both nature and reason,
and because the human intelligence, being too weak to arrive there by
its own efforts, is unable to travel to the heights of understanding unless
it is carried there by an all-powerful and supernatural force.[6]

It is to demonstrate that the changing facts of science need neither grace nor
authority to be established that Pascal here insists, in very Catholic fashion, that
the unalterable truths of faith, "made visible" in Scripture by the Church's teaching, need both.

In another essay, on the mathematical mind and the art of rhetoric, written
probably in 1657, Pascal presses his distinction rather differently in a discussion
of the power of rational argument:

I do not speak here of divine truths, which I would not dream of
bringing down to the level of the art of persuasion, because they are
infinitely above nature: God alone can put them into the soul, and in
whatever way pleases him. I know that it is his will that they should
enter the mind from the heart, and not enter the heart from the mind.
This is to humble the arrogant power of the reason, which pretends
that it should be the judge of those things which the will chooses, and
to cure the weakness of the will, which is always corrupted by its pol-
luting attachments.[7]

Between the writing of these two passages, Pascal had not only undergone the
night of fire. He had also read a great deal of Augustine—hence, no doubt, the
appearance here of "the heart" and "the will"—because he had become involved
in the theological controversy that had at its centre, almost by chance, the community of Port Royal.

Although Pascal did not stop working on mathematical and scientific problems until the last few months of his life, his personal priorities were rearranged
for good by what happened to him on 23 November 1654. In January 1655 he
made his first retreat at Port Royal des Champs, staying for a fortnight with the
"gentlemen of the barns", who now became his friends. From this retreat there
survives a reported conversation between Pascal and one of the priests among
the *solitaires*, a nephew of Mère Angélique, Antoine de Saci. This record, only
about ten pages long, was written by the priest's secretary, impressed by Pascal's
presence at Port Royal—"I need not explain who he was, this man admired not

only by the whole of France but by the whole of Europe" [8]—but not so over-come that he failed to catch the precise quality of Pascal's intellectual excitement a few weeks after the night of fire. The discussion concerned two contrasting philosophers, the pagan Epictetus and the celebrated French essayist of the six-teenth century, Montaigne. The thought of each was well known to Pascal but unknown to de Saci. With sharp forensic skill, Pascal set Epictetus's optimistic reliance on human reason to deliver a sound moral life against Montaigne's relaxed, pessimistic scepticism: those who rely on reason, Montaigne had observed, never agree, so reason is demonstrably an unsound guide, truth is undiscoverable and religion can be bracketed off from civilised life as a mere cause of contention among the educated. So Epictetus, Pascal says, "knowing man's duty but not knowing his powerlessness, is lost in pride", while Montaigne, "knowing man's powerlessnes but not his duty, sinks to a cowardly inertia".[9] While to Epictetus the human mind is evidently too strong to need to bother with the idea of God, to Montaigne it is evidently too weak. (These radically incompatible views, often held by the same person, have become so common among the educated in our own world as to be now quite unremarkable.)

The cleverness of the way the contrast has been presented becomes clear when Pascal looks at the possibility of reconciling one with the other. "It might seem", he says, "that, since one [of these accounts] is true exactly where the other is false,

> it ought to be possible to form a perfect moral system by combining them. But instead of peace there results from such a combination only war and general destruction. ... They break and annihilate each other to make way for the truth of the Gospel. It is the Gospel that brings contraries into accord through a skill entirely divine, and, uniting all that is true while banishing all that is false, makes the real wisdom of heaven where opposites, irreconcilable in human teaching, are harmo-nised. ... This is the new and astonishing union that only God is able to teach and that only he is able to achieve and that is nothing less than the image and the result of the ineffable union of two natures in the one person of Christ.[10]

What Pascal will later call *misère de l'homme*, the poverty of man, may be trans-formed into the glory of man, but only through grace, only in Christ. In the "Con-versation with M. de Saci", it is de Saci rather than Pascal who refers several times to Augustine. Indeed, Pascal at this point apologises for straying from philosophy, which he knows something about, into theology, which is de Saci's subject. But

before long, circumstances drew Pascal not only into reading Augustine extensively and with passionate attention, but into writing in defence of the very truth
that was still "new and astonishing" to him in January 1655.

In the course of that year, the storm raised by the official questioning of the
orthodoxy of Jansen's *Augustinus* that had been slowly gathering for more than a
decade broke over the nuns and their friends. The story is complicated and
needs careful unravelling, as does the relation of Pascal both to Port Royal and to
its embattled theological supporters.

In 1643, the year of Saint-Cyran's death and three years after the publication
of Jansen's *Augustinus*, a book called *De la fréquente communion* appeared and was
read by many influential Parisians and their wives, who would never have contemplated attempting the *Augustinus*. The book was by Antoine Arnauld, youngest brother of Mère Angélique and more than twenty years her junior. It argued
for conversion to a new seriousness among worldly Catholics accustomed to
taking their religion lightly, particularly for a new seriousness in the approach to
the sacraments of penance and the Eucharist. That anyone in the Church should
object to such a book might seem strange. But Arnauld argued his case from an
Augustinian understanding of grace, inspired by Jansen and Saint-Cyran, that
appeared close to Calvin's in its insistence on our absolute dependence on grace
for any good action, and also on its irresistible power. What had become of
human freedom to respond, or not, to God? What had become of the merit we
might earn in the sight of God by our own efforts? The only variety of Protestantism well known in France was Calvinism. One long-term objective of both
Richelieu and Mazarin was to rid France of Huguenots once and for all. Another
was to neutralize the exemplary rigour of Port Royal, more and more admired
even at court, but which the two cardinals and the Jesuits, at the centre of power
in France, saw as a divisive wedge driven into the government-controlled unity
of the national church. Arnauld's book presented the enemies of Port Royal
with a golden opportunity to make progress toward both objectives by accusing
Arnauld and his mentor, Jansen, of heresy.

Neither Saint-Cyran nor Arnauld nor anyone else connected with Port Royal—
where Jansen had never been and where the nuns had almost certainly not read
his book—remotely resembled an actual Calvinist, as their theological opponents must have known perfectly well. The Port Royal community was famous
for its eucharistic orthodoxy and its devotion to the Blessed Sacrament, and
both the orthodoxy and the devotion were the theme and motive of Arnauld's
work. But Arnauld was a bleak, tactless character, trained as a lawyer and entirely
without the winning charm of Saint-Cyran; the aged and much revered Vincent

de Paul regarded Arnauld as a self-righteous menace and threw his considerable weight against him. Without Arnauld's persistence—he continued to write, more and more combatively, for Jansen and against the Jesuits—and his stubborn insistence on his own unbending correctness, it would have been more difficult even for the Jesuits and the government not to leave the harmless nuns in peace. There was a dogmatic extremeness, impervious to mystery, in Arnauld, and perhaps in Jansen, which destroyed Augustine's careful balance between grace and freedom and was certainly not orthodox.[11]

In 1649 five propositions, all of a strongly anti-Pelagian colour and said to be taken from the *Augustinus*—whether they were really to be found in the book was disputed for decades—were condemned as heretical by the theological faculty at the Sorbonne. The Pope, Innocent X, who disliked Mazarin, had the issue examined with unusual care by a committee of cardinals. In 1653 he at last concurred with the condemnation of the five propositions, no doubt partly because Mazarin had just achieved the final putting down of rebellion in Paris and, like most seventeenth-century Popes, Innocent wanted to appear more powerful than he was by emerging from controversy on the winning side. His decision cleared the way for the Sorbonne to expel Arnauld from the theological faculty: this plan had the full support of Mazarin, now back in firm control of France, who saw the Jansenists as a dissident faction to be extirpated, and also had the support of the Jesuits, because to them Port Royal was a threat, a magnetic centre of rigour and reform altogether outside their influence.

With Arnauld's expulsion looming, in January 1656 the gentlemen of the barns asked Pascal, the most intelligent supporter they had and brother of a nun in the community, for help. The result was the *Provincial Letters*, eighteen pieces of attacking journalism, written and published over the next fourteen months. Pascal was by no means a trained theologian. To write the *Letters*, he had to read Arnauld's books, some recent Jesuit writing to find out what the Jansenists were up against, and a good deal of Augustine. Whether he read much, if any, of the *Augustinus* is not clear and, significantly, mattered little then and matters not at all now. Although the object of Pascal's campaign was the Jesuits rather than the government, the two were so closely intertwined that it was brave to write the letters and difficult to find printers willing to take the risk of publishing them. Pascal's anonymity was, except among his friends, sustained until well beyond the appearance of the last letter.

The *Provincial Letters* are a masterpiece of satirical writing, witty, urbane, persuasively readable but also passionately felt. The assumption of the persona of a naïve gentleman recounting to a provincial friend with bemused astonishment the quarrel at the Sorbonne was a stroke of genius, making possible the constant juxtaposition of simple, traditional Christian faith and the sophisticated accommodations of the Jesuits to the lives and values of the worldly. The underlying subject of all the letters is grace, the precise definition of which was the current theological bone of contention. From Pascal's treatment of the subject, something quite different emerges: grace as a word, inadequate as human words always are, for the undeserved love of God for us and for our love of him, love from the broken and contrite heart with which we approach him in the sacrament of penance and in which we receive his forgiveness—for the sacrament of penance was the real focus of the quarrel.

The Jesuits had developed a system—known as "casuistry", once a respectable word but deprived of its innocuousness by Pascal—for use in the confessional, designed for flexibility and adaptation to the circumstances and character of the sinner. Pascal mocks it both for being new and for taking out of Christian life the reality of God's challenge to the truthfulness of the soul. In the fifth letter, he has a Jesuit explain that

> "as directors of consciences we scarcely read the Fathers and refer in our writings only to modern casuists.... There are 296 of them, of whom the earliest was only eighty years ago." "So all this has come into the world since your Society?" [Pascal innocently asks]. "Thereabouts." "That's to say, Father, that at your arrival Saint Augustine, Saint Chrysostom, Saint Ambrose, Saint Jerome and the others just disappeared." [12]

One would not expect Pascal to regard the everyday guidance of souls as an area in which the scrapping of authority in favour of a modern, progressive approach is permissible. Worse, the Jesuit system is easy on the sinner. Here there is an edge to Pascal's mockery because he regards this moral suppleness as genuinely dangerous. He also recognises it as driven by the Jesuits' greediness for power. In the same letter, he says of them:

> You must realise that it is not their object to corrupt morals; that is not their policy. But nor is it their sole aim to reform them. That would be bad policy. This is how they think. They have a good enough opinion of themselves to believe that it is useful and almost necessary for the good of religion that they should be trusted everywhere and govern the consciences of all. And as the strict principles of the Gospel are appropriate

for governing some kinds of people, they use them at those times when they will be helpful to themselves. But since these same principles do not suit the intentions of most people, in these cases they leave them to one side, so as to have something with which to satisfy everyone.[13]

The tone is gentle, but the attack is fierce; behind the Jesuits' resentment of Jansenist rigour, Pascal has detected the resentment of those whose creeping relativism is shown to be what it is by the clarity of absolute standards of goodness and truth.

The first ten of the eighteen *Letters* are those "written to a provincial gentleman". They come to a crushing climax when the Jesuit of the reported conversations finds himself saying:

> This is how our [Jesuit] Fathers have dispensed people from the *burdensome* [Pascal's italics] obligation of having here and now to love God. . . .
> It was reasonable that in the law of grace of the New Testament, God should remove the annoying and difficult obligation that there used to be in the rigorous law, of performing an act of perfect contrition to be justified. . . . Otherwise, indeed, Christians, who are the children, would not nowadays put themselves back into the good graces of their Father more easily than the Jews, who were slaves, obtained mercy from their Lord.[14]

To which it is scarcely surprising to find Pascal replying:

> This is to break "the great commandment on which hang the whole law and the prophets"; to strike at the heart of devotion; to deprive people of the spirit that gives life; you are saying that the love of God is not necessary to salvation; and you even go so far as to pretend that "this dispensation from loving God is the advantage that Christ brought into the world."[15]

The next six letters are addressed directly to "the Reverend Jesuit Fathers", and the last two, the longest and most seriously argued, to the young Louis XIV's Jesuit confessor, Père Annat. In letter 17 Pascal replies to the dismissive deduction that since he, the anonymous writer of all the letters, is a heretic, nothing he says deserves to be believed by anyone since "you say that it is enough of a reply to all my fifteen Letters to say fifteen times that I am a heretic."[16] Pascal's defence is threefold and powerful. In the first place, he is a faithful Catholic, a dutiful parishioner who does not miss Mass, an ordinary layman with nothing to gain or lose from the dispute; he is not a priest, not a theologian, and has no position at either Port Royal or the Sorbonne:[17] these are not only the words of his assumed persona but, truthfully, his own. Secondly, there is no heresy dividing the French church; the Jansenists as well as the Jesuits are orthodox Catholics, and those who make a full confession of their Catholic faith are, he insists on the authority of Saint Gregory the Great, to be believed. Thirdly, since all agree in condemning what is not orthodox in the five propositions, the real question is one of fact—whether the propositions are to be found in Jansen's book—and not of truth: the faith itself is not at issue. With debating skills that must have infuriated the Jesuits, Pascal summarises the argument to make his opponents appear merely stupid:

> To put the matter in two words: either Jansen's teaching on grace was orthodox [i.e., that of Saint Augustine and Saint Thomas Aquinas], in which case he has made no mistake at all; or he taught something different, in which case he has no defenders at all. . . . If it is found that he taught something different, you will have the glory of having understood him best, but they will not have the misfortune of having made a mistake in faith.[18]

In the last letter, he presses the argument home by showing that the Pope may well have been deceived as to what was or was not, in fact, in the *Augustinus*: Popes, being human, can of course be wrong as to matters of fact, though not as to matters of faith. Pascal's examples are telling:

> It was in vain that you [the Jesuits] obtained from Rome the decree against Galileo, which condemned his opinion as to the movement of the earth. It will not be this that will prove that it stays still; and if there are reliable results of experiments to prove that it turns, all men together could not stop it turning, nor stop themselves being turned with it. . . . The King of Spain did better to believe Christopher Columbus, who had just come back [from the new world], rather than the judgement of the Pope who had never been there.[19]

This is the scientist speaking, the young man who had defended the existence of the vacuum, proved by experiment, against the authority of Descartes and the venerable past. The distinction he is making here is one best made by a scientist. He would have been delighted to know that when Galileo was accused by his students of cowardice for abandoning, under pressure from the Church, his assertion that the earth revolved around the sun, his defence was that one does not die for a fact, which someone else would sooner or later establish in any case. And Pascal clearly was cheered to be able to quote Augustine making the same distinction twelve hundred years earlier: We must not expose Scripture to the ridicule of unbelievers, Augustine said, by insisting that everything in it is literally true, for example, that the moon is greater than the stars, "because, once they knew that we believe things in Scripture which they know for a fact to be false, they would laugh at our belief in other things that are more hidden, like the resurrection of the dead and eternal life." [20] As Newman said in the nineteenth century, also referring to Galileo: "Religious truths, unlike scientific truths, cannot take care of themselves." [21]

Pascal's forensic brilliance can dazzle the reader into missing the quieter, more positive, thoroughly Augustinian confidence in the truth of the love of God, the joy of conversion and the interaction of freedom and grace that underlies all the *Letters*. Laying to one side of the actual life of any Christian the clashing terminology that he knows is being used to attack "persons more than errors",[22] Pascal says simply:

> The only way of bringing into agreement these apparent contradictions that ascribe our good deeds now to God and now to ourselves is to recognise that, as Saint Augustine says, "our [good] actions are our own, because of the free will that produces them, and they are also God's, because of his grace, which makes our will produce them." [23]

The impenetrable mystery of grace, which is also the common sense of Christians, had been left thus unresolved, after protracted argument, by the Council of Trent's justification decree. Pascal in the course of his research discovered that this was so, and, in one of his "Writings on Grace", rough drafts of a more properly theological discussion of the issue than he published in the *Letters*, concluded, sensibly:

> Let us learn from this pure teaching [of the Fathers and of the Council of Trent] to defend at the same time both the capacity of [human] nature against the Lutherans, and its incapacity against the Pelagians ... without wrecking free will by grace like the Lutherans, and without wrecking grace by free will like the Pelagians.

And let us never think that to escape only one of these mistakes is enough to keep us in the truth.[24]

He wrote later in a single-sentence note: "To make of a man a saint, there must certainly be grace, and whoever doubts this does not know what a saint is, nor what a man is."[25]

Jansen was caricatured in the baldness of the five propositions. It is nevertheless probably true, as it is certainly true of Calvin, that he had extrapolated from the anti-Pelagian writings of Augustine, read with new attention after the Lutheran Reformation, firm, excluding teaching on grace that Augustine had left in the mysteriousness, not for us to understand, of God's dealings with human beings: "Some men try hard to discover in our will what good is particularly our own, owing nothing to God; how they can find this out, I just do not know."[26] Saint Anselm in his third Meditation, praying, "Lord, my heart is before you. I try, but by myself I can do nothing; do what I cannot",[27] is as Augustinian as Pascal, with the same emphasis on the sinner's dependence on God, and no one has ever accused Saint Anselm of heresy. If Jansen and then Arnauld had laid themselves open to the charge of overdefinition, Pascal never did, and in France in the 1650s, the issue was in any case, as he was fully aware, the excuse rather than the reason for the onslaught on the defenders of Jansen. Balthasar was surely correct to conclude:

> It is much more important to show clearly how far in Jansenism, despite its narrowing, the greatness and breadth of Augustinianism was sought, sighted and actually realized, than to nail Pascal to a condemned theological position and to derive from this the right to ignore him. Pascal comes to Port Royal from something of his own that is greater, and he finally passes beyond Port Royal to something of his own that is greater yet.[28]

The *Provincial Letters* stopped in March 1657. Their quality had naturally made matters worse rather than better. They were widely read. They polarised opinion. They greatly magnified the scale of the dispute. In vain had Pascal written, correctly, at the end of the last completed letter, that only the Jesuits had anything to gain from proving that Jansen, "a doctor and bishop who died in the communion of the Church" had perhaps been not wholly orthodox, when his propositions "are condemned by everyone without exception in the very sense in which you have explained you want them condemned. Isn't this enough?" says Pascal.[29] The Jesuits, worsted in the argument and tumbled from the moral high ground, were furious; so were their many supporters and penitents. Just before the first letter appeared, Arnauld was sacked by the Sorbonne; soon his doctorate was removed; he remained in disgrace until years after Pascal's death. Mazarin compelled the gentlemen of the barns and the boys in their school to leave Port Royal. In 1656, the year of most of the *Letters*, the new Pope, Alexander VII, issued a bull condemning Jansenism and requiring the priests and religious of France to sign a formulary forswearing it, but Mazarin, hedging his bets and keen to maintain Gallican independence of Rome, allowed its promulgation to be delayed for four years. A black cloud hung over the Port Royal nuns but did not yet burst. In 1659 a savage Jesuit response to the *Letters*, the *Apology for the Casuists*, was put on the Index of Forbidden Books; but the *Provincial Letters*, which had been translated into Latin and English and were now being read all over Europe, had been on the Index since September 1657. In 1660 the royal council ordered all copies to be burned. No French government was going to support what could be made to appear a dissident, quasi-Protestant faction in the national church, a faction that was, at the very least, embarrassing the prosperous and powerful, the *honnêtes hommes*, the *gens du monde*, who sent their sons to Jesuit schools and had their paths through life made comfortable by their Jesuit confessors—nor, in the seventeenth century's choppy waters of religious controversy, blown into breakers everywhere by the gales of secular power, was Rome.

* * *

Meanwhile, Pascal, while the dispute hung fire, continued with his mathematical work and wrote the occasional essay in defence of the Jansenists. He was also, as only his family and a few friends knew, assembling material for a major book, *On the Truth of the Christian Religion*, to be written for his intelligent contemporaries, whose disdainful or careless scepticism, or, more commonly, complacent nominal Christianity, really frightened him. He got nowhere near the completion of the book. Always disabled by severe headaches and stomach pain—his sister said that he could never digest ordinary food and could drink only tepid liquid in small sips—he died in the summer of 1662, just thirty-nine years old, his last months a torture of suffering made only more painful by the medical practices of the day. He left not his book but notes for his book, isolated sentences, paragraphs of varying length, some pieces several pages long, work sketched, work unfinished, work giving a degree of insight into his mind and soul that the completed book would almost certainly not have allowed us. He wrote on large pieces of paper and cut them into different-sized strips. When he died, he had threaded about half the strips on string in twenty-eight bundles, each with a provisional title. He left the rest in a disorder which has since been differently sorted by each of a number of editors. There are, so far, 969 fragments; new ones occasionally surface. But Pascal's *Pensées*, however the fragments are arranged and read, is one of the great books of the world and the first written by a profoundly orthodox Christian to confront head on what we easily recognize as modernity, both in its overconfidence in human capacity and in its nervous anxiety that human life means nothing.

The objective of the planned book is no longer narrowly controversial, no longer the product—as the *Provincial Letters* were, however splendidly they rose above it—of a specific quarrel. The objective now is to bring people to God, through Christ, in the Church. Pascal was writing not only for "the philosophers and *savants*" who relied solely on reason to make sense of the world and their lives, but also for the lazy, the self-indulgent, the educated but thoughtless, the bored who filled their lives with distraction, the simply indifferent. In his day, such people belonged to a small, privileged minority, a few of whom were already convinced that philosophy, science and the use of reason were well on the way to solving all human problems. The people for whom Pascal was writing have vastly increased in proportion, as well as in number, in all the countries belonging to the civilisation of the first world, in the three and a half centuries since his death. And the *Pensées*, bought and read by thousands, particularly in the twentieth century, has survived his mathematical and scientific works for the reason he himself so well understood: progress has left behind his science, but nothing leaves the truth behind.

The enterprise of which the *Pensées* are all we have may be understood as a supremely intelligent exploration of the perception of the truth that had struck Pascal so forcefully on the night of fire. In the last of the *Provincial Letters*, after deploring the "imaginary contradictions" theologians make between freedom and grace, he wrote:

> According to this great saint [Augustine], whom the Popes and the Church have given us as the authority in this matter, God changes the human heart by a celestial sweetness which fills it, and which, surpassing all human delight, makes us on the one hand aware of our mortality and our nothingness and on the other able to discover the grandeur and the eternity of God.[30]

Human wretchedness, poverty, fallenness; the power, eternity and glory of God; Christ, who shed his glory to join our wretchedness and so to make possible God's saving of us from our sinful selves: the contrast and its resolution in Christ is the subject of Pascal's planned book. "Not only", he wrote, "do we know God only through Jesus Christ, but we know ourselves only through Jesus Christ; we know life and death only through Jesus Christ. Outside Jesus Christ we do not know what our life is, or our death, or God, or ourselves."[31]

However the *Pensées* are arranged, it soon becomes clear to the reader that Pascal intended to begin his book with an account of the human condition— "our mortality and our nothingness", "the wretchedness, poverty, of man without God", *misère de l'homme sans Dieu* —discoverable by anyone prepared to think clearly about it. Although he was certain that it is impossible for us by using our reason alone to arrive at Christian truth, nevertheless he was accustomed to, and entirely in favour of, thinking. He knew that imperfect human beings can produce nothing perfect out of themselves. "It is in vain that you seek in yourselves the cure for your wretchedness. All your brilliance can take you only to the recognition that it will never be in yourselves that you will find truth or goodness."[32] Philosophy, ungrounded in the God who is truth and who has given us the capacity to recognize, if only in part, his truth, is beset by inevitable epistemological uncertainty and is bound to lead to scepticism and also to endemic disagreement. Philosophical argument cut loose from revelation will deliver only 280 kinds of sovereign good, annihilating the phrase's meaning. On the other hand, although man is no more than "a thinking reed", he can think, and therefore he should.

Man alone in creation is conscious of his condition, knows that he will die, knows that in relation to the infinite spaces of the universe he is as nothing, the earth on which he lives no more than a tiny speck. Against the scale of a creation recently vastly expanded in human perception by the telescope, Pascal sees the relative, temporary littleness of the *civitas terrena* with a clarity even sharper than Augustine's:

> Let man think of himself as wandering in this remote outpost of nature, and from this little prison where he finds he has been put, I mean the universe, let him learn to value at their real worth the earth, kingdoms, cities, himself. What is man in infinity?[33]

At the same time, the even more recent revelations of the microscope have shown man the equally humbling mysteries of the infinitely small. Pitched as we are between ungraspable extremes, we can but yield to awe:

These extremes touch and are joined by the force of their travel in opposite directions, and they meet in God and only in God. So let us understand our scope: we are something, and we are not everything. What we have of being takes from us knowledge of first principles, which are born from nothing; and the little being that we have hides from us the sight [understanding: *vue*] of infinity.[34]

"We are something" because if we think at all we find in ourselves, for all our weakness, frailty and fallibility, a trace of God, a possibility of recovering our openness to his glory. We know about the glory of God because we have lost it, the innocence of paradise, the closeness to God in whose image we were made. With Augustine, Pascal sees the revealed mystery of original sin as the only account of our nature that can explain us to ourselves. Original sin is "the nub, the knot (*nœud*) of our condition". It shocks us. It seems deeply unjust. "Nothing hits us harder than this doctrine; and nevertheless, without this mystery, the most incomprehensible of all, we are incomprehensible to ourselves." It is not discoverable through "the arrogant efforts of our reason", but only in the "simple submission of reason" to "the inviolable authority of religion", which teaches us "two equally constant truths of faith, that man in the state of creation or of grace is raised above the whole of nature, made into the likeness of God and sharing in his divinity; and that in the state of corruption or of sin he has fallen from that state and is made into the likeness of the animals."[35] It is instructive to compare Pascal's response to the apparent injustice of our inherited loss of closeness to God, our inherited culpability and our inherited punishment, with that of Milton, Pascal's exact contemporary. Milton's heroic effort to "justify" God's treatment of us is a campaign that ends in the proud truce of Adam's "paradise within ... happier far", or in Jesus's human defiance of Satan in *Paradise Regained*. It is the very opposite, both intellectually and emotionally, of Pascal's submission to God revealed in Christ and to the teaching authority of the Church. For Milton, original sin, as a description of the human condition, is a scandal to be surmounted or recovered from, to be left behind as we face the human future confident in our own strength. For Pascal, it is not only the revealed, therefore the loved, truth that explains us to ourselves; it is also confirmed by the evidence we find if we look within ourselves or look without at the mess that our greed, selfishness, laziness and pride—our *libido dominandi*—makes of all enterprises of the *civitas terrena*.

The "both ... and" of Pascal's "two equally constant truths of faith" is of critical importance:

Those who lose their way lose their way only for lack of one of these two things. It is possible to know God without knowing our misery, or our misery without knowing God; but it is not possible to know Jesus Christ without knowing both.[36]

Knowledge of God without knowledge of our wretchedness delivers pride. Knowledge of our wretchedness without knowledge of God delivers despair. Knowledge of Jesus Christ centres us, because in him we find both God and our wretchedness.[37]

The despair of knowing our wretchedness without knowing God may not be the grand desolation of the thoroughgoing atheist (or of the existentialist taking as a justification for nihilism those *Pensées* intended only to alarm with the accuracy with which they describe man without God). It is more likely to be merely "fickleness, boredom, anxiety".[38] In a fragment labelled *Misère*, Pascal says:

The only thing that consoles us for our miseries is diversion, and yet it is the greatest of our miseries. For it is this above all which stops us reflecting about ourselves, and which takes us unnoticeably to perdition.[39]

Diversion (the very opposite of conversion)—distraction, work, games and entertainment—fill up the days so that thought is avoided. Conversely, and the observation catches Milton perfectly, "those who have known God without knowing their own misery have glorified not him but themselves.... That is the result of knowledge of God that manages without Jesus Christ."[40] Pascal knew that already more common than either despair or arrogance (or the combination imagined in Milton's Satan) was mere indifference, the indifference of suspended judgement, of the relativism that supposes all religion no more than the result of "habit, education, custom, local tradition and other such things, which, although they carry along the majority of ordinary people who teach religion on this weak basis, are overturned by the slightest breath of scepticism".[41] "Anyone who imagines he can stay neutral", committing himself neither to Christian truth nor to scepticism, "is a perfect example of a sceptic. This neutrality is of the essence of the sceptical party; whoever is not against them is perfectly and precisely for them; this is their strength."[42] That Pascal recognised not the progress of science but this sheer carelessness as to our life and its meaning, our fate and our death as the great contemporary danger to people's faith is one among many marks of his extraordinary farsightedness.

Naturally, however an editor arranges the *Pensées*, there is more coherence in what would have been the first section of Pascal's book than in the rest. His urgent sense of the scale of the difference it makes whether or not Christianity is true is the reason for this first section, the basis of the argument, being a description of human life that anyone can recognise. It is also the reason for his taking further in the *Pensées*, into an exploration of the nature of faith, his old distinction between observation of the material world, the use of reason, and the acceptance in grace of the truth of God revealed in Christ. The ascending order of these three modes of knowledge, so like Plato's ascending order of the three modes of beauty, and therefore of love, in the *Symposium*, has now become crystal clear. Equally clear, and as personally searching as in Plato, is the challenge of the three kinds of value that they imply. Observation of the material world belongs with the valuing of wealth and power, of greatness as recognised in the *civitas terrena*. Deduction from facts and abstract reasoning, as of the scientist, the mathematician or the philosopher, belong with the valuing of intellectual greatness: "Great geniuses have their power, their fame, their victory, their splendour, and have no need at all of worldly greatness, which means nothing to them. They are recognised not with the eyes but with the mind, and that is enough."[43] This is a kind of knowledge and a kind of recognition with which Pascal was personally familiar; they were perhaps for him, as for any Christian of outstanding intellectual gifts, always the great temptation. He can also mock them. Metaphysical proofs of the existence of God, he says, are too complicated to be of any use after the brief moment in which people understand the argument: "an hour later they are afraid they got it wrong."[44] Meanwhile:

Saints have their power, their fame, their victory, their splendour, and do not need either worldly or intellectual greatness, which mean nothing to them and which can neither add nor take away. They are recognised by God and the angels and not by the senses nor by investigating minds. God is enough for them....

Jesus Christ, without possessions or any outward show of knowledge, is in his own order of holiness. He made no discoveries; he never reigned; but he was humble, patient, holy, holy, holy to God, terrible to devils, without sin. O with what great pomp and wonderful magnificence has he come in the eyes of the heart, where wisdom is perceived.[45]

"The eyes of the heart": the phrase is Paul's, and Augustine's—Christians, Augustine wrote, should "look into Scripture, the eyes of their heart on its heart"[46]—as is Pascal's order of holiness, which is the order of love. "Jesus Christ,

Saint Paul, follow the order of love (*la charité*), not that of the intellect; because they wanted to warm, not to instruct. Saint Augustine the same."[47]

> From all bodies together no one could successfully make a single little thought: this is impossible, of another order. From all bodies and minds no one could successfully draw an impulse of real love (*un mouvement de vraie charité*): this is impossible, of another order, supernatural.[48]

What moves us to tears, to prayer, to love? Pascal poses the question and answers it exactly as Augustine had. There is a choice, which is both God's and our own. "Everyone loves; the question is, what does he love? Consequently we are not told not to love, but to choose what to love. But how can we choose unless we are first chosen?"[49] That is Augustine. In the most famous sentence in the *Pensées*, Pascal wrote: "The heart has its reasons, of which the reason knows nothing; we are aware of this in a thousand things." Less familiar is the rest of this single fragment:

> I am saying that the heart naturally loves the universal being, and naturally loves itself: but which it loves depends on which it is committed to; it hardens itself against one or the other, at its choice. You have rejected one and held on to the other. Is it on account of reason that you love yourself?[50]

The question cuts with a moralist's, a psychologist's, knife, sharpened for Pascal by Augustine. Elsewhere, Pascal analyses the choice between the self and God with a swift argument characteristic in its mixture of common sense, logic and revealed truth:

> Whoever does not hate in himself his self-love, and the instinct that carries him into making himself his God, is really blind. Who doesn't see that nothing is so contrary to justice and truth? For it is false that we deserve [to be God]; and it is both unjust and impossible to get there, because everyone wants the same thing. It is therefore a manifest injustice into which we are born, from which we cannot detach ourselves, from which we must detach ourselves.
>
> However, no [other] religion has noticed that this was a sin, nor that into it we were born, nor that we are obliged to resist it, nor has thought of giving us the remedy for it.[51]

So much for the eighteenth century's long-lived assumption that "self-love and social are the same." [52]

The *Pensées* are rooted in a sensible, everyday realism that shows Pascal always keeping in mind the people he hoped would read his book, everyday people, literate, educated, but not necessarily scholars, theologians, scientists or mathematicians. Even the "wager", the famous experiment in probability theory (a professional interest that he had applied, among his grand friends, to the practicalities of gambling), ends with the simplest of recommendations. Since, he says, you have everything to gain and nothing to lose by taking a chance on Christianity being true, try it. Learn from others who have turned to the Church, have behaved as if they believed until they did. "What harm will come to you from taking this course? You will be faithful, honest, humble, grateful, kind, a sincere, true friend, ... and you will realise in the end that you have bet on something certain, something infinite, for which you have lost nothing." [53]

The attitude of this highly sophisticated lay intellectual toward the Church, which, as an instrument of government in seventeenth-century France, was treating him and his friends with bullying menace, is one of straightforward confidence and devotion. "There would be too much obscurity if the truth had no visible signs. One admirable sign of its being is always there in the visible assembly of the Church." [54] "The history of the Church should properly be called the history of truth." [55] There is no paradox here, but a profoundly Augustinian sense of what the Church is and of what she is not. She is not the *civitas Dei* but a *corpus permixtum* in which the judgement between those who are truly of God and those who only appear to be must always be left to God. [56] On the other hand, the Church is, for faithful Catholics, in the sacraments, most of all in the Eucharist, the visibility, the reality, of Christ's presence in the world. "It is impossible for those who love God with all their heart not to recognise the Church insofar as she is evident. It is impossible for those who do not love God to be certain of the Church." [57] In a wonderful letter Pascal wrote to his friend the Duc de Roannez's sister, who was hesitating as to her vocation to Port Royal, he applies to the hiddenness of God and to our perception of him a tripartite division of the kind that appealed to him. This one he uses only here. God stayed hidden, he writes, under the veil of nature that covers us, until the Incarnation; then he was even more hidden under the cover of his humanity. Finally he chose to live in the strangest and most impenetrable hiding place of all, in the bread and wine of the Eucharist. Many pagans, Pascal goes on, penetrated the veil of nature and discovered through its visibility an invisible God. Christian heretics know and worship God in Jesus Christ the man. "But to recognise him in the bread of the Eucharist belongs only to Catholics; only to us does God grant this much light." [58]

It is impossible in a short space to do full justice to the scope and penetration of the *Pensées*. Only Pascal's Old Testament scholarship now seems dated, as his long view of the continuing existence and fidelity of the Jews, whom he regards with both awe and sympathy, certainly does not. In whatever order the fragmentary text is arranged or read, Christ is always at its centre, the focus of Pascal's graced and thankful gaze. A beautiful meditation, called by Pascal himself "The Mystery of Jesus", begins with the lonely figure in the garden of Gethsemane, where "Jesus will be in agony until the end of the world. We must not sleep during this time." [59] But, like the disciples in the garden, we do sleep. However: "While his disciples slept, Jesus achieved their salvation. He has done this for each of the just while they slept, both in the nothingness before their birth and after their birth in their sins." [60] Later in the meditation, Jesus speaks, as he does in one or two of George Herbert's poems. What he says is simple, everyday, nevertheless unexpected:

Be comforted; you would not seek me if you had not found me. . . .
Let yourself be guided by my rules; see how well I have guided the
Virgin and the saints, who have let me work in them. . . . I am present
to you through my word in Scripture, through my spirit in the Church,
through my power in the priests, through my prayer in the faithful. [61]

"You would not seek me if you had not found me" is a clue to be held onto by any wanderer in the labyrinth that the *Pensées* can seem to be. It will take him, if he does not let go of it, to the evident truth of another memorable sentence: "There are only two kinds of people one can call reasonable, those who serve God with all their heart because they know him and those who seek him with all their heart because they do not know him." [62] To the seeking and finding of God, his of us, ours of him, Pascal often returns. Because of his experience in the night of fire, because also of his understanding of what was really at issue in the Jesuit-Jansenist dispute about grace, he knew the recognition of God in Christ to be at the very heart of the conversion of anyone to the truth. It is this knowledge, almost the reverse of the concentration on the hidden God thought to be central to the *Pensées* by those who have read only a few of them, that informs his delicate sense of the exact relation between the darkness—ours—of resistance, and the light—given us by God—of faith. Here is one example:

It was not right for Christ to appear in a fashion obviously divine and able absolutely to convince everyone; but nor was it right for him to come in a fashion so hidden that he could not be recognised by those who would sincerely seek him. He wanted to make himself perfectly knowable by them, and so, to appear revealed to those who seek him with all their heart, and hidden from those who evade him with all their heart, he tempers our knowledge of him, by making the stamp of who he is visible to those who are seeking him and not to those who are not.[63]

Pascal's unique combination of range, intelligence, warmth, balance and urgency is evident on almost every page of the *Pensées*, giving the book a relevance to all periods not wholly Christian, a relevance that it shares with the *City of God*: the Christian consensus not yet arrived at in Augustine's day had, in Pascal's, recently disintegrated. Some of the best writing of each could well be by the other. A chapter on original sin in the *City of God* is about Adam, about the philosophers of Augustine's time and about anyone's proud abandonment of "the basis on which the mind should be firmly fixed, to become, as it were, based on oneself and so remain. . . . This then is the original evil: man regards himself as his own light, and turns away from that light which would make man himself a light if he would set his heart on it."[64] Pascal criticises, on precisely the same grounds, the philosophers of his own time in a fragment headed "Against the philosophers who have God and not Jesus Christ". "Their only inclination is to win men's esteem", he says. "They have known God and their sole desire has been, not that men should love God, but that they should stop at loving them; they want themselves to be the chosen object of men's happiness."[65] Pascal on the philosophers who have turned aside from Christianity without taking the trouble to understand it could as well be Augustine on Porphyry, to whom in the *City of God* he writes: "You profess to be a lover of virtue and wisdom. If you were a genuine and faithful lover, you would have recognised Christ 'the power and the wisdom of God', instead of shying away, inflated with the swollen pride of useless learning, from his saving humility."[66] This is the lesson Augustine and Pascal both learned, and both taught.

*　　*　　*

The last year of Pascal's life was full of sadness and suffering, borne, according to the moving account of his elder sister, with extraordinary patience and thoughtfulness for others, and profound Catholic faith. For months before he died, he must have known that he was now too ill for the completion of his book to be a possibility. Together with this private disappointment, he had to cope with the misery that resulted from a public assault on Port Royal.

Shortly before Mazarin's death in March 1661, Louis XIV, the ruthless twenty-three-year-old who now took full personal command of the government of France, announced that Jansenism was to be exterminated from his country. A new formulary of orthodoxy, repudiating the five propositions, was drawn up, to be signed by all priests and religious. In April the oppression of Port Royal began in earnest: no more postulants were allowed into the community; the seventy girls the nuns in Paris were educating were sent home; Père Singlin was sacked from the position as the nuns' spiritual director that he had innocuously held since the imprisonment of Saint-Cyran more than twenty years before. In June the nuns were coerced into signing the formulary that had been designed only to cow them: Antoine Arnauld recommended this compliance. In August Mère Angélique, now seventy, died in the midst of the destruction of her life's work. Early in October Jacqueline Pascal died, her brother was convinced, of a broken heart. At the end of the same month, the nuns were required to sign a fiercer formulary; Pascal, who wrote that the formulary repudiated not just Jansen but "grace itself, Saint Augustine, Saint Paul",[67] quarrelled with Arnauld because he again told the nuns to comply, which they did at the end of November. Pascal took no further part in the defence of Port Royal; he was now too ill, and no doubt also too depressed by the triumph—not completed until the final destruction of the community by Louis XIV forty years later—of power over blameless lives, perhaps all this time resented only because too-well defended by intellectuals, including Pascal himself.

In the following June, Pascal, desperately ill and in much pain, was moved to his sister's house. He died, on 19 August 1662, nursed by his sister and niece, and absolved and anointed by a simple parish priest who had heard his confession several times, was deeply impressed by him and was able truthfully to assure the dubious Church authorities that his death had been that of a faithful Catholic. His enemies had, therefore, to leave undisturbed his modest grave in the church of Saint Étienne-du-Mont, in the heart of Abelard's old Latin Quarter, since the nineteenth century overshadowed by the Panthéon, the imposing deconsecrated temple to secular glory where Voltaire, Rousseau, Napoleon's marshals and Victor Hugo grandly lie.

Of all the great intellectuals of his period (who included Francis Bacon, René Descartes, Thomas Hobbes, John Milton, Benedict de Spinoza, Gottfried Leibniz, Sir Isaac Newton and John Locke), Pascal alone wrote, from the heart of the Church for the heart of the Church, of "the beauty ever ancient and ever new", a phrase in the *Confessions* quoted in the *Pensées*, the beauty revealed in Christ that he had seen on the night of fire. The truth he tried so hard to write down for a time from which faith was seeping away was of course ancient. In no way did he attempt to alter or extend it. But, as he wrote himself: "It should not be said that I have said nothing new; the arrangement of the material is new. In tennis both players hit the same ball, but one places it better." [68]

1. The paper text is given in Blaise Pascal, *Oeuvres complètes*, ed. Jacques Chevalier, Bibliothèque de la Pléiade 34 (Paris: Gallimard, 1954), pp. 553–54. All translations from Pascal are my own. Different editions of the *Pensées* notoriously number them differently. References here are to the numbers given in the Pléiade *Oeuvres Complètes* (*OC*).

2. Jn 20:18.

3. Jn 17:3.

4. Jn 17:25.

5. Pascal, *Pensée* 195, OC 1137.

6. Pascal, *Préface pour le traité du vide*, OC 530.

7. Pascal, *De l'esprit géométrique et de l'art de persuader*, OC 592.

8. Pascal, *Entretien avec M. de Saci*, OC 560.

9. Ibid., p. 572.

10. Ibid.

11. See Hans Urs von Balthasar, *Theo-Drama*, trans. Graham Harrison, vol. 2 (San Francisco, 1990), pp. 231–34.

12. Pascal, letter 5, in *Les Provinciales*, OC 713.

13. Ibid., pp. 704–5.

14. Pascal, letter 10, in *Les Provinciales*, OC 777.

15. Ibid., p. 778.

16. Pascal, letter 17, in *Les Provinciales*, OC 866.

17. Ibid., pp. 867–68.

18. Ibid., p. 875.

19. Pascal, letter 18, in *Les Provinciales*, OC 900.

20. Ibid., p. 899.

21. Quoted in Ian Ker, *John Henry Newman* (Oxford, 1988), p. 677.

22. Pascal, letter 18, in *Les Provinciales*, OC 892.

23. Ibid., p. 888.

24. Pascal, *Écrits sur la grace*, OC 1044.

25. Pascal, *Pensée* 654, OC 1295.

26. Augustine, *De peccatorum meritis et remissione* 2.18.28, quoted in Peter Brown, *Augustine of Hippo* (London, 1988), p. 374.

27. Anselm, *Prayers and Meditations*, trans. Benedicta Ward (London, 1973), p. 237.

28. Hans Urs von Balthasar, *The Glory of the Lord: A Theological Aesthetics*, vol. 3, trans. Andrew Louth et al. (San Francisco and Edinburgh, 1986), pp. 173–74.

29. Pascal, letter 18, in *Les Provinciales*, OC 901.

30. Ibid., p. 887.

31. Pascal, *Pensée* 729, OC 1310.

32. Pascal, *Pensée* 483, OC 1225.

33. Pascal, *Pensée* 84, OC 1105–6.

34. Ibid., p. 1108.

35. Pascal, *Pensée* 438, OC 1207–8.

36. Pascal, *Pensée* 602, *OC* 1280–81.
37. Pascal, *Pensée* 75, *OC* 1103.
38. Pascal, *Pensée* 199, *OC* 1137.
39. Pascal, *Pensée* 217, *OC* 1147.
40. Pascal, *Pensées* 731 and 5, *OC* 1310 and 1090.
41. *Pensée* 438, *OC* 1205.
42. Ibid., p. 1206.
43. Pascal, *Pensée* 829, *OC* 1341.
44. Pascal, *Pensée* 5, *OC* 1089–90.
45. Pascal, *Pensée* 829, *OC* 1341–42.
46. Augustine, *De doctrina christiana* 4.5.8.
47. Pascal, *Pensée* 72, *OC* 1102.
48. Pascal, *Pensée* 829, *OC* 1342.
49. Augustine, sermon 34.
50. Pascal, *Pensée* 477, *OC* 1221.
51. Pascal, *Pensée* 434, *OC* 1204.
52. Alexander Pope, *Essay on Man*, 4.396.
53. Pascal, *Pensée* 451, *OC* 1216.
54. Pascal, *Pensée* 786, *OC* 1329.
55. Pascal, *Pensée* 778, *OC* 1328.
56. Pascal, *Pensée* 819, *OC* 1337.
57. Pascal, *Pensée* 764, *OC* 1323.
58. Pascal, letter 4 to Mademoiselle de Roannez, *OC* 510.
59. Pascal, *Pensée* 736, *OC* 1313.
60. Ibid.
61. Ibid., pp. 1313–14.
62. Pascal, *Pensée* 335, *OC* 1179.
63. Pascal, *Pensée* 483, *OC* 1227–28.
64. Augustine, *City of God* 14.13, trans. Henry Bettenson (London, 1972).
65. Pascal, *Pensée* 379, *OC* 1187–88.
66. Augustine, *City of God* 10.28.
67. Pascal, *Écrit sur la signature*, *OC* 1075.
68. Pascal, *Pensée* 65, *OC* 1101.

CHAPTER FOURTEEN

SAMUEL JOHNSON

A fter the resounding victory of revolution in the middle of the seventeenth century—and the thud of its failure, cleverly dulled by Charles II—England, as if exhausted by religious and political passions, settled for a monarchy more or less under parliamentary control, and a moderately Protestant national church, to which neither Catholics nor various dissenting sects belonged. Memories of the Gunpowder Plot of 1605, and dimmer memories, coloured by myth, of Catholics as traitors and spies for a foreign power in Elizabeth's reign, together with fear of Louis XIV's Catholic autocracy across the English Channel and its attractions as a model for Charles and his less-cautious brother and heir, made hatred of "Popery" the only cause liable to ignite, in the cause of "liberty", both mob emotion and the organised self-interest of the ruling class. So powerful was this combination of irrational prejudice and reasonable fear that it was possible, twice in thirty years and each time without bloodshed, except in Catholic Ireland and then in Scotland, for a foreigner to be imported into England as sovereign of Britain, while legitimate kings—James II in 1688 and then his son James Stuart in 1714—were pushed aside, mostly on account of their Catholicism. To understand why England, having restored its monarchy, its bishops and the power of its aristocracy in the House of Lords, nevertheless preferred a Dutch and then a German king to the direct male heirs of Charles I is to understand how deep Protestant dislike of the Catholicising prelates of Charles's reign had been and also how firm was becoming English antagonism to the totalitarian might of Louis XIV's France, where both Charles II and James II had spent eleven formative years. Better a Protestant, even from abroad, than a French-influenced Catholic monarch, it was almost universally felt. Best of all was the Protestant Queen Anne, English and a Stuart, who reigned between the Dutch William III and the German George I, and whose general, Marlborough, inflicted such damage on the power of France that thirty years of European peace followed his campaigns.

Such were the foundations of eighteenth- and early nineteenth-century Britain. These conditions supported the Whig ascendancy and the steadily increasing commercial and then industrial wealth of the country that first harnessed capital to technological advance. They also underpinned the defeat of France in the far-flung wars of the 1750s and 1760s that made of North America and India British imperial possessions. They ensured, above all, that English political institutions long ago inoculated against revolution survived the incendiary examples of America in 1775, France in 1789 and most of Europe in 1848.

And what became, during this period of notable English prosperity and self-confidence, of writing in the Christian tradition? The intellectual atmosphere of the times was inimical to its continuing vitality in two different ways. The undemandingness of the Church of England, its clergy often motivated more by place-seeking than by religious zeal, presented little challenge to the souls of writers. A wide spectrum of belief and unbelief was acceptable; "enthusiasm" and "superstition" were not acceptable, even if the former had produced *Paradise Lost* and *The Pilgrim's Progress*, books at least owned by almost all Englishmen who could read, and the latter was the derogatively labelled faith of the past that refused altogether to wither away. Writing in *The Spectator* in 1711, Addison spoke for a whole age when he said:

> Enthusiasm has something in it of madness, superstition of folly. Most of the sects that fall short of the church of England have in them strong tinctures of enthusiasm, as the Roman-catholic religion is one huge overgrown body of childish and idle superstition.[1]

The Church of England of this period took much of its colour, a grey, "evidence"-based unassertiveness, from the complacent triumphalism of the Enlightenment, the second and weightier enemy of the writing of Christian tradition. In Britain, as in France and Germany, rationalism had commandeered the frontiers of thought to the extent that the "progress" plainly under way became inextricably associated in many minds with brisk, modern contempt for the mysteries of orthodox Christianity, now safely consigned to the past.

"God said, *Let Newton be!* and all was light":[2] Pope's line catches English pride in the supreme physicist of the period, while political thought absorbed and developed the state's appropriation of spiritual authority that Henry VIII had initiated. Hobbes, born in the year of the Armada (1588), dying in the year of the fabricated Popish Plot (1679), was a moral relativist and a political absolutist:

> Every man, for his own part, calleth that which pleaseth, and is delightful to himself, GOOD; and that EVIL, which displeaseth him; inasmuch that while every man differeth from other in constitution, they differ also one from another concerning the common distinction of good and evil.[3]

The only hope of achieving an orderly society in the consequent chaos of competing desires, Hobbes explained in *Leviathan*, is a ruthless autocracy that will dictate the religion of all its members. Locke, nearly half a century younger, was milder and more optimistic in both respects. He understood that without God, man "could have no law but his own will; no end but himself. He would be a god to himself, and the satisfaction of his own will the sole measure and end of all his actions."[4] But Locke's God was the distant deity of the Enlightenment, his Jesus no more than a rationally acceptable moral example. Toleration, in a Lockean state, should be withheld from atheists, who were certain to lack moral foundation for their behaviour, but extended to all Christians except Papists, whom he thought bound to be enemies of the civil authority. (How he proposed to identify or to deal with atheists he did not say.) No less reliant on reason for the underpinning of their enlightened ideas were the slightly later Gibbon, who saw in the adoption of the Christianity he came to scorn the sole reason for the collapse of the Roman Empire; Adam Smith, who based *The Wealth of Nations* on the secular realism of his belief that self-interest is the only human motive worth consideration; and David Hume, whose lucid demolition of what he took to be an already-crumbling Christianity dazzled even a Europe accustomed to the fireworks of Voltaire.

In an intellectual atmosphere in which reason, and ascertainable and then usable facts, appeared to have defeated the truth of revelation, which cannot be proved and therefore requires belief, serious Christian faith of a kind Pascal would have recognized was rare among major writers. Very few of them, on the other hand, took lack of belief to the logical conclusions of Hobbes. The assumption that good and evil, truth and falsehood, beauty and ugliness are terms whose meaning is guaranteed by the existence of absolutes beyond the opinions of individual people survived decades and centuries of dwindling belief in God. Voltaire himself took this assumption to be necessary: he knew that there had to be some kind of absolute, if only as a philosophical postulate, to guarantee the meaning of good and evil, and some kind of general belief in God to hold moral chaos at bay. Not that he was a Hobbesian, or a Schopenhauerian, pessimist. He seriously thought that in "all the children in the world ... you will find nothing ... but innocence, sweetness and modesty" and that nature has given human beings no destructive instincts whatever.[5] His "nature", in no need of redeeming grace, is not the nature of Edmund or Iago; one wonders whether he knew any children. He hated and despised both Pascal and Augustine. In his *Philosophical Dictionary* of 1767, he described original sin as "the wild and fantastic invention of an African both debauched and repentant ... who spent his life contradicting himself".[6] Voltaire's confidence in the human race, and the formless God of his deism—Christ, for orthodox Christians, is the form of God—both survive in the minds of many secular humanists who deny all religious connexions.

The most powerful English book of the early eighteenth century, exceptional in every respect, is Jonathan Swift's *Gulliver's Travels*, savage in its assault on cruelty, lies, colonial exploitation and all kinds of misuse of power, and equally savage in its exposure of the folly and the chilling pride of excessive confidence in reason. Swift, dean of Saint Patrick's Cathedral in Dublin, was a cleric in the Church of England (in Ireland the church of the Protestant ascendancy), much loved by the common people of Dublin, whom he cared for with practical generosity and defended against English oppression with his terrifying pen. *Gulliver's Travels* is without doubt a Christian masterpiece, but Christianity remains no more than implied in its black depiction of human fallibility, a world of original sin unlit by revelation, a negative image that never attains positive development. The differences between Catholic and Protestant, correctly observed by Swift to divide the Church of England itself, are reduced to mere absurdity, the ludicrous excuse for war between England and France. The Christian quality of the moral insight that informs the whole work, particularly in its rare gleams of kindness and old-fashioned common sense—among the book's very few heroes are Socrates and Thomas More[7]—has therefore, in Swift's own time and ever since, often been missed. It was comprehensively missed by Swift's younger contemporary Dr. Johnson, who found the one-off oddness of *Gulliver's Travels*—"no rules of judgement [could be] applied to a book written in open defiance of truth and regularity"[8]—altogether beyond him.

Johnson, nevertheless, was the central Christian writer of eighteenth-century England, a critic of his times as well as of the writing of the past, who sought to reconnect his world to what is valuable because permanently true, living because never killed by the transient ideas that appear to be associated with "progress". A measure of the chasm between him and Voltaire is Johnson's remark, "No man is more naturally good than a wolf is."[9]

* * *

Samuel Johnson, born in 1709, shared many of the literary assumptions—which turned out to be transient ideas—of his contemporaries; where his judgement falters, as over *Gulliver's Travels*, it is by these ideas that he is confused, as the word "regularity" in the condemnation just quoted shows. Rational enquiry into the proprieties of both literature and life the eighteenth century reckoned to have only recently begun, or, more accurately, been resumed after long centuries of postclassical barbarism. Literary criticism conducted in a classical spirit—these writers were not called Augustan for nothing—had been reinvented by John Dryden; for all Johnson's justified doubts about Dryden's own plays, he praises without reservation Dryden's essay *Of Dramatick Poesie*: "The structure of dramatic poems was not then generally understood.... A writer who obtains his full purpose loses himself in his own lustre. Of an opinion which is no longer doubted, the evidence ceases to be examined."[10] Johnson himself shared with contemporary scholars in France the encyclopaedic impulse to achieve both correctness and completeness of information: his *Dictionary*, his edition of Shakespeare's plays and his last major work, the *Lives of the English Poets*, remain to this day three quite different, and lastingly valuable, triumphs of almost (he had a little help with the first two) single-handed labour and judgement.

The Christianity of such a man at such a time was bound to seem to him defensible as wholly rational; how otherwise could it be held to be true by an educated man? "He that thinks reasonably must think morally", Johnson, forgetting that the best reasoners in Shakespeare are his villains, conceded to the playwright who, as we have seen, seemed "to write without any moral purpose".[11] But Shakespeare worked in what Johnson took to be a still-naïve intellectual climate. Johnson's *Preface* to his edition of the plays is a fine defence of Shakespeare's powers of observation and capacity to hold an audience or a reader, though Johnson has to concede to his contemporaries that the poet lacked learning:

> The English nation, in the time of Shakespeare, was yet struggling to emerge from barbarity.... The contest about the original benevolence or malignity of man had not yet commenced. Speculation had not yet attempted to analyse the mind, to trace the passions to their sources, to unfold the seminal principles of vice and virtue, or sound the depths of the heart for the motives of action.[12]

The astonishing last sentence, written as if Augustine had never existed, illustrates the gulf of ignorance opened by the Reformation between Protestant England and its Catholic past. Johnson spent time and effort translating into Latin some of the great Collects in the Book of Common Prayer, clearly unaware that Cranmer had translated them in the first place, out of the ancient, though not classical, Latin of the missal.

Johnson himself wrote and lived, in the rackety surroundings of hard-bitten Georgian London, with the utmost seriousness of pious Christian intention. He tried his hand at both drama (an unperformably static tragedy, *Irene*) and the Latinate satire popular in his youth. "The Vanity of Human Wishes", his most considerable poem, written in 1749 in imitation of Juvenal, is an intensely gloomy survey of human ambition and frustration, concluding with a moving prayer for love, patience and faith—really for a firm belief that the truth of God will in the end transform to happiness the unavoidable unhappiness of human life. In 1750–1752, to earn some money and to give himself some relief from his work on the *Dictionary*, he wrote very nearly all of the 209 essays published twice weekly as *The Rambler*. Ten editions of these essays, written, although Johnson was often ill at the time, with unfailing punctuality and almost unfailing judgement and sense, appeared in book form before Johnson's death. A slightly later (1823) editor said of the book, "It was recommended by the friends of religion and literature, as a book by which a man might be taught to think." [13] The *Rambler* essays are in the tradition of the *Tatler* and *Spectator* but have an intellectual range well beyond that of Addison and Steele. The single most interesting *Rambler* essay is no. 96, "Truth, Falsehood, and Fiction, an Allegory", which tells of the apparent triumph of Falsehood over Truth in the contemporary world and of the divine compassion that invested Truth with the mantle of Fiction and returned her to the world, where "she now went out again to conquer with more success." [14] The epigraph of the essay is two lines from one of Boethius's poems in *The Consolation of Philosophy*: "If Plato's muse tells the truth, / To learn is to remember what has been forgotten." [15] Boethius may have been thinking of Plato's theory of the soul's knowledge forgotten at birth; Johnson was certainly not. His idea in this essay, which connects fiction, storytelling and image-making to truth rather than to falsehood is of striking originality and depth; had he applied it to Shakespeare, it might have helped him to sort out what was to him the unresolvable puzzle of Shakespeare's incorrect greatness.

An early *Rambler* essay (no. 7) gives a fair indication of the quality of Johnson's Christianity, which filled his soul with certainty but also with dread:

> The great task of him who conducts his life by the precepts of religion, is to make the future predominate over the present, to impress upon his mind so strong a sense of the importance of obedience to the divine will, of the value of the reward promised to virtue, and the terrors of the punishment denounced against crimes, as may overbear all the temptations, which temporal hope or fear can bring in his way.... The great art, therefore, of piety, and the end for which all the rites of religion seem to be instituted, is the perpetual renovation of the motives

to virtue, by a voluntary employment of our mind in the contemplation of its excellence, its importance, and its necessity.[16]

This is earnestness of moral purpose indeed and is likely to strike a Catholic, an Augustinian Catholic in particular, as Pelagian in its emphasis on obedience in the apparently total absence of a sense of grace: Should not God rather than virtue be the object of contemplation in the second sentence quoted? Johnson wrote a number of prayers, however, in which his conviction of his need for undeserved grace is equally clear. In his prayer for the outset of *The Rambler*, he wrote:

> Almighty God, the giver of all good things, without whose help all labour is ineffectual, and without whose grace all wisdom is folly; grant, I beseech Thee, that in this my undertaking, thy Holy Spirit may not be withheld from me; but that I may promote thy glory, and the salvation both of myself and others.[17]

Johnson was a devoted churchman, a regular communicant—even at home during his last illness—and a man whose kindness to the waifs and strays of his motley, quarrelsome household impressed everyone he knew. He was also frightened all his life of death and of the judgement of God. "As I cannot be *sure*", he said in the last year of his life to a merry Oxford cleric, "that I have fulfilled the conditions on which salvation is granted, I am afraid I may be one of those who shall be damned." "(Looking dismally.)", Boswell adds.[18] Twenty-five years earlier, he had warned himself in *Rasselas*: "You are only one atom of the mass of humanity, and have neither such virtue nor vice, as that you should be singled out for supernatural favours or afflictions." [19] But in vain. Of his own salvation no Christian can ever, of course, be sure; it is, all the same, a sign of the theological meagreness and unnourishing legalism of the Church of England of his time that his faithful Christian life, his own genuine virtue, perceptible to all his friends, brought Johnson so little cheerful resignation to the will of God, so little peace of mind. No wonder Blake, the visionary autodidact who loved much that was Christian but lived entirely outside the orthodox tradition, hated the church he knew for its bleak repressiveness.

Johnson regarded Thomas More as "the person of greatest virtue these islands ever produced".[20] He had a particular fondness for Shakespeare's *Henry VIII* and said that Queen Katherine was "his favourite" character in the whole of Shakespeare.[21] His not unsympathetic portrait of Wolsey in "The Vanity of Human Wishes", victim of his own pride and of the fickleness of the king, owes much to the play. Nevertheless, Johnson's Christianity had in it a strain of passionate loyalty to monarchy as the source of authority in the church, and to this loyalty there was a paradoxical—but in England, inescapable—logic. Since Henry VIII's rejection of the authority of Rome, the English monarch had governed the national church. Violent lurches of royal religious policy, including Mary Tudor's return of England to the Roman obedience, had each occasioned resolute resistance and martyrdoms or, later, at least considerable sacrifices. But in the absence of papal authority, the authority of the monarch was an essential constituent of the church to a Christian who believed, as Johnson did, that without the discipline of regular, public observance the individual Christian would soon be lost. "To be of no church is dangerous", he wrote of Milton. "Religion, of which the rewards are distant, and which is animated only by Faith and Hope, will glide by degrees out of the mind, unless it be invigorated and re-impressed by external ordinances, by stated calls to worship, and the salutary influence of example." [22] External ordinances have to be laid down by an authority that expects obedience; Milton, Johnson wrote, "an acrimonious and surly republican, ... hated monarchs in the state, and prelates in the church, for he hated all whom he was required to obey." [23] Power over the church must, according to a Christian of Johnson's stamp, be divinely guaranteed; the monarch in England must therefore have the sanction of God. Early in his life, Johnson took this logic as far as a commitment to the Stuart cause sufficiently devoted to prevent him proceeding to a degree in George II's Oxford because he could not in conscience swear an oath of loyalty to the Hanoverian king. This Test Act oath, on the pattern of Henry VIII's oath—the refusal of which led to Thomas More's execution—was from 1673 to 1829 imposed on all graduates and officeholders to ensure loyalty to the monarchy and to keep Catholics out of university education and public life. (In 1755 Johnson's friends obtained for him, to give his *Dictionary* appropriate scholarly weight, an Oxford M.A. without the imposition of an oath. In 1765 and 1775 he received doctorates from Dublin and Oxford respectively.)

Boswell reports a conversation in which Johnson defended Jacobites as, at least, necessarily Christian:

A Jacobite, Sir, believes in the divine right of Kings. He that believes in the divine right of Kings believes in a Divinity. A Jacobite believes in the divine right of Bishops. He that believes in the divine right of Bishops believes in the divine authority of the Christian religion. Therefore, Sir, a Jacobite is neither an Atheist nor a Deist. This cannot be said of a Whig; for *Whiggism is a negation of all principle*.[24]

This by no means implies that an orthodox English Christian must necessarily be a Jacobite; it does imply that in Johnson's view, such a Christian is likely to be a Tory. In his *Dictionary* he defined a Tory as "one who adheres to the antient [ancient] constitution of the state, and the apostolical hierarchy of the church of England." The divine right of kings was no doubt for him associated with the quasi-sacramental tradition of royal "touching" for scrofula, "the King's Evil": as a small child he had himself been "touched" by Queen Anne. The Stuarts, like the French monarchy, made much of this late medieval custom; to demonstrate loyalty to James I, it is accurately, if unhistorically, described by Shakespeare in *Macbeth*. Neither William III nor the Hanoverian kings "touched" for scrofula, and the rite died with the exiled Stuarts. Johnson took no part whatever in the Jacobite rising of 1745, distanced himself (at least to Boswell) from the remaining nonjuring clergy (those who had refused oaths of loyalty to the foreign kings of 1688 or 1714), and, like most Englishmen with Jacobite sympathies, finally abandoned the Stuart cause after Bonnie Prince Charlie's disappointing appearance in London, as an unappealing drunk, in 1750. George III, king from 1760, not only behaved like an English monarch worthy of respect but in 1762 awarded Johnson a handsome royal pension. This, for the rest of Johnson's life, protected him from the poverty in which he had lived and worked from boyhood in fierce independence. It would not, he said, "be decent for me to drink King James's health in the wine that King George gives me money to pay for".[25]

But Johnson's Tory high churchmanship, the stiffening all his life of his Christianity as of his politics, narrowed his human and historical sympathies less than would have been likely in either the seventeenth or the nineteenth centuries. He condemned the English as well as the Spaniards for their treatment of native peoples in the Americas and loathed the institution of slavery. He took personal, costly trouble over the poor people he took in, organised a subscription for Milton's destitute granddaughter, deeply though he disapproved of Milton's politics and religion, and at his death left his faithful black servant, Francis Barber, a generous income for the remaining seventeen years of his life. More surprisingly still, he reveals often, in his writing and in his conversation reported by Boswell, an informed fellow-feeling for the Catholic Church that sits oddly with his Enlightenment assumption that civilisation had only recently recovered from the benighted interval soon to be called the Middle Ages.

Actual persecution of Catholics had stopped in the reign of Charles II, which saw the last martyrdoms of English priests. The eighteenth century, caring less than the seventeenth about every Christian issue, including the truth of revelation, on the whole merely ignored Catholics, so long—this is very English—as they behaved as coolly about their religion as everyone else was expected to behave about his. Dryden and Pope were both Catholics, Pope from birth, Dryden after an opportune conversion in the brief reign of James II. In the work of neither is there anything, beyond the ordinary moral assumptions of a Christian society, that even approaches the already-current question of whether trinitarian Christianity is or is not true. Johnson in his *Lives of the English Poets* is unimpressed by the Christianity of either, not because it is Catholic but, as it were on the contrary, because it strikes him as shallow. He tries to give Dryden the benefit of the doubt as to the genuineness of his conversion, saying that "it is natural to hope that a comprehensive is likewise an elevated soul, and that whoever is wise is also honest." [26] But he is not convinced: "When he professed himself a convert to Popery, he did not pretend to have received any new conviction of the fundamental doctrines of Christianity",[27] a sentence that suggests what Johnson would expect of a real conversion. As for Pope, Johnson famously regarded the *Essay on Man*, the closest Pope came to serious reflection on the human condition, as decorated emptiness: "Never were penury of knowledge and vulgarity of sentiment so happily disguised." [28]

So far was Johnson from agreeing with Addison as to "the Roman-catholic religion" being "one huge overgrown body of childish and idle superstition" that he shocked Boswell more than once by defending the fullness of Catholic faith. Hearing of a parson "who had given up great prospects in the Church of England on his conversion to the Roman Catholic faith, Johnson ... exclaimed fervently, 'God bless him'", a response Boswell excuses on the grounds that Johnson "warmly admired every man who acted from a conscientious regard to principle, erroneous or not" [29] (which is like Robert Bolt in *A Man for All Seasons* persuading a twentieth-century audience that Thomas More died for freedom of conscience rather than for the unity of the Church). On the tour of Scotland that Johnson and Boswell undertook in 1773, Johnson, according to his own account, was saddened by the ruins of old churches and abbeys, destroyed by what he called "the ruffians of reformation", and by reflecting that English cathedrals were in almost as bad a state: "The ruins of the cathedral of Elgin afforded us another proof of the waste of reformation. Let us not however make too much haste to despise our neighbours. Our own cathedrals are mouldering by unregarded dilapidation." Well might he add: "It seems to be part of the despicable philosophy of the time to despise monuments of sacred magnificence." [30] When Goethe visited Assisi ten years later, he avoided the basilica in favour of the remains of a Roman temple, as if Saint Francis were best forgotten. By contrast, Johnson's visit to Iona drew from him a noble tribute to the power of things unseen:

Whatever withdraws us from the power of our senses; whatever makes the past, the distant, or the future predominate over the present, advances us in the dignity of thinking beings. Far from me and from my friends, be such frigid philosophy as may conduct us indifferent and unmoved over any ground which has been dignified by wisdom, bravery, or virtue. That man is little to be envied ... whose piety would not grow warmer among the ruins of Iona.[31]

Johnson's feeling for the Catholic Church was more than nostalgic. Boswell records a conversation of 1769 in which Johnson startled him by saying that he preferred the Popish to the Presbyterian religion and then spoke warmly of "apostolical ordination" and of a liturgy "in which [the people] know they are to join", and frostily of the Thirty-nine Articles, a product of "the clamour of the times". The astonished Boswell, a lowland Scot, a more or less lapsed Presbyterian, and too young to remember any Stuart, asked Johnson the usual questions of those brought up on standard anti-Catholic prejudice: Purgatory? Praying for the dead? The idolatry of the Mass? The worship of saints? Johnson's answers to these questions show not only sympathy but accurate information. He saw "nothing unreasonable" in the idea of Purgatory, "a very harmless doctrine" since "the generality of mankind are neither so obstinately wicked as to deserve everlasting punishment, nor so good as to merit being admitted into the society of blessed spirits". (Article 22 of the Thirty-nine Articles calls "the Romish Doctrine of Purgatory ... a fond thing vainly invented".) Johnson thought praying for the dead equally harmless and prayed all his life "so far as it may be lawful", as one prayer cautiously says, for the souls of his parents, his brother and his wife. As for the Mass and the other notorious examples of "superstition": "Sir, there is no idolatry in the Mass. They believe God to be there, and they adore him.... They do not worship Saints; they invoke them; they only ask their prayers." Boswell, more and more amazed, tried asking about confession. "Why," Johnson replied, "I don't know but that is a good thing." Boswell recounts this conversation with some embarrassment and adds, unconvincingly, that Johnson "might have reasoned differently if one had taken the other side". But he concedes that Johnson always "had a respect for 'the old religion'" and had said on another occasion that he could believe in the sincerity of any convert from Protestantism to Popery because "he parts with nothing: he is only super-adding to what he already had."[32] At age seventy-five and close to death, Johnson said to Boswell:

A good man of a timorous disposition, in great doubt of his acceptance with God, and pretty credulous, may be glad to be of a church where there are so many helps to get to Heaven. I would be a Papist if I could. I have fear enough; but an obstinate rationality prevents me. I shall never be a Papist, unless on the near approach of death, of which I have a very great terror.[33]

It is not impossible, but will never be certain, that he did become a "Papist" in the last weeks of his life. The last prayer he wrote, a few days before he died, refers to "my late conversion", but this may mean only conversion to a calm acceptance of death. It is, in any case, at least permissible to suggest that the sacramental routine of ordinary Catholic life would have consoled and cheered a Christian in whose faith there was so much more fear than hope. And, given the depth of the faith he already had and the weight of Catholic thought of which he knew nothing, his obstinate rationality might have been less disturbed than he imagined.

"The poet must divest himself of the prejudices of his age or country; he must consider right and wrong in their abstracted and invariable state; he must disregard present laws and opinions, and rise to general and transcendental truths, which will always be the same."[34] These words are spoken by the philosopher Imlac, describing his self-education as a poet in Johnson's *History of Rasselas, Prince of Abyssinia*, the gentle fable Johnson wrote in a week to pay for his mother's funeral in 1759, the same year as was written Voltaire's abrasive *Candide*. Johnson's literary judgement was not always free of the constriction of "present opinions", in particular of the limits implied by Pope's definition of "true wit" as "what oft was thought but ne'er so well express'd".[35] Imlac says: "The plants of the garden, the animals of the wood, the minerals of the earth, and meteors of the sky, must all concur to store [the poet's] mind with inexhaustible variety; for every idea is useful for the enforcement or decoration of moral or religious truth."[36] Behind this programme is no doubt the figure of Shakespeare, on whose plays Johnson was working at the time. Johnson's *Preface* to his edition, with many of his notes, did much to rescue Shakespeare from the neoclassical embarrassment that had dimmed perception of him after mid-seventeenth-century Protestant disapproval had lifted. (During the Commonwealth, the plays, known to have been the favourite reading of Charles I in prison, were denounced as "prelatical trash".) Nevertheless, the recommendation of "enforcement or decoration of moral or religious truth" would seem certain seriously to handicap Johnson's sense of what Shakespeare actually achieved. That Shakespeare's plays embody rather than preach truth was a notion almost beyond Johnson's grasp. F. R. Leavis said: "For Johnson a moral judgement that isn't *stated* isn't there."[37] This is often so and explains, for instance, Johnson's blindness to what *is* there in *Gulliver's Travels*. Yet in Shakespeare's case, Johnson's critical instincts were even stronger than his principles. In recognising that Shakespeare, more than any other poet he had read, rose "to general and transcendental truths, which will always be the same", he was doing exactly this himself. Throughout the *Preface*, his instincts are at war with his principles. To take just one example, while his principles support his praise of Shakespeare for his "practical axioms" and also his regret that there are not more of them, his instinct leads him at once to a contrary and more perceptive judgement:

> [Shakespeare's] real power is not shown in the splendour of particular passages, but by the progress of his fable, and the tenor of his dialogue; and he that tries to recommend him by select quotations, will succeed like the pedant in *Hierocles*, who, when he offered his house to sale, carried a brick in his pocket as a specimen.[38]

It is an oblique approach to the organic life of the plays, but an approach it certainly is.

The truths "which will always be the same" are for Johnson, as for Shakespeare, the truths of orthodox Christianity. In the world of "our present misery", in which the consequences of sin are everywhere evident, "the sentiments and worship proper to a fallen and offending being, we have all to learn, as we have all to practise."[39] In one of the sermons he wrote for others to preach, he said: "We cannot make truth; it is our business only to find it."[40] And he knew that to hold to Christian truth in an intellectual climate of increasing scepticism required courage, loyalty of heart, and the recognition, familiar to Pascal, that truth is not the same as fact. When Boswell said that "it was a pity that truth was not so firm as to bid defiance to all attacks, so that it might be shot at as much as people chose to attempt, and yet remain unhurt", Johnson replied: "Then, sir, it would not be shot at. Nobody attempts to dispute that two and two make four."[41] There is no virtue in the acknowledgement of a fact. Faith, on the other hand, is itself a virtue. The collision between Christianity and destructive rationalism in the eighteenth century was the old collision, familiar to Augustine, between love of self and obedience to God, for "if we try to build ourselves up, we build a ruin."[42] Johnson said:

> Hume and other sceptical innovators are vain men, and will gratify themselves at any expense. Truth will not afford sufficient food to their

vanity; so they have betaken themselves to error. Truth, sir, is a cow which will yield such people no more milk, and so they are gone to milk the bull. If I could have allowed myself to gratify my vanity at the expense of truth, what fame might I have acquired. Every thing which Hume has advanced against Christianity had passed through my mind long before he wrote.[43]

Pascal's *Pensées* appeared in English in 1688. On Johnson's fifty-ninth birthday, which filled him with anxiety, Johnson wrote in his journal, "How the last year has passed I am unwilling to terrify myself with thinking.... I this day read a great part of Pascal's Life."[44] Whether or not this "Life" was actually the *Pensées*, and with or without Pascal's example, Johnson always knew that the learning of the truths of God is to be valued above the factual learning of the sciences. Pascal wrote: "Knowledge of external things will not console me for ignorance of morality in times of affliction, but knowledge of how to live will always console me for ignorance of physical science."[45] In Johnson's *Life of Milton*, written toward the end of his life, he deplored the "modern" system of education Milton set up in his school, with its Baconian emphasis on the sciences. Johnson writes that in the lives of people one by one, "the first requisite is the religious and moral knowledge of right and wrong.... We are perpetually moralists, but we are geometricians only by chance." "Geometry", Pascal wrote to Fermat, the most distinguished mathematician of his time, "[is] the most beautiful craft in the world, but in the end it is only a craft."[46] Johnson went on:

If I have Milton against me, I have Socrates on my side. It was his labour to turn philosophy from the study of nature to speculations upon life, but the innovators whom I oppose are turning off attention from life to nature. They seem to think that we are placed here to watch the growth of plants, or the motions of the stars. Socrates was rather of opinion, that what we had to learn was, how to do good, and avoid evil.[47]

Johnson was no doubt wholly unaware of what Augustine, late in his life, had written in the *Enchiridion* about a line in Virgil's *Georgics*: "Happy is he who can discover the causes of things",[48] the things being earthquakes and tidal waves. Augustine said:

We should not suppose that it is necessary to happiness to know the causes of the great physical convulsions, causes which lie hid in the most secret recesses of nature's kingdom. . . . But we ought to know the causes of good and evil in ourselves as far as man may in this life know them, in order to avoid the mistakes and troubles of which this life is so full.[49]

Johnson died in 1784. Two years after his death, a biographical essayist wrote: "One of the great features of Johnson's character, was a degree of bigotry, both in politics and in religion, which is now seldom to be met with in persons of a cultivated understanding." [50] It was becoming steadily rarer, and therefore more difficult, for an intellectual to believe that the central doctrines of the Christian faith were true. In 1789 the French Revolution upset all the securities of Johnson's century, and very soon everything he thought and felt seemed to have been left behind by the chaotic swirl of ideas in a new age, a new world. He remains, particularly for his work on Shakespeare, an indispensable literary critic. But he is even more indispensable as a man and a writer in the Christian tradition who, when the enterprise was already eccentric, and in England was confused by national ecclesiastical politics, built his life and his work in the discipline of the truth.

1. Joseph Addison, *The Spectator*, no. 201 (20 October 1711), in *British Essayists* (London, 1823), 7:258.
2. Alexander Pope, "Epitaph Intended for Sir Isaac Newton".
3. Thomas Hobbes, *Elements of Law* 1.7.3, quoted in Richard Tuck, *Hobbes* (Oxford, 1989), pp. 52–53.
4. Quoted in John Dunn, *Locke* (Oxford, 1984), p. 75.
5. Quoted in Richard Price, *Augustine* (London, 1996), p. 58.
6. Ibid.
7. *Gulliver's Travels*, pt. 3, chap. 7.
8. Samuel Johnson, *Lives of the English Poets* (London, 1793), 3:234.
9. Quoted in Pat Rogers, *Samuel Johnson* (Oxford, 1993), p. 27.
10. Johnson, *Lives of the English Poets* 2:62.
11. Samuel Johnson, *Preface to Shakespeare*, in *Prose and Poetry*, sel. Mona Wilson (London, 1966), p. 497.
12. Ibid., pp. 505, 510.
13. A. Chalmers, preface to *The Rambler*, in *British Essayists* (London, 1823), 16:xix.
14. *British Essayists* 17:197.
15. Boethius, *The Consolation of Philosophy* 3.11, quoted in Latin in Johnson; my translation.
16. *British Essayists* 16:37, 39.
17. *The Works of Samuel Johnson*, ed. Arthur Murphy (London, 1806), 12:442.
18. James Boswell, *The Life of Samuel Johnson* (London, 1823), 4:267.
19. Samuel Johnson, *The History of Rasselas, Prince of Abyssinia*, ed. D.J. Enright (London, 1976), p. 142.
20. Quoted in Anthony Kenny, *Thomas More* (Oxford, 1983), p. 2.
21. Boswell, *Life of Samuel Johnson* 4:208.
22. Johnson, *Lives of the English Poets* 1:123.
23. Ibid., p. 124.

24. Boswell, *Life of Samuel Johnson* 1:367.

25. Ibid., p. 366.

26. Johnson, *Lives of the English Poets* 2:37.

27. Ibid., p. 57.

28. Ibid., 4:114–15.

29. Boswell, *Life of Samuel Johnson* 4:257.

30. Samuel Johnson, *A Journey to the Western Islands of Scotland*, in *Prose and Poetry*, pp. 672–73.

31. Ibid., p. 776.

32. Boswell, *Life of Samuel Johnson* 2:105–7.

33. Ibid., 4:258.

34. Johnson, *History of Rasselas*, p. 62.

35. Alexander Pope, "Essay on Criticism", 298.

36. Johnson, *History of Rasselas*, p. 61.

37. F. R. Leavis, *The Common Pursuit* (London, 1962), p. 111.

38. Johnson, *Preface to Shakespeare*, p. 491.

39. Johnson, *Lives of the English Poets* 1:142.

40. Quoted in Rogers, *Samuel Johnson*, p. 33.

41. Boswell, *Life of Samuel Johnson* 3:17.

42. Augustine, sermon 169.

43. Boswell, *Life of Samuel Johnson* 1:378.

44. Johnson, *Journal* 18 September 1768, in *Samuel Johnson: Selected Writings*, ed. Patrick Cruttwell (London, 1968), p. 508.

45. Blaise Pascal, *Pensée* 196, in *Oeuvres complètes*, ed. Jacques Chevalier, Bibliothèque de la Pléiade 34 (Paris: Gallimard, 1954), p. 1137.

46. Quoted in Marvin R. O'Connell, *Blaise Pascal* (Grand Rapids, Mich., 1997), p. 175.

47. Johnson, *Lives of the English Poets* 1:83–84.

48. Virgil, *Georgics* 2.490; my translation.

49. Augustine, *Enchiridion*, chap. 16, trans. S. D. Salmond (Edinburgh, 1883), p. 185.

50. Joseph Towers, *An Essay on the Life, Character, and Writings, of Dr. Samuel Johnson* (London, 1786), quoted in J. C. D. Clark, *Samuel Johnson* (Cambridge, 1994), p. 243.

CHAPTER FIFTEEN

SAMUEL TAYLOR COLERIDGE

When Johnson died, William Wordsworth was fourteen, an orphaned but well-cared-for schoolboy in Westmoreland, and Samuel Taylor Coleridge, a charity child boarding at Christ's Hospital in the heart of London, was twelve. They met eleven years later, gifted young men with boundless hopes for themselves and their writing, and the effect they had on each other transformed both English poetry and English criticism.

They were very different, much more different than at first either of them realised, in both temperament and intellectual capacity. When they met in 1795 and then for a few intense years shared their lives, work and ambitions, they were already sufferers from different kinds of emotional damage, the scars of which never faded and the consequences of which eventually broke their friendship. Wordsworth, as an impressionable boy of twenty-one, carried away in the new dawn of the Revolution with enthusiasm for a France liberated from centuries of oppression, had fallen in love with a Frenchwoman, fathered her child and then abandoned her in a France that had become more and more terrifying and England's official enemy. Beginning the long process of suppressing his guilt, Wordsworth was now living with his devoted sister Dorothy and starting to write the poems of love for the natural world, observation of simple people and careful protection of his own feelings from injury that were to include the works for which he has been famous ever since.

Coleridge, the spoiled tenth and last child of an adored father who was the parson and schoolmaster in the Devon market town of Ottery Saint Mary, had been torn from his world at the age of nine on his father's death. The excellent classical education he received at Christ's Hospital was supposed to be completed at Cambridge as a preparation for the life as a clergyman his father had planned for him. But the university in 1791 was as feverishly exciting for Coleridge as France, at exactly the same time, was being for Wordsworth. Cambridge, like Oxford, was a clerical institution. Nevertheless, advanced opinion, among fellows of colleges as well as undergraduates, was at the time radical, libertarian, utopian and often actually atheist. Coleridge was caught up in every current of controversy and worked less hard than he should have done on account of more than the usual student quantity of alcohol, late nights and debts. In his second year, he left Cambridge in a panic, joined the army under an assumed name and had to be rescued by his brothers. By this time he reckoned he was a determinist in philosophy, a republican in politics and a Unitarian in religion. He never completed his degree.

The determinism was derived from David Hartley, a mid-eighteenth-century Cambridge philosopher whose fashionable materialist psychology was built on Locke's theory of perception as the mere receiving of sense impressions by the blank mind. Hartley's influence on Coleridge was powerful for a couple of years but was then dissolved forever in the light of Coleridge's instinctive sense of the active, creative powers of the mind, the freedom of the will and his own moral accountability. His republicanism was equally youthful, equally short-lived and the very opposite of violent: he dreamed of an egalitarian society in which there would be no need for power because no one's private interests or property would need protection from anyone else. The route to this notoriously unrealisable ideal from the heavily political, heavily commercial England he knew was, for him, a matter not of reform, still less of revolution, but simply of escape, of sailing across the Atlantic with a few friends to start a new society on the banks of the Susquehanna. The idea foundered before it could be put into effect, but not before Coleridge had become engaged to the sister-in-law of his fellow-utopian Robert Southey. When he married, still not quite twenty-three, the Susquehanna vision had evaporated, and he had quarrelled, though only temporarily, with the stolid Southey.

Unitarianism was a dissenting sect with its roots in the civil war period and a flourishing future in nineteenth-century New England. In its brief English heyday, it held Coleridge for rather longer than determinism or pantisocracy, the theory backing the projected commune. Unitarians dispensed with everything apparently irrational in orthodox Christian belief, that is, the Trinity, the Incarnation and Resurrection of Christ, man's redemption in Christ and all sense of the sacramental. Only a conviction of the existence of God and an earnest respect for the moral example set by Jesus remained. It was not so much this bloodless belief that attracted Coleridge as the liberal causes—no less Christian in inspiration, it should be noted, than the principles of the American Bill of Rights, drawn up in 1791—in which Unitarians were preaching, to considerable effect, up and down the country: the abolition of the slave trade, pacifism in all circumstances, freedom of the press and freedom of scientific enquiry. It was as a young Unitarian preacher that Coleridge first discovered that he could use well, in formal circumstances, his quite extraordinary gift for talking. In the personally dreadful years to come, this gift, and his commitment to deliver public courses of lectures on politics, on education and above all on Shakespeare and other poets, several times probably saved Coleridge's life.

Wordsworth and Coleridge each found in the other something he badly needed. Wordsworth found in Coleridge's acutely perceptive admiration and encouragement confirmation that he himself was a poetic genius and that his sense of beauty, particularly the beauty of the mountains and lakes of his childhood, could be enough to smother his guilt, inform his work, nourish his soul, protect him from emotional risk and be proclaimed to the world as a pattern for contented living. Coleridge found in Wordsworth an intellectual companion to listen to his passionate talk; a strong, calm hero figure against whom his own storms of emotional need and insecurity could harmlessly break; and a fellow poet alongside whom the mould of eighteenth-century correctness in verse—the heroic couplet with its neat closures, decorous high diction and decorative classical reference—could be shattered by work of new vitality and closeness to the spoken language of every day. The friendship produced *Lyrical Ballads*, published anonymously in 1798 as a joint enterprise. All but four of its poems were by Wordsworth, but the friends had written one each of the two best poems, which frame the original collection: "The Rime of the Ancient Mariner" and "Lines Written a Few Miles above Tintern Abbey". Subsequent editions of the work appeared, under Wordsworth's name alone, in 1800 and 1802, with many more (fifty-five by 1802) of Wordsworth's poems and one of Coleridge's four replaced by another.

In December 1800 Coleridge wrote from Greta Hall near Keswick, where he and his family were living to be near the Wordsworths in the Lake District, in a letter to an acquaintance:

> Wordsworth & I have never resided together—he lives at Grasmere, a place worthy of him, & of which he is worthy—and neither to Man nor Place can higher praise be given.... As to our literary occupations they are still more distant than our residences—He is a great, a true Poet—I am only a kind of a Metaphysician.—He has even now sent off the last sheet of a second Volume of his Lyrical Ballads.[1]

The hero worship is still there. Clouded by separation and misunderstanding, and later further darkened by Coleridge's insupportable behaviour and Wordsworth's unkindness, it never altogether faded. But already in 1800 the "great", the "true Poet", whose very presence in his life had by now persuaded Coleridge that he himself was not really a poet at all, was not behaving like a great or a true friend. "His" *Lyrical Ballads* still contained Coleridge's "Ancient Mariner", one of the masterpieces of the whole European Romantic movement. This poem Wordsworth moved from the beginning of the collection to the end of the new first volume, saying in a note,[2] which was printed before Coleridge saw it, that "the Author was himself very desirous that it should be suppressed", which was not the case, and pointing out several "great defects" in the poem. Perhaps Wordsworth never appreciated the particular quality of "The Ancient Mariner"; certainly his poetic principles, set out—very much in the emphatic first person—in the famous preface to the 1800 *Lyrical Ballads*, had almost no bearing on it. The poem is a haunting ballad, written in unforgettable mock medieval stanzas, telling of the voyage through nightmare and blessing that follows the mariner's sudden, pointless shooting of the friendly albatross in the land of mist and snow, the agony of his guilt, the beginning of his recovery in the love for the beautiful sea snakes that catches him unawares, and the repeated penance of his retelling of the story. It is a narrative of loneliness, of a soul lost and found and lost again, of sin and grace and helpless longing and rescue. It is, uncannily, the story of Coleridge's life, written when he was twenty-five and had nearly forty more years to live. It has nothing to do with Wordsworth's programme for making "the incidents of common life interesting", using "the manners of rural life" and "a language arising out of repeated experience and regular feelings".[3]

The *Lyrical Ballads* enterprise was weighted toward Wordsworth from the outset, and not only on account of the greater bulk of his work. The poems written by both friends, in the golden period (1797–1798) when the Coleridges were living at Nether Stowey in Somerset and Wordsworth and Dorothy nearby at Alfoxden, were, with the exception of "The Ancient Mariner", closely intertwined in both matter and manner. Coleridge's two great conversation poems, "This Lime-Tree Bower My Prison" and "Frost at Midnight", were, unaccountably, left out of *Lyrical Ballads*, although each of them responds to Wordsworth's inferior "Lines Left upon a Seat in a Yew-Tree", which was included. In both these quiet, moving personal meditations, Coleridge is trying out Wordsworth's sense of nature as the all-consoling, all-justifying reality that will keep the soul steady. In "This Lime-Tree Bower", "the Almighty Spirit" communicates his presence through the beauty of the natural world to those capable of perceiving it:

> Henceforth I shall know
> That Nature ne'er deserts the wise and pure,
> No Plot so narrow, be but Nature there,
> No waste so vacant, but may well employ

> Each faculty of sense, and keep the heart
> Awake to Love and Beauty![4]

In "Frost at Midnight", written seven months later, Coleridge, beside his sleeping baby, contrasts his own bitterly lonely London schooldays with the childhood he plans for his son:

> But *thou*, my babe! shalt wander like a breeze
> By lakes and sandy shores, beneath the crags
> Of ancient mountain, and beneath the clouds,
> Which image in their bulk both lakes and shores
> And mountain crags: so shalt thou see and hear
> The lovely shapes and sounds intelligible
> Of that eternal language, which thy God
> Utters, who from eternity doth teach
> Himself in all, and all things in himself.
> Great universal Teacher! he shall mould
> Thy spirit, and by giving make it ask.[5]

Nature is enough for Wordsworth, who is in Coleridge's loving eyes "wise and pure"; the childhood he hopes will mould his son's spirit is Wordsworth's childhood among the Cumbrian fells Coleridge had not yet even seen.

The poem that concluded the first *Lyrical Ballads*, and ever since has been the most familiar summary of Wordsworth's sense of the sufficiency of nature to meet the needs of the soul, is "Tintern Abbey". In his evocation of "A presence that disturbs me with the joy / Of elevated thoughts",

> A motion and a spirit, that impels
> All thinking things, all objects of all thought,
> And rolls through all things,[6]

Wordsworth seems close to Coleridge's "Almighty Spirit", or even to the God of "Frost at Midnight". A little later he echoes closely the "Nature ne'er deserts" line of "This Lime-Tree Bower":

> And this prayer I make,
> Knowing that Nature never did betray
> The heart that loved her,[7]

but the lines that immediately follow show not only how passive is his notion of
the mind "fed" by nature compared to the active response from the soul already
hoped for by Coleridge, but also how strong an element of escape from the
unpleasant impact of other people there is in Wordsworth's aspiration to an undisturbed happiness bestowed by "Nature":

> 'Tis her privilege,
> Through all the years of this our life, to lead
> From joy to joy; for she can so inform
> The mind that is within us, so impress
> With quietness and beauty, and so feed
> With lofty thoughts, that neither evil tongues,
> Rash judgements, nor the sneers of selfish men,
> Nor greetings where no kindness is, nor all
> The dreary intercourse of daily life,
> Shall e'er prevail against us, or disturb
> Our cheerful faith that all which we behold
> Is full of blessings.[8]

Even thus baldly summarised, the story of the *Lyrical Ballads* suggests the underlying reality of the relationship between Wordsworth and Coleridge. As Wordsworth's confidence, capacity to work, and grip on his own literary career, his
own deployment of his poetic talent, increased with Coleridge's admiration and
support, Coleridge's confidence, capacity to work and personal grip declined. It
was not only that Wordsworth's growth in psychological strength sapped Coleridge's. Wordsworth, with Dorothy's help, learned how to detach himself from
the existence of his mistress and daughter in France. In 1802 he married, in a
considered fashion and, as it turned out, notably happily, a childhood friend
who was willing to share her husband's affection with his sister. Meanwhile,
Coleridge's hastily undertaken marriage became increasingly wretched; his wife,
left out of years of high-flown talk and poetic aspiration, was more and more
neglected by Coleridge, who travelled about England and then in Germany with
and without the Wordsworths, while babies at home were born and raised, one
dying in his absence. By the time of Wordsworth's marriage, Coleridge was hopelessly in love with Wordsworth's sister-in-law, Sara Hutchinson. This unconsum-
mated, unrequited passion haunted him for the rest of his life. But even this
might not have become the last straw that eventually broke the back of the
friendship had it not been for Coleridge's increasingly frightening dependence

on opium, then readily available as an ordinary medicine, mixed with brandy as laudanum.

From the depths of his misery over Sara and his marriage, and from his own certainty that nature by itself could never anchor the distressed soul—"O Sara! we receive but what we give, / And in *our* Life alone does Nature live"[9]—he wrote in 1802 a long, desperate verse letter to his love, much of which soon became his last considerable poem, "Dejection: An Ode". In the course of the next decade, Coleridge's life became more and more destructively affected by opium. He spent two years in the wartime Mediterranean, working for months for the governor of Malta. On his return in 1806, his separation from his wife (and for many years from his children) became definite. Guilt over this only added to his guilt over his addiction, then neither named nor clearly understood, which was ruining his self-respect, his health and his capacity to organise any sensible kind of literary career. Early in this wretched period of Coleridge's life, Wordsworth underlined the widening gulf between them by completing the several thousand lines, in thirteen books, of *The Prelude*. The poem is addressed to Coleridge. On a series of winter evenings at the end of 1806, Wordsworth read it aloud to his wife, his sister, his sister-in-law Sara and Coleridge, who could now see that Sara had merely joined the other women in a closed circle admiring and protecting Wordsworth.

The Prelude tells the story, on an epic scale, of Wordsworth's developing sense of himself, in relation to the landscapes of his childhood—to London, France, Dorothy and Coleridge—the "growth of a poet's mind", as Wordsworth's wife later subtitled it. The dominant note in the entire poem, a note already struck in "Tintern Abbey", is of complacency; Wordsworth is delighted to be himself and has turned everything that has happened to him into a source of his present strength and confidence. His youthful love affair appears only obliquely as a romantic tale told of others. Sometimes the poem recalls forlorn human beings observed by the poet—a blind man with a written account of his life pinned to his chest, a labourer in a sunny London square with a sickly baby in his arms—but a cool distance is sustained between the poet and these figures. Years later Coleridge talked of "this peculiarity of utter non-sympathy with the subjects of [Wordsworth's] poetry".[10] Most of *The Prelude* records the feelings of a young man, unremarkable except for his gift for easy, flowing, sometimes vivid and moving blank verse. He strikes the reader as educated but not seriously thoughtful, equipped much as one would expect, with a little history, a little idealism and a flat, rational, late eighteenth-century assumption—which can be touched into life only by the beauty of nature—that there is a deity. The human world, particularly in cities and for the poor, is a dreadful place, but nature remembered from childhood, nature seen with the right vision—and this, in contrast to Coleridge, is with Wordsworth a matter of willpower and self-control—cures the poet's sense of evil, which is always evil perpetrated by others. The upshot of the whole work is Wordsworth's pride in himself as one of the "higher minds" that are "truly from the Deity":

> hence the highest bliss
> That can be known is theirs, the consciousness
> Of whom they are habitually infused
> Through every image, and through every thought,
> And all impressions; hence religion, faith,
> And endless occupation for the soul
> Whether discursive or intuitive;
> Hence sovereignty within and peace at will.[11]

And the poem ends with a verse paragraph addressed to Coleridge (previously mentioned several times, with a forbearing compassion that strikes the reader as loftily patronising), hoping that the pair of them as "Prophets of Nature" can rescue their contemporaries from a "fall back to old idolatry" by setting a shining example that will

> Instruct them how the mind of man becomes
> A thousand times more beautiful than the earth
> On which he dwells.[12]

Coleridge responded, not only to *The Prelude*, but to the domestic hearth of the readings, from which he now felt terminally excluded, with a poem to Wordsworth that was not published for more than twenty years (a couple of more desperate poems[13] to Wordsworth, written in Latin in Coleridge's notebook at about this time, were not published at all). In "To William Wordsworth", Coleridge manages to pay a generous tribute to his friend's "ever-enduring" greatness, contrasting it bitterly with his own failure:

> Sense of past Youth, and Manhood come in vain,
> And Genius given, and knowledge won in vain.[14]

He and Wordsworth can no longer be regarded as a prophetic pair; his own unhappiness has nothing to do with Wordsworth's strength; he is beset with

> the poisons of self-harm! And ill
> Such intertwine beseems triumphal wreaths
> Strewed before *thy* advancing![15]

Nevertheless, in contrast to the "tranquil sea" of Wordsworth's poem, Coleridge still pictures in his own mind:

> momentary Stars of my own birth,
> Fair constellated Foam, still darting off
> Into the darkness.[16]

And there is a brave assertion of his independence in the judgement implied in his two lines on Wordsworth's account of his return from France:

> So summoned homeward, thenceforth calm and sure
> From the dread Watch-Tower of man's absolute Self.[17]

Nearly thirty years later, in the closing months of his life, Coleridge, in his last lines of serious verse, wrote on the ancient Delphic advice, "Know Thyself":

> Γνωθι σεαυτον!—and is this the prime
> And heaven-sprung adage of the olden time!—
> Say, canst thou make thyself?—Learn first that trade;—
> Haply thou mayst know what thyself had made.
> What hast thou, Man, that thou dar'st call thine own?
> What is there in thee, Man, that can be known?
> Dark fluxion, all unfixable by thought,
> A phantom dim of past and future wrought,
> Vain sister of the worm,—life, death, soul, clod—
> Ignore thyself, and strive to know thy God![18]

The Augustinian tone of these lines, and the contrast between them and the proclamation of "man's absolute Self" that drives the entire *Prelude*, signal what had already in 1806 become the unbridgeable chasm between the minds, the souls, of Coleridge and Wordsworth. Coleridge was a Christian, still feeling his way toward the full orthodoxy of belief that he would, now before very long, gratefully reach: the story of the rest of his life is the story of a major writer in the Christian tradition who, because of self-delusion, lack of application, dependence on the huge range of his reading, infinite capacity to talk, and the muddle that his desk must always have been, nearly failed to be a major writer at all. Wordsworth, during the whole period in which he was a good poet, was not a Christian but an eccentric eighteenth-century deist with a clear allegiance only to the beauty of nature, in his own response to which he found what would now be called "the sacred". When, in the 1820s, Wordsworth wrote eighteen "Ecclesiastical Sketches" (sonnets), his subject was the Church of England. The poems are lit by an occasional spurt of anti-Catholic animus; otherwise, they are bland exercises, the last of which ends with a satisfied vision of the future where

> The living Waters, less and less by guilt
> Stained and polluted, brighten as they roll,
> Till they have reached the Eternal city—built
> For the perfected Spirits of the just![19]

In the same decade, Coleridge, closer to Augustine than he knew, wrote in his notebook of the

> extreme peril of *Security* / we must cling like Infants, who are still in the arms or in the clutch of an Alien, tho' their arms are round their Mother's Neck. In a state of triumph and security the first Adam dreams, of *becoming* a God, and the secure Christian will too easily mistake God for himself.—That the spiritual Life in him is Christ (= God manifested in the Flesh) and not Himself, he can only continue to know by reminding himself of his *base*, his *Nature*, being the *Contrary* to God.[20]

The friendship creaked on for four more years. In 1808 Coleridge was so lonely, ill and miserable in London that, he told Thomas De Quincey, he could not write to Grasmere for fear of disgusting the Wordsworths. He added with generosity: "That there is such a man in the World as Wordsworth, and that such a man enjoys such a Family, makes both Death & my inefficient Life a less grievous Thought to me."[21] In the following year he wrote in his notebook: "Chained by a darling passion or *tyrannic* Vice in Hell, yet with the Telescope of an unperverted Understanding descrying and describing Heaven and the Road thereto to my companions, the Damn'd! O fearful fate!"[22] In 1809–1810 Coleridge, to the astonishment of the sceptical Wordsworths, managed, in their house and with Sara Hutchinson as his secretary, to produce twenty-eight almost regular weekly numbers of *The Friend*, a serious periodical essay on the lines of *The Rambler*. When Sara, without warning, left the house and the district, Coleridge collapsed, fled to London and found the refuge he expected denied him because Wordsworth had written to warn his hosts of his behaviour. The friendship was never restored. For six more muddled years, Coleridge just survived his addiction, managing to give occasional courses of brilliant lectures, managing to write *Biographia Literaria* in a few confused months of 1815 and recording his guilt, his fears, his isolation and his frequent despair in the letters and notebooks eventually published in the twentieth century. In 1816 a young doctor, James Gillman, living with his wife and children in Highgate, then just outside London, took in the very ill Coleridge as a patient for a month. For eighteen years, until Coleridge's death in 1834, Dr. Gillman cared for him with extraordinary kindness, controlling the opium problem and providing stability, affection and safety. In the prose gloss Coleridge added, probably in 1813, to "The Ancient Mariner" for its republication in 1817 appears the magical sentence:

In his loneliness and fixedness he yearneth towards the journeying Moon, and the stars that still sojourn, yet still move onward; and every where the blue sky belongs to them, and is their appointed rest, and their native country and their own natural homes, which they enter unannounced, as lords that are certainly expected and yet there is a silent joy at their arrival.[23]

On Christmas Day 1827, for the first time since he was a boy of nineteen, Coleridge, now fifty-five, received Holy Communion at his parish church in Highgate.

* * *

Early in 1798, with "The Ancient Mariner" begun but not completed, Coleridge, aged twenty-five, wrote in a letter:

To the cause of Religion I solemnly devote all my best faculties—and if I wish to acquire knowledge as a philosopher and fame as a poet, I pray for grace that I may continue to feel what I now feel, that my greatest reason for wishing the one & the other, is that I may be enabled by my knowledge to defend Religion ably, and by my reputation to draw attention to the defence of it.[24]

Through the chaos and unhappiness of the next eighteen years, through the comparative calm thereafter, through the weakening of his ambition as a poet in the face of Wordsworth's strength, and through the vast range of the philosophical knowledge that he acquired, borrowed, mangled and then largely left behind, Coleridge never abandoned this resolution. It is the clue to his writing life, as to his life.

In 1799 he jotted down in his notebook: "Socinianism [Unitarianism] Moonlight—Methodism &c. A Stove! O for some Sun that shall unite Light & Warmth."[25] This was an image he returned to several times in his interior journey toward the sun of full, trinitarian and sacramental Christian faith. The kinds of emotional and intellectual nourishment that sustained him on this journey were various and in some ways ill-assorted. All that he thought and felt about poetry—Wordsworth's along with that of others, though Wordsworth, while using it here and there, failed to follow (in any sense) Coleridge's thought—reached coherent meaning for him only in relation to his developing perception of God. His ten months in Germany in 1798–99, during which he learned German well and became the first Englishman to read Immanuel Kant, Friedrich Schelling, and A. W. and Friedrich von Schlegel with enthusiastic insight, filled his head with philosophical terminology and the aesthetic theories of Romanticism: again, he took from all this what helped him toward God, as well as taking much, from A. W. Schlegel in particular, that helped him to understand Shakespeare. Deeper than his fascination with poetry or his submission to the torrent of German Romantic philosophy was the agony of his conscience, his remorse over his failed marriage, his grief over his misplaced love, and the torture of his addiction, with its endlessly repeated resolutions and relapses. His conscience led him to his certainty of the judgement of God and eventually also to his belief in God's mercy, incarnate, with the justice and wisdom of God, in the figure of Christ on the Cross.

Despite the difference between Coleridge's chronic weakness of character and Augustine's exceptional robustness, there is much in this journey, and much in Coleridge's soul and rare intelligence, that is reminiscent of Augustine's soul and Augustine's intelligence. Coleridge's youthful interest in philosophy, and then his passion for German metaphysics with its lasting impact on a receptive mind of material both powerful and distracting in relation to trinitarian Christianity, both had parallels in Augustine's life. Augustine's enthusiasm for Cicero was overtaken, when he was much the same age as Coleridge in Germany, by his intoxication with Neoplatonism in Milan, where the orderly mind of the dead Plotinus was exciting the young as Kant's did in Germany fourteen centuries later. Coleridge recognised the parallel. In *Biographia Literaria* he attributes his "final re-conversion to the whole truth in Christ" to both "a deeper insight into my own heart" and "the difference of my metaphysical notions from those of [the] Unitarians", "even as according to [Augustine's] own confession the books of certain Platonic philosophers (*libri quorundam Platonicorum*) commenced the rescue of Saint Augustine's faith from the same error aggravated by the far darker accompaniment of the Manichaean heresy".[26] (The slightly inaccurate quotation suggests that Coleridge read the *Confessions* in Latin and that he read it closely enough almost to remember actual phrases.) There is even a parallel between the constant tug in Augustine of Monica's prayers for his conversion and Coleridge's memory of his father's faith, his father's church, and a simplicity that would never fail to absorb his own complexity. In May 1798, before he went to Germany, he wrote to his friend Thomas Poole when both of them were dealing with painful domestic problems: "I have had lately some sorrows that have cut more deeply into my heart than they ought to have done—& I have found Religion & *commonplace Religion* too, my restorer & my comfort—giving me gentleness & calmness & dignity."[27] On the same day, he wrote to his brother George, who had succeeded their father as vicar of Ottery Saint Mary, about an old man whose daughter had drowned herself: "Good old Man! he bears it like one in whom Christianity is an habit of feeling in a still greater degree than a conviction of the understanding."[28] For Coleridge himself to pull, by the exercise of the will in obedience to God, his reasoning power into harmony with the habit of feeling—*credo ut intelligam*—was the work of decades, though he always knew that faith was more than "the conviction of the understanding". In consonance with both Pascal and Johnson, he wrote in the same section of the *Biographia* in which he compared himself to Augustine that he had always known that the existence of God "could not be intellectually more evident without becoming morally less effective; without counteracting its own end by sacrificing the *life* of faith to the cold mechanism of a worthless because compulsory assent."[29]

In 1802, with German philosophy now expanding in his mind to strengthen but also to confuse his beliefs, he nevertheless wrote to George, who had certainly never heard of Kant or Schelling, of "the Change which has taken place in me", meaning that his conversion from Unitarianism was complete:

My Faith is simply this—that there is an original corruption in our nature, from which & from the consequences of which, we may be redeemed by Christ—not as the Socinians say, by his pure morals or excellent Example merely—but in a mysterious manner as an effect of his Crucifixion—and this I believe—not because I *understand* it; but because I *feel*, that it is not only suitable to, but needful for, my nature and because I find it clearly revealed.—Whatever the New Testament says, I believe—according to my best judgment of the meaning of the sacred writers.[30]

But Coleridge was never going to rest in a simple personal faith held in common with his clerical brother. He was by nature "a kind of Metaphysician", a thinker and a critic (a judge of his own time) even before Wordsworth's self-confidence had convinced him that he was not primarily a poet. Inescapably an intellectual, a brilliant child of the Enlightenment as well as of the parsonage, Coleridge knew that much effort lay ahead if he were to "defend Religion ably", that is, to persuade an increasingly sceptical, increasingly worldly, educated English public that it was possible for a highly intelligent, rational person to believe in the truth of Christian revelation.

As his faith in salvation in Christ, for years a fitful light in the darkness of his worst period, became steadier and more confident, his ambition, in an England losing its Christian bearings, became exactly the same as Pascal's. He planned to produce, as his *opus maximum*, a great defence of Christianity. He called it "Christianity the one true Philosophy", or "a large theological work on Revelation", or "Logosophia: Or on the Logos, Divine and Human", or simply "Assertion of Religion". It was intended "finally" to be "a revolution of all that has been called *Philosophy* or Metaphysics in England and France since the era of the commencing predominance of the mechanical system at the Restoration of our second Charles".[31] It was never completed or even roughly shaped as a coherent whole. But, with many characteristic indirections, borrowings and confusions, writing toward it did take place.

His first attempt was *The Friend*. In the prospectus he sent out to possible subscribers in 1809, he said that he had been encouraged to embark on a series of essays, "upholding the [altered to 'some'] Principles both of Taste and Philosophy, adopted by the great Men of Europe from the Middle of the fifteenth till toward the Close of the seventeenth Century", by finding that his many notebook entries tended, "miscellaneous as they were, to one common End (... *what we are and what we are born to become*)." He conceded that in upholding these principles, "I must run Counter to the Prejudices of many of my readers (*for old Faith is often modern Heresy*)."[32] The intention is a remarkable one: the period whose principles he wants to restore includes the Reformation—Luther was a particular hero of Coleridge's—but it extends back to include the brief peak of the Catholic classical Renaissance, the "taste and philosophy" of the Florentine Platonists, Erasmus and Thomas More. And by "old Faith" it is clear that he means genuine, orthodox, Christian faith, which by implication he is distinguishing from the attenuated, "enlightened" beliefs of contemporary England.

A little way into the first of his "periodical Essays", he begins at the very beginning, with Adam (man) hearing the voice of God and choosing to disobey it—that is, with conscience and with sin and the suffering it causes—as universal human experience:

> Whatever humbles the heart and forces the mind inward, whether it be sickness, or grief, or remorse, or the deep yearnings of love (and there have been children of affliction, for whom all these have met and made up one complex suffering) in proportion as it acquaints us with "the thing, we are," renders us docile to the concurrent testimony of our fellow-men in all ages and in all nations.[33]

He is writing, of course, about himself, with a swift reference to a passage about moral tangle in Shakespeare's *Rape of Lucrece*. But he goes on:

> From PASCAL in his closet, resting the arm, which supports his thoughtful brow, on a pile of demonstrations, to the poor pensive Indian, that seeks the missionary in the American wilderness, the humiliated self-examinant feels that there is Evil in our nature as well as Good, an EVIL and a GOOD for a just analogy to which he questions all other natures in vain. It is still the great definition of humanity, that we have a conscience ... which we may stupify but cannot delude; which we may suspend, but cannot annihilate; although we may perhaps find a treacherous counterfeit in the very quiet which we derive from its slumber, or its entrancement.[34]

Whether or not he was aware of it, and probably he was not, Coleridge is here drawing a distinction, which pervades all his writing on Christianity, between what is about and for everyone, from Pascal to the poor Indian, and what—for example, Wordsworth's quieting of the conscience in the entrancement of the response to beauty—is available only to the very few. (Had Wordsworth's programme for a happy life been of general application, everyone growing up in unspoiled mountain country would be both virtuous and wise.)

If the subscribers thought that an orderly exposition was to follow the first issue, they would have been, as was always the case with Coleridge's projects, disappointed. Religion, philosophy, political thought, personal reminiscence and literary criticism were jumbled together in essays not at all easy to read, though always conveying a sense of breadth of learning and depth of thought and sometimes reaching clear expression in passages of piercing insight. A stranger who had taken the trouble to understand the scale of what Coleridge was trying to do wrote encouragingly, after fifteen issues:

> It constitutes the greater part of those grateful feelings which the Friend has inspired in me, that I perceive in it a decided & energetic opposition to the proud & weak wisdom of modern philosophy—that darkness of a false & insufficient light; & an acknowledgement of that pure & essential light, which shone once, & is for ever[,] from whence the rays of the other borrowed supply a set of men, the produce & the disgrace of extended knowledge, with twilight to talk of passions which they do not feel, & wisdom "which they do not understand".[35]

But there were too few like him. A month after receiving this letter, Coleridge wrote the unnumbered essay that comes between nos. 20 and 21. Here he draws again his crucial distinction between genuine Christian faith, the fallenness of man, man's rescue in Christ, and the freedom of the will, and the varieties of materialism, determinism, atheism, or the optimism of "the pious Deists of the last Century", then prevailing in England. The essay also reveals that *The Friend* was in financial trouble, partly caused by Grasmere's distance from London and problems with the post, but partly by a falling-off of subscribers because, as Coleridge admits, he was pleasing too few of his readers, making demands on their patience and intelligence that, unsurprisingly, they found excessive. No doubt (as would have been the case at any time in the two centuries since) it irritated many that Coleridge's opinions could not be packaged, and therefore welcomed or dismissed, as either liberal or conservative (to use slightly anachronistic but appropriate labels). He was passionate in defence of the powerless and maltreated; of the poor; of press-ganged soldiers and sailors; and of the uneducated, most of all of slaves in America, while the appalling trade continued to enrich English merchants. But he was no Jacobin, as he makes quite clear in *Biographia Literaria*: mob politics horrified him, as did the quenching of the Christian in the secular, protoutilitarian reform movements of the day. On the other hand, he had too keen a sense of the non-identity of the city of God with the *civitas terrena* ever to be a straightforward Tory. He was writing, though not at all simply, as a Christian, and the time was already past when an educated public could cope readily with Christianity and wide-ranging intelligence combined.

The underlying problem was identified by another friendly stranger who wrote in response to the unnumbered essay, sending some money to help keep the periodical afloat, "as behoves them who care for the Truth":

> I could not in consistency with the opinion I have long been com-
> pelled to entertain of the present generation of my countrymen form
> any strong hopes of the popularity of a work which requires in the
> outset the laborious thought of a zealous and vigorous student and
> which only promises to bring us back at last to where we were an
> hundred and fifty years ago.[36]

It had been hard for Augustine, in the *City of God*, to persuade sceptical pagans in a crumbling empire of the truth of Christian revelation. It was no less hard now for Coleridge to persuade of the same truth sceptical post-Christians in an imperial England of ever-increasing confidence in commercial and industrial progress. Three months later, *The Friend*, though not only, as we have seen, for this reason, collapsed after a final half-dozen random essays. It was a considerable achievement, and not only on account of the hard come by perseverance that produced it. But its most valuable section, to which we will shortly return, was written as an addition from Coleridge's Highgate haven in 1818 when he was preparing the essays for book publication. Meanwhile, his life reached new depths of humiliation and squalor, out of which he managed, in three frantic months of 1815, to write most of *Biographia Literaria*, the prose work for which he is best known, particularly among those who regard his Christianity as of no interest.

Biographia Literaria is a notorious muddle, inconsistent as to the kind of book it is intended to be and a proportion of it translated or paraphrased from German writers, especially Schelling, without acknowledgement. Later in the century, Leslie Stephen wrote that it seemed to have been "put together with a pitch-fork".[37] Very much Coleridge's own are the passages of detailed literary criticism—penetrating on Shakespeare, about whose single lines and words Coleridge wrote as no one had written before, and cautiously discriminating on Wordsworth—and firm, in truthful, painful report in the distancing of himself and his own views from what became of the *Lyrical Ballads* and its preface. The famous passage concluding chapter 13, on the imagination, which owes a good deal to the

Germans, connects, in summary definition, the creative perceptiveness of the poet to that of any human being, and both to the eternal act of creation in God:

> The IMAGINATION then I consider either as primary, or secondary. The primary IMAGINATION I hold to be the living Power and prime Agent of all human Perception, and as a repetition in the finite mind of the eternal act of creation in the infinite I AM. The secondary I consider as an echo of the former, co-existing with the conscious will, yet still as identical with the primary in the *kin* of its agency, and differing only in *degree*, and in the *mode* of its operation.[38]

The context in which these sentences appear is typical: a long letter, which Coleridge pretends to have been written by a friend, asks for clarity; the definition is hedged about with promises of future development that never materialized. But the great definition stands. It has had a long and mostly cloudy afterlife in the writing of those who found Coleridge's formulation illuminating but wished the imagination to have nothing to do with God, and the poetic imagination to have little to do with the mental life of ordinary people. It has been the very quality of the literary comment in this hopelessly disorganised book that has made it possible for readers largely to ignore the fact that the *Biographia* is primarily, like Augustine's *Confessions*, a study of the soul in relation to God and only secondarily a fight for Coleridge's soul in relation to Wordsworth's. The book ends with a lyrical paragraph about faith, expanded from a marginal note Coleridge had scribbled in a book by the seventeenth-century German mystic Jakob Böhme. The paragraph ends:

> Religion passes out of the ken of Reason only where the eye of Reason has reached its own Horizon; and ... Faith is then but its continuation ... to preserve the Soul steady and collected in its pure *Act* of inward Adoration to the great I AM, and to the filial WORD that re-affirmeth it from Eternity to Eternity, whose choral Echo is the Universe.[39]

Although the completion of his *opus maximum* remained among the broken promises Coleridge was always making to himself, to his correspondents and to his unknown readers, he did, after his life became comparatively orderly, comparatively "steady and collected", in Dr. Gillman's house, finish several works that had the defence of Christianity at their heart. The first of these was the *Statesman's Manual: A Lay Sermon* of 1816, the recommended manual being the

Bible, and this work's companion [second] *Lay Sermon ... on the Existing Distresses and Discontents* of the following year. These are lengthy essays of criticism, in the full sense of judgement, of the ideas and social problems of contemporary England in the light of what Coleridge felt to be the best that he could discover in the past. They were intended for what Coleridge a little later was to call "the clerisy", "the Learned and Reflecting of all Ranks and Professions, especially among the Higher Class",[40] and they are readily understandable, free of technical philosophy and in places passionately eloquent, though, as usual, not well organised. Coleridge's target is poverty, the poverty of the spirit produced by the current state of education, and the actual poverty of those starved into factory labour or rural slums by the recently concluded war, by rapid industrialisation, and by the cruelties of land enclosures, particularly in the highlands of Scotland.

On education in Regency England, Coleridge had things to say to which attention was certainly paid later in the nineteenth century, but which had been almost entirely forgotten by the late twentieth. He is shocked by the consequences of mere literacy—by what, already, people were reading who had been taught only to read—and by the thinness of a Christianity that, deprived of substance and mystery (in effect, of both truth and beauty), is deprived of all but moral injunction. He condemns "the plan of poisoning the children of the poor with a sort of *potential* infidelity under the '*liberal idea*' of teaching those points only of religious faith, in which all denominations agree."[41] It is not only the children of the poor who are starved of spiritual nourishment. "In the present day we hear much, and from men of various creeds, of the *plainness* and *simplicity* of the Christian religion: and a strange abuse has been made of these words ... by men who would fain transform the necessity of believing *in* Christ into a recommendation to believe him."[42] The principal enemy is, as ever, emasculated Unitarianism. But unreflecting, everyday complacency in the Church of England is just as pernicious:

> Alas!—the main hindrance to the use of the Scriptures, as your Manual, lies in the notion that you are already acquainted with its contents. ... Truths of all others the most awful and mysterious and at the same time of universal interest, are considered as so true as to lose all the powers of truth, and lie bed-ridden in the dormitory of the soul.[43]

He sees this dire attenuation of Christianity's saving truth as attributable mainly to the Enlightenment; on Voltaire and Hume, and on the frivolous self-centredness encouraged by both, he writes with real anger in these essays. It is in this context that he delivers his resonant definition of "symbol":

> A hunger-bitten and idea-less philosophy naturally produces a starveling and comfortless religion. It is among the miseries of the present age that it recognizes no medium between *Literal* and *Metaphorical*. Faith is either to be buried in the dead letter, or its name and honours usurped by a counterfeit product of the mechanical understanding, which in the blindness of self-complacency confounds SYMBOLS with ALLEGORIES. Now an Allegory is but a translation of abstract notions into a picture-language.... On the other hand a Symbol is characterized ... above all by the translucence of the Eternal through and in the Temporal. It always partakes of the Reality which it renders intelligible; and while it enunciates the whole, abides itself as a living part in that Unity, of which it is the representative.[44]

This passage has profound christological and eucharistic implications. It should be pondered by all those who think that nothing but empty space lies between a fundamentalist and a metaphorical understanding of Christianity.

While Coleridge was writing the lay sermons, he was preparing the essays of *The Friend* for book publication. As well as tidying and rearranging the original texts, he added a long section called "On the Grounds of Morals and Religion", which he later described to his son Derwent as outweighing "in point of *value* ... all my other works, verse or prose".[45] The eleven short essays of this section are unsurprisingly uneven in both manner and quality, but they do contain some of the most impressive thought that Coleridge had yet achieved. They address the question set out in the first paragraph: "Since the commencement of this edition, the question has repeatedly arisen in my mind, whether morality can be said to have any principle distinguishable from religion, or religion any substance divisible from morality?"[46] This has become an increasingly pressing question in the almost two centuries since Coleridge was writing these essays. His answer, elaborated at length, was of course in the negative, as the answer to this question is bound to be if the unity that supports the whole of Christian belief holds firm, the unity in God of truth with goodness and beauty. Several times in these essays Coleridge insists on the connexion, perceptible by anyone, between the heart and God. There is no one who does not recognise his own conscience, ignore it as he may:

Is not a true *efficient* conviction of a moral truth, is not "the creating of a new heart", which collects the energies of a man's whole being in the focus of the conscience, the one essential miracle, the same and of the same evidence in the ignorant and the learned . . . ? Is it not emphatically that leading of the Father, without which no man can come to Christ?[47]

Faced, as Augustine and Pascal (and scarcely anyone in the Christian centuries between them) had been, by a world blind and deaf to the scale of the difference it makes whether or not Christianity is true, Coleridge in the last of these essays returns as they did, and, like Augustine, with the support of Plato (and, pushing him a little, of the Wordsworth of the *Immortality Ode*), to our most basic instinct-ive sense of the miracle of being. Our wonder that there is anything at all is where we begin:

Hast thou ever raised thy mind to the consideration of EXISTENCE, in and by itself, as the mere act of existing? Hast thou ever said to thyself thoughtfully, IT IS! heedless in that moment, whether it were a man before thee, or a flower, or a grain of sand? . . . If thou hast indeed attained to this, thou wilt have felt the presence of a mystery, which must have fixed thy spirit in awe and wonder.[48]

It is typical of Coleridge that eleven years later, perhaps thinking he had not made the point clearly enough for Derwent, now a clergyman, he added in Derwent's copy of this book:

Here do we stop? Woe to us if we do! Better that we had never begun. A deeper yet must be sought for. Even the Absolute Will, THE GOOD, the superessential Source of BEING; and in the eternal Act of Self-affirmation, the I AM, The Father—who with the only-begotten Logos . . . and with the Spirit proceeding, is the One only God from ever-lasting to everlasting.[49]

But the whole section in any case ends with a kind of hymn to God, who is

the substantiating principle of all true wisdom, the satisfactory solution of all the contradictions of human nature, of the whole riddle of the world. This alone belongs to and speaks intelligibly to all alike, the learned and the ignorant, if but the *heart* listens.[50]

Aids to Reflection, published in 1825, is yet another generically peculiar book, the result of Coleridge's unmethodical methods of getting anything written at all. The most widely read of his books for the rest of the nineteenth century, it was intended to be a short annotated selection from the writings of Robert Leighton, a seventeenth-century Anglican (the word "Anglican" becoming current in Coleridge's time) divine, beleaguered archbishop of Glasgow under Charles II in a largely Presbyterian Scotland. Coleridge was devoted to Leighton's writings because they had helped to stabilise his faith in the darkest years of his life. In the upshot, Coleridge used Leighton as no more than a prop or impetus, soon altogether left behind, for writing of his own that, oddly divided into numbered "Aphorisms" and passages of "Comment", further developed his defence of Christianity in the intellectual climate of advancing science, which Coleridge both understood and did not fear. The book was meant for the young—Coleridge in the early 1820s was regularly spellbinding, in hours of talk, a group of young men who had gathered around him—and was intended to teach them to think properly, so that they would come to see that only Christianity made sense of human life and of themselves in particular. "You have been bred", Coleridge tells such young men at the end of his preface,

> in a land abounding with men, able in arts, learning, and knowledges manifold, this man in one, this in another, few in many, none in all. But there is one art, of which every man should be master, the art of REFLECTION. If you are not a *thinking* man, to what purpose are you a *man* at all? ... Or to what end was man alone, of all animals, endued by the Creator with the faculty of *self*-consciousness? [51]

This being Coleridge, the book travels, on an inevitably zigzag path, full of interruptions and indirections, all the way from this recommendation of self-discovery to the total dependence of the self on God. The third section, "Aphorisms on Spiritual Religion", has in it some of the most penetrating and inspiriting pages Coleridge ever wrote. He knew, as Pascal had known, how difficult it had become for an educated person to arrive at real Christian conviction in the face of the consensus of the times:

> There is nothing in religion farther out of Nature's reach, and more remote from the natural man's liking and believing, than the doctrine of Redemption by a Saviour, and by a crucified Saviour. It is comparatively easy to persuade men of the necessity of an amendment of

conduct; it is more difficult to make them see the necessity of Repentance in the *Gospel* sense, the necessity of a change in the *principle* of
action; but to convince men of the necessity of the Death of Christ is
the most difficult of all.[52]

(This is close to Pascal's three-stage progression from the pre-Christian sense of
the absolute to the Catholic recognition of Christ in the Eucharist.) Yet, as
Coleridge says elsewhere in *Aids to Reflection,* "Christianity and REDEMPTION are
equivalent terms." [53] The very truth that is most essential to Christian faith, our
redemption in Christ and our dependence on grace for all that is good in us, is
also the truth that is hardest to believe; it is now, therefore, that which is most
likely to be left out, smoothed away, risen above in a world in which man's
confidence in reason and in his own powers is constantly increasing.

It is fascinating to watch Coleridge in this book confronting the old, apparent
paradox—we are free, yet we are totally dependent on the grace of God—which
can be resolved only in faith, and to see his long-learned love of God, together
with his capacity to think, taking him, as similar qualities had taken Pascal, to
fully Augustinian conclusions. Shall he who has come to hope in Christ

refer the first movements and preparations to his own Will and Understanding, and bottom his claim to the Promises on his own comparative exellence? If not, if no man dare take this honor to himself, to
whom shall he assign it, if not to that Being in whom the Promise
originated, and on whom its Fulfilment depends? [54]

What follows from this is as inescapable for Coleridge as it had been for Augustine: "Thus then the Doctrine of Election is in itself a necessary inference from
an undeniable fact—necessary at least for all who hold that the best of men are
what they are through the grace of God." [55] Against all those, Unitarians, and
Pelagians within the Church of England, who were at the time recommending
only the morality of Christianity, having left behind, they thought, the naïveté
of its mysterious but central truth, Coleridge writes here in orthodox solidarity
with the central tradition of the Church. "On the doctrine of Redemption depends
the *Faith,* the *Duty,* of believing in the Divinity of our Lord." [56] On believing,
that is, that "God so loved the world that he sent his only Son, so that everyone
who believes in him might not perish but have eternal life." [57]

If, against the scepticism of the times, we are to respond with our whole
selves to God in Trinity, to Christ's question "But you, who do you say I am?" [58]

we must begin from an awareness of that from which we need to be redeemed, the universal sinfulness of the human race. "Original sin. Is there any such Thing?" Coleridge asks, and goes on, "That is not the question. For it is a fact acknowledged on all hands almost: and even those who will not confess it in words, confess it in their complaints." [59] If you doubt its existence, look honestly at yourself and at your own capacity to do what you know to be right:

> From what you know of yourself; of your own Heart and Strength; and from what History and personal Experience have led you to conclude of mankind generally; dare you *trust* to it? Dare *you* trust to it? To *it*, and to it alone? If so, well! . . . But if not, if you have had too good reason to know, that your heart is deceitful and your strength weakness: if you are disposed to exclaim with Paul—the Law indeed is holy, just, good, spiritual; but I am carnal, sold under sin; for that which I do, I allow not; and what I would, that I do not—in this case, there is a Voice that says, Come unto *me*: and I will give you rest. This is the Voice of Christ: and the Conditions, under which the promise was given by him, are that you believe *in* him, and believe his words. [60]

Again and again Coleridge returns to this requirement to believe *in* Christ. "I believe Moses, I believe Paul; but I believe *in* Christ." [61] "Did Christ come from Heaven, did the Son of God leave the Glory which he had with his Father before the World began, only to *show* us a way to life, to *teach* truths, to *tell* us of a resurrection? Or saith he not, I *am* the way, I *am* the truth, I *am* the Resurrection and the Life!" [62] At just such a critical point, Coleridge writes, "I should expect to hear a troubled murmur: How can I comprehend this? How is this to be proved?"

> To the first question I should answer: Christianity is not a Theory, or a Speculation; but a *Life*. Not a *Philosophy* of Life, but a Life and a living Process. To the second: TRY IT. It has been eighteen hundred Years in existence: and has one Individual left a record, like the following? "I tried it and it did not answer." [63]

As Pascal said at the end of his discussion of the wager: "Now what harm will come to you from taking this course?" [64]

Coleridge feared that the time was past when such writing was likely to command much approval or assent. His conclusion to *Aids to Reflection* begins with the rueful expectation that his efforts are likely to be written off as "Visionary Ravings, Obsolete Whimsies, Transcendental Trash, &c. &c".[65] Undaunted, he presses on to castigate both the atheist materialism that reduces the created world to "a lifeless Machine whirled about by the dust of its own Grinding",[66] and the aesthetic squeamishness that has influenced the young in particular "even to shrink from the personal pronouns as applied to the Deity".[67] This leads him to echo Pascal's Memorial in an attack on Wordsworth, which his respectful parenthesis does nothing to blunt:

> But many do I know, and yearly meet with, in whom a false and sickly *Taste* co-operates with the prevailing fashion: many, who find the God of Abraham, Isaac, and Jacob, far too *real*, too substantial; who feel it more in harmony with their indefinite sensations
> > "To worship NATURE in the hill and valley,
> > Not knowing what they love—"
> and (to use the language, but not the sense or purpose of the great Poet of our Age) would fain substitute for the Jehovah of their Bible
> > "A sense sublime
> > Of something far more deeply interfused,
> > Whose dwelling is the Light of setting suns,
> > And the round Ocean and the living Air. . . ."
> And this from having been educated to understand the Divine Omnipresence in any sense rather than the alone safe and legitimate one, the presence of all things to God![68]

Coleridge ends the whole book in a flurry of grapeshot and promises. He is trying to establish a central position between two different pairs of contraries: on the one hand, literal as opposed to metaphorical interpretations of the Bible, and on the other hand, Protestant emptying-out of the mystery and reality of Christian truth as opposed to (Roman) Catholic superstition and idolatry. These pairs do not match each other. To detach one from the other with some hope of clarity required new thought on the nature of the Church and also on the correct approach to the Bible, the authority of which Protestants had from the Reformation preferred to the authority of any church. Coleridge is fully aware of the kind of thought needed to sort out the issues *Aids to Reflection* leaves confused; he here promises later unravelling, particularly in what he calls "my Treatise on the Church and Churches",[69] to be properly grounded in ecclesiastical history. At the time of writing this conclusion, he was also planning six essays supplementary to *Aids to Reflection*, one of which, to be "on Church and State", was no doubt the intended "Treatise". What he actually wrote was, as usual, considerably less than he promised. Two short books did get written. One, *On the Constitution of the Church and State*, he published in 1829, with a revised and tidied second edition the following year. The other, probably written a little earlier, was an essay in the form of seven "Letters to a Friend", after Coleridge's death edited and published, in 1840, by his son-in-law and nephew Henry Nelson Coleridge, under the title *Confessions of an Inquiring Spirit*.

This most appealing and sensible little book explains that properly Christian reading of the Bible is a matter of allowing its truth to discover the reader, a very different thing from the rigid conviction that every sentence of Scripture is to be taken as fact. The Holy Spirit speaks through Scripture to the receptive soul—"Whatever [in the Bible] *finds* me, bears witness for itself that it has proceeded from ... the same Spirit, which ... in all ages entering into holy souls maketh them friends of God",[70] and "it is the spirit of the Bible, and not the detached words and sentences, that is infallible and absolute."[71] What he is describing is traditional Benedictine *lectio divina*. But of course it will not be arrived at by a reader of Scripture who embarks on the whole Bible untaught, "unaided by note or comment, catechism or liturgical preparation". What this reader will arrive at will be "*his* religion. For he has found it in his Bible, and the Bible is the Religion of Protestants!"[72] There is, in other words, no safe Christianity outside the Church. In a sustained attack on the dismantling of Christian teaching in favour of reliance on Scripture alone, Coleridge defends, alongside "sacred Writings" outside Scripture, "the institution and perpetuity of a visible Church" to be revered as "the most precious boon of God, next to Christianity itself".[73] The "scheme", he says,

> that the Bible is the sole source; that it not only contains, but constitutes the Christian Religion; that it is, in short a Creed ... was brought into currency by and in favour of those by whom the operation of grace, the aids of the Spirit, the necessity of regeneration, the corruption of our nature, in short, all the peculiar and spiritual mysteries of the Gospel were explained and diluted away.[74]

We are back with believing *in* Christ, with the real Creed, determined for all Christians at Nicaea, "shared by Greeks and Latins, 'Romanist and Protestant'—this and only this is the *ordo traditionis, quam tradiderunt Apostoli iis quibus committebant ecclesias* (the order of tradition, the inherited order, which the Apostles handed on to those to whom they entrusted the churches)." It is no surprise to find Coleridge quoting Augustine, in Latin, here: "This is that *rule of faith* ... of which St Augustine says;—*noveritis hoc esse Fidei Catholicae fundamentum super quod edificium surrexit Ecclesiae* (you will have recognised anew that this is the basis of the Catholic Faith on which has risen the edifice of the Church)." [75] Entirely, also, in the spirit of Augustine is Coleridge's warning that insistence on the factual veracity of unbelievable or unedifying passages in the Old Testament only makes easier its enemies' attacks on Christian truth itself.

Coleridge was far too intelligent not to realise that his belief in the necessity of a doctrinal tradition, a teaching authority to sustain orthodoxy for Christian people, was taking him close to a recognition of the claim of the (Roman) Catholic Church to be that authority, the guardian of that tradition. An Englishman born in the eighteenth century, the son of a good country parson, his instincts led him to regard this closeness as thoroughly alarming. A thoughtful notebook entry of 1806 lets us watch him examining carefully the Thirty-nine Articles, the founding document of the Church of England, drawn up early in Elizabeth's reign (1562) and reiterated by Charles I, the product of the two periods of the English church looked back to with most reverence in the nineteenth century. Coleridge is as dubious about the Articles as Johnson had been, picking up precisely the spirit of both compromise and overconfidence in which they were framed. "The C. of England's founders differed among themselves" and yet had to assert the self-sufficiency of a national church defined by what distinguished it from the Roman Catholic Church. The unsolved question of authority is what strikes Coleridge most forcibly. The canon of Scripture itself, the very Bible that the Articles refer to as the ultimate authority, was settled by "Tradition & critical deductions", that is, a foundation of orthodox decision whose antecedent authority is therefore "a *necessity*" (Coleridge's italics): there is an unresolved problem here, which "lays open to the Roman Catholics an unarmed place". But it is not the only problem. Article 20 says: "The Church hath ... authority in Controversies of Faith": Coleridge finds this statement "objectionable from the extreme looseness & nugatoriness of the definition of the word, Church.... Who is to decide? ... Who chuses & who gives lawful authority in the congregation? The King?—One man?—And what if he be an Infidel, or Heretic—& send such as himself. And who is to determine whether he has nor no?" Coleridge concludes this note, "On what or whom is the practical authority finally built? This may be considered as one of the two or three main vantage grounds of the R. Catholics, from which their Fire commands the Eng. Church." [76] This was the issue for which More had died and the issue on which, not long after Coleridge's death, Newman, after years of suffering, left the Church of England, which he loved as Coleridge loved it.

Closer to Coleridge's heart, and closer to the heart of faith, was an issue that could, just, remain blurred for a devoted Anglican. In *Aids to Reflection* Coleridge sees a line separating the orthodox from the "latitudinarian" dividing both Protestants and Roman Catholics among themselves, the Jesuits attacked by Pascal in the *Provincial Letters* being the Catholic latitudinarians. In his conclusion, Coleridge discusses the sixth chapter of Saint John's Gospel, the mystery of the Incarnation and the mystery of the Eucharist, and, in an explanatory footnote of his own, swerves in two consecutive sentences from a bland *via media* description of the Church of England to a thoroughly Catholic view of the Eucharist:

> The Church of England in this as in other doctrinal points, has preserved the golden mean between the superstitious reverence of the Romanists, and the avowed contempt of the Sectarians, for the Writings of the Fathers, and the authority and unimpeached traditions of the Church during the first three or four Centuries. And how, consistently with this honorable characteristic of our Church, a minister of the same could, on the sacramentary scheme now in fashion, return even a plausible answer to Arnauld's great Work on Transubstantiation, (not without reason the Boast of Catholicism,) exceeds my powers of conjecture.[77]

Despite his perception of the problem of doctrinal authority, despite his hard-won trinitarian and sacramental orthodoxy, Coleridge never lost a deep and blinding anti-Roman prejudice that Johnson, born in the reign of Queen Anne and attached to the old Stuart cause, never had. In Coleridge this prejudice was strengthened (possibly deliberately, since Coleridge was in general one of the most learned Englishmen ever) by an extraordinary ignorance of the Christian Middle Ages. In *Aids to Reflection*, he writes, very well, of the gap between academic theology and popular superstition in the Church, the gap between Aquinas, say, and the victims of Chaucer's Pardoner, as if this were the whole Christian story from the early councils to the Reformation:

> Too soon did the doctors of the Church forget that the *Heart*, the *Moral* Nature, was the beginning and the end; and that Truth, Knowledge and Insight were comprehended in its expansion. This was the true and first apostasy—when in Council and Synod the divine Humanities of the Gospel gave way to speculative Systems, and Religion became

a Science of Shadows under the name of Theology, or at best a bare Skeleton of Truth, without life or interest, alike inaccessible and unintelligible to the majority of Christians.[78]

Coleridge by this time had read, with great enthusiasm, the first translation of the whole of Dante's *Divine Comedy* into English.[79] But here he writes as if the tradition of Augustine, Benedict, Bede, Anselm and Bernard had never existed to support, as well as to be ordered and abstracted from by, the Scholastic philosophers. In *Confessions of an Inquiring Spirit*, Coleridge even wrote of the state

> into which the Latin Church sunk deeper and deeper from the sixth to the fourteenth century; during which time religion was ... merely objective and superstitious,—a letter proudly emblazoned and illuminated, but yet a dead letter that was to be read by its own outward glories without the light of the Spirit in the mind of the believer.[80]

Newman's anguish, both before and after he became a Roman Catholic, suggests that it was necessary for an English Christian of Coleridge's stamp to go on thinking this kind of thing in order to avoid the wrenchingly painful consequences of a more accurate view. (In fairness to Coleridge, it should also be said that the great scholarly recovery of medieval texts—Migne and his *Patrologia Latina* and much work in England, too—had not begun in his lifetime. The regaining of an accurate sense of medieval piety had to wait until the twentieth century.)

When Coleridge, already ill and mortally tired five years before his death, came to write his "treatise" *On the Constitution of the Church and State*, the burning topic of the day was the emancipation of Catholics from some of the civil disabilities imposed on them ever since Elizabeth's reign. Several times in the 1820s, Parliament had foiled attempts to pass a Catholic Relief Act, the purpose of which was to calm Ireland. As Coleridge, who at first opposed and then cautiously supported Catholic relief, put it, "three-fourths of the sum total of His Majesty's Irish subjects are Roman Catholics, with a papal priesthood, while three-fourths of the sum total of His Majesty's subjects are Protestants."[81] A "papal priesthood" is the significant phrase here: for centuries after the papacy was any kind of threat as a foreign power, Englishmen assumed that it must be. Early in 1829, a Catholic Relief Bill, hedged about with precautions—including the severe limiting of the franchise in Ireland—was finally passed by the Commons, then by the Lords, and at last signed by a reluctant George IV under extreme pressure from the Duke of Wellington. Coleridge's book was published at the end of the year and so had no effect on the debate, but the acute contentiousness of the issue while he was writing, and his own ambivalence, much affected his work.

On the Constitution of the Church and State is a wide-ranging, deeply confused book, its degree of confusion suggested by the range of people, all across and beyond the spectrum of English Christianity, who quarried it for helpful phrases and aspirations in the next generation. What Coleridge was attempting here was an ambitious discussion of the nation, the state and "the church" (by which he means various things, distinguished from each other with more energy than clarity), as all of them were and as all of them could be if brought closer to their "idea" or ideal condition. A vision of nation and church as an organic whole, led in every parish by a parson and teacher on the model of Coleridge's father or George Herbert's *Priest to the Temple*, inspires the first part of the book. Coleridge calls the parson

> a nucleus round which the capabilities of the place may crystallise and brighten; a model sufficiently superior to excite, yet sufficiently near to encourage and facilitate, imitation; *this* unobtrusive, continuous agency of a Protestant Church Establishment.... [T]he clergyman is with his parishioners and among them; he is neither in the cloistered cell, nor in the wilderness, but a neighbour and family man, whose education and rank admit him to the mansion of the rich landholder, while his duties make him the frequent visitor of the farmhouse and the cottage.[82]

This rural idyll of the parson's life Coleridge expands to include the teacher, the doctor, the lawyer: all belong to "a permanent class" for which Coleridge coins the term "clerisy". This class, from which Catholic priests are disqualified on the grounds of celibacy and loyalty to a foreign power, must be led from the universities by a small number "at the fountain heads of the humanities"; the much larger number of lesser "clerks" were to "preserve the stores, to guard the treasures, of past civilisation, and thus to bind the present with the past" as well as to secure and guide the moral health and prosperity of "the whole community".[83]

It is a noble, unrealistic picture painted by Coleridge largely for contrast with the current condition of the Church of England, fractured not only by the recent loss of all the followers of the Wesleys into Methodism, but by the acceptance, at least since 1689, of the existence of the dissenting sects beyond its pale. In a furious passage, he rages against the irreparable loss of the unity of the Elizabethan church and the financial management of what has become, instead of the church, "religion, a *noun of multitude*", by a parliament of which the members are not necessarily Anglicans, not necessarily even Christians. As for education, detached from the church for the sake of Dissenters, it has become a secular, utilitarian enterprise directed solely to the increase of national prosperity through the imparting of "those attainments, which give a man the power of doing what he wishes in order to obtain what he desires.... But enough! I will ask only one question. Has the national welfare, have the *weal* and happiness of the people, advanced with the increase of the circumstantial prosperity?"[84] He answers the question with a terrifying indictment of the social evils and cruelties delivered by a modern industrialised society.

Perhaps it is not too late to restore a sense of Christian responsibility to the "clerisy". By suggesting that it is only by chance that the clerisy happens to be connected to a Christian church, Coleridge intends to jolt his reader into an understanding of what he is hoping for:

> In relation to the National Church, Christianity, or the Church of Christ, is a blessed accident, a providential boon, a grace of God, a mighty and faithful friend, the envoy indeed and liege subject of another state, but which can neither administer the laws nor promote the ends of this other State, which is *not* of the world, without advantage, direct and indirect, to the true interests of the States, the aggregate of which is what we mean by the WORLD. [He adds a snappish footnote:] What we ought to mean, at least.[85]

Here Coleridge seems close to Augustine's distinction between the *civitas Dei* and any part of the actual Church that is bound to belong also to the *civitas terrena*. It would have helped Coleridge considerably if he had read the *City of God*, for there is a fuzzy slippage of definition later in the book when he distinguishes "Christianity", "the great redemptive process which began in the separation of light from Chaos ... and has its end in the union of life with God", from "the Christian Church", which within three pages he describes both as "no state, kingdom, or realm of this world; nor ... an Estate of any such realm, kingdom or state; but ... the appointed opposite to them all *collectively*"—so far so Augustinian—and also as a "city built on a hill and not to be hid—an institution consisting of visible and public communities ... the Church visible and militant under Christ".[86] Coleridge needs, to keep him straight, Augustine's great, clarifying distinction between the *civitas Dei* and the *corpus permixtum* that the Church is always certain to be. He does not have it and slides from the *civitas Dei* to the whole Church as distinct from the national church without noticing that there is a difference.

The key to his difficulty is that the discussion is constantly limited by its Englishness. It was too late, and had been too late since the civil war period, for the English church to be either a coherent, united part of "one Catholic Church" or a united, national, Protestant church. Further, because of Coleridge's background and precise historical circumstances, it was impossible for him, almost all the time, to regard what was once the unity of Latin Christendom—*securus iudicat orbis terrarum*, "what the whole world decides is safe", the phrase of Augustine's that electrified Newman—as more than the preposterous imposition of papal power. He even defines one of the three essential characteristics of "the Church of Christ" as "the absence of any visible head or sovereign ... the non-existence, nay the utter preclusion of any head or personal centre of unity, of any single source of universal power."[87] The need for an authority to protect orthodoxy, a need that he clearly understood in his criticism of the Thirty-nine Articles, has vanished. But not entirely. Muddle in and between his many distinctions persists to the end of the book. Its last, short section, however, "On the Third Possible Church or the CHURCH OF ANTICHRIST", while castigating the papacy, and blaming it entirely for the destruction of unity at the Reformation, nevertheless concedes a great deal not only to the merits of doctrinal unity then broken but to (Roman) Catholic doctrine itself:

> It is ... my full conviction that the rites and doctrines, the *agenda et credenda* [things to be done and things to be believed], of the Catholics, could we separate them from the adulterating ingredients combined with, and the use made of them, by the sacerdotal Mamelukes of the Romish monarchy, for the support of the Papacy and papal hierarchy, would neither have brought about, nor have sufficed to justify, the convulsive separation under Leo X. Nay, that if they were fairly, and in the light of sound philosophy, compared with either of the two main divisions of Protestantism, as it now exists in this country [attenuated deism and Calvinist fundamentalism] ... an enlightened disciple of John and Paul would be perplexed, which of the three to prefer as the least unlike the profound and sublime system, he had learnt from his great masters.[88]

Suddenly, with a respectful nod in the direction of Aquinas, Coleridge, abandoning the Anglican *via media* to a void between two extremes, is astonishingly close to the Newman who found the Roman Catholic Church, while far from perfect, the "least unlike" contemporary heir of the Church of the apostles. There is here a hint of Coleridge being able, as faithful Catholics at the time of the Reformation and since have been able, to distinguish between the "idea" of the Church and deplorable episodes in her actual government. (Perhaps from time to time he remembered that, as he reports in *Biographia Literaria*, in Rome in 1806, under a different kind of actual government of the Church, he was rescued from possible French imprisonment "by the kindness of a noble Benedictine, and the gracious connivance of that good old man, the present Pope [Pius VII]".)[89] In his "AntiChrist" section, he adds, even more remarkably, recalling his impression of the poverty and ignorance of the lesser clergy in parts of Catholic Europe he had visited, that he is aware of pressure within the Catholic Church for measures to deal with backwardness and superstition:

> I feel it as no small comfort and confirmation, to know that the same view of the subject is taken, the same conviction entertained, by a large and increasing number in the Catholic communion itself, in Germany, France, Italy, and even in Spain; and that no inconsiderable portion of this number consists of men who are not only pious as Christians, but zealous as Catholics.[90]

This is a brief moment only, for Coleridge could approve of the Catholic Church wholeheartedly only if she were to modify unrecognisably the authority of the Pope himself. Nevertheless, it is there, at the end of Coleridge's long, chaotic writing career, as an omen for Newman, and therefore more for the Second than for the First Vatican Council. Toward the end of his life, Coleridge wrote in his notebook, in almost the words Newman was later to use, that "there is no consistent Medium, no abiding-place for the Mind, between Atheism, and the Catholic faith."[91] Three weeks before he died, according to Henry Coleridge, he said: "I think I could have conformed to the then dominant Church before the Reformation", but added, from long habit, "The errors existed, but they had not been riveted into peremptory articles of faith before the Council of Trent."[92]

Four and a half years after finishing his last book, Coleridge died at peace in Dr. Gillman's house. His remaining characteristic regret was that he had never written more than bits of his great work in defence of orthodox Christianity. A fortnight before his death, he said sadly: "I own I wish life and strength had been spared to me to complete my Philosophy. For, as God hears me, the originating, continuing, and sustaining wish and design in my heart were to exalt the glory of his name."[93] In many ways he had already done this—in his poems, in his published books; and in the millions of words of his letters, notebooks, lectures and talk, edited and published by patient scholars over the century and a half since his death. It is a reflection not on him but on the twentieth century that in recent decades he has been remembered more vividly and with more gratitude as a Romantic poet and literary critic than as a Christian writer, as if the cruel 1825 attack of Hazlitt, who had once revered him, were justified: "All that he has done of moment, he had done twenty years ago: since then, he may be said to have lived on the sound of his own voice."[94] Newman was reluctant to acknowledge Coleridge's influence and distanced himself, with fastidious distaste, from a man notorious in prim Victorian circles for his broken marriage and his addiction. His character was deeply flawed; there was much waste in his life; his work in many respects was unsatisfyingly indeterminate. Nevertheless, this lonely, damaged man, never not aware of his need for God, living without malice, without conceit and with much kindness in the wreckage of his loves and hopes wrote with more warmth, more brilliance of intellect and imagination, and more powerful personal conviction, in defence of Christian truth than anyone else in the nineteenth century.

1. *Collected Letters of Samuel Taylor Coleridge*, ed. Earl Leslie Griggs (Oxford, 1956–1971), 1:371.
2. Quoted in Richard Holmes, *Coleridge: Early Visions* (London, 1989), p. 285n.
3. William Wordsworth, preface to *Lyrical Ballads* (1800), in *Wordsworth: Poetry and Prose*, sel. W. M. Merchant (London, 1955), pp. 222–23.
4. S. T. Coleridge, "This Lime-Tree Bower My Prison", lines 60–65.
5. S. T. Coleridge, "Frost at Midnight", lines 54–64.
6. William Wordsworth, "Lines Written a Few Miles above Tintern Abbey", lines 101–3.
7. Ibid., lines 122–24.
8. Ibid., lines 124–35.
9. S. T. Coleridge, "A Letter to —", lines 296–97, in *Poetical Works*, ed. J. C. C. Mays (Princeton, 2001), vol. 1, pt. 2, p. 689.
10. S. T. Coleridge, *Table Talk* (Oxford, 1917), pp. 210–11.
11. Wordsworth, *The Prelude* (1805), 13.106–14.
12. Ibid., 13.446–48.
13. Coleridge, *Poetical Works*, nos. 374 and 430.
14. Coleridge, "To William Wordsworth", lines 69–70, in *Poetical Works*, pp. 816–19.
15. Ibid., lines 80–82.
16. Ibid., lines 98–100.
17. Ibid., lines 39–40.
18. Coleridge, "Know Thyself", in *Poetical Works*, p. 1154.
19. William Wordsworth, "Conclusion", lines 11–14, *Ecclesiastical Sketches*.
20. Quoted in Kathleen Coburn, *The Self Conscious Imagination* (Oxford, 1974), pp. 71–72.
21. Coleridge, *Collected Letters* 3:670.
22. *The Notebooks of Samuel Taylor Coleridge*, ed. Kathleen Coburn et al. (New York and London, 1957–2002), 3:3539.
23. Coleridge, *Poetical Works* 1:393.
24. Coleridge, *Collected Letters* 1:221.

25. Coleridge, *Notebooks* 1:467.
26. S. T. Coleridge, *Biographia Literaria*, ed. James Engell and W. Jackson Bate (Princeton and London, 1983), 1:205.
27. Coleridge, *Collected Letters* 1:246.
28. Ibid., p. 247.
29. Coleridge, *Biographia Literaria* 1:203.
30. Coleridge, *Collected Letters* 2:443.
31. Ibid., 5:1228.
32. S. T. Coleridge, *The Friend*, ed. Barbara E. Rooke (Princeton and London, 1969), 2:17.
33. Ibid., p. 7.
34. Ibid., pp. 7–8.
35. Ibid., p. 500.
36. Ibid., p. 502.
37. Quoted in Coleridge, *Biographia Literaria* 1:xliii.
38. Ibid., p. 304.
39. Ibid., 2:247–48.
40. S. T. Coleridge, *Lay Sermons*, ed. R. J. White (Princeton and London, 1972), p. 3.
41. Ibid., p. 40.
42. Ibid., p. 176.
43. Ibid., p. 25.
44. Ibid., p. 30.
45. Coleridge, *Friend* 1:407n.
46. Ibid., p. 409.
47. Ibid., p. 431.
48. Ibid., p. 514.
49. Ibid., p. 515n.
50. Ibid., p. 524.
51. S. T. Coleridge, *Aids to Reflection*, ed. John Beer (Princeton and London, 1993), pp. 9–10.
52. Ibid., pp. 160–61.
53. Ibid., p. 307.
54. Ibid., p. 171.
55. Ibid., p. 173.
56. Ibid., p. 184.
57. Jn 3:16.
58. Lk 9:20.
59. Coleridge, *Aids to Reflection*, p. 285.
60. Ibid., pp. 198–99.
61. Ibid., p. 359.
62. Ibid., p. 316.
63. Ibid., p. 202.
64. Blaise Pascal, *Pensée* 451, in *Oeuvres complètes*, ed. Jacques Chevalier, Bibliothèque de la Pléiade 34 (Paris, 1954), p. 1216.
65. Coleridge, *Aids to Reflection*, p. 383.
66. Ibid., pp. 400–1.
67. Ibid., p. 404.
68. Ibid., pp. 404–5.
69. Ibid., p. 408.
70. S. T. Coleridge, *Confessions of an Inquiring Spirit*, ed. H. N. Coleridge (London, 1840), p. 10.
71. Ibid., p. 73.
72. Ibid., p. 85.
73. Ibid., p. 65.
74. Ibid., pp. 51–52.
75. Ibid., p. 80.

76. Coleridge, *Notebooks* 2:2888.
77. Coleridge, *Aids to Reflection*, p. 387.
78. Ibid., p. 192.
79. The translation was by H. F. Cary (London, 1805–1814).
80. Coleridge, *Inquiring Spirit*, p. 90.
81. S. T. Coleridge, *On the Constitution of the Church and State*, ed. John Colmer (Princeton and London, 1976), p. 150.
82. Ibid., pp. 75–76.
83. Ibid., pp. 43–44.
84. Ibid., pp. 61–64.
85. Ibid., p. 55.
86. Ibid., pp. 114–16.
87. Ibid., p. 118.
88. Ibid., pp. 134–35.
89. Coleridge, *Biographia Literaria* 1:216.
90. Coleridge, *Constitution of the Church and State*, p. 136.
91. Quoted in Coburn, *Self Conscious Imagination*, p. 65.
92. Coleridge, *Table Talk*, ed. Carl Woodring (Princeton and London, 2000), 1:295.
93. Ibid., p. 296.
94. William Hazlitt, "Mr. Coleridge", in *The Spirit of the Age* (London, 1910), p. 196.

CHAPTER SIXTEEN

JOHN HENRY NEWMAN AND
MATTHEW ARNOLD

In his faith in God, Creator, incarnate Word and Holy Spirit, and in the unity of goodness, truth and beauty to be discovered only in and through God, Coleridge was alone among the English literary figures of his lifetime. "A hooded eagle among blinking owls",[1] Shelley called him: the owls were smaller but they could see the atheist light, even if it made them blink. Many heard him talk in the last rambling, magnetic years of his life at Highgate; many more read his books. But the poets, novelists, philosophers and critics of the next two generations, some of whom became the influential sages of Victorian England, paid little attention to his Christianity. Meanwhile, churchmen sometimes referred to his vision of the Church of England as an organic whole binding the nation together; if they did, the reference was likely to be in support of whichever competing notion of the church or churches in England they happened to favour. One notable churchman and academic, F.D. Maurice, acknowledged a considerable debt to Coleridge. Inscribing in 1842 a copy of his book *The Kingdom of Christ* to Coleridge's son, he wrote: "The power of perceiving that by the very law of the Reason the knowledge of God must be *given* to it; that the moment it attempts to create its Maker, it denies itself ... I received from him."[2] Maurice's book brought unity, even within the Church of England, no nearer. In general, in this fractious and factional period, faith itself, however much threatened by an increasingly secular intellectual atmosphere, often appeared to be of less importance to the clergy of the established church than their precise place on the scale of churchmanship that went from High to Low with an almost antidoctrinal Broad patch in the middle. The dean of Chester, said the young Protestant Newman, "has no *views*, and in consequence is like a ship without a rudder". He added, "To *become* a Romanist seems more and more impossible.... Somehow my own confidence in my own views seems to grow."[3]

It was, in other words, too late for the Church of England to become what it had never been but what Queen Elizabeth's settlement had intended it to be, an inclusive church, both Protestant and Catholic enough for every English Christian to feel at home in it. Seventeenth-century dissenting sects, now joined by an increasing number of Methodist refugees from a church identified more and more with the landowning classes and the Tory party, demonstrated that the national church had never been Protestant enough for many, while Roman Catholics, self-excluded from the church by their loyalty to Rome and to the sacraments, were still excluded also from public life, the universities and much else. Worse, from the point of view taken by Coleridge, divisions of opinion within the Church of England were becoming more rather than less marked as a religious revival took shape in the 1820s and 1830s. Was the Bible, open to almost as many different interpretations as there are Christians, or the national church, a dependency of the sovereign state, to be taken as the ultimate authority? This question was perceived by Coleridge to be incapable of solution. A clearheaded observer would have noticed that not much more than patriotism and an optimistic view of the coherence of a short historical tradition held the Church of England together, along, of course, with a shared, indeed a self-identifying, hatred of Rome. In the years of liberal pressure for the relief of Catholics, it was rare indeed for a clergyman to take such a line as that of Sydney Smith, who wrote in 1824 in the Whig *Edinburgh Review*, which he had helped to found in 1802, in bold defence of Catholics:

> It is hardly possible for any nation to show a greater superiority over another than the Americans, in this particular, have done over this country. They have fairly and completely, and probably for ever, extinguished that spirit of religious persecution which has been the employment and the curse of mankind for four or five centuries,—not only that persecution which imprisons and scourges for religious opinions, but the tyranny of incapacitation, which, by disqualifying from civil offices, and cutting a man off from the lawful objects of ambition, endeavours to strangle religious freedom in silence, and to enjoy all the advantages, without the blood, and noise, and fire of persecution.[4]

If Coleridge read this, he must have been torn between his longing to see Christianity restored to vitality in England through the renewal of a united, national and "Catholic" church and a reluctant recognition that Smith's implied approval of the separation of church and state was a much to be desired ideal. Six years later, in *On the Constitution of Church and State*, Coleridge himself wrote, at his most Augustinian:

The Christian Church, I say, is ... the *sustaining, correcting, befriending* Opposite of the world! the compensating counterforce to the inherent and inevitable evils and defects of the STATE, *as* a State. ... And for these services the Church of Christ asks of the state neither wages nor dignities. She asks only protection, and *to be let alone.*[5]

In reality, however, there was no hope of disentangling the nineteenth-century Church of England from the state, just as there was no hope of it becoming the inclusive church of the whole nation. Much commoner than the aspirations of either Coleridge or Sydney Smith was a hardheaded utilitarian conviction that the main purpose of the national church was to keep the nation in order. Horrified by the course of events in atheist revolutionary France, which appeared to demonstrate that king, nobility, bishops and Christianity stood or fell together, bishops warned of the chaos that weakening of the church would bring. "Of this we may all be well assured, that when religion shall have lost its hold on men's consciences, government will lose its authority over their persons, and a state of barbarous anarchy will ensue",[6] wrote the bishop of Llandaff in 1806. Twenty-five years later the bishop of Gloucester justified the state's hold over its subjects' religious life on the grounds that "religious motives are the only effectual security for their orderly and virtuous behaviour, and for the peace and prosperity of the commonwealth." [7]

In an atmosphere of alarm that the glue of Christianity might fail to hold together a rapidly industrialising society in which radical opinion was everywhere gaining ground, the Church of England, far from closing ranks, produced ideas for renewal that were deeply divisive. In 1833, the year before Coleridge's death, conflicting winds blew straws across the church. Thomas Arnold, forcefully Protestant headmaster of Rugby, proposed in his widely read *Principles of Church Reform* that all the Protestant churches and sects should be gathered into a single organisation, in effect a new church, with uniform religious practise: this was the only way to restore the cohesion of England as "a Christian country". Questions of belief were not important enough to be allowed to hinder the scheme. In contrast, in this same year, Newman, whose confidence in his earlier views was fading, published the first Tract of the Oxford Movement. This was a passionate campaign conducted by academic clerics in the university to restore the self-confidence of the Anglican Church—now so called, particularly by its more Catholic members—as the right, the correct, the only true *via media* between the excesses of Roman Catholicism on the one hand and of Protestant dissent on the other. As reformers of the church in which they were both ordained, Arnold and Newman shared little but anti-Roman defensiveness. By 1841, when Thomas Arnold delivered his inaugural lecture as Regius Professor of Modern History at Oxford, he had identified the Tractarians as destructive Catholicising enemies of his simple, healthy programme for English Christianity, which had nothing more controversial in view than straightforward moral improvement:

> Belief in the desirableness of an act differs widely from belief in the truth of a proposition.... All societies of men, whether we call them states or churches, should make their bond to consist in a common object and a common practice, rather than in a common belief; in other words, their end should be good rather than truth.[8]

Elsewhere in Oxford, truth was becoming more, not less, of an issue. Also in 1841, Newman the man who had been the staunchest and most learned defender of the Anglican *via media*, and, in the university church of Saint Mary's, one of the most effective preachers in England since Donne, published Tract no. 90, an attempt to interpret the Thirty-nine Articles as consonant with (Roman) Catholic truth. He incurred instant ecclesiastical obloquy and a silencing order from his bishop. It took Newman four more years finally to bring himself to the point of no return. From 1842 he lived in retirement with a few like-minded friends in a village outside Oxford, accused (like Nicholas Ferrar at Little Gidding two centuries earlier) of "founding a monastery", and worked at a justification of the extent, the accretion over the centuries, of Catholic teaching, his *Essay on the Development of Christian Doctrine*. At last, on 9 October 1845, he was received into the Catholic Church by a visiting Italian priest and soon afterward published the *Essay*.

Newman's conversion, which was an event of immense consequence, unforeseeable at the time, for the whole Catholic Church, unsurprisingly horrified both Protestant England and most of the rest of the Oxford Movement. He was accompanied or followed into "apostasy" by some of the Movement's lesser lights, but not by John Keble or Edward Pusey, who between them were responsible for most of the Catholic practices that survive to this day in the ritualist, or Anglo-Catholic (the term was first used in the late 1830s), wing of the Church of England. Years later, Newman wrote, tellingly, of Keble: "I do not find *why* he holds so much of the Roman doctrine, yet not more,—unless he asserts the right of believing what he pleases."[9] It was, in the end, the kind of obedience to the whole truth suggested by contrast in this remark that brought Newman to the final step. It required a great deal of courage. His love of the English church, his loyalty to many friends, and his security within the ancient beauty of clerical Oxford life had all to be abandoned. He had four and a half decades as a Catholic ahead, decades of frequent difficulty and pain. He was henceforward isolated from the company of intellectual equals. The Catholic Church in England could offer him none, either among the Irish or among the descendants of recusants—both cut off from the best of English education for generations—and still less among Newman's fellow converts from Anglicanism, inclined to rabid ultramontane bigotry. In 1850 the Catholic hierarchy was restored in England, to the accompaniment of hysterical opposition in Parliament and beyond. Cardinal Wiseman, the first Archbishop of Westminster, was a gentle Anglo-Irishman baffled by Newman and embarrassed by the celebrity that Newman did nothing to encourage. Wiseman's successor, Cardinal Manning, was a narrow-minded convert to Catholicism and on occasion a bully, who came to regard Newman as an actual enemy. Meanwhile, the wider Catholic Church of Newman's maturity was struggling with "modernism" from an entrenched textbook neo-Thomism that provided Newman with little theological life to share, even in Rome, where he spent a lonely period studying for the Catholic priesthood. Newman blamed, with some reason, the lack of theological vitality in nineteenth-century Catholicism on the disappearance of German intellectuals into Protestantism and beyond and on Napoleon's destruction of monasteries, schools and faculties of theology.

In a long life, Newman wrote half a dozen books and a large number of sermons, lectures and polemical pieces. Of all his books, the one most read has been the *Apologia pro Vita Sua*, his account, in response to a furious attack in 1864, of the conversion that had taken place twenty years earlier. The *Apologia* was written in two months as a series of weekly pamphlets. In a book review, Charles Kingsley, author of the sickly children's fable *The Water Babies* and professor of modern history at Cambridge, a post for which he was even less qualified than Thomas Arnold had been at Oxford, called the Catholic Church, past and present, "a heap of lies" and accused Newman of deceit, in particular of having masqueraded as a Protestant clergyman while he was already a Roman Catholic. "Truth for its own sake", Kingsley famously wrote,

> had never been a virtue with the Roman clergy. Father Newman informs us that it need not, and on the whole ought not to be; that cunning is the weapon which Heaven has given to the saints wherewith to withstand the brute male force of the wicked world which marries and is given in marriage.[10]

Ignoring Kingsley's terror of celibacy, Newman was stung to the defence both of Catholic truth and of his own integrity. ("The controversy was not a very fruitful one", Lytton Strachey said, "chiefly because Kingsley could no more understand the nature of Newman's intelligence than a subaltern in a line regiment can understand a Brahmin.")[11]

The *Apologia* has often been compared to Augustine's *Confessions*, which had reappeared in 1838, newly edited by Pusey, as the first volume in the Oxford Movement's *Library of the Fathers*. But it is very different. Newman was as certain as Coleridge or Pascal or Augustine himself that Christian truth is no mere matter of rational proof. Told by a future bishop that some people were certain of Christianity because they had strictly proved its truth, Newman said, "No one is certain for this reason."[12] *Cor ad cor loquitur*, "heart speaks to heart", was the phrase Newman chose as his motto when, to his own and most other people's astonishment, he was in 1879 made a cardinal by Pope Leo XIII. "That there is one truth ... , that the mind is below truth, not above it, and is bound, not to descant upon it, but to venerate it; that truth and falsehood are set before us for the trial of our hearts"[13], he had written in the *Essay on the Development of Christian Doctrine*. But the *Apologia* is the story of his intellectual conversion from the Anglican church to the Catholic Church, not the story, as Augustine's was, of the pull of his heart to God. Understandably in the circumstances, there is more self-justification than self-knowledge in his account; the book does not have the personal depth, and for this reason will never have the timeless attractiveness, of the *Confessions*. Much of it is concerned to demonstrate, through an account of Newman's own troubled departure from the Church of England, that the Anglican *via media* as the true descendant of the church of the apostles cannot be grounded in properly understood historical evidence.

The founders of the Oxford Movement, and their Anglo-Catholic followers (as we shall see in the case of T. S. Eliot), looked back, for their model, to the church of Hooker, Lancelot Andrewes and Laud. It was research into the much more distant past, however, in particular into the sustaining of orthodoxy against the great heresies of the fourth and fifth centuries, that led Newman to suspect, to be afraid and eventually to be certain that the truest descendant of the early Church was, as she had all along claimed, the Church of Rome. Authority and consensus epitomised in Augustine's phrase *securus iudicat orbis terrarum* struck him as incontrovertible and, since he was a Protestant at the time, also as shattering: "By those great words of the ancient Father, interpreting and summing up the long and varied course of ecclesiastical history, the theory of the *Via Media* was absolutely pulverized."[14] Before long he was writing: "Whatever line of early history I look into, I see as in a glass reflected our own Church in the heretical party, and the Roman church in the Catholic. This is an appalling fact." [15] Both history and observation of the contemporary battlefield in the Church of England prompted his question: "Is it not very clear that the English Church subsists *in the State*, and has no internal consistency (in matter of fact, I do not say in theory) to keep it together?" [16]

It is necessary to remember how profoundly "the Roman church", now associated not only with a sinister foreign power but with "low democracy" [17] (Newman's phrase) and the possibility of Irish rebellion, was feared and hated in nineteenth-century England to appreciate the horror Newman felt at the inescapable logic of his discoveries. He hung on to his own antipapalism as long as he could to keep him from the step he dreaded. His beloved Church of England, after all, had been founded as an anti-Roman church. "He who could not protest against the Church of Rome was no true divine in the English Church." [18] Newman also knew that his own eminence by the 1840s meant that his defection to Rome was likely to do serious harm to the institution that had formed his life and his mind. But the demand made on him by the truth was in the end inexorable, and by the time he told the story in the *Apologia*, the issue had become stark:

> There are but two alternatives, the way to Rome and the way to Atheism: Anglicanism is the halfway house on the one side, and Liberalism is the halfway house on the other. How many men were there, as I knew full well, who would not follow me now in my advance from Anglicanism to Rome, but would at once leave Anglicanism and me for the Liberal camp. It is not at all easy (humanly speaking) to wind up an Englishman to a dogmatic level. [19]

That last sentence suggests the degree to which Newman thought mere lukewarmness, ignorance of ecclesiastical history, complacency and inattention infected the church he eventually brought himself to abandon as, "if truth be a real objective thing, ... a system *short of* truth". [20] "They want only so much religion as will satisfy their natural perception of the propriety of being religious", [21] he wrote of his contemporaries. And, on the progress-achieving entrepreneurs and administrators of Victorian England, perhaps consciously almost quoting Augustine on republican Rome, he wrote: "They fell back, with closed affections, and haughty reserve, and dreariness within, upon their worldly integrity, honour, energy, prudence, and perseverance; they made the most of the natural man, and they 'received their reward'."[22]

Here we approach the Newman who deserves his place in the story of writing in the Christian tradition not so much for the painfully arrived at clarity with which he left the Anglican church for the Roman Catholic Church but for his criticism, his judgement, of his own time, for his awareness of the rarity of actual belief in the truth of Christianity among his contemporaries, and for his unfailing sense of the difference it makes whether or not Christianity is true. The Gospel, he wrote, must always be preached "as a witness against the world".[23] It is not, in other words, as a Catholic against an alien background of Protestantism, but as a Christian against an alien background of relativist, materialist individualism that Newman will always be a writer with whom to be reckoned.

In the fifth and final section of the *Apologia* as pruned and ordered for book publication, there is a single sentence on the condition of the human world, from which can be deduced only that "the human race is implicated in some terrible aboriginal calamity":

> To consider the world in its length and breadth, its various history, the many races of man, their fortunes, their mutual alienation, their conflicts, and then their ways, habits, governments, forms of worship, their enterprises, their aimless courses, their random achievements and acquirements, the impotent conclusions of long-standing facts, the tokens so faint and broken of a superintending design, the blind evolution of what may turn out to be great powers or truths, the progress of things, as if from unreasoning elements, not towards final causes, the greatness and littleness of man, his far-reaching aims, his short duration, the curtain hung over his futurity, the disappointments of life, the defeat of good, the success of evil, physical pain, mental anguish, the prevalence and intensity of sin, the pervading idolatries, the corruptions, the dreary hopeless irreligion, that condition of the whole race, so fearfully yet exactly described in the Apostle's words, "having no hope and without God in the world."—all this is a vision to dizzy and appal; and inflicts upon the mind the sense of a profound mystery, which is absolutely beyond human solution.[24]

We are all faced with this challenge of universally experienced human reality. Either we turn toward God's redeeming love for the world, revealed in Christ, or we turn to our own intelligence, our own opinions, our own will. That these are the only alternatives for someone born into what was once the Christian world, Newman was always convinced. In 1841, in *The Tamworth Reading Room*, he attacked Sir Robert Peel's educational ideals, satirising the Prime Minister's views with characteristic sarcasm:

> Another age has come in, and Faith is effete; let us submit to what we cannot change; let us not hang over our dead, but bury it out of sight. Seek we out some young and vigorous principle, rich in sap, and fierce in life, to give form to elements which are fast resolving into their inorganic chaos; and where shall we find such a principle but in Knowledge?[25]

If this attack has a prescient ring of the Internet age, it also echoes Pascal, or Johnson, or Coleridge, on the proper place of the scientific triumphs that none of them either scorned or feared. Newman, indeed, in the generation that saw published Charles Darwin's *The Origin of Species*, roundly opposed those "who would set knowledge against itself, and would make truth contradict truth, and would persuade the world that, to be religious, you must be ignorant, and to be intellectual, you must be unbelieving".[26] However:

> that the mind is changed by a discovery, or saved by a diversion, and can thus be amused into immortality,—that grief, anger, cowardice, self-conceit, pride, or passion, can be subdued by an examination of shells or grasses, or inhaling of gases, or chipping of rocks, or calculating the longitude, is the veriest of pretences which sophist or mountebank ever professed to a gaping auditory.[27]

In all the work for education that Newman undertook as a Catholic, constantly frustrated as he was by lack of understanding in the Catholic Church, in England, in Ireland and in Rome, his efforts were informed by the urgent sense that if the context for intellectual life were not Christian, intellectual life itself would become— had already become—a substitute for Christianity. A Catholic Oxford was his model for the Catholic university he helped, against dispiriting odds, to found in Dublin, where Trinity College, the university of the Protestant ascendancy, had a distinguished history. But for his inspiration he looked much further back than to the Schoolmen's Oxford of the late Middle Ages. In an essay of 1858 he divides the educational history of the Church into three periods—"Now, St Benedict has had the training of the ancient intellect, St Dominic of the mediaeval; and St Ignatius of the modern"—and summarises the three, somewhat unfairly, as "Poetry, Science,

Practical Sense". But "this important *proviso* has to be borne in mind, ... that what the Catholic church once has had, she never has lost."[28] And in an essay of the following year, he vigorously defends the Latin education of the pre-Scholastic medieval world from Victorian contempt for the "monkish" dark ages, seeing "the Colleges in the English Universities" as "lineal descendants or heirs of the Benedictine schools of Charlemagne"[29] and registering precisely the inflected *romanitas* that Benedict himself shared with Virgil. Cardinal Manning and the suspicious Irish bishops and the Rome of Pius IX did their best to foil all Newman's efforts. Manning said: "I see much danger of an English Catholicism of which Newman is the highest type. It is the old Anglican, patristic, literary, Oxford tone transplanted into the Church."[30]

Newman described more clearly than anyone else in the nineteenth century what those sustaining the Christian tradition now had to contend with: an increasingly widespread consensus

> that truth and falsehood in religion are but matter of opinion; that one doctrine is as good as another; that the Governor of the world does not intend that we should gain the truth; that there is not truth; ... that no one is answerable for his opinions; that they are a matter of necessity or accident; that it is enough if we sincerely hold what we profess.[31]

This diagnosis of a casual negligence, which has since become even more common, is in the *Essay on the Development of Christian Doctrine*. Nearly forty years later, in the great speech Newman made as an old man in Rome, accepting the cardinalate, he returned to the reason for his years of struggle in the intervening decades:

> Liberalism in religion is the doctrine that there is no positive truth in religion, but that one creed is as good as another, and this is the teaching which is gaining substance and force daily. It is inconsistent with any recognition of any religion as *true*.... Revealed religion is not a truth, but a sentiment and a taste; not an objective fact, not miraculous, and it is the right of each individual to make it say just what strikes his fancy.... There is much in the liberalistic theory which is good and true; for example, not to say more, the precepts of justice, truthfulness, sobriety, self-command, benevolence, which are among its avowed principles, and the natural laws of society. There never was a device of the Enemy, so cleverly framed, and with such promise of success.[32]

What Newman meant by "liberalism" in this speech and elsewhere is evident. But the word in his time was being used in a number of different senses. Discrimination between them required a degree of intelligence and balance that few shared, and this was the underlying reason for the overwhelming distrust of Newman in the Catholic Church during his lifetime. Many Catholics regarded him as a "liberal", in the first place because his writing as a Catholic, while incontrovertibly orthodox, was never expressed in the categories or the terminology of neo-Scholasticism, in the second half of the nineteenth century regarded by Rome as intrinsic to orthodox theology. Second, his emphasis (Coleridgean, however little he cared for the parallel) on the intuitive response to divine truth, on the need of the broken heart to be mended in Christ, appeared dangerously subjective, though it was not. Third, his measured justification of the development of Christian doctrine appeared to undermine the current, narrow Roman view of revelation as complete and unchangeable, though it did not. Fourth, he was, at the time of the First Vatican Council in 1869–1870, uncertain of the wisdom of the declaration of papal infallibility—"I think its definition inexpedient and unlikely; but I should have no difficulty in accepting it, were it made"[33]—and certain that the Pope would "be stronger and firmer than he has been for a long while"[34] without his temporal power, which, as it turned out, was lost for good (in both senses) as the Council ended. On these last two issues, Cardinal Manning regarded Newman as practically heretical. In all the circumstances, it was bold indeed for Leo XIII, soon after becoming Pope, to confer the red hat on Newman nine years after the Council. "My cardinal!" the Pope said. "It was not easy. It was not easy. They said he was too liberal, but I had determined to honour the Church in honouring Newman."[35] The Second Vatican Council, almost a century later, saw the Church's wholehearted acceptance of that honour with the eventual emergence into papal approval of such theologians as de Lubac and Balthasar.

Newman was an Augustinian by temperament, learning and experience. As an Anglican who became a Catholic, and as a student of the whole history of the Church, he was able to take a longer view of the relation of the Church to the world than that of most of his Catholic contemporaries. Although he continued to regard the Church of England as a "breakwater against infidelity",[36] his keen sense of all states as powers of the *civitas terrena* and his bitter knowledge of England led him to describe "Establishment" as "making emphatically Christ's Kingdom a Kingdom of this world".[37] And he once said, "I am not at all sure that it would not be better for the Catholic religion every where, if it had no very different status from that which it has in England."[38] A generation younger than Coleridge, clearer-headed and a much better historian, Newman took Coleridge's organic vision of the Church of England to its logical conclusion: only the Roman Catholic Church was an organic whole that should and could be everywhere free of the control of the state; it was, unlike the Anglican and unlike the Orthodox churches, "the one faithful representative . . . of that free-spoken dauntless Church of old".[39] He knew, of course, that in the world of his time, this was not everywhere the case. The Catholic fidelity of the people of Ireland and Poland, subject to Protestant and Orthodox imperial rule, was then exemplary. It would take the terrible upheavals of the twentieth century to detach the Church, even in theory, from her identification with old structures of monarchist, aristocratic or plutocratic power in many countries, and the process is even yet not complete. One of the best defences ever written of the possibility of faithful Catholic loyalty to the Church in calm combination with loyal obedience to the just requirements of the *civitas terrena* is Newman's *Letter to the Duke of Norfolk*, written in 1875 in reply to a pamphlet by William Gladstone, then temporarily out of office as Prime Minister. Gladstone had attacked the Catholic Church for enslaving English converts to a foreign power: "No one can become her convert without renouncing his moral and mental freedom, and placing his civil loyalty and duty at the mercy of another."[40] Newman's *Letter* demolishes this charge from a thoroughly Augustinian understanding of the relations between Church and state in a condition of unconfusion beneficial to both.

It was always more remarkable that Newman, one of the most intelligent Englishmen of his century, was a Christian than that he became a Catholic. In his last, most difficult book, *An Essay in Aid of a Grammar of Assent*, he set himself to explain, for intellectuals certain, by now, of the impossibility of Christian belief, the difference between real and notional assent to Christian truth. It is a Coleridgean project, for Newman's "real" assent turns out to engage the imagination in Coleridge's full, creative sense. Meanwhile, religion, the life of a Christian within the sacramental reality of the Church ("TRY IT", as Coleridge had written), is in this book sharply distinguished from theology, which deals with abstract ideas that command "notional" assent. This is a distinction at least as old as the conflict between Abelard and Saint Bernard.

It is not at all surprising that Newman should have much in common with both Coleridge and Pascal. The consonance between them is not a matter of influence but of inevitable similarity between three men of rare intelligence who reflected, and reflected on, their own sudden or gradually developing certainty in the trinitarian God. They all believed that the shocked or suffering fallen soul, with any degree of self-knowledge, would discover, by trying Christianity, not that Christianity seems true because it meets human need, but that it meets human need because it is true. That Christ is the way, the truth and the life is what, in the end, they knew. As Coleridge wrote:

> *Evidences* of Christianity! I am weary of the word. Make a man feel the *want* of it; rouse him, if you can, to the self-knowledge of his *need* of it; and you may safely trust to its own Evidence—remembering only the express declaration of Christ himself: "No man cometh to me, unless the Father leadeth him!" [41]

* * *

In the literary England of his time, so resplendent with talent and achievement in remarkable variety, Newman, in the clarity of his allegiance to Christian truth, was a countercultural figure. For almost all the writers of the period, the demand-ingness of Christianity, the compelling pull of its unity of truth, goodness and beauty, was a challenge ignored when it was not scorned as a relic of outgrown credulousness. In a lecture on Emerson delivered in America in 1883, Matthew Arnold praised Emerson for the optimistic, inchoate, Godless transcendentalism of his *Essays*, "the most important work done in prose", "as Wordsworth's poetry is, in my judgement, the most important work done in verse, in our language, during the present century." [42] Arnold opened this lecture with romantic, soft-focus memories of the Oxford of "forty years ago, when I was an undergradu-ate", that included an equivocal tribute to the now-octogenarian Newman. "His genius and his style are still things of power", but—this is an emphatic "but"— "he has adopted, for the doubts and difficulties which beset men's minds to-day, a solution which, to speak frankly, is impossible." [43] The note struck in this lecture is characteristic not only of Arnold but of a great deal of the critical writing of the second half of the English nineteenth century and much of the twentieth: "Poetry" and "style", later the intensity or subtlety of life evoked on the page, must carry a weight they cannot bear because Christianity is "to speak frankly, impossible". Newman, with the extremeness he sometimes allowed him-self, said: "Poetry is the refuge of those who have not the Catholic Church." [44]

The great novelists of the period, concerned with the collisions of goodness with evil, truthfulness with lies, altruism with selfishness and love with power—without which there is no human story—assumed either that Christianity is true or that it is not. The moral judgement acute in all of these writers has its only anchor in the Christianity they took for granted or rejected, but none of them is interested in the confrontation of God and the soul, or in redemption from sin in Christ, or in the dark into which we vanish if neither of these phrases has any meaning. Facing the real consequences, for meaning and for hope, of the abandonment of the God who "so loved the world" had to wait, in England, until the twentieth century. Instead, in the nineteenth century, a consensus developed that adequate sense could be made of everything if one regarded Jesus as no more than an exemplary teacher of morality in the absence of God, who was in turn no more than a consoling figment (fiction) of the human imagination. Confined as we are by time and death, there is no light for us from the *civitas Dei*, but only from the human purposes of the *civitas terrena*, where, as always, in Newman's words: "the sole object . . . of the social and political world everywhere, is to make the most of this life." [45] George Eliot in 1854 translated Feuerbach's 1841 *The Essence of Christianity*; such was the difficulty of "winding up an Englishman to a dogmatic level" that almost no one for two generations took on board the full implications of the book's central thesis: "The turning point of history will be the moment when man becomes aware that the only God of man is man himself." [46] That this sentence, like Nietzsche's "God is dead, and we have killed him", can bear a full Christian interpretation has a depth of irony that it would have laid waste his entire case for either Nietzsche or Feuerbach to contemplate.

If the result of divorcing goodness from truth was unclear to the English nineteenth century, the result of divorcing beauty from either, but particularly from truth, and of taking it in isolation to be meaning itself, was foggier still. For a great deal of confusion in some key writing of the time, Wordsworth was ultimately responsible. Hazlitt was not far wrong when he wrote in 1825: "Mr. Wordsworth's genius is a pure emanation of the Spirit of the Age. Had he lived in any other period of the world, he would never have been heard of." [47] It was Wordsworth, not Coleridge, who encouraged the drift toward the identification of beauty with "poetry", and the confused and confusing promise, sketched by Shelley and preached wholeheartedly by Matthew Arnold, that "poetry" could be regarded as the single, saving human "value".

Shelley and Keats, the most gifted poets of the generation that followed that of Wordsworth and Coleridge, died so young that it is a shock to remember that they were born only eight and six years respectively before Newman, who lived until 1890. Keats wrote almost all the poems for which he is remembered before his twenty-fourth birthday. In his "I have lov'd the principle of beauty in all things", [48] there is no confusion between "beauty" and "poetry", the latter of which he knew to be words on the page produced by talent and hard work. With a modest education and little knowledge of Christianity, he was, nevertheless, as several of his letters and his last, unfinished poem, "The Fall of Hyperion", show, already thinking and feeling his way toward questions of truth, goodness and meaning that might have taken him in a Coleridgean direction from his instinctive "Beauty is truth, truth beauty".[49] His youthful improvisation, in a letter, about the world as "a vale of soul-making" proposes in all innocence "a grander system of salvation than the chrystiain religion";[50] yet there is in it a strong intuition of the presence and power of God in a human world of suffering that he knew much about. Shakespeare was almost literally his Bible: "I never quite despair, and I read Shakespeare—indeed, I shall, I think, never read any other Book much."[51] His distrust of what he called "the wordsworthian or egotistical sublime" was defined in terms of the contrast he felt between Wordsworth and Shakespeare "the camelion [sic] Poet",[52] invisible behind the imagined reality of his characters and the rich vitality of their language.

Shelley, more privileged, better educated and more sophisticated than Keats, and sufficiently self-aware to know that Keats was the better poet—Shelley was generous enough to admit it—was much more representative of "the spirit of the age". A defiant radical as a boy, he got himself sent down from Oxford for publishing a seven-page pamphlet demonstrating *The Necessity of Atheism* ("QED", he put at the end). He remained a rebel against all kinds of convention for the rest of his short, chaotic life, allowing in most things, including his nearly nine hundred pages of poetry, the emotion of the moment to outrun his considerable intelligence. After Shelley's death, Coleridge regretted that he had never met him, acknowledging the "flashes of the true spirit" in his work and saying that he could have laughed Shelley out of the atheism they had once shared: "Could he only have had some notion of order, could you only have given him some plane whereon to stand, and look down upon his own mind, he would have succeeded."[53] It is a perceptive comment, and Shelley's major contribution to criticism, to the judgement of the present in the light of the past, his essay *A Defence of Poetry*, could have done with just such a steadying hand.

The essay, the kind of ambitious muddle that a brilliant undergraduate produces, was written in 1821, the year before Shelley's death, but not published until 1840. His social criticism is acute as well as keenly felt:

> We have more moral, political, and historical wisdom than we know
> how to reduce into practice; we have more scientific and economic
> knowledge than can be accommodated to the just distribution of the
> produce which it multiplies.... The cultivation of those sciences which
> have enlarged the limits of the empire of man over the external world

has for want of the poetical faculty proportionally circumscribed those of the internal world; and man, having enslaved the elements, remains himself a slave.[54]

Few would dispute his diagnosis of the injustices of industrial capitalism, which "tend as they have in modern England to exasperate at once the extremes of luxury and want".[55] But his proposed cure is wild to the point of unintelligibility, confusing as it does poetry as ordinarily understood, the work of poets, with "the poetical faculty", which turns out to mean the quality in human beings that reconciles them to the world, gives them pleasure and increases their capacity to feel with, and have compassion for, other people (that these three are not always compatible does not occur to Shelley). "The great secret of morals is love", and "[t]he great instrument of moral good is the imagination; and poetry administers to the effect by acting upon the cause." [56] It is as a consequence of these statements that Shelley is able to conclude the essay with the famous sentence: "Poets are the unacknowledged legislators of the world." [57]

There may seem to be agreement between all this and Samuel Johnson's wise Imlac in *Rasselas*: "[The poet] must write as the interpreter of nature, and the legislator of mankind, and consider himself as presiding over the thoughts and manners of future generations; as a being superiour to time and place." But Imlac's poet "must consider right and wrong in their abstract and invariable state";[58] Shelley's poet "would do ill to embody his own conceptions of right and wrong, which are usually those of his place and time, in his poetical creations which participate in neither".[59] For Shelley, brought up on Hume and on Godwin's certainty of the perfectibility of man, has altogether dispensed with the Christian framework within which Johnson always wrote, and poetry is for him, while essential to the new morality of "love", far above what he regards as the always relative morality of "right and wrong". In his *Treatise on Morals*, he writes: "That is called good which produces pleasure; that is called evil which produces pain." [60] In *A Defence of Poetry*, he detaches Shakespeare from his Christian world, contrasting him favourably with Calderón, whom he accuses of "the substitution of the rigidly-defined and ever-repeated idealisms of a distorted superstition for the living impersonations of the truth of human passions".[61] In a context that is predictably anti-Catholic in the ordinary English fashion, he lists the "poetic" benefactors of mankind:

It exceeds all imagination to conceive what would have been the moral condition of the world if neither Dante, Petrarch, Boccaccio, Chaucer,

Shakespeare, Calderón, Lord Bacon, nor Milton had ever existed; if Raphael and Michael Angelo had never been born; if the Hebrew poetry had never been translated; if a revival of the study of Greek literature had never taken place.[62]

He fails to notice that, with the exception of Milton and the sceptical Bacon (an odd choice for this list in any case), what he is describing here is the bearing on "the moral condition of the world" of the writing—and painting and sculpture—of Catholic tradition with its antecedents in the Old Testament and in pagan but God-fearing Greece. Milton, Shelley has already said, he admires because "he has so far violated the popular creed ... as to have alleged no superiority of moral virtue to his God over his Devil. And this bold neglect of a direct moral purpose is the most decisive proof of the supremacy of Milton's genius."[63] In "the utter anarchy and darkness" of earlier centuries, Shelley's Dante was the poet of love, not of Christian truth, and "the first religious reformer" on account of his dislike of various Popes.

A Defence of Poetry collapses into a paradoxically self-centred description of poetic inspiration as liberation from the self, shot through with Wordsworthian wishful thinking—"Poetry is the record of the best and happiest moments of the best and happiest minds"[64] (Wordsworth's "spots of time")—and even with blasphemy: The sins of poets "have been washed in the blood of the mediator and the redeemer, Time".[65] The upshot of the essay is a proto-Nietzschean aspiration toward an art that will be life-enhancing but without moral content as ordinarily understood, condemnation of the "abjectness" of Christian morality and an underlying celebration of the conclusive freeing of civilised humanity from the oppression of churches and the claim of Christianity to be true.

* * *

Matthew Arnold, a generation younger than Keats and Shelley, was born in 1822 and died in 1888. If he read *A Defence of Poetry*—in his one essay on Shelley he does not mention it—he must have approved of much of it, for the claims for poetry that Shelley scattered recklessly through his essay became in Arnold's mature and measured writing the liberal philosophy of high culture as a substitute for religion that survived Arnold by almost a century. This was above all a literary enterprise. Arnold wrote, in a number of books and essays of varying lengths, widely read at the time and since, of poetry as "a criticism of life", of the great poetry of the past as all that can rescue people from the ugliness and faithlessness of modern life: "More and more mankind will discover that we have to turn to poetry to interpret life for us, to console us, to sustain us."[66] In *The Function of Criticism at the Present Time*, published in 1865, he defined criticism as "a disinterested endeavour to learn and propagate the best that is known and thought in the world".[67] More than any other writer or thinker, Arnold was responsible for the extravagant advancement of literary criticism—the appreciation and judgement of works of literature, poetry in his case, also novels as time went by—to become criticism, judgement, itself. As the framework of truth, one in God with goodness and beauty, melted away, the relative judgements of literary criticism claimed an absoluteness they could not sustain. When, in the last third of the twentieth century, literary theory gradually and then rapidly eroded this claim, until both literary criticism and judgement of any kind of value had been thoroughly discredited in much of the intellectual world, the sheer power of thought about literature to achieve this destruction from its position of perceived centrality still had a distant connexion to Arnold. He would have been horrified by these consequences of his attempt to fill with poetry the space left by discredited, no longer believed, religion. For Arnold wanted it both ways, wanted to eat his cake and have it too: he was certain that Christianity was not true, but he wanted to retain what he found to be good and beautiful in its tradition. His distinction between "Hebraism" (strict morality) and "Hellenism" (aesthetics and freedom of the spirit) in that tradition signalled the uncoupling of goodness and beauty from each other, while both were uncoupled from the truth that tethers the very words to reliable meaning. He could not have predicted that a hundred years after his death, goodness and beauty would have gone the way he staked out for truth.

Matthew Arnold was Thomas Arnold's son, temperamentally very different from his father. A talented poet of plangent nostalgia, his poetic models are clear from an early letter: "Those who cannot read Greek should read nothing but Milton and Wordsworth."[68] In his famous poem "Dover Beach", he mourns Christianity's passing, an evident fact about which no one could do anything; he hears the "melancholy, long, withdrawing roar" of "the sea of faith" and takes an intensely gloomy view of the apparently promising world that

> Hath really neither joy, nor love, nor light,
> Nor certitude, nor peace, nor help for pain;
> And we are here as on a darkling plain
> Swept with confused alarms of struggle and flight,
> Where ignorant armies clash by night.[69]

He had found it easy, nevertheless, to slip the leash of his father's Broad Church Christianity, and in the above lines "ignorant" is the most characteristic word. A classicist who shared the nineteenth century's passion for the congenially pre-Christian Greeks, he spent most of his life as an inspector of schools, seeing for himself the worthy, dispiriting efforts of the dissenting churches to educate in ugly surroundings the children of industrial, commercial England. Fastidious distaste, a gentlemanly shrinking from the mess of the human condition, colours his judgement often. He wrote lastingly influential essays on the poetry of Wordsworth, Byron, Shelley and Keats, rating Wordsworth very highly, partly, one cannot help deducing, because he approved of Wordsworth's orderly life—the Arnold family knew the Wordsworths in the Lake District—and found the lives of the others shockingly untidy and immoral. His judgement of Keats's poetry is warm and sympathetic, though he calls the publication of his letters "inexcusable" and the private immediacy of his love letters "underbred and ignoble".[70] "What a set!" he wrote of Shelley and his friends, "and Lord Byron with his deep grain of coarseness and commonness, his affectation, his brutal selfishness—what a set!"[71] (Perhaps he did not know of Byron's extraordinary kindness to Coleridge. Perhaps he would not have approved of it.) On Coleridge, who had done much more than any English predecessor to connect the faculty of imagination to the meaning of life, on the one hand, and to the work of poets, on the other, Arnold never wrote an extended piece, regarding him as "wrecked in a mist of opium".[72] "How little either of his poetry, or of his criticism or of his philosophy, can we expect permanently to stand?" He admitted some admiration for Coleridge's intellectual effort but described it as "not a moral effort, for he had no morals".[73]

The snobbery and priggishness in all this have a depressing Englishness; so, more seriously, does Arnold's partial, prejudiced view of history. Civilisation, according to this view, began with the Greeks, weakened with the Romans and disappeared altogether in the Middle Ages, to reawaken at the Renaissance and be taken forward by Protestantism into secular modernity, "while Catholicism threw itself violently across its path".[74] This Whig picture of the past explains Arnold's edgy attitude toward Shakespeare, about whose plays he wrote almost nothing, though Shakespeare was the subject of an early, awed sonnet and has his due place in Arnold's lists of great writers. The classicist's disdain appears early: Shakespeare "has not the severe and scrupulous self-restraint of the Ancients, partly, no doubt, because he had a far less cultivated and exacting audience."[75] Several years later, Arnold wrote of the Catholic Church that she was "indisputably the Church of the past and, in the past, the Church of the multitude. . . .

Catholicism suggests,—what shall I say?—all the pell-mell of the men and women of Shakespeare's plays." [76] That Catholic Christianity is the religion of foreigners and peasants who have not caught up even with the Enlightenment is an ordinary English opinion. In his dismissal of the Oxford Movement—"Liberalism prevailed; it was the appointed force to do the work of the hour; it was necessary, it was inevitable that it should prevail. The Oxford movement was broken, it failed" [77]—Matthew Arnold was echoing his father's recoil from Catholicising clergy.

The Enlightenment is Arnold's spiritual home. He has a thoroughly eighteenth-century confidence in reason: "What is binding on one man's conscience is not binding on another's. . . . But the prescriptions of reason are absolute, unchanging, of universal validity." [78] By the time he wrote his most celebrated essay, *Culture and Anarchy*, in 1869, "reason" has become "reason and the will of God", which he sets out to establish as the "plain grounds on which a faith in culture . . . may rest securely". [79] (The reader's suspicion, or hope, that "the will of God" might mean something recognisable to a Christian is rapidly dispelled.) The essay contains much splendid and deserved criticism of the England of his time: the upper and middle classes are described respectively as Barbarians and Philistines (Arnold's lasting usage), and his scorn for the puritanical dedication to commercial and industrial success for which (yet again) "we have had our reward" [80] is very like that of Wordsworth and Shelley. He is particularly disdainful toward the dissenting churches, accusing them of encouraging complacency in a grim moral perfectionism—"their idea of human perfection is narrow and inadequate" [81]—but not for a moment noticing that his attack on them is grounded in complacency of a different kind, that is to say, pure cultural snobbery:

> Notwithstanding the mighty results of the Pilgrim Fathers' voyage, they and their standard of perfection are rightly judged when we figure to ourselves Shakespeare or Virgil,—souls in whom sweetness and light, and all that in human nature is most humane, were eminent,— accompanying them on their voyage, and think what intolerable company Shakespeare and Virgil would have found them! [82]

(They would not.) Arnold concedes that "morality" is of course necessary, but it has little connexion with his "will of God", which turns out to be no more than a construct of rationalist optimism, "the universal order which seems to be intended and aimed at in the world, and which it is a man's happiness to go along with or his misery to go counter to". [83] We have to remember that Hegel was in the air that all intellectuals, whether or not they had read him, breathed in the mid-nineteenth century and that Marx's *Das Kapital*, not that Arnold would have heard of it, had appeared two years before *Culture and Anarchy*. Arnold believed both in the *Zeitgeist*, which he called "the Time-Spirit", and in human perfectibility. The culture that will achieve human perfection he sees as composed partly of "Hebraism", which gives it "strictness of conscience"; partly of "Hellenism", which gives it the aesthetic sense; and "spontaneity of consciousness" [84] (very Nietzschean, this phrase), summarised as "the two noblest of things, sweetness and light".[85] Both Hebraism and Hellenism were present in Christianity, but, now that reason has disposed of Christianity's truth, what remains of it is valuable only for the example of humility set by Jesus (beautiful) and for his moral teaching (good). As for "the final aim of both Hellenism and Hebraism", it is "no doubt the same: man's perfection or salvation".[86]

That Arnold can regard "perfection" and "salvation" as interchangeable terms shows how completely he had distanced himself from any sense of human sinfulness, from the soul's need for forgiveness or grace, from the figure of Christ on the Cross. The distance was a decision, but given Arnold's sanguine acceptance of the power of the *Zeitgeist*, scarcely a choice. In 1880 he restated his lifelong effort to replace religion with poetry in these words: "Our religion has materialised itself in the fact [ironically, as with Feuerbach and Nietzsche, a description of the Incarnation], the supposed fact; it has attached its emotion to the fact, and now the fact is failing it. But Poetry attaches its emotion to the idea; the idea is the fact." [87] And the truth?

Arnold remained uneasy about his campaign to replace religion with culture, in relation both to the Bible, evidently full of goodness and beauty if not of truth, and to the mass of the people, "the Populace", still in his view stuck with an unnourishing Christianity or with nothing but respectability and the work ethic to replace it. His *Literature and Dogma* (1873), a long and badly argued book much read in its time, is a valiant attempt to deal with both these anxieties. The Bible is to be read for its "poetry", as if it were a literary work like any other; in this way it will be included in the "culture" that is to replace religion. Whereas long ago Augustine had placed classical culture as valuable only in relation to the truth of Christianity, Arnold wishes to place the Bible, and a doctrineless Christianity, as valuable only in relation to "culture". In order to do this, in order to empty Christian doctrine of its force, he has to assert, astonishingly, that Christianity is technical, scientific and difficult to understand, whereas literary culture is easy to come by, easy to understand and a matter of subjective response that will somehow always be good. With dire mock humility, he describes his own reliance on "letters; thrown upon reading this and that—which anybody can do".[88] "The good of letters is, that they require no extraordinary acuteness such as is required to handle ... the doctrine of the Godhead of the Eternal Son."[89] The sleight of hand here is the identification of dogma, of the familiar statements of the Creed, the assertions without which there is no Christianity, with sophisticated theological scholarship (the rebarbative result of what he calls "mediaeval ignorance")[90] that is beyond the grasp of almost everyone. So Christian doctrine is difficult, while "letters", "the judgement which forms itself insensibly in a fair mind along with fresh reading", is easy. It became clear over the next two or three generations, however, that the reverse was true. Orthodox Christianity continued to be as it had always been, an ocean in which children can paddle and wise scholars never plumb the depths, while those who took Arnold seriously and actually attempted to replace Christian truth with literary culture were facing and posing intellectual demands that only a tiny minority were able or willing to meet. Most people who abandoned Christianity merely understood the liberal consensus to be giving them permission to follow any impulse in their lives, their reading, their watching, that made them feel better, or feel something. This long-term consequence of his effort to stay abreast, even ahead, of the Time-Spirit, in the light of which, he was sure, any reader would see the Christian tradition to have crumbled away, would certainly have shocked Arnold. In *Literature and Dogma*, he reckons to have saved morality, "the three-fourths of life which is *conduct*" by redefining religion as "morality touched by emotion".[91] His demonstration, by quotation from classical authors and the Bible, of the difference between morality and religion is intended to show the addition of "feeling" to rules of conduct; what it really shows is the addition of God.

On God, *Literature and Dogma* is equivocal. Arnold goes as far as to say that God is "the *not ourselves*, that element wherein religion has its being" or "the Eternal *not ourselves* that makes for righteousness";[92] but that this is a very long way he never admits. His purpose is to disentangle "the saving doctrine of Jesus" from "what is called 'orthodox doctrine' ... an immense literary misapprehension".[93] "Faith" he redefines as "a recognition of what is perfectly clear", suggesting that Newman's statement that "Faith is, in its very nature, the acceptance of what our *reason* cannot reach" is refuted by Jesus saying "If I tell you the truth, why do ye not believe me?"[94] Indeed, the closer Arnold comes to grappling with actual Christianity in his attempt to show that literary methods applied to the Bible are a decisive improvement on the dogmatic theology of "an age which ... had neither the resources nor the faculty for such a criticism",[95] the more his plain ignorance of Christianity is revealed. On Newman's faith in the patristic recognition of truth in the Bible, he says: "Born into the world twenty years later, and touched with the breath of the 'Zeit-Geist', how would this exquisite and delicate genius have been himself the first to feel the unsoundness of all this!" [96]

"We do not at all despair of finding some lasting faith to minister to the diseased spirit of our time",[97] Arnold wrote in *Culture and Anarchy*, the implication always being that culture was the hope and anarchy the alternative. It was an enterprise to which he dedicated a disinterested, hard-working—in its way, noble—life. But in the end, the faith he recommended amounts to not much more than faith in the self-cultivation of the individual, in "the ever-increasing efficacy and ... the general harmonious expansion of those gifts of thought and feeling, which make the peculiar dignity, wealth and happiness of human nature".[98] Those for whom "poetry" could achieve this turned out to be few and far between; meanwhile, the kind of self-esteem that Arnold encouraged is more likely to blind the soul to self-knowledge than to open the eyes of the heart to God. As Newman observed, "A system of doctrine has risen up during the last three centuries in which faith or spiritual-mindedness is contemplated and rested on as the end of religion instead of Christ. And in this way religion is made to consist in contemplating ourselves instead of Christ." [99]

1. P. B. Shelley, "Letter to Maria Gisborne", line 208.
2. Quoted in Basil Willey, *Nineteenth Century Studies* (London, 1949), p. 3.
3. Quoted in Ian Ker, *John Henry Newman: A Biography* (Oxford, 1988), p. 108.
4. Sydney Smith, *Edinburgh Review*, July 1824.
5. S. T. Coleridge, *On the Constitution of the Church and State*, ed. John Colmer (Princeton and London, 1976), pp. 114–15.
6. Quoted in Edward Norman, *Church and Society in England 1770–1970* (Oxford, 1976), p. 20.
7. Ibid., p. 95.
8. Quoted in Willey, *Nineteenth Century Studies*, p. 63.
9. Quoted in Ker, *John Henry Newman*, p. 323.
10. Quoted in John Henry Newman, *Apologia pro Vita Sua*, ed. Ian Ker (London, 1994), p. xi.
11. Lytton Strachey, *Eminent Victorians* (1918; London, 1928), p. 26.
12. Quoted in Owen Chadwick, *Newman* (Oxford, 1983), p. 28.
13. Quoted in Ker, *John Henry Newman*, p. 312.
14. Newman, *Apologia*, p. 116.
15. Quoted in Ker, *John Henry Newman*, p. 243.
16. Ibid., p. 124.
17. Ibid., p. 188.
18. Newman, *Apologia*, p. 148.
19. Ibid., p. 186.
20. Ibid., p. 188.
21. Quoted in Ker, *John Henry Newman*, p. 181.
22. Ibid., p. 361.

23. Ibid., p. 99.
24. Newman, *Apologia*, p. 217.
25. Quoted in Ker, *John Henry Newman*, p. 207.
26. Ibid., p. 433.
27. Ibid., p. 209.
28. John Henry Newman, *Rise and Progress of Universities*, ed. M. K. Tillman (Leominster and Notre Dame, Ind., 2001), pp. 366, 368.
29. Ibid., p. 466.
30. Quoted in Ker, *John Henry Newman*, p. 609.
31. Ibid., p. 312.
32. Ibid., p. 721.
33. Ibid., p. 589.
34. Ibid., p. 498.
35. Ibid., p. 715.
36. Ibid., p. 510.
37. Quoted in Willey, *Nineteenth Century Studies*, p. 82.
38. Quoted in Ker, *John Henry Newman*, p. 538.
39. Ibid., p. 687.
40. Ibid., p. 681.
41. S. T. Coleridge, *Aids to Reflection*, ed. John Beer (Princeton and London, 1993), pp. 405–6.
42. Matthew Arnold, "Emerson", in *Essays in Criticism*, 2nd series, *The Works of Matthew Arnold* (London, 1903–1904), 4:376–77.
43. Ibid., p. 349.
44. Quoted in Ker, *John Henry Newman*, p. 322.
45. Ibid., p. 678.
46. Quoted in Henri de Lubac, *The Drama of Atheist Humanism* (1944), trans. E. M. Riley et al. (San Francisco, 1995), p. 30.
47. William Hazlitt, *The Spirit of the Age* (London, 1910), p. 252.
48. *The Letters of John Keats*, ed. Maurice Buxton Forman (Oxford, 1952), p. 468.
49. John Keats, "Ode to a Grecian Urn", line 49.
50. Keats, *Letters*, pp. 334–36.
51. Ibid., p. 31.
52. Ibid., pp. 226–27.
53. Quoted in Richard Holmes, *Coleridge: Darker Reflections* (London, 1998), p. 456.
54. P. B. Shelley, *Shelley's Prose*, ed. David Lee Clark (London, 1988), p. 293.
55. Ibid., p. 292.
56. Ibid., pp. 282–83.
57. Ibid., p. 297.
58. Samuel Johnson, *The History of Rasselas, Prince of Abyssinia*, ed. D. J. Enright (London, 1976), pp. 61–62.
59. Shelley, *Shelley's Prose*, p. 283.
60. Ibid., p. 187.
61. Ibid., p. 284.
62. Ibid., p. 292.
63. Ibid., p. 290.
64. Ibid., p. 294.
65. Ibid., p. 295.
66. Matthew Arnold, "The Study of Poetry", in *Works* 4:2.
67. Matthew Arnold, *The Function of Criticism at the Present Time*, in *Essays in Criticism*, 1st series, vol. 3 of *Works*, p. 42.
68. *The Portable Matthew Arnold*, ed. Lionel Trilling (New York, 1949), p. 621.
69. Matthew Arnold, "Dover Beach", lines 21, 25, 33–37.
70. Matthew Arnold, "John Keats", in *Works* 4:74–75.

71. Matthew Arnold, "Shelley", in *Works* 4:175.
72. Matthew Arnold, "Byron", in *Works* 4:150.
73. Matthew Arnold, "Joubert", in *Works* 3:300.
74. Arnold, *Function of Criticism*, p. 38.
75. Matthew Arnold, preface to *Poems* (1853), 1.11, quoted in Stefan Collini, *Arnold* (Oxford, 1988), p. 48.
76. Matthew Arnold, "Pagan and Mediaeval Religious Sentiment", in *Works* 3:215.
77. Matthew Arnold, *Culture and Anarchy*, vol. 6 of *Works*, p. 31.
78. Arnold, *Function of Criticism*, p. 11.
79. Arnold, *Culture and Anarchy*, p. 4.
80. Ibid., p. 22.
81. Ibid., p. 25.
82. Ibid.
83. Ibid., p. 10.
84. Ibid., p. 124.
85. Ibid., p. 20.
86. Ibid., p. 121.
87. Arnold, "Study of Poetry", p. 1.
88. Matthew Arnold, *Literature and Dogma*, vol. 7 of *Works*, p. 390.
89. Ibid., p. 7.
90. Ibid., p. xxvii.
91. Ibid., pp. 20–21.
92. Ibid., p. 268.
93. Ibid., p. 176.
94. Ibid., p. 233; Jn 8:46: "And if I say the truth, why do ye not believe me?" (AV).
95. Arnold, *Literature and Dogma*, p. 284.
96. Ibid., p. 337.
97. Arnold, *Culture and Anarchy*, p. 166.
98. Ibid., p. 11.
99. Quoted in Ker, *John Henry Newman*, p. 155.

CHAPTER SEVENTEEN

G. M. HOPKINS AND EMILY DICKINSON

In Oxford, where Newman had been an undergraduate in the 1820s and Arnold in the 1840s, another gifted, impressionable boy was reading the classics in the 1860s. Gerard Hopkins (he disliked his middle name and only ever used its initial M) loved for the rest of his life, as they did, the beauty of the city, the gentle landscape surrounding it, and the particular atmosphere of the university in the nineteenth century—clerical, scholarly, far from London, insulated in many ways from the urban ugliness of industrial England. He went to Arnold's lectures. Arnold was the first layman to be Oxford Professor of Poetry and the first to lecture in English rather than Latin. Nearly twenty years later, Hopkins defended Arnold in a letter to Robert Bridges:

> I do not like your calling Matthew Arnold Mr. Kidglove Cocksure. I have more reason than you for disagreeing with him and thinking him very wrong, but nevertheless I am sure he is a rare genius and a great critic.[1]

The student Hopkins was writing his own verse, but his priority was not poetic ambition, as a letter he wrote to a schoolfriend in 1864 makes clear. He is urging his friend, Coleridge's grandson, to come up to Oxford soon, because Oxford is

> the head and fount of Catholicism in England and the heart of our Church. Beware of doing what I once thought I could do, *adopt an enlightened Christianity*, I may say, horrible as it is, *be a credit to religion*. This fatal state of mind leads to infidelity, if consistently and logically developed. The great aid to belief and object of belief is the doctrine of the Real Presence in the Blessed Sacrament of the Altar. Religon without that is sombre, dangerous, illogical, with that it is—not to speak of its grand consistency and certainty—*loveable*. Hold that and you will gain all Catholic truth.[2]

The nineteen-year-old writer of this letter had received, as was quite normal at the time, a confused religious upbringing in the Church of England, High at home from his respectable middle-class parents, and Low from his fierce headmaster at Highgate School, where he was also given an excellent classical education. In his letter to Ernest Coleridge he shows, as his two references to "logic" suggest, after a few months of immersion in Oxford's Anglo-Catholicism, a passionate but accurate sense of Newman's "I do not see any medium between disowning Christianity, and taking the Church of Rome."[3] This was the very year of Newman's *Apologia pro Vita Sua*.

A little over two years later, Hopkins visited Newman at the Birmingham Oratory and found him, in response to Hopkins's anguish over his now decided-on conversion, cheerful, practical and surprisingly "unserious";[4] Hopkins had expected, and got, a horrified reaction from his parents to the idea of his becoming a Catholic. With long experience of emotional young converts, Newman cooled Hopkins's sense of drama and received him into the Catholic Church in October 1866. Manning confirmed him in London a fortnight later. Newman told Hopkins to go back to Oxford and work hard for his degree: the university had just, at last, decided to allow Catholics to take BA degrees. Manning told another undergraduate convert at exactly this time that "as a Catholic now, it was plainly his duty not to return to Oxford."[5] Hopkins went back to Oxford, worked hard through his final year, and was awarded a First-class degree in Latin and Greek with philosophy, the highest goal attainable by a humanities student in England. In 1868 he joined the Jesuit novitiate. A little over twenty years later, in June 1889, he died of typhoid in Dublin at the age of forty-four.

Hopkins was small, dutiful, as a boy high-spirited, fragile in health, independent-minded but vulnerable, devoted to a few friends and to the beauty of the natural world. He needed the steady routine of a demanding, regular life. Eighteen months after becoming a Catholic, having completed a short retreat at the Jesuit house near London, he noted in his journal: "Home, after having decided to be a priest and religious but still doubtful betw. St Benedict and St Ignatius."[6] A week later, Newman wrote to him: "Don't call 'the Jesuit discipline hard': it will bring you to heaven. The Benedictines would not have suited you."[7] Newman had observed Hopkins working unhappily for a year as a teacher in his Oratory school: perhaps he thought Hopkins more in need of what, ten years before, he had called the "practical sense" of Saint Ignatius than of the "poetry" of Saint Benedict.[8] His advice was, nevertheless, bad. The Jesuits did their best to sustain Hopkins, were never unkind, never forbade him to write poetry, and gave him what seemed appropriate work. But his choice of religious order wrecked both his health and his confidence. He was happy in Wales for a few months in Oxford in 1878–1879, and now and then at Stonyhurst; these were the times and places that produced his most positive and vigorous poetry. He also set himself nobly to parish work in the heartbreaking slums of Liverpool. But he was no good at preaching and worse at teaching—the task, because of his degree, usually given him—and he found upsetting the frequent and unpredictable moves of Jesuit life, which he feared even more often than they happened. His final five years in Dublin, as the only English Jesuit teaching in the run-down college that was the current result of Newman's efforts to found a Catholic university for Ireland, were the most desolate of his life. Catholic Ireland was philistine, edgy and resentful of all Englishmen. As professor of Latin and Greek, Hopkins was expected to function as a lecturer and administrator; he was bad at both jobs, felt he was living as neither priest nor religious, and became severely depressed while his health gradually collapsed during the months before his final illness. The affectionate support of a stable monastic community, the daily habit of office in the same choir, even the changing seasons altering the same walks in the same woods: all of these, in a Benedictine monastery such as Ampleforth or Downside, or, perhaps best of all because without a school, at the Cistercian Mount Saint Bernard, would have suited him much better. In temperament he was not unlike Saint Aelred, though an abbot he would never have become. During the confinement of his tertianship at Manresa House in 1881, when he had been a Jesuit for thirteen years, he wrote in a letter: "My mind is here more at peace than it has ever been and I would gladly live all my life, if it were so to be, in as great or a greater seclusion from the world and be busied only with God."[9]

Yet, for all the sadness and frustrations of his lonely life, Hopkins's faith, together with his brave, clear intelligence and an outstanding gift for words and rhythm, delivered some of the greatest poems in English of the entire Christian tradition. He thought it necessary, though no one had told him it was, to burn all he had so far written—he forgot one or two pieces—when he became a Jesuit and to write no more verse. The chance remark of a superior that it would be good to have a poem on a disaster at sea that had cost over sixty lives in December 1875 released Hopkins's suppressed creative energy. The result of this sudden permission, for so it was taken by the scrupulous Hopkins, to attempt a poem, and also of years of reflection on how to write verse, was "The Wreck of the Deutschland", a long poem on the shipwreck and especially on the drowning of five Franciscan nuns on their way to exile in Canada as a result of Bismarck's banishment of all religious orders from Germany.

The poem is a quite extraordinary technical achievement, written in an eight-line stanza of Hopkins's invention, regularly rhymed, with heavily stressed lines, the number of stresses differing according to the stanza pattern, but the number of syllables varying widely. Hopkins called this exact counting of stresses rather than syllables "sprung rhythm" and used it, more or less freely, more or less intensely, in all the rest of his poems, though the stanza of the "Deutschland" never appeared again. Nothing like this poem had ever been seen or heard before in English poetry, for which the iambic pentameter had been the natural line, the iambic foot the natural unit—the default setting, as it were—for centuries. Chaucer, Spenser, Shakespeare, Milton, Dryden, Pope, Wordsworth, Coleridge, Keats, Tennyson and Arnold wrote almost always in iambics. No wonder the very few people who read the "Deutschland" in Hopkins's lifetime, with a single exception, found the poem so difficult, so unfamiliar, that that was all they found it. Actually, as became clear only decades after the poet's death, what is difficult about the poem is not its rhythm, which reveals, when the stanzas are read aloud, its capacity to make sense of clotted syntax and crammed-together words and meanings of words. A single example, with Hopkins's helpful stress, will demonstrate this:

> But wé dream we are rooted in earth—Dust!
> Flesh falls within sight of us, we, though our flower the same,
> Wave with the meadow, forget that there must
> The sour scythe cringe, and the blear share come.[10]

If these lines are read naturally, the stresses fall easily as the sense deepens. The contrast between earth, which is living, and dust, which is dead, is reinforced by the juxtaposition of two strongly stressed monosyllables; in the last line quoted, there are six stresses, falling heavily on every word except "the" and "and". Further, as one rereads, there is the density of colliding or amplifying meanings in "wave" and "share", of the faint pun in "flower", of the transitive-intransitive doubt in the surprising use of "cringe". The lines yield much to attention; then they are hard to forget.

But what is genuinely difficult in "The Wreck of the Deutschland" is its tremendous devotional intensity, a challenge to both the mind and the feelings almost impossible to meet without some grounding in the Catholic faith. There are ten stanzas in the first part of the poem, and twenty-four in the second, which tells the story of the shipwreck through the night of 7–8 December, the vigil and feast of the Immaculate Conception, a dogma of the Church declared as recently as 1854 but through the ages dear to the hearts of Franciscans and Jesuits and, long ago, to Hopkins's particular theological mentor, the fourteenth-century Oxford philosopher Duns Scotus. The seed-stanza of the whole poem, the first to be written, is stanza 12:

On Saturday sailed from Bremen,
    American-outward-bound,
  Take settler and seamen, tell men with women,
    Two hundred souls in the round—
O Father, not under thy feathers nor ever as guessing
The goal was a shoal, of a fourth the doom to be drowned;
    Yet did the dark side of the bay of thy blessing
Not vault them, the million of rounds of thy mercy not reeve even them in?[11]

From this reference to Psalm 90, said every day in the Office—*scapulis suis obumbrabit tibi, et sub pennis eius sperabit*[12] (He will shadow you with his wings, and under his feathers you will hope)—and from this concern, this prayer, for all who suffered the disaster, as well as from the invented stanza-shape, the whole poem developed. The second part of the poem, as thrilling and terrifying as the storm that drove the ship onto the sandbank where it broke up, focuses on the five nuns—five as the wounds of Christ, imprinted on the body of Saint Francis, were five—and then on "the chief sister, a gaunt woman 6 ft high, calling out loudly and often 'O Christ, come quickly!' till the end came"[13], as the *Illustrated London News* reported. At the very height of the storm, as the nun is drowning, she meets Christ in her death:

Ipse, the only one, Christ, King, Head;
  He was to cure the extremity where he had cast her;
    Do, deal, lord it with living and dead;
Let him ride, her pride, in his triumph, despatch and have done with his doom
    there.[14]

At this point Hopkins remembers the *cor rectum* and *oculus simplex* of Scripture:[15]

    Ah! there was a heart right!
      There was single eye!
  Read the unshapeable shock night
    And knew the who and the why;
Wording it how but by him that present and past,
Heaven and earth are word of, worded by?[16]

The suffering and death of the tall nun and her companions are pulled by the poem into the Passion and death, the sacrifice and Resurrection of Christ, and so into redemption. But the "Comfortless unconfessed of them" [17] are not forgotten by the poet, in the mercy of God and in the care of Mary for the lost, and there is, in stanza 33, a swift, profound evocation of Christ's descent among all the dead on Holy Saturday:

> With a mercy that outrides
> The all of water, an ark
> For the listener; for the lingerer with a love glides
> Lower than death and the dark;
> A vein for the visiting of the past-prayer, pent in prison. [18]

The first part of the poem, meanwhile, became a resounding, complex exploration of, and prayer of thanksgiving for, Hopkins's faith in God—terrifying, loving Father; loved, consoling Son; in the Holy Spirit—the Trinity revealed in Christ, ending in stanza 10 with reference to the representative conversions of Saint Paul, "once at a crash", and of Saint Augustine, "a lingering-out sweet skill". [19] "It is an ode and not primarily a narrative", [20] Hopkins wrote later, arguing for the unity of the whole poem. The brevity and terror of our life: "We dream we are rooted in earth—Dust!"; the annihilating swirl of the natural world, so beautiful, so destructive; the saving love for us of God in Christ: these are at the core of this first great piece, as they are at the core of all Hopkins's poems. "I think that the trivialness of life", he had written, in the year of his conversion, to Ernest Coleridge, "is, and personally to each one, ought to be seen to be, done away with by the Incarnation . . . (the greatness of which no saint can have ever hoped to realise)." [21] It is a wholly characteristic remark, from the very core of Christian faith.

It is not surprising that "The Wreck of the Deutschland" baffled those who saw it. Robert Bridges, Hopkins's friend from his time at Oxford, and a fellow poet, failed altogether to cope with it. He was unsympathetic to Hopkins's Christianity and could not—any more than could (less forgivably) the Jesuit editor of *The Month*, who rejected it for publication—get beyond the poem's metrical surprisingness. Defending the poem against the objections of Bridges, Hopkins wrote that his sprung rhythm was not arbitrarily odd. "Why do I employ sprung rhythm at all? Because it is the nearest to the rhythm of prose, that is the native and natural rhythm of speech, the least forced, the most rhetorical and emphatic of all possible rhythms." [22] In the same letter, he said:

> You ask may you call it "presumptious jugglery". No, but only for this reason, that *presumptious* is not English.

I cannot think of altering anything. Why shd. I? I do not write for the public. You are my public and I hope to convert you.

You say you wd. not for any money read my poem again. Nevertheless I beg you will. Besides money, you know, there is love.[23]

The broken paragraphs suggest the depth of his disappointment. He converted Bridges neither to any understanding of Catholicism nor to any understanding of his revolution in verse-making. He had simply to accept this. In 1881 he wrote to Bridges: "I always think ... that your mind towards my verse is like mine towards Browning's: I greatly admire the touches and the details, but the general effect, the whole, offends me, I think it repulsive."[24] More desolating even than this (rightly perceived) antipathy to his work was Hopkins's sense that Bridges, the closest friend of his entire adult life, was so certain that Christianity was not true that he even doubted the integrity of Hopkins's faith. In 1882 Hopkins wrote about a Corpus Christi procession Bridges had witnessed:

It is long since such things had any significance for you. But what is strange and unpleasant is that you sometimes speak as if they had in reality none for me and you were only waiting with a certain disgust till I too should be disgusted with myself enough to throw off the mask.[25]

In Hopkins's lifetime only Canon Dixon, an Anglican priest who had briefly taught Hopkins at Highgate, and also a poet, responded, up to a point, to the strength and distinction of "The Wreck of the Deutschland". Returning a bundle of Hopkins's work in 1880, he wrote:

I have read them many times with the greatest admiration: in the power of forcibly & delicately giving the essence of things in nature, & of carrying one out of one's self with healing, these poems are unmatched.... The Deutschland is enormously powerful: it has however such elements of deep distress in it that one reads it with less excited delight though not with less interest than the others.[26]

It was about the failure of Dixon's own poems to attract attention that Hopkins had written in 1876:

Fame whether won or lost is a thing which lies in the award of a random, reckless, incompetent, and unjust judge, the public, the multitude. The only just judge, the only just literary critic, is Christ, who prizes, is proud of, and admires, more than any man, more than the receiver himself can, the gifts of his own making.[27]

This disregard for the approval of the *civitas terrena* in favour of unembittered confidence in the *civitas Dei* was something that Hopkins knew that he, a priest and religious, should achieve in relation to his own unpublished, uncomprehended work. With selfless perseverance he held always to the priorities of his youth, but a letter to Dixon of 1881, painful to read in its transparent honesty, shows how difficult this fidelity had been:

My vocation puts before me a standard so high that a higher can be found nowhere else. The question then for me is not whether I am willing (if I may guess what is in your mind) to make a sacrifice of hopes of fame (let us suppose), but whether I am not to undergo a severe judgment from God for the lothness I have shewn in making it, for the reserves I may have in my heart made, for the backward glances I have given with my hand upon the plough, for the waste of time the very compositions you admire may have caused and their preoccupation of the mind which belonged to more sacred or more binding duties, for the disquiet and the thoughts of vainglory they have given rise to. A purpose may look smooth and perfect from without but be frayed and faltering from within. I have never wavered in my vocation, but I have not lived up to it.[28]

Hopkins completed about fifty more poems in the thirteen years between the "Deutschland" and his death. More than thirty of them are sonnets of one sort or another, many of these pushing the principles of sprung rhythm against the conventional constraints of the form to invigorating effect. With the encouragement of Duns Scotus's emphasis on *haeccitas*, the "thisness" of every individual being in God's creation—for Hopkins a golden insight of medieval philosophy on which he had fallen with delight in 1872—he harnessed his own delicate observation of the infinite detail of the natural world, recorded in his journal, to his love of Christ. "It may come to nothing or it may be a mercy from God",[29] he wrote of his discovery of Scotus. In the sonnet that is a tribute to Scotus and a lament for the modern encroachment of "a base and brickish skirt" on the beauty of Oxford, he says of his medieval predecessor: "Of realty the rarest-veined unraveller." [30] Certainly Hopkins's lexical range, his plunder of the English language to catch the very particularity, flow and stillness, light and shadow he saw in God's creation, in poems such as "Pied Beauty", "Spring", "Hurrahing in Harvest", "Inversnaid", "That Nature Is a Heraclitean Fire", gives weight to his judgement of Wordsworth and "the Lake School": "They were faithful but not rich observers of nature." [31] Even Wordsworth's best poems—Hopkins particularly admired the "Immortality" ode—could not place, as Hopkins's did, both the beauty of the natural world and the poet's passionate response to it in doctrinally secure relation to God. Only the full Catholic sense of the Incarnation and of our Lady's representative place in the order of all things could unite for Hopkins his aesthetic and spiritual capacities in his belief in the immanence of a transcendent God. Balthasar, in the only essay on an English writer in *The Glory of the Lord*, takes Hopkins as in this respect exemplary:

> Here the whole world order—and within it the whole of aesthetics—depends on the inextricable linkage of Christ and Mary: on the interweaving, by grace, of the human act of assent into the redeemer's own act of assent, which is one with the assent of the love of the Trinity. Thus is Mary everywhere present in the work of Hopkins and indeed compared to the air we breathe [the title of a poem]: in her the whole of creation is worthy of God, is objectively, and without any dialectic "as if", beautiful. [32]

Almost all Hopkins's poems of celebration are explicitly or implicitly Christ-centred, because what they celebrate is the Incarnation. The sonnet "Spring" begins as a poem of simple rejoicing in beauty precisely evoked: "Thrush's eggs look little low heavens". Then:

> What is all this juice and all this joy?
>   A strain of the earth's sweet being in the beginning
> In Eden garden.—Have, get, before it cloy,
>   Before it cloud, Christ, lord, and sour with sinning,
> Innocent mind and Mayday in girl and boy,
>   Most, O maid's child, thy choice and worthy the winning. [33]

In "Hurrahing in Harvest", the exhilaration of a walk in windy reaped fields becomes a hymn to Christ and an illustration of Coleridge's line "O lady! we receive but what we give."[34] The last four lines of Hopkins's sonnet, not in any way difficult to grasp, show the effectiveness of sprung rhythm at its simplest: five-stress lines with from eight to fifteen syllables according to inseparable movement and sense:

> These things, these things were here and but the beholder
>   Wanting; which two when they once meet,
> The heart rears wings bold and bolder
> And hurls for him, O half hurls earth for him off under his feet.[35]

A much-anthologised sonnet begins: "The world is charged with the grandeur of God."[36] The loading of "charged" with electricity and responsibility is beyond any of Hopkins's contemporary poets; the poem develops the full implications of both senses of the word: we spoil God's world; in constant creation God renews it. Hopkins's finest achievement in this vein is "The Windhover", also much discussed, often by critics who ignore its dedication "To Christ our Lord". Christ is not directly referred to in the poem, but his glory and heroic sacrifice in the shedding of his blood on the Cross are caught in the exact evocation of the soaring and miraculously stalled flight of a hawk high in the air. The packed resonance of this poem, in which every word more than earns its place, has the density of Shakespeare's lines from the sonnet that begins "Like as the waves make towards the pebbled shore", with their distant recall of the Incarnation and Crucifixion of Christ:

> Nativity, once in the main of light,
> Crawls to maturity; wherewith being crowned
> Crooked eclipses 'gainst his glory fight,
> And time that gave doth now his gift confound.[37]

"Sunt lacrimae rerum et mentem mortalia tangunt" (There are tears in things, and mortality touches the soul).[38] In a number of poems, beauty's transience, which has haunted poets always, is taken up by Hopkins into his faith in the eternal truth of God's love. "The Leaden Echo and the Golden Echo", of which Hopkins said, "I never did anything more musical",[39] contrasts the despair of mortality with the safety of fleeting beauty in the everlastingness of God. The poem begins:

How to keep—is there any any, is there none such, nowhere known
    some, bow or brooch or braid or brace, lace, latch or catch
    or key to keep
Back beauty, keep it, beauty, beauty, beauty, ... from vanishing away?

But the leaden echo—"O there's none; no no no there's none"—is cancelled by the golden:

Give beauty back, beauty, beauty, beauty, back to God, beauty's self and
    beauty's giver.
See; not a hair is, not an eyelash, not the least lash lost; every hair
Is, hair of the head, numbered.[40]

A poignant sonnet, "To what serves mortal beauty?" (here, in particular, human beauty is meant), answers the question, fraught with danger for the celibate, with self-control, and then with prayer:

Merely meet it; own,
Home at heart, heaven's sweet gift; then leave, let that alone.
Yea, wish that though, wish all, God's better beauty, grace.

But earlier in the poem there is also the grateful response:

See: it does this: keeps warm
Men's wits to the things that are.[41]

Hopkins was already in Dublin in the summer of 1885 when he wrote this carefully restrained poem. It was probably in this same year that he wrote the so-called terrible sonnets, six poems that record the agony of his struggle with severe depression. They have been much misunderstood. They are not about loss of faith but record the black depths of a fight against despair, in the certainty, but without the consolation, that only in God is the hope of rescue. The desolate prayers:

Comforter, where, where is your comforting?
Mary, mother of us, where is your relief?[42]

are, however, answered. In the sestet of the sonnet "Patience, hard thing!" there is the underlying trust of a deeply unhappy man sustained nevertheless by faith:

> We hear our hearts grate on themselves: it kills
> To bruise them dearer. Yet the rebellious wills
> Of us we do bid God bend to him even so.
> And where is he who more and more distils
> Delicious kindness?—He is patient. Patience fills
> His crisp combs, and that comes those ways we know.[43]

As the honey of God's patience sweetens and soothes the force of "grate" and "bruise", so, in "My own heart let me more have pity on" God's "smile":

> 's not wrung, see you; unforeseen times rather—as skies
> Betweenpie mountains—lights a lovely mile.[44]

(The coinage "betweenpie" fuses the meaning of "betweentimes" and "pied" or "dappled".) These are moments of grace, of unquenchable light in the crowding darkness.

And it was three years later, in the summer before his death, that Hopkins wrote "That Nature is a Heraclitean Fire and of the Comfort of the Resurrection", the single poem that most perfectly captures both his unfailing responsiveness to the hurtle of mortal beauty into oblivion and his faith in the oblivion-cancelling Resurrection of Christ. The poem asks, and answers, the deepest, simplest question confronting anyone who might or might not respond to the challenge of belief in Christ—Is this true?

> Man, how fast his firedint, his mark on mind, is gone!

Or is this?

> Flesh fade, and mortal trash
> Fall to the residuary worm; world's wildfire, leave but ash;
> In a flash, at a trumpet crash,
> I am all at once what Christ is, since he was what I am, and
> This Jack, joke, poor potsherd, patch, matchwood, immortal diamond,
> Is immortal diamond.[45]

As Hopkins wrote in a single line of an unfinished poem: "There's none but truth can stead you. Christ is truth." [46]

* * *

So Victorian England, the philistine England of commerce and industry bemoaned by Matthew Arnold; the England of Thomas Carlyle, Charles Kingsley's hearty Protestantism and John Stuart Mill's utilitarian secularism; the England of soft Pre-Raphaelite nostalgia and the beginnings of fin-de-siècle decadence, produced, against all the odds, a great Catholic poet unaffected by any of them. Without Newman's example, Hopkins might not have become a Catholic. Like Newman, he took the step for the sake of the truth. In a remarkably firm letter, to a celebrated Oxford Anglican cleric who had tried to hold him in the Church of England, he wrote, just after his reception into the Catholic Church:

> I must have decided as I have done if I had waited till after my Degree for a leisure time of thought, but since the only claim the Church of England made on my allegiance was by a theory of 20 years prevalence among a minority of her clergy, it is not wonderful that the claims of the Catholic Church broke down my efforts to wait that time many months beforehand.[47]

He certainly did not become a Catholic for the aesthetic reasons of which he was accused by his father at the time of his conversion. To his father's charge, he replied: "I am surprised you shd. say fancy and aesthetic tastes have led me to my present state of mind: these wd. be better satisfied in the Church of England, for bad taste is always meeting one in the accessories of Catholicism."[48] As one would expect from his poems, his own taste was sure, perceptive, uncluttered by the assumptions of the day. At age twenty, in a rambling student letter, he wrote: "Do you know, a horrible thing has happened to me. I have begun to *doubt* Tennyson"; later in the same letter: "Inconsequent conclusion: Shakespeare is and must be utterly the greatest of poets"; and later still, on a new Arnold essay, "As is so often the case, in censuring bad taste he falls into two flagrant pieces of bad taste himself."[49] Of Arnold's *Empedocles on Etna* poems, he wrote, justly: "They seem to have all the ingredients of poetry without quite being it";[50] and on his contemporaries' enthusiasm for the Greeks, he wrote to Bridges, who shared it: "Believe me, the Greek gods are a totally unworkable material; the merest frigidity, which must chill and kill every living work of art they are brought into."[51]

Of course, Victorian England had no idea what it had produced in Hopkins. In a late letter (1886) to Bridges, Hopkins wrote, one imagines with considerable sadness in the circumstances:

By the bye, I say it deliberately and before God, I would have you and Canon Dixon and all true poets remember that fame, the being known, though in itself one of the most dangerous things to man, is nevertheless the true and appointed air, element, and setting of genius and its works. What are works of art for? to educate, to be standards. Education is meant for the many, standards are for public use. To produce then is of little use unless what we produce is known, if known widely, the wider known the better, for it is by being known it works, it influences, it does its duty, it does good.... A great work by an Englishman is like a great battle won by England. It is an unfading bay tree.[52]

Perhaps Bridges remembered this letter, though he had little idea, ever, of the quality of what Hopkins had written. In any case, when the Victorian world had shattered in the Great War, Bridges in 1918, now Poet Laureate, published the poems that he had kept for the thirty years since Hopkins's death, apologising to the end for their "Oddity and Obscurity" and particularly for the "faults of taste" (among which he included "perverted Marianism"), "which few as they numerically are yet affect my liking and more repel my sympathy than do all the rude shocks of his purely artistic wantonness".[53] Nevertheless, we owe Bridges much more gratitude than reproach: but for him, Hopkins's poems would almost certainly have been known only to God.

Over the next ten or twelve years, it became evident to some that a couple of sentences about Shakespeare in Coleridge's *Biographia Literaria* had been vindicated, most surprisingly, in the work of an obscure Jesuit priest who had died decades earlier. Coleridge had written:

Images however beautiful, though faithfully copied from nature, and as accurately represented in words, do not of themselves characterize the poet. They become proofs of original genius only as far as they are modified by a predominant passion; or ... when a human and intellectual life is transferred to them from the poet's own spirit.[54]

Balthasar wrote of the rhythm that holds together the flying words in "That Nature Is a Heraclitean Fire" that "it sweeps the whole cultivated world of beauty of the Victorian age into the dustbin."[55] This is as true of the poetry of Newman himself—"The Lake School expires in Keble and Faber and Cardinal Newman",[56] Hopkins said—as it is of a good deal of the work of Wordsworth, Arnold, Tennyson, Bridges and everyone else Hopkins labelled "Parnassian". But it is not sprung rhythm, nor even the Shakespearean vitality of Hopkins's grip on the English language that make his poems "proofs of original genius", but the "predominant passion" that moved his spirit to deploy these resources in exactly the way he did. Balthasar, later in his essay, said:

> It is precisely the duty of the one who ascends to Christ in faith, hope and love to interpret all the forms of God's revelation in Christ throughout the universe, and this task is achieved by Hopkins the poet. What has to be interpreted is not concepts (of "universal", abstract truths), but images (of the unique, personal, divine-human truth), and here poetry is the absolutely appropriate theological language, and Hopkins brings the great English tradition back into the Church by his own creative achievement.[57]

In 1881–1882 Hopkins made some headway with "a great ode on Edmund Campion S.J."[58] He never finished it, and nothing of it survives. This connexion with the world of Shakespeare's youth (Hopkins knew that Shakespeare had used some of Campion's writing[59]) with the martyred Jesuits and "The Phoenix and the Turtle" would have been perfectly appropriate. As it was, Hopkins had done enough to deserve a place of particular honour in the story of writing in the Christian tradition, as one hopes he knew. "Since, as Solomon says," he wrote to Dixon, "there is a time for everything, there is nothing that does not some day come to be, it may be that the time will come for my verses."[60]

* * *

How many Flowers fail in Wood—
Or perish from the Hill—
Without the privilege to know
That they are Beautiful—

How many cast a nameless Pod
Upon the nearest Breeze—
Unconscious of the Scarlet Freight—
It bear to Other Eyes—[61]

At the same time that Hopkins in England was writing poetry two or three people read and no one understood, an equally remarkable poet was writing in

America in an isolation even more extreme than his. Emily Dickinson, the author of the above wistful lines, wrote hundreds of poems unlike any that had ever been written before. Whereas Hopkins was cut off from "the spirit of the age" by his Catholicism, his priesthood and his bold technical inventiveness, Emily Dickinson, a recluse by her own choice in her parents' house, was not only cut off from almost all ordinary human company and an audience for her work, but also separated by a wide historical distance from the tradition of Catholic Christianity.

She was born in 1830, in Amherst, Massachusetts, a small, respectable town in the heart of Puritan New England. She lived in Amherst all her life, except for a single year as a student at nearby Mount Holyoke, the pioneering college for women, and at Amherst she died in 1886. A lively, witty girl of acute intelligence and painfully acute sensibility, she suffered in her early thirties an emotional disaster, probably the loss of a man she loved, possibly only the realisation that she would never marry, and thereafter saw almost no one outside her family, though she corresponded with several people, some of whom she never met. She always read widely and absorbed Shakespeare with particular intensity. She sent a few poems to a friendly, bemused correspondent, T. W. Higginson, a Unitarian minister in Cambridge, Massachusetts, who treated her as kindly as Bridges treated Hopkins, and with as little understanding. Half a dozen of her poems were printed in her lifetime. At her death, nearly two thousand poems, many fair-copied and strung together in bundles like Pascal's *Pensées*, many in various stages of composition, were found in her room. Batches of these poems, tidied by Higginson and others—her eccentric dashes, her capital letters, and her occasionally "incorrect" scansion were at first considered too odd to stand—were published over decades. Only in 1955 did her work as she had left it finally appear, and in 1960 its devoted editor, Thomas H. Johnson, produced a definitive text of every poem. The "scarlet freight" of her work therefore struck, puzzled and enthralled the ordinary reader of poetry even longer after her death than the proper publication of Hopkins's poems after his.

Old Christianity in old Massachusetts was grimly Calvinist; the dark retributive clouds of the Salem witch trials and of Nathaniel Hawthorne's *The Scarlet Letter*, written when Emily Dickinson was twenty, had not altogether lifted from her sky. During her lifetime, Unitarianism—liberal, rationalist and optimistic—became the religion of the New England elite in Harvard and Boston, while the soft mists of Emerson's transcendentalism (a mild emanation from German philosophy, Wordsworth and a misunderstood Coleridge) floated over both. Out of this mixed religious atmosphere Emily Dickinson collected a terrifying sense of

God, a more terrifying sense of his absence, and an occasional, consoling sense of Christ, each often impossible to disentangle in her poems from a man, or men, feared, lost or loved. An orthodox Christian she was certainly not. From her New England surroundings, Catholic Christianity was remote to the point of complete incomprehension. In early American history, Catholicism had been associated with foreign powers, French and Spanish, then, more equivocally, with the distant English monarchy and its state church, from all of which the virtuous republic managed to wrest, one way or another, its expanding Protestant land. Every wave of revivalism in the American nineteenth century was Protestant, while the rapidly increasing Catholic population was mostly composed of newly arrived Irish and German immigrants, their faith still regarded as "un-American" in almost all of the older states of the Union. The dreadful carnage of the Civil War, killing hundreds of thousands of Americans while Emily Dickinson was writing in peaceful Amherst, delivered, eventually, the victory of Protestant, republican virtue over a backward-looking slave-owning aristocracy. Disorderly, cosmopolitan New York and Chicago were hundreds of miles away, their famous twentieth-century Catholic mayors (and the first Catholic president of the United States, from Massachusetts) decades in the future.

Emily Dickinson's poems, short, swift and packed, in their apparent simplicity, with their passionate registration of fear, loss, love and celebration, each held in a quite astonishing intellectual grip, are not in any ordinary sense devotional. In them she responds to, through, and with the simplest elements of everyday experience—the weather, the seasons, the sea, trees, birds and most of all, death— but also to, through and with the broken pieces of Christianity about her. Sometimes her response is positive:

> It is an honorable Thought
> And makes One lift One's Hat
> As One met sudden Gentlefolk
> Upon a daily Street
>
> That We've immortal Place
> Though Pyramids decay
> And Kingdoms, like the Orchard
> Flit Russetly away.[62]

More often it is negative, a response from bereftness:

Those—dying then,
Knew where they went—
They went to God's Right Hand—
That Hand is amputated now
And God cannot be found—

The abdication of Belief
Makes the Behavior small—
Better an ignis fatuus
Than no illume at all—[63]

She knew well, as the sixth and seventh lines here show, the scale of the consequences of the absence of God. Sometimes she is as appalled as Pascal's frightened unbeliever by the meaninglessness of a Godless universe. In the second half of a terrifying poem that begins "It was not Death, for I stood up, / And all the Dead, lie down—", she records an icy nothingness:

As if my life were shaven,
And fitted to a frame,
And could not breathe without a key,
And 'twas like Midnight, some—

When everything that ticked—has stopped—
And Space stares all around—
Or Grisly frosts—first Autumn morns,
Repeal the Beating Ground—

But, most, like Chaos—Stopless—cool
Without a Chance, or Spar—
Or even a Report of Land—
To justify—Despair.[64]

The combination of claustrophobia and dizzying space is no less terrifying here:

I saw no Way—The Heavens were stitched—
I felt the Columns close—
The Earth reversed her Hemispheres—
I touched the Universe—

And back it slid—and I alone—
A Speck upon a Ball—
Went out upon Circumference—
Beyond the Dip of Bell—[65]

Other poems record a kind of stunned numbness:

"*Speech*"—is a prank of *Parliament*—
"*Tears*"—a trick of the *nerve*—
But the Heart with the heaviest freight on—
Doesn't—always—move—[66]

She fought these paralysing fears and times of depression with courage, resource-fulness and the confidence she managed to sustain in the quality of her work and in the mysterious value of her solitary introspection:

Adventure must unto itself
The Soul condemned to be—
Attended by a single Hound
Its own identity.[67]

She knew that somewhere in her soul there was an instinct for an absolute meaning beyond the meanings of every day. She said, in a letter to Higginson accepting her "Barefoot-Rank" as an unpublished poet: "The Sailor cannot see the North, but knows the Needle can."[68] Many poems rejoice in the limitless beauty of her limited world. Others record the impact of a presence that can be only the presence of God:

He fumbles at your Soul
As Players at the Keys
Before they drop full Music on—
He stuns you by degrees—
Prepares your brittle Nature
For the Ethereal Blow
By fainter Hammers—further heard—
Then nearer—Then so slow
Your Breath has time to straighten—
Your Brain—to bubble Cool—

> Deals—One—imperial—Thunderbolt—
> That scalps your naked Soul—
>
> When Winds take Forests in their Paws—
> The Universe—is still—[69]

Or, more quietly and steadily, in an explanation for the constancy of her solitude:

> The Soul that hath a Guest
> Doth seldom go abroad—
> Diviner Crowd at Home—
> Obliterate the need—
>
> And Courtesy forbid
> A Host's departure when
> Upon Himself be visiting
> The Emperor of Men—[70]

The freight of ambiguity in "Himself", conveying both the host who stays at home for his guest and the fragment of God that is the soul in each of us, is characteristic of her writing. And "freight", as in "How many Flowers fail", and in the frozen quatrain just quoted, is a word she uses herself with a full sense of its heaviness:

> That Love is all there is,
> Is all we know of Love;
> It is enough, the freight should be
> Proportioned to the groove.[71]

The hesitant comma in the penultimate line suggests both that what we know is enough and that what we can bear is enough for us.

Much that Emily Dickinson wrote repays reading and rereading for this kind of subtlety and for the awe one soon feels for the working of so extraordinary an intelligence in such a richly complex use, both delicate and laden, of the simplest words, deployed in the short lines and steady rhythms of the simplest hymns. All but two of these quotations are complete poems; none of her poems has a title. Her work has a compressed lucidity in common with the best of William Blake's *Songs of Innocence* and *Songs of Experience*, but there is nothing in her poems resembling either Blake's Swedenborgian distortions of Christianity or the invented mythologies of his later work. In the nakedness of a soul before God, before death, before the beauty and terror of the world in which each of us is briefly alive, and in her attachment to the Christian tradition that, in her loneliness, without sacraments or ancient liturgy, gave her shaky but real support, her work has no parallel.

> How brittle are the Piers
> On which our Faith doth tread—
> No Bridge below doth totter so—
> Yet none hath such a Crowd.

> It is as old as God—
> Indeed—'twas built by him—
> He sent his Son to test the Plank,
> And he pronounced it firm.[72]

1. *The Letters of Gerard Manley Hopkins to Robert Bridges*, ed. C. C. Abbott (Oxford, 1935), p. 172.
2. *Further Letters of Gerard Manley Hopkins*, ed. C. C. Abbott, 2nd ed. (Oxford, 1956), pp. 16–17.
3. Quoted in Ian Ker, *John Henry Newman: A Biography* (Oxford, 1988), p. 300.
4. Quoted in Robert Bernard Martin, *Gerard Manley Hopkins: A Very Private Life* (London, 1991), p. 145.
5. Ibid., p. 154.
6. G. M. Hopkins, journal entry dated 7 May 1868, quoted in Gerard Manley Hopkins, *Poems and Prose*, ed. W. H. Gardner (London, 1985), p. 110.
7. Hopkins, *Further Letters*, p. 408.
8. John Henry Newman, *Rise and Progress of Universities*, ed. M. K. Tillman (Leominster and Notre Dame, Ind., 2001), pp. 366, 368.
9. *The Correspondence of Gerard Manley Hopkins and Richard Watson Dixon*, ed. C. C. Abbott (Oxford, 1935), p. 75.
10. G. M. Hopkins, "The Wreck of the Deutschland", st. 11, lines 5–8.
11. Ibid., st. 12.
12. Ps 90(91):4; the psalm is said daily at Compline.
13. Hopkins, *Further Letters*, p. 443.
14. Hopkins, "Wreck of the Deutschland", st. 28, lines 5–8.
15. Ps 124(125):4; Lk 11:34.
16. Hopkins, "Wreck of the Deutschland", st. 29, lines 1–6.
17. Ibid., st. 31, lines 3–4.
18. Ibid., st. 33, lines 1–5.
19. Ibid., st. 10, lines 5–6.
20. Hopkins, *Letters*, p. 49.
21. Hopkins, *Further Letters*, p. 19.
22. Hopkins, *Letters*, p. 46.
23. Ibid.
24. Ibid., p. 137.

25. Ibid., p. 148.
26. Hopkins, *Correspondence*, pp. 32–33.
27. Ibid., p. 8.
28. Ibid., p. 88.
29. Hopkins, *Poems and Prose*, p. xxiii.
30. G. M. Hopkins, "Duns Scotus's Oxford", lines 5, 12.
31. Hopkins, *Correspondence*, p. 98.
32. Hans Urs von Balthasar, *The Glory of the Lord: A Theological Aesthetics*, vol. 3, trans. Andrew Louth et al. (San Francisco and Edinburgh, 1986), pp. 390–91.
33. G. M. Hopkins, "Spring", lines 9–14.
34. S. T. Coleridge, "Dejection: An Ode" 4.1.
35. G. M. Hopkins, "Hurrahing in Harvest", lines 11–14.
36. G. M. Hopkins, "God's Grandeur", line 1.
37. Shakespeare, Sonnet 60.
38. Virgil, *Aeneid* 1.462.
39. Hopkins, *Correspondence*, p. 149.
40. G. M. Hopkins, "The Leaden Echo", lines 1–2, 14; "The Golden Echo", lines 19–21.
41. G. M. Hopkins, "To what serves mortal beauty?" lines 3–4, 12–14.
42. G. M. Hopkins, "No worst, there is none", lines 3–4.
43. G. M. Hopkins, "Patience, hard thing!", lines 9–14.
44. G. M. Hopkins, "My own heart let me more have pity on", lines 13–14.
45. G. M. Hopkins, "That Nature Is a Heraclitean Fire", lines 10, 18–23.
46. G. M. Hopkins, "On the Portrait of Two Beautiful Young People", line 20.
47. Hopkins, *Further Letters*, p. 33.
48. Ibid., p. 93.
49. Ibid., pp. 215, 219, 331.
50. Ibid., p. 58.
51. Hopkins, *Letters*, p. 217.
52. Ibid., p. 231.
53. Quoted in F. R. Leavis, *New Bearings in English Poetry* (1932; London, 1963), p. 131.
54. S. T. Coleridge, *Biographia Literaria*, ed. James Engell and W. Jackson Bate (Princeton and London, 1983), 2:23.
55. Balthasar, *Glory of the Lord* 3:362.
56. Hopkins, *Correspondence*, p. 99.
57. Balthasar, *Glory of the Lord* 3:391.
58. Hopkins, *Letters*, p. 135.
59. Hopkins, *Correspondence*, p. 94.
60. Ibid., p. 95.
61. Emily Dickinson, *The Complete Poems*, ed. Thomas H. Johnson (London, 1970), no. 404.
62. Ibid., no. 946.
63. Ibid., no. 1551.
64. Ibid., no. 510, lines 13–24.
65. Ibid., no. 378.
66. Ibid., no. 688.
67. Ibid., no. 822, lines 13–16.
68. Ibid., quoted in introduction, p. vii.
69. Ibid., no. 315.
70. Ibid., no. 674.
71. Ibid., no. 1765.
72. Ibid., no. 1433.

CHAPTER EIGHTEEN

GEORGE SANTAYANA, WALLACE STEVENS
AND T. S. ELIOT

In 1889, three years after Emily Dickinson's death, a twenty-five-year-old Spaniard was appointed to teach philosophy at Harvard College. George Santayana was born and raised a Catholic, spending his early childhood in Avila. From the age of nine he had lived and been educated in Boston and then at Harvard. A promising young philosopher, he had in 1888 completed his doctorate at Harvard after two years' study in Germany and a shorter spell in Oxford. He taught at Harvard for twenty-three years, with academic leave in Cambridge (England) in 1896–1897 and at the Sorbonne in 1905–1906. In 1907 he became a full professor at Harvard. But he was never wholly settled or happy there and chose not to renounce his Spanish citizenship. In 1912 he resigned his post, from England, and never crossed the Atlantic again, living in England through the years of the 1914–1918 war, then briefly in Paris, and finally, through the decades of a long old age, in Rome, where, at nearly eighty-nine, in 1952 he died.

Santayana was a poet and a literary critic, but primarily a philosopher. As a philosopher of the late nineteenth century, dedicated to rational thought, he decided early that he did not, and could not, believe that Christianity was true. Nevertheless, he brought to Harvard something it was entirely without, a knowledge and love of European Catholicism as a venerable intellectual home for minds of the highest distinction, deserving, at the very least, awareness and respect. "In feeling and in legal allegiance I have always remained a Spaniard", he wrote late in his life. "My first philosophical enthusiasm was for Catholic theology." [1] It was an enthusiasm that never left him and that deepened at the end of his life, as we shall see, to something approaching the conviction he had long regarded as impossible in the modern "life of reason". It was also both what made him unhappy as he attempted, with considerable success, to live the "life of reason" at Harvard and what makes him a figure of major importance in the story this book is attempting to tell. For among the students he taught and befriended at Harvard at the end of the nineteenth and the beginning of the twentieth centuries were two young men who became, in very different ways, the great modern poets in English of the Christian tradition.

In public, Santayana analysed with moderation and some sympathy the religious atmosphere, or rather its absence, that had depressed him at Harvard:

> Harvard College had been founded to rear Puritan divines, and as Calvinism gradually dissolved, it left a void there and as it were a mould, which a philosophy expressing the same instincts in a world intellectually transformed could flow into and fill almost without knowing it. . . .
> In academic America the Platonic and Catholic traditions had never been planted; it was only the Calvinist tradition, when revived in some modern disguise, that could stir there the secret chord of reverence and enthusiasm. Harvard was the seminary and academy for the inner circle of Bostonians, and naturally responded to all the liberal and literary movements of which Boston was the centre. In religion it became first Unitarian and afterwards neutral.[2]

What filled the empty mould left by defunct Calvinism was a bland version of nineteenth-century German philosophy, stemming from Kant and Hegel, that Santayana, from an irreducibly Catholic standpoint given him by his early training, regarded as only plausibly high-minded while in reality it subverted the ancient demandingness of truths it had turned inside out. "German philosophy", he wrote in 1915,

> has inherited from Protestantism its earnestness and pious intention; also a tendency to retain, for whatever changed views it may put forward, the names of former beliefs. God, freedom, and immortality, for instance, may eventually be transformed into their opposites, since the oracle of faith is internal; but their names may be kept, together with a feeling that what will now bear those names [vital energy, personality, the endlessness of human progress] is much more satisfying than what they originally stood for.

(No wonder, since this analysis has considerable force, Coleridge found the process of disentangling Christian truth from the seductions of German philosophy so protracted and so difficult.) That Santayana here has New England as well as Germany in mind quickly becomes clear; he goes on:

> If these new thoughts should satisfy and encourage us as the evanescent ideas of God, freedom, and immortality satisfied and encouraged our

fathers, why should we not use these consecrated names for our new conceptions, and thus indicate the continuity of religion amid the flux of science? ... Whether candid [Emerson is his American example] or disingenuous, this habit has the advantage of oiling the wheels of progress with a sacred unction.[3]

What Santayana suffered at Harvard was the absence of a single, secure intellectual tradition. Instead, there was the careless accommodation of personal views of all kinds—"granted industry, sobriety, and some semblance of theism, no professor was expected to agree with any other"—and no expectation of discipline or depth in the learning of "absent-minded youths, ill-grounded in the humanities, and not keenly alive to intellectual interests".[4] The number of students a professor could attract was of more importance than their quality, and a cheerful worldliness of wealth and business ambition prevailed as an unquestioned good. All this occasionally drove Santayana to private fury, as in his letters to William James, his tutor and later his chief supporter at Harvard, where Santayana cannot always have been a popular colleague:

> You tax me several times with impertinence and superior airs. I wonder if you realize the years of suppressed irritation which I have passed in the midst of an unintelligible, sanctimonious and often disingenuous Protestantism, which is thoroughly alien and repulsive to me. ... I object to and absolutely abhor ... the assertion that all the eggs indiscriminately are good because the hen has laid them.[5]

He found the academic atmosphere in England different but no more sympathetic. Of the Oxford he knew in the 1880s he wrote: "All in England was a matter of culture, of the pathos of distance, of sentimental religiosity. ... Even the learned and gifted that I saw in Oxford were saturated with affectations."[6] And of English liberalism he wrote, memorably, that "it does not go very deep; it is an adventitious principle, a mere loosening of an older structure." It opens "to all who felt cramped and ill-suited ... that sweet, scholarly, tenderly moral, critically superior attitude of mind which Matthew Arnold called culture."[7] He was no less velvety and no less sharp about the Church of England, in a letter of 1896:

> The more I see of the Church of England the more I admire it, not, you conceive, philosophically or as a thing possible for myself, but as a masterpiece of social diplomacy, by which everything passes off with a

vague dignity, a sense of spiritual elevation is attained, and no harm is done. A real religion, on the other hand, raises the imagination to a higher power, but makes it inapt, and an encumbrance to a man in the business of the world.[8]

This was the man who gave to the young Wallace Stevens, a student at Harvard from 1897 to 1900, not only the certainty that to believe Christianity is true was no longer possible, and the certainty that the vocation of the poet was the highest possible calling in a world that had lost religious conviction, but also a sense of the substance and value of the Catholic faith as "a real religion" that remained in the back of Stevens's mind for the rest of his life. Santayana was also the man who gave to the young T. S. Eliot, a student at Harvard from 1907 to 1910, some of his education in philosophy, his precise appreciation of how the poet's emotions "must at all hazards find or feign their correlative objects",[9] and perhaps above all his awareness of his need for a sustaining tradition in which to live and think and write.

* * *

Wallace Stevens was born in Reading, Pennsylvania, in 1879 to a family of Dutch and German provenance, farmers in Pennsylvania for several generations. His father had left the land to become a schoolteacher and then a lawyer and modest businessman in Reading, not a large city. Stevens's background was, compared to that of many of his Harvard contemporaries, almost that of a country boy; certainly it was provincial, small-town America that he knew best—not patrician, Bostonian New England, but long-farmed land nonetheless, settled by hard-working northern Europeans, with little churches, Lutheran or Presbyterian (in poems of his middle and old age, he remembered both), and rural graveyards where forgotten ancestors lay. Years later, he would make of the park and the river in the New England city where he lived for most of his life something like the countryman's own patch of familiar land in all the weathers of each returning season. He did well at Harvard, becoming an undergraduate literary figure of some note, and was encouraged by Santayana. In a letter he wrote in 1945, he said:

I doubt if Santayana was any more isolated at Cambridge than he wished to be. While I did not take any of his courses and never heard him lecture, he invited me to come to see him a number of times and, in that way, I came to know him a little. I read several poems to him and he expressed his own view of the subject of them in a sonnet which he sent me, and which is in one of his books.... I always came away from my visits to him feeling that he made up in the most genuine way for many things that I needed.[10]

After Harvard, Stevens never saw Santayana again. He tried literary hackwork for a few months in New York, gave it up for law school, became a lawyer, eventually specialising in insurance work, and, after several more years in New York, in 1916 moved with his wife—he married in 1909, after a long courtship, Elsie Moll, a fragile, beautiful girl from a modest Reading family—to Hartford, Connecticut, the insurance capital of the United States, where he worked steadily and very successfully in the same large insurance company until his death in 1955. He was therefore "a man in the business of the world", in Santayana's phrase, and by late middle age a rich man, able, for instance, to buy paintings of the first quality from France. He was also, all his life to its end, a poet of most unusual dedication and single-mindedness who managed, without it becoming "inapt" or "an encumbrance", to raise his imagination "to a higher power", the ambiguity of which phrase he would have appreciated. This double achievement of two quite different and quite separate ends suggests, correctly, rare self-motivation and self-sufficiency in a lonely man who never allowed the two worlds in which he lived to mix and who seems, in a long, disappointing, though kind and faithful marriage, to have shared little of either world with his wife or with their only child.

He knew early this division in himself. As a boy of nineteen, alone in New York in the summer vacation from Harvard, Stevens wrote in a single entry in his journal:

> The feeling of piety is very dear to me. I would sacrifice a great deal to be a Saint Augustine but modernity is so Chicagoan, so plain, so unmeditative. I thoroughly believe that at this very moment I get none of my chief pleasures except from what is unsullied. The love of beauty excludes evil.... The only practical life of the world, as a man of the world, not as a University Professor, a Retired Farmer or Citizen, a Philanthropist, a Preacher, a Poet or the like, but as a bustling merchant, a money-making lawyer, a soldier, a politician, is to be if unavoidable a pseudo-villain in the drama, a decent person in private life.... I'm completely satisfied that behind every physical fact there is a divine force. Don't, therefore look *at* facts, but *through* them.[11]

(The capital letters for the noble occupations tell their own tale.) It is not fanciful to see here the influence of Santayana on an impressionable student to whom "the meditative" in any case came naturally. Where, in Harvard in 1899, was he likely to have heard of Saint Augustine? Probably from a man who wrote of his own father's unquestioned, unquestioning Catholic faith: "Of inner unrest or faith suddenly born out of despair my father had absolutely no notion. Could he ever have read the Confessions of his patron saint, Saint Augustine?" [12]

Stevens in his years alone in New York haunted Saint Patrick's Cathedral, occasionally attended Mass and spent hours "in the dark transept where I go now and then in my more lonely moods". [13] In the summer of 1902, still only twenty-two, he identified in his journal another division in himself, contrasting the God he encountered in the cathedral with the divine presence he sensed, walking in the country, behind the beauty of the earth. "The priest in me worshipped one God at one shrine; the poet another God at another shrine. The priest worshipped Mercy and Love; the poet, Beauty and Might.... As I went tramping through the fields and woods I beheld every leaf and blade of grass revealing or rather betokening the Invisible." [14] He had no one to connect the two for him, as they had been connected, for example, for Hopkins. He makes the same contrast in a warm letter of 1907, encouraging Elsie to join a (presumably Protestant) church:

> One can get a thousand benefits from churches that one cannot get outside of them.... Don't *care* about the Truth. There are other things in Life besides the Truth upon which everybody of any experience agrees, while no two people agree about the Truth.... I am not in the least religious. The sun clears my spirit, if I may say that, and an occasional sight of the sea, and thinking of blue valleys, and the odor of the earth, and many things. Such things make a god of a man; but a chapel makes a man of him. Churches are human.—I say my prayers every night—not that I need them now, or that they are anything more than a habit, half-conscious. But in Spain, in Salamanca, there is a pillar in a church (Santayana told me) worn by the kisses of generations of the devout. One of their kisses are worth all my prayers. [15]

The last record of what it is fair to call the Catholic streak in his youthful mind, given him by Santayana, is in another letter to Elsie, written shortly before their marriage. He was now nearly thirty and, still alone in New York, had spent a Sunday morning wandering about in Manhattan, "stopping once to watch three flocks of pigeons circling in the sky" and then sitting for a while in an Evangelical chapel.

> It happens that last night at the Library I read a life of Jesus and I was interested to see what symbols of that life appeared in the chapel. I think there were none at all excepting the gold cross on the altar. When you compare that poverty with the wealth of symbols, of remembrances, that were created and revered in times past, you appreciate the change that has come over the church. . . . And one turns from this chapel to those built by men who felt the wonder of the life and death of Jesus—temples full of sacred images, full of the air of love and holiness—tabernacles hallowed by worship that sprang from the noble depths of men familiar with Gethsemane, familiar with Jerusalem—I do not wonder that the church is so largely a relic. Its vitality depended on its association with Palestine, so to speak.[16]

Behind both these passages stands the Santayana who at just this time (in 1905–1906) wrote in *The Life of Reason* of the careless atheists of the day:

> They are proud of how much they have rejected, as if a great wit were required to do so. . . . They have discarded the machinery in which their ancestors embodied the ideal; they have not perceived that these symbols stood for the life of reason and gave fantastic and embarrassed expression to what, in itself, is pure humanity; and they have thus remained entangled in the colossal error that ideals are something adventitious and unmeaning, not having a soil in mortal life nor a possible fulfilment there.[17]

If ideals have "a soil in mortal life" but the possibility that Christianity is true is now closed to a rational mind, then the role of the poet—and here Santayana comes close, though from a more rigorous direction, to Arnold—becomes of supreme importance. The poet may be able to meet the spiritual need revealed by the loss of religious faith, a need that certainly was not met by thinned German philosophy.

In 1900 Santayana had published a collection of critical essays under the title *Interpretations of Poetry and Religion*. In his preface, he wrote:

Religion and poetry are identical in essence, and differ merely in the way in which they are attached to practical affairs. Poetry is called religion when it intervenes in life, and religion, when it merely supervenes upon life, is seen to be nothing but poetry. It would naturally follow from this conception that religious doctrines would do well to withdraw their pretentions to be dealing with matters of fact.[18]

The claim to truth has distinguished religion from poetry but should never have been made, for it was no more than "the natural but hopeless misunderstanding of imagining that poetry in order to be religion, in order to be the inspiration of life, must first deny that it is poetry and deceive us about the facts with which we have to deal—this misunderstanding has marred the work of the Christian imagination and condemned it, if we may trust appearances, to be transitory." [19] No wonder Stevens told Elsie, beset with the claims of different sects in Protestant Reading, not to "*care* about the truth". In the last essay in *Interpretations of Poetry and Religion*, Santayana concluded that "the great function of poetry is . . . to build new structures, richer, finer, fitter to the primary tendencies of our nature, to the ultimate possibilities of the soul",[20] and exactly this became the project of Stevens's life as a poet.

So Santanyana opened to the young Stevens a glimpse of the European Catholic past but also closed for him, for almost all Stevens's life, the possibility that Christianity might be true. Both gestures—they were little more than gestures, in the student life of a boy admiring an older, foreign academic—are caught, as if in a snapshot, in Santayana's swift comments in the autobiography he wrote in 1945 on the minor English poet Lionel Johnson, a Catholic convert heading for alcoholism and an early death, whom he had known in Oxford in 1887: "He was not a traditional Catholic, accepting good-naturedly a supernatural economy that happened to prevail in the universe, as political and domestic economy prevail in one's earthly fortunes. Nor was he a philosopher, enduring the truth." [21] But Santayana also, without doubt, at least contributed to Stevens's lasting conviction that it was the duty of the serious poet to write toward "the ultimate possibilities of the soul", to meet in some fashion the spiritual need, the spiritual poverty, of people living in the wreckage of the religion of the past.

Stevens's first great poem, "Sunday Morning",[22] written in 1914–1915 and published in Harriet Monroe's magazine *Poetry* in 1915, is a woman's meditation, but "anybody's meditation", Stevens said later, "on religion and the meaning of life".[23] It is an elegy, in feeling and in shape not unlike a Keats ode, with eight fifteen-line stanzas in fluent, resonant, unrhymed iambic pentameters, on the lost possibility that Christianity might be true. The beauty of the earth, the seasons, the weather, trees, birds, fruit, rivers—simple, natural beauty, as in Emily Dickinson's poems—is affirmed as all the beauty there is. "There is not any haunt of prophecy", and no "imperishable bliss", for

> Death is the mother of beauty; hence from her,
> Alone, shall come fulfilment to our dreams
> And our desires.

The poem ends with an unforgettably beautiful stanza that begins:

> She hears, upon that water without sound,
> A voice that cries, "The tomb in Palestine
> Is not the porch of spirits lingering.
> It is the grave of Jesus, where he lay."

and ends with the pigeons, perhaps, of that Sunday in Manhattan:

> And, in the isolation of the sky,
> At evening, casual flocks of pigeons make
> Ambiguous undulations as they sink,
> Downward to darkness, on extended wings.

The total effect of the poem is as ambiguous as the pigeons' flight. Its notes of celebration are constantly deepened by chords of sadness, and its lines on the Incarnation, in the third stanza, seem to the reader briefly, but lastingly, as positive as the lines on the Resurrection are negative:

> Jove in the clouds had his inhuman birth.
> No mother suckled him, no sweet land gave
> Large-mannered motions to his mythy mind
> He moved among us, as a muttering king,
> Magnificent, would move among his hinds,
> Until our blood, commingling, virginal,
> With heaven, brought such requital to desire
> The very hinds discerned it, in a star.

The mind of God might be "mythy", but he moved (it) among us until his muttering became the incarnate Word: the effect on the reader of this statement, withdrawn later in the poem, is lasting nonetheless, like the effect of Milton's list of flowers for Lycidas's nonexistent bier, or of Mulciber falling from the sky: "Thus they relate, erring". In "Sunday Morning", the young man in the church and the young man tramping the fields are both still present, unreconciled.

In 1923 *Harmonium*, Stevens's first book, was published. He was forty-four when it appeared; by then, he had been writing poems for a quarter of a century. *Harmonium* is a rich collection of poems, relaxed and confident in manner, often celebratory, yet often desolate, the poet's moods sometimes, as in "Sunday Morning", colliding in the harmonies of the book's title, sometimes separated into poems of, as it were, a single melody. Its longest poem, "The Comedian as the Letter C",[24] is a self-mocking narrative from which the poet emerges as a figure more absurd than grandly able to fulfil "the great function of poetry". Another long poem, "Le Monocle de Mon Oncle"[25]—Stevens's bizarre titles sometimes suggest an embarrassment at the emotional weight of his poems—is a tired, middle-aged lament:

> I am a man of fortune greeting heirs;
> For it has come that thus I greet the spring.

and a disillusioned reflection on, one may reasonably guess, the failure of his marriage to move from romantic passion into intimate companionship. The poem begins with a bitter apostrophe, recalling prayers to our Lady, to an ideal both held and destroyed:

> "Mother of heaven, regina of the clouds,
> O sceptre of the sun, crown of the moon,
> There is not nothing, no, no, never nothing,
> Like the clashed edges of two words that kill."
> And so I mocked her in magnificent measure.
> Or was it that I mocked myself alone?

The powerful ambiguity of the third line haunts the rest of the poem. In the seventh of twelve long stanzas, there is another equivocal, beautiful reference to the Incarnation:

The mules that angels ride come slowly down
The blazing passes, from beyond the sun.
Descensions of their tinkling bells arrive.
These muleteers are dainty of their way.
Meantime, centurions guffaw and beat
Their shrilling tankards on the table-boards.
This parable, in sense, amounts to this:
The honey of heaven may or may not come,
But that of earth both comes and goes at once.
Suppose these couriers brought amid their train
A damsel heightened by eternal bloom.

This figure reappears in another exquisite *Harmonium* poem, "To the One of Fictive Music".[26] Here she is even more "an anticipation of perfection", even more reminiscent of the ancient, consoling Madonna, given "fantastic and embarrassed expression"—the phrases are Santayana's—because her music is "fictive", made by the poet, who can make up his words, but not his mind, about her. This poem, too long to quote in its entirety, begins:

Sister and mother and diviner love,
And of the sisterhood of the living dead
Most near, most clear, and of the clearest bloom.

The poet refers forlornly, in passing, to the "difference that heavenly pity brings", but ends:

Unreal, give back to us what once you gave:
The imagination that we spurned and crave.

(Is it possible to pray to a listener of whose reality one is not certain? Of course it is.)

The shorter poems in *Harmonium* include some famous pieces—for example, "The Snow Man", "The Emperor of Ice-Cream", "The Death of a Soldier" and "Valley Candle"—registering in different ways ultimate nothingness or the finality of death. One of them, "Of Heaven Considered as a Tomb",[27] ends with a poignant evocation of the poet's solitary call to the silent dead, for a moment colouring their blankness:

Make hue among the dark comedians,
Halloo them in the topmost distances
For answer from their icy Elysée.

Another short anthology piece, "Anecdote of the Jar",[28] ruefully mocks the grandiose effort of the poet, who attempts with his few words to make "the slovenly wilderness" surround the hill on which he places his jar: "The jar was gray and bare." That the poem briefly triumphs over its own bleakness is true of this as of a number of Stevens's short pieces throughout his writing life.

Harmonium was little noticed and little read. After its discouraging failure, Stevens wrote scarcely any new poems for nearly ten years.

* * *

The attention of the literary world was elsewhere. The years 1922–1923 were the *anni mirabiles* of modernism. In Europe, in the emotional and spiritual dereliction that followed the 1914–1918 war, there appeared in 1922 James Joyce's *Ulysses* and Paul Valéry's *Charmes*, the latter a collection of poems that included Valéry's "Le Cimetière marin", a long, beautiful, difficult elegy for the death of Christianity and the millions dead in the war; the poem's Pindaric epigraph could have been *Harmonium*'s: "My soul, do not seek immortal life, but exhaust the realm of the possible." In 1923 Rainer Maria Rilke's *Duino Elegies* and *Sonnets to Orpheus* were published, demonstrating (to those who could read German) the astonishing victory of a poet's efforts to generate his own sufficient, Godless meaning in the ruins of faith and of everyday political life. Joyce, Valéry and Rilke, building masterpieces from the rubble of the past, which included broken pieces of the Christianity each had rejected, had all received a strict, orthodox Catholic upbringing. Another central writer at this extraordinary moment in literary history had not. T. S. Eliot's *The Waste Land* was published in London, in the first issue of his literary quarterly, *The Criterion*, in December 1922.

Eliot was born in 1888, nine years after Stevens, in Saint Louis, Missouri, on the Mississippi River, far to the west and south of the patrician New England to which his father's family, seventeenth-century arrivals from England, belonged. His grandfather was a Unitarian minister; his first cousin, Frederick Eliot, became president of the American Unitarian Society; and a more distant relative, Charles Eliot Norton, was the presiding genius of the liberal, vaguely Protestant, Harvard described by Santayana, where Eliot was an undergraduate from 1907. Eliot left America for Germany early in 1914 and, after a spell in Paris, arrived in

Oxford as an advanced student of philosophy in the autumn of that year, when war between Germany and both France and England had begun. Except for short visits, he never returned to America, and in 1927 he became a naturalised Englishman and a convert to the Anglican church. With, thereafter, a profound loyalty to the short period in the history of the Church of England that had been almost Catholic—the period of Lancelot Andrewes, Donne, Archbishop Laud, Nicholas Ferrar and Charles I—and a personal commitment to the Anglo-Catholic *via media* first defended and then abandoned by Newman, Eliot had found himself a tradition. Perhaps Santayana at Harvard had contributed to his powerful sense both that a tradition was what he needed and that the liberal Unitarianism in which he had been brought up was too lacking in nourishment to sustain either his writing or his life. In a short early poem, "Cousin Nancy",[29] he mocked both the conventions of aristocratic New England and the frivolous breaking of them by the "modern" young. Over the last three lines, Arnold and Emerson, neglected, preside nonetheless:

> Upon the glazen shelves kept watch
> Matthew and Waldo, guardians of the faith,
> The army of unalterable law.

But Christianity of any colour was not what the young Eliot, after five years in England, meant by "tradition". In his famous essay of 1919, "Tradition and the Individual Talent", he locates himself—the essay is about himself as a poet—in the European literary tradition and announces that consciousness of this tradition is essential to the new poet, whose work, if "really new", will alter the whole tradition by joining it; knowledge of the tradition "cannot be inherited, and if you want it you must obtain it by great labour".[30] The process of learning the tradition, so as, however subtly, to refigure all of it, involves the self-abnegation of the poet: "The progress of an artist is a continual self-sacrifice, a continual extinction of personality."[31] The composition of poems themselves also requires self-abnegation: "Poetry is not a turning loose of emotion, but an escape from emotion; it is not the expression of personality, but an escape from personality."[32]

If this hugely influential essay is an exercise in self-advertisement, it is also an exercise in self-admonition, possibly even self-delusion. Eliot's first volume of poems, *Prufrock and Other Observations*, twelve poems in all, headed by "The Love Song of J. Alfred Prufrock" (like "Sunday Morning", first published in *Poetry* in 1915) appeared in 1917. It is clear from these early poems that Eliot had a gift for indelibly memorable, unparaphrasable lines. It is also clear, and clearer still from his second, even shorter, collection (including four poems in French) three years later, that escaping from his personality was, as it would remain, an aspiration rather than an achievement. The poems in these two books are brilliant, brittle, world-weary, cynical and—with one exception, "La Figlia Che Piange"—ruthlessly destructive of anything that could be described as "romantic", either sexually or in affiliation to the past. This clever, sophisticated young American had surveyed European civilisation and found in it no more of a congenial home than he had found in the New England he had left. This is hardly surprising. In England, Eliot had joined a generation of young men who fought, suffered and very often died in a terrible war beyond his own experience. The "Prufrock" volume is dedicated to a Frenchman of his own age, whom Eliot met and left in Paris and was then killed in the Dardanelles. None of these early poems explicitly refers to the war, but together they are, among many other things, a report from the London of the home front and of the war's aftermath; of winter and fog and drabness; of shallow encounters and shallow conversation; and of the presence, horrible to a poet desperate to be assimilated to a steady world, of stray foreigners, refugees and, worst of all (in Eliot's notorious view), Jews, rootless after the convulsion of the war. Eliot in 1915 entered into what quickly became a miserably unhappy marriage: sexual disgust is a recurring note in these poems. As for Christianity, two poems in the second volume—"The Hippopotamus" and "Mr Eliot's Sunday Morning Service"—written in dismissive, rhymed ballad-stanzas, the second with an extreme cleverness of diction ("polyphiloprogenitive" and "piaculative" [33] are invented words, though of obvious meaning), treat the Church as a sick, romantic temptation to be inspected, with contempt, at a hygienic distance. Positive emotion may be escaped from in all these poems, but only into negative emotion.

Negative emotion, compounded of these same elements of cold distrust of people displaced by the war, sexual revulsion and fascination with, and fear of, surrender to love, to death and to belief informs the jagged sections of Eliot's first masterpiece, *The Waste Land*.[34] A long poem, considerably longer before it was pruned by Eliot's generous poetic mentor Ezra Pound, *The Waste Land* throws together, in a prevailing mood of fitfully lit despair, fragments—"These fragments I have shored against my ruins",[35] runs a line at the poem's end—from the European literary tradition, the whole of which the poem is, presumably, intended slightly to alter. London is the outer edge of Dante's Inferno, with occasional glances forward to Purgatory. Echoes and thefts from Scripture, from Shakespeare and from many other texts abound, broken and scattered. Remembered couplings of high literary glamour—Dido and Aeneas, Tristan and Isolde, Antony and Cleopatra, Elizabeth and Leicester—are undercut with present sexual squalor. The war, for once explicitly present, has thrown long-absent soldiers back to their wives, only to make the wives' wretched lives more wretched. Glancing references to Augustine, to Buddha and to the Upanishads suggest conceivable redemption, or at least purgation, in ascesis, but a mysterious reminiscence of the road to Emmaus is quickly cancelled in a Boschlike nightmare. *The Waste Land* is a poem of complex desperation, removed by a vast emotional distance from the unafraid, lyrical grief for lost Christian belief that appears occasionally in Stevens's early poems.

Eliot, publishing his own work as a director of Faber and Faber from 1925, was careful in his *Collected Poems* to date every collection and every substantial individual poem, as if to chart for the reader the progress of his soul toward the settled Anglican conviction at which he arrived in 1928. His last poem of fear and despair, "The Hollow Men" of 1925, culminates in a fractured phrase from the Anglican Lord's Prayer: "*For Thine is the Kingdom* / For Thine is / Life is / For Thine is the".[36] In "Journey of the Magi" (1927), the desolate old men of "Gerontion" (1920) and "The Hollow Men" have become the deeply disturbed Magi, recognising in the birth at Bethlehem what is also "our death", the death of "the old dispensation".[37] Then all these old men are replaced, in "A Song for Simeon" (1928), by the consoled Simeon, knowing "the time of sorrow"[38] that is ahead but awaiting his own death lightly, in the full spirit of the *Nunc dimittis*. Eliot is now an early Stuart Anglican; Lancelot Andrewes, from whom he took the resonant opening of "Journey of the Magi", is his model. Of Andrewes he wrote:

> Latimer, the preacher of Henry VIII and Edward VI, is merely a Protestant; but the voice of Andrewes is the voice of a man who has a formed visible Church behind him, who speaks with the old authority and the new culture.[39]

Andrewes's church, as Eliot explains at the start of his tribute, was formed by Elizabeth I as a political compromise three years after Andrewes was born; "the old authority" is a curious phrase to use of a bishop necessarily, if not "merely", Protestant.

It is in the preface to his collection of essays, entitled *For Lancelot Andrewes*, published in 1928, that Eliot declared that he was "classical in literature, royalist in politics, and Anglo-Catholic in religion".[40] This position had been difficult for Dr. Johnson to sustain in the middle of the eighteenth century; in the twentieth it was easier, if only because by then most people in the English literary world cared little about any of these three loyalties. Two poignant passages from letters Eliot wrote in this same year show the depth of his need for the security his adopted loyalties gave him. On Shrove Tuesday, he wrote to Paul Elmer More, an American friend, theologian and classical scholar, of those "'for whom religion is wholly unnecessary":

> They may be very good, or very happy, they simply seem to miss nothing, to be unconscious of any void—the void that I find in the middle of all human happiness and all human relations, and which there is only one thing to fill. I am one whom this sense of void tends to drive towards asceticism or sensuality, and only Christianity helps to reconcile me to life, which is otherwise disgusting.[41]

Two months later, he wrote to Herbert Read, fellow poet and fellow critic, a Yorkshireman who had been a soldier throughout the war and who much later died three miles from where he was born:

> Some day I want to write an essay about the point of view of an American who wasn't an American, because he was born in the South and went to school in New England as a small boy with a nigger drawl, but who wasn't a southerner in the South because his people were northerners in a border state and looked down on all southerners and Virginians, and who so was never anything anywhere and who therefore felt himself to be more a Frenchman than an American and more an Englishman than a Frenchman and yet felt that the U.S.A. up to a hundred years ago was a family extension.[42]

Here is the key to Eliot's feeling for England: in America the "family extension" had been spoiled, diluted, sullied by foreigners. In 1934, in *After Strange Gods*, his protofascist blood-and-soil lectures delivered in Virginia (and left out of his list of prose works in his 1963 *Collected Poems*), he told his audience:

> I think that the chances for the re-establishment of a native culture are perhaps better here than in New England. You are farther away from New York; you have been less industrialized and less invaded by foreign races.[43]

As late as 1949 he wrote:

> It would appear to be for the best that the great majority of human beings should go on living in the place in which they were born. Family, class and local loyalty all support each other; and if one of these decays, the others will suffer also.[44]

In telling contrast, Stevens, in a little piece on Connecticut, written at the very end of his life, said:

> There are no foreigners in Connecticut. Once you are here you are or you are on your way to become a Yankee.... Going back to Connecticut is a return to an origin. And as it happens, it is an origin which many men all over the world, both those who have been part of us and those who have not, share in common: an origin of hardihood, good faith and good will.[45]

There is here an exemplary "Americanness" toward which Eliot felt neither sympathy nor loyalty.

*   *   *

"Ash-Wednesday",[46] the poem of Eliot's conversion, was published in 1930. Tentative, oblique and thoroughly Christian, it gently stacks images and prayers of light and consolation against darkness, nightmare and horrors of a kind familiar from his earlier work, always uncertainly, as if the light might yet not overcome the dark. The rose of Dante's paradise now shines:

> The single Rose
> Is now the Garden
> Where all loves end
> Terminate torment
> Of love unsatisfied
> The greater torment
> Of love satisfied
> End of the endless
> Journey to no end[47]

But after moments of blessing, desolation returns, and Eliot loads with negative ambiguity the phrase from the *Salve Regina* with which he ends the glimpsed redemption of part 4, "And after this our exile", managing to imply an absent comma after "this".

The line is one of many quotations in "Ash-Wednesday" from Catholic prayers, from the Mass, from the Good Friday liturgy and from the preliminary prayer of the penitent, "Bless me father", at confession. The whole poem's quiet conclusion is a prayer to our Lady (in strange coincidence recalling Stevens's prayer "To the One of Fictive Music"):

Blessèd sister, holy mother, spirit of the fountain, spirit of the garden,
Suffer us not to mock ourselves with falsehood
Teach us to care and not to care
Teach us to sit still
Even among these rocks,
Our peace in His Will
And even among these rocks
Sister, mother
And spirit of the river, spirit of the sea,
Suffer us not to be separated

And let my cry come unto Thee.[48]

The last line is from the Anglican liturgy (where it is, of course, addressed to God); "Our peace in His will" is Dante's; the penultimate line is from the priest's prayer at Communion in the Mass, "et a te nunquam separari permittas", and is the phrase quoted twice by Pascal in the Memorial.

Why did Eliot, with his consciousness of the European tradition, his love for Virgil and Dante and his respect for Pascal (he wrote an appreciative introduction to the *Pensées* in 1931), not become a Roman Catholic? The answer, given by himself, is that Englishness mattered most to him. In 1931, in "Thoughts after Lambeth", an essay on the current state of the Church of England, he wrote:

With all due respect, the Roman Church is in England a sect. It is easier for the Church of England to become Catholic, than for the Church of Rome in England to become English.[49]

And in *After Strange Gods*, he mentioned Hopkins with this jarring comment:

> To be converted, in any case, while it is sufficient for entertaining the hope
> of individual salvation, is not going to do for a man, as a writer, what his
> ancestry and his country for some generations have failed to do.[50]

This sentence casts a revealing light on Eliot's priorities. In 1949 he expanded,
with special pleading, his defence of his own choice:

> In England, the main cultural tradition has for several centuries been Angli-
> can. Roman Catholics in England are, of course, in a more central Euro-
> pean tradition than are Anglicans; yet, because the main tradition of England
> has been Anglican, they are in another aspect more outside of the tra-
> dition than are Protestant dissenters. . . . It is always the main religious body
> which is the guardian of more of the remains of the higher develop-
> ments of culture preserved from a past time before the division took place.
> Not only is it the main religious body which has the more elaborated the-
> ology; it is the main religious body which is the least alienated from the
> best intellectual and artistic activity of its time.[51]

Some of this is untrue, notably "the more elaborated theology". All of it is, to say
the least, tendentious. What of Milton, Bunyan, Blake, Wordsworth (at his best),
Byron, Shelley, Keats and Arnold? What, nearer home for the "classical" Eliot, of
Dryden and Pope, the former a convert and the latter a born Roman Catholic?
Only Herbert, Swift, Johnson and Coleridge really support Eliot's case. With Coleridge the later Eliot, in his concern to convert educated England to an Anglican
consensus, had most in common. But Coleridge he despised, dismissing both the
Shakespeare criticism and *Biographia Literaria* almost without qualification, having
pronounced that Coleridge "had no vocation for the religious life. . . . He was condemned to know that the little poetry he had written was worth more than all he
could do with the rest of his life. The author of *Biographia Literaria* was already a
ruined man. Sometimes, however, to be a 'ruined man' is itself a vocation."[52] The
cruelty of this is exceeded only by its inaccuracy. Perhaps Eliot had not noticed
that Coleridge was the greatest Anglican writer on Christian life and the Christian church since the seventeenth century because he had not read the *Lay Sermons*,
Aids to Reflection or *On the Constitution of the Church and State*. Perhaps he had not
read them because he had collected from Arnold, whom he regarded as "rather a
friend than a leader",[53] a lofty snobbery he found congenial. Eliot wrote of Arnold:

"It is a pleasure, certainly, after associating with the riff-raff of the early part of the [nineteenth] century, to be in the company of a man *qui sait se conduire*." [54] As for Newman, whose life and writing had definitively changed the relation of English Catholics to "the main tradition of England", Eliot mentions him occasionally, and with respect, but as if Newman had never left the Anglican church.

In 1935 Eliot wrote *Murder in the Cathedral*, as notable a success as it was hard to achieve, a non-Shakespearean English play in verse. He must have found the subject at least as difficult as the form he chose: Thomas Becket was a Roman Catholic martyr, killed, if less deliberately, in the cause for which Thomas More was martyred four centuries later. The twelfth century was sufficiently different from the sixteenth for Becket's martyrdom to have defeated Henry II and naturally allowed Eliot to establish a fully Catholic atmosphere. But Eliot hedged his bets by giving the murdering knights some strong arguments for what would be Henry VIII's successful detachment of the English church from Rome.

Eliot, in the same year, developed some writing left over from the finished play and called the result "Burnt Norton", the first poem of what, seven years later, was completed as his last major poetic work, *Four Quartets*. [55] These poems have an unassailable place near the summit of twentieth-century English poetry. They are full, as is always the case with Eliot, of lines hard to forget. They are also generally regarded as a Christian masterpiece, the last poem, "Little Gidding", and one passage in "The Dry Salvages" perhaps rightly. But, though the sexual revulsion, the Boschlike horror and the moments of sheer nastiness of much of the earlier poetry have disappeared, the whole work's impact on the reader is still one of desolation, anxiety and fear, only now and then resolved into fleeting affirmations of the positive. "Now and then" is an apposite phrase. "Burnt Norton", retaining some of *Murder in the Cathedral*'s emphasis on the *kairos*, the significant moment at which the sacrifice of the self is required, is a meditation on time, which delivers an exalted version of Wordsworth's insistence on the sustaining quality of remembered, irrecoverable "spots of time", moments of apprehended beauty, here a rose garden, or the vision of a rose garden never entered, children laughing, water. The fourth and fifth lines of the poem are already despairing:

> If all time is eternally present
> All time is unredeemable. [56]

And almost at the end of this first movement—there are five in each "Quartet"— there is a famous statement, as the memory of a magical moment vanishes, that appears also in *Murder in the Cathedral*:

Go, said the bird, for the leaves were full of children,
Hidden excitedly, containing laughter.
Go, go, go, said the bird: human kind
Cannot bear very much reality.[57]

Glimpses of release from the constriction of time and from the urban wasteland reinvoked here are given only to the soul that can

Descend lower, descend only
Into the world of perpetual solitude,
World not world, but that which is not world,
Internal darkness, deprivation
And destitution of all property,
Desiccation of the world of sense,
Evacuation of the world of fancy,
Inoperancy of the world of spirit.[58]

This is the way of abnegation of some late medieval mystics, or perhaps Saint John of the Cross's "dark night". But there is no consoling suggestion of the eventual presence of God, only a brief recovery, at the poem's end, of that "spot of time":

There rises the hidden laughter
Of children in the foliage
Quick, now, here, now, always—
Ridiculous the waste sad time
Stretching before and after.[59]

"Burnt Norton" is a ruined house in Gloucestershire, not that it appears in the poem. "East Coker", the title of the second poem, is a village in Somerset that Eliot's forefathers left for Massachusetts in the seventeenth century: this poem is a home-coming to the ancestral ground under his feet he so much needed, and a resonant verse-paragraph in the first movement recalls his walk into the village. But the poem, earthy, even muddy, has no note of security, let alone exhilaration. Physical life "whirled in a vortex" toward "destructive fire", everyone and everything pulled toward death—as in Hopkins, but with no countervailing promise of resurrection—is powerfully presented, with echoes of Ecclesiastes's "A time to be born and a time to die".[60] Sixteenth-century peasants, evoked, dancing at a wedding, with phrases from Sir Thomas Elyot, who died in 1546, end in "Dung and death"; the rich and powerful of today end in death; "the laughter in the garden" recurs, but as

> echoed ecstasy
> Not lost, but requiring, pointing to the agony
> Of death and birth.[61]

Eliot himself, dissatisfied in two substantial passages with his efforts as a poet, is lost, like Dante beginning the *Commedia*, "in the middle of the way", and

> not only in the middle of the way
> But all the way, in a dark wood, in a bramble,
> On the edge of a grimpen, where is no secure foothold,
> And menaced by monsters, fancy lights,
> Risking enchantment. Do not let me hear
> Of the wisdom of old men, but rather of their folly,
> Their fear of fear and frenzy, their fear of possession,
> Of belonging to another, or to others, or to God.
> The only wisdom we can hope to acquire
> Is the wisdom of humility: humility is endless.[62]

The fourth movement—each "Quartet" has a kind of Andante at this point, as each has a rhymed, formal lyric at the start of its second movement—is a grim, five-stanza, tightly rhymed and metred summary of Christian doctrine on the Incarnation, Atonement, original sin, Purgatory and the Eucharist. This declaration conveys no warmth; it is distanced from the reader by stark medical imagery and a tone of voice more angry than anguished, as if all this is true but its very truth is resented. It is a statement of faith as far removed as it could be from "the wisdom of humility". The whole poem ends more quietly, even with a tentative hope

> For a further union, a deeper communion
> Through the dark cold and the empty desolation. . . .[63]

"Further" and "deeper", the reader cannot help wondering, than what?

The third Quartet, "The Dry Salvages", is a poem of water and also of America rather than England—of the great river, the Mississippi of Eliot's childhood, and the foggy, treacherous coast of Massachusetts. The second movement's lyric is an awkward near-sestina on the endless destructiveness of the sea, with the barest suggestion, not even in a completed sentence, of consolation at its end:

> Only the hardly, barely prayable
> Prayer of the one Annunciation.[64]

This is at once succeeded by a bleak, plodding passage of doubt and regret, explicit as prose is explicit. The third movement comes alive, but only to suggest the journey of every human being toward death—"(And the time of death is every moment)"—while the fourth, the Andante, is, suddenly, a simple, moving prayer to our Lady for the sea's dead. In the fifth, the sinister fortune-telling of *The Waste Land* reappears, to be cancelled in the miracle of the Incarnation:

> But to apprehend
> The point of intersection of the timeless
> With time, is an occupation for the saint—
> No occupation either, but something given
> And taken in a lifetime's death in love,
> Ardour and selflessness and self-surrender.[65]

The strenuous abstract nouns of the last line are too much for nearly everyone: "For most of us" there are only the remembered, perhaps saving, "spots of time", and

> These are only hints and guesses,
> Hints followed by guesses; and the rest
> Is prayer, observance, discipline, thought and action.

The hint half-guessed, the gift half-understood, is the Incarnation. "The rest" is a great deal, almost all of life—as if Christian faith were only a matter of very occasional Wordsworthian moments—and is dimmed in another list of exhortatory abstract nouns. However, there follows a Christian assertion more definite than any in the *Quartets* so far, now of the redemption of time and of the freedom, which means responsibility, given to all of us by the coming of Christ:

> Here the impossible union
> Of spheres of existence is actual,
> Here the past and future
> Are conquered, and reconciled,

> Where action were otherwise movement
> Of that which is only moved
> And has in it no source of movement—
> Driven by daemonic, chthonic
> Powers.

But the poem ends only with Eliot again longing for his place in his own ground:

> We, content at the last
> If our temporal reversion nourish
> (Not too far from the yew-tree)
> The life of significant soil.[66]

In the last Quartet, "Little Gidding", Eliot is back in England, in the Huntingdonshire village where Nicholas Ferrar's community took Anglican life in the 1620s and 1630s to a high point of holiness revered by Eliot not least for the visit of Charles I, "a broken king". The trajectory of *Four Quartets* sank to the earth of "East Coker" from the air of "Burnt Norton", widened to the death-bringing waters of "The Dry Salvages" and now rises to the "pentecostal fire" of a place "Where prayer has been valid". Only this, only "the communication of the dead", "what the dead had no speech for, when living", makes Little Gidding "the world's end", the edge of death, that the poet needs it to be. For, as the varying music of *Four Quartets* suggests over and over again, the world, reality, is redeemed for him only in pure transcendence.

> There are other places
> Which also are the world's end, some at the sea jaws,
> Or over a dark lake, in a desert or a city—
> But this is the nearest, in place and time,
> Now and in England.[67]

(There is an inscription over the door of the little chapel that survives at Little Gidding: "This is none other than the gate of heaven.")[68]

The rhymed lyric that begins the second movement and the rhymed Andante that is the fourth are both weak sections of the poem; it is as if the other ways in which Eliot writes with such felicity have given rhyme an inevitable irony or distance. But the second part of the second movement, in the other *Quartets* discursively prosaic, is here the most memorable, the most realised, passage of the whole work—an encounter, in a deserted, air-raided London street (this is 1942), with "a familiar compound ghost".[69] The ghost, described with a quotation from Dante's meeting with his old teacher Brunetto Latini halfway down the circles of hell, is "some dead master", partly Dante himself, partly Virgil (there is a reference to Palinurus, who "left [his] body on a distant shore" and whose spirit met Aeneas in the underworld). The ghost's message to the poet is a deeply gloomy prediction of the irritations, the miseries and the remorse of old age, until the last line and a half:

> From wrong to wrong the exasperated spirit
> Proceeds, unless restored by that refining fire
> Where you must move in measure, like a dancer.[70]

The refining fire is purgatorial—though Purgatory was closed to Latini, who was condemned to hell—but also, in this poem, pentecostal; the dance suggests Dante's paradise. The whole passage is arranged on the page in Dantesque tercets, though the arrangement has little bearing on the long sentences, and the lines are unrhymed.

The third movement begins with long prosy lines full of abstract nouns; the effect is of daylight bathos after the high emotion of the dawn meeting with the ghost. But the lines shorten with a quotation from the fourteenth-century mystic Julian of Norwich:

> Sin is Behovely, but
> All shall be well, and
> All manner of thing shall be well.

The prayer at first seems forlorn in the immediate context, but it leads the reader into a meditation on the English civil war and on the deaths of Charles I, Strafford and Laud, and then of their enemy, Milton, with the assertion that all of them are now "folded in a single party":

> We cannot revive old factions
> We cannot restore old policies
> Or follow an antique drum.[71]

There is nothing in the poem to underpin this sudden reconciliation, or self-admonition, and five years later the royalist, Anglo-Catholic Eliot wrote, while explaining the antipathy to Milton that he shared with Johnson, "The fact is simply that the Civil War of the seventeenth century, in which Milton is a symbolic figure, has never been concluded." [72]

The last movement of "Little Gidding" recapitulates, in a kind of trance, the leading motives (the music is as Wagnerian as that of *The Waste Land*) of all four *Quartets*: the hope for achieved poetry that is personal but also impersonal, "Every poem an epitaph"; the hope that death aquires meaning in the uniting of personal history with national history; the hope that the moments of blessing remembered in "Burnt Norton" are redeemed into an eternity where Julian of Norwich will be right and Dante's vision at the end of the *Paradiso* will come true in

> A condition of complete simplicity
> (Costing not less than everything)
> And all shall be well and
> All manner of thing shall be well
> When the tongues of flame are in-folded
> Into the crowned knot of fire
> And the fire and the rose will be one. [73]

Four Quartets, as the last movement of "Little Gidding" suggests, is best understood as a work of personal conclusion, as a series of oblique, provisional replies to the questions: What is a poet, this particular poet, trying to do? Where are roots to be sunk that will hold? What can, truthfully and with prayer, be believed? A suffering Christian who chose to sink his roots in the Anglo-Catholic *via media*, for which Little Gidding is the image and the model, wrote these poems, which are never forgotten by anyone who has read them carefully. Thus to describe them as notes toward the autobiography of a soul is only to acknowledge that they are a conclusive demonstration of the definition of a poem given by Eliot twenty years before he wrote them:

> It is a concentration, and a new thing resulting from the concentration,
> of a very great number of experiences which to the practical and active
> person would not seem to be experiences at all. [74]

It was in the same essay that he said: "The progress of an artist is a continual self-sacrifice, a continual extinction of personality." [75] But impersonal *Four Quartets* is not, and this is just as well. These poems include the reader in "a very great number of experiences", among them rare glimpses of the love and mercy of God that were the poet's own and for which he finds words of which no reader would ever have thought.

Eliot as impersonal judge—as a critic of literature, society, belief and other people's aspirations—was, by contrast, a shutter-out, a chilling excluder. In 1927, the year before he joined the Anglican church, he wrote: "The majority of people live below the level of belief or doubt. It takes application and a kind of genius to believe anything." [76] Six years later, with convert ruthlessness, he wrote: "A poet may borrow a philosophy or he may do without one.... If you find that you must do without something, such as religious faith or philosophic belief, then you must just do without it." [77] (What he meant by "philosophic belief" is far from clear, particularly as Wordsworth and Shelley are his examples of poets who had "a philosophy".) The question a Christian asks in relation to both these remarks is, "What of the grace of God?" He receives a positive reply from very few passages in *Four Quartets*; a sense of sustaining confidence in the fullness of faith in Christ, or of devoted awe before the truth that "the world is charged with the grandeur of God", he does not receive.

After *Four Quartets*, Eliot wrote more essays and four ambitious, awkward plays, but no more major poems: only a handful of slight "occasional verses" follow the *Quartets* in his carefully dated *Collected Poems*. He glancingly refers to himself as an "old man" several times in the *Quartets*, though he was only fifty-four when he wrote "Little Gidding" and had more than twenty years to live, as the most distinguished literary figure in England. In 1948 he received both the Order of Merit, the grandest honour conferred by the English monarch, and the Nobel Prize for literature.

* * *

Meanwhile, in Hartford, Connecticut, receiving no prizes and scarcely any recognition until he was over seventy, Stevens, after the almost poemless period that followed the publication of *Harmonium*, continued quietly to devote his private time to writing. Though they lived in different worlds—Stevens never crossed the Atlantic, and his keen sense of Europe, particularly France, was nourished only by books, paintings and postcards from friends—the poetic careers of Eliot and Stevens followed strangely parallel courses; that is, until Eliot's stopped. "The Love Song of J. Alfred Prufrock" and "Sunday Morning", each revealing a startling new talent to the world, had been published in the same magazine in the same year; eight years later, *The Waste Land* and *Harmonium* appeared within months of each other, the electric crackle of the first subduing to near inaudibility the deeper music of the second. The year 1942, which saw the publication of the completed *Four Quartets*, also saw the publication, much less noticed even in America, of Stevens's longest and equally remarkable poem, *Notes toward a Supreme Fiction*.

Between 1935 and the appearance of *Notes*, Stevens, always more prolific than Eliot, published three books, amounting to more than 150 pages, of poems. The titles of these books, *Ideas of Order*, *The Man with the Blue Guitar* and *Parts of a World*, accurately suggest the poet, alone with the resources of his intelligence and his imagination—blue, in Stevens, is always the colour of the imagination—strumming, picking out his own tunes, to make some sense, his own sense, of a world of chaos and spiritual poverty (a key Stevens word) but also of beauty and perceived possibilities of order. The earth is reality—rich, full and green in summer in the South, but bare and cold in the North in winter; it is what the poet, like all of us, has for the play, the work, of his imagination, which is of the unreal yet perhaps more real. These are the terms, ordinary and recognisable by anyone, of Stevens's poems, Stevens's mind. Whereas Eliot needed Christianity to "fill the void" and because life is "otherwise disgusting", Stevens thought and wrote his experimental way toward something that would, perhaps, confirm that his responsiveness to beauty, his love for the earth and his sense that poetry was for him a serious, lifelong vocation all had somewhere, somehow, a sufficient meaning. In some notes he wrote in a letter of 1940 to help a friend with a few difficult poems in *Ideas of Order*, Stevens said:

> I ought to say that it is a habit of mind with me to be thinking of some substitute for religion. I don't necessarily mean some substitute for the church, because no one believes in the church as an institution more than I do. My trouble, and the trouble of a great many people, is the loss of belief in the sort of God in Whom we were all brought up to believe. Humanism would be the natural substitute, but the more I see of humanism the less I like it.

Later in the letter, he says: "What keeps me alive is the fury of the desire to get somewhere with all this, in the midst of all the other things that one has to do." [78]

Stevens's best critic, Helen Vendler, was right to call him "a poet knowable in the instance only when he is known in the whole", [79] and it is possible here only to indicate, with a very few poems as signposts, his path, with many experimental directions and many dead ends, through this middle period of his writing, which should also include the more than fifty poems of *Transport to Summer*

(1947). One piece in *Parts of a World* is called "Of Modern Poetry";[80] it catches
well Stevens's sense of where he has no choice but to be. It begins:

> The poem of the mind in the act of finding
> What will suffice. It has not always had
> To find: the scene was set; it repeated what
> Was in the script.
> 　　　　　　　　Then the theatre was changed
> To something else. Its past was a souvenir.

("Souvenir" carries its full French meaning, "memory", as well as its narrower
English "something you have to remind you".) Later in this short poem, the
poet appears on the "new stage":

> 　　　　　　　　　　　The actor is
> A metaphysician in the dark, twanging
> An instrument, twanging a wiry string that gives
> Sounds passing through sudden rightnesses. . . .

Sometimes a "sudden rightness" is only of the certainty that there is no whole,
no single truth. In "On the Road Home":[81]

> It was when I said,
> "Words are not forms of a single word.
> In the sum of the parts, there are only the parts.
> The world must be measured by eye";
>
> It was when you said,
> "The idols have seen lots of poverty,
> Snakes and gold and lice,
> But not the truth";
>
> It was at that time, that the silence was largest
> And longest, the night was roundest,
> The fragrance of the autumn warmest,
> Closest and strongest.

The collection *Ideas of Order* takes its title from a grander, more expansive moment of similar certainty, "The Idea of Order at Key West",[82] in which a girl singing beside the twilit Florida ocean becomes an image for the poet making his own, provisionally satisfying, pattern of the chaos of the real. The poem ends ("Ramon" is a notional Spaniard to whom it is addressed):[83]

> Oh! Blessed rage for order, pale Ramon,
> The maker's rage to order words of the sea,
> Words of the fragrant portals, dimly-starred,
> And of ourselves and of our origins,
> In ghostlier demarcations, keener sounds.

These lines very faintly suggest, in the word "portals", a possible transcendence, a meaning beyond the ordering song of the girl, the ordering words of the poet. The suggestion, in due course, will become less faint.

In this middle period of Stevens's creative life, there is no consistent line that can be traced through his poems—only many poems, long and short, more or less successful in the pleasure they give or the resonance they leave, as they catch a mood or a moment: "what still is / The look of things".[84] In the 1940 letter quoted above, he said: "People ought to like poetry the way a child likes snow & they would if poets wrote it."[85] In "The Man with the Blue Guitar", a sequence of thirty-three short poems, their reflective four-beat lines arranged in pairs, Stevens is "a metaphysician in the dark / Twanging an instrument", certain, some of the time, that

> Poetry
>
> Exceeding music must take the place
> Of empty heaven and its hymns,[86]

yet always yearning for a different, a cancelling, conviction:

> Believe would be a brother full
> Of love, believe would be a friend,
>
> Friendlier than my only friend,
> Good air. Poor pale, poor pale guitar ...[87]

Perhaps it is not necessarily poetry, which can seem, like snow, "a finikin thing of air", that is itself the answer: always, though it appears only rarely in these several books, these many poems, Stevens is haunted by the old truth that used to be believed:

> The lean cats of the arches of the churches.
> That's the old world. In the new, all men are priests.
> . . . .
> If they could gather their theses into one,
> Collect their thoughts together into one,
> Into a single thought, thus: into a queen,
> An intercessor by innate rapport,
> Or into a dark blue king, *un roi tonnerre*,
> Whose merely being was his valiance,
> Panjandrum and central heart and mind of minds—
> If they could! Or is it the multitude of thoughts,
> Like insects in the depths of the mind, that kill
> The single thought? The multitudes of men
> That kill the single man, starvation's head,
> One man, their bread and their remembered wine?[88]

The single thought, the single man, the figure of Christ, never altogether left him, even in the major poem of which the first assumption is "The death of one god is the death of all".

Is it—might it be—possible for the poet to make, for himself and even for others, out of the words that are all he has, something that does not otherwise exist in which to believe? *Notes toward a Supreme Fiction*[89] is Stevens's longest, most ambitious attempt to answer this question, not necessarily in the affirmative. A controlled, brave exercise in thought that cannot be paraphrased, *Notes* consists of three sets of ten poems, each set circling around an attribute of the supreme fiction: "It Must Be Abstract", "It Must Change", and "It Must Give Pleasure" (that is, it must be absolute, must act and must attract us). The whole poem is an extraordinary feat, as extraordinary as *Four Quartets*, never explicitly self-deprecating as Eliot's poem is, but, in the simplicity of its approach to difficult hopes and fears, considerably humbler. Its best passages are no less memorable, no less moving. Two such passages, not typical, because most of the poem keeps its fictive distance from "looking for what was, where it used to be", revert to "the single man, starvation's head". In the ninth poem of "It Must Be Abstract", what is abstract becomes incarnate:

He comes,

Compact in invincible foils, from reason,
Lighted at midnight by the studious eye,
Swaddled in revery, the object of

The hum of thoughts evaded in the mind,
Hidden from other thoughts, he that reposes
On a breast forever precious for that touch,

For whom the good of April falls tenderly,
Falls down, the cock-birds calling at the time.
My dame, sing for this person accurate songs.

He is and may be but oh! he is, he is,
This foundling of the infected past, so bright,
So moving in the manner of his hand.

Yet look not at his colored eyes. Give him
No names. Dismiss him from your images.
The hot of him is purest in the heart.[90]

And in the third poem of "It Must Give Pleasure", the God of the Old Testament appears, terrifying as in "Sunday Morning", but now "the tomb in Palestine" is remembered differently:

An effulgence faded, dull cornelian

Too venerably used. That might have been,
It might and might have been. But as it was,
A dead shepherd brought tremendous chords from hell

And bade the sheep carouse. Or so they said.
Children in love with them brought early flowers
And scattered them about, no two alike.[91]

Was Stevens, in *Notes*, coming closer to the God of truth, goodness and beauty (it must be abstract; it must change; it must give pleasure), to God revealed in Christ?

Of course not, the unbelieving critic will reply, since there is no such God. The Christian cannot so reply; he might reply instead that God is coming closer to Stevens. In the eight-line apostrophe, or dedication to "the supreme fiction", that he put at the head of his poem, someone is addressed. The lines begin and end:

> And for what, except for you, do I feel love?
> . . . .
> The vivid transparence that you bring is peace.[92]

Does anyone so address "poetry"—in embarrassed letters of this period Stevens both affirms and denies that the supreme fiction is "poetry"—or something he has made (up) by himself?

Stevens was sixty-three when he finished *Notes* in 1942. Half of his poems, and all the prose he wished to appear in a book (*The Necessary Angel*, 1951) were written between 1942 and his death in 1955. He held to his routine to the very end, stubbornly walking to the office across Elizabeth Park, watching the ducks, watching the Connecticut River, dividing his day between work and work like a monk decades in the habit of the *opus Dei* and ordinary labour. His prose is bold, idiosyncratic and often moving, with the uninhibited freshness, almost naïveté, of a wise old man who has read—his references are wide but informal—and thought for many years in isolation from both the literary and the academic worlds. He worked hard at writing these lectures; they must have greatly surprised and puzzled his audiences.

The first, "The Noble Rider and the Sound of Words", discloses a good deal of the thought behind *Notes*. It makes what seem at first sight extravagant claims for "the imagination" as the poet's, and anyone's, resource against "the pressure of reality", a reality growing ever more inimical to the imagination because of "the spirit of negation . . . so active, so confident and so intolerant"[93] and because of the dreadfulness of the times. Typically, Stevens says:

> When one is trying to think of a whole generation and of a world at war,
> and trying at the same time to see what is happening to the imagination,
> particularly if one believes that that is what matters most, the plainest state-
> ment of what is happening can easily appear to be an affectation.[94]

Both extravagance and affectation disappear if one translates Stevens's "imagination" as "the soul", or perhaps as "the invisible", in us and beyond us, which, as in Plato, has a reality beyond the reality of the visible. Of "Virgil, Dante, Shakespeare, Milton",

Stevens says, the poet "will wonder at those huge imaginations, in which what is remote becomes near, and what is dead lives with an intensity beyond any experience of life." [95] Coleridge is over Stevens's shoulder in this lecture, but so, confusingly, is I. A. Richards, a resolutely atheist critic whose *Coleridge on Imagination* (1934) Stevens had just read. So, as always, is Santayana: there is still, as there is in *Notes*, an evasion, "the hum of thoughts evaded in the mind", of the never quite abandoned possibility that the imagination, the soul, the invisible, has also to do with the truth.

In the most demanding of these lectures, "Imagination as Value" (1949), Stevens circles nearer and nearer to God, or at least to the relation between the imagination, the soul and God. It is now Pascal who is over his shoulder. He quotes Pascal's sister's account of her dying brother's reception of the last sacraments and his prayer: "Let God never forsake me",[96] but he withdraws at once from the implications of the story. As to truth, he cannot make up his mind:

> If the imagination is the faculty by which we import the unreal into what is real, its value is the value of the way of thinking by which we project the idea of God into the idea of man.[97]

It may seem impertinent, in both senses, to suggest that "invisible" and "visible" would make what is being said here clearer than "unreal" and "real". But a little later, Stevens says: "The imagination is the power that enables us to perceive the normal in the abnormal, the opposite of chaos in chaos." [98] Conceding, his examples being Arthur Rimbaud and Franz Kafka, that in "arts and letters" the modern consensus identifies the imagination with "the abnormal", he therefore concludes:

> It is natural for us to identify the imagination with those that extend its abnormality. It is like identifying liberty with those that abuse it. A literature overfull of abnormality ... gives the reason an appearance of normality to which it is not, solely, entitled.[99]

This is, by any standards, a sane, steadying, central observation. It is made with the evident assistance of Pascal, but it is also wholly characteristic of Stevens in old age, as are the last words of this lecture—slight, modest, immensely grand:

> The chief problems of any artist, as of any man, are the problems of the normal and ... he needs, in order to solve them, everything that the imagination has to give.[100]

Nearly one hundred poems of Stevens's old age were published in *The Auroras of Autumn* (1950), *The Rock* (the last section of his *Collected Poems*, 1954) and, after his death, in *Opus Posthumous*. They include "An Ordinary Evening in New Haven" (a bare meditation nearly as long as *Notes*) and a number of short poems that are among his greatest. Some of these look, as simply as possible in the manner now natural to him, at "The Plain Sense of Things" or "Local Objects" or "The River of Rivers in Connecticut", as three are called. In two, "Large Red Man Reading" and "The Planet on the Table", Stevens looks back with some satisfaction on his life's work, on poems that "spoke the feeling" [101] for the most ordinary things or bore

> Some affluence, if only half-perceived,
> In the poverty of their words,
> Of the planet of which they were part. [102]

In some he comes nearer than he had ever come before to what, in a letter to a Franciscan nun who had written to him about his poems and whom he never met, he called "a centre":

> Your mind is too much like my own for it to seem to be an evasion on my part to say merely that I do seek a centre and expect to go on seeking it. I don't say that I shall not find it or that I do not expect to find it. It is the great necessity even without specific identification. [103]

This was in 1948. In 1952 he wrote to his Irish friend Thomas MacGreevy, a devoted Catholic:

> At my age it would be nice to be able to read more and think more and be myself more and to make up my mind about God, say, before it is too late, or at least before he makes up his mind about me. [104]

In "Prologues to What Is Possible", [105] a poem of this time, he writes of "an ease of mind that was like being alone in a boat at sea":

As he traveled alone, like a man lured on by a syllable without any meaning,
A syllable of which he felt, with an appointed sureness,
That it contained the meaning into which he wanted to enter,
A meaning which, as he entered it, would shatter the boat and leave the oarsmen
 quiet

As at a point of central arrival, an instant moment, much or little,
Removed from any shore, from any man or woman, and needing none.

In "St Armorer's Church from the Outside",[106] he writes in the ruins of the
past, without using the word "God", of his own sense of God, of "A sacred
syllable rising from sacked speech":

> An ember yes among its cindery noes,
> His own: a chapel of breath, an appearance made
> For a sign of meaning, in the meaningless.

And in two of the most beautiful poems he ever wrote, God at last comes very close
to him. In "The World as Meditation",[107] the soul waiting for God becomes Penel-
ope waiting for Ulysses, an old married pair long separated. The poem ends:

> She would talk a little to herself as she combed her hair,
> Repeating his name with its patient syllables,
> Never forgetting him that kept coming constantly so near.

In "Final Soliloquy of the Interior Paramour",[108] in "the intensest rendezvous"
a pair without names become as one:

> We feel the obscurity of an order, a whole,
> A knowledge, that which arranged the rendezvous.
>
> Within its vital boundary, in the mind.
> We say God and the imagination are one ...
> How high that highest candle lights the dark.

If Stevens's imagination is his soul, the invisible in himself at one with the invisible God, there is no obscurity here. Nor is there any obscurity in his acknowledgement of the grace of God in a passage from "The Sail of Ulysses", a poem
of 1954, too late to be included in *Collected Poems*:

> Yet always there is another life,
> A life beyond this present knowing,
> A life lighter than this present splendor,
> Brighter, perfected and distant away,
> Not to be reached but to be known,

Not an attainment of the will
But something illogically received,
A divination, a letting down
From loftiness, misgivings dazzlingly
Resolved in dazzling discovery.[109]

During Stevens's last illness, in the summer of 1955, he was received into the Catholic Church by a chaplain at the hospital of Saint Francis in Hartford, which he had chosen in April of that year for an operation that revealed advanced cancer. His godparents were an insurance company colleague whom he had known for many years, and the colleague's wife. Stevens's reception into the Church was not made public (or even entered in the diocesan records; the archbishop of Hartford wanted to avoid "the impression that anyone who came to the hospital would be urged to become a Catholic").[110] This last decision, of no interest to most of Stevens's critics, was of long preparation. His lifelong love of France and of the Spanishness of Florida and Cuba, and the Catholic friends of his old age, the Franciscan nun and Thomas MacGreevy, had some bearing on this homecoming. The distant figure of Santayana, whom Stevens had not seen for nearly half a century, had more.

Santayana had been living in a convent in Rome since 1941. In 1946, at the age of eighty-three, he published *The Idea of Christ in the Gospels*. This book is a small gold tessera in the mosaic that is the writing of the Christian tradition. Long familiarity with Scripture and the liturgy produces, from a mind trained in scepticism but devoted to the tradition of the Church, a lucid, engaged account of the revelation of God in Christ. The old philosopher some of the time remembers that he is supposed to be dealing ironically, that is, across an Arnoldian gap, with a truth that is only ideal. But, while Arnold sails past Christianity in a small boat, Santayana here stands on the mainland of Catholic faith, a figure confident against the expanses of sea and sky, and the impact of this book as a whole is the impact of orthodox, Augustinian belief:

> The gifts of grace, like those of nature, require active acceptance and exercise, but such acceptance and quick response are a part of those gifts; the flighty convert has not been fully converted; the lazy artist has never been truly inspired.[111]
>
> [Christ's] pity and sympathy are the more profound in that he understands our nature and possibilities far better than we do. We know what we suffer, but he knows what we miss.[112]

It was moralistic insolence in Milton to profess to justify the ways of God to man. The justification of God's ways is that he has chosen them. What ultimate reason can any of us give for loving anything except that we love it?[113]

Christ, being God, reflects God's whole glory. For us, also, there is no difference between God entering into us and our attaining our special perfections and reflecting our appointed part of the good. . . . However brief or troubled [the spirit's] career might be, it would be justified if ever the same light touched it that shone in Christ.[114]

Stevens may or may not have read this book. Whether he did or not, Santayana in these last years of both their lives was often in his mind. In "Imagination as Value", writing for an audience at Columbia University, Stevens thinks of Rome as a useful example:

In this town [New York], no single public object of the imagination exists, while in the Vatican City, say, no public object exists that is not an object of the imagination.[115]

A few pages later, he remembers his time at Harvard: "What is the residual effect of the years we spend at a university, the years of imaginative life?" And in his next paragraph, he says:

There can be lives ... which exist by the deliberate choice of those that live them. To use a single illustration: it may be assumed that the life of Professor Santayana is a life in which the function of the imagination has had a function similar to its function in any deliberate work of art or letters. We have only to think of this present phase of it, in which, in his old age, he dwells in the head of the world, in the company of devoted women, in their convent, and in the company of familiar saints, whose presence does so much to make any convent an appropriate refuge for a generous and human philosopher.[116]

Two years later this thought became the greatest poem of Stevens's old age, "To an Old Philosopher in Rome",[117] which finds both the poet and his subject "On the threshold of heaven", its opening words. Here, in a simple room, because "It is poverty's speech that seeks us out the most", the most ordinary things become the "portal" of Key West transformed:

It is a kind of total grandeur at the end,
With every visible thing enlarged and yet
No more than a bed, a chair and moving nuns,
The immensest theatre, the pillared porch,
The book and candle in your ambered room.

The candle is the candle of the soul:

A light on the candle tearing aginst the wick
To join a hovering excellence, to escape
From fire and be part only of that of which

Fire is the symbol: the celestial possible.

Stevens did not know that in this very year, 1951, in the last autumn of his life, Santayana gave his friend and editor Daniel Cory a sealed envelope, to be opened after his death, containing twenty pages entitled "On the False Steps in Philosophy". In the course of a steady attack on Hegel, Santayana had here written:

If once the Father has existed and created a world ... the idea of that creation will have been raised for ever from the realm of essence to the realm of truth.... Our participation in truth is final and intimate, and raises us, as far as it goes, above our mortal condition.[118]

* * *

Stevens and Eliot never met. Eliot never mentioned Stevens in print and perhaps knew little of his work. Possibly the title for Eliot's book *Notes towards the Definition of Culture* (1948) has an echo in it of which he was conscious. Stevens, in turn, was wary of Eliot. In 1940, writing to his friend Henry Church, who was considering endowing a chair of poetry and finding a good candidate for it, he said: "It is possible that a man like T. S. Eliot illustrates the character, except that I regard him as a negative rather than a positive force." Ten years later he wrote: "Eliot and I are dead opposites and I have been doing about everything that he would not be likely to do." At the very end of both their writing lives, however, in the last of several odd coincidences, each of them was asked to write an introduction to a volume of the Bollingen Foundation's edition of the works of Valéry in English translation. Eliot's introduction to the pieces collected under

the title *The Art of Poetry*, is, as one would expect, a practised public performance, very much in the first person, by a judicious critic who had been writing
this kind of piece for forty years. He is sympathetic to Valéry as a poet and guard-
edly sympathetic to his prose: "The one complaint which I am tempted to lodge
against Valéry's poetics, is that it provides us with no criterion of *seriousness*."[119]

In their meditative inwardness, not expressed in the first person, Stevens's short
prefaces to the two most substantial of Valéry's six Socratic *Dialogues* are quite
different. He had never before been asked to do anything like this; he worked
hard on the *Dialogues* during his last winter, when he was already ill. "It was a
great pleasure", he wrote to his Bollingen editor, enclosing the finished pieces,
"to be asked to take part in this job."[120] In his first paragraph there is a sentence
about a passage in "Eupalinos, or The Architect" that suggests his delighted
surprise at the appositeness of this task: "Socrates speaks of the chance that had
placed in his hands an object which became, for him, the source of reflections
on the difference between constructing and knowing."[121] It was a difference, if
it was a difference, about which Stevens had been reflecting all his writing life.
Now, at last, he knew that it was a difference.

It is eerie to watch Stevens finding in Valéry's writing so much that he might
have written himself. Valéry's Socrates talks, for instance, of "the best use for that
part of our strength that is unnecessary for living, and seems to be reserved for the
pursuit of an object that infinitely transcends us".[122] In Socrates's *Timaeus*-like account
of God's creation of the universe, there is a passage to which Stevens returns twice
in his brief preface, which he titled "Gloire du long Désir, Idées":

> If, then, the universe is the effect of some act; that act itself, the effect
> of a Being, and of a need, a thought, a knowledge, and a power which
> belong to that Being; it is then only by an act that you can rejoin the
> grand design, and undertake the imitation of that which has made all
> things. And that is to put oneself in the most natural way in the very
> place of God.[123]

Stevens interprets this passage as "not meaning that [man] becomes God but that
he puts himself in the very place of God: *la place même du Dieu*. It follows that
for Eupalinos and for men like him what they do is their approach to the
divine."[124] The place where God is has become the place where the supreme
fiction is, after all, the truth. The last sentence of the second preface, to Valéry's
"lesser" work "Dance and the Soul", in which the dancer's name is Athikte,

runs: "Man has many ways to attain the divine, and the way of Eupalinos and the way of Athikte and the various ways of Paul Valéry are only a few of them." [125]

Four months later Stevens died, after receiving, like Pascal, the last sacraments of the Church.

1. George Santayana, *The Birth of Reason and Other Essays*, ed. Daniel Cory (New York, 1968), p. 134.
2. George Santayana, *Selected Critical Writings*, ed. Norman Henfrey (Cambridge, 1968), 2:46.
3. Ibid., p. 172.
4. Ibid., 1:22.
5. Ibid., p. 7.
6. Ibid., p. 279.
7. Ibid., 2:21.
8. *The Letters of George Santayana*, ed. Daniel Cory (New York, 1955), p. 49.
9. George Santayana, *Interpretations of Poetry and Religion*, ed. W.G. Holzberger and H.J. Saatkamp, Jr. (Cambridge, Mass., 1989), p. 165.
10. *Letters of Wallace Stevens*, ed. Holly Stevens (New York, 1966; London, 1967), pp. 481–82.
11. Ibid., p. 32.
12. Santayana, *Selected Critical Writings* 1:279.
13. Stevens, *Letters*, p. 58.
14. Ibid., p. 59.
15. Ibid., p. 96.
16. Ibid., pp. 139–40.
17. George Santayana, *The Life of Reason* (London, 1905–1906), pp. 9–10.
18. Santayana, *Interpretations of Poetry and Religion*, p. 3.
19. Ibid., pp. 71–72.
20. Ibid., p. 161.
21. Santayana, *Selected Critical Writings* 1:319.
22. Wallace Stevens, *Collected Poems* (New York, 1954; London, 1955), pp. 66–70.
23. Stevens, *Letters*, p. 250.
24. Stevens, *Collected Poems*, pp. 27–46.
25. Ibid., pp. 13–18.
26. Ibid., pp. 87–88.
27. Ibid., p. 56.
28. Ibid., p. 76.
29. T.S. Eliot, *Collected Poems 1909–1962* (London, 1963), p. 32.
30. T.S. Eliot, *Selected Essays* (London, 1932), p. 14.
31. Ibid., p. 17.
32. Ibid., p. 21.
33. Eliot, *Collected Poems*, p. 57.
34. Ibid., pp. 63–79.
35. *The Waste Land*, line 430.
36. Eliot, *Collected Poems*, p. 92.
37. Ibid., p. 110.
38. Ibid., p. 111.
39. Eliot, *Selected Essays*, p. 334.
40. Quoted in John Hayward, introduction to *T.S. Eliot: Selected Prose* (London, 1953), p. 11. Eliot did not reprint his preface in *Selected Essays*.
41. Quoted in Christopher Ricks, *T.S. Eliot and Prejudice* (1988; London, 1994), p. 173.
42. Quoted in Herbert Read, *The Cult of Sincerity* (London, 1953), p. 101.

43. Quoted in Northrop Frye, *T. S. Eliot* (London, 1963), p. 10.

44. T. S. Eliot, *Notes towards the Definition of Culture* (London, 1949), p. 52.

45. Wallace Stevens, *Opus Posthumous*, 2nd ed. (New York, 1989; London, 1990), p. 304.

46. Eliot, *Collected Poems*, pp. 95–105.

47. T. S. Eliot, "Ash Wednesday", pt. 2, in ibid., p. 98.

48. Ibid., pt. 6, p. 105.

49. Eliot, *Selected Essays*, p. 372.

50. Quoted in Ricks, *T. S. Eliot and Prejudice*, p. 44.

51. Eliot, *Definition of Culture*, pp. 74, 80.

52. T. S. Eliot, *The Use of Poetry and the Use of Criticism* (1933; London, 1964), p. 69.

53. Eliot, *Selected Essays*, p. 396.

54. Eliot, *Use of Poetry*, p. 105.

55. Eliot, *Collected Poems*, pp. 189–223.

56. T. S. Eliot, "Burnt Norton", pt. 1.

57. Ibid.

58. Ibid., pt. 3.

59. Ibid., pt. 5.

60. Eccles 3:2 (AV).

61. T. S. Eliot, "East Coker", pt. 3.

62. Ibid., pt. 2.

63. Ibid., pt. 5.

64. T. S. Eliot, "The Dry Salvages", pt. 2.

65. Ibid., pt. 5.

66. Ibid.

67. T. S. Eliot, "Little Gidding", pt. 1.

68. See Stephen Prickett, *Narrative, Religion and Science* (Cambridge, 2002), p. 223.

69. Eliot, "Little Gidding", pt. 2.

70. Ibid.

71. Ibid., pt. 3.

72. Eliot, *Selected Prose*, p. 134.

73. Eliot, "Little Gidding", pt. 5.

74. Eliot, *Selected Essays*, p. 21.

75. Ibid., p. 17.

76. Quoted in F. R. Leavis, *New Bearings in English Poetry* (1932; London, 1963), p. 181.

77. Eliot, *Use of Poetry*, pp. 99, 113.

78. Stevens, *Letters*, pp. 348, 350.

79. Helen Vendler, *Words Chosen out of Desire* (Knoxville, Tenn., 1984), p. 57.

80. Stevens, *Collected Poems*, pp. 239–40.

81. Ibid., pp. 203–4.

82. Ibid., pp. 128–30.

83. Stevens, *Letters*, p. 823.

84. Wallace Stevens, "A Postcard from the Volcano", in *Collected Poems*, p. 159.

85. Stevens, *Letters*, p. 349.

86. Stevens, *Collected Poems*, p. 167.

87. Ibid., pp. 175–76.

88. Wallace Stevens, "Extracts from Addresses to the Academy of Fine Ideas", in *Collected Poems*, p. 254.

89. Stevens, *Collected Poems*, pp. 380–408.

90. Ibid., pp. 387–88.

91. Ibid., p. 400.

92. Ibid., p. 380.

93. Wallace Stevens, *The Necessary Angel* (1951; London, 1960), p. 17.

94. Ibid., p. 20.

95. Ibid., p. 23.
96. Ibid., p. 135.
97. Ibid., p. 150.
98. Ibid., p. 153.
99. Ibid., pp. 153–54.
100. Ibid., p. 156.
101. Wallace Stevens, "Large Red Man Reading", in *Collected Poems*, p. 424.
102. Wallace Stevens, "The Planet on the Table", in *Collected Poems*, p. 533.
103. Stevens, *Letters*, p. 584.
104. Ibid., p. 763.
105. Stevens, *Collected Poems*, pp. 515–17.
106. Ibid., pp. 529–30.
107. Ibid., pp. 520–21.
108. Ibid., p. 524.
109. Stevens, *Opus Posthumous*, p. 128.
110. Charles M. Murphy, *Wallace Stevens* (New York, 1997), p. 94.
111. George Santayana, *The Idea of Christ in the Gospels* (New York, 1946), p. 95.
112. Ibid., p. 100.
113. Ibid., p. 207.
114. Ibid., p. 251.
115. Stevens, *Necessary Angel*, pp. 140–41.
116. Ibid., pp. 146–48.
117. Stevens, *Collected Poems*, pp. 508–11.
118. Santayana, *Birth of Reason*, p. 167.
119. T. S. Eliot, introduction to *The Art of Poetry*, by Paul Valéry (New York and London, 1958), p. xxiii.
120. Stevens, *Letters*, p. 878.
121. Wallace Stevens, preface to *Dialogues*, by Paul Valéry (New York, 1956), p. ix.
122. Quoted in ibid., p. x.
123. Valéry, *Dialogues*, p. 145.
124. Stevens, preface to ibid., p. xviii.
125. Ibid., p. xxviii.

CHAPTER NINETEEN

RUSSIA I

Pushkin to *The Devils*

Consciously, ruthlessly, and with a success both greatly admired and bitterly resented by his people, Peter the Great in the early years of the eighteenth century took Russia into the mainstream of European history, nations, events and ideas. In 1721 the tsar's chancellor, conferring new titles on his master after a successful military campaign, proclaimed: "He has brought us out of the darkness of ignorance on to the stage of glory before the eyes of the whole world and, as it were, transformed us from non-existence into being, bringing us into the society of political nations",[1] as if Russia had scarcely existed until it was recognized as "a power" by the West. Earlier in the same year, as part of the process here loyally described, Peter had abolished the patriarchate of Moscow and replaced it with a Holy Synod of church officials entirely responsible to himself, with a lay chief procurator—his job similar to that invented as "vicegerent in spirituals" for Thomas Cromwell by Henry VIII—as his eyes and ears at meetings of the Synod. This arrangement for the government of the Russian church remained in place until 1917. Meanwhile, in his campaign to wrest Russia out of "the darkness of ignorance", by which was meant a poor and primitive level of education transmitted by the church and disconnected from the intellectual traditions of the West, Peter imposed on the sons of his at first dubious nobility an up-to-date training in mathematics, navigation, science and Latin (only because it was still the international language of science), but no theology. There were many in Orthodox Russia who regarded all this with deep suspicion and some who described Peter as the Antichrist.

By the nineteenth century, the question of whether to look forward with the West or backward to Russia's past was the constant preoccupation of educated Russian life. There was attraction to the lure of Western progress and secular thought, and there was horrified resistance to them. The conflict, which was both intellectual and emotional, divided writers and thinkers from each other, particularly among the "men of the 1840s" who thought of themselves as either

"Westernizers" or "Slavophiles", each with a rose-tinted and historically uninformed view of the traditions to which they thought they belonged. But it also raged within individuals, most fiercely in the two greatest Russian writers, Leo Tolstoy and Fyodor Dostoyevsky.

One of the most momentous decisions in the whole of history, the granting of papal permission for the liturgy of newly converted Slavs (in Moldavia, Serbia and Bulgaria) to be conducted in Slavonic, was made, withdrawn, and made again by a hard-pressed ninth-century pope, John VIII, anxious to secure the support of the emperor in Constantinople against Saracen invaders and anxious to rescue Saint Methodius, with his brother Saint Cyril the apostles of the Slavs, from the enmity of German missionary bishops accusing him of heresy. A hundred years later, when the grand duke of Kiev decided that Byzantine Christianity was preferable, for himself and his people, to their existing paganism and also to Latin Christianity or Islam, the Russian church, its liturgy and gospels in Slavonic, was born into a spirit, never lost, of stubborn isolation from the languages and the already long history of the Latin and Greek churches, not yet separated from each other. The persistent streak of virulent anti-Semitism in Russian Orthodoxy also dates from its very beginning, in particular from the mass conversion of the enemy Khazar people, north of the Caucasus, to Judaism. Furiously resisting the brief accommodation with Rome reached by Constantinople in the desperate fifteenth century, the Russian church established its autocephalous independence under the metropolitan of Moscow, rather than Kiev, in 1448, this office becoming a patriarchate in 1589. In the following century, Kiev, now in the Catholic kingdom of Poland-Lithuania, had to cope with a large part of the Western Russian church accepting the authority, though not the liturgy, of Rome (the Uniate or Greek Catholic Church), while efforts by Patriarch Nikon to reform the Russian liturgy along Greek lines produced in Muscovite Russia a lasting schism. The Old Believers, without bishops of their own until the nineteenth century, regarded Greek reforms as un-Russian, indeed, Western. Meanwhile, increasingly powerful tsars often bullied and sometimes murdered Patriarchs and drove into the dark corners of Russian memory the old, hidden, contemplative monastic tradition of eleventh-century Kiev. Against Jews, against schismatic sects and above all against the Roman Catholicism of Poland and the West, Russian Orthodoxy has been embattled always.

When Peter the Great imposed on his nobles modern European education, his brand-new capital (Saint Petersburg) and what was supposed to be a tightly organized government bureaucracy, he took charge of the Russian church in the spirit of contemporary Protestant rule in northern Europe. In 1697–1698 he had visited for several months the Dutch Republic and England, both of them ruled by William of Orange. The tsar was impressed by William and by the naval and commercial efficiency of both countries; he was no less impressed by the firm state control of the church explained to him in England by Bishop Burnet, a learned propagandist for the kind of Whig, latitudinarian Protestantism that was still upsetting Dr. Johnson half a century later. Peter used his absolute power to build, with serf (slave) labour, a semblance of the modern states he had seen in the West: they had developed over centuries from the enterprise of merchants, craftsmen and inventors from a law-abiding urban middle class that did not exist in Russia. Similarly, Peter used his absolute power over the Russian church to run its finances in the interests of the state, to reduce the number of monasteries and prescribe their work and to force parish priests to become government spies. His most effective eighteenth-century successor, Catherine the Great, strengthened the state's grip on the church, dissolved half of the remaining monasteries and steered the small Russian elite even further in the direction of secular European education, manners, ambitions and ideas. Where Peter's model had been bourgeois England and Holland, Catherine's was the cultured absolutism of Frederick the Great's Prussia and ancien régime France. Four years before the French Revolution, she strengthened the class rights of the Russian nobility and further depressed the condition of the serfs, the vast majority of the Russian population, still bought and sold with the land they worked.

The result of all this was that by the nineteenth century, the Russian church was separated from the nobility by a huge gulf of incomprehension, poverty and illiteracy. The privileged landowning class, even the often-impoverished country gentry, in two or three generations became thoroughly westernized, speaking French to each other, educating, when they could afford it, their sons in German universities, affecting English upper-class habits and manners. In high society (unsurprisingly, Enlightenment Europe being what it had joined), the prevailing attitude to religion was that Christianity belonged to the peasants, to an illiterate, barbarous past of superstition and consoling ceremony, which no civilised person could any longer take seriously. Earnest German Pietism and fashionable Freemasonry became popular among the Petersburg aristocracy. The Russian church had neither the independence nor the intellectual resources to provide a counterweight to all this. The parish clergy, married, bound to the land, looking always for security within the church for their sons and sons-in-law, were peasants among peasants, badly trained, without power or influence in the secular state, in roughly the condition of the parish clergy in the Latin Church in the eleventh century, before the Gregorian reform. During the nineteenth century, a spiritual revival took place in the Russian monasteries, under the influence of a late revival of the study of the Greek Fathers of the Church at Mount Athos. Many new monasteries were founded; one, the Optino monastery not far from Moscow, with its succession of wise and saintly monk-teachers (elders), became a magnet for the few noblemen and intellectuals who were anxious to establish some connexion between their lives and the Orthodox piety of the peasants who flocked to the elders. (Tolstoy visited the Optino monastery several times and characteristically decided that the elders were "vainglorious".) Meanwhile, at the summit of the church, his aura of holiness carefully sustained to inspire devotion and loyalty, was the sacred figure of the tsar. In 1914 whole regiments of Russian soldiers knelt to receive the tsar's blessing as they set off for the Great War, while Rasputin, a devilish parody of the saintly monk, was the most powerful man in still-absolutist Saint Petersburg.

* * *

The short, glorious story of great Russian writing began after Napoleon had invaded Russia and failed to conquer it—after, that is, Russia had faced and repelled a terrifying incursion from the "enlightened" West. Of this achievement the westernized aristocracy was as proud as were the soldiers and the peasants who had harried Napoleon's ragged, freezing retreat. After imitative beginnings in the two previous centuries, literary writing in Russian became, with Alexander Pushkin, for the first time a means of identifying the country to itself in its own language; Pushkin has been a hero ever since to every Russian able to read. The first masterpieces of Russian literature, by Pushkin himself, Nikolai Gogol and Mikhail Lermontov, were all written, in the 1820s, 1830s and 1840s, under heavy censorship, particularly oppressive under the unpredictable Tsar Nicholas I, who on his accession in 1825 had put down a hopeless, romantic rebellion by a handful of disaffected young noblemen (the "Decembrists") and thereafter managed to keep the authoritarian lid screwed tightly down on Russia. Pushkin and Lermontov, Byronic heroes themselves—each was killed in a duel, Pushkin at thirty-seven, Lermontov at twenty-seven—wrote, in *Eugene Onegin* and *A Hero of Our Time*, of pointless, murderous duels and of Byronic heroes who in Russia became weary, cynical, overeducated, overtravelled "superfluous men" aware of the backwardness and constriction of Russian society yet unable to do anything to loosen the rigidity of its structure or bridge its chasms. Pushkin, toward the end of his short life, wrote some prose stories cryptically critical of the cruelty and fantasy of Russian military and aristocratic life, to support which millions of serfs laboured in archaic poverty.

Gogol, an even more gifted writer of prose than either Lermontov or Pushkin, and a sharp exposer of both cruelty and fantasy, was neither a soldier nor an aristocrat, but the son of a minor Ukrainian landowner and a devoutly Orthodox mother. He came to Saint Petersburg from his distant western home to work and write. His agonised stories, particularly "Diary of a Madman" and "The Overcoat", reveal the misery of the new urban poor in what had become of Peter the Great's gleaming modern city and the starved lives of humble clerks at the lowest levels of its bureaucracy. His play *The Government Inspector*, funny and acute, is a fierce satirical attack on the hypocrisy, corruption and inefficiency of what had become of this huge bureaucracy in small provincial towns. It could have got him into serious trouble, but after a tense moment of hesitation, the tsar applauded the first performance: there have been countless productions and performances all over Russia ever since. Gogol's masterpiece, the novel *Dead Souls*, extends satire and fantasy to the vast expanses of the Russian countryside, where Chichikov, an exploiter of the dishonesty and greed of landowners, travels and trades in the names of dead serfs, counted as alive until the next census. The idea for the novel was Pushkin's. When it was published, after difficulties with the censor, in 1842, Pushkin was dead and Gogol had decided that *Dead Souls* was only the first part of a three-part novel: two further parts would demonstrate to Russia, whose terrible condition the first part had described, that its salvation was certain and lay in a return to the Orthodox faith that waited deep in its heart. For ten years, living mostly abroad, Gogol struggled, dissatisfied and unhappy, with this project. At last, under the influence of a fanatical priest, he burned all he had written of the rest of *Dead Souls* and died, of extreme fasting and hysterical penance, ten days later.

Between them, Pushkin the court nobleman and Gogol the anguished professional writer had set an example that their great successors in the century after their deaths were all to follow. One of their contemporaries, Vissarion Belinsky, firebrand consumptive son of an impoverished naval doctor, saw exactly what they had achieved, particularly in *Eugene Onegin* and *Dead Souls*, and saw that in a society built on the lie that a European state had been constructed in Russia for the benefit of all its citizens, only the truth told by writers had any chance of waking the conscience of the powerful before destruction overcame the whole nation. In a short, hectic life—he died in 1848 at thirty-seven—Belinsky veered wildly from one extreme view to another, all derived from the West, as to the best political model for the Russian future. But on what was wrong with his country, and how its writers could reveal it, his words became a clarion call for the rest of the nineteenth century. When Gogol turned toward the revival of Orthodoxy as his passionately believed-in goal for Russia, Belinsky rounded on him in his "Letter to Gogol", a document later much feared by the secret police.

The letter does two things with equal vehemence. It proclaims the unique power of the truth-telling writer: "Only our literature, in spite of a barbarous censorship, shows signs of life and forward movement. That is why the calling of the writer is so honoured among us. . . . The Russian people is right. It sees in writers of Russia its only leaders, defenders, and saviours." At the same time, the letter, attacking Gogol, announces that writers must lead, defend and save the Russian people "from the darkness of Russian autocracy, Orthodoxy, and nationalism", from a darkness in which the church, corrupt, ignorant and cruel, keeps the country back from "education, civilization, and humane culture" and is an intrinsic justifying component of "a land where men buy and sell other men without even the cant of the Americans, who say that negroes are not men . . . a country where there are no guarantees of personal liberty or honour or property; not even a police state, only huge corporations of official thieves and robbers." [2] It is not surprising that this letter, written in 1847, became the inspiration of Russian writers thereafter. The letter is echoed, far in the future, in Alexander Solzhenitsyn's 1971 Nobel Prize lecture, which a different Russian autocracy, a different barbarous censorship, did not allow him to deliver:

> Writers can *defeat the lie*. . . . Once the lie is shattered the nakedness of violence is revealed in all its repulsiveness. . . . In Russia the most popular proverbs are those about *truth*. Insistently these proverbs express the people's deep and bitter experiences, sometimes with striking force: "One word of truth is of more weight than all the rest of the world." [3]

But the other proclamation of Belinsky's letter yoked the saving truth to the demolition not only of autocracy and nationalism but also of Christianity, and the conjunction reinforced what already seemed self-evident to Belinsky and his friends, the "men of the forties", that light, progress, reform and revolution— any or all of which could be achieved only by attention to what the West could teach—must necessarily mean consigning Russian Christianity to the darkness of the past.

One of these friends, Mikhail Bakunin, a disaffected son of the nobility, became the model for violent anarchist wreckers all over Europe: "First destroy; and then we shall see."[4] But also among these friends were two major Russian writers, both privileged aristocrats and both highly educated in the most modern ideas and schemes for a better future for mankind, which Russia needed more desperately than did any of the countries caught up in the failed revolutions of 1848–1849. One was the essayist, journalist and autobiographer Alexander Herzen. Brought up in Moscow high society, in trouble with Nicholas I's censors from his student days, imprisoned for a year in Petersburg and banished to a remote provincial town to work, with conspicuous lack of success, in a bureaucracy every bit as dishonest and incompetent as that lampooned in *The Government Inspector*, Herzen left Russia for good in 1847. He witnessed the defeat of the Paris revolution of 1848 and then settled in London. There he published *The Bell*, the first dissident periodical to criticise the tsarist government in detail and by name, and welcomed Russian exiles of every sort who turned up in England. Herzen was a highly intelligent critic of all that was oppressive, cruel and doomed in Russia's ruling class, but also of the likely consequences of a destructive, ideologically driven revolution, whether anarchist or Marxist. A free spirit, sustained all his life by old wealth and the civilised values of old Europe, with faith in nothing but the innate goodness and noble instincts of individuals, he thought a revolution in Russia both desirable and one day inevitable. He was on the side of the downtrodden peasants at home, as in Paris he had been on the side of the downtrodden urban poor. But he was suspicious of all grand projects likely to sacrifice countless lives for a distant utopian future, and he loathed Karl Marx. Like Belinsky, he regarded Christianity as part of the cruel machinery of the autocratic state; he knew too little about it not to see it as another dangerous ideology, one now happily outgrown, careless of the fate of individuals and organised only in the interests of bullying power. Herzen's leading ideas; his sense of the complexity of human life, never susceptible to sweeping solutions; and his love for and hope in people one by one were closer than he knew to the Christian principles he thought he despised. "If only people wanted, instead of liberating humanity, to liberate themselves, they would do much for the liberation of man",[5] he wrote. It is a notion of freedom not far from Augustine's.

His friend and fellow nobleman, Ivan Turgenev, was brought up on his mother's large, tyrannically run estate—his grandmother smothered a serf boy for breaking a cup—and was a student of Hegel's followers at the university in Berlin. Like Herzen, he was banished to the country in his youth for his writing; he also left Russia in disgust and also died abroad. His novels were the first Russian works to be read and admired in the West, and he was a friend, as Herzen was not, of the celebrated writers of the time in France and England—for Turgenev was no impassioned campaigner or political thinker, but a truth-telling artist of great delicacy and skill. His novels record, with impartial perception, the frustrated lives of the "superfluous men", the disillusion of the westernised idealists of his own generation and class, their hopes for Russia having come to so little; the bleak destructiveness of their successors, the nihilists of the 1860s; and the unbridgeable gulf between all of them and the peasants. His judgement is mild, detached, humane; in his books the only characters he plainly dislikes are heartless, ambitious bureaucrats, working their way up the system for their own selfish ends. He presents his most famous character, Bazarov, the out-and-out materialist rebel of the novel *Fathers and Sons*—"Show me a single institution of contemporary life, private or public, which does not call for absolute and ruthless repudiation"[6]—with enough sympathy to have caused fury from the right on the novel's publication. On the other hand, he makes the older generation's case against Bazarov with enough sympathy to have caused equal fury from the left. He describes with wry understanding "men of the forties" like himself, some of whom have retreated to their estates and attempted to improve the lot of their peasants despite or across the peasants' mulish incomprehension, pilfering, drunkenness and deep conservatism. Occasionally these liberal landowners achieve, with patient effort, a little success against all the odds. *Fathers and Sons*, published in 1862, shows that the emancipation of the serfs, at last decreed in 1861 by the new tsar, Alexander II, had, at least immediately, made the serfs' lives even more difficult. The serfs were hardly delighted to discover that their freedom meant paying rent to the masters on top of working the masters' land no less punishingly hard than before: in the grinding poverty of Russian villages, nothing had improved by 1897 when Anton Chekhov wrote his story "Peasants".

Old-fashioned Christian belief, which is how he always sees it, Turgenev treats with melancholy respect. The young heroine of *Home of the Gentry*, brought up by a devout peasant nurse, decides to become a nun when she loses her one chance of a happy marriage. Lavretsky, who loves her but must let her go, watches the peasants in the village church: "'What can replace for them the comfort of the church?' thought Lavretsky and made his own attempt to pray; but his heart had become hard and embittered and his thoughts were far away."[7] An old German musician in the same novel, poor, disappointed and good, reads "the Bible, a Protestant collection of psalms and the works of Shakespeare in Schlegel's translation".[8] In *Fathers and Sons* Turgenev mocks only very lightly the confusion of Christianity with pagan superstition in the touching figure of Bazarov's mother and ends the novel with a memorable picture of the dead nihilist's old parents at his grave and the questions: "Are those prayers of theirs, those tears, all fruitless? Is their love, their hallowed selfless love, not omnipotent? Oh yes!"[9] But the tone of the passage remains wistful, as if the scale of the positive reply to the questions is too much for the novelist to face. Bazarov's chief opponent, a highly civilised, faintly ridiculous "man of the forties" who eloquently pleads the lasting value of European culture against Bazarov's contempt (and fights him in a comic parody of the murderous duels that killed Pushkin and Lermontov) disappears to elegant retirement in Dresden. "He is a Slavophile in outlook: as is well known, this is considered *très distingué* in the best society. He reads nothing Russian but on his writing-desk there is a silver ashtray in the shape of a peasant's bast shoe." Occasionally he visits the Russian church, where "he leans in some corner against the wall, motionless and lost in thought, with lips tightly compressed; then at long last he will suddenly recollect himself and begin almost imperceptibly to cross himself."[10]

This short description, Turgenev taking swift, acute leave of a character we are fond of despite, or because of, his loyalty to a past that will not long survive the onslaught of the Bazarovs, is an indication of how dangerous it is to divide nineteenth-century Russians into the two categories "westerniser" and "Slavophile", one thoroughly secular, European and modern, the other devoted to "autocracy, Orthodoxy and nationalism". The character of old Kirsanov defends European civilisation with deep loyalty, lives in Germany and is no tsarist or nationalist; but his Slavophilism is more than an affectation, his residual feeling for Orthodoxy real. All this was true of Turgenev himself, even if none of his opinions was passionately held. In his own narrative voice, he says, recounting Lavretsky's family history in *Home of the Gentry*, "How could one demand convictions of a young man fifty years ago when we haven't grown up sufficiently to have them even today?"[11] Between the youth of Russia as a European nation, open to every brand-new idea or ideology from the West and without the West's long experience of scepticism, and the old age of Russia as a huge peasant country ruled by an autocrat and sustained by unchanging Orthodoxy, there was space for a mix of ideas and hopes that the familiar division into two categories misleadingly oversimplifies. This is particularly true of both Tolstoy and Dostoyevsky.

* * *

Tolstoy was born only ten years after Turgenev (and, more surprisingly, only twenty-nine years after Pushkin) but lived until 1910. Like both of them, he was a rich nobleman. He was patchily educated but all his life read everything he could find to support the preoccupations of the moment. He inherited a large estate and many hundreds of serfs, and as a young man led the life—described by Pushkin and Lermontov and in several different versions by himself—of a self-indulgent Russian aristocrat of the time, though never without a bleeding con-science and a severely critical eye. An officer in a grand regiment, he served in the Caucasus and in the Crimean War, travelled in the West and spent years in Saint Petersburg in a social whirl of clubs, gambling, champagne and casual love affairs. He wrote always, and when he settled to marriage and children in the country, he produced in a little over ten years his two long masterpieces of enthralling imaginative grip on a huge range of characters—*War and Peace*, his vast narrative account of Russia in the Napoleonic period, and *Anna Karenina*. Both novels have in them, along with much else, profound observation of the challenges, difficulties and rewards of marriage, of family life, of birth and death, of loyalty and betrayal, and of love both constructive and destructive, all in the privileged world with which Tolstoy was familiar. The novels also have a strong moral tone, of a conventional Christian kind: the epigraph to *Anna Karenina*, whose heroine is destroyed by her abandonment of her loveless marriage, is from Saint Paul quoting the Old Testament: "Vengeance is mine; I will repay." [12]

Tolstoy married in 1862, the year of *Fathers and Sons*, and in the following year began writing *War and Peace*. The European intellectual atmosphere of the moment, to which Tolstoy, like most educated Russians, was fully awake, crack-led with the modern, the utilitarian, the scientific, the materialist, the socialist. Auguste Comte and Pierre-Joseph Proudhon, the father of French anarchist social-ism, had written their major works. John Stuart Mill's essay *On Liberty* was pub-lished in 1859, his *Utilitarianism* in 1861. Darwin's *Origin of Species* appeared in 1859, as did Marx's first sketch for *Das Kapital*. Herbert Spencer's *First Principles*, using Darwin to support an atheist "evolutionary philosophy", appeared in 1862. In 1863 Renan's reductive and destructive *Vie de Jésus* was read with enthusiasm throughout Europe. Bazarov was only abreast of current Western thought; a pro-vincial bluestocking in *Fathers and Sons* scoffs: "They tell me you've begun to sing the praises of George Sand [novelist and famously "liberated" woman, a friend of Turgenev].... She hasn't a single idea about education or physiology or anything. I am convinced she's never even heard of embryology, and in these days—how can one get on without that?" [13]

Tolstoy's attitude to this atmosphere was deeply ambivalent. A European rational-ist who regarded traditional Christianity as a relic of the past now evidently impos-sible to believe in, he became almost as fierce a repudiator as Bazarov of the old institutions of church and state. He sympathised with much in revolutionary social-ism, certain, with Rousseau, that civilization had warped and distorted the natural goodness of mankind. On the other hand, scientific materialism struck Tolstoy as terrifyingly lacking in nourishment for the soul, and he knew that it provided no context for the moral imperatives he sought for years to justify: these imperatives were derived from Christianity, and Christianity he regarded as irrational nonsense. Two characters in his great novels, characters gentler than he ever was, reflect himself in his struggle in the 1860s and 1870s toward establishing the religion he had set himself in 1855 to found, "a religion corresponding to the present development of mankind: the religion of Christ purged of dogmas and mysticism—a practical religion not promising future bliss but giving bliss on earth".[14]

Pierre Bezukhov in *War and Peace* is a very rich landowner—therefore, in Russia, a man with power over thousands of serfs. A well-meaning liberal, he is deceived by dishonest stewards into thinking his "reforms" are improving the lives of his peasants; in reality, he is making their lives worse. But what he feels within himself is all-important to him. Searching for a reason for living, he has read much and drifted into modish Freemasonry. "Pierre was delighted with his visit to his estates and quite recovered the philanthropic mood in which he had left Petersburg, and wrote enthusiastic letters to his 'brother-instructor' as he called the Grand Master."[15] Like Tolstoy at the time he was writing this book, Pierre wants to educate his peasants in vaguely Masonic eighteenth-century deism in order to rescue them from the superstitions of Christianity. These superstitions are evident in the "people of God", the pilgrims and beggars welcomed to the back door by the only devoutly Orthodox character among the gentry in *War and Peace*, Princess Mary, shut away in the country with her exacting ("Western") mathematician father. Pierre tells his friend Prince Andrew, Mary's brother, of the rational education he is giving his serfs, who "were growing up and dying with no idea of God and truth beyond ceremonies and meaningless prayers". Prince Andrew is sceptical: the peasants are incapable of improvement, not worth Pierre's time except as labourers increasing his wealth. But Pierre is sure he is, for himself, right: "The main thing is that I know, and know for certain, that the enjoyment of doing this good is the only sure happiness in life."[16] (There may be a distancing irony in Tolstoy's account of Pierre's side of this conversation. Probably there is not.)

Pierre relapses into the idle, dissipated life Tolstoy knew well and also into superstition of his own: in 1812 Masonic number-cryptology convinces Pierre that he has a divine mission to assassinate the invading Napoleon, who is Antichrist under the mark of the beast. Events, the battle of Borodino, the burning of Moscow, and Pierre's capture and near-execution by the French shake him out of this and out of the last traces of his old complacency. At last, amid the icy hardships of the French retreat, Pierre meets Platon Karataev, an old Russian peasant and fellow prisoner about to be shot for falling behind on the march. Karataev, from the depths of ancient, simple, Christian faith, teaches Pierre a cheerful acceptance of the will of God.

It took Tolstoy himself years to disentangle acceptance (or, in his own case, strenuous doing) of what he took, largely from Christianity, to be the will of God, with which he could cope, from actual Christian faith, with which he could not. Levin, another rich landowner and Tolstoy's alter ego in *Anna Karenina*, written in the 1870s, searches, more desperately than Pierre—as Tolstoy became more desperate—for the meaning of life. The painful death from consumption of Levin's brother mirrors exactly the death, witnessed by Tolstoy, of his own favourite brother in 1860. The dying man receives the last sacraments to please Levin's wife: "I went through that farce for her sake. She is so sweet, but you and I can't deceive ourselves." [17] Tolstoy's brother's death terrified Tolstoy and haunted him for the rest of his life. Levin, though happily married and temporarily successful in his efforts to calm his soul by sharing the physical labour of his peasants, is, toward the end of the novel, close to suicide. Bazarov of *Fathers and Sons*, knowing himself to be a meaningless speck in a meaningless universe, could set his teeth in bitter defiance. Levin cannot: "I cannot live without knowing what I am and why I am here. And that I can't know, so therefore I can't live. In infinite time, in infinite matter, in infinite space an organic cell stands out, will hold together awhile and then burst, and that cell is Me." [18] He is rescued, as Pierre was, by hearing of an old peasant (also called Platon) who "is an upright old man. He thinks of his soul. He does not forget God." Levin asks: "Not forget God? And how does he live for his soul?" and the peasant he is talking to replies, "Why, that's plain enough: it's living rightly, in God's way." [19] This conversation becomes the saving light for Levin, of whom Tolstoy says shortly afterward, "It seemed to him now that there was not a single article of faith which could disturb the main thing—belief in God, in goodness, as the one goal of man's destiny." [20]

Whose goodness? The goodness of God or the goodness of Levin? The passage provokes this question. And when, two years after *Anna Karenina*, Tolstoy published *A Confession*, recording in plain autobiography his own suicidal despair and his own conversion, the question had not evaporated. For Tolstoy the rationalist, recounting his journey from childhood faith through youthful worldliness—the young man who needs praise and gets it from high society for ambition, extravagance, adultery, anger and revenge—to adult terror in the face of death, which reveals life to be "a senseless evil", [21] has now arrived at a faith that turns out to be faith in his own moral effort. His observation of the Russia of his time has led him to the conclusion that only the idle rich have time to be atheists; they behave badly, but the educated who profess Christianity behave worse. The peasants, who all believe, are, on the other hand, good (he ignores the fact that, as other Russian writers demonstrate, for every one Platon there were always twenty peasants brutalised by poverty into chronic drunkenness and violence). Therefore he loved the peasants and loathed the nobility, including himself. "It was more important and necessary for me to feel that I was good than to admit that 2 + 2 = 4."[22] In *The Death of Ivan Ilyich*, the story that is Tolstoy's concentrated distillation of *A Confession*, a prosperous bureaucrat on his deathbed furiously hates his wife, daughter, doctor and footman—everyone he knows except the peasant nursing him—until the last moments of consciousness, when he feels sorry for his son and wife and tries to ask their forgiveness. Then he dies in a "light" that has overtaken terror, "knowing that whoever was concerned would understand".[23] His family? God?

Tolstoy tried for a short time to live the peasants' observant Christian life. But the substance of Christian belief—the Incarnation, the Resurrection, the revelation of the Trinity in Christ—he could no more accept after his conversion than before it, and soon, in a self-sufficient refusal of dependence on God or on the Church, he reverted to his plan of founding a rational religion of his own, since all existing religions were in any case only the work of their founders. *A Confession* strikes the reader as more an account of a nervous breakdown followed by a recovery of health and self-confidence than a record of a Christian conversion. The short essay "Religion and Morality", written in 1893 for a German ethical society, confirms this impression. Here, with a wildly unhistorical swipe at Russia's "state religion ... reduced to this level by Augustine and improperly called Christian",[24] he insists that his stoic communitarian morality must be firmly separated from Church, sacraments, grace and faith. But he knows that morality needs the backing of religion. "To allege that social progress produces morality is the same as suggesting that the construction of stoves produces heat. Heat is produced by the sun.... Morality proceeds from religion in just the same way." "The unfortunate Nietzsche, who has lately become so famous ... cannot be refuted."[25] But since Christianity can no longer be believed in, a new religion must be put in place to back a morality that remained Christian. (Tolstoy here agrees with Matthew Arnold; they admired each other's writing on religion.) Everyone should obey the rules Tolstoy himself had derived from the Sermon on the Mount, and "the kingdom of heaven on earth would be attained."[26] He could not see, as Nietzsche saw, that "[w]hen one gives up Christian belief one thereby deprives oneself of the *right* to Christian morality. For the latter is absolutely *not* self-evident." [27] Nor could he see that his driving purpose, to achieve "bliss on earth", is neither Christian nor, properly, even religious. "The desire for universal welfare", he once wrote, "is that which we call God." [28]

No one observed more accurately than Tolstoy the frailty and fallibility of human beings. But he clearly thought he could deal with his own frailty and fallibility by an effort of his own mind, his own will, and that everyone else, if properly instructed, could do the same. Of the immensity of the human soul, as the delineation of Pierre in particular makes clear, Tolstoy had no doubt. But God was always somewhere within that soul, not its maker or its home. The much younger writer Maxim Gorky, who knew Tolstoy well in his old age, said: "With God he has very suspicious relations; they sometimes remind me of the relations of 'two bears in one den'." [29] The remark, to an English reader, suggests Milton.

In 1898 Nicholas II gave permission for the Doukhobors, a Russian peasant sect cruelly persecuted by both church and state, to emigrate to Canada. To raise money to make their departure possible, Tolstoy, at the age of seventy, wrote his third and last long novel, *Resurrection*. The book is a moral tract and a fine novel, telling the story of the sin, guilt, penitence and salvation—of course through his own efforts—of yet another wealthy Russian nobleman, now at the centre of a single narrative as Pierre and Levin had not been. Nekhlyudov, a juryman at a trial, recognises the prisoner, a prostitute wrongly convicted of murder, as a country girl he had years before seduced and abandoned. He tries, and fails, to save her, saving his own soul in the process. She will have none of this: "She would not let him make use of her spiritually as he had done physically": [30] Tolstoy was still a great, and honest, writer of fiction. In this book the murky depths of late tsarist society—the city underworld, the corrupt courts, the prisons, the dreadful trains taking convicts to Siberia—are vividly and shockingly presented. Although Tolstoy was by then the most famous living Russian, the novel was savagely cut by the censors; on its appearance, nevertheless, its author was unsurprisingly excommunicated by the Holy Synod.

The title of the book, a gesture of defiance in itself, is as misleading to an ordinary Christian as *Paradise Regained*, and for a similar reason. Nekhlyudov's regeneration has nothing to do with the Resurrection of Christ or the grace of God. It is a conversion to a new, more accurate view of the terrible condition of Russia and to a utopian hope for a regained paradise that, like Milton's, will be achieved by taking Jesus as a model for obedience, unselfishness and love. One of Tolstoy's epigraphs, all four from the Gospels, is a verse from Luke: "The disciple is not above his master: but everyone that is perfect shall be as his master." [31] With Nekhlyudov's cure comes renewed confidence in his own perfectibility, "a paradise within thee, happier far": [32]

> The free spiritual being, which alone is true, alone powerful, alone eternal, had already awakened in Nekhlyudov. And he could not but trust it. However vast the disparity between what he was and what he wished to be, everything appeared possible to this newly awakened spiritual being. [33]

There is much that is Christian in the book because there is much that is about the closeness of goodness to truth, and the real evils that Nekhlyudov comes to understand are evil indeed. He learns to see through the hypocrisy and complacency of the powerful to the careless cruelty that condemns the poor and unlucky to the humiliated wretchedness of shaved, fettered and unrescuable victims of an unjust society. Tolstoy's rage, provoked, for example, by "all sorts of crimes committed by persons in high places, who occupied, not prison cells, but presidential chairs in various official institutions", [34] is not unlike King Lear's. Tolstoy's devastating portrait of the chief procurator of the Holy Synod, a cynical official who uses all the coercive means of unaccountable government to enforce the unity of the national church, seems to set Voltairean contempt against the possibility of actual Christian faith:

> At the bottom of his heart he really believed in nothing, and found such a state very convenient and agreeable, but fearing that the people might some day arrive at the same state he considered it his sacred duty (as he called it) to try to save them from it. [35]

But Tolstoy in old age was no more able than Belinsky (or Bazarov) to distinguish autocracy and nationalism from Orthodox Christianity. A harmless old priest administering the oath in the district court is mercilessly guyed, and a long, corrosive passage describes with cynical, mocking destructiveness and inaccuracy a eucharistic liturgy celebrated in the prison. The only Christians in the whole book, and there are many, who escape attack are a Doukhobor-like group sentenced to deportation and an old tramp who believes in "the Spirit" in himself but in no one else and sees himself as exactly like Jesus. There is also a brief, sympathetic portrait of a senior Petersburg bureaucrat, the assistant public prosecutor in the senate appeal court, to which Nekhlyudov manages, in vain, to take his victim's case. This bureaucrat, like Tolstoy, "like all of his set and generation, had, as his intellect developed, without the least effort shaken off the fetters of the religious superstitions in which he had been reared." Anxious, later, about the hypocrisy of his constant attendance at the Orthodox ceremonies that are a daily part of his official life, he reads Hegel and the Slavophile writers of the 1840s in order to see whether Christianity might after all be true, though "he had already decided the answer". The result is "a sort of peace of mind and a vindication of the religious teaching in which he had been brought up and which his reason had long since discarded", a condition familiar to many who for one reason or another "go along" with a Christianity they know is false:

> He adopted the usual sophisms, such as the incapacity of the individual intellect to grasp the truth; that the truth is only revealed to an aggregate of men; that it can only be known through revelation; that revelation is in the keeping of the Church; and so on.... He thought he believed, and yet he knew with his entire being that this faith of his was farther than anything else from being "right". And this was why his eyes always looked sad.[36]

This man's plight, which Tolstoy was too truthful to accept for himself, is an indication of the intellectual weakness of Russian Orthodoxy, distant as it was from the Catholic tradition until the end of the nineteenth century. The Hegelian Slavophiles could provide an intelligent man with no more than a romantic dream of Russia before Peter the Great and an endorsement of the "religious superstitions" from which Tolstoy spent much of his life trying to liberate his peasants.

So Nekhluyodov finds ways of forgiving himself and persuading himself that he is doing good. As with Pierre and Levin, and Tolstoy, the good he does is his own; at the end of the book, he has not overcome the terror of death. A young prisoner dies of consumption, like Tolstoy's brother forty years before, and Nekhlyudov asks himself: "'Why had he suffered? Why had he lived? Does he understand now what it's all for?' ... and it seemed to him that there was no answer, that there was nothing but death." [37] Tolstoy had it in mind to write a sequel to *Resurrection*, the story of "the peasant life of Nekhlyudov". He never tried it, perhaps because it would have been as impossible to imagine as "the peasant life of Count Leo Tolstoy". In 1910, at eighty-two years old and in a rage with his wife, Tolstoy set out from home on what he had long intended to be the pilgrim road of the devout peasant. Eleven days later, he died in the stationmaster's house at a country halt with the press and film-cameras of the world watching the door. The irony was characteristic of his entire life. He was buried in a wood on his estate with no religious ceremony.

Yet if we know, as we do, that Nekhlyudov and Pierre and Levin, and Tolstoy himself, remain fallible, that the degree to which they feel better by resolving to do good is a matter of the moment, of mood and self-persuasion, and also a matter of staving off the fear of death, it is because Tolstoy tells us so. Both he and his characters will always move us because Tolstoy was one of the greatest truth-tellers of all writers, his peculiar relation to Christianity conditioned both by the circumstances of nineteenth-century Russia and by his own intractable temperament.

* * *

Conditioned, but not determined. When Dostoyevsky died in 1881, at home in Saint Petersburg with his family, thirty thousand people came to his funeral at the Alexander Nevsky monastery. In the course of a life beset by hardships of a kind the patrician Tolstoy had never experienced, Dostoyevsky had faced every intellectual and spiritual challenge of Russia in the time they shared and had arrived at a very different conclusion, a very different hope.

Dostoyevsky was born seven years before Tolstoy, though his novels, written, like Tolstoy's masterpieces, in the 1860s and 1870s, give the impression that he was younger. His father was a doctor in the pauper hospital in Moscow; his mother was a devout Christian. His paternal ancestors had been priests for generations. He received a modern education in Moscow; his mother died when he was sixteen; two years later, his father was murdered. By 1849, a year of hypersensitivity to any suggestion of dissidence, he was a qualified engineer and a struggling writer, briefly considered a genius by Belinsky, of Gogol-like stories. He was arrested, imprisoned and condemned to death by Nicholas I's secret police for reading Belinsky's letter to Gogol to a group of young radical socialists planning an illegal printing press. He had put himself in the power—he thought forever—of a nihilist terrorist called Speshnyov, "my own Mephistopheles", by borrowing money from him. After ten months in the Peter and Paul Fortress in Petersburg, Dostoyevsky was reprieved from the firing squad at the last minute, a searing experience (shared by Pierre in *War and Peace*) that recurs in various forms in his novels. Fettered and chained, he was then marched with fellow convicts nearly two thousand miles to a prison at Omsk in western Siberia, where he spent four years, followed by five years of compulsory service in a Siberian regiment, where he began again to write. On his return to European Russia, epileptic and rheumatic, he lived restlessly and unhappily for years, suffering a miserable marriage, a frantic love affair, chronic debt, anxiety and an addiction to gambling. He travelled extensively in western Europe after 1867 with his second wife, who eventually managed to cure his gambling and sort out his debts. They returned to Petersburg in 1871, and there, at last, he lived an orderly family life, respected and loved by a large public.

To have written during, as a result of, and in spite of all this, half a dozen great books, all of them censored and four of them very long and produced to the stressful deadlines of serial publication, was a feat of psychological resilience and intellectual control that has perhaps no parallel in the history of literature. He did complain. "Do you know", he wrote from Germany to his niece in 1870, "that I am absolutely *aware* that if I could have spent two or three years at that book—as Turgenev and Tolstoy can—I could have produced a work of which men would still be talking in a hundred years from now."[38] The book was *The Idiot*, and a hundred years later, they were.

When Dostoyevsky, at twenty-eight, was arrested, he had followed the ordinary path—described by Matthew Arnold writing of Levin, as "in Russia, as in France, among all young men of the upper and cultivated classes more a matter of course, perhaps, more universal, more avowed, than it is with us"[39]—from childhood Christianity to utopian atheism. Out of this ordinary path he was shaken for good—but by no means, yet, into calm or confident Orthodoxy—by his years in prison. He described these years through a colourless first-person narrator who is and is not himself in *Memoirs from the House of the Dead*, serially published in 1861–1862. The tone of this book, surprising to a reader familiar with Dostoyevsky's later novels, is level, though not without firm judgement of cruelty, and fair to prisoners, officers, orderlies and the townspeople of Omsk. The physical privations, hunger, cold and filth of the prison are vividly described; so is the particular misery of the very few gentry prisoners, of whom the narrator is one as Dostoyevsky had been, among the mass of peasant convicts with their automatic hatred for the oppressor class. This

profoundest of gulfs ... is *fully* seen only when the *nobleman* is suddenly compelled, by the power of laws external to himself, to become one of the common people. Otherwise, you may associate all your life with the people, you may come into contact with them every day for forty years together, in the civil service, for example, in any of the accepted formal relationships, or even simply in a friendly way, as a benefactor and in a certain sense a father—you will never know the essence of them. It will all be an optical illusion, no more.[40]

So much for "the peasant life of Nekhlyudov". Only in Dostoyevsky's last years, and in journalism rather than in his novels, did he, with bursts of rabid nationalism and anti-Semitism, pin his hope for the future on the peasants because they had some Christian faith, however primitive, while the intelligentsia had almost none.

In *The House of the Dead*, "the most delicate inner feeling" or the coarsest insensitivity might appear in any convict: "education itself furnishes no criterion here."[41] The hellish darkness of prison life is occasionally lit by piety irrespective of religion. The Muslims, who are allowed their prayers and their religious holidays, as is the one Jew, comically but sympathetically described, are gentle and friendly. One of them, a Tartar boy from Daghestan, is taught to read and write Russian by the narrator. They read the New Testament, the only book allowed in the prison; the boy is moved by Jesus's teaching and loves him, as do his brothers, as "God's great and glorious prophet".[42] The narrator is equally impressed by the Catholic piety of an old Polish soldier, a peasant, who disappears for two years and returns mad, a butt of mockery; "I felt very sad."[43] And the narrator himself, his accustomed misery increased by the beauty of a spring day, is profoundly moved by preparation for Easter and by standing at the liturgy with other fettered convicts and receiving Communion after the priest's words, "Accept me, O Lord, even as the thief."[44]

In Omsk, Dostoyevsky's adult faith in Christ dawned. But as a free man and an intellectual assailed by the competing ideas of the 1860s, he was unable to settle, untroubled, into Orthodox belief and practice. He was faced by the Russian dilemma that reason belonged to the West, but faith belonged to the Orthodox, but to peasants, to the naïve, to the pre-rational. His sense of this dilemma explains his much-misunderstood sentence in a letter written on his release from prison in 1854: "If anyone could prove to me that Christ is outside the truth, and if the truth really did exclude Christ, I should stay with Christ rather than with the truth." He had been educated to believe that reason establishes what is true. In the same letter, he said: "I am a child of the age, a child of unbelief and doubt, up till now, and till the grave shall cover me"; but also: "There is nothing lovelier, deeper, more appealing, more rational, more human and more perfect than the Saviour."[45] With the help of no Latin theology, closed to both Dostoyevsky and Tolstoy because Latin theology was Roman and hated, Dostoyevsky had, like Tolstoy, to work out his own justification for that "rational". By "staying with Christ", he chose a route on which Tolstoy turned his back.

First he plumbed the depths of current European "truth". The first thirty pages of Dostoyevsky's short book *Notes from Underground* are a Nietzschean rant (though Nietzsche had not yet begun to write: later, he much admired this book) of "cold, venomous and, above all undying resentment", uttered by an "offended, browbeaten and derided" victim of the driving ideas of the time.[46] These are the confident ideas of the Enlightenment, developed in Darwinian dissolution of the line between man and the rest of creation, in Comte's positivism, in utilitarian optimism and in, above all, utopian socialism. Where is the peaceful world enlightened self-interest was supposed to deliver? "Look around you: everywhere blood flows in torrents, and what's more, as merrily as if it was champagne. There's our nineteenth century!"[47] Dostoyevsky was writing in the decade of the Crimean War, the ghastly battle of Solferino and the American Civil War. And the future?

> "Then," (this is all of you speaking) "a new political economy will come into existence, all complete, and also calculated with mathematical accuracy, so that all problems will vanish in the twinkling of an eye, simply because all possible answers to them will have been supplied."[48]

But man is free—this is the book's cry of protest—and he will wreck any utopia reason organises for him:

> Shower man with all earthly blessings ... give him such economic prosperity that he will have nothing left to do but sleep, eat gingerbread, and worry about the continuance of world history—and he, I mean man, even then, out of mere ingratitude, out of sheer devilment, will commit some abomination.[49]

The underground man rails against all who announce "with a laugh, 'You know, as a matter of fact volition doesn't exist!' " all who would have each of us "some unprecedented kind of generalized human being" rather than a person "with real flesh and blood *of our own*",[50] therefore capable of evil (but therefore also capable of good). These embittered pages record a struggle, far from concluded here, toward recognition of original sin; the freedom of the will to admit dependence on, or to reject, the grace of God; and the absolute value of the person before God: an Augustinian understanding of the relation between man and God. Augustine himself, then and always, was as unknown to Dostoyevsky as he was to Tolstoy.

*   *   *

At the lowest point of his personal life, in 1865, Dostoyevsky began to write *Crime and Punishment*. He was in Wiesbaden, deep in debt. His first wife, and his brother who left a widow and children for Dostoyevsky to support, had recently died. His seizures were worse. He had sold his next, unwritten book for an advance and borrowed from Turgenev. He paid some of his debts and lost all the rest of this money at roulette. One way or another, by friends and with luck (though not at roulette), he was rescued. And he rescued himself. With enormous effort he kept up the long, regular instalments of *Crime and Punishment* for periodical publication, interrupting them to dictate another novel (*The Gambler*) in three weeks to meet the date tied to the wasted advance. By the time *Crime and Punishment* was published as a book, a popular success that sold well, he had married the girl he had hired to take his dictation of *The Gambler*. Much younger than he, she was devoted, sensible and firm, and his life was now set in a gradually steadier course.

Crime and Punishment explores the motives and the fate of a clever young man of the 1860s who translates into murder the freedom to act established as irreducibly human by the "underground man". Raskolnikov needs money because he is in debt, to prevent his mother and his sister sacrificing their lives for him and because he has decided that he deserves a brilliant future. His victim is a horrible old woman, a pawnbroker who profits from the sufferings of the poor and mistreats her simple, harmless sister. Like Macbeth, Raskolnikov is drawn on the day of the murder in a stunned daze toward his crime, "slavishly and stubbornly, fumbling for some valid objections in all directions, as though someone were compelling and pushing him to do it".[51] He has to murder the harmless sister as well as the old woman. He is careful and leaves no clues; there is nothing to connect him to the crime. The rest of the book, crowded with other characters— including a cold, rational capitalist and a deeply sinister, vicious immoralist, Svidrigaylov, a dark alter ego of Raskolnikov—is the story of Raskolnikov's growing recognition both of the truth of what he has done and of his compulsion to confess. In a charged conversation, ostensibly theoretical, civil but terrifying, with an examining magistrate almost sure of his guilt, Raskolnikov develops a Nietzschean thesis. There is a division between the great mass of ordinary people and the very few "who possess the gift or talent to say *a new word*". The very few "all transgress the law and are all destroyers", particularly "of the present in the name of a better future". There is a "law of nature" yet to be discovered, by which many millions will produce "a man of genius", and thousands of millions "a great genius, the crowning glory of mankind". When successful, this genius will "begin executing".[52] Behind this conversation lurks the Russian vision of the Antichrist, the man-god—the very reverse of the God-man, who is Christ alone. Both will come into clearer focus later in Dostoyevsky's work.

Meanwhile, Raskolnikov eventually confesses his crime to Sonia, a destitute girl forced into prostitution by the plight of her wretched family. He is drawn to her but scorns her for her "feeble-minded" belief in God. When she responds to his confession with pity rather than recoil, he tries his thesis on her: "He who dares much is right ... and he who dares more than anyone is more right than anyone." But when Sonia cries in horror: "You have turned away from God, and God has struck you down and handed you over to Satan", he agrees with her. In a striking premonition of Nietzsche's madman proclaiming the death of God ("and we have murdered him"), Sonia orders him to "stand at the cross-roads ... bow down to all the four corners of the world—and say to all men aloud, I am a murderer." [53]

Raskolnikov does not lose his "underground" conviction, reproaching himself not for the murder but for his confession and his failure to kill himself, until the last paragraphs of the book. After a year in prison (Omsk again), treating roughly the devoted Sonia who has followed him to Siberia, he turns conclusively to her, to her love and to the New Testament he had asked her for but not yet opened. "Life had taken the place of dialectics, and something quite different had to work itself out in his mind." [54] Only in Russia, which had joined the tradition of European reason, that is, "dialectics", after it had become atheist, could reason appear so starkly as the enemy of faith.

Dostoyevsky's next novel, *The Idiot*, was written in Germany, Switzerland and Italy, where he was travelling with his young wife, fleeing creditors, the censors, his liberal friends who knew by now that he had deserted the secular cause, and fresh grief: his first, beloved, child died in Geneva in 1868. Nevertheless, he finished the book in sixteen months. He had set himself an extraordinarily demanding challenge: "the portrayal of a truly perfect and beautiful human being". He knew how difficult this would be: "What is beautiful is what is ideal, but the ideal, in Russia just as much as in civilized Europe, has not been secure for some time now. There is really only one positively beautiful figure: Christ." [55] The only literary precedent was the figure of Don Quixote, to whom there are occasional, anchoring references in the novel, as there are to Pushkin's chivalric ballad "The Poor Knight". But Cervantes solved the problem by making his hero (also) comic. Dostoyevsky approached, and solved, the problem quite differently. Prince Myshkin, his central character, firmly set in the messy social and political reality of contemporary upper-class Russia, is an outsider because he has lived in Switzerland for years, being treated for severe epilepsy. He is an orphan, a penniless prince at the end of his family line, who is suddenly left a lot of money. Partly, but only partly, because of his illness and his strange, secluded past—as a child he was much punished by one of his guardians but much loved by the other, now a nun—he is without the ordinary human desires for sex, power, money and social success, but also without the (Tolstoyan) desire to be good, or to feel that he is good. Into the space left by these absences in his nevertheless human and believable personality, Dostoyevsky puts an uncluttered openness to others, disinterested fellow feeling and the uncanny perceptiveness of a mind and heart unclouded by self-interest. Not in the usual sense in the least "an idiot", he is nevertheless a gentlemanly version of the Russian "holy fool", a humble teller of the truth, apologetic often for not expressing himself as well as he would like, always wholly unconscious of his qualities.

A grotesque and violent story, driven by the desires and ambitions he does not share, rages intensely round Myshkin, pulling him, because of his ready sympathy, into its vortex. Two highly strung women, both beautiful, one an impressionable society girl romantically seeking a husband, the other a hysterical victim of predatory men and addicted to the drama of her own suffering, collide in their need for his loving responsiveness, which each mistakes for passion. His alter ego, Rogozhin, wild and careless but not deliberately evil like Svidrigaylov in *Crime and Punishment*, is a rich, boorish merchant, bound to Myshkin in what Rogozhin takes to be rivalry for the love of the second woman. A frantic meeting between the two women, and Rogozhin's unassuagable erotic possessiveness, propel the novel toward its climax, the murder the reader understands to be by now inevitable. Myshkin disappears into the illness from which he emerged at the outset, the world too much for his rare spirit.

Myshkin's Christlike quality is always evident to the reader but is touched on only occasionally and glancingly by Dostoyevsky. Myshkin tells other characters, in passing, of things he has seen and heard. He describes, to a footman who is moved by his account, an execution he saw in Lyons, saying how much more dreadful than mere murder—this is very early in the book—judicial murder seems to him:

> Possibly there are men [there had been Dostoyevsky] who have sentence of death read out to them and have been given time to go through this torture, and have then been told, You can go now, you've been reprieved. . . . It was of agony like this and of such horror that Christ spoke.[56]

Later in this long book, there is a short scene of powerful intensity. Myshkin and Rogozhin are alone in Rogozhin's oppressive house, the atmosphere between them heavy with Rogozhin's misplaced jealousy. On the wall there is a reproduction of Holbein's painting of the dead Christ. (Dostoyevsky himself was painfully struck, no doubt partly because the subject is one that does not appear in Orthodox iconography, by the original, which he saw in Basel while he was writing *The Idiot*. By an odd coincidence, the young Hopkins, travelling in Switzerland before joining the Jesuits, was struck, though not painfully, by the same painting a month later. Nietzsche, the same age as Hopkins, arrived in Basel to teach classical philology the following year.) Rogozhin says: "I like looking at that picture", and the implication is that the painting confirms his lack of faith, his certainty that God is dead. Myshkin tells him briefly of four people he met by chance during the week before: a civilised atheist he talked to on a train, a peasant who, with a prayer to God for forgiveness, had murdered his friend for a watch, a drunken soldier who sold him the worthless tin cross from his neck for a few coppers, and a young peasant woman who crossed herself at her baby's first smile and explained: "Well, sir, just as a mother rejoices seeing her baby's first smile, so does God rejoice every time he beholds from above a sinner kneeling down before him." This last tale suddenly deepens Myshkin's observation of the atheist on the train:

> He doesn't believe in God. One thing struck me, though: he didn't seem to be talking about that at all. . . . Before, too, whenever I met unbelievers and however many of their books I read, I could not help feeling that they were not talking or writing about that at all, though they may appear to do so. I told him this . . . but he did not understand what I was talking about.[57]

Credo ut intelligam: there is a depth at which faith and (mere) reason do not meet.

Much in *The Idiot*, including this perception, is further and more confidently developed in one or other of the two great novels Dostoyevsky was yet to write. The disreputable gang of young nihilists who try to deceive Myshkin out of a large sum of money—he is, by ordinary standards, absurdly generous throughout the book—are a preliminary version of the more terrifying and older conspirators of *The Devils*. "Rights" is their much-vaunted watchword, but their only belief is that might is right. Myshkin sees a dire warning for the future in the annihilation of conscience in these young men, who are "different" from the most hardened criminal, who "still knows that he *is* a criminal".[58] One of the gang is a seventeen-year-old intellectual, dying of consumption, another proto-Nietzschean: "I wanted to be a leader of men—I had a right to. . . . I wanted to live for the happiness of all men, for the discovery and proclamation of the truth." [59] He mocks Myshkin in a feverish mixture of admiration and hatred and reads out a long explanation of his reasons for making a free choice of suicide because it is the only free choice he has. He has also been shattered by the real death evident in Rogozhin's Holbein: the terror induced by the painting was followed by a nightmare in which Rogozhin came into his room through a locked door in a ghastly parody of the resurrected Christ. It was this experience that decided him for suicide in the face of blind, inevitable, death-dealing nature. But there is another boy in *The Idiot*, a bright, perceptive free spirit who promises, from the unhappiness he says he and Myshkin share, to be Myshkin's faithful servant for ever. His successor in *The Brothers Karamazov* even has the same name, Kolya.

* * *

In 1869, the year that *The Idiot* was completed, a particularly shocking murder took place in Moscow. At the instigation and with the help of a young wire-puller, setting up from Geneva revolutionary cells of five in Russia, a radical student was killed by the other four members of his cell. Dostoyevsky, still living abroad and still harried by creditors, was attempting to order a plethora of competing, proliferating ideas for what he intended to be his last, vastly ambitious, novel. Under the impact of the murder story, he divided the ideas and the scheme and wrote not one but two more huge novels, very different in organisation and in tone.

The first, *The Devils* (sometimes translated as *The Possessed*), was written in Russia in 1871–1872, when the murderers of the student were still at large. It develops, to terrifying effect, the vicious cruelty of Svidrigaylov and the nihilism of Raskolnikov and *The Idiot*'s gang of hooligans into a worst-case prophecy of the future of Russia. The plot of the novel is complicated, difficult to grasp at first reading, melodramatic and chillingly violent. So are the plots of *Hamlet* and *King Lear*, and the comparison is not adventitious, for this is the most Shakespearean of all Dostoyevsky's works. "Shakespeare", Dostoyevsky wrote in his notebook when he was writing *The Devils*, "is a prophet, sent by God, to proclaim to us the mystery of man and of the human soul." [60] The understanding of evil in the souls of those who have abandoned God, the understanding, in particular, of the depths of contempt for other human beings in such souls, is what

Dostoyevsky in this novel above all shares with Shakespeare. His central character, Stavrogin, is explicitly compared to Prince Hal, fooling disingenuously with the devoted riffraff he has collected about him. But Stavrogin, whose mother thinks he is more like Hamlet, has also the heartless sexual power of Edmund and the arrogant aloofness of Coriolanus. He is the antithesis of Prince Myshkin. Whereas Myshkin is "the wretched little prince, a sickly idiot"[61] but in his responsiveness to others is always alongside the suffering, however little they deserve his understanding, Stavrogin is fatally attractive, clever, controlled and absolutely unresponsive to others, the empty space in his soul just that, a terrifying void. Myshkin is close to Christ; Stavrogin is close to the devil (and perhaps to Dostoyevsky's "own Mephistopheles" in his radical youth). He is a descendant of the "superfluous men" of earlier in the century, a rich landowner with nothing useful to do, who has tried dissipation (he has seduced a child—the chapter known as "Stavrogin's Confession" was cut out by the censors and is absent from standard editions of the novel), Petersburg society, duels (he has killed a man) and finally, international terrorism. He destroys in the course of the novel the lives of four very different women. By the time he returns to the provincial town of his childhood, his playing with current ideas—atheism, socialism, organisation of revolutionary cells set up by exiled Russians in Geneva—has come together with his magnetic personality to create a band of disparate admirers in a conspiracy of terror that will destroy all of them, except one. Peter Verkhovensky is Stavrogin's henchman, Iago translated into contemporary Russia, a manipulative liar, spy and double agent driven by malice, by both admiration and hatred for Stavrogin and by thirst for power. It is he who organises, with destructive efficiency, the multiple catastrophe that is the climax of the book, his success demonstrating, like Iago's, the ease with which combustible materials—here, the modish, readily deceived upper classes, oppressed factory workers and a peasant with a grudge, happy to become a hired murderer, as well as the muddled conspirators—can be assembled and set alight by sheer malevolence. Like Iago, he survives his achievements. He disappears on a train, leaving the murder and suicide of others behind him.

High society in the town, and all we see of the church, are as corrupt as those who seek to destroy them. In an atmosphere of louche, hectic frivolity, encouraged by the conceit of the governor's wife, who thinks she can control the sinister hangers-on it amuses her to befriend, a party of fashionable young people visits a monastery. They gloat, on the way, over a wretched anonymous suicide in an inn; they gloat over a thoroughly unpleasant "holy fool" exploited for money by the local monks.

Against so much that is negative and violent in the book, there are set a few gentle passages, particularly concerning Shatov, the only one of Stavrogin's disciples to have taken seriously Stavrogin's moment of playing with Slavophilism (as he played with every other fashionable idea), and two of the women, both called Mary, one of them Shatov's wife, who are among the victims of Stavrogin's careless cruelty. The complexity, lies, deceit and mere talk of the whole book form the murky backdrop for the warmth and light of the passage describing the return of Shatov's wife and the birth of her baby, Stavrogin's child. This scene is shadowed by the reader's knowledge that Shatov will shortly be killed, in one of the most chilling murders in literature. Almost as horrifying, though more melodramatic, is the suicide of the other revolutionary with whom we have some sympathy, Kirilov, this book's Nietzschean character:

> Man is not yet what he will be. A new man will come, happy and proud. To whom it won't matter whether he lives or not.... He who conquers pain and fear will himself be a god. And that other God will not be.... Then history will be divided into two parts: from the gorilla to the annihilation of God, and from the annihilation of God to—

"To the gorilla?" puts in the scantly delineated narrator of the novel.[62] Kirilov, like Rogozhin with his Holbein, is haunted by the death, unfollowed by Resurrection, of Christ on the Cross: "And if that is so, if the laws of nature did not spare even *Him*, if they did not spare their own miracle, and made even Him live in the midst of lies and die for a lie, then the whole planet is a lie. What, then, is there to live for?"[63]

In the stark evocation of mounting horror that is *The Devils*, one other major character gives the reader some relief. Stepan Verkhovensky, the malevolent Peter's father, is an ageing "man of the forties", "a liberal without any aim whatever",[64] vaguely in favour of art and of the peasants (of whom he knows nothing) and vaguely against Christianity. A salon dilettante who has read Tolstoy, he believes in God, "*mais distinguons*, I believe in him as a Being who is conscious of himself in me only.... I'm an ancient pagan, like the great Goethe, or like an ancient Greek."[65] He has been dependent for years, stranded as if in a Chekhov play, on the charity of a rich, wilful widow (Stavrogin's mother); he keeps bound copies of Herzen's *The Bell* and likes to think of himself as watched by the police because dangerously abreast of new ideas. He is the only truly comic figure in all Dostoyevsky. An innocent at large—"The enthusiasm of our modern youth is as bright and pure as it was in our time"[66]—he flees the conflagration in the town, setting out on "his last pilgrimage" like a character in *Waiting for Godot*, with a suggestion of Mr. Toad. "He sighed vaguely, put down his bag beside a willow, and sat down to rest. As he was sitting down, he felt shivery and wrapped himself in his rug; becoming aware of the rain, he put up his umbrella.... 'And there's a great idea in the open road too!'" [67] Exhausted and ill, he is rescued by a kind, evangelising woman and undergoes a touching, faintly absurd, deathbed conversion. But it is he who asks his new friend to read him the story of the devils cast by Jesus out of the maniac and into the Gadarene swine—the epigraph to the novel—and he compares the sick man to Russia, and the swine to his son; "*et les autres avec lui*", he adds, in his habitual drawing-room French, "and perhaps I at the head of them all." [68]

Meanwhile, Stavrogin, the devils gone out of him to destroy his followers, hangs himself in his mother's house, where, as a boy, he was taught by Stepan Verkhovensky.

1. Quoted in Lindsey Hughes, *Peter the Great* (New Haven and London, 2002), p. 146.
2. Quoted in Isaiah Berlin, *Russian Thinkers* (London, 1979), pp. 172–73.
3. Alexander Solzhenitsyn, *Nobel Prize Lecture*, trans. Nicholas Bethell (London, 1973), pp. 53, 55.
4. Quoted in Berlin, *Russian Thinkers*, p. 103.
5. Ibid., p. 200.
6. Ivan Turgenev, *Fathers and Sons*, trans. Rosemary Edmonds (London, 1965), p. 128.
7. Ivan Turgenev, *Home of the Gentry*, trans. Richard Freeborn (London, 1970), p. 188.
8. Ibid., p. 32.
9. Turgenev, *Fathers and Sons*, p. 295.
10. Ibid., pp. 293–94.
11. Turgenev, *Home of the Gentry*, p. 45.
12. Rom 12:20.
13. Turgenev, *Fathers and Sons*, p. 142.
14. Leo Tolstoy, *A Confession and Other Religious Writings*, trans. Jane Kentish (London, 1987), p. 12.
15. Leo Tolstoy, *War and Peace*, trans. Louise and Aylmer Maude (Oxford, 1941), vol. 1, bk. 5, chap. 10.
16. Ibid., chap. 11.
17. Leo Tolstoy, *Anna Karenina*, trans. Rosemary Edmonds (London, 1954), p. 527.
18. Ibid., p. 823.
19. Ibid., p. 829.
20. Ibid., p. 834.
21. Tolstoy, *Confession*, p. 47.
22. Ibid., p. 60.
23. Leo Tolstoy, *The Death of Ivan Ilyich and Other Stories*, trans. Rosemary Edmonds (London, 1960), p. 160.
24. Tolstoy, *Confession*, p. 136.
25. Ibid., pp. 149, 145.
26. Leo Tolstoy, *Resurrection*, trans. Rosemary Edmonds (London, 1966), pp. 565–66.
27. Friedrich Nietzsche, *Twilight of the Idols*, trans. R.J. Hollingdale (London, 1968), p. 69.
28. Quoted in George Steiner, *Tolstoy or Dostoevsky* (1960; London, 1967), p. 235.

29. Ibid., p. 240.
30. Tolstoy, *Resurrection*, p. 321.
31. Lk 6:40.
32. John Milton, *Paradise Lost*, 12.587.
33. Tolstoy, *Resurrection*, p. 141.
34. Ibid., p. 367.
35. Ibid., p. 383.
36. Ibid., pp. 364–66.
37. Ibid., p. 561.
38. Quoted in Steiner, *Tolstoy or Dostoevsky*, p. 294.
39. Matthew Arnold, "Count Leo Tolstoi", in *Works* (London, 1903), 4:203–4.
40. Fyodor Dostoyevsky, *Memoirs from the House of the Dead*, trans. Jessie Coulson (1956; Oxford, 1983), pp. 308–9.
41. Ibid., p. 307.
42. Ibid., p. 76.
43. Ibid., p. 244.
44. Ibid., p. 273.
45. Quoted in A. Boyce Gibson, *The Religion of Dostoevsky* (London, 1973), p. 22.
46. Fyodor Dostoyevsky, *Notes from Underground*, trans. Jessie Coulson (London, 1972), p. 21.
47. Ibid., p. 31.
48. Ibid., p. 33.
49. Ibid., pp. 37–38.
50. Ibid., pp. 34, 123.
51. Fyodor Dostoyevsky, *Crime and Punishment*, trans. David Magarshack (London, 1951), p. 90.
52. Ibid., pp. 277–80.
53. Ibid., pp. 431–33.
54. Ibid., p. 558.
55. Quoted in Hans Urs von Balthasar, *The Glory of the Lord: A Theological Aesthetics*, vol. 5, trans. Andrew Davies et al. (San Francisco and Edinburgh, 1991), p. 190.
56. Fyodor Dostoyevsky, *The Idiot*, trans. David Magarshack (London, 1955), p. 48.
57. Ibid., pp. 250–55.
58. Ibid., p. 374.
59. Ibid., p. 332.
60. Quoted in Steiner, *Tolstoy or Dostoevsky*, p. 157.
61. Dostoyevsky, *Idiot*, p. 547.
62. Fyodor Dostoyevsky, *The Devils*, trans. David Magarshack (London, 1953), p. 126.
63. Ibid., p. 614.
64. Ibid., p. 47.
65. Ibid., p. 51.
66. Ibid., p. 483.
67. Ibid., pp. 627, 638.
68. Ibid., p. 648.

CHAPTER TWENTY

RUSSIA II

The Brothers Karamazov to Solzhenitsyn

D ostoyevsky's last and greatest novel, *The Brothers Karamazov*, completed only three months before his death, took two years and four months to write but was his whole life in the making. As a boy of ten, he saw a performance he never forgot of *The Robbers*, Friedrich von Schiller's Shakespearean *Sturm und Drang* play about fratricidal jealousy, treachery and suicide. When Dostoyevsky was eighteen, his father was murdered. In prison in Omsk, he met a young officer, who later turned out to be innocent, convicted of killing his own father. All these came together in the plot of the novel, which concerns the murder of a father by one of his four sons and the wrongful conviction of another son. Through the complexities and the manifold inwardness—for we learn a great deal about each son—of a very long narrative, suspense is remarkably sustained: not until four-fifths of the way through the novel does the reader discover which son is the murderer. But the final formation and placing in relation to each other of the ideas, hopes and terrors that had all his life jostled for first place in Dostoyevsky's mind go, in the intricate workings of this book, much deeper than the plot.

The three legitimate sons of old Karamazov, a monster of lust, greed, selfishness and contempt, are rounded characters, entirely believable as individuals and as brothers, but in each of them there predominates one element of those to be found, if often reduced to the merest trace, in every human being. The eldest, Mitya, a soldier, the most neglected of the three as a motherless child, lives passionately through his senses, a prey to temptations familiar for much of his life to Dostoyevsky. His half-brother Ivan is an intellectual, a modern rationalist in search of a utopian programme, feeling acutely the cruelty of the human world: Dostoyevsky's daughter said that Ivan was her father's "retrospective portrait of himself as a young man".[1] Both Mitya and Ivan are drawn with much more sympathy than the characters in earlier Dostoyevsky novels who share some of their failings. Ivan, for example, is set off against a brittle nihilist, Rakitin, whose manipulative cruelty shows Ivan's disastrous influence on the illegitimate brother, Smerdyakov, treated as a servant by old Karamazov, to be angry carelessness rather than intentional evil. The third legitimate son, Ivan's full brother Alyosha, is a novice in a monastery. In him qualities of the soul predominate.

Alyosha has less in common than his brothers with Dostoyevsky himself at any period of his life, or with any earlier Dostoyevsky character. He shares neither the isolation in goodness of the Sonia of *Crime and Punishment*, the mysterious otherworldliness of the "idiot" Prince Myshkin nor the Slavophile stubbornness of the lonely Shatov. Describing Alyosha early in the novel, Dostoyevsky says:

> He was to a certain extent a young man of our own times, that is, honest by nature, demanding truth, seeking it, believing in it, and, believing in it, demanding to serve it with all the strength of his soul.... Alyosha merely chose a path leading in the opposite direction to that of all the others, but with the same ardent desire for swift achievement.... If he had decided that there was no immortality and no God, he would at once have become an atheist and a Socialist.[2]

On the scale of the consequences of that "merely", of the choice between Christian truth and the apparently rational, utopian choice of "all the others", hangs much of the novel. The starkness of these alternatives is not just youthful; it is wholly characteristic of educated Russians in the later nineteenth century.

Alyosha is the product of new discoveries, new experiences, of the ageing, now-famous and widely admired Dostoyevsky. A large public was reading his frequent articles, *Diary of a Writer*, published at first in a reactionary Slavophile periodical and then by Dostoyevsky himself, in which he responded to current ideas and events and worked through much preparation for *The Brothers Karamazov*. Many people wrote to him or came to see him for advice. He became a friend of the chief procurator of the Holy Synod, the very man later damningly attacked by Tolstoy in *Resurrection*. More importantly for the novel, a young philosopher, only twenty when Dostoyevsky met him in 1873, became not only a friend but in many respects the model for Alyosha. Vladimir Soloviev was an extraordinarily gifted academic and writer, the son of a Moscow University professor with friends among the aristocracy, a kind of Orthodox Christian Dostoyevsky had never before known well: he also had a Saint Francis–like personal simplicity and saintliness. He knew the elders of the Optino monastery, where the ancient Russian tradition of monastic life and teaching had been revived fifty years before on the model of the eighteenth-century Saint Tikhon of Zadonsk, always admired by Dostoyevsky, and Saint Seraphim of Sarov. This was the underground current of Russian contemplative austerity, almost lost forever under the impact of Peter the Great and Catherine the Great's westernizing. When, in May 1878, Dostoyevsky's three-year-old only son (called Alyosha) died of the epilepsy he had inherited from his father, Soloviev took the brokenhearted Dostoyevsky to stay for a week at Optino, where Dostoyevsky met and talked at length to the elder of the day, Father Amvrosy.

A month later he started to write *The Brothers Karamazov*, beginning the action in a monastery, and taking Father Zossima, the monastery elder and Alyosha's beloved mentor, as the father figure against whose goodness the moral dereliction of old Karamazov looks all the blacker. (There are other father figures in the book, including the old servant who gave Mitya what care he had as a child.) Later, book 6 of the twelve into which the novel is divided tells us of Father Zossima's early life, a life exactly like that of the young Tolstoy and many of his characters: a pious childhood; then the excitement, glamour and false values of the Cadet Corps; Petersburg high society; and the Imperial Guard. After years of this "honourable", pleasure-filled existence, his heart and mind are changed forever by a foolish duel—the duel is a leitmotif in the lives of Russian writers and in their books—and his own impatient bullying of a soldier-servant. He learns, with the help of a mysterious stranger burdened with his own guilt, of truthfulness, penitence and the love and forgiveness of God, and he becomes a monk. By the time we meet him, he is a wise and venerable figure, drawing to the monastery every day a crowd of peasants and others who come for his help and advice and for healing. He has all the sympathy and intuition of Myshkin but with the solid strength given him by decades of monastic formation and discipline. He is bitterly resented by some of the other monks, in particular by a fanatical old bigot, Father Ferapont (whose blinkered ferocity tells us a good deal about what Dostoyevsky did and did not admire in the Russian church of his time).

It is through Father Zossima's eyes, in a long, fraught scene in his monastery, that the reader, who as yet knows almost nothing of him, nevertheless first sees the Karamazov family. The elder's implied judgement of the dissolute old father, of the clever Ivan and the recklessly emotional Mitya, as well as of his own young disciple Alyosha, remains in the reader's mind for the rest of the book. Ivan, who has written a speculative thesis, taken with a pinch of salt by the elder, about the ideal relation between church and state, is reported by an ageing liberal (much less endearing than Stepan Verkhovensky) to have announced that, since there is no immortality, "everything is permitted". Father Zossima notices that Ivan is suffering real pain because, fully understanding the implications of this statement, he cannot decide whether or not it is true. "Thank the Creator", Zossima tells him, "who has given you a heart capable of such agony.... God grant that your heart's answer will find you still on earth." [3] As for Mitya, the elder, at the end of the scene he astonishes everyone by suddenly prostrating himself at the young man's feet. Hundreds of pages later (on the next day), Zossima, close to death, explains to Alyosha that he had seen in Mitya's face "the great suffering that is in store for him".[4] He then quotes the verse from Saint John's Gospel, laden with tragic prophecy but also with hope, that Dostoyevsky used as the epigraph to the novel: "Except a corn of wheat fall into the ground and die, it abideth alone: but if it die, it bringeth forth much fruit." [5]

The anguish of indecision that the elder saw in Ivan underlies three chapters of conversation between Ivan and Alyosha in book 5 of the novel, which Dostoyevsky called "Pro and Contra". Ivan is close to the revolutionary nihilism rife among the educated young in Russia: we have already seen, in a long evening at old Karamazov's after the meeting in the monastery, the effect Ivan's talk has had on the intelligent, loutish peasant, his half-brother Smerdyakov, and Ivan's certainty that there will be a revolution. He says of Smerdyakov, "First-class material when the time comes.... At first there will be fellows like him. The better ones will come after." [6] (Fifteen years after 1917, Nicholas Berdyaev wrote: "The relationship between Smerdyakov and Ivan is an excellent type of the relationship between 'the people' and the intelligentsia at a time of revolution." [7])

But doubt tortures Ivan. He responds acutely to the freshness and beauty of creation, "the sticky little leaves that open up in the spring", and he plans to travel to Europe, the source, for him as for Dostoyevsky, of much more than nihilism: "I know very well that I'm only going to a graveyard, but it's a most precious graveyard—yes, indeed! Precious are the dead that lie there." Alyosha seizes on both these signs of the positive in his brother: "Half your work is done, Ivan: you love life. Now you must try to do the second half and you are saved ... to raise up your dead who have perhaps never died at all." [8] As the conversation goes on, the reader realises, with Alyosha, that what he is up against in Ivan is not a rejection of God's existence but a rejection of God as the creator of a world of hideous cruelty that nothing, certainly not "forgiveness", can ever put right. "I hasten to return my ticket of admission.... It is not God that I do not accept, Alyosha. I merely most respectfully return him the ticket." Ivan is a long way from Nietzschean joy in freedom from the moral restraint that was once anchored in the existence of God: his agonised justification for "returning his ticket" is a catalogue of horror—incidents of cruelty to young children taken from newspaper reports, a kind of cruelty that haunted Dostoyevsky always and that is not to be called "bestial", since that is "very unfair and insulting to the beasts". In hysterical triumph Ivan gets Alyosha to agree, for an instant, that a particularly disgusting perpetrator of this kind of cruelty ought to be shot: it is a moment of victory for Ivan because he wants to detach Alyosha from his Christian loyalty: "You're dear to me. I don't want to let you go and I won't give you up to your Zossima." But Alyosha pulls himself together and remembers not only that judgement is, in the end, for God and not for us, but that Christ "gave his innocent blood for all and for everything. You've forgotten him, but it is on him that the edifice is founded and it is to him that they will cry aloud: 'Thou art just, O Lord, for thy ways are revealed.' "[9] It is this swift summary of what is essential to Christianity that provokes Ivan's "poem", "made up about a year ago" and never written down, the legend of the Grand Inquisitor that Ivan calls "an absurd thing" but that occupies the twenty pages[10] of which Dostoyevsky said he was most proud.

Ivan's story tells of Christ's appearance in sixteenth-century Seville, the time and place of the Catholic Church at her cruellest, pitilessly clearing southern Spain of its Muslims and Jews. Christ heals the sick and raises the dead. The Grand Inquisitor, a terrifying figure borrowed from Schiller's *Don Carlos* (as some of the plot of this novel is borrowed from *The Robbers*), has Christ arrested. Then he harangues him as a heretic who, on the next day, will be burned at the stake. The Inquisitor's tremendous diatribe appears for a while to be an attack on the Catholic Church, an institution that deprives the faithful of their freedom in order to make them happy. To achieve this, the Church is exercising the very powers, prophetic of all use of God in the interests of human *libido dominandi*, that Christ refused when he was offered them in the wilderness by the devil: the power to feed the hungry ("Feed them first and then demand virtue of them"); the power to seize men's souls by incontrovertible miracles; and temporal power, not yet complete, over the whole world. The eventual result will be childlike happiness for obedient millions—entertained, controlled, spied-on, entirely without freedom—and freedom and grief only for the rulers "who have taken upon themselves the curse of the knowledge of good and evil". Then there will be, for the great mass of the people, no truth, no immortality and no sin, and for the rulers who have "*corrected your work*", the Inquisitor tells Christ, defiance: "Judge us if you can and if you dare." By now it has dawned on Alyosha, who springs to the defence even of Rome, which should not be defined only by its entanglement with earthly power, that what is being described is the kingdom of the devil and that the meaning of the story is that the Inquisitor does not believe in God. On the modern reader (who may have caught the eerie pre-monition of Bertolt Brecht's "Erst kommt das Fressen; dann kommt die Moral") it has dawned, with the recognition of prophecy fulfilled, that Ivan's nightmare vision is a premonition of Leninist and Stalinist Russia, of the Communist regime that in its seventy years of spied-on, freedomless oppression killed tens of millions of Russians in the name of "the world state and universal peace", the Inquisitor's phrase.

Christ, to whom all this is addressed, says nothing. Then "he suddenly approached the old man, and kissed him gently on his bloodless, aged lips. That was all his answer." And Ivan's tale ends with the old man letting the silent Christ go, into "the dark streets and lanes of the city". So Ivan, though he tries to turn Alyosha's response aside with a flippant denial that his poem meant anything and a chilling resolve to "live" as a self-indulgent Karamazov but only "to thirty—and then dash the cup to the floor", has still not made up his mind. His legend, indeed, shows him as close to Shatov in *The Devils*, who was sure of Christ, unsure, until just before his death, of God. In the rush of events that follow in this novel, Ivan Karamazov never makes up his mind about either.

*   *   *

The next day, Father Zossima dies an exemplary death, and Alyosha is plunged into a spiritual crisis "causing a violent shock, but finally strengthening his mind for the rest of his life and giving it a definite aim".[11] It is not the elder's expected death that causes the crisis but the crushing disappointment that follows: Alyosha the devoted disciple, with all the pious people of the town, expects Father Zossima's holiness to be confirmed with a traditional miracle, the incorruptible body of the saint. When ordinary decomposition quickly sets in, Father Ferapont and all the elder's enemies are gleeful; Alyosha is shattered, his faith evaporating before "the blind, dumb and pitiless laws of nature" that strike him suddenly as they had struck Rogozhin and Kirilov. Rakitin sneers at his naïve expectation: "But damn it all, a thirteen-year-old schoolboy doesn't believe in that now."[12] Dostoyevsky resolves Alyosha's crisis with the complex economy characteristic of his writing at its best.

Rakitin and the deeply shaken Alyosha together visit Grushenka, the beautiful woman in disreputable circumstances with whom both Mitya and old Karamazov are obsessed. Rakitin's intention is to organise the seduction, and therefore spiritual downfall, of Alyosha: he fails, after a scene of sharp sexual tension unpleasantly heightened by Rakitin, because Alyosha's compassion for Grushenka dissolves her automatic predatoriness into friendly affection. (The scene is a realistic parallel to Kundry's failed seduction of Parsifal under Klingsor's malicious auspices in Richard Wagner's *Parsifal*, written in the same three years as *The Brothers Karamazov*.) With no pious intention, perhaps by the grace of God, Alyosha has done something good here. Back beside Father Zossima's coffin, listening sleepily to the monk who has inherited care of him reading the story of Jesus's miracle at the wedding in Cana from Saint John's Gospel, Alyosha dreams that he sees Father Zossima greeting him in forgiveness. Alyosha, decisively restored to faith and obedience, leaves the monastery according to the elder's last instruction to him, for his "sojourn in the world". The whole episode has been a lesson in Christian freedom, connected to Ivan's Legend of the Grand Inquisitor because the incontrovertible miracle was one of the temptations Jesus resisted. Miracles cannot be commanded; they, like faith, are given; coercion is profoundly incompatible with both. Dostoyevsky wrote in one of his last notes: "The Saviour did not descend from the cross because he did not wish to convert men through the compulsion of an outward miracle, but through freedom of belief." [13] The thought, as we have seen, occurred frequently to Pascal: "It was not right for Christ to appear in a fashion obviously divine and able absolutely to convince everyone; but nor was it right for him to come in a fashion so hidden that he could not be recognised by those who would sincerely seek him." [14]

The "world" to which Alyosha returns is the world of his suffering brothers. Mitya on this same night is lost in a tangle of passion, desperation, money, violence and blood, with every motive to kill his father and the opportunity to do it. His night culminates in a wild party at a country inn with his dearly loved Grushenka and a crowd of drunken peasants. Here Mitya is arrested for his father's murder. On his headlong dash to the inn, it occurs to Mitya that he is hurtling toward hell. Echoing other stories told earlier in the novel, one by Ivan before his legend and one by Grushenka, his coachman tells him that Christ on Holy Saturday set free all the sinners in hell, but, though hell will fill again with "the great men, the rulers, the chief judges, and the rich", "the Lord will forgive you for your being simple-hearted." [15] There is a Tolstoyan note here; but Mitya, unlike Pierre or Levin, feels worse rather than better at the peasant's words and prays frantically for forgiveness. At his arrest he cries out, truthfully, as the reader discovers only much later, "I nearly did kill him! But, then, I didn't kill him. My guardian angel saved me." [16] As with Alyosha, a dream, from inside himself but revealing the hidden truth about a choice long made, resolves Mitya's crisis. Still in the inn, exhausted by questioning and about to be remanded in prison, he falls asleep on a chest and dreams of a burned-out village in the steppe, starving women and a crying baby at a milkless breast. "Why?" he asks in the dream, "why are they so black with black misfortune?" "He wanted to do something for everyone so that the baby should cry no more." He wakes from the nightmare, which is a release in him of compassion and love, calmed, remembering Grushenka's promise to stay with him always and finding a pillow under his head that someone, feeling sorry for him, has put there. At once he accepts the punishment that is in store for him, "not because I killed him but because I wanted to kill him and, perhaps, would, in fact, have killed him."[17]

So, after six hundred pages, the novel reaches the end of the fourth day of the story; another third of the book is to come.

Alyosha, having recovered his own peace of mind, now has to fight for the peace of mind of both his brothers. Mitya, hysterical in his prison cell the day before his trial, is sure of God, despite the insidious cynicism of Rakitin, here as elsewhere Alyosha's enemy. Rakitin is a purveyor of what were already standard atheist clichés. In the monastery, he had produced the bland solution to the problem of morality untethered to God, to truth: we have, naturally, "the strength to live for virtue . . . , in love for liberty, equality and fraternity". Mitya can deal with this: "Rakitin says that one can love humanity without God. Well, only a little snivelling half-wit can maintain that!"[18] but is in despair nonetheless, partly because Ivan has shown his certainty of Mitya's guilt by planning his escape after he is convicted. Alyosha gives Mitya the strength he needs simply by telling him he is certain of his innocence (which the reader at this point is not).

Ivan before the trial is in far worse shape than Mitya, uncertain as ever of everything except what he feels, without yet knowing, to be his own guilt for his father's death. Alyosha cannot rescue him as he rescued Mitya, through confidence in his innocence. As the rational Ivan descends into madness, he has to face the truth: Smerdyakov killed their father because Ivan prompted him to: "You was brave enough then, sir. Everything, you said, is permitted, and look how frightened you are now!"[19] And all along Ivan wanted not Smerdyakov but Mitya to kill, to have killed, their father. Whereas both Alyosha and Mitya were delivered from crisis by dreams that surfaced from their own distant choices, Ivan is pushed into madness by a hallucination reaching him from the choice neither he nor the reader, till now, has realised that he has made. The devil visits him, in the guise of a figure familiar to everyone who has read some of the writing of nineteenth-century Russia: a down-at-heel sponger, with presentable manners, faded connexions with high society, and no remaining family or responsibilities. This banal apparition talks and talks in uncannily Nietzschean fashion, even of the ghastly entrapment of eternal recurrence (an idea Nietzsche reached in 1882, two years after this novel was finished). Just one passage, on the figure he does not call the *Übermensch*, will give the flavour of the apparition's talk:

> Since there is neither God nor immortality, anyway, the new man has a right to become a man-god, though he may be the only one in the whole world, and having attained that new rank, he may lightheartedly jump over every barrier of the old moral code of the former man-slave, if he deems it necessary.[20]

There are echoes in the devil's conversation of the underground man, of the gang of hooligans in *The Idiot* and of Kirilov in *The Devils*, but the horror of this scene, because of the sympathy for Ivan that Dostoyevsky has taken such care to build in the reader, is fresh and chilling, like the draught from a door opened into the night. By the time Alyosha arrives, with the news that Smerdyakov has killed himself, Ivan is raving: Alyosha understands that his condition is the result of his knowledge that the truth is required of him at the trial and his simultaneous lack of faith in God, who guarantees the power of truth over lies.

Mitya's trial, recounted in one hundred riveting pages, is itself a masterpiece of realist fiction. In one of the brief stories of kindness and gratitude that light the blackness of Karamazov life, a character witness for Mitya, an old German doctor not unlike Turgenev's musician in *Home of the Gentry*, tells how he once gave the neglected little boy a pound of nuts and taught him the names of the Trinity in German. Twenty-three years later, Mitya walked into his study and greeted him with "*Gott der Vater, Gott der Sohn* ... I've come to thank you for the pound of nuts." [21] After this story, darkness closes on the possibility of the truth prevailing in the courtroom. Ivan tells the truth but is evidently mad, and collapses. The self-dramatising woman of this novel, once engaged to Mitya but now in love with Ivan, lies to ensure Mitya's conviction. Two speeches by lawyers, both very long, enthral the reader and muddle the jury. The public prosecutor wonders how Russia can have become indifferent to such horrors as parricide. One of his answers to his own question has in it a good deal of Dostoyevsky's own insight into the condition of nineteenth-century Russia, unshared by any other country: "Our cynicism, the premature exhaustion of the intellect and the imagination of our society, which is still so young and yet has grown so decrepit before it has had time to grow old." [22] This speech is a demonstration, written with great skill, of how, with every fact in place, the truth can nevertheless be entirely subverted by descriptive tone (in this case, supercilious) and prior judgement (in this case, wrong). The defence speech, made by a famous

Petersburg advocate, is a grander rhetorical affair but turns out to be no more than an elaborate plea in mitigation since this lawyer, too, assumes that Mitya is guilty. After all this, and even after the innocent Mitya's impassioned appeal to them, the verdict of "guilty" returned by the jury is no surprise, particularly as Mitya is a gentleman: "Our dear old peasants have stood up for themselves." [23] (Trial by jury was less than twenty years old in Russia; politics and class prejudice were delivering many bad verdicts.)

At the end of the book, Alyosha has lost Ivan to mental breakdown and Mitya to a Siberian prison—"he understood", as did Dostoyevsky, "how hard it must be for a man like Mitya to pass over all at once into the company of thieves and murderers" [24]—or possibly to an escape to the wilds of America. Alyosha has not lost his group of boys, his friends and disciples, his connexion with whom is a thread bound into the skein of the whole novel. The funeral of Ilyusha, one of these boys who has died in squalid poverty but surrounded by his friends and held in the love of his useless, touchy but devoted father (another contrast to old Karamazov), is the very last event in the book. The leader of the group is Kolya, a more developed version of the boy of the same name in *The Idiot*. Although the hope for the future placed in these boys by Alyosha (and Dostoyevsky) seems fragile, even sentimental, against the dark future foreseen for Russia in all Dostoyevsky, especially in *The Devils*, the relationship between Alyosha and Kolya is composed as finely as anything in the novel. Kolya is a bright, precocious adolescent, "fourteen really—I shall be fourteen in a fortnight", with a heavily concealed kind heart, who has picked up from Rakitin every hackneyed opinion current among the disaffected young. "I'm a socialist. . . . It's when all are equal, all hold property in common, there are no marriages, and religion and laws are according to everyone's liking, and, well, all the rest of it." "If there were no God he'd have to be invented." Only mathematics and science are worth studying; classics "are nothing but a police measure". "Christianity has been useful only to the rich and powerful to keep the lower classes in slavery." [25] Alyosha's taming of this boy is beautifully drawn. Kolya patronises Alyosha, taking him to be naïve after years in the monastery. Alyosha, amused but hiding his amusement, treats Kolya as an adult, astutely separating him from his opinions: "Don't be like everyone else, even if you are the only one who is not." [26] ("Alyosha", the reader may remember, "merely chose a path leading in the opposite direction to that of all the others.") The result is a friendship good for both of them, confirmed for the reader when Alyosha echoes Father Zossima's perception of Mitya: "Listen, Kolya, I can't help feeling that you'll be very unhappy in life." [27]

* * *

The Brothers Karamazov has been, with good reason, compared to Dante's *Divine Comedy*. Each of these great works, completed shortly before the writer's death, is a summation of the writer's life, of his world and of his long reflection on that world. Just as Dante himself, both in his narrative and in the reality that his narrative distances, had travelled through each region of the soul, so Dostoyevsky had known the inferno that pulls Ivan into its depths, the purgatory of recognised and healed sin up which Mitya has to climb, and the glimpses of paradise to which Father Zossima's life and death have shown Alyosha the way. It is not surprising that, just as Dante's *Inferno* has always been the most read, most familiar section of his poem, so Ivan has been the most remembered, most referred to, of the Karamazov brothers, with his Legend of the Grand Inquisitor often taken to cancel conclusively what is positive and Christian in the novel. Many commentators have regarded book 6, Alyosha's account of Father Zossima's life, with a number of passages from the elder's "discourses and sermons", as a literary excrescence, a moralising essay dislocating the complex narrative flow of the novel. But for the reader of Dante who is thoroughly engaged by the climb of Purgatory and never afterward forgets the light of paradise, Father Zossima's teaching of Alyosha is no more eclipsed by Ivan than are Mitya's sufferings. After completing the book, Dostoyevsky wrote: "You might search Europe in vain for so powerful an expression of atheism. Thus it is not like a child that I believe in Christ and confess him. My hosanna has come forth from the crucible of doubt."[28] This is quietly true of Alyosha's youthful crisis of faith, and more strongly true of the long life of Father Zossima himself, to whom Dostoyevsky gives, in the "discourses" reported by Alyosha, some of the most powerful passages of prophecy he ever wrote. He foresees an intellectual consensus in which the spiritual will be "utterly rejected, dismissed with a sort of triumph, even with hatred". He also foresees that freedom will come to mean no more than the freedom of the market:

> We are assured that the world is getting more and more united and growing into a brotherly community by the reduction of distances and the transmission of ideas through the air. Alas, put no faith in such a union of peoples. By interpreting freedom as the multiplication and the rapid satisfaction of needs, they do violence to their own nature, for such an interpretation merely gives rise to many senseless and foolish desires, habits and most absurd inventions.[29]

All this will lead to increasing greed, increasing isolation and, among those wishing "to live a life based on justice by their reason alone", the abolition of the sense of sin.[30] In a world that has dispensed with God, man's true knowledge of himself is bound to disappear.

An intelligent stance counter to the world here so accurately foretold must be a matter of adult understanding, adult faith "come forth from the crucible of doubt", and this Dostoyevsky well knew. That Father Zossima is a monk, responsible from within a long tradition for the upbringing of Alyosha, might suggest that Dostoyevsky also knew that those taking such a stance would need the security and support of the Church. But the vulnerable fragility of Alyosha's group of boys is a very tentative hope for the future. It was sketched by Dostoyevsky when he was exhausted and close to death, but perhaps he also had some premonition that the destructive violence described in *The Devils* would before long wreck such support as the church in Russia could provide for the faithful, in any case neither widespread nor impressive among the educated. In the event, the 1917 revolution delivered the tragically brief liberation of the church from state control: under the provisional government, an all-Russian church council abolished the Holy Synod and restored the patriarchate, the bishops electing the metropolitan of Moscow as patriarch. Two days before this election, Lenin gained control of Moscow; before the council was dissolved in 1918, the saintly metropolitan of Kiev had been murdered by the Bolsheviks. By 1922 the patriarch was barred from office and under house arrest; in the same year the metropolitan of Petrograd (Saint Petersburg) and three of his priests were tried and shot. In 1914 there were over a thousand monasteries in Russia; twenty-five years later there were none, and what was left of the church was riven by schism, reminiscent of Donatist Africa, caused by different views of the merits of accommodation to Stalin's wishes. Dostoyevsky was far from foreseeing the planned destruction of the church by the state, a policy never before contemplated, except by the emperor Diocletian in 303, by any European government. Indeed, his confidence in the "God-bearing" strength of Russian Christianity, in contrast to the secular West ("The West has lost Christ and that is why it is dying"),[31] led him to the excesses, particularly in *Diary of a Writer* and his notebooks, from which a case can be built against him as a bigoted Slavophile. In his famous speech in honour of Pushkin, delivered in 1880 at the high, concluding moment of his public celebrity, his rhetoric on Russia's mission to the world leaves the realism of his novels far behind:

> Oh, the people of Europe do not know how dear they are to us. And
> I believe that we (that is to say, of course, not we but the Russians of

the future) will all eventually understand, every single one of us, that to become a real Russian will mean precisely this: to strive to bring conciliation to the contradictions of Europe, to show a way out of the sorrows of Europe in our own Russian soul, universally human and all-uniting; to find a place in it, with brotherly love, for all our brothers, and finally perhaps to speak the final word of the great harmony of all, of the brotherly unison of all the nations according to the law of the gospel of Christ.[32]

This is a dream that perhaps only Shatov, in all Dostoyevsky's novels, might have had. It has no bearing whatever on Pushkin. More significantly, until the very last word, it could be the programme for Lenin's world revolution. The best comment on the Slavophile fantasy it represents was written by Dostoyevsky's friend Soloviev in 1889:

If we believed the Slavophiles ... we should have to regard the Russian people as some sort of Pharisee, righteous in its own eyes, extolling its own virtues in the name of humility, despising and condemning neighbour peoples in the name of brotherly love, and ready to wipe them off the face of the earth to ensure the complete triumph of its own gentle and pacific nature.[33]

(This has about it a prescient ring of the Warsaw Pact, but also of the America of George W. Bush.)

In the great novels, however, Dostoyevsky is at a considerable distance from the wishful thinking of either the romantic Slavophiles or the liberals, Herzen for example, who hoped so much from the peasant commune as a model for government. Dostoyevsky owned no land, lived among peasants only in prison and had no Tolstoyan vision of their exemplary goodness. Born and brought up in Moscow, widely travelled in Europe and living in Saint Petersburg for the last nine years of his life, he was a sophisticated urban intellectual who would have concurred, however sadly, with the sympathetic but pessimistic view of the peasants—destitute, drunk, violent, almost entirely ignorant of Christianity—given by Chekhov, grandson of a serf and for years a country doctor, in 1897. Chekhov describes typical village women:

Marya and Fyokla would cross themselves and prepare to take the sacrament once a year, but they had no idea what it meant. They hadn't taught their children to pray, had told them nothing about God and never taught them moral principles: all they did was tell them not to eat forbidden food during fast days. In the other families it was almost the same story: hardly anyone believed in God or understood anything about religion.[34]

A church so faintly present in the lives of the mass of the people could not have sustained the only completely inaccurate forecast Dostoyevsky puts into the mouth of Father Zossima: "An unbelieving leader will never achieve anything in Russia."[35]

On the whole issue of the church, past, present and future, Dostoyevsky, in fact, was in a peculiarly Russian fix, best analysed by Nicholas Berdyaev in his *Dostoievsky*, written in French in 1932. Berdyaev was a highly educated philosopher born in 1874, and was, as a young man, an atheist and a socialist. He became an Orthodox believer, with several other intellectuals, in the last decade before the revolution, wrote critically of the state's control of the Russian church, was exiled by Nicholas II, was twice imprisoned by Lenin and in 1922 was exiled to Paris, where he lived for the rest of his life, observing Russia from the West, and the West from his Russian experience. He was born before Dostoyevsky began to write *The Brothers Karamazov* and died five years before the death of Stalin. He was well placed to understand the complicated mixture of love and bafflement with which Dostoyevsky regarded the Russian church and the awe and ignorance with which Dostoyevsky regarded the West. For Dostoyevsky's courage in his long journey from the creation of the underground man to the creation of Alyosha, and for Dostoyevsky's perception of the magnitude of the choice facing modern man, Berdyaev has profound admiration. He places Dostoyevsky in parallel and in contrast to Nietzsche:

> The thing which Dostoievsky and Nietzsche knew is that man is terribly free, that liberty is tragic and a grievous burden to him. They had seen the parting of the ways in front of mankind. . . . The road of liberty can only end either in the deification of man or in the discovery of God; in the one case, he is lost and done for; in the other, he finds salvation and the definitive confirmation of himself as God's earthly image. . . . The only solution to the problem of man is in Jesus Christ.[36]

Berdyaev is also impressed by the accuracy of Dostoyevsky's understanding of the coming revolution, through which he himself had lived: "It took place in the way he said it would. . . . *The Devils* was not a novel about the present but about the future." [37] Berdyaev had seen come true Peter Verkhovensky's feverish vision of the future, in which he failed to interest the icy Stavrogin:

> Every member of the society spies on the others, and he is obliged to inform against them. Everyone belongs to all the others, and all belong to everyone. All are slaves and equals in slavery.... We'll have a few fires—we'll spread a few legends. Every mangy little group will be useful. I shall find you such keen fellows in each one of these groups that they'll be glad to do some shooting and be grateful for the honour.... There's going to be such a to-do as the world has never seen. Russia will become shrouded in a fog, the earth will weep for its old gods. [38]

Berdyaev is clear that Dostoyevsky always admired, loved and envied the long, civilised past of the West that Russia did not share, Ivan Karamazov's "most precious graveyard". [39] He quotes Versilov, a character in the weak novel *A Raw Youth*, which Dostoyevsky wrote between *The Devils* and *The Brothers Karamazov*:

> No one can love Russia more than I do, but I can never reproach myself because Venice and Rome and Paris with all their art and learning and history are yet more delectable to me. How dear they are to a Russian!— those old foreign stones, those miracles of God's ancient world, those ruins of holy marvels: they are more dear to us than even to them. [40]

The tone is nostalgic, the tense a past tense. Russians in the eighteenth century— and in the nineteenth, when many more of them travelled to the West—joined an already-secular culture: the "old foreign stones" they saw through the Enlightenment eyes of those to whom they were no more than beautiful relics of a dead faith. No wonder Dostoyevsky, with many other Russian intellectuals, looked homeward for living Christianity and "found in the people the God they had lost", entertaining even what Berdyaev describes as "belief in the people more than in God ... a pagan tendency in the very bosom of Orthodoxy, a narrow and exclusive religious nationalism, foreign to Western Christianity and purely negative in its attitude towards Catholicism." [41]

Dostoyevsky's uninformed horror of the Catholic Church, reinforced by anti-Polish prejudice, increased in blind intensity as he grew older. Dostoyevsky gives Prince Myshkin a jarringly uncharacteristic tirade against Rome, which he accuses of "preaching Antichrist", of believing "that the Church cannot exist on earth without universal temporal power"; "the Pope seized the earth, an earthly throne and took up the sword"; out of the Catholic Church came atheism.[42] (This outburst is provoked by the news that Myshkin's old benefactor has become a Catholic, a dire fate awarded by Dostoyevsky also to the society girl who thought herself in love with Myshkin, and by Tolstoy in *War and Peace* to Pierre's spoiled, selfish wife, Hélène.) The terrifying vision of the future drawn by Ivan's Grand Inquisitor begins with a similar identification of the Catholic Church with universal temporal power. Even Father Zossima says: "In Rome, of course, a State has been proclaimed instead of a Church for the last thousand years."[43] But, in Berdyaev's words, Dostoyevsky both failed to notice that "there was no liberty in the Byzantine imperial theocracy"[44] (a lack of liberty reinforced in Russia by Peter the Great) and at the same time "had an extremely inadequate and entirely exterior knowledge of Catholicism".[45] The temporal power of the papacy, which would have appalled Augustine and did appal Dante, had in any case meant for centuries little more than bad administration of the papal states; by 1861 its area of control had shrunk to Rome itself, and by 1870 to the Vatican City. That Catholics who had studied the whole history of Christianity, Newman for example, thought this a blessing for the Church was something of which Dostoyevsky was unaware, as he was unaware of the long, and still living, Latin intellectual tradition, which had for centuries been thought of almost entirely as a threat by the Russian church.

Vladimir Soloviev, the young man who had taken Dostoyevsky to Optino and been the model for Alyosha, was the most remarkable of the rare Russian thinkers then, or ever, prepared to approach the history of the Church with an open mind. Balthasar, who gives Soloviev the only whole chapter devoted to a Russian in *The Glory of the Lord*, rates very highly the "skill in the technique of integrating all partial truths in one vision" in this trained philosopher, who used everything he had learned in his pursuit of a coherent Christian theology grounded in both Plato and the Trinity.

Five weeks after Dostoyevsky's death, Tsar Alexander II was assassinated, after two failed attempts on his life in the previous year (parricide was not a distant topic for Russians in 1880). Soloviev pleaded for remission of the death penalty for the murderers and a little later organised a petition to the new tsar on behalf of the Jews, who were being bullied more than ever. He was sacked from Moscow University. He then began to study seriously the theology of the Church in both the Orthodox and the Catholic traditions. By the mid-1880s he had become convinced that the reuniting of the ancient Church, which had been divided in two for nearly a thousand years, could and should be achieved with the loss of nothing essential to either tradition. He began discussions with Joseph Strossmayer, a Croatian bishop who had been a professor of canon law in Vienna and had opposed, but then accepted, the declaration of papal infallibility at the Vatican Council in 1869–1870. Strossmayer was working toward uniting the southern Slavs across the religious divide, an effort that years after his death came to temporary fruition in the kingdom of Yugoslavia. The ecclesiastical discussions came to nothing. Soloviev was working on a huge history of Christianity, which he never finished. Most of his thought about the Church is to be found in *The Spiritual Foundations of Life*, on which he worked from 1882 to 1884. In 1889 he published, in France, *Russia and the Universal Church*, in which he made his case for the reunion of the whole Church as "an objective and universal ecclesial form".[46] Sound history and steady judgement support his case. He recalled how the Byzantine church, after the great doctrinal councils, separated itself from Rome and lost its freedom to the emperors in Constantinople, bequeathing this servitude to Russia. He did not criticise Peter the Great for setting up the Holy Synod since the Old Believer schism had demonstrated that there was in Russia "the cruel lack of any decisive ecclesiastical court of appeal".[47] But nationalism is Orthodoxy's lasting obstacle to the reunion of the Church (and even to unity within Orthodoxy), while Rome's arrogation of temporal power and use of war and other means of coercion in the imposition of "faith" (Soloviev is here in consonance with Dostoyevsky, though he knows, as Dostoyevsky did not, that both are now in the past), and the Protestants' abandonment of the "universal ecclesial form", have been equally insurmountable obstacles. As soon as this book was published, there was a furious response in Russia, and Soloviev was forbidden by the Holy Synod to write on religious subjects. He was received into the Catholic Church in 1896, a fact always denied by the Orthodox, and died, exhausted by feverish overwork, four years later.

Soloviev's analysis is by no means superficial. It rests on a profound Augustinian understanding of what the Church is. Like Augustine, Soloviev, a Platonist all his life, was converted from philosophy to Christianity by the Incarnation. "In Christ what was sought was given to us, the ideal became fact.... The Word became flesh, and it is this new spiritualized and divinized flesh that remains the divine substance of the Church."[48] "That which is fresh and original in Christianity does not lie in general conceptions but in positive facts, not in the speculative content of its ideal structure, but in this idea's embodiment in a person."[49] Dostoyevsky, here most sharply distinguishing his Christianity from Tolstoy's, wrote in his notebook several years before he met Soloviev:

> It is possible to argue, and even to assert, that Christianity will not fall to the ground if Christ is regarded as no more than a man, as a philosopher who goes about doing good.... [But] we know that Christ,

considered as merely man, is not the Savior and the source of life; we know that no science will serve to realize the human ideal and that, for mankind, peace, the source of life and salvation and the indispensable condition for the existence of the whole world, is contained in the saying: "The Word was made flesh", and in faith in that saying.[50]

Like Augustine, and with his help, Soloviev never confused the Church with the *civitas Dei*, the eschatological kingdom of God. The Church, he wrote, is "a plenitude in the process of coming to be";[51] she is to be believed in as a truth and as a whole, despite her failings and her fracture as a human institution: "the enduring limitations of sinners do not damage the dignity of the Church as a whole."[52] Augustine's *corpus permixtum* is "not only the assembly of believers; it is, before all else, that which assembles them",[53] and we should never "confuse the bed with the stream".[54] "Of course, not everything in the visible Church is divine, but the divine is already something visible within it."[55] Further, so many centuries after Augustine, who had been himself part of the process, Soloviev recognised, with Newman, that acknowledgement of the development of doctrine was essential to a proper understanding of the Church: "The visible forms of the divine, though always present in the Church, were at first very rudimentary and imperfect, just as the visible form of a seed is rudimentary and imperfect", so we should not "reject the more fully revealed forms of God's grace in the Church [the full-grown tree], preferring absolutely a return to the structure of the primitive Christian community".[56] Soloviev's vision of the developed form, and of the essential oneness, of the Church, which inspired the constantly rebuffed efforts of Pope John Paul II to open serious ecumenical discussion with the Orthodox churches, looked back to Augustine and the Greek Fathers as Newman and his twentieth-century Catholic successors looked back to the Greek Fathers and Augustine. Soloviev wrote:

The fresh and original character can never be taken from Christianity; it is not at all necessary in establishing this to demonstrate, in the face of all historical fact and all sound human understanding, that the ideas of Christian dogma come on to the scene as something entirely novel, fallen from Heaven, so to speak, in their perfected shape. Nor would this be a view shared by the great fathers of the Church.[57]

That a Russian should have written on the Church in this Catholic, though always historical, always critical, fashion is astonishing. That he should have been silenced in Russia is not. Soloviev in his last years, disappointed of all his hopes, lonely and ill, collapsed into visionary apocalyptic prophecy, culminating, in the year he died, in *Three Conversations*, where a fable of the future, to which we shall return in a later chapter, foresees a ruler of the world who "does not know that he is the Antichrist . . . until the moment when he consciously puts himself above Christ because Christ was no more than his predecessor, who died and was not resurrected."[58] This is the nightmare of Tolstoy's dream come true. It has a frightening bearing on what was said to be taking place in Russia after the revolution, and an even more frightening bearing on what actually took place. It is also not without relevance to the self-righteous rhetoric, identifying the national interest with world rule and both with the will of God, to be heard in present-day America. Soloviev's Antichrist says: "World peace is assured forever. Every attempt to disturb it will instantly meet with irresistible opposition; for from now on there is only a single central power on earth. . . . That power is mine."[59]

* * *

The revolution came, and then civil war. In 1917 a soldier said to the British ambassador in the revolutionary streets of Petersburg: "Yes, we need a republic, but at the head there should be a good Tsar."[60] Soon there was Lenin. Between 1918 and 1921 ten million Russians died in the civil war; more died from famine and disease than from violence; more died at the hands of the Cheka, Lenin's secret police, than in the fighting. A gifted generation of Russian poets, born in the decade 1885–1895, suffered the full impact of the revolution, the civil war, Lenin's terror, Stalin's terror: their lives or the lives of those close to them ended in suicide, execution or disappearance to the prison camps of Siberia. In 1971 Alexander Solzhenitsyn wrote of the Russian writers of his century: "The tree fellers did their work. They left . . . just two or three trees, missed out apparently by accident."[61] One of the very few who survived to die in old age, after decades of grief and guilt, was Boris Pasternak, whose single great novel, *Doctor Zhivago*, written in the last years of Stalin's rule, is about the life of a poet in the times through which Pasternak had lived.

The story begins in 1901, twenty years after the death of Dostoyevsky and recognisably in his world. Ideas that in *The Devils* and *The Brothers Karamazov* seemed powerful have become, in ageing members of the intelligentsia, almost frivolous in the lightness with which they are bandied about. The boy Zhivago's uncle, "a priest who had been unfrocked at his own request", "had been both a Tolstoyan and a revolutionary idealist and was still travelling on".[62] When Uncle

Kolya argues with "one of those disciples of Tolstoy in whom the teacher's restless thoughts grow shallow past redeeming and settle down to a long, unclouded rest", Kolya protests: "But Tolstoy says that the more a man devotes himself to beauty the further he moves away from goodness." To which his opponent replies: "And you think it's the other way round—the world will be saved by beauty, is that it?—Dostoyevsky, mystery plays and what not?" [63] Pasternak makes us see how little purchase this kind of talk had on the revolution brewing in the streets of Moscow; Uncle Kolya disappears to Switzerland to write about aesthetics. More like characters in Dostoyevsky's own novels are Zhivago's thirteen-year-old friend Nicky, who is "sick and tired of being a child" and thinks: "God exists, of course. But if He exists, then I am he", [64] and "a slovenly old chatterbox" on whom the orphaned adolescent Zhivago is "foisted". This character "lived in sin with his ward and therefore saw himself as a disrupter of the established order and a champion of progressive thought". [65] He is Stepan Verkhovensky gone to seed.

But the weight of the novel as a whole is not, as it always is in Dostoyevsky, in the souls of its characters, but in the events that threaten to crush the soul out of individuals in whom alone, one by one, there is the life, the love, the responsiveness, the possibility of creating something new, which are Pasternak's priorities. He is an artist at an observant distance from events, and so, for all the suffering through which he is dragged by these events, is his principal character, who is a poet as well as a doctor and is at first exhilarated by the new freedoms promised by the revolution. Zhivago writes in his diary that he prefers Pushkin and Chekhov to Gogol, Tolstoy and Dostoyevsky because of "their shy unconcern with such high-sounding matters as the ultimate purpose of mankind or their own salvation". [66] The climax of Zhivago's own life, which has been wrecked by war and the actual consequences of the revolution, by the shock of poverty to which his bourgeois family in Moscow is reduced in his absence, and by the shock of passion that has destroyed his affectionate marriage, is a gentle twelve-day respite from events, spent with the woman he loves in a dilapidated house miles from anywhere in the winter snow. The house is called Varykino. Here, Zhivago's writing of the twenty-five poems that are printed as the last section of the novel, the peace of his love and his sense of the Passion and Resurrection and judgement of Christ are all as one. Lara is taken away to safety by the rich, and now, in 1921, cynically powerful man who long ago seduced and debauched her. Zhivago never sees her again, writes no more poems and scarcely lives, though eventually with a new humble wife and two more children, until, in Moscow in 1929, before the worst years of Stalin's terror, he dies of a broken heart. "Small cardiac haemorrhages" he describes as "the common disease of our time. I think its causes are chiefly moral. The great majority of us are required to live a life of constant, systematic duplicity." [67]

That truth has to do with people one by one, with love, and with God, and that the lie has to do with people as an undifferentiated mass, and with power, is the central perception of the novel. The lie, before the revolution, was the means by which the rich used and abused the poor. Capitalism, like much else copied from the West, arrived late and crude in Russia, adorned with the cachet of "science". Luzhin, a monster of selfishness, explains to Raskolnikov in *Crime and Punishment*:

> If, say, I've been told in the past, "love thy neighbour as thyself", and I did, what was the result of it? The result of it was that I tore my coat in half to share it with my neighbour, and both of us were left half naked.... But science tells us, "Love yourself before everyone else, for everything in the world is based on self-interest." ... And economic truth adds that the more successfully private business is run, and the more whole coats, as it were, there are, the more solid are the foundations of our social life and the greater is the general well-being of the people. Which means that by acquiring wealth exclusively and only for myself, I'm by that very fact acquiring it for everybody. [68]

In Lenin's Russia a different version of Western science, another economic "truth", had made of the victims of such as Luzhin powerful purveyors of a new lie. In *Doctor Zhivago* the poor, radical student who marries Lara and becomes Strelnikov, the terrifyingly competent Red Army commander in the civil war, is the polar opposite not of Zhivago himself but of Lara's old seducer. He strikes Zhivago, in Nietzschean fashion, as "a finished product of the will".[69] Pasternak says of him: "He had an unusual power of clear and logical reasoning, and he was endowed with great moral purity and sense of justice." On the other hand, "in order to do good to others he would have needed, besides the principles which filled his mind, an unprincipled heart,—the kind of heart that knows of no general cases, but only of particular ones, and has the greatness of small actions." [70] On the night before his desolate suicide, Strelnikov talks to the once-privileged Zhivago, in the Varykino house that Lara has just left:

> None of this can mean anything to you. You couldn't understand it. You grew up quite differently. There was the world of the suburbs, of

the railways, of the slums and tenements. Dirt, hunger, overcrowding, the degradation of the worker as a human being, the degradation of women. And there was the world of the mothers' darlings, of smart students and rich merchants' sons; the world of impunity, of brazen, insolent vice; of rich men laughing or shrugging off the tears of the poor, the robbed, the insulted.[71]

But Strelnikov is a pitiless killer, hanging peasants and burning villages in the cause of the new truth. Violence sustained the old order: a tsarist cavalry charge kills unarmed demonstrators early in the novel. Violence will sustain the new. A hundred years before Pasternak wrote *Doctor Zhivago*, Herzen had written: "Which will finish us off? The senile barbarism of the sceptre or the wild barbarism of communism; the bloody sabre, or the red flag?"[72] Pasternak gives to the unsophisticated Lara the identification of the new lie:

It was then [1917] that falsehood came into our Russian land.... People imagined that it was out of date to follow their own moral sense, that they must all sing the same tune in chorus, and live by other people's notions, the notions which were being crammed down everybody's throat.[73]

The phrase "their own moral sense" suggests the formed conscience of the taken for granted Christian past, or, not noticeably different, of the educated liberal present. Lara has had almost no Christian upbringing. Of the miserably abused girl early in the book Pasternak tells us:

Lara was not religious. She did not believe in ritual. But sometimes, to enable her to bear her life, she needed the accompaniment of an inward music and she could not always compose it for herself. That music was God's word of life and it was to weep over it that she went to church.[74]

Zhivago and his friends, on the other hand, are enlightened rationalists, educated to an all-around, thoroughly Western confidence, doomed even as it is described. This is Zhivago as a medical student in 1912:

In his twelve years at school and college he had studied the classics and Scripture, legends and poets, history and natural science, reading all these things as if they were the chronicles of his house, his family tree.

> Now he was afraid of nothing, neither of life nor of death; everything in the world, each thing in it, was named in his dictionary.[75]

Pasternak's family was Jewish. His parents were highly civilised, highly educated and comfortably assimilated into cultured Moscow society, as similar Jews were at the time in London or Berlin or Vienna. Pasternak's father, a distinguished impressionist painter, was asked by Tolstoy to illustrate *Resurrection*. In the novel, Zhivago's lifelong friend Misha Gordon suffers, as a boy, the added pain of incomprehension that anti-Semitism inflicts on the secular Jew:

> He could not understand how it was that if you were worse than other people you could not improve yourself by trying. What did it mean to be a Jew? What was the purpose of it? What was the reward or the justification of this unarmed challenge which brought nothing but grief?[76]

There is a hint here of a remarkable passage later in the book, in which the adult Misha sees Christianity as the possibility of freedom, for people one by one, from the imprisonment of nationhood, in its way as harsh as imprisonment in the exploitation of Lara's girlhood or in the tyranny of singing "the same tune in chorus":

> The Gospels are an offer, a naive and tentative offer: "Would you like to live in a completely new way?" ... What the Gospels tell us is that in this new way of life and of communion, which is born of the heart and which is called the Kingdom of God, there are no nations, but only persons.[77]

Later still, implausibly, Pasternak gives Lara the same thought about the Jews:

> It's so strange that these people who once brought about the liberation of mankind from the yoke of idolatry, and so many of whom now devote themselves to its liberation from injustice, should be powerless to achieve their own liberation from themselves, from the yoke of their loyalty to an obsolete, antediluvian designation which has lost all meaning.[78]

Pasternak's own faith is given to the Zhivago who writes the Varykino poems. There is one hint of it earlier in the novel. When Zhivago almost dies of typhoid in the destitute Moscow of 1918, he dreams of himself as the Christ of Holy Saturday:

He had always wanted to describe how for three days the black, raging, worm-filled earth had assailed the deathless incarnation of love. . . . Near him, touching him, were hell, corruption, dissolution, death; yet equally near him were the spring and Mary Magdalene and life.[79]

There is a suggestion here of Hamlet, and also of the poet—"he had always wanted to describe"—both strangely identified with Christ. The suggestions become firm in the first of Zhivago's poems, "Hamlet".

In the 1930s, with Russia in Stalin's cruel grip, and the ideological constriction of the Writers' Union making the writing of his own poetry impossible, Pasternak had both earned his living and preserved some private truthfulness of spirit by translating literature, particularly Shakespeare's plays. On *Hamlet*, Pasternak wrote, the vocations of Christ and of Hamlet mingling in his mind with the almost impossible vocation of the truth-telling poet:

From the moment the ghost appears, Hamlet renounces himself in order to "do the will of him who sent him". *Hamlet* is not a drama of characterlessness, but of duty and self-sacrifice. When it transpires that an abyss separates appearance and reality, it isn't important that the reminder of the world's falsehood should come in a supernatural form. . . . It is far more important that a chance occurrence turns Hamlet into the judge of his own time, and servant of the future. *Hamlet* is a drama of high calling, imposed heroism, and incontrovertible destiny.[80]

All three vocations are there in Zhivago's poem, where Hamlet comes out on the stage and prays, "Father, if it be possible, / Let this cup pass from me." For the reader of Balthasar there is a striking consonance between this poem and the analogy, in the first volume of *Theo-Drama*, between the three Persons of the Trinity and the author, the actor and the director of a play. The poem ends with a Russian proverb:

To live your life is not as simple as to cross a field.[81]

Here the "you" addressed is still God the Father, God the playwright, God who has summoned the poet to his calling.

Without knowledge of Russian, it is impossible to catch the nuances of language and metaphor in the Varykino poems, some explicitly Christian in reference and some not, which take us in a carefully ordered sequence through a year from one Holy Week to the next. In the last four poems, which are entirely faithful to the Gospel accounts, Zhivago and Lara have disappeared behind Jesus, surrounded by enemies in Jerusalem; Mary Magdalene, penitent and forgiven, anointing him for his burial—"I break my life before you / Like an alabaster box" [82]—and suffering the emptiness between his death and his Resurrection; and finally Jesus in the garden of Gethsemane, where, with "Hamlet", the cycle of poems began. The last two stanzas of the last poem leave the reader with Christ as the "servant of the future" and the only judge of Zhivago's, or Pasternak's, time, as of all time:

> "You see, the passage of the centuries is like a parable
> And catches fire on its way.
> In the name of its terrible majesty
> I shall go freely, through torment, down to the grave.
>
> "And on the third day I shall rise again.
> Like rafts down a river, like a convoy of barges,
> The centuries will float to me out of the darkness.
> And I shall judge them." [83]

There was too much truth in *Doctor Zhivago* for it to be published in the Russia of Stalin's successors. It was published in Milan in 1957 and in English translation in 1958. In that year Pasternak became world-famous and was awarded the Nobel Prize for Literature. He was expelled from the Writers' Union, which for a quarter of a century had bullied him into near-silence and caused the deaths of most of his fellow poets; he was also forced to renounce the Nobel Prize. In 1960 he died. Zhivago's poem "Hamlet" was read at his graveside.

In 1987 *Doctor Zhivago* having circulated for years in the dangerous underground of samizdat reproduction, was at last published in Russia, in accordance with Mikhail Gorbachev's policy of glasnost (candour, openness).

* * *

One Russian writer, a generation younger than Pasternak, had, by an accident of permission, a major truth-telling work published in Russia in 1962. Alexander Solzhenitsyn, born in the midst of the civil war in 1918, was a decorated officer of the Russian army who had fought the Nazis for four years when he was arrested in 1945 for writing dissident letters to a friend. He spent the next four years in a forced-labour camp, four more years in a special prison for intellectuals and then three years in exile in southeastern Kazakhstan near the Chinese border. *One Day in the Life of Ivan Denisovich*, the book published in 1962, is a simple, spare account of life in a forced-labour camp in the period after the Second World War. The war, which had brought suffering and loss on an immense scale to Russia, had also been a relief. At the end of *Doctor Zhivago*, Misha Gordon and another of Zhivago's old friends, both prisoners in the Gulag of the 1930s, meet in the army in 1943: "When the war broke out, its real horrors, its real dangers, its menace of real death were a blessing compared with the inhuman power of the lie." [84] Stalin restored the power of the lie with a vengeance after the defeat of the Nazis, as Solzhenitsyn's book, which had a very great impact in Russia, shows with calm clarity. Its central character is a peasant soldier, sent to the Gulag because he had escaped from the Germans, who had taken him prisoner: there were many thousands like him. He had signed a confession of "treason"; the alternative was to be shot. In the camp there is one educated convict, finding, as both Solzhenitsyn and Dostoyevsky had done, prison life particularly hard. He is a naval captain given a twenty-five-year sentence because a British admiral had sent him a gift in gratitude for his work as a wartime liaison officer on a British cruiser. The prison conditions described, exactly a hundred years later than *Memoirs from the House of the Dead*, are worse in almost every respect: less food, less contact with the outside world, more severe punishments, less possibility of a little choice here and there, and of course no religion. The only book in the prison, as in Dostoyevsky's Omsk, is the New Testament, but now it is a fragmentary handwritten copy, read and hidden every day by a young Baptist sentenced to twenty-five years for being a Baptist. The central character says to this boy: "It works out all right for you: Jesus Christ wanted you to sit in prison and so you are—sitting there for his sake. But for whose sake am *I* here? Because we weren't ready for war in '41?" [85] The meaninglessness of almost all the "crimes", the savage arbitrariness of almost all the sentences, and the huge numbers of prisoners implied by the book are all much worse than in the life described in *Memoirs from the House of the Dead*.

It suited Nikita Khrushchev in 1962 to allow the publication of *One Day in the Life of Ivan Denisovich* because the propaganda line of the moment was that the Gulag camps were Stalin's and no longer existed. (They did. In 2003 there were still several thousand old Gulag prisoners trapped in the Arctic because it had never been possible for them to put together the train fare home.) Khrushchev's patronage was still assumed by the same brave, nervous publisher, the following year, of Solzhenitsyn's story "Matryona's House". If *One Day in the*

Life showed Russia that prison was worse under Stalin than under Nicholas I, "Matryona's House", though Solzhenitsyn pushed its date back a few years, showed Russia that village life was worse under Khrushchev than in the days of serfdom. The story is true. As a recovering convict in 1956, Solzhenitsyn taught in a village school only one hundred miles from Moscow. He lodged with an old peasant woman, desperately poor, hard-working, humble, unselfish and good. She was killed in an accident caused by the greed, jealousy and drunken incompetence of what was left of her family after war, and the deaths of her six children had ruined her life. The collectivised village suffers more injustice than the village in Chekhov's "Peasants": fuel, the peat dug by the peasants, is for the bosses and the factory workers; to stay alive, the peasants have to steal it; to fetch it home, the women have to haul it; there are no horses to pull sleds or to plough. Matryona's faith is much the same as that of Bazarov's mother or of the women in "Peasants", a matter of what brings good or bad luck, with special dates, the feasts of the Church, marked by the lighting of icon lamps. But Matryona has a vague sense that God presides over her life, and Solzhenitsyn ends the story: "None of us who lived close to her perceived that she was that one righteous person without whom, as the saying goes, no city can stand. Nor the world." [86]

"Matryona's House" is very like the moral tales of Tolstoy's old age, though told with less narrative expertise. A samizdat historian wrote that "for a million people Christianity began with reading 'Matryona's House'." [87] Whether or not this is true, it seems clear that Solzhenitsyn's own, Tolstoyan, Christianity became firmer with his writing of this story and that its publication turned him into a second Tolstoy both in other people's eyes and in his own. His early childhood in his mother's family had been Orthodox; educated in a provincial school and university in Rostov through the 1920s and 1930s, he became a bright, successful student and an exemplary young Communist. The dissident letters for which he was consigned to the Gulag criticised Stalin for having deviated from the path of pure Leninism. While the camp of *One Day in the Life* destroyed forever his confidence in the success or justice of what the revolution had achieved, it was much discussion with other educated convicts in the special prison, described in *The First Circle*, that introduced him to the possibility that an educated adult in communist Russia might believe in God. In *Cancer Ward*, the book that records Solzhenitsyn's stay in a hospital in Tashkent that cured the cancer from which, in exile, he almost died, there are more discussions, more stories of the horrific 1930s. There is little left here, even among the educated, of Russia's past: a small volume of Tolstoy's late tales, one or two lines of Pushkin lodged in people's memories. An old Bolshevik, close to death, bitterly regrets allowing himself ever to be deceived by the rhetoric of the phrase "as one man": he tells of the lies and tricks of the Party, which, for example, "disappeared" to death or the Gulag the one abstainer in a small-town vote that was supposed to represent "the whole Soviet nation as one man". "We were individual human beings, and then suddenly we were 'as one man'." [88] Neither the old Bolshevik nor Kostoglotov, the central character of *Cancer Ward*, has any sense that belief in the irreducible value, and freedom, of the individual human being has to do with belief in God. Nor, in either of these major books—although in *The First Circle* Solzhenitsyn is clearly travelling from Leninism toward an atavistic nationalism connected to Christianity—is there any sign of real understanding of Christian doctrine or of the Church. Lenin and Stalin had tried to eliminate the possibility of such understanding, particularly from the education of the clever: much in Solzhenitsyn's career shows how successful they were.

For the courage and quality of his truth-telling, Solzhenitsyn was quickly seen as dangerous to the Party and the government. Both *The First Circle* and *Cancer Ward*, and some brief, acute prose poems about the true condition of Russia, had to be published abroad, while smuggled and samizdat copies, from 1967 on, increased his fame at home. This fame, and a growing conviction that his vocation—for which God had preserved him through the war, prison and cancer—was to be a prophet for Russia, gave him the confidence openly to defy the Party's authority. In 1967 he wrote a letter to the Fourth Congress of Soviet Writers, attacking censorship, which was more savage than under the tsars; attacking persecution of writers by the Writers' Union; and ending, boldly and provocatively, with his own resolution to write as he had to, "from the grave even more successfully and incontrovertibly than in my lifetime".[89] In 1969 he was expelled from the Writers' Union. In 1970 (only twelve years after Pasternak) he was awarded the Nobel Prize for Literature but not allowed to receive it. In 1972 he wrote another open letter, this time to the Patriarch of Moscow, criticising the Russian church with scorn for its hypocrisy, its weakness and its failure to stand up to the government department supervising it: "A church dictatorially ruled by atheists is a sight not seen in two thousand years." [90] This letter, in which there is a note of the self-righteousness that fame was strengthening in Solzhenitsyn, understandably caused much anger and distress in the church, struggling, as it had been struggling for fifty years, to keep the liturgy, the sacraments and some Christian teaching alive for the people in the face of the state religion of atheism and of clever persecution, relaxed during the war, then renewed by Stalin and reinforced by Khrushchev. Finally, in 1974, Solzhenitsyn replied to a legal summons in terms recalling Thomas More's speech at his trial, in reference, that is, to a real justice beyond law: "In the circumstances created by the universal and unrelieved illegality enthroned for many years past in our country ... I refuse to acknowledge the legality of your summons and shall not report for questioning to any agency of the state."[91] He was, as he presumably expected if not intended, arrested and imprisoned at once on the capital charge of treason but was deported the next day. He spent the next twenty years in the West, mostly in America.

It is beyond dispute that Solzhenitsyn was a hero, for almost half the Soviet state's duration, of resistance to Soviet oppression through the power of truth told in writing. The claim he made in his undelivered Nobel Prize lecture is incontrovertible: "Works which have drawn upon the truth and presented it to us in live, concentrated form capture us and draw us compulsively in. And never, even centuries later, will anyone be able to refute them."[92] As he wrote more and more, in his dedication to recording accurately the sufferings of Russia since 1914, his books lost the "live, concentrated form" of, particularly, *One Day in the Life of Ivan Denisovich*, and he became increasingly an historian, to use an ancient distinction, who tells us what did happen, rather than a poet, who tells us what does happen. He also became a preacher, consciously picking up the responsibility for Russia and the world that both Tolstoy and Dostoyevsky in different ways reckoned they held. He shares with the later Tolstoy a strong sense of God, an equally strong sense of his own mission, and little, if any, sense of dependence on the grace that is given through Christ. One prayer of his was published, though not in Russia. It begins: "At the height of earthly fame I gaze with wonder at the path that has led me through hopelessness to here—to where I have been able to convey to mankind some reflection of Thy radiance."[93] He shares with the later Dostoyevsky a passionate, atavistic confidence in the Christianity of the Russian people. He traced the roots of the 1917 revolution to the seventeenth-century schism of the Old Believers, regarding the Old Believers' resistance to the Greek reform of the liturgy as entirely justified. In 1975 he visited a community of Old Believers in Alaska and approved of their refusal to allow him into their church because he did not belong to the sect. This visit reinforced both his angry scorn for the disunited Orthodox churches in exile and his messianic hopes for Russia. "In the Russia of the Old Believers the Leninist revolution would have been impossible", he wrote in this year, and also, almost in the words of Dostoyevsky's Pushkin memorial speech, that it was now the mission of Russia, after its spiritual suffering and spiritual growth, to be for the benighted West "a voice from the future".[94]

Solzhenitsyn knew little about the West before his exile. He bitterly disapproved of almost everything he found there, and by 1990, as Communism crumbled in Russia, was warning his countrymen against contamination from Western democracy, party politics, the mass media and consumerism and recommending a moral programme of self-denial and an unrealistic political structure to be built upward from the village commune to an authoritarian summit by the election of incorruptible, partyless representatives. Meanwhile, Western liberals had realised, when the awe and adulation surrounding Solzhenitsyn on his arrival had subsided, that he was no Herzen or Turgenev, no liberal sceptic presentable in Western universities or corridors of power, but an awkward, embattled, tactless prophet, entirely convinced of his own rightness on every subject and set on returning Russia, by his own strength of character, to its condition before the disastrous efforts of the patriarch Nikon and Peter the Great.

So, from the Byronic Pushkin, the European Romantic poet who gave Russia its literary voice after Napoleon's invasion from the West had been seen off, to Solzhenitsyn, a Russian writer who knew no other language and wished that the Russian mind and imagination had never been opened to the West, the short history of great Russian writing has described a strange circle. By the time Solzhenitsyn returned to his country in 1994, "the pressures of the marketplace", wrote Anatol Lieven, a keen observer of Russia, "have proved a more effective censor than the Soviet state ever was. Solzhenitsyn's works are no longer printed in his own country; nor for that matter are the great majority of other Russian classic writers."[95] Among Russians at present, preoccupied with survival in an atmosphere of raw, often criminal, capitalism and overwhelmed with the heady availability of Western junk culture, the books of the great Russian writers are valued less than at any time since the publication of *Eugene Onegin* in 1831. Nevertheless, for Russians and for all of us, the genius of these writers, and particularly of Dostoyevsky, with their profoundly mixed feelings for and against the West and for and against their troubled Orthodox inheritance, has made its own powerful contribution to the story of writing in the Christian tradition and, in a different realm from that of Peter the Great's victories, on "the stage of glory before the eyes of the whole world".[96]

1. Quoted in A. Boyce Gibson, *The Religion of Dostoevsky* (London, 1973), p. 192.
2. Fyodor Dostoyevsky, *The Brothers Karamazov*, trans. David Magarshack (London, 1958), p. 26.
3. Ibid., pp. 78–79.
4. Ibid., p. 334.
5. Jn 12:24.
6. Dostoyevsky, *Brothers Karamazov*, p. 153.

7. Nicholas Berdyaev, *Dostoievsky* (Paris, 1932), trans. Donald Attwater (London, 1934), p. 153.
8. Dostoyevsky, *Brothers Karamazov*, pp. 268–89.
9. Ibid., pp. 278–88.
10. Ibid., pp. 288–308.
11. Ibid., p. 386.
12. Ibid., pp. 398, 400.
13. Quoted in George Steiner, *Tolstoy or Dostoevsky* (1960; London, 1967), p. 238.
14. Blaise Pascal, *Pensée* 483, in *Oeuvres complètes*, ed. Jacques Chevalier, Bibliothèque de la Pléiade 34 (Paris, 1954), pp. 1227–28.
15. Dostoyevsky, *Brothers Karamazov*, p. 485.
16. Ibid., p. 558.
17. Ibid., pp. 595–98.
18. Ibid., p. 693.
19. Ibid., p. 733.
20. Ibid., p. 764.
21. Ibid., p. 794.
22. Ibid., pp. 816–17.
23. Ibid., p. 889.
24. Ibid., p. 895.
25. Ibid., pp. 617, 629, 646–49.
26. Ibid., p. 654.
27. Ibid.
28. Quoted in Henri de Lubac, *The Drama of Atheist Humanism* (1944), trans. M. Riley et al. (San Francisco, 1995), p. 296.
29. Dostoyevsky, *Brothers Karamazov*, p. 369.
30. Ibid., pp. 370–71.
31. Quoted in de Lubac, *Drama of Atheist Humanism*, p. 304.
32. Quoted in Hugh Seton-Watson, *The Russian Empire 1801–1917* (Oxford, 1967), p. 741.
33. Quoted in ibid., p. 261.
34. Anton Chekhov, "Peasants", sec. 8, in *The Kiss and Other Stories*, trans. Ronald Wilks (London, 1982).
35. Dostoyevsky, *Brothers Karamazov*, p. 370.
36. Berdyaev, *Dostoievsky*, pp. 62–63, 56.
37. Ibid., pp. 133–34.
38. Fyodor Dostoyevsky, *The Devils*, trans. David Magarshack (London, 1953), pp. 418, 422.
39. Dostoyevsky, *Brothers Karamazov*, pp. 268–69.
40. Quoted in Berdyaev, *Dostoievsky*, p. 173.
41. Ibid., pp. 184–85.
42. Fyodor Dostoyevsky, *The Idiot*, trans. David Magarshack (London, 1955), p. 585.
43. Dostoyevsky, *Brothers Karamazov*, p. 72.
44. Berdyaev, *Dostoievsky*, p. 79
45. Ibid., p. 200.
46. Quoted in Hans Urs von Balthasar, *The Glory of the Lord: A Theological Aesthetics*, vol. 3, trans. Andrew Louth et al. (San Francisco and Edinburgh, 1986), p. 337.
47. Ibid., p. 335.
48. Quoted in ibid., p. 287.
49. Quoted in ibid., p. 322.
50. Quoted in de Lubac, *Drama of Atheist Humanism*, pp. 304–5.
51. Balthasar, *Glory of the Lord* 3:330.
52. Ibid., p. 331.
53. Quoted in ibid., p. 332.
54. Quoted in ibid.
55. Quoted in ibid.

56. Quoted in ibid., p. 333.
57. Quoted in ibid., p. 322.
58. Quoted in Czeslaw Milosz, *Emperor of the Earth* (Berkeley, 1981), p. 25.
59. Quoted in Hans Urs von Balthasar, *Theo-Drama*, trans. Graham Harrison, vol. 4 (San Francisco, 1994), p. 447.
60. Quoted in George Walden, *Times Literary Supplement*, 24 March 2000.
61. Alexander Solzhenitsyn, *Nobel Prize Lecture*, trans. Nicholas Bethell (London, 1973), p. 17.
62. Boris Pasternak, *Doctor Zhivago*, trans. Max Hayward and Manya Harari (1958; London, 1996), pp. 13, 17.
63. Ibid., pp. 46–47.
64. Ibid., pp. 25–26.
65. Ibid., p. 45.
66. Ibid., p. 259.
67. Ibid., pp. 431–32.
68. Fyodor Dostoyevsky, *Crime and Punishment*, trans. David Magarshack (London, 1951), p. 167.
69. Pasternak, *Doctor Zhivago*, p. 224.
70. Ibid., p. 226.
71. Ibid., p. 411.
72. Quoted in Isaiah Berlin, *Russian Thinkers* (London, 1979), p. 198.
73. Pasternak, *Doctor Zhivago*, p. 363.
74. Ibid., p. 53.
75. Ibid., p. 87.
76. Ibid., p. 22.
77. Ibid., p. 117.
78. Ibid., p. 272.
79. Ibid., p. 188.
80. Boris Pasternak, *People and Propositions*, trans. Anne Pasternak Slater (London, 1990), quoted in John Gross, *After Shakespeare* (Oxford, 2002), pp. 80–81.
81. Pasternak, *Doctor Zhivago*, p. 467.
82. Ibid., p. 503.
83. Ibid., p. 507.
84. Ibid., p. 453.
85. Alexander Solzhenitsyn, *One Day in the Life of Ivan Denisovich*, trans. Ralph Parker (London, 1963), p. 140.
86. Alexander Solzhenitsyn, *Stories and Prose Poems*, trans. Michael Glenny (London, 1973), p. 47.
87. Quoted in Michael Scammell, *Solzhenitsyn* (London, 1985), p. 930n.
88. Alexander Solzhenitsyn, *Cancer Ward*, trans. Nicholas Bethell and David Burg (London, 1971), pp. 464–65.
89. Quoted in Scammell, *Solzhenitsyn*, p. 587.
90. Quoted in ibid., p. 765.
91. Quoted in ibid., p. 836.
92. Solzhenitsyn, *Nobel Prize Lecture*, p. 13.
93. Quoted in Scammell, *Solzhenitsyn*, p. 641.
94. Quoted in ibid., p. 921.
95. Anatol Lieven, in *The Tablet*, 11 June 1994.
96. Quoted in Lindsey Hughes, *Peter the Great* (New Haven and London, 2002), p. 146.

CHAPTER TWENTY-ONE

D. H. LAWRENCE, F. R. LEAVIS, SAMUEL BECKETT, SIMONE WEIL AND SAUL BELLOW

"The truth will set you free."[1] In the twentieth century, false narratives purporting to be the truth, and partial narratives taken for the whole truth, were forced on, and believed in by, countless people who were persuaded to place in them their hopes for different kinds of freedom. Power, driving and driven by narratives guaranteeing history's delivery of a socialist utopia or the unassailable supremacy of the German nation, killed, tortured, starved to death or otherwise destroyed the lives of tens of millions. Within and beyond the countries and times where these horrors, unparalleled in any past century, took place, grand scientific narratives, generally absorbed rather than read or properly understood, appeared to account for the human mess in ways that absolved people one by one from moral responsibility, which, unless blunted by the optimism of utilitarian compromise, means answerability to God. Charles Darwin, having rubbed out the line that divides mankind from the rest of creation, appeared to sanction as "natural" the capitalist and imperialist competitiveness that sends the weakest to the wall and impelled the mass slaughter of the 1914–1918 war. Sigmund Freud, having rubbed out the relation between the soul and the will of God, appeared to sanction as "healthy" and reveal as possible a morally neutral liberation from unhappiness, guilt and the tangle of the past in any human life now dedicated to self-fulfilment. In different ways these lies and partial truths, all promising one or another version of freedom, were coloured through and through by determinism and all replaced God with one or another version of progress, to be learned and worshipped. A sense of positive proof, a lowest common denominator of scientific respectability, underpinned all of them.

The herald of positive proof to be taken on trust by almost everyone, much less brilliant than Marx, Darwin or Freud, and now much less famous, was born in the eighteenth century. In 1825 Auguste Comte wrote:

From the very nature of the human mind, every branch of our knowledge has necessarily to pass through three successive theoretical states:

the theological or fictitious state, the metaphysical or abstract state, and the scientific or positive state.[2]

Religion, in this sweeping account of human history, was left behind by rationalist philosophy, which in turn was left behind by the practical certainties of science. Comte's ascending scale is the exact reverse of that of Pascal, who saw material wealth and power (recognised by everyone) as of less value than the intellectual achievements of abstract reasoners (recognised by their peers), and these in turn as of less value than the greatness of saints in Christ's "own order of holiness" (who are "recognised by God and the angels and not by the senses or by investigating minds.")[3] Pascal in the seventeenth century was already suspicious of the identification of progress with improvement. Comte in the nineteenth was delighted to find his forward-looking contemporaries agreeing that "the hopeless outmodedness of the reign of God" could be left behind in "the long minority of mankind".[4]

"Faith", Comte wrote, "that is to say, the disposition to believe spontaneously, without previous demonstration, the dogmas proclaimed by a competent authority, is a fundamental virtue, the immutable and indispensable basis of social order."[5] But faith must now be placed not in God but in science. If the development of Comte's vision—scientists as "spiritual fathers" and Comte himself as the new pope—descended to parody, even to craziness, it has nevertheless to be admitted that some of his predictions have come uncomfortably close to fulfilment. "Temporal power will be exercised by those in charge of industrial enterprises"; they will "preside over the habitual improvement of our material lot".[6] Henri de Lubac, writing in Nazi-occupied Paris in 1944, in the deep night that had overtaken civilised Europe, thought Comte's variety of atheism the most to be feared because of its flat, everyday plausibility and its appeal to the greed and laziness that are in every human being. Science works. Therefore its grand narratives command people's faith, even if these narratives reduce us to mere specks of biochemical accident in a meaningless universe. Meanwhile, the very same kind of faith in "dogmas proclaimed by a competent authority", though the dogmas were different, had driven the murderous nightmare that had become Russian reality since 1917 and was soon to overtake the satellite states of the Warsaw Pact.

One grand narrative produced in the nineteenth century, a powerful influence on writers in particular, was philosophical rather than historical or scientific, though it foreshadowed remarkably the theories of both Darwin and Freud. Arthur Schopenhauer's *The World as Will and Representation* was published in 1819 and, much enlarged, republished in 1844. Schopenhauer's vision of a Godless, meaningless, ceaselessly cruel universe in which the competitive struggle of the will to life delivers nothing but suffering was in stark contrast to the historical optimism of Hegel. "The Hegelians," Schopenhauer wrote, "who regard the philosophy of history as the main purpose of all philosophy, should be referred to Plato, who untiringly repeats that the object of all philosophy is the unchangeable."[7] Hegel reckoned that he had rethought Christianity in terms of historical progress for the nineteenth century: without Hegel, no Marxism. Schopenhauer was an atheist. Nevertheless, as Schopenhauer himself well knew, there is much in common between his perception of the raging drive of the will to life—in human beings, Augustine's self-will or self-love—and the Christian recognition of original sin in a fallen world. Schopenhauer's only ethical prescription, for renunciation of the will together with compassion for fellow sufferers from the misery inflicted by the nature of things, is so close to Christian ethics that Schopenhauer was compelled to a deep ambivalence as to how renunciation of the will was to be achieved. The dilemma he was in is that renunciation of the will cannot, by definition, be achieved by the will. "The state in which the character is withdrawn from the power of motives does not proceed directly from the will, but from a changed form of knowledge.... [This is] that which in the Christian church is very appropriately called *new birth* or *regeneration*, and the knowledge from which it springs, the *effect of divine grace*."[8] But since, according to Schopenhauer, there is no God, he is driven to a single exception to his account of everything: "What the Christian mystics call *the effect of grace* and the *new birth*, is for us the only direct expression of the *freedom of the will*.... Necessity is the kingdom of nature; freedom is the kingdom of grace."[9] A little later he says: "Our state is originally and essentially an incurable one, and ... we need *deliverance* from it.... Salvation is to be gained only through faith, in other words, through a changed way of knowledge. This faith can come only through grace, and hence as if from without."[10] *Also wie von Aussen*: if Schopenhauer realised that this equivocal phrase leaves his atheism in ruins, he never admitted it. To this "as if" we will return. In one of his 1844 supplementary chapters, he says, resolved to remain in Plato's cave facing the shadows on the wall:

> The actual, positive solution to the riddle of the world must be something that the human intellect is wholly incapable of grasping and conceiving; so that if a being of a higher order came and took all the trouble to impart it to us, we should be quite unable to understand any part of his disclosures.[11]

It was this almost-Christian strain in Schopenhauer against which Nietzsche revolted, and with the help of which Wagner, to Nietzsche's disgust, arrived at the Good

Friday peace of part of the third act of *Parsifal* and at Hans Sachs's renunciation of his own self-will in the third act of *Die Meistersinger von Nürnberg*, where Wagner has Sachs actually quoting some phrases from Schopenhauer's passage on necessity as the kingdom of nature and freedom as the kingdom of grace.

But Schopenhauer's conviction that reality amounted to no more than a vortex of destructive competitiveness—from which the good or lucky man escapes to suffer less, rather than into the will of God—was the conviction that prevailed over most of those Schopenhauer affected. Nietzsche, more resolutely atheist but much more religious in temperament, transformed Schopenhauer's destructive will to life into the will to power, Augustine's *libido dominandi*, and radically countervalued it as good. Nietzsche's hectic optimism, recommending in the face of nihilism heroic self-surmounting, the very opposite of renunciation of the will, penetrated more deeply into the intellectual atmosphere of the twentieth century than Schopenhauer's resigned pessimism. Erich Heller, in *The Disinherited Mind*, his very perceptive book on German thought, regarded Schopenhauer and his disciple, the great historian Jacob Burckhardt, as representing "the true aristocracy of the nineteenth century". Of Burckhardt he wrote:

> Like Schopenhauer, he accepts an *order of things* identical with that accepted by the Christian believer. It is the only order of things in which the religion of Christ can make sense; and if it is the true order of things, it is, at the same time, a profoundly senseless pattern *without* the religion of Christ. To look upon man, as Schopenhauer and Burckhardt did, as the fallen creature, on sin and evil as constituent and ineradicable factors in human history, on human affairs as pathological, without believing in the reality, existence, possibility and indeed the definite offer of spiritual health, must needs create a profound spiritual predicament.[12]

This predicament, Heller adds, "they bore nobly, and with a strength of spirit and character which is rare among human beings." By contrast, he detects in Nietzsche, as in Rilke, a very different solution to "the whole excruciating problem that besets the spiritually disinherited mind of Europe", a response that he defines as "a *religio intransitiva*":

> Neither Rilke nor Nietzsche praises the praiseworthy. They praise. They do not believe the believable. They believe. And it is their praising and believing itself that becomes praiseworthy and believable in the act of worship.[13]

German intellectuals in 1914 welcomed the war as a cause filling the void left by the death of God. "At long last," Rilke wrote, "a God, the God of hosts." [14]

* * *

In the liberal England of Mill's utilitarian consensus and Arnold's hope that culture would gently replace Christianity, no one was much concerned by the danger of the "truths" in the name of which the twentieth century's appalling cruelties were to be inflicted. Nietzsche was read by few people outside Germany until after his death in 1900. Having had its revolution, England since 1660 had managed to contain radical intellectuals with little difficulty, mostly by paying them no serious attention. Marx and Engels lived and wrote for decades in the security of a society tolerant of foreign scholars and particularly benign to Germans. Both of them died peacefully in London, while British socialism retained a Christian tinge until well into the twentieth century. Meanwhile, the seepage into English life of Comte's atheist confidence in the triumph of science as power seemed to those who noticed it (among whom Mill was the best informed and a cautious admirer) no more than confirmation of the inevitable march of progress. In the long run, Comte's positivism, underpinning industrial capitalism and a mass society of usually docile wage earners who exercise leverage as organised labour and even more as consumers, has been, except among intellectuals, more successful in the whole Western world than either Marxism or Nietzsche's liberation from all (other) values of the self-creating, self-surmounting individual.

By the early twentieth century, the best English writing was far removed from the Christian tradition. Henry James represented the actual achievement of the replacement of Christianity with culture, his later novels demonstrating for how few people this enterprise was likely to deal with the real problems of life and death. Joseph Conrad, as an exiled Pole, had a keen, un-English sense of the gathering menace in post-Dostoyevskian Russia and its waiting terrorist exiles. He had been brought up as a Catholic, but there is little trace of Christian hope in his bleak, brave scepticism. Both James and Conrad disliked Dostoyevsky's novels, and D. H. Lawrence, the one major English novelist of the period with a naturally religious temperament, saw in them only the Nietzschean *ressentiment* of the underground man: Dostoyevsky "is like the rat, slithering along in hate".

Lawrence was born in the Nottinghamshire coalfield in 1885, his family united and divided by the social and emotional tensions he described in *Sons and Lovers*. The religion of his childhood was the nonconformist Christianity of Congregational chapels, strongly biblical and strongly independent of the established church, with a powerful strain of respectability and self-improvement. Through a hard-won, secular education, an early spell as a schoolteacher, and twenty years of pro-lific writing, the imagery of the Bible, the language of the Authorized (King James) Version, and the independence and the self-improvement stayed with him. The con-strictions of respectability and any possibility that Christianity might be true he left behind early and for good. His two great novels, *The Rainbow* and *Women in Love*, were written just before and during the 1914–1918 war. *Women in Love* was revised just after it. Together they explore the lives of the most interesting characters in three generations of a single family, presenting with complexity and vividness the impact of modern England on his own sensibility. Nothing written at the time has the power of Lawrence's analysis of the society in which he grew up and tried to live, until, in 1919 at the age of thirty-four, he abandoned it, except for brief vis-its, for the rest of his short life. After ten years of feverish wandering all over the world; feverish writing of some remarkable stories, travel books, criticism and sev-eral more novels; and feverish married life, he died of tuberculosis in the south of France in 1930, still only forty-four.

The Rainbow and *Women in Love* are novels of loss. They tell the story of the destruction, by the arrival of mines, factories, railways and the black sprawl of workers' housing—all that had horrified the Charles Dickens of *Hard Times*—of the centuries-old roots of English rural life in the rhythms of the seasons and the Christian year. Tom Brangwen, the patriarch, is a figure out of Thomas Hardy, Gabriel Oak in middle age imagined with a deeper inwardness than Hardy could manage. Tom's faith in the God who made and sustains the universe is pre-literate, pre-theological, almost pre-Christian, but it is safe, true and moving:

> During the long February nights with the ewes in labour, looking out from the shelter into the flashing stars, he knew he did not belong to himself. He must admit that he was only fragmentary, something incom-plete and subject. There were the stars, in the dark heaven travelling, the whole host passing by on some eternal voyage. So he sat, small and submissive in the great ordering.[15]

Lawrence leaves the reader to make the connexion between this trust in things as they are and Tom's goodness; his steady marriage to a foreign woman, always mys-terious to him; the warm security he gives her fatherless daughter; and the nobil-ity of his giving of this daughter, in turn, in marriage to his resented nephew. This pair, the second Brangwen generation, more educated and further from the land, is divided over what is now an explicit Christianity very much of its time and place.

Will Brangwen's late-Victorian Anglicanism, romantically tied to medieval church architecture and Pre-Raphaelite aestheticism, strikes his wife, whose own religion is a kind of pagan celebration of fecundity and motherhood, as both ludicrous and threatening. Their daughter Ursula, of Lawrence's own generation and in *The Rainbow* the figure most like him, retains from her childhood the soaring Old Testament language in which she articulates her adolescent emotions to herself, but she, like both her parents, shies away from Christian doctrine. By the book's end, she is overwhelmingly oppressed by the inexorable ugliness of industrial England defeating the remembered land of her childhood, her grandfather:

> She saw the dun atmosphere over the blackened hills opposite, the dark blotches of houses, slate roofed and amorphous, the old church-tower standing up in hideous obsoleteness above raw new houses on the crest of the hill ... a dry, brittle, terrible corruption spreading over the face of the land, and she was sick with a nausea so deep that she perished as she sat.[16]

She sees over this desolation a rainbow shine—when she was a child, her grandfather was drowned in a real flood—and the book's last paragraph holds out a biblically phrased but not in the least Christian promise of a redeeming, destructive newness. "She saw in the rainbow the earth's new architecture, the old, brittle corruption of houses and factories swept away, the world built up in a living fabric of Truth, fitting to the over-arching heaven." [17]

Ursula becomes one of the four central characters of *Women in Love*, though the Lawrence-figure is now the hypersensitive, prickly intellectual Rupert Birkin, whom Ursula learns to love. The presence, so evident in *The Rainbow*, of biblical language and imagery as artist's materials in a collage of exaltation have now almost disappeared. Although the richness of its writing and the unforgettable vitality of many of its scenes can dazzle the reader into thinking otherwise, *Women in Love* is a despairing book. An abyss of meaninglessness, opened, no doubt, partly by the 1914–1918 war, which Lawrence escaped through ill health, gapes under its characters' feet. Violence pervades the story. The relationship between Ursula's sister Gudrun and Birkin's friend Gerald, a cruel industrialist (the friendship is accounted for only by Birkin's subliminal homosexuality) is horrifyingly bleak, as is Gerald's death in utter Alpine cold. The differing values of lesser characters, from the paternalist charity of Gerald's father to the modish cultural chatter of society highbrows and the nihilist creativeness of the sinister German Jew to whom Gudrun escapes, are in turn analysed to destruction. What is presented as positive, the relationship between Birkin and Ursula, has the demandingness of unrealisable theory: a man and a woman must respond to each other from pure "singleness", each like a star in its own orbit (we are very far from the real stars in the real sky that reassured Tom Brangwen). At the end of the book, they leave the England they cannot bear for an apparently childless and workless isolation with each other. Lawrence, proposing, at thirty, this uprooted marriage as the answer to all human questions, was not too young to appreciate the anchorage in ordinariness, in daily occupation and obligation that sustains real marriages: he had already created the marriage of Tom and Lydia Brangwen. But Birkin, who has had one moment of ecstatic union, with nature rather than with Ursula, is allowed, in his excluding misery at Gerald's death, a final vision only of "the eternal creative mystery", or evolution, disposing of mankind altogether and replacing him "with a finer created being".[18]

By the time Lawrence, in New Mexico in 1925, gave a direct account of his beliefs in an essay called "Reflections on the Death of a Porcupine", he had thoroughly absorbed Nietzsche, and existence has become the universal struggle for ascendancy. Escape from this "existence" into "being", also called "heaven", is achievable only through getting "vitality . . . absorbing it from living creatures lower than ourselves".[19] "You will know that any creature or race is still alive with the Holy Ghost, when it can subordinate the lower creatures or races, and assimilate them into a new incarnation."[20] "The Kingdom of heaven is the Kingdom of conquerors."[21] "Life is more vivid in me, than in the Mexican who drives the wagon for me."[22] Although Lawrence, with his prophetic sensitivity, had the year before felt, with fear, the imminence of the barbarism then collecting strength in Germany, he shows here how easy was the slide, in an intellectual of religious temperament starved of any serious Christian formation, not only into lazy thought decked with Christian terminology but into proto-fascism. At this point in his life, he wrote what he reckoned to be his most important novel, *The Plumed Serpent*. Its central character, a Spanish-Mexican aristocrat, is sickened by life as seen by Schopenhauer:

> I can't *find God* in the old sense. I know it's a sentimentalism if I pretend to. But I am nauseated with humanity and the human will; even with my own will. I have realized that *my own will*, no matter how intelligent I am, is only a nuisance on the face of the earth, once I start exerting it. And other people's wills are even worse.[23]

He is also sickened by the imposition of European (Catholic) power on the Mexican Indians, so much closer to "life" than their conquerors. What is presented as positive in this book is a return to the service of sinister pagan gods in blood-lust and fertility dances.

In the year he visited Germany, Lawrence wrote a little essay called "Books". In it he praises the courage of Christians in "the flood of barbarism" that followed the fall of the Roman Empire:

> But, bless your life, there was Noah in his Ark with the animals. There was young Christianity. There were the lonely fortified monasteries, like little arks floating and keeping the adventure afloat.... The monks and bishops of the Early Church carried the soul and spirit of man unbroken, unabated, undiminished over the howling flood of the Dark Ages.[24]

He makes no connexion between the "adventure" and the truth, and his conclusion suggests the pride, the submission to "history" and the muddle in which he thought and wrote:

> I know the greatness of Christianity: it is a past greatness.... If I had lived in the year 400, pray God, I should have been a true and passionate Christian. The adventurer. But now I live in 1924, and the Christian venture is done. The adventure is gone out of Christianity. We must start on a new venture towards God.[25]

* * *

The best English literary critic of the twentieth century, F. R. Leavis, considered Lawrence the greatest novelist of his time. He also considered him to be an exemplary, and perhaps the last, writer able to sustain, in creative use of the English language, a quasi-religious connexion with what Leavis called "the living principle", or, more often, simply "life". These judgements seem surprising, until one realises how badly Leavis needed Lawrence to validate his whole approach to literature and to criticism.

Leavis was born ten years after Lawrence, in 1895. He served in a Quaker ambulance unit throughout the 1914–1918 war, a copy of Milton always in his pocket. Writing later of the 1920s, he said: "In those early years after the great hiatus, as in a dazed and retarded way I struggled to achieve the beginning of the power of articulate thought about literature, it was Santayana ... and Matthew Arnold who really counted."[26] His first book, *Mass Civilization and Minority Culture* (1930), had a thoroughly Arnoldian title and picked up where Arnold had left off the project of preserving "the best that has been said and thought" as a substitute for evidently exhausted Christianity. Leavis recognised from the outset, as Arnold had not, that this was a project only for the few, the "minority" upon whom "depends our power of profiting by the finest human experience of the past; they keep alive the subtlest and most perishable parts of tradition."[27] To defining the tradition and educating those who were to keep it alive, Leavis devoted the rest of his long working life: his last book, *Thought, Words and Creativity*, his second devoted entirely to Lawrence, appeared in 1976, two years before his death. He saw himself as contending always with the hostile forces that had driven Lawrence from England: a philistine civilisation Leavis called "technologico-Benthamite" and a snobbish cultural establishment that regarded him as a ranting moralist. His educational campaign nevertheless succeeded to a remarkable degree. Generations of his Cambridge pupils taught English literature and his kind of attention to the detail of great writing to thousands of students in universities and schools. Thousands more learned from his books and from his periodical, *Scrutiny*, how to read seriously and how to teach others to read. His judgements established a canon of works—and it is, strictly speaking, a canon rather than a tradition—that formed the national literary syllabus. In the last decades of the century, his influence quickly faded, as literary theory overtook literary criticism and dissolved his, and soon any, canon. Although his lifetime's work represents the best that could be made of Arnold's post- or para-Christian enterprise, almost no one reads him now.

Leavis said, and repeated often, that "unique literary values" or "a realm of the exclusively aesthetic" do not exist; that "a real literary interest is an interest in man, society and civilization, and its boundaries cannot be drawn";[28] that criticism must always be "responsible"; and that maturity, "relevance" and responsibility are the qualities in literature that the critic is to seek. He must look for them in literature because "the other traditional continuities have so completely disintegrated; ... if the literary tradition is allowed to lapse, the gap is complete."[29] But if Christianity, as Leavis thought, belongs irretrievably to the past, what are relevance and responsibility to? What is maturity for? He came close to the *religio intransitiva* of Nietzsche and Rilke. But only close.

Considering tragedy, to counter Santayana's false deduction that Shakespeare's own view of existence can be found in Macbeth's despairing nihilism, Leavis wrote, after a rare mention and rebuttal of Nietzsche:

> The sense of heightened life that goes with the tragic experience is conditioned by a transcending of the ego—an escape from all attitudes

545

of self-assertion. "Escape", perhaps, is not altogether a good word, since it might suggest something negative and irresponsible.... Actually the experience is constructive or creative, and involves a recognizing positive value as in some way defined and vindicated by death. It is *as if* we were challenged at the profoundest level with the question, "In what does the significance of life reside?", and found ourselves contemplating, for answer, a view of life, and of the things giving it value, that makes the valued appear unquestionably more important than the valuer, so that significance lies, clearly and inescapably, in the willing adhesion of the individual self to something other than itself.[30] [Italics mine.]

Here is another "as if", as loaded and as equivocal as Schopenhauer's. Leavis is writing about God, but it is impossible for him to admit that he is doing so.

Leavis wrote, occasionally, with clearly focussed warmth on Christian writers, notably on Hopkins, whose quality as a poet he was the first to recognise fully, and on John Bunyan. On "the incomparable end" of Bunyan's masterpiece, he wrote: "*The Pilgrim's Progress* must leave us asking whether without something corresponding to what is supremely affirmed in that exaltation, without an equivalently sanctioned attitude to death that is at the same time 'a stimulus to further living' ... there can be such a thing as cultural health."[31] In a lecture entitled "Literature and Society", however, he sidestepped the implications of this admission (what, outside Christian faith, could be "an equivalently sanctioned attitude to death"?) by saying: "If *The Pilgrim's Progress* is a humane masterpiece, that is in spite of the bigoted sectarian creed that Bunyan's allegory, in detail as in sum, directs itself to enforcing."[32] This is not true: the burden falling from Christian's back at the foot of the Cross has the same meaning, which is neither bigoted nor sectarian, as Coleridge's albatross falling from the ancient mariner's neck; it cannot in either case be abstracted so as to make the story merely "humane".

Leavis's essays on Hopkins—two on his poems, one on his letters—are less equivocal. He knows that Hopkins's Catholic faith and Hopkins's writing are as one: "Hopkins's religious interests are bound up with the presence in his poetry of a vigour of mind that puts him in another poetic world from the other Victorians. It is a vitality of thought, a vigour of the thinking intelligence, that is at the same time a vitality of concreteness."[33] "It is a habit of seeing things as charged with significance, 'significance' here being not a romantic vagueness, but a matter of explicit and ordered conceptions regarding the relations between God, man and nature."[34] In this essay, written in 1944, Leavis contrasts Hopkins's Christian poetry with Eliot's: "Hopkins's habit is utterly remote from Eliot's extreme discipline of continence in respect of affirmation." [35] The implication of the contrast is that now, Hopkins's faith being, as Arnold thought Newman's, "a solution which, to speak frankly, is impossible",[36] Eliot's habit must be the better of the two. But when, thirty years later, Leavis, at eighty, wrote his remarkable hundred-page commentary on *Four Quartets* in *The Living Principle* (1975), he detected beneath the poems' rare moments of personal affirmation "an essential nihilism". He explains:

> The reality that Eliot seeks to apprehend being spiritual, he assumes
> that the spiritual must be thought of as the absolutely "other"—the
> antithetically and excludingly non-human. In *Four Quartets*, for all the
> creative energy devoted to establishing the approach to apprehending,
> the painfully developed or enforced offer of apprehension is illusory:
> the real to be apprehended is nothing.[37]

Leavis much expands this and calls it "a severe adverse criticism". He grounds it in Eliot's "fear of life and contempt (which includes self-contempt) for humanity. This combination of fear and contempt commits him to a frustrating and untenable conception of the spiritual. By 'untenable' I mean one that cannot without his implicitly contradicting it be served by a poet." Behind this judgement is the countervailing figure of Lawrence, unmentioned but clearly present. "In demonstrating his supreme respect for his creativity, the artist demonstrates his allegiance to what he knows to be other than himself. The demonstration is the assertion of spiritual values, spiritual significance, spiritual authority; the resulting evidence their vindication." [38] Behind even Lawrence is a remark of William Blake's that Leavis quoted many times: "Tho' I call them Mine, I know that they are not Mine." Here Leavis adds, "Blake ... meant that when the artist is creatively successful the creativity to which the achievement belongs is not his, though, while transcending the person he is, it needed his devoted and supremely responsible service." [39] Toward the end of his last book, on Lawrence, he says: "We didn't create ourselves; and the sole access to the promptings to be gathered from the unknown—from which life and creativity enter us—is by the wellhead, which is deep below our valid thought. Submission to the promptings is escape from the ego and its will." [40]

All this raises immense questions. What does the artist know "to be other than himself"? To what does he owe "his devoted and responsible service"? What is "the unknown" from which life and creativity "enter us"? There are only two possible answers: the unconscious, and God. Leavis avoids either answer, with a lurking "as if"—"This faith can come only through grace, and hence as if from without"[41]—that he never acknowledges. He has dispensed with the Christian context that was, however eccentrically, Blake's and was centrally Coleridge's when he defined the imagination as "a repetition in the finite mind of the eternal act of creation in the infinite I AM".[42] Leavis's criticism of *Four Quartets* could be grounded not on what is negative in Eliot and positive in Lawrence, but on the lack in *Four Quartets* of a full Christian sense of the significance of the incarnation of God in Christ: Eliot does not share, or the poems do not show that he shares, Hopkins's "explicit and ordered conceptions regarding the relations between God, man and nature"; therefore "the vitality of concreteness" in his poems is negative rather than positive. Unsurprisingly, this is not a connexion Leavis makes. On the contrary, his overrating of the "spiritual values", even "spiritual authority", of creativity in Lawrence leads him to ask too much of Eliot because he finds too much in Lawrence. One poet, one novelist, any artist, cannot rescue spiritual values; Leavis, disliking the "desperation" he identifies (probably rightly) as "the great drive behind his creativity", demands of Eliot "more than a matter of mere personal affirmation",[43] requires of him a Lawrentian confidence in the spiritual authority of his own creativeness. But Eliot, seen in a Christian context, is no more than a struggling soul having to learn, like the rest of us, to answer with faith the given truth. As Heller most pertinently wrote, in his analysis of the *religio intransitiva*:

> Without that all-pervasive sense of truth which bestows upon happier cultures their intuition of order and reality, poetry ... will be faced with ever increasing demands for ever greater "creativeness".... With every new gain in poetic creativity the world as it is, the world as created without the poet's intervention, becomes poorer; and every new impoverishment of the world is a new incentive to poetic creativeness. In the end the world as it is is nothing but a slum to the spirit, and an offence to the artist.[44]

Leavis never abandoned his hope, forlorn though he knew it to be, in "ever greater 'creativeness'", the hope that carries with it, as it did in both him and Lawrence, an inevitable disdain for almost everyone and almost everything in "the world as it is". His hope, and in particular his long dedication to the project of replacing Christianity with a literary canon that would save people capable of reading well from the dereliction of meaninglessness, has a Schopenhauerian nobility. Certainly, both his hope and his dedication have at their very core a

Schopenhauerian equivocation. To what should we submit in order to "escape from the ego and its will"? Into what is our escape? The will of God? The truth that commands our obedience? Are we helped by "grace, and hence as if from without"? If not, the escape will be only into the further reaches of the self and into the chilling satisfactions of Wordsworth's "higher minds", rightly understood by Coleridge as "the dread Watch-Tower of man's absolute self".[45]

A deeply-buried nostalgia for Christianity is detectable in Leavis. His knowledge of it, as the living whole he perceived in Hopkins, was as fragmentary, as ordinarily English, as the knowledge of it possessed by his heroes, Blake, Dickens and Arnold as well as Lawrence. It is not insignificant that in *Thought, Words and Creativity* he travels backward through Lawrence's best novels, ending his commentary with *The Rainbow*. But Tom Brangwen's trust in God belongs to irrecoverable childhood; trust in "creativity" has to replace it for a sophisticated adult intellectual. The last pages of Leavis's last book are intensely gloomy. With an astonishing nod of approval in the direction of Birkin's/Lawrence's curious conviction that "even if human life ... was eliminated from the world, new life would be generated in the universe", he ends with a forlorn hope:

> We have the incitement, which is irresistible, of the life-courage in the product of his [Lawrence's] creativity, and that makes it inevitable for us to carry on the creative effort with all our intelligence, courage and resource. Who can be sure? Logic and automatism, impossible as it now seems, may yet be robbed of their final victory; the decisively new and unforeseen may yet reward us.[46]

* * *

No doubt because of his resolute Englishness—inconsistent, since two of the three novelists discussed in *The Great Tradition* were foreigners—Leavis failed altogether to notice Samuel Beckett, who obscurely published an obscure poem in 1930, the year of Leavis's first book, but who was by 1960 a famous writer and a most striking example of "the decisively new and unforeseen".

Beckett was born into a middle-class Irish Protestant family in 1906. An exceedingly clever, self-contained boy, he grew up as the masterpieces of modernism were being written. He was sixteen in the year of *The Waste Land*, Rilke's *Duino Elegies* and Joyce's *Ulysses*; before he was twenty-one, Kafka's *The Trial*, Thomas Mann's *The Magic Mountain* and the whole of Marcel Proust's *À la recherche du temps perdu* had been published. A brilliant undergraduate linguist at Trinity College,

Dublin, he found himself at twenty-two the visiting *lecteur* in English, a two-year appointment, at the École Normale Supérieure in Paris. He soon became a friend and disciple of Joyce. At the École Normale he met Thomas MacGreevy, the Irish Catholic with whom Wallace Stevens warmly corresponded during the last years of Stevens's life. MacGreevy, until his death in 1967, was one of Beckett's closest friends. Beckett disliked teaching, abandoned his subsequent job at Trinity College after four terms, and travelled restlessly through his twenties, living for periods in London, Germany and France, returning to Ireland as little and to Paris as much as he could, writing, earning almost nothing, existing on a small allowance from his disapproving family. His first novel, *Dream of Fair to Middling Women*, unpublishable at the time and not published till after his death, was written in Paris in 1932. He later called it "the chest into which I threw my wild thoughts".[47] It has, indeed, in a glitteringly resourceful prose licenced by the example of Joyce, then working on *Finnegans Wake*, a wildness he later cut down and eventually out of everything he wrote until, in old age, his texts became so short that they approach the silence that always had for him a blessedness. But it also has, in youthful, unpared form, the essential qualities of his later work: beauty, great (Irish) humour, the freight of the written past of Europe deployed with light erudition in several languages, and above all a sense of the absurdity, brevity, futility and grief of all human life.

The hero of *Dream of Fair to Middling Women*—as of *More Pricks Than Kicks*, a collection of stories including sections of *Dream* published in 1934—is a wryly observed version of Beckett, a young Irishman sharing his initials in reverse, Belacqua Shuah. "Shuah" means "depression" in Hebrew; Belacqua is the name of Dante's idle friend whom he and Virgil meet sitting in a disconsolate heap at the foot of the mountain of Purgatory, unable to start the climb, "for I put off repenting till the end".[48] As a student learning Italian, Beckett discovered Dante and read and reread him for the rest of his life. Beckett's later characters are stuck in Limbo, at the outer edge of the Inferno, even more obviously than they are waiting to leave Belacqua's rocky shelf. Vladimir and Estragon in *Waiting for Godot* listen to "all the dead voices",[49] and Pozzo echoes Virgil's advice to Dante, who feels sorry for the grieving souls whose lives have been lived too dimly for either heaven or hell, "Let us not speak of them, but look and pass on."[50] (This is the canto from which Eliot stole for *The Waste Land* the line: "I had not thought death had undone so many."[51])

When the Second World War began, Beckett, still a struggling and almost unknown writer, at once left the safety of neutral Ireland, where he was visiting his widowed mother, for Paris. In Germany for several months in 1936–1937, he had failed to respond more than distantly, locked as he was in a Joycean detachment from politics and his own inturned unhappiness, to the gathering persecution of Jews and the bullying of the expressionist painters he admired. Now he chose to share the fear and privations of what, by the summer of 1940, became Nazi-occupied Paris. In 1941 he was working for a Resistance group; in 1942 Alfred Péron, another member of the group, a Jew and Beckett's oldest (since 1926) French friend, was arrested by the Gestapo. Péron died in 1945 as a result of his treatment in the Mauthausen concentration camp. Paul Léon, Joyce's secretary, was arrested by the Nazis in 1941 and died in Silesia in 1942. Beckett and his companion, later his wife, fled Paris just in time to avoid capture and spent the rest of the war at Roussillon in the Vaucluse, where he worked again for the Resistance and where the villagers, because he was called Samuel, assumed he was Jewish. In 1945 he worked for the Irish Red Cross in a field hospital in Normandy, helping the bombed-out people of the ruined town of Saint-Lô. By 1946, when he began the astonishingly productive four years that saw him write *Mercier and Camier*; the trilogy of monologue novels, *Molloy, Malone Dies* and *The Unnamable*; and *Waiting for Godot* (described as a fourteen-week "marvellously liberating diversion" [52]) Beckett had witnessed a good deal of the kind of wartime suffering that most of his countrymen were spared.

In 1946, in Ireland, he had experienced a kind of revelation from within himself, fragmentarily described later by the old, failed writer who is the sole character in the short play *Krapp's Last Tape* (1958). "What I suddenly saw then ... clear to me at last that the dark I have always struggled to keep under is in reality my most—." [53] From then on he wrote, without answers, without philosophy, of "the dark" in the soul, particularly in the soul of the lost, the dispossessed and the maimed—those who live in the lower depths of the human condition. He had also become a French writer. He said that it was easier to escape "style" in French than in English; it was certainly easier in French to escape the influence of Joyce. When he translated, or, more accurately because of his extraordinary inwardness with both languages, rewrote, his works of 1946–1950, his English writing had lost the compulsive wordplay caught from *Finnegans Wake* and gained a purity and power entirely his own. He is, at least in *Godot*, both warmer and funnier in his mother tongue, and two of his best later pieces, *All That Fall* (1956), a play for radio, and *Krapp's Last Tape* itself were first written in English.

Beckett is famous for the difficulty of his work, which has evoked an immense quantity of commentary and explanation, and for the unconsoled darkness of his vision. The trilogy novels, their prose of startling beauty, are indeed a demanding and often grim read, as is the spooky, sometimes cruel, sometimes manically logical novel *Watt*, which he wrote in English at Roussillon during the war. *Endgame* is a play of despair, lit with occasional shafts of painful humour. His late, brief plays have a plangent sadness. But the reader or watcher of any of these is helped little by commentary; the reader has only to read, the watcher to watch and listen. The power of the writing is overwhelming—or not. Which it is will depend on the reader or watcher, not on the presence or absence of critical help. All this is most true of *Waiting for Godot*, his most loved, most often performed work, the masterpiece that, after many years of failure to find publishers and a readership, made him in the 1950s swiftly one of the most celebrated writers in the world.

Godot was written when the roads of Europe had very recently been wandered by countless thousands of the displaced, uncertain of the next safe lodging, the next meal, desperate to avoid the next beating, the next bullying official. "A country road. A tree. Evening." Two old men, connected for decades in a relationship of affection, irritation, routine and dependence, as in an old marriage, wait. They call each other "Didi" and "Gogo": only in Vladimir's ruminations do their full names, Vladimir and Estragon, appear. Their supplies are down to a carrot, a few turnips and some radishes. They pass the time, bickering, remembering or forgetting this and that, reflecting (Vladimir reflects; Estragon sometimes responds), and swapping invective, anguish and devices for passing the time, including an elegiac lament ("All the dead voices"). In each of the play's two acts, two successive evenings, another pair of old men, Pozzo and Lucky, connected vertically rather than horizontally since Pozzo is a master and Lucky his man, come and go. Pozzo is a figure of hollow power, rapidly diminishing as he loses his belongings; in the second act, he is blind. He is a meretricious orator, like the European dictators recently defeated: "Is everybody ready? Is everybody looking at me?" [54] But he has the persuasive force to convert, in seconds, Vladimir and Estragon's pity for Lucky to contempt. "Remark that I might just as well have been in his shoes and he in mine. If chance had not willed otherwise. To each one his due"; [55] the empty conceit of this, as of the statement "From the meanest creature one departs wiser, richer, more conscious of one's blessings", [56] strikes us, not them. Lucky, hired "nearly sixty years ago" to teach Pozzo "beauty, grace, truth of the first water", [57] Pozzo treats like a dog: "Basket!"; "I've never known him refuse a bone before." [58] Lucky speaks only once. His speech, a crazed, unpunctuated parody of an academic lecture that rises in a crescendo of incoherence until his hat is taken off, is a broken threnody for a God-forsaking post-Enlightenment world, "the dead loss per caput since the death of Bishop Berkeley" (Voltaire in the French text, Samuel Johnson in

Beckett's first translation), a world of distraction where "in spite of the strides of physical culture"—the concentration on health and sport—man can only "waste and pine waste and pine".[59] "The crisis started", Beckett said over lunch in Germany in 1967, "with the end of the eighteenth century. The encyclopaedists were all mad, *tous fous* . . . ils déraisonnent! They gave reason a responsibility which it simply can't bear, it's too weak." [60] Dr. Johnson, for whom God was God, as he was for Dante, was the eighteenth-century figure Beckett most loved.

Vladimir and Estragon are as much an interdependent, foundered pair as Adam and Eve after the Fall. All Vladimir and Estragon know is that they must wait for Godot. A little exchange, repeated several times in the second act, is at the play's heart:

> ESTRAGON. Let's go.
> VLADIMIR. We can't.
> ESTRAGON. Why not?
> VLADIMIR. We're waiting for Godot.
> ESTRAGON. Ah![61]

(His "Ah!" is of recollection and/or of sorrow.) They talk about suicide comically, hopelessly. At the end of each act:

> VLADIMIR. Well? Shall we go?
> ESTRAGON. Yes, let's go.
> *They do not move.*[62]

When Pozzo and Lucky collapse in a pratfall heap in act 2, another interdependent, foundered pair, Vladimir says, grandly, comically, truthfully:

> To all mankind they were addressed, those cries for help still ringing in
> our ears! But at this place, at this moment of time, all mankind is us,
> whether we like it or not.[63]

When Pozzo responds to being called first "Abel!" and then "Cain!", Estragon, who has forgotten, as he forgets nearly everything, that he is called Pozzo, says: "He's all humanity." [64] Very early in the play, Vladimir, talking of the two thieves crucified with Christ—"One of the thieves was saved. It's a reasonable percentage" [65]—strikes a note whose resonance never altogether dies away. The tree, the only thing on the stage apart from the characters and what they carry, deepens this note. When Beckett sketched the tree for a Dublin production of *Godot* in 1988, he drew it as a cross, arms slightly raised, as in Michelangelo's late drawings. The tree anchors the appointment kept, "He said by the tree."[66] Vladimir, grand again, says: "We are not saints, but we have kept our appointment. How many people can boast as much?" To which Estragon replies: "Billions."[67] Between the first act—when the tree looks dead—and the second, the tree has acquired leaves (as, far away and long ago, the trees flanking the figure of Christ in Piero della Francesca's painting of the Resurrection are bare on the left, but covered in leaves on the right). "Yesterday evening it was all black and bare. And now it's covered with leaves", Vladimir says, "In a single night." Estragon answers, "It must be the Spring."[68] And almost at the end:

ESTRAGON. And if we dropped him? (*Pause.*) If we dropped him?
VLADIMIR. He'd punish us. (*Silence. He looks at the tree.*)
Everything's dead but the tree.[69]

It is while "doing the tree", staggering on one leg, that Estragon suddenly says: "Do you think God sees me?" and then cries "(*at the top of his voice*), 'God have pity on me'", to which Vladimir responds "(*vexed*), 'And me?'".[70] Toward the end of both acts, when Pozzo and Lucky have gone, a boy appears to tell Vladimir and Estragon that Mr. Godot won't come this evening "but surely tomorrow".[71] In both acts, Vladimir gives the boy a message for Mr. Godot: "Tell him you saw us"; "Tell him you saw me."[72] Lurking here there is Bishop Berkeley's *esse est percipi* (to be is to be perceived), and an echo of Saint Anselm's prayer to Saint John the Evangelist:

Cry, groan from the depths of your soul in his sight, "You see me....
Sir, see me, and know me, look and have pity upon me!"[73]

Some of the boy's words very faintly suggest Christ: "I mind the goats, sir."[74] And when Vladimir asks him: "Are you a native of these parts? (*Silence.*) Do you belong to these parts?" he replies, "Yes, sir."[75] At the play's end, just before a final music-hall joke, Vladimir says: "We'll hang ourselves tomorrow." (*Pause.*)

VLADIMIR. Unless Godot comes.
ESTRAGON. And if he comes?
VLADIMIR. We'll be saved.[76]

A heavy and specific Christian interpretation of *Waiting for Godot*, like any other heavy and specific interpretation, is neither appropriate nor helpful. The play is (also) very funny and is scored with as much detailed care for the stage directions as for the dialogue. The visual jokes never fail, while Pozzo stamping on Lucky's hat—"There's an end to his thinking!"[77]—has the impact of a violent blow. The indications *Pause, silence* and *long silence* should be observed as exactly as different "rests" in music. Often the audience is poised between laughter and tears, as in the fourth act of *King Lear*, where two other old men are beached on the shore of the wide world. "When we are born, we cry that we are come / To this great stage of fools",[78] says the mad Lear to the blind Gloucester, much as Vladimir says: "Down in the hole, lingeringly, the gravedigger puts on the forceps. We have time to grow old. The world is full of our cries."[79] Beckett's scoring is always light, suggesting the balance of a string quartet. The play perhaps strikes us as Emil Nolde's painting *Christ and the Children* struck Beckett in Hamburg in 1936: "Feel at once on terms with the picture, and that I want to spend a long time before it, and play it over and over again like the record of a quartet." In the same notebook he wrote: "The art (picture) that is a prayer sets up prayer, releases prayer in onlooker: i.e., *Priest*: Lord have mercy upon us. *People*: Christ have mercy upon us."[80]

Beckett always loved both music, especially that of Schubert, and painting. Reviewing in 1945 a book by Thomas MacGreevy on Jack Yeats—the old Irish painter who was both a friend and a hero of his own—he wrote: "He is with the great of our time ... because he brings light, as only the great dare to bring light, to the issueless predicament of existence",[81] a phrase that neatly describes the not yet written *Godot*. When MacGreevy sent Stevens his book in 1948, Stevens's response included the remark: "Your essay on Mr. Yeats is right on the rightness of his realism.... Kate O'Brien says in one of her novels that in Ireland God is a member of the family. So, in Mr Yeats' house, reality is a member of the family."[82] Beckett always refused to explain or identify Godot, who promises to come, who does not come, who must be waited for. Who is he? If he is "a member of the family", it is not surprising that he has a nickname, even a clown's name, on the lines of "Charlot" (Charlie Chaplin in France) or Pierrot, as Christ is a clown, mocked and sad, in some of the paintings of Georges Rouault, another painter Beckett admired. What is certainly true is that nowhere in Beckett's work is there the sense that God, apparently absent from "the issueless predicament of existence", must now be replaced by the efforts of the artist. There is an immense difference, a difference almost of opposites, between Beckett's awareness of his own impoverishment (and the plight of impoverished, lost, grotesquely forlorn humanity), and the confidence in "an ever greater creativeness", or self-surmounting, of Nietzsche, Rilke, Lawrence and Leavis, in a world that has become, in Heller's words, "a slum to the spirit and an offence to the artist". It is the difference between contempt and compassion. The *religio intransitiva* of self-generated divinity was not for Beckett. In a review Beckett wrote for Eliot's *Criterion* in 1934, he said of Rilke: "He has the fidgets, a disorder which may well give rise, as it did . . . on occasion, to poetry of a high order. But why call the fidgets God, Ego, Orpheus, and the rest." [83] No wonder Beckett loved Schopenhauer, from 1930 when he first read him, for his "intellectual justification of unhappiness", [84] for the clarity of his account of the "issueless predicament", and for his assault on "Wahn", that is, illusion, particularly perhaps the illusion of ambition, achievement and competitive success. Very low-spirited, in Paris in 1937, Beckett wrote to MacGreevy that he

> found the only thing I could read was Schopenhauer. Everything else I tried only confirmed the feeling of sickness. It was very curious. Like suddenly a window opened on a fug. I always knew he was one of the ones that mattered most to me. [85]

Like Schopenhauer, Beckett saw the human race as locked into suffering that somehow seems deserved, "the unintelligible terms of an incomprehensible damnation". [86] In his first published prose piece, a short book on Proust (1931), scattered with references to Dante and Schopenhauer, he wrote: "The tragic figure represents the expiation of original sin, of the original and eternal sin of him and all his 'socii malorum' [companions in calamity], the sin of having been born." [87] "Suppose we repented?" Vladimir says early in *Godot*. "Repented what? . . . Our being born?" [88] Estragon suggests. Like Schopenhauer also, Beckett rejected the escape of suicide, a fashionable topic and sometimes a reality among Parisian intellectuals in his youth. "Let's go. We can't." [89] Or, in the famous last phrases of *The Unnamable*, "you must go on, I can't go on, I'll go on." [90] The force of this "must" is as distant, as mysterious, as the force of "obligation" in Beckett's self-description in his brief *Dialogues* on painters, written in the same year as *Godot*, where he says that

> there is nothing to express, nothing with which to express, nothing from which to express, no power to express, no desire to express, together with the obligation to express. [91]

Does the obligation come, like Schopenhauer's grace, "as if from without"? As *Godot*, if he comes, will come? In any case, in Beckett as in Schopenhauer, there is nothing for it, nothing for the issueless predicament but the resignation of the will, and compassion for "the others". "Was I sleeping", Vladimir asks himself, "while the others suffered?" [92]

After *Godot*, Beckett lived for forty years in Paris, shy of fame, appalled (a word Vladimir relishes) by the Nobel Prize he was awarded in 1969, his quiet kindness, loyalty and generosity unfailing. He travelled a little to supervise productions of his plays; visited America once to make a short silent film, called *Film*, with Buster Keaton; retreated when he could to a tiny house he had built in the Marne; and wrote more and more briefly and poignantly of the old, the damaged, the sad, the "socii malorum", each of his voices representing "all humanity". He spent his last months in a modest home for the elderly in Montparnasse, a copy of Dante and a life of Dr. Johnson by his bed, a single tree in the yard outside his window. He died on Christmas 1989 and was buried, without ceremony and before the world knew of his death, in Montparnasse cemetery, a few hundred yards from the École Normale where the silent Irish boy had arrived more than sixty years before.

His subject was always what Pascal called "misère de l'homme sans Dieu". There is no proof that Beckett read Pascal. They are kindred spirits nonetheless. "Consolez-vous: ce n'est pas de vous que vous devez l'attendre, mais au contraire, en n'attendant rien de vous, que vous devez l'attendre." [93] This *pensée* is untranslatable because *attendre*, as in *En attendant Godot*, means both "wait for" and "expect": "Be consoled; it is not from yourself that you should expect consolation, but on the contrary, it is in expecting (waiting for) nothing from yourself that you should wait for it." A maxim of the seventeenth-century philosopher Geulincx, *ubi nihil vales, ibi nil velis* (Where you can do nothing, wish for nothing), Beckett always cherished; Geulincx's work, he wrote to MacGreevy, appealed to him on account of "its saturation in the conviction that the Sub Specie Aeternitatis vision is the only excuse for remaining alive." [94] The very last piece he wrote, slowly and with difficulty in the year of his death, is a three-page sequence of short, broken lines. It ends:

> glimpse—
> seem to glimpse—
> need to seem to glimpse—
> afaint, afar away over there what—
> folly for to need to seem to glimpse afaint,
>   afar away over there what—
> what is the word—
>
> what is the word. [95]

This is more tentative, fainter and further away than Stevens's "ember yes among the cindery noes", but Beckett also was, perhaps, "a man lured on by a syllable without any meaning".[96]

* * *

"It is God who looks for man.... The attitude which makes salvation possible is not like activity of any kind.... It is waiting.... Waiting for goodness and truth is something more intense than any searching."[97]

Simone Weil, who wrote of *Attente de Dieu*, "waiting for God", without any shadow of an "as if", began her studies at the École Normale in October 1928, a month before Beckett, three years older, arrived in the same building to take up his post as *lecteur*. They probably never met, nor is there much likelihood that either was ever aware of the other's existence. Simone Weil, a Jewish refugee from Nazi-occupied France, left her parents safe in New York in 1942 and travelled to London to work for General de Gaulle and the Free French. She died at age thirty-four, in a Kent sanatorium in August 1943 of heart failure and incipient tuberculosis, aggravated by self-neglect and starvation. She had, in solidarity, been eating only what the poorest in occupied France were surviving on. (Two years later, Beckett, awarded the Croix de Guerre by de Gaulle for his Resistance work, visited Ireland and wrote: "My friends [in France] eat sawdust and turnips while all of Ireland safely gorges."[98])

Simone Weil's mother was born at Rostov-on-Don in tsarist Russia in 1879 to a middle-class Jewish family that was assimilated, nonreligious and cultivated; the family moved to France in 1882. Simone Weil's father, a doctor in Paris when he married, came of a long-assimilated Jewish family of merchants in Alsace. Their exceptionally intelligent daughter, born in 1909, received the very best, entirely secular, education available in Third Republic France and the impact, at home, of the most modern ideas about health, hygiene and exercise (as mocked in Lucky's speech). As a child, and for the rest of her short life, she was often ill, prone to depression, violent migraines and psychosomatic disorders, as, in his youth, was Beckett. Always younger and more brilliant than her classmates, she attended the Lycée Henri Quatre for three years and was taught philosophy and classical and French literature by Alain (Emile Chartier), the most celebrated teacher in Paris. At the École Normale she studied philosophy for three more years, her only brush with Christian thought a single course of lectures given by Étienne Gilson, the great Thomist.

Unlike Beckett, who sustained his detachment until he risked his life against the Nazis, Weil was deeply involved in politics from her adolescence to her death. In the left–right maelstrom of French intellectual life in the 1930s, she was always of the left. Feeling passionately for the poor—factory hands, miners, the unemployed—she worked, wrote, marched and spoke at meetings, at first with Marxist sympathies. She never joined the Communist party. Visiting Germany in 1932, she felt acutely the impending horror: "Germany Waiting", she called the essay she wrote for a Marxist journal. "Hitler", she wrote, three months before he became chancellor, "means organized massacre, the suppression of all freedom, all culture." [99] She was already aware of the similar impact on people's lives of Nazism and Stalin's communism. Antitotalitarian to her bones, she was shocked when Stalin's Russia in 1933 closed its borders to refugees from Germany; she persuaded her parents to shelter fleeing communists in their flat, including briefly Leon Trotsky himself. A highly qualified teacher, she gave up good teaching posts to work on assembly lines in factories for several months in 1934 and again in 1935. With characteristic extremeness, she was utterly horrified by shop-floor life, regarding it as unmitigated slavery. The experience, which she felt had branded her as a slave herself, made her less rather than more Marxist, since she saw that the real oppression of the workers was not in the ownership of the means of production but in the means of production itself, in Auguste Comte's triumph of the theology of science. In 1935 she saw, as Beckett did, Charlie Chaplin's *Modern Times* and said that only Charlot understood the plight of downtrodden workers. A brief encounter in 1936, as an anarchist journalist, with the cruelties of the Spanish civil war—she had to be rescued after burning her leg with boiling oil—confirmed her horror of all war, but in 1939 she abandoned pacifism at the outbreak of the Second World War, and after the fall of France and the Vichy statute forbidding Jews professional work, including teaching, she left Paris with her family for the south, reaching Marseilles in 1941.

Meanwhile, her compassion for the sufferings of the poor, and then her susceptibility to beauty—"God's snare for the soul" [100] she later called it—had unexpectedly opened her heart to the possibility that Christianity might have some connexion with truth. In the summer of 1935, broken in body and spirit by her factory work and on holiday with her parents in Portugal, she watched a procession of candle-bearing peasant women singing ancient hymns for the safety of the village fishing boats. She wrote (in agreement with Nietzsche but reversing his judgement): "There I was suddenly certain that Christianity is above all the religion of slaves, that slaves cannot but adhere to it, and myself among the others." [101] In 1937 she spent "two marvellous days" at Assisi and found herself, alone in the little church of Saint Francis's vision, compelled, for the first time in her life, to her knees. In 1938, almost incapacitated by shattering headaches, she stayed for Holy Week at Solesmes, the Benedictine monastery famous for the austere beauty of its liturgy. A young English Catholic introduced her to the poems of George Herbert. Five months later, not for the first or last time in a migraine-racked depression so profound that "I asked myself with anguish whether to die wasn't for me the most imperative of duties", she was reciting the poem that begins "Love bade me welcome: yet my soul drew back" when Christ himself visited her, "his presence more personal, more certain, more real than that of a human being ... like the love glimpsed through the tenderest smile of a loved being. From that moment the name of God and the name of Christ were more and more irresistibly mingled in my thoughts." [102]

The moment was like that of Pascal's conversion—"Certainty. Certainty. God of Jesus Christ" [103]—except that Simone Weil, unlike Pascal with years of faithful Catholic practice behind him, was totally unprepared for it. It was not her soul that drew back from the implications of this moment, but her ferociously clear, ferociously trained, secular intellect. She now began to read the history of the Christian Middle Ages, the history and sacred texts of other religions, and for the first time, the Old Testament in its entirety. Without guidance, and accustomed to using her formidably equipped mind with an independence of judgement that she had developed over years—"I have an extremely rigorous conception of intellectual probity" [104]—she came to a set of conclusions that held her back decisively from baptism into the Church. By the time she met, in Marseilles in June 1941, an intelligent and sympathetic priest, the Dominican Joseph-Marie Perrin, she was convinced that there was an unbridgeable gulf between the Church and the religion of Christ, between orthodox dogma and the truth. From her shocked reading of the Old Testament, she had conceived an intense antipathy to the religion and history of Israel; from her shocked reading of Christian history, she had conceived an intense antipathy to the Rome of both empire and papacy, in particular to the Church of the Crusades and the Inquisition, of anathemas and the definition of heresy. During her time in Marseilles, she worked in the Dominicans' library on classical Greek authors familiar from her youth and became increasingly sure that they, particularly Plato, Sophocles and (in an idiosyncratic reading of the *Iliad*) Homer, had much more in common with Christianity than either Judaism or the actual Church. "The Romans and the Hebrews", she wrote at the end of her essay on Homer, "have been admired, read, imitated in deeds and in words, cited every time there was need to justify a crime, throughout twenty centuries of Christianity." [105] She told Father Perrin that she loved

God, Christ, the Catholic faith, the saints, the liturgy and "the six or seven Catholics of genuine spirituality whom chance has led me to meet.... But I have not the slightest love for the Church." [106] There remained to her death these two empty spaces in her thinking: she had no sense of the Jewish roots of Christianity and no sense of the essential connexion between the Church, however imperfect as a human institution, and the faith. Father Perrin must have tried, and failed, to persuade her to dismantle her resistance to both. She thanked him for telling her that it would be a pity if she, through her own fault, missed something important; this, she told him, made her see "the duty of intellectual probity in a new light. I had thought of it only as opposed to faith." [107] But he could not alter her certainty that "it is necessary and ordained that I should be alone, a stranger and an exile in relation to every human circle without exception." [108]

Young, proud and pathologically fastidious—there was anorexic self-harm in the illness that killed her—she saw the Church as a temptation to the same kind of "social enthusiasm" that, in fascism, Nazism and Communism, was killing and persecuting millions of people. More specifically, the French church of her lifetime, "the sacristy atmosphere", in Balthasar's words, in which it "withdrew, genteel and offended, from the secularized modern world", [109] and its association both with right-wing nationalism and with sentimental naïveté, offended her deeply. "It was the fashion before 1940", she wrote in L'Enracinement, her programme for France's future written in London at frenetic speed, "to talk about 'eternal France.' Such words are a sort of blasphemy.... France is something which is temporal, terrestrial. Unless I am mistaken, it has never been suggested that Christ died to save nations." [110] Love of the Church struck her as an analogous, even a connected, idolatry: "I am afraid", she wrote to Father Perrin, "of the Church patriotism which exists in Catholic circles. By patriotism I mean the feeling one has for a terrestrial country." [111]

Father Perrin became a friend: Simone Weil's exalted view of friendship, as a chaste and equal closeness and distance in God, has much in common with that of Saint Aelred, of whom she knew nothing. Four months after she left Marseilles, she wrote in New York a letter to a priest she did not know, another Dominican, Father Couturier, recommended to her by Jacques Maritain as "open-minded", in order to be told whether or not she could be considered a Catholic. The "Letter to a Religious" is long, passionate and confused, for all its intellectual qualities, and very far from orthodox. Her prejudice against both Judaism and the Church blind her to the crucially connected history of both and therefore to the uniqueness of God's revelation of himself in Christ. Her reading had led her to the conclusion that the gods of India, Egypt, Persia and Greece were more Christian than the God of Israel. Only a few books in the Old Testament—Isaiah, Job, parts of Ezekiel and the Psalms, and some of the Wisdom books—are "assimilable by a Christian soul".[112] All mystics of all religions "are connected almost to the point of identity. They constitute the truth of each tradition."[113] Catholics, misled by the metaphor "the body of Christ", regarded not Jesus but the Church as God incarnate: "But there is a small difference: Christ was perfect but the Church is sullied with a quantity of crimes."[114] Christianity is divided into "two distinct religions, that of the mystics and the other." "The other" is totalitarian: "Israel and Rome have left their mark on Christianity, the official religion of the Roman Empire, which was something like Hitler's dream."[115]

There is much in all this—the rejection of Israel, the division between the mystics and everyone else, and the gnostic syncretism—that fits the pattern set by Marcion and Mani, the major heretics of the second and third centuries. No wonder Weil loved and admired the Cathars, the medieval Manichaean sect bullied and finally eradicated by the Church. At this point, aged thirty-three, Simone Weil had reached a position not unlike that of Augustine at much the same age: Augustine, classically educated in an entirely secular world and exceedingly clever and a philosopher by training, had also been horrified by the barbarism of some of the Old Testament when he first read the Bible, and he also had been seduced by the dualist perfectionism of the Manichees. Had Weil read the *Confessions* and, especially, the *City of God*, she would have learned from Augustine something of which she had no idea: a balanced, orthodox view of the Church as *both* human and fallible *and* divine and to be believed in, not the idol of blind "patriotism", but the *corpus permixtum* of which the sorting, the judgement, belongs only to God, a Church in which "the mystics" and everyone else are not only included but, to mortal eyes, inextricably mixed. In the *City of God* she would have found solid reinforcement for her distrust of "eternal France". Perhaps, even more important, Augustine, or Pascal, would have persuaded her that there is a difference between provable facts and truth. In her "Letter to a Religious", she wrote: "The value of such propositions as 'Jesus Christ is God' or 'The consecrated bread and wine are the body and blood of Christ' is not strictly speaking of the order of truth, but of a superior order, because it is a value not graspable by the intelligence.... And truth, in the strict sense, belongs to the domain of the intelligence."[116]

But, with no sense of how much she and Augustine shared in the legacy of Plato, and indeed with no sense of the tradition to which her own insight into Christian truth belonged, she thought of Augustine as a "narrow Catholic" who had made the Church "the instrument of a totalitarian power".[117] A short paragraph in her New York notebook begins: "Rome and Israel introduced into Christianity, mixed with the spirit of Christ, the spirit of the Beast. Israel, which slew Christ, is the very form of the Church as St Augustine conceived it." But the paragraph ends: "All pure good proceeds from Christ. All good has its source in God." [118] A few pages earlier, she wrote: "There is only one unique source of light. Dim light does not consist of rays coming from another source, which is dim; it is the same light, degraded.... Christ is the key.... The true is the contact of the good with the intelligence." [119] (This is Anselm's "intelligible beauty".) Augustine could have helped her to understand her love for Plato and for the good in other religions in the spirit suggested here. But after a few more months of thought, mostly about the dereliction of France and of Europe, she was dead.

She was always a French intellectual improbably pulled by the touch of Christ into truth she had been educated out of confronting as true. Her writing, almost all of it collected and published as various books only after her death, has much in common with the work of the great Russians, who also encountered Christianity with the resources of only a secular education. She saw, in her agonised, intense life and in the dreadful times in which she lived, what they in their different ways had also seen. Her abhorrence of violence and her insistent identification with the poor were Tolstoyan: Simone Weil on the Renault car-part assembly line must have cut as odd a figure as Count Tolstoy scything incompetently in a line of peasant haymakers. Her anti-ecclesiastical veneration for the Cathars was like Tolstoy's for the Doukhobors or Solzhenitsyn's for the Old Believers. Her love for Christ and her fear of any kind of ideology was like Pasternak's, whose cultured, secularised Jewish background was very similar to her own. Her adopted privations, Franciscan generosity and early death were like Soloviev's. But she had most in common with Dostoyevsky.

Like Dostoyevsky, she saw the Catholic Church as the oppressive, even diabolical, continuation of the Roman Empire. Her desire for the presence of Christ in the Eucharist to be brought "into those places most polluted with shame, misery, crime and affliction, into prisons and law-courts, into shelters for the poor and wretched" [120] was met in the Easter liturgy described in *Memoirs from the House of the Dead* and is in extreme contrast to the guyed prison liturgy and the wretched lawcourt priest in Tolstoy's *Resurrection*. Her own longing for the saving renunciation of the will no doubt owed something to the Schopenhauer she had read as a philosophy student at the École Normale: "Compassion is natural to man if the obstacle of the feeling of 'I' is removed. It is not compassion that is supernatural, but the removal of that obstacle." [121] This "removal" was most perfectly imagined in Prince Myshkin. The puzzle of Dostoyevsky's choice of "Christ rather than the truth" is resolved in Weil's "Christ likes us to prefer truth to him because, before being Christ, he is the truth. If one turns away from him to go towards the truth, one will not travel far before falling into his arms." [122] Most Dostoyevskian of all is the chasm that in Ivan Karamazov separates the disciplined rationalist anguished by the suffering of the innocent from his own vision of the silent Christ. At the end of her life, Weil stared into this chasm. In April 1943 she wrote to Maurice Schumann, who four months later read the prayers at her graveside:

> I feel a tearing apart, which gets worse all the time, both in my mind and in the depths of my heart, on account of my inability to think at the same time of the truth of the affliction of mankind, the perfection of God and the connection between the two. [123]

In her London notebook, kept in these months, she unconsciously summarises the Legend of the Grand Inquisitor in two consecutive sentences:

> The silence of Christ under blows and mockery is the twofold silence of truth and affliction in this world.
>   "All this power and the glory thereof is delivered unto me", said the Father of Lies. [124]

The silenced Word on the Cross she always found easier to love than the resurrected Word of Easter. "If the Gospel omitted all mention of the resurrection of Christ, faith would be easier for me.... The Cross has the same effect on me as the resurrection has on others." [125]

Weil's was a rare spirit. For all the prejudices and complexities that kept her from the Church where she belonged, and that she might well, one day, have reached, much that she wrote is close to the heart of Christian truth, in particular her emphasis on waiting for, attention to, God, mirrored in attention to intellectual problems, however minor, mirrored in attention to other people—mirrored in, but not to be replaced by.

> Love is a divine thing. If it enters a human heart it breaks it. The human heart was created in order to be broken in this way. It is the saddest waste if it is broken by anything else. But it prefers to be broken by anything rather than by the divine love. [126]

Augustine said that God wants to give us something, but our hands are full. In her last long letter to her parents, written from her hospital bed two weeks before her death, she compares herself, "in spite of the École, the *agrégation*, all the praise of my 'intelligence'", to the fools in Shakespeare. She had seen *King Lear* in London:

> In this world, only those fallen to the last degree of humiliation, far below lies, not only beyond the consideration of society, but regarded by everyone as deprived of the prime human dignity, reason—only they have the possibility of speaking the truth. All the rest lie.
>
> In *Lear* this is striking. Even Kent and Cordelia attenuate, mitigate, sweeten, veil the truth, dodge with it, as long as they are not compelled either to speak the truth or to lie.[127]

She is clearly thinking even more of Edgar than of the Fool. But Edgar is a prince in disguise and so—in Weil's strangeness, her illnesses, her addiction to the victimhood of what Beckett called "the dark"—was she. "True faith", she wrote, "implies great discretion, even in relation to itself. It is a secret between God and us and we ourselves have almost no part in it."[128]

* * *

Beckett saw his Jewish friends disappear into Hitler's camps. After the war, he absorbed with everyone else the facts of the Shoah and the facts of the parallel history of murder and suffering in Stalin's Russia. In the first draft of *Godot*, Vladimir already had his Russian name; Estragon was called Lévy. The play has an Old Testament tinge, a colour that distantly recalls the liturgy of Advent, when Christians are reminded that they also are "the people that walked in darkness"[129] until the Messiah comes. Weil died before the catastrophe of the Final Solution became known to the world. Obsessed though she always was with "malheur", affliction and "déracinement" (uprootedness), the misery of the oppressed, she never wrote sympathetically of the affliction of the Jews through the centuries. This refusal of sympathy, which occasionally led her into actual anti-Semitism, was perhaps connected to the element of self-harm that killed her. Nevertheless, much that she wrote, because of the depth of her Christian intuition, has an instinctive connexion with the Jewish sense of God.

In one of her 1942 essays on the Greeks, *Intuitions pré-chrétiennes*, she quotes from Sophocles's *Antigone*. Antigone's crime has been to bury, against Creon's order, her brother, killed attacking Creon's city, while her other, honoured, brother defended it:

ANTIGONE.   The God of the Dead at least desires equality.
CREON.   But not that the good should win an equal share with the bad.
ANTIGONE.   Who knows if this is sacred in the world below?
CREON.   Never at any time is the enemy, even when dead, a friend.
ANTIGONE.   I was born not to share in hate but to share in love.

Weil comments:

> This verse spoken by Antigone is splendid; but Creon's reply is even more splendid, for it shows that those who share only in love and not in hate belong to another world and have nothing to expect from this world but a violent death: "Descend then, since you have such need to love, love those who are below." It is only among the dead, in the other world, that one is free to love. This present world does not authorize love.[130]

Again, in the *City of God* she would have found extended confirmation of her sense of a critical collision here, between the laws of the *civitas terrena* and the eschatological justice of the *civitas Dei*, "another world". (This is the dialogue of which George Steiner wrote, astonishingly: "The transcendent absolutes to which Antigone appeals ... are, in a radical sense, secular.")[131]

Balthasar's remarkable essay "Tragedy and Christian Faith", written in 1965, is included in the section called "Night" in his third volume of *Explorations in Theology*. One passage, concerning the Jews in relation to the Church, "who is half immaculate bride and half harlot, ever ready anew for every backsliding and betrayal of her Lord", almost uncannily echoes Weil's perception of the collision in the *Antigone*. In a profoundly serious attack on the anti-Semitism of the Church down the ages, Balthasar sees the Israel of the Old Covenant and the Jewish people always in

> the role of the Servant of Yahweh, deprived of power, disfigured and put to shame, who suffers vicariously for the arrogant and disobedient persons who persecute him. And this poor figure is persecuted now by the Church and by Christianity, which holds (incomprehensibly) that it may or must do this in the name of the Servant of Yahweh and has no idea, in its pious heartlessness, that it thereby only brings to fulfillment the original unity of the prophecy: the unity between the collective Servant of Yahweh as the holy people of Israel and the personal Servant of Yahweh, Jesus, who comes from Israel and recapitulates this collective suffering in himself in eternal solidarity with Israel.

From a truly Christian perspective, which rests on Augustine's distinction between the actual Church and the eternal *civitas Dei*, Balthasar expects that the "renewed encounter between the Lord and his people is to be only eschatological. Everything that happens before that is only of interim value. This means that the whole Church, too, as long as she continues to be separated from Israel, has only interim value." His clinching illustration is very striking to the reader of *Waiting for Godot*: "Jesus openly makes a promise to the thief on his right and says nothing to the thief on his left. But in order that the thief on the right may win the promise, Jesus unites himself in secret with the thief on the left in the solidarity of being rejected."[132] "I was born not to share in hate but to share in love."

After an impressive debate, free of any trace of anti-Semitism, the English House of Commons in 1847 decided (the bill failed in the House of Lords) to take out of its oath of loyalty to the Crown the Christian element that barred Jews from membership of the Commons. Disraeli supported the measure not on Gladstone's grounds of religious liberty but because: "The Jews ... profess a true religion. It may not be in your more comprehensive form. I do not say it is the true religion; but although they do not profess all that we profess, all that they do profess is true."[133] The slide here from "your" to "we" and "they" perhaps signals Disraeli's own uncertain hold on any particular belief. It is a tribute to at least official tolerance in nineteenth-century England that Disraeli, baptized in London in 1817 at the age of twelve, became Queen Victoria's favourite Prime Minister, while Felix Mendelssohn, baptized in Berlin in 1816 at the age of seven, became her favourite composer. Both their lives have much to do with the emergence from discrimination and oppression of prosperous Jewish families into the cultured haute bourgeoisie in most countries of post-Napoleonic Europe, even, as was the case with the Pasternaks and the Weils, in Russia and France. This emergence was made easier, of course, by the growing intellectual consensus, to which many Jews, notably Marx and Freud, contributed, that all religion had been left behind in the continent's superstitious childhood.

After the unexampled horror inflicted on Europe's Jews by the very nation in which secularised Jews had been most successful, some Jewish writers in England and America have been among those most nostalgic for the God to whom Jews have been indissolubly connected by tradition, learning and observance for thousands of years, in what all Christians must recognise as Disraeli's "true religion". In England George Steiner, an extraordinarily wide-ranging literary critic and thinker, has, in ten books in over forty years, come closer and closer to admitting that unless there is, actually *is*, God, to guarantee as real our perceptions of truth, goodness, beauty and meaning, then even the greatest masterpieces of literature are no more than word games played against the silence of an accidental universe. Steiner, born in Paris in 1929 to parents who had left Vienna in 1924, was educated at home to high European culture in three languages—French, English and German—and to secular, classical and philosophical rigour in the French Lycée in Manhattan. His family, like the Weils, left Nazi Europe for New York. Steiner, though his range has been over the whole of European literature, has as powerful a sense of the canon of great works "inexhaustible to meditation"[134] as Leavis had. A generation younger, he has lived to be horrified by the derelictions of literary theory, and, on this account as well as on account of a more philosophical education and temperament, has had to face explicitly, as Leavis never did, the underlying, immense question of real—real?—value in supreme works of art, a question he knows to be theological.

Steiner's *Real Presences* (1989) is subtitled *Is there anything in what we say?* In its attempt to answer this question, the book is anguished, subtle and deeply evasive. Unable to leave what he calls "that in being which is not ours" as undefined as Leavis left his "well-head", he writes of a "postulate of transcendence", a possibility, on which we may bet, in the spirit of Pascal's wager, that meaning is not illusion. "The meaning of meaning is a transcendent postulate. To read the poem responsibly ('respondingly'), to be answerable to form, is to wager on a reinsurance of sense."[135] The bracket takes the force out of Leavis's "responsibly", as does the reduction, which is the theme of the whole book, to the aesthetic in "answerable to form". Pascal's wager was about living, not about reading. If God is a postulate only raised in great art, what about the countless millions excluded by lack of education, lack of sensibility and lack of opportunity from high aesthetic perception? We are back with Arnold, with Leavis's "mass civilization and minority culture". In his autobiographical book *Errata* (1997), Steiner, closer than ever to Leavis, wrote that great teaching "will . . . aim to elicit and cultivate a meritocracy of the unpredictable, founded on the conviction that the *dignitas*, the validation of our species on this planet, consists in the disinterested advances out of animality made by the creative spirit."[136] Steiner does know that this is not enough. In *Errata*, as in the essays of *No Passion Spent* (1996) and the yet more anguished, more subtle, more deeply evasive *Grammars of Creation* (2001), he returns often, with a characteristic mixture of embarrassment and courage—for he thinks of himself as inescapably an atheist—to the wager on transcendence. Knowing that most of the masterpieces on whose meaning he has staked his critical and teaching life have been created in "explicit engagement with transcendence", he has nevertheless, in the end, to leave "the God-hypothesis" as no more than that.[137] It is impossible for him, a twentieth-century intellectual, to return to his ancestral connexion with the God of Israel; it is more impossible for him to turn to the Christianity that he repeatedly insists alone delivered the Shoah. "How", he asks at the end of *Errata*, "can 'the totally Other' act on us, let alone give any signal of its utterly inaccessible existence?"[138] thus denying real meaning, and any value grounded in the existence of God, to both Old and New Testaments. In *No Passion Spent*, he writes, with warmth and honour, of Socrates and Jesus as if their deaths can be understood in the same way. Like other Jews (including Simone Weil) educated to the view that nobody thought properly between Aristotle and Descartes, Steiner finds in Plato, particularly in *The Symposium*, a vindication of his sense of the possibly ultimate value of love. But in the end, both Plato and the Evangelists play only what he has to call "the language-games of the sacred".[139] Steiner's wager is no more than a shot in the dark, an "as if" blinder even than Schopenhauer's, whose atheological sense of original sin he shares, calling it the "working metaphor".[140] Belief he abandons to others—to "reinsure", one of his favourite words for his bet, is defined in the *Oxford English Dictionary* as "to devolve the risk of an insurance on another insurer"—though he doubts that any intelligent belief has survived the twentieth century.

Steiner, with Augustine though not because of him, recognises that the goodness, beauty and truth of even the greatest works of art is relative to the goodness, beauty and truth of God: "there is aesthetic creation because there is *creation*".[141] God, however, is not there. Another incisive Jewish critic of our time campaigned for the soul of man and the ideal as the object of longing but was less embarrassed by this central dilemma. Allan Bloom, with tremendous élan, rattled the cages of value-free American academia with his *The Closing of the American Mind* (1987), defending the study of great writing with as much intellectual energy as Steiner. The purpose of his attack on "the new language of value relativism",[142] which destroys the possibility of even talking about good and evil, is to return, in the spirit but without the belief of Dr. Johnson, "the search for a good life" to its proper place as "the real motive of education"[143] and to rescue the humanities from ignorance and contempt:

> All that is human, all that is of concern to us lies outside of natural science.... The kinds of questions children ask: Is there a God? Is there freedom? Is there punishment for evil deeds? Is there certain knowledge? What is a good society? were once also the questions addressed by science and philosophy. But now the grownups are too busy at work, and the children are left in a day-care center called the humanities, in which the discussions have no echo in the adult world.[144]

He knows what a life of faith was:

> My grandparents found reasons for the existence of their family and the
> fulfillment of their duties in serious writings, and they interpreted their
> special sufferings with respect to a great and ennobling past. Their sim-
> ple faith and practices linked them to great scholars and thinkers who dealt
> with the same material, not from outside or from an alien perspective,
> but believing as they did, while simply going deeper and providing guid-
> ance.... This is what a community and a history mean, a common expe-
> rience inviting high and low into a single body of belief.[145]

He also knows what is not a life of faith: "These sociologists who talk so facilely
about the sacred are like a man who keeps a toothless old circus lion around the
house in order to experience the thrills of the jungle."[146] But his last, long,
impassioned book, *Love and Friendship* (1992), heroically dictated through months
of the illness from which he was dying, is a new Arnoldian attempt to replace
the "serious writings" that are Scripture with the works of literature that will
teach people to live with imagination, with the longing for the ideal that he
calls "eros": some nineteenth-century novels, Shakespeare's plays about love, and
above all Plato's *Symposium* (again). He recognises, with Heller, the *religio intransitiva* of the nineteenth century: "longing, not the object of longing.... The
emptiness at the top haunts this literature."[147] He consistently defends Plato
against Nietzsche, the beauty of the truth against the ugliness of the truth, although
he is always inclined to write about Nietzsche as if Christianity had never been:
"Socrates is alive and must be overcome. It is essential to recognize that this is
the issue in Nietzsche."[148] The subject of that sentence should be Christ. We
have already seen that when, at the end of Bloom's last book, Diotima's account
of the ascent of love reaches the form of the good, it is impossible for him to
follow her because, he says, he is "a philosopher, who is by definition a doubter".[149]

* * *

Allan Bloom's friend Saul Bellow wrote in his foreword to *The Closing of the
American Mind*: "The soul has to find and hold its ground against hostile forces,
sometimes embodied in ideas which frequently deny its very existence, and which
indeed often seem to be trying to annul it altogether."[150] If the soul, Bellow
always knew, without the intellectual panic of Steiner or the philosopher's insou-
ciance of Bloom, then God.

Bellow, who died in April 2005, was the best American novelist of the second half of the twentieth century. Born in Canada in 1915 to Jewish parents who had left tsarist Russia eighteen months earlier, he was two generations closer to traditional, observant Jewish life than Simone Weil or George Steiner. " 'Wie Gott in Frankreich'" (like God in France), he wrote, "was the expression used by the Jews of Eastern Europe to describe perfect happiness", because in France no one would bother God, especially not in Paris, "the heavenly city of secularists".[151] His father, once a rabbinical student in Vilnius, was a moderately successful trader in Saint Petersburg, in trouble with the tsarist police for living outside the Jewish pale. In Lachine, Quebec, and then Chicago, where the family lived from 1924, he was poor, but "all for Americanism", telling his children "you're free either to run yourself into the ground or improve your chances."[152] The immigrant back streets of Chicago in the Depression were a far cry from the French Lycée in Manhattan in the 1940s, though both Steiner and Bellow, fourteen years older, were students at the University of Chicago.

As a child, Bellow spoke Yiddish and learned Hebrew. At age eight, he was very ill in a Protestant hospital in Canada for six months. There, he recalls, "A missionary lady came and gave me a New Testament for children. I read that. I was very moved by the life of Jesus, and I recognized him as a fellow Jew." Many children in his ward died. He got better, and felt that "I'd better make it worth the while of whoever it was that authorized all this. I've always had some such feeling."[153] Like Lawrence, he was the least strong and most gifted child in the family, his mother's favourite son. She died when Bellow was sixteen. As a schoolboy and a student, he read all the books he could lay his hands on—Plato, Shakespeare, Dostoyevsky, T. S. Eliot; novels in quantity; and the great purveyors of what were supposed to be liberating truths, Marx, Lenin (the progress of the Russian Revolution was of keen interest to his family, who had left behind friends and relatives), Nietzsche, Freud and Schopenhauer (at seventy-five, Bellow still had the Schopenhauer he "bought for two dimes and read when I was a high school junior"). "So you had the Bible and the Patriarchs, cheek by jowl with Russian novelists and German philosophers and revolutionary activists and all the rest. . . . You were really pitched headlong into a kind of mental chaos and you had to make your way."[154] Also like Lawrence, Bellow had to make his way in resolute contention with a complacent world of assumed cultural superiority. Leavis, Lawrence's champion, noticed Bellow no more than he noticed Beckett. In 1952 Leavis wrote of Theodore Dreiser, one of Bellow's early heroes, in the lofty tones of Eliot: "He ... clearly belongs to no tradition. He represents the consequences of the later influxes from Europe and the sudden polyglot agglomeration of big raw cities, and may with some point be said to belong to the culturally dispossessed." [155] The beloved Chicago of Bellow's youth was a big raw city; culturally dispossessed he was not.

Over more than fifty years, Bellow wrote a dozen novels and a number of dazzling stories, all packed with vivid life, all readable and enjoyable by anyone who can read, and all about the outer and inner lives of central characters not unlike himself, liberal and endlessly interested, never Marxist. He was caught by history and personal fate between the exhilarating, threatening challenges of twentieth-century America and the patient certainties of the long Jewish past, at home in neither because too acutely familiar with their conflicting magnetic fields. For all the rich exuberance of his books, there is in Bellow's work not only the element of piety of his dedication to writing through years of poverty and in the face of scorn from his father and brothers, but a thread of certainty that the truth of every life lies between the soul and God. In his second novel, *The Victim* (1947), the central character says:

> "I know what really goes on inside me. I'll let you in on something. There isn't a man living who doesn't. All this business, 'Know thyself'! Everybody knows but nobody wants to admit.... 'Repent!' That's John the Baptist coming out of the desert.... There's another thing behind that 'repent'; it's that we know what to repent. How? ... *I* know. Everybody knows." [156]

Decades later, Corde, the mild academic hero of *The Dean's December* (1982), who is deeply depressed by the violence and squalor of downtown Chicago, says: "The worst of it I haven't gotten around to at all—the slums we carry around inside us. Every man's *inner* inner city." [157] This sure knowledge is always counter to the competitive prosperity of successful America: "As if everybody were saying 'This is life, this is what I give myself to. There is no other deal. No holding back, go with the rest.' Then a man like Corde came haunting around. He would never put his chips on the mortal roulette squares, good enough for everybody else." [158]

For all his reading and all his prodigious talent, Bellow was not seduced by the *folie de grandeur* of the *religio intransitiva*. "Frightening, the lives some of these geniuses led", says a sensible character in the story "The Gonzaga Manuscripts". "They knew that if by their poems and novels they were fixing values, there must be something wrong with the values.... If you throw the full responsibility for meaning and for the establishing of good and evil on poets, they are bound to go down." [159] The Arnoldian project has been tried, and it has failed. Moses Herzog, the most sympathetic and most carefully explored of all Bellow's central characters, an intellectual losing his grip on the complexities of his emotional life, says:

> The people who come to evening classes are only ostensibly after culture. Their great need, their hunger, is for good sense, clarity, truth—even an atom of it. People are dying—it is no metaphor—for lack of something real to carry home when day is done. [160]

Remembering his vanished childhood, Herzog approaches what is for everyone, culture or no culture, the central question: "All children have cheeks and all mothers spittle to wipe them tenderly. These things either matter or they do not matter. It depends upon the universe, what it is." [161] Does everything mean something or nothing mean anything? "The living man", Bellow said in a lecture in 1977, "is preoccupied with such questions as who he is, what he lives for, what he is so keenly and interminably yearning for, what his human essence is, and instead of the bread of thought he is offered conceptual stones and fashionable non-ideas." [162] Bellow's character Mr. Sammler, an old Jew left for dead by the Nazis and now living, but not happily, in Manhattan, thinks there is nowadays too much "explaining":

> The roots of this, the causes of the other, the sources of events, the history, the structure, the reasons why. For the most part, in one ear out the other. The soul wanted what it wanted. It had its own natural knowledge. It sat unhappily on superstructures of explanation, poor bird, not knowing which way to fly. [163]

At the end of this book, Mr. Sammler prays by the body of his dead friend:

> He did meet—through all the confusion and degraded clowning of the life through which we are speeding—he did meet the terms of his contract. The terms which, in his inmost heart, each man knows. As I know mine. As all know. For that is the truth of it—that we all know, God, that we know, that we know, we know, we know. [164]

In Vladimir's words, "We have kept our appointment."

In 1976 Bellow delivered his Nobel Prize lecture, six years after Solzhenitsyn had been prevented from delivering his. In its free American fashion, Bellow's is as Russian as Solzhenitsyn's:

> There were European writers in the nineteenth century who would not give up the connection of literature with the main human enter-prise. The very suggestion would have shocked Tolstoy and Dos-toyevsky. But in the West, a separation between great artists and the general public took place. Artists developed a marked contempt for the average reader and the bourgeois mass.... What would writers do today if it occurred to them that literature might once again engage those "central energies", if they were to recognize that an immense desire had arisen for a return from the periphery, for what is simple and true?[165]

What they would do is what Bellow all his writing life tried to do, against Western enemies of the soul all the more powerful for their apparent benignity, their almost universal acceptance. In 1993 he wrote:

> The powers of soul, which were Shakespeare's subject (to be simple about it) ... have no footing at present in modern life and are held to be sub-jective. Writers here and there still stake their lives on the existence of these forces. About this, intellectuals have little or nothing to say.[166]

Or, as in Steiner's case, what they say is so hedged about with qualification and hesitation that nothing is actually staked. There is no "as if" in Bellow, but, in Mr. Sammler's words, "the belief that there is the same truth in the heart of every human being, or a splash of God's own spirit, and that this is the richest thing we share".[167] "We have an idea of truth", Pascal wrote, "unconquerable by any amount of scepticism."[168]

1. Jn 8:32.
2. Quoted in Henri de Lubac, *The Drama of Atheist Humanism* (1944), trans. Edith M. Riley et al. (San Francisco, 1995), p. 139.
3. Blaise Pascal, *Pensée 829*, in *Oeuvres Complètes*, ed. Jacques Chevalier, Bibliothèque de la Pléiade 34 (Paris, 1954), p. 1341.
4. Quoted in de Lubac, *Drama of Atheist Humanism*, p. 166.
5. Ibid., p. 239.
6. Ibid., pp. 249–50.

7. Arthur Schopenhauer, *The World as Will and Representation*, trans. E. F. J. Payne (New York, 1966), 2:443.
8. Ibid., 1:403.
9. Ibid., p. 404.
10. Ibid., p. 407.
11. Ibid., 2:185.
12. Erich Heller, *The Disinherited Mind* (London, 1975), p. 79.
13. Ibid., p. 171.
14. Quoted in Amos Elon, *The Pity of It All* (London, 2002), p. 304.
15. D. H. Lawrence, *The Rainbow* (1926; London, 1928), p. 33.
16. Ibid., p. 466.
17. Ibid., p. 467.
18. D. H. Lawrence, *Women in Love* (London, 1921), p. 505.
19. D. H. Lawrence, "Reflections on the Death of a Porcupine", in *Selected Essays* (London, 1950), p. 66.
20. Ibid., p. 69.
21. Ibid., p. 71.
22. Ibid., p. 65.
23. Quoted in F. R. Leavis, *Thought, Words and Creativity* (London, 1976), p. 53.
24. D. H. Lawrence, "Books", in *Selected Essays*, p. 47.
25. Ibid., p. 48.
26. F. R. Leavis, *Anna Karenina, and Other Essays* (London, 1967), p. 177.
27. F. R. Leavis, *For Continuity* (Cambridge, 1933), p. 15.
28. F. R. Leavis, *The Common Pursuit* (London, 1952), p. 200.
29. Leavis, *Anna Karenina*, p. 223.
30. Leavis, *Common Pursuit*, pp. 131–32.
31. Ibid., p. 210.
32. Ibid., pp. 188–89.
33. Ibid., p. 48.
34. Ibid., pp. 51–52.
35. Ibid., p. 50.
36. Matthew Arnold, "Emerson", in *Essays in Criticism*, 2nd series, vol. 4 of *The Works of Matthew Arnold* (London, 1903–1904), pp. 376–77.
37. F. R. Leavis, *The Living Principle* (London, 1975), p. 203.
38. Ibid., p. 205.
39. Ibid., p. 185.
40. F. R. Leavis, *Thought, Words and Creativity*, p. 128.
41. Schopenhauer, *The World as Will and Representation* 1:407.
42. S. T. Coleridge, *Biographia Literaria*, ed. James Engell and W. Jackson Bate (Princeton and London, 1983), 1:304.
43. Leavis, *Living Principle*, pp. 220, 222.
44. Heller, *Disinherited Mind*, pp. 170–71.
45. S. T. Coleridge, "To William Wordsworth", lines 39–40, in *Poetical Works*, ed. J. C. C. Mays (Princeton, 2001), vol. 1, pt. 2, pp. 816–19.
46. Leavis, *Thought, Words and Creativity*, p. 156.
47. Quoted on dust jacket text by John Calder for Samuel Beckett, *Dream of Fair to Middling Women* (London, 1993).
48. Dante, *La divina commedia*, Purgatorio 4.132.
49. Samuel Beckett, *Waiting for Godot* (London, 1965), p. 62.
50. Ibid., p. 33; Dante, *Inferno* 3.51.
51. T. S. Eliot, *The Waste Land*, line 63; Dante, *Inferno* 3.57.
52. Quoted in Anthony Cronin, *Samuel Beckett: The Last Modernist* (London, 1996), p. 390.
53. Samuel Beckett, *Krapp's Last Tape*, in *The Complete Dramatic Works* (London, 1986), p. 220.

54. Beckett, *Waiting for Godot*, p. 30.
55. Ibid., p. 31.
56. Ibid., p. 29.
57. Ibid., p. 33.
58. Ibid., p. 27.
59. Ibid., pp. 43–44.
60. Quoted in Cronin, *Samuel Beckett*, p. 557.
61. Beckett, *Waiting for Godot*, p. 68, etc.
62. Ibid., pp. 54, 94.
63. Ibid., p. 79.
64. Ibid., p. 83.
65. Ibid., p. 11.
66. Ibid., p. 14.
67. Ibid., p. 80.
68. Ibid., p. 66.
69. Ibid., p. 93.
70. Ibid., pp. 76–77.
71. Ibid., pp. 50, 91.
72. Ibid., pp. 52, 92.
73. *The Prayers and Meditations of Saint Anselm*, trans. Benedicta Ward (London, 1973), p. 169.
74. Beckett, *Waiting for Godot*, p. 51.
75. Ibid., p. 50.
76. Ibid., p. 94.
77. Ibid., p. 45.
78. William Shakespeare, *King Lear*, 4.6.80–81.
79. Beckett, *Waiting for Godot*, pp. 90–91.
80. Quoted in James Knowlson, *Damned to Fame* (London and New York, 1996), pp. 220, 222.
81. Quoted in Cronin, *Samuel Beckett*, p. 141.
82. Wallace Stevens, *Letters* (London 1967), p. 597.
83. Quoted in Cronin, *Samuel Beckett*, p. 203.
84. Quoted in Knowlson, *Damned to Fame*, p. 122.
85. Ibid., p. 248.
86. Samuel Beckett, *The Unnamable*, quoted in Cronin, *Samuel Beckett*, p. 375.
87. Samuel Beckett, *Proust and Three Dialogues with Georges Duthuit* (London, 1965), p. 67.
88. Beckett, *Waiting for Godot*, p. 11.
89. Quoted in Cronin, *Samuel Beckett*, p. 557.
90. *The Beckett Trilogy* (London, 1979), p. 382.
91. Beckett, *Proust and Three Dialogues*, p. 103.
92. Beckett, *Waiting for Godot*, p. 90.
93. Pascal, *Pensée 657*, *Oeuvres complètes*, p. 1296.
94. Quoted in Cronin, *Samuel Beckett*, p. 239.
95. Ibid., p. 587.
96. Wallace Stevens, "St. Armorer's Church from the Outside" and "Prologues to What Is Possible", in *Collected Poems* (New York, 1954; London, 1955), pp. 529–30, 515–17.
97. Simone Weil, "Formes de l'amour implicite de Dieu", in *Oeuvres*, ed. F. de Lussy (Paris, 1999), p. 753; my translation.
98. Quoted in Cronin, *Samuel Beckett*, p. 343.
99. Weil, *Oeuvres*, p. 54.
100. Ibid., p. 734.
101. Ibid., p. 771.
102. Ibid., p. 797.
103. Pascal, *Oeuvres complètes*, p. 554.
104. Weil, *Oeuvres*, p. 770.

105. Ibid., p. 552.
106. Simone Weil, letter to Fr. Perrin, 19 January 1942, in *Waiting on God*, trans. Emma Craufurd (London, 1959), p. 19.
107. Weil, *Oeuvres*, p. 774.
108. Weil, letter to Fr. Perrin, p. 23.
109. Hans Urs von Balthasar, *My Work in Retrospect*, trans. Brian McNeil et al. (San Francisco, 1993), p. 38.
110. Simone Weil, *The Need for Roots*, trans. Arthur Wills (New York, 1931), p. 131.
111. Weil, letter to Fr. Perrin, p. 21.
112. Weil, *Oeuvres*, p. 1007.
113. Ibid., p. 1000.
114. Ibid., p. 997.
115. Ibid., p. 999.
116. Ibid., p. 1001.
117. Simone Weil, *First and Last Notebooks*, trans. Richard Rees (Oxford, 1970), p. 130.
118. Ibid., p. 120.
119. Ibid., p. 98.
120. Weil, *Oeuvres*, p. 754.
121. Weil, *First and Last Notebooks*, p. 210.
122. Weil, *Oeuvres*, p. 772.
123. Ibid., p. 1224.
124. Weil, *First and Last Notebooks*, p. 341.
125. Weil, *Oeuvres*, pp. 1003–4.
126. Ibid., p. 324.
127. Ibid., p. 1236.
128. Ibid., p. 755.
129. Is 9:1.
130. Simone Weil, *Intimations of Christianity among the Ancient Greeks*, ed. and trans. Elisabeth Chase Geissbuhler (London, 1957), p. 9.
131. George Steiner, *Antigones* (London, 1984), p. 271.
132. Hans Urs von Balthasar, *Creator Spirit*, trans. Brian McNeil, Explorations in Theology, vol. 3 (San Francisco, 1993), pp. 405–6.
133. See David Vital, *A People Apart: The Jews in Europe 1789–1939* (Oxford, 1999), p. 180.
134. I. A. Richards, *Coleridge on Imagination* (London, 1934), p. 171.
135. George Steiner, *Real Presences* (London, 1989), p. 216.
136. George Steiner, *Errata* (London, 1997), p. 116.
137. George Steiner, *Grammars of Creation* (London, 2001), pp. 279–80.
138. Steiner, *Errata*, p. 167.
139. George Steiner, *No Passion Spent* (London, 1996), p. 388.
140. Steiner, *Errata*, p. 169.
141. Steiner, *Real Presences*, p. 201.
142. Allan Bloom, *The Closing of the American Mind* (New York, 1987), p. 141.
143. Ibid., p. 34.
144. Ibid., pp. 356, 372.
145. Ibid., p. 60.
146. Ibid., p. 216.
147. Allan Bloom, *Love and Friendship* (New York, 1993), p. 184.
148. Bloom, *Closing of the American Mind*, p. 308.
149. Bloom, *Love and Friendship*, pp. 517–18.
150. Saul Bellow, foreword to Bloom, *Closing of the American Mind*, p. 17.
151. Saul Bellow, *It All Adds Up* (New York, 1994), p. 239.
152. Ibid., p. 294.
153. Ibid., pp. 288–89.

154. Ibid., p. 300.
155. Leavis, *Anna Karenina*, p. 155.
156. Saul Bellow, *The Victim* (London, 1988), p. 203.
157. Saul Bellow, *The Dean's December* (New York, 1982), p. 229.
158. Ibid., p. 86.
159. Saul Bellow, *Mosby's Memoirs and Other Stories* (London, 1971), p. 123.
160. Saul Bellow, *Herzog* (London, 1965), p. 28.
161. Ibid., p. 33.
162. Bellow, *It All Adds Up*, p. 129.
163. Saul Bellow, *Mr. Sammler's Planet* (London, 1972), pp. 3–4.
164. Ibid., p. 313.
165. Bellow, *It All Adds Up*, p. 94.
166. Ibid., p. 113.
167. Bellow, *Mr. Sammler's Planet*, p. 189.
168. Pascal, *Pensée* 273, in *Oeuvres complètes*, p. 1159.

CHAPTER TWENTY-TWO

CZESŁAW MIŁOSZ AND POPE JOHN PAUL II

There was one Augustinian writer who lived, in his own country, through both of the most horrific implementations of the nineteenth century's great lies, who also lived for more than forty years in California, and who never abandoned his sense that the supremely important question is whether or not the revelation of God in Christ is true. He was above all a poet; he was also a novelist, an essayist, an historian, a literary critic, and, though never a professional philosopher, a wide-ranging thinker of power and depth. In 1997, at the age of eighty-six, he wrote:

> Instead of leaving to theologians their worries, I have constantly med-itated on religion. Why? Simply because someone had to do this. To write on literature or art was considered an honorable occupation, whereas anytime notions taken from the language of religion appeared, the one who brought them up was immediately treated as lacking in tact, as if a silent pact had been broken.[1]

After listing the losses to "the human imagination" of a Christian frame giving meaning to life, death and judgement; of the line between man and the rest of nature; of "the supreme position" of "the notion of absolute truth"; of trust in Providence, he ended this short reflection:

> After two thousand years in which a huge edifice of creeds and dogmas has been erected, from Origen and Saint Augustine to Thomas Aqui-nas and Cardinal Newman, when every work of the human mind and of human hands was created within a system of references, the age of homelessness has dawned. How could I not think of this? And is it not surprising that my preoccupation was a rare case?[2]

This is an adult, Catholic perception of "the age of homelessness", as distant from the fragments of childhood Bible-reading retained in the memory of D. H. Lawrence as it is from the secular assumption that rational thought can take place only if God is dispensed with.

Czesław Miłosz was born in 1911, of Polish and Lithuanian ancestry, in Lithuania, then a province of tsarist Russia and always "on the very borderline between Rome and Byzantium".[3] His Polish father, educated in a Russian school and then at the German-speaking university of Riga, was a civil engineer. He built bridges for the tsar's army in the First World War, travelling with his family to Siberia. They were in a Volga town when the 1917 Russian Revolution took place. Miłosz's mother belonged to the landowning gentry of rural Lithuania. After the war, "between the ages of seven and ten," Miłosz wrote, "I lived in perfect happiness on the farm of my grandparents in Lithuania."[4] His grandfather was "a gentleman of the eighteenth century",[5] civilised, tolerant and mild. This land of lost content, almost untouched by the German occupation of 1914 and by the subsequent war against Lenin's Russia that Poland won, and almost untouched by even the nineteenth century but doomed on account of its place on the map of Europe to decades of destruction and suffering, has haunted Miłosz's poetry always. It is most poignantly remembered in his autobiographical novel *The Issa Valley*, written in exile ten years after the end of the Second—and for Poland, infinitely more dreadful—World War.

Lithuania was the last corner of Europe to be converted to Latin Christianity: Chaucer's Knight, in the prologue to *The Canterbury Tales*, has in the 1390s just come back to England from a crusade in pagan Lettow.[6] The peaceful countryside of Miłosz's childhood, a land of peasant farmers, hunters and foresters, village priests and Jewish traders (in *The Issa Valley* a Christian forester, possessed by the guilt of a foolish murder, goes to a rabbi for help), was not altogether free of pagan superstition. Where would the spirits, and the priests and the rabbis, "take refuge when the earth was ploughed up by the tracks of tanks, when those who were about to be executed dug their own shallow graves by the river; and when, in blood and tears, Industrialization rose up, surrounded by the halo of History?"[7] Miłosz was able to return to his valley in 1991, seventy years after his magic boyhood. Half a century of collective farming in the Soviet Socialist Republic that Lithuania became in 1940 had felled the forests and fruit trees of his youth, and his river was poisoned by chemical factories upstream:

> Among the many definitions of Communism, perhaps one would be the most apt: enemy of orchards.... Orchards under Communism had no chance, but in all fairness let us concede they are antique by their very nature. Only the passion of a gardener can delight in growing a great variety of trees, each producing a small crop of fruit whose taste pleases the gardener himself and a few connoisseurs.[8]

It would be easy to jump to the conclusion that the old poet is here implying an analogy between the growing of orchards and the writing of poems. But this would be a mistake. All through his long writing life, Miłosz resisted the romantic drive to elevate the poet and his creativity to a unique relation to, or responsibility for, meaning. Not for him the *religio intransitiva*, or the nearly despairing hope of Leavis or Steiner that a "decisively new and unforeseen" burst of creativity will somehow rescue us from nihilism. On the contrary, Miłosz knew that in everyone, however dreadful the circumstances of his life, there is the possibility of contact with, and love for, the good, the true and the beautiful, the possibility of the touch of God. In a brief prose poem published in 1998, he wrote:

> Our civilization poisoned river waters, and their contamination acquires a powerful emotional meaning. As the course of a river is a symbol of time, we are inclined to think of a poisoned time. And yet the sources continue to gush and we believe time will be purified one day. I am a worshipper of flowing and would like to entrust my sins to the waters, let them be carried to the sea.[9]

This "well-head" is not accessible only to the poet or only to the highly educated. In *The Captive Mind*, a masterly analysis, written in 1951–1952, of the killing of the soul in Stalin's empire, he wrote: "Never has there been a close study of how necessary to a man are the experiences which we clumsily call aesthetic. Such experiences are associated with works of art for only an insignificant number of individuals."[10] For most people, aesthetic experiences are part of being ordinarily alive, to the variety and strangeness of crowded city streets as much as to the seasonal rhythms and festivals of the countryside. Miłosz was attacking the uniform drabness imposed on cities, as on fields, by Soviet rule, starving every life of "the feeling of *potentiality*, of constant unexpectedness, of a mystery one ever pursues".[11]

Miłosz eventually went to school and then to university in the ancient city of Wilno (this is his spelling, the Polish spelling, for Vilnius, since the collapse of Soviet Communism at last the capital city of independent Lithuania). Wilno, a city of the Russian empire from 1795, had been for centuries the Latin city furthest east in Europe. Between 1832 and 1920 Russia kept closed the Catholic, Renaissance university of Wilno for fear of academic encouragement of Polish insurrection. From 1920 to 1939 Wilno was part of independent Poland, and Miłosz and his mother had to be smuggled over the border into Lithuania for the summer holidays. Miłosz received a classical and Catholic education in a Jesuit school. His account of his schooldays in *Native Realm*, the autobiography he wrote in France in 1959, tells of a conflict between two powerful teachers that he felt as a conflict for the allegiance of his adolescent mind and that was, in truth, the conflict between the two Romes, the classical and the Catholic, and therefore between the two cities of the *City of God*. The fierce Jesuit priest and the rigorous, rationalist Latin master, educated in enlightened Habsburg Poland—he describes them as much like the celebrated opponents who fight for Hans Castorp's soul in Thomas Mann's *The Magic Mountain*, published in 1924 while Miłosz was at school—took respectively a pessimistic and an optimistic view of both human nature and the European future. The boy caught between them, whose favourite subject was biology because of his childhood passion for birds, fish and plants, found the sceptical irony of the classicist more attractive than the nervous puritanism of the priest. But he also found the priest's pessimism more convincing than the classicist's optimism, and he was intelligent enough, and sufficiently well-informed about Darwin, to notice that there were no rational grounds for the classicist's confidence in unaided human reason: "On what did he base his conviction that 'here the animal ends and here man begins'?"[12] This serious boy, "striving to build intellectual bridges between two dissociated entities", was separated from his schoolfriends by "an intensity [that] won me the position among them of a Jew among *goyim*."[13] The school book "to which I owe a large part of my education" was a manual of Church history that "contained the history of Europe in its entirety".[14] He found in this textbook descriptions of the ancient heresy that a little later so strongly attracted Simone Weil and that centuries earlier had for years held the young Augustine. The Manichaean sense of collision in man between the evil realm of necessity and the distant freedom of God as "the object of our desires" perhaps never altogether left Miłosz. But in the religious crisis with which he was still struggling as a law student, he turned "to two books: the *Confessions* of St. Augustine and William James' *Varieties of Religious Experience*". Augustine confirmed the validity of a kind of intelligent introspection under the eye of God with which Miłosz was already familiar—he had noticed as a schoolboy the dubious element of pride in his own newly shriven soul: "Of what value then is virtue?"—while James taught him something else. "The intricacy and richness of St Augustine's experiences were a fact, just as the religious ecstasy of many average men and women, as described by James, was a fact."[15] He was moving decisively toward the Catholic and pessimistic pole of his education and away from the rationalist and optimistic. He had identified in himself what was terrifying in the world, Nietzsche's world, in which God was dead:

I was, it could be feared, a potential executioner. Every man is whose "I" is grounded in a scientific way of thinking. The temptation to apply the laws of evolution to society soon becomes almost irresistible. All other men flow together into a "mass" subordinated to the "great lines of evolution", while he, with his reason, dominates those "great lines." He is a free man; they are slaves. If I should have confessed a sin, this was it.[16]

His sense of the innate flaw, the sinfulness latent in himself as in everyone, was already thoroughly Augustinian. So was his sense of awe at the miracle of being alive at all: "I did not have the makings of an atheist, because I lived in a state of constant wonder, as if before a curtain which I knew had to rise someday." [17] Both the wonder—the "distant curtain" reappears in a poem written more than half a century later[18]—and the awareness of "a barrier deep in myself", the darkness of the will,[19] stayed with him for the rest of his life.

In Catholic Wilno there were a few Protestants, a few Muslims and a few Russian Orthodox, but after Catholicism, "Judaism held second place".[20] Miłosz was astonished to discover later in his life that he had grown up in total ignorance that the Wilno of his youth had been for centuries "mother Vilna", the northern centre of Jewish and particularly Hasidic culture and literature. Books printed there in Hebrew and Yiddish he read in New York in English translation when the Jewish world of Wilno, Lithuania, and the whole of Poland had been obliterated forever by the Nazis. There were many Jewish students at the university. But these young leftist intellectuals were reading Aldous Huxley, H. G. Wells and Sigmund Freud, disowning their religion as "provincial": "from general ideas about the equality of men they drew the conclusion that the past does not count." [21] Further, the nineteenth-century Catholic theology taught in Miłosz's school was strongly liturgical and wholly of the New Testament; his Jesuit teacher "never opened the Old Testament with us".[22] Not only would direct knowledge of the great texts of the Hebrew Bible have shown these Christian boys how much they shared with their Jewish friends, but the priest "could also have shown us that Judaism, contrary to its rival beliefs in antiquity, with their cyclical vision of the world, conceived of Creation in a dynamic way, as a dialogue, a perpetual upsurging of constantly modified questions and constantly modified answers, and that Christianity has inherited this trait.... He would have accustomed us to history." [23]

Miłosz, however, accustomed himself to history and learned in his youth to distinguish knowledge of the troubled past of Europe from pseudo-scientific faith in any predictive ideology adorned with "the halo of History". Brought up to a sense of pride in the long-lost commonwealth of Poland-Lithuania with its mixed population and religious freedom, and appalled as a student by the careless cruelties of Polish anti-Semitism, he hated and feared romantic Polish nationalism. "The Jews helped to form a complex in me thanks to which, at an early age, I was already lost for the Right.... My allergy to everything that smacks of the 'national'" has "weighed heavily upon my destiny."[24] When in 1999 he wrote a history of the fragile independent Poland of 1921–1939 with much evidence of the Polish anti-Semitism of the period, he was depressed to find that "all my reviewers simply ignored the subject ... letting the discomfiting skeleton rest quietly in the closet."[25] His hero was Adam Mickiewicz, the greatest Polish poet of the nineteenth century, like himself born in Lithuania and educated in Wilno (just before, as Miłosz just after, Russia closed the university). Mickiewicz spent most of his life in exile and never visited Warsaw. His masterpiece, the wry and beautiful epic poem *Pan Tadeusz*, is set in the Lithuania of his childhood. Always sympathetic to the oppressed Jews of oppressed Poland, Mickiewicz after 1848 wrote a Christian socialist manifesto proclaiming among much else: "To the Jew, our elder brother, esteem and help on his way to eternal good and welfare, and in all matters equal rights."[26] In 1855 he helped to organise a Jewish as well as a Polish legion to fight the Russians in the confusion of the Crimean War, and he died that same year near Constantinople in the arms of his friend Armand Lévy, whom he had persuaded to return to the faith of his fathers. In his *History of Polish Literature* (1969), Miłosz called Mickiewicz, as he might have called himself, "a posthumous child of the old *Respublica*".[27] As a young Lithuanian poet in the 1930s, Miłosz felt closest to Jewish poets writing in Polish, for them as for him their mother tongue but not, at least in sentiment, their native language. The Marxism of most of them he could not share: his mind was not "a clean slate" on which "another faith" could be written:

> Through my heretical tendencies I remained at bottom a Catholic, in the sense that I carried in my memory the whole history of the Church.... My imperviousness to the usually rather shallow progressive-atheist arguments was like the chess-player's contempt for cards.... What was I, with my liking for St. Augustine, doing here?[28]

In 1934–1935 Miłosz spent a year in Paris on a scholarship to study literature. There he became a friend and disciple of his cousin Oscar Miłosz, who was a generation older, a diplomat at the Lithuanian legation, a distinguished French poet, and half-Jewish. The Polish embassy, by contrast, struck the young Miłosz as snobbish and ineffectual; nothing was done by its staff for the thousands of unemployed Poles then miserably wandering the streets of Paris, returning drunk every night to a closed slum camp. Oscar Miłosz had a deep and accurate sense of foreboding about the near future. There would be a war in 1939; it would last five years. "You will survive", he told his cousin.[29] Oscar Miłosz himself died, mercifully, in the spring of 1939.

* * *

When in 1939 Poland was infamously divided between Nazi Germany and Soviet Russia, a division followed a week later by Hitler's invasion and the outbreak of the Second World War, Czesław Miłosz was in Warsaw to witness the total collapse of independent Poland after bloody military defeat. He left for the east, where, in the summer of 1940, quietly conquered Lithuania—"not a single shot was fired"—was annexed to the Soviet Union after an "election": "ninety-nine per cent for a single slate".[30] That summer Miłosz undertook a long, difficult and extremely dangerous journey to return to Warsaw, certain that National Socialism, "too pure an evil", could not last, certain that "Lenin's more diabolical sheaf of good and evil" had a contrasting and terrible durability.[31] He was in Warsaw for the remaining four years of the hideously cruel Nazi occupation. Many of his friends were among the hundreds of thousands killed or taken to forced-labour camps or concentration camps. He saw the burning of the Warsaw ghetto in 1943 and the catastrophe of the Warsaw uprising in 1944, when the Russian army stood by and watched the slaughter of a quarter of a million Poles by the already defeated Germans and then watched the Germans dynamite the city, street by street. "You remember", Miłosz wrote decades later, "therefore you have no doubt: there is a Hell for certain."[32] The Nazi Government-General eliminated the jobs, in offices, schools and universities, of the Polish educated class, banned the publication of all books and magazines, and abolished the entire educational system. Poles were to be taught only to count to one hundred and to read simple instructions: "a race of slaves has no need for learning."[33] Like most of his kind who managed to survive, Miłosz lived from day to day by black-market trading and occasional labouring. As a clandestine system of education and publication developed, with a little money trickling in from the Allies, he wrote articles and poems, edited anthologies and translated for the Resistance press. He translated an attack on the Vichy government, written and published in Canada by Jacques Maritain, one copy of which had reached Warsaw.

Like Pasternak in Stalin's Moscow, he translated Shakespeare, *As You Like It* for a secret theatre company: "bucolic Shakespeare proved to be first-rate therapy."[34] All this was dangerous, but no more dangerous than everyday existence in a city where distant racial policy sanctioned random cruelty of the most inhuman and banal kind. Runaway Jewish children from the ghetto were shot in the streets and their corpses left in the gutter. "Causing someone's death" Miłosz wrote in 1943, "is dissociated from the reek of demonism, pangs of conscience, and similar accessories of Shakespearean drama. Young men in perfectly clean uniforms can then shoot people while gnawing on a ham sandwich."[35]

Miłosz was first and last a poet. To write a poem in occupied Warsaw required what he much later called "a nearly superhuman effort ... while juggling with despair".[36] The poems published in Warsaw in 1945 as the collection called *Rescue* are the fruit of this effort, words ordered by an imagination indelibly bruised. "Campo dei Fiori" is a searing lament for the burning of the Warsaw ghetto, expressed in the analogy of the burning in Rome in 1600 of the heretical Dominican priest Giordano Bruno. The six "Voices of Poor People" probe the extremity of desolation with words of anguish but also of beauty, beauty for which the poet can feel only guilt. A stanza from "The Poor Poet" reads:

I poise the pen and it puts forth twigs and leaves, it is covered with blossoms
And the scent of that tree is impudent, for there, on the real earth,
Such trees do not grow, and like an insult
To suffering humanity is the scent of that tree.[37]

A different tree, or the same tree unadorned, appears in "A Poor Christian Looks at the Ghetto", a poem that confesses to a greater guilt, that of all Christians for the fate of the Jews:

Bees build around the honeycomb of lungs,
Ants build around white bone.
Torn is paper, rubber, linen, leather, flax,
Fiber, fabrics, cellulose, snakeskin, wire.
The roof and the wall collapse in flame and heat seizes the foundations.
Now there is only the earth, sandy, trodden down,
With one leafless tree.[38]

The bravest of all these feats of truthfulness and love achieved in almost unimaginable circumstances is the series of twenty short, apparently simple, poems called

"The World", of which Miłosz much later wrote that their "primerlike" qua-
trains "exemplify the effort to resist the temptation of utter despair".[39] The poems
are of innocence, home, the earth, and above all, of their reality—a father and
mother, two children, a house in deep country, pictures on its walls, books (one
is perhaps Augustine, perhaps Mickiewicz), an atlas with a map of Europe where
"Warsaw stands, open from all sides, / A city not very old but quite famous",[40]
flowers and birds, the forest, God. One poem, "Love", begins:

> Love means to learn to look at yourself
> The way one looks at distant things
> For you are only one thing among many.
> And whoever sees that way heals his heart,
> Without knowing it, from various ills—
> A bird and a tree say to him: Friend.[41]

The effect is of the Ancient Mariner blessing the water snakes. The most poignant words of all come at the end of the last poem: "Warsaw, 1943".

In the same city in the same year, the year of the burning of the ghetto,
Miłosz wrote a series of essays in the form of letters to his closest friend at the
time, Jerzy Andrzejewski. These were at last published in Poland in 1990. One
was translated for the 2001 anthology of Miłosz's prose *To Begin Where I Am*. Ten
helter-skelter pages of prose—"Slow down, slow down", Miłosz says to himself,
in vain—reveal, in the midst of horrors, a keen historical perceptiveness of a
deeply Catholic colour. It is the hubris, the baseless pride and optimism of the
Europe that abandoned Catholicism for faith in truthless progress, that has brought
devastation. "The fundamental argument that has been going on for centuries in
the bosom of Western civilization [is] between the pessimistic and optimistic
conceptions of man." The Reformation detached each man from "the bonds of
the Church ... and the assistance of the sacraments", the means of grace; "that
was the germ of faith in man as the judge of his own actions." Then there was
the optimist and Protestant Jean-Jacques Rousseau, then "the optimist and Protestant Nietzsche, summoning man to total liberation from the chains of 'slave
morality'.... 'Let truth die, let life triumph!' (And so it did, poor, mad philol-
ogist.) ... The path that leads from Luther to Rosenberg [Hitler's leading ideol-
ogist] ... is by no means crooked, while Rosenberg is separated from Catholicism
by an abyss." The letter ends with a premonition of the rootless, shiftless relativism of the late twentieth century:

Without religious and metaphysical underpinning, the word *man* is too ambiguous a term, is it not? From the moment it is deprived of traits such as an immortal soul and redemption through Christ, does it not disintegrate into a vast number of possibilities ... ?

And even here, in the depths of 1943, Miłosz cannot identify himself with Polish nationalism; there must be "a standard different from that of patriotic exaltation".[42]

In January 1945, satisfied that the Germans had utterly destroyed any possibility of material Polish resistance to Soviet power, the Russians arrived in Warsaw. In his novel *The Seizure of Power*, Miłosz, in exile in the early 1950s, vividly described the postwar chaos that made possible the gradual but rapid tightening of Stalin's grip on Poland. A professor without a university is translating Thucydides. The first quoted passage of his translation begins: "Words had to change their ordinary meaning and to take that which was now given them."[43] The imposition of totalitarian power and the unclear alternatives it poses—to join it, to compromise with it, to sustain a private resistance to it, to leave one's country to its depredations—are explored in the novel, as they are with more rigour and more inwardness in *The Captive Mind*. Inevitability made intellectually respectable as "the Spirit of History" stalks the book as that which above all has to be resisted. A Jewish communist has doubts, is inclined to leave or betray the Party: "Where would he find sense or reason if by his decision he tried to prove that history had neither sense nor reason?"[44] The professor reflects on a young Marxist: "The new world in which she believed was a cruel world because it lacked respect for the complexity of man, respect which perhaps ought to be called piety. ... You could only be for or against. Nuances meant nothing."[45] Miłosz was a socialist in 1945, but not a Marxist; a Catholic, but not a nationalist. A wise old man in the novel knows that these nuances will not be preservable and refuses to give advice: "Can you say to anyone: 'Work here, with the Socialists or the peasants,' when you know in advance that in the end this must either lead him to orthodox Stalinism, if he behaves himself, or to prison, if he doesn't?"[46] As for the nationalist Right, the same old man says: "All the reactionaries among the *émigrés* will, of course, appropriate to themselves the monopoly of being 'pure'. ... According to them, whoever cares only for his own money is always innocent."[47] And the Right's nostalgia for the irrecoverable past is sarcastically dissected by a clever Party interrogator:

Ah, a mystical faith. Admirable. The only possible way of dreaming about a resurrection of the Middle Ages. I know. A cathedral, and all around it small houses inhabited by craftsmen. Order. Each man in his place. By hereditary right. A cobbler with cobblers, a Jew with the Jews in the ghetto. A little bit of Berdyaev. A little bit of T. S. Eliot. Enchanting.[48]

Reactionary nostalgia has always got short shrift from Miłosz. Of the nineteenth century, he wrote elsewhere:

Ethereal pastoral duets were sung at the rectory; the peace of books and flowers by the window protected the island of poetic fantasies from the world. However, close by, in the industrial city, human phantoms reeled and fell to the streets from hunger.[49]

For six years Miłosz tried to preserve within himself his own complexity, the nuances of what he thought, felt and believed, against the closing vice of the Stalinist regime. He spent four of those years in Washington, as second secretary in the embassy of People's Poland: the Communist government was keen to show off an apparently compliant writer. He found Americans, as Herzen had found western Europeans a century earlier, bland, shallow, careless and uninterested in the world beyond the Elbe. "Americans accepted their society as if it had arisen from the very order of nature; so saturated with it were they that they tended to pity the rest of humanity for having strayed from the norm. . . . Millions of people who cared about money."[50] But he also found blessed confirmation of childhood memory and experience in the wilds of Pennsylvania, Vermont and Maine and a refreshingly uncomplicated friendliness in country people:

None of us "Easterners", regardless of how long he may have lived in France or England, would ever be a Frenchman or an Englishman, but here, at barn dances where everybody, both grownups and children, danced together, one could forget. I realized then that the popular legend about America, cut off by an ocean as if by the waters of Lethe, was justified.[51]

In 1951 he took the exceedingly difficult decision to defect to the West, abandoning his country, his own suffering people, and above all his daily connexion with his own language, the very stuff of his life as a writer. He lived in Paris, a Paris of Marxist intellectuals who treated him with contempt: "A writer, who fled from a country where Tomorrow was being born (if the system is bad, then it is good enough for Eastern barbarians) was guilty of a *social blunder*." [52] In 1960 he wrote an angry essay telling the story of a French boy, Gilbert Brognart, from a mining town in the Pas-de-Calais, swept by chance into the war in Nazi Poland and then into a slave-labour camp in Siberia, where he died in 1951 after eleven years in prison. He was much the same age as Miłosz's cousin, shipped at fifteen by the Nazis to a concentration camp, where he died two years later. The fury of the essay, written because the boy's fate was of no interest to any French writer of the time, is reflected in its title, "Brognart: A Story Told over a Drink". [53]

The truth about Stalinist Europe told in the searing inner biographies of *The Captive Mind* was in Paris unwelcome, even despised, while the warm reception of the book in McCarthyite America, particularly in the South, depressed Miłosz no less: "I had believed that by coming out against human degradation, by this alone, I was already on the side of the Negroes." [54] Where in the West was there any intelligent understanding of the complexity that he carried in his soul, that he *was*? The woundedness, honesty and courage of the last pages of *Native Realm* have lost none of their force after nearly half a century. There is an alert conscience: "I had to consent in advance to defeat, which is dangerous because then we are tempted to exult in our inner readiness to accept the cross." [55] There is also Pascal's recognition of the devices people use to shield themselves from reality, from truth:

> Many of my contemporaries may regard such thrashing about as the neurotic unhinging of a modern Hamlet. Their jobs and their amusements prevent them from seeing what is really at stake. I was not a philosopher. Events themselves threw me into my century's towering philosophical pressures, into the vortex of its hardest and most essential questions. Perhaps these exceeded my grasp, but they mobilized all my energies.
>
> Westerners like to dwell in the empyrean of noble words about spirit and freedom; but it is not often that they ask someone whether he has enough money for lunch. [56]

In France Miłosz wrote *The Captive Mind*, *The Issa Valley*, *The Seizure of Power* and *Native Realm*. All these books are works of great power (though *The Issa Valley* has not yet been translated as well as it deserves to be), and the first and last should be read by anyone interested in "what is really at stake" in the modern world.

From the desolation of his years in Paris, Miłosz was rescued by his discovery of the quintessentially European beauty, marked by the passage of long centuries of farming and quiet building and craftsmanship, of *la France profonde*. "After a few years of groping in the dark, my foot once again touched solid ground."[57] The masterpiece of his French exile—a line in its verse preface declares: "Novels and essays serve but will not last"[58]—is a long poem, *A Treatise on Poetry*, completed in 1956. The poem, though much longer and much easier to grasp, is, among other things, a reply to *The Waste Land*. Like Eliot's poem, it is in five parts; also like Eliot's poem, it is a lament composed among ruins. But the ruins are not literary. "A real 'wasteland'", Miłosz wrote in *The Captive Mind*, "is much more terrible than any imaginary one."[59]

Each section of the poem evokes a time and a place and the Polish poets—in the last two sections, Miłosz himself—who were trying to deal with, or escape, both. The poets (although the first section has a moving tribute to Joseph Conrad) are unfamiliar to an ordinary English reader, but we are told enough, particularly with the addition of helpful factual notes, about each of them for their work and their fate to be clear. The first section, "Beautiful Times", is set in Cracow, the ancient Polish capital, in 1900–1914. The decadent elegance of the *belle époque*, over which its imminent end looms, is elegantly, yet sadly, presented in Cracow, a Habsburg city for most of the period from the eighteenth-century partition of Poland until the collapse of the Russian empire in 1918. It was not only in Cracow that the poetry of the period was, as Miłosz briskly says: "A stand-in / For religion, and such it will remain." Of one poet he writes: "His praise was as if in a world of as if."[60] The second, much longer section, "The Capital", is about Warsaw in the twenty years of Polish independence, 1918–1939, a city of mixed peoples under both the lasting menace of Russia, which had ruled it for more than a century, and, in this eerie pause between war and war, the gathering menace of Germany. Of this Warsaw, to be completely destroyed, the poem declares:

> Yet you exist. With your blackened ghetto,
> The somnolent anger of your unemployed,
> Your women's tears and their prewar shawls.[61]

"Yet you exist": in *The Issa Valley*, the boy Thomas's grandmother, close to death, thinks: "If all that is born passes away without leaving a trace, then only God could rescue the past from insignificance."[62] But traces of the past survive also in the memory of the living. Thomas learns from his much-loved grandfather: "No one lives alone; he is speaking with those who are no more, their lives are incarnated in him." The thought is "the seed sown",[63] and *A Treatise on Poetry* is, like very many of Miłosz's later poems, a fixing in time of the traces of the dead. The poets evoked one by one in "The Capital" were Miłosz's older contemporaries, all of them condemned to exile, to violent death, or to later dishonesty under the pressure of the times, when, for example, supporters of the Far Right became dutiful patriotic Communists. The country child of *The Issa Valley*, now a city schoolboy reading books about explorers and jungles, appears in this section, unaware of the catastrophe to come:

> He is the future reader of our poets.
> Impervious to crooked fences, the calling of crows
> In cloudy skies, he lives among his marvels.
> And, if he survives destruction, it is he
> Who will preserve with tenderness his guides.[64]

The few lines recording the last of these guides in "The Capital" demonstrate the whole poem's exact immediacy, to which translation and an English reader's ignorance are scarcely barriers:

> The last poem of the epoch went to print.
> Its author, Władysław Sebyła,
> Liked to take his violin from the wardobe,
> Putting its case by the volumes of Norwid.
> He kept the collar of his blue uniform
> Unbuttoned (He worked for the railway at Praga).
> In that poem, as if it were his last will,
> Poland is the ancient, two-faced god
> Swiatowid, listening as the drums beat closer
> On plains to the east, plains to the west,
> While in its sleep the country dreams of bees
> Buzzing through noons in Hesperidian groves.
> Was it for this they shot him in the head
> And buried his body in a Smolensk forest?[65]

(It helps, but only a little, to know that Cyprian Norwid was Poland's Hopkins, a profoundly Catholic poet who died abroad, his work almost unread, in 1883 and whose poems were discovered in the twentieth century. Many will know that "a Smolensk forest" is Katyn, where more than twenty-two thousand Polish officers, prisoners of war, were executed on Stalin's orders in 1940 and that the

Russians pretended for decades that this was a Nazi massacre.) "The Capital" ends with a desperately sad little lyric about a simple, nameless pair of lovers in the doomed city.

The third and longest section, "The Spirit of History: Warsaw 1939–1945" faces the "hardest and most essential questions" of the double catastrophe that overcame Poland. "The Spirit of History is out walking", destroying. "Who are you, Powerful One?" The blind destructiveness of the will to life in all nature is given philosophical respectability as it becomes the will to power:

> And you, is it just that you,
> in a reasonable frock like Hegel's,
> Have chosen for yourself a different name?

Schopenhauer, Darwin and Nietzsche, unnamed, shadow this enquiry. So does Augustine:

> We have not been taught. We do not know at all
> How to unite Freedom and Necessity.[66]

A terrifying, craven hymn, terrifying because it is a hymn, to the Spirit of History as dialectical materialism, ends:

> "Spare us, do not punish us. Our offense
> Was grave: we forgot the power of your law.
> Save us from ignorance. Accept now our devotion."[67]

And the poem then crashes into a painfully controlled threnody for the Jews of the ghetto and the death camps, and also for the Christian peasants, whose folk songs, carols and music are broken and gone, lit with memories of Mickiewicz and his hopes. The section ends very quietly:

> The wind was blowing. I sat on the road at noon,
> Thinking and thinking. Beside me, potatoes.[68]

The fourth section, "Natura" is a private and beautiful meditation from a boat on a lake in "Pennsylvania 1948–1949", where the poet waits for darkness to see a beaver and reflects on the healing forgetfulness of America:

> You will hear not one word spoken of the court
> Of Sigismund Augustus on the banks of the Delaware River.[69]

But "I remember everything",[70] though the memories here, except in some bitter verses on Paris, drift gently. This section, which echoes a couple of lines from Eliot's *Four Quartets* and quotes two phrases from Stevens, wry about the possibilities of poetry in "The Comedian as the Letter C", is also a demonstration of the undefeatedness of poetry. It ends with a resolution:

> Let names of months mean only what they mean.
> Let the *Aurora's* cannons be heard in none
> Of them, or the tread of young rebels marching.
> We might, at best, keep some kind of souvenir,
> Preserved like a fan in a garret. Why not
> Sit down at a rough country table and compose
> An ode in the old manner, as in the old times
> Chasing a beetle with the nib of our pen?[71]

The last section, shorter, begins with this ode, to an American October, purged of the revolution that "October" meant throughout the Communist world, remembering only, in the Hudson Valley, fragments of American history. The whole poem concludes as in 1950, at the end of his Washington job, Miłosz leaves America for Europe—"the most painful decision of my life", he said in *Native Realm*, "though none other was permissible."[72] The poet on the Atlantic voyage is almost, but not quite, despairing:

> The ship's body, creaking, carries the freight
> Of our foolishness, vagueness, and hidden faith,
> The dirt of our subjectivity, and the homeless
> White faces of the ones who were killed in combat.[73]

In *Native Realm* Miłosz attributes to his terrible experiences in Warsaw the decisive breaking of a poetic and personal shell, a breaking that made possible the poetry he wrote after the war: "by fusing individual and historical elements in my poetry, I had made an alloy that one seldom encounters in the West."[74] *A Treatise on Poetry*, a shining example of this alloy, deserves to rank among the great poems of the twentieth century, with Eliot's *Four Quartets* and Stevens's *Notes toward a Supreme Fiction*. Longer and much more direct than either, as moving and as memorable, even in translation, as either, it has the purity and candour that marked Miłosz's poetry for the rest of his life.

* * *

In 1961 Miłosz, already fifty years old, moved from France to California, where he became professor of Slavic languages and literatures at the University of California in Berkeley and lived for almost all the rest of his life, with visits to Europe and, after the collapse of Communism, a new home in Cracow. He never stopped writing poetry: in his *New and Collected Poems 1931–2001*, there are 550 pages of poems written after he settled in America, among them scarcely a poem that is dull or unapproachable. He also wrote much prose: his *History of Polish Literature*, written in English, was published in 1969; his impassioned essays on some Polish, Russian and other writers, *Emperor of the Earth: Modes of Eccentric Vision*, was published in 1977. *Visions from San Francisco Bay*, a book recording the impact on him of life in California; and *The Land of Ulro*, a personal meditation on the plight of the modern soul, were published in Polish, though not in Poland, in 1969 and 1977 respectively, and translated into English only after, in 1980, he was awarded the Nobel Prize. In 1981–1982 he gave the Charles Eliot Norton lectures, published as *The Witness of Poetry*, at Harvard. In his old age, he continued to write prose, often shorter pieces, sometimes alongside poems.

Visions from San Francisco Bay is a remarkable book, a self-portrait of an exiled poet who carries within him the weight of European devastation inflicted by two centuries of history and who has nursed his own complexity to survive the murderous simplifications of both Right and Left. Now he faces the "boundless immensities" [75] of ocean and mountains, the racing capitalist success of prosperous America, the routine violence of its films and television watched by millions every day, and the cults, drugs, flower-power and mindless self-indulgence of its spoiled children in 1960s San Francisco. There are passages of desolation in this book. The immigrant American, isolated in his grief for the European past and his distaste for the "heritage" present, finds it impossible, sometimes, not to catch from his intellectual contemporaries a Schopenhauerian despair: mankind is alone "in the face of limitless space, in motion yet empty, from which no voice reaches down speaking a language I can understand".[76] The Catholic who has fought and won the battle to sustain in himself the distinction between his own faith and the pull of Polish nationalism identified with faith is cut to the Augustinian quick by the easy American confusion of the *civitas Dei* with the *civitas terrena*:

God everywhere, like the products for daily hygiene and medications, God on the dollar, In God We Trust, the national God, guarantee of the established order, helping those who believe in him, multiplying their sheep and cattle, their machines.... Unfortunately the substance of that God is withering away; his name, uttered from pulpits and tribunals, is as empty as the names of the gods in the Roman Empire and serves only as a demonstration of loyalty to traditional values.[77]

The hazards, so evident to Augustine, of justifying imperial might by the appropriation of God to guarantee its virtue have grown more acute in the decades since this was written. Giving the America of the Constitution its due, and out of his own experience of totalitarian regimes, Miłosz wrote in this book: "No less amazing [than the striking of fire and the shaping of the wheel] is the idea that the power of the state should have limits prescribed by law and that nobody should be thrown in prison on the whim of men in uniform."[78] Even after the trauma of the terrorist attacks in America of 11 September 2001, it is shocking to know that many of the hundreds of uncharged, untried men and boys kept in Guantanamo Bay for years were thrown in prison on the whim of Americans in uniform. In his *History of Polish Literature*, Miłosz quoted Cyprian Norwid:

A man is born on this planet to give testimony to the truth. He should, therefore, know and remember that every civilization should be considered as a means and not as an end—thus, to sell one's soul to a civilization and at the same time to pray in church is to be a pharisee.[79]

In *Visions from San Francisco Bay*, a complex man exercises complex judgement. Never forgetting that "in the countries ruled by Marxists, the Prince of Lies put on a performance that made all his previous exploits pale by comparison", he knows that any perversion of the Judaeo-Christian "flight of the arrow, the Covenant with God" into "a static reality", "the dream of building the Kingdom of God here and now with our own hands", even if in the much less horrible form of "a life of getting and spending", is an offence against truth and a danger to the soul.[80] He loves, and describes beautifully, rural America, its kind people, its cheerful parades. "Anyone who knows from experience, as I do, how important certain of the less obvious human virtues can be will not frivolously call a certain heavy decency and unselfishness plain stupidity, even if they are accompanied by mental limitations.... America is the legitimate heir to the Judaeo-Christian civilization."[81] But disinherited this heir also is. In a short chapter entitled "On Catholicism", Miłosz laments the loss from the Catholicism of West Coast America, infected with the optimism and materialism of the science on which California depends, of the realities of sin and grace. Sin, here, "is being broken down into clusters of psychological and sociological determinants", while "I suspect, a few exceptions aside . . . that the imagination of those who attend Mass every Sunday is not different from that of those who never set foot inside a church." The loss is of

> the warm, human presence of a God who took on flesh in order to experience our hunger and our pain, so we would not be doomed to strain our eyes upward but could be nourished by words spoken by lips like our own. And the God-man is not one of us in our moments of pride and glory, but he is one of us in misfortune, in slavery, and in the fear of death. The hour when he agreed to accept suffering conquers time; centuries of change and passing civilizations are insignificant, short-lived, and no wasteland of cement, glass, and metal will make man different from those men Christ addressed in Galilee.[82]

This reply to the kingdom, the power and the glory that are not God's but man's, and also to his own fear that "no voice reaches down speaking a language I can understand", is in this book clouded with doubt and grief. But the reply is in this book—as is an incident from his childhood that he never forgot:

> Once, a very long time ago, walking down a street in a Polish village, I grew thoughtful at the sight of ducks splashing about in a miserable puddle. I was struck because nearby there was a lovely stream flowing through an alder wood. "Why don't they go over to the stream?", I asked an old peasant sitting on a bench in front of his hut. "Bah, if only they knew!"[83]

The poems of Miłosz's first years in California are hectic, brilliant, tender and desolate; to catch in words the crowded past is both demanded of him and impossible. "*Ars Poetica?*" (1968) registers the shock of the poem that asks to be written:

> In the very essence of poetry there is something indecent:
> a thing is brought forth which we didn't know we had in us,
> so we blink our eyes, as if a tiger had sprung out
> and stood in the light, lashing his tail.

The demand does not come from within. The poem ends:

> ... poems should be written rarely and reluctantly,
> under unbearable duress and only with the hope
> that good spirits, not evil ones, choose us for their instruments.[84]

In "On Angels", written in 1969, the year of *Visions from San Francisco Bay*, it is clear from where the demand comes: messengers deliver it from Dante's heaven:

> There, where the world is turned inside out,
> a heavy fabric embroidered with stars and beasts,
> you stroll, inspecting the trustworthy seams.
> . . . .
> I have heard that voice many a time when asleep
> and, what is strange, I understood more or less
> an order or an appeal in an unearthly tongue:
>
> day draws near
> another one
> do what you can.[85]

The essays collected in *Emperor of the Earth* reflect Miłosz's effort to "do what he could" not only in poems but in critical prose to address the "the vital tasks" that no longer seemed to interest Western intellectuals: the question of whether or not there is life for the soul, and "the riddle of Evil active in History".[86] Poland may always have been peripheral to Western civilisation, a frontier land ignored or bullied by the centre, but Miłosz begins his preface to this book by quoting a Polish friend: "We are now like the Dalmatians in the collapsing Roman Empire. They cared when the others wouldn't give a damn." [87] There is one piece on a French writer; it is an acute, wholly sympathetic but not uncritical account of Simone Weil, some of whose writing Miłosz had translated into Polish in 1958 to show both nationalist and Marxist Poland "that the choice between Christianity as represented by a national religion and the official Marxist ideology is not the only choice left to us today." [88] Most of the book is on Polish and Russian writers. Some of his subjects are famous everywhere: Dostoyevsky, on whose anguished struggle with nihilism, evil, truth and the silent figure of Christ Miłosz writes with deep understanding and fine-tuned, very Catholic, discrimination; Pasternak, on whom he justly says that, for all the truthfulness and tentative hope of *Doctor Zhivago*, "there is no trace

... of that polemic with the anti-Christian concept of man which makes the strength of Dostoevsky. ... Pasternak's Christianity is atheological."[89] Yet "Pasternak's and Solzhenitzyn's works ... 'judge' all contemporary literature by reintroducing a hierarchy of values, the renunciation of which threatens mankind with madness."[90] Other subjects are unfamiliar to the ordinary Western reader. There is a masterly essay on Lev Shestov, a Russian exile who died an old man in Paris in 1938 and wrote with austere force for years on the distance between Christian truth and truths ascertainable by reason. There is a long account, from a book published only in Polish, of the extraordinary Polish writer Stanisław Brzozowski, who died at thirty-two in exile in Florence in 1911. This exceedingly gifted and independent-minded young man, in constant revolt against the complacency and intellectual laziness of the nationalist Polish gentry, was familiar with Russian, French, German, Italian and English literature and thought. He travelled rapidly yet critically through every great idea, every grand narrative of his time. "Everywhere", says Miłosz, "he attacks reduction, the main principle of every scientism: 'man is no more than...'."[91] A dissident Catholic from his youth, Brzozowski regarded the neo-Scholasticism of his time as a kind of rationalist totalitarianism. But shortly before his death, he was reconciled to Catholicism by the writings of Newman.

The most remarkable essay in Miłosz's *Emperor of the Earth* is on Soloviev, in particular on the fable of the Antichrist in Soloviev's last work, *Three Conversations*, written in 1899–1900. This terrifying vision, of an emperor of the earth made possible by the collapse of real Christian belief and the transfer of its eschatological hope in Christ to actual hope in a human ruler, Miłosz describes as a prophecy arising from Soloviev's perception of the great error of the Russian intelligentsia's "religion of humanity". "Their unlimited ethical demands [were] addressed, however, not to an individual but to a social milieu responsible for the pollution of an inherently good human nature."[92] Soloviev himself "is one of those pessimistic philosophers who hold that every ego repeats the act of the fallen angel: it cannot be otherwise in the order of Nature except through the intervention of divine grace."[93] "Man is confronted with one all-important either/or: either Christ was resurrected and thus victorious over the powers of Hell, or he was not resurrected. Soloviev counsels those who choose the latter to become Buddhists instead of constantly quoting the Gospels."[94] Writing in 1971, Miłosz sees Soloviev's vision as a prophecy that has begun, in a way quite different from that of Soviet totalitarianism, to come true also in the liberal, optimistic and simplistic West. The last few pages of the essay on Soloviev contain some sharp analysis of the perils of muddled thinking in America in particular. What is really terrifying about Soloviev's Antichrist is that he "deserves admiration precisely as a benefactor of man"; he "strives for and attains much good, deceiving not only others but himself as well." The lie upon which his rule is founded "is tantamount to demanding that both what is God's and what is Caesar's be rendered unto Caesar", and—this is the essay's conclusion—"Were such a superman to step forward, promising an end to all alienation, and love and peace, we may be certain that millions of mortals, indifferent to truth and untruth, would pay him divine homage." [95] In the thirty years since this was written, confidence in the "global" success of the American way of life and confidence in God have become so confused that a right-wing fundamentalist president is able almost to command this kind of homage. Michael Ignatieff, an Anglo-American academic but a Russian born in Canada, said in 2003: "We do have an ideology and, like all ideologies, it doesn't believe it is one. It just believes that it is The Truth. Bush believes in it to a degree which is astonishing. So far as he is concerned, America's way is God's way." [96] But, as Miłosz wrote in his Soloviev essay, "The historic role of Christianity consisted of reminding people of the tragic quality of human existence. Man wants to be good, but he is not good; he wants to be happy, but he is not happy; he wants to live, but he knows he must die." [97] These are reminders America, with so many valid reasons for its pride, apparently does not care to hear: ninety-four percent of Americans say they believe in God; yet two-thirds of them do not know who delivered the Sermon on the Mount.

The Land of Ulro's title is taken from Blake, who wrote that in the land of Ulro, "They rage like wild beasts in the forests of affliction". This was Miłosz's most inward prose work. In 1984, seven years after its publication in Polish, he called it, in an introduction for the English translation, "a bizarre tangle ... [my] one maverick work".[98] The book is a lament for "the precipitous decline" of the twentieth century, "one so remarkable in its constancy as to be without historical analogy",[99] by a man who has read and thought all his life with the passion of those dedicated to the ancient monastic "ordering rhythm" of "the office and of litanies, Gregorian chant, the daily reading of the breviary and the lives of the saints". Defining "this category" of devoted readers, not necessarily Christians of course, he adds that it "is not coincident with the category of 'poets' and 'artists'".[100] His own most beloved books, his heroes of the spirit, are those a reader of his earlier prose would expect: Augustine, Pascal, Swedenborg, Blake, Mickiewicz, Dostoyevsky, Soloviev, Weil, and his cousin Oscar Miłosz. Fully recognising the eccentricity, one way or another, of all of these except Augustine and Pascal in relation to Christianity, he calls them "an unorthodox tradition".[101] But it is a tradition of those who, though they may sometimes have doubted God's existence, never doubted the scale of the difference made by his existence and by his incarnation in Christ.

In *The Land of Ulro*, there is much fresh thought on Dostoyevsky. Miłosz has a Catholic's reservations about Dostoyevsky's partial and prejudiced sense of the Church; in a later (1997) note, he wrote: "The conclusion of *The Brothers Karamazov* [Alyosha and his twelve schoolboys] allows us to doubt whether the destructive forces, which he observed, had found an effective counterweight in his mind." [102] But he profoundly admires him as the only novelist who "made use of fiction to render the fundamental antinomy facing modern man". [103] That is to say, in deciding what is the source of truth, we have to choose between God and ourselves. If we choose ourselves, "truth" becomes constructed, fragile, variable, temporal, transient and relative, but relative to nothing. On Ivan Karamazov, Miłosz writes: "The moment God has been 'invalidated', the distinction between good and evil, truth and falsehood, has become groundless, and Nature, obedient to its laws, becomes supreme." [104] Then there is mere mortality, the dead Christ in the Holbein painting that haunted Dostoyevsky, the unredeemed misery of the human world. For a long time the Christian ethical tradition "of self-discipline, self-denial, and sacrifice" survived Christianity itself—to the scorn of Nietzsche above all—but Miłosz writes: "By themselves, deprived of religious sanction, [these notions] not only proclaimed their vacancy; eventually they would become an object of contempt among the young, those whose education had given them nothing but that void." Alongside Alastair MacIntyre at much the same time, Miłosz adds: "No one of sound mind, who has lived long in a country of the West, can have any illusions as to the utter failure of secular humanism, a failure sponsored by the very successes of that same humanism." [105] The result is the desolation of the denied soul, the desolation foreseen by Nietzsche—"So you killed God and think you can get away with it?" in Miłosz's words—and the futile attempts of the imagination "to wage a defense by fortifying itself on its own territory, that of art and literature". This desolation, with its subtext of "as if", is better described by Miłosz in two powerful paragraphs than it is by those, for example Leavis and Steiner, who suffered it all their lives. And Miłosz recognises in Beckett its bleakest expression: "Anyone wishing to plumb the essence of our modern civilization should turn to its most honest writer, Samuel Beckett." [106]

In Miłosz's earlier books, he described the unspoken, unspeakable deprivation of ordinary people in Stalin's empire. In *The Captive Mind*, for example, he wrote:

> The resistance against the new set of values is ... emotional. It survives but it is beaten whenever it has to explain itself in rational terms. A man's subconscious or not-quite-conscious life is richer than his vocabulary. His opposition to this new philosophy of life is much like a toothache. Not

only can he not express the pain in words, but he cannot even tell you which tooth is aching.[107]

That the soul is no less deprived in the West is the theme of *The Land of Ulro*, and in its last thirty pages Miłosz rises to the challenge he sets himself in these words: "Now, after long consideration, I can summon the courage to offer my own vision of man, which is neither that of a Beckett nor possibly that of any other writer practising in the West today." [108]

Man is either in the hands of God—he uses Pascal's words: "not the God of the philosophers but the God of Abraham, Isaac and Jacob"—or alone in a meaningless universe. It is now very difficult to say this. An exile from his country and his language for twenty-six years when this was written, he describes himself also as a "self-exile from the 'respectable society' of Western intellectuals, because I dared to offend their most hallowed assumptions, which I took to be a compilation of historical, geographical, and political ignorance." He watches with amazement "the citizens of Ulro" taking devoted care of their bodies (Lucky's speech, again) while they "seem to take for granted that their souls are vigorously healthy." [109] They are not. Miłosz's students at Berkeley live in "an atmosphere of tolerance vis-à-vis all creeds, cults, persuasions of thought, provided they be sufficiently loose, syncretic". Homage is done only to "creativity"—a lowest common denominator descended from the hopes of Arnold, Leavis and Steiner—and "by 'creativity' is meant excretion for the sake of excretion, the more tempting for being conducted outside of truth and falsehood, good and evil, beauty and ugliness." [110] Dostoyevsky's "tragedies, those morality plays of good versus evil, ... have been validated by time." The collapse of tsarism did not "mean the end of willful arrogance, greed, the lust for power";[111] in a world of original sin no arrangement of the *civitas terrena* will be free of them. Weil is a heroine not for the self-immolation of her Manichaean life but for her unfailing attention to human suffering and for her absoluteness for the truth of Christ.

Finally Miłosz arrives at an honest and rueful, yet nevertheless hopeful, confession of an ineradicable faith, presented in dense, complex pages that deserve to be read fully and carefully. The whole book is, as he says at the end, "both childish and adult, both ethereal and earthbound".[112] For example, on consecutive pages, he writes:

My ecstatically religious childhood would have passed without leaving a trace if I had not observed, early in life, that it was not within my power to live without offering constant prayer to God.

And:

> A man like me ... is constantly visited by a voice imputing his own
> deficiency as the real source of his internal manoeuvres; by a voice
> which accuses him of *willing* belief in the absence of any real belief.
> And to this unquitting voice he replies with a mental shrug: So?[113]

As was said long ago: *fides voluntatis est*, faith is of the will. But also *credo ut intelligam*, I believe that I may understand.

The 1981–1982 lectures published as *The Witness of Poetry* are a straightforward plea no less moving than the subtle densities of *The Land of Ulro* for poets and readers to return to the confidence they once had in the objective reality of the actual world and the reliability of the languages in which poets catch that reality. Underlying the argument and appearing from time to time with a lack of embarrassment brave in the Harvard of the 1980s is Miłosz's faith:

> The world exists objectively, despite the shapes in which it appears in
> the mind and despite the colors, bright or dark, lent it by the happi-
> ness or misfortune of a particular man. That objective world can be
> seen as it is; yet we may surmise that it can be seen with perfect impar-
> tiality only by God.[114]

(This irresistibly recalls Coleridge: "Hast thou ever said to thyself thoughtfully, IT IS!?" and his insistence on "the presence of all things to God".)[115] Miłosz knows, and says, that the draining away of confidence in both reality and language is the draining away of belief in God. "When poets discover that their words refer only to words and not to a reality which must be described as faithfully as possible, they despair."[116] They will then be engaged only in what Steiner calls "the language-games of the sacred", and their despair, in Miłosz's words, "goes against the grain of our civilization, shaped as it is by the Bible and, for that reason, eschatological to the core".[117] The hope at the end of the last lecture is that humanity might turn again, as for centuries it has turned, to the contemplation of "its entire past, searching for a key to its own enigma" and that then "the world which exists objectively—perhaps as it appears in the eyes of God, not as it is peceived by us, desiring and suffering—will be accepted with all its good and evil."[118]

In the third lecture, Miłosz quotes a Polish poem, by Wisłowa Szymborska, on the death of a very young woman poet. It contains the lines:

Here a heavy heart, there *non omnis moriar,*
Three little words, like three little plumes of light.[119]

"I shall not altogether die": this trust in the eternal reality of God, or doubt, or prayer—Horace's phrase (in Horace referring of course only to fame) can also mean "may I not altogether die"—recurs again and again in Miłosz's own poems of the last thirty years of the twentieth century, poems long and short, in verse, in prose, in single lines that dissolve the distinction. The poems are laden with memory and with grief for those known well and those scarcely known or seen just once, killed, imprisoned, disappeared and scattered, as well as for the country of his childhood, the city of his youth, and the Lithuanian language in which he, like the other great Lithuanian poets, does not write. Remembered times and places haunt these poems: the five-year-old playing by Red Cross tents in a wartime field in 1916; the boy among the fish, birds and animals in the valley of his grandparents' manor; and the young provincial in Paris, the "capital of the world" in the 1930s, ashamed of his distant, doomed province. And always there are people, named and unnamed, dead. In 1997 Miłosz wrote: "I think that, could I start anew, every poem of mine would have been a biography."[120] Are the dead lost except to his own memory? If so, the responsibility of the survivor, the old poet, is heavy. A very late poem is called "Persons":

I meditate now on the insufficiency of language.
I am very old and, together with me, words, unpronounced, will disappear,
In which persons who died long ago might have had their home,
While I am unable to make them appear with the oval of that, their only, face.[121]

"No one but me remembers their names any more", he says of two spinster sisters, old and poor, whom he used to visit in Wilno.[122] But perhaps the dead are not lost. In a poem written in 1980 to a friend killed in the 1939 bombardment of Warsaw, he writes:

And this is what tormented me in those years I lived after you; a question:
Where is the truth of unremembered things?[123]

In God? Sometimes his faith is almost sure. The powerful sequence of long poems "From the Rising of the Sun", full of people remembered here and here only, ends with the beautiful poem "Bells in Winter", flecked with phrases from the Latin Mass and shadowed by Swedenborg's prediction of the end of the

world. But the Judgement, though it will come, will come at some indetermin-
able moment, soon or distant:

> And the form of every single grain will be restored in glory.
> I was judged for my despair because I was unable to understand this.[124]

A fragment written a little later says:

> Not to know. Not to remember. With this one hope:
> That beyond the River Lethe, there is memory, healed.[125]

As time went by and more was written—more than half of Miłosz's *New and
Collected Poems* were written after he was seventy—the question, the hope, the
prayer never faded; it became, sometimes, starkly simple:

> Theologians are silent. And philosophers
> Don't even dare ask: "What is truth?"
> And so, after the great wars, undecided,
> With almost good will but not quite,
> We plod on with hope. And now let everyone
> Confess to himself—"Has he risen?" "I don't know."[126]

But, looking at a photograph of a girl long dead:

> He addresses her,
> Perfectly certain
> That she hears him.[127]

And, refusing to take himself entirely seriously, he watches the elderly academic
lecturing on Dostoyevsky and Conrad:

> the old professor's passionate tone
> Is a bit ridiculous as if the fate of the world depended on truth.[128]

And it does. As he wrote in a slightly earlier poem:

> P.S. Really I am more concerned than words would indicate.
> I perform a pitiful rite for all of us.
> I would like everyone to know they are the king's children
> And to be sure of their immortal souls.[129]

It would be quite wrong to give the impression that the poems of Miłosz's old age are slack, naïve, or lacking in the acute perception of objective reality, of people one by one as themselves and of things as things, that marked all his work. Two lines from a very late poem might be an epigraph for everything he wrote:

> The Prince of This World governs number.
> The singular is the hidden God's dominion.[130]

Memories of his childhood always anchored his sense of the particular and transient as real and eternal, somewhere, somehow. His discovery "in Dutch paintings [of] the images of interiors just like those in my childhood home"[131] produced a memorable poem, "Realism", both pleading for and vindicating the restoration of confidence in objective reality on which he had lectured at Harvard:

> We are not so badly off, if we can
> Admire Dutch painting. For that means
> We shrug off what we have been told
> For a hundred, two hundred years....
> Splendor (certainly incomprehensible)
> Touches a cracked wall, a refuse heap,
> The floor of an inn, jerkins of the rustics,
> A broom, and two fish bleeding on a board.
> Rejoice! Give thanks![132]

Wallace Stevens at seventy bought a still life by Tal Coat. "I have given it a title of my own: *Angel Surrounded by Peasants*. The angel is the Venetian glass bowl on the left with a little spray of leaves in it. The peasants are the terrines, bottles and the glasses that surround it. This title alone tames it as a lump of sugar might tame a lion."[133] Stevens wrote a poem, "Angel Surrounded by Paysans", in which "the angel of reality" is "the necessary angel of the earth, / Since, in my sight, you see the earth again".[134] As Miłosz said in one of the Harvard lectures: "The very fact of naming things presupposes a faith in their existence and thus in a true world, whatever Nietzsche might say."[135]

In 1991 Miłosz, at eighty, published an essay in Polish, which was translated into English with the title "If Only This Could Be Said"—ironic, since he does say it—for the 2001 selection of his essays, *To Begin Where I Am*. The essay[136] is a brief, transparently honest confession in both senses, that is, a confession of faith and a confession of sinfulness, doubt and hesitancy, likely to be recognised with deep fellow-feeling by any intelligent, self-aware Catholic whose friends—in Miłosz's case, liberal West Coast academics—regard faith as "something held by others that they have rejected for themselves". In the long past, at least the Christian rites of passage—baptism, marriage, a funeral in church—held people's lives in a frame everyone recognised; now each has become a testing option, though most people turn with relief to a Christian funeral rather than "an almost impossible improvisation at a time when, at best, one can come up with a moment of silence and the playing of a Mozart recording". In that long past, "when religion was a matter of custom, very few people would have been able to say what and how they believed"; one thinks of Tom Brangwen under the stars. Now, the sexual free-for-all and "the rupture of the link between sex and fertility" have made hay of the "inhibitions and self-imposed prohibitions without which monogamous ties are impossible". Repression and guilt had their hazards, but "do they not have a fundamental significance for culture, as a school of discipline?" As for death, it has become both an embarrassment and a constant "areligious" anxiety:

> Here, perhaps, is where I part ways with many people with whom I would like to be in solidarity but cannot be. To put it very simply and bluntly, I must ask if I believe that the four Gospels tell the truth. My answer to this is: "Yes." So I believe in an absurdity, that Jesus rose from the dead? Just answer without any of those evasions and artful tricks employed by theologians: "Yes or no?" I answer: "Yes," and by that response I nullify death's omnipotence. If I am mistaken in my faith, I offer it as a challenge to the Spirit of the Earth. He is a powerful enemy; his field is the world as mathematical necessity, and in the face of earthly powers how weak an act of faith in the incarnate God seems to be.

The faith declared in the rest of the essay strikes the reader as far from weak. It is both tentative—in the words Miłosz, almost silent in the face of the mystery of God's love, manages to find—and deeply rooted in a thoroughly Augustinian acknowledgement of the miracle of grace. On the discipline of sacramental confession he says:

> Man cannot know his own true evil; all he can do is trust in divine mercy, knowing that the sins he confesses to will almost certainly be nothing but a mask and a disguise. In other words, I am with all those people who have proclaimed their distrust of Nature (it's contaminated) and relied solely on the boundless freedom of the divine act, or Grace.

Long ago, with his Polish and neo-Scholastic upbringing, he assumed this sense of total dependence on grace to be somehow Protestant. Later, "with great relief", he understood that it was a component of ancient and orthodox belief misleadingly overdefined for purposes of polemical contrast at the Reformation. Further, the apparent contradiction between our freedom and the grace of God is one of the great mysteries of Christianity that human reason cannot resolve and that, with Augustine, we do best to acknowledge as such: "The breathtaking casuistic distinctions developed by Catholics attempting to capture the riddle of free will and grace in Aristotelian-Thomist language do not seem convincing to me." The essay ends with a grateful recognition of what is always the rescue from "human aloneness" in the "communion between 'Eve's exiles'" that is the Church, and with a simple declaration:

> Ought I to try to explain "why I believe"? I don't think so. It should suffice if I attempt to convey the coloring or tone. If I believed that man can do good with his own powers, I would have no interest in Christianity. But he cannot, because he is enslaved in his own predatory, domineering instincts, which we may call *proprium*, or self-love.... This complete human poverty, since even what is most elevated must be supported and nourished by the aggression of the perverse "I" is, for me, an argument against any and all assumptions of a reliance on the natural order.... The more we rid ourselves of illusions, the closer we are to the truth, which is cruel. Yet it would be incomplete if we were to overlook the true "good news," the news of victory.

"The soul", in Augustine's words, "needs to be enlightened by light from outside itself." [137]

There is a most impressive consistency in the hundreds of poems and translations and more than a dozen books of prose written in Miłosz's very long life of fidelity to the calling for which he always believed himself preserved. His responsiveness was itself a gift, nourished by his ordinary Catholic practice: "Had I not been raised in the Roman Catholic rite, mine would have been a pitiable fate. For that rite liberates the feminine in us, a passivity which makes us receptive to Christ or poetic inspiration." [138] (How much muddled debate on "creativity" that sentence blows away.) Miłosz survived much, far more than most of us have to face. Like everyone old and honest—"Old age is a vocation, an order which everyone enters in turn" [139]—he knew he had not done enough. "I am ashamed, for I must believe you protected me", runs a line in a very late poem, "Prayer". [140]

As a small child he survived the attack of a revolutionary peasant who threw a grenade through his bedroom window: "Why it failed to explode is not for us to judge. It hit a wall, bounced to the floor, and rolled over to Thomas's bed, where the decision to explode or not to explode ripened inside it." [141] As a very old man, in the last poems he published, he resigned to God his own complex history, in solidarity with the complex history of everyone, in the spirit that moved all his work. The final piece in *New and Collected Poems* ends:

> We were miserable, we used no more than a hundredth part
> of the gift we received for our long journey.
>
> Moments from yesterday and from centuries ago—
> a sword blow, the painting of eyelashes before a mirror
> of polished metal, a lethal musket shot, a caravel
> staving its hull against a reef—they dwell in us,
> waiting for a fulfillment.
>
> I knew, always, that I would be a worker in the vineyard,
> as are all men and women living at the same time,
> whether they are aware of it or not. [142]

Czesław Miłosz died in Cracow, at the age of ninety-three, on 14 August 2004.

* * *

There was another Polish writer, only nine years younger, who also, in his own words, "participated in the great experience of my contemporaries—humiliation at the hands of evil" [143] and who was for more than half a century most consciously "a worker in the vineyard" as priest, bishop, archbishop and, for twenty-six years, Pope.

Karol Wojtyła was three months old in August 1920, when Poland defeated the Red Army and saved itself from Soviet rule by the Lithuanian Feliks Dzerzhinski, the most terrifying of all Lenin's henchmen after Stalin. Through the nineteen years of precarious independence in which Miłosz was a schoolboy, a student and a young poet, Wojtyła grew up in Wadowice, a prosperous Galician town where a fifth of the population was Jewish and where Jews and Catholics lived together in an amity that had prevailed for generations. This area of Poland, part of or close to the Austro-Hungarian empire for more than a century, was very different from the much-larger areas under Russian or Prussian domination or menace. The Habsburg government in Vienna had ruled a multiracial, polyglot empire in the nineteenth century with difficulty but with comparative tolerance and fairness. The ancient university, the Jagellion, in Cracow was never closed, though no archbishop was appointed between 1831 and 1879 for fear of a powerful figurehead for Polish nationalism. Wojtyła's father (his mother died when he was nine) for many years served loyally in the Habsburg imperial army. He gave his younger son, born four years after the death of the venerable Franz Josef, emperor since 1848, and two years after the abdication of the last emperor, Karl, the Habsburg names Carol and Jozef. The boy's best friend at school was a Jew, Jerzy Kruger, whose father was the leading lawyer in the town. Wojtyła was brought up in an atmosphere that was devoutly Catholic but not nationalistic; the family spoke German, the language of the Habsburg army, as well as Polish, and poetry in both languages was read at home. The virulent anti-Semitism of independent Poland, translated into new excluding legislation after Jozef Pilsudski's death in 1935, horrified Wojtyła's father and those who influenced opinion in Wadowice. Karol Wojtyła's parish priest declared from the pulpit that anti-Semitism was un-Christian, and his high-school teacher read out to his class, with its several Jewish pupils, Mickiewicz's 1848 pledge of respect for "the elder brother in the faith of Abraham". As a young priest, Wojtyła refused to baptize a Jewish boy orphaned by the Shoah and cared for in Cracow throughout the war by a devout Catholic couple: they had promised the child's parents to "return him to his people".[144]

When catastrophe overtook Poland in September 1939, Wojtyła had completed his first year studying Polish language and literature and campaigning for the fair treatment of Jewish students at the Jagellion University. In that one year of ordinary academic study, this highly intelligent eighteen-year-old was introduced, he wrote nearly sixty years later, to "the mystery of language which brings us back to the inscrutable mystery of God himself".[145] In another sentence of this account, there is a note of the actor, the poet and the priest, all of which he became, and also of Balthasar's *Theo-Drama*: "The word, before it is ever spoken on the stage, is already present in human history as a fundamental dimension of man's spiritual experience."[146] Wojtyła's friend Jerzy Kruger had, because of anti-Semitic bullying, left the University of Warsaw after one month; escaped Nazi Poland; and forty years later, now an Italian engineer, became the intermediary in the first diplomatic discussions between John Paul II's Vatican and Israel.

In the university of Nazi-occupied Cracow, "Lectures", wrote Wojtyła, who was attending them, "lasted only until 6 November 1939. On that day the German authorities assembled all the teachers in a meeting which ended with the deportation of those distinguished scholars to the Sachsenhausen concentration camp",[147] where most of them died. This was part of the Nazi abolition of all Polish education beyond that fit for slaves. Cracow as a city suffered less dreadfully than Warsaw from the years of Nazi occupation, but its people suffered the same terror, the same designed and arbitrary cruelty. There had been no ghetto in Cracow. Now the ancient Jewish community was confined to a ghetto and then taken in batches of thousands to Auschwitz or Belzec. Several hundred were hidden by local Catholics; if caught, the rescuers were summarily hanged or shot. Many priests were deported to camps; the cathedral, where Polish kings, and Mickiewicz, were buried, was closed; the medieval royal castle became the headquarters of the Nazi governor-general, Hans Frank. From 1940 to 1945 Wojtyła worked as a serf labourer, mining limestone in a quarry and then hauling buckets in a chemical factory. Meanwhile, like Miłosz in Warsaw, he wrote and translated plays, including *Oedipus the King*, for a clandestine theatre company in which he acted and directed. In 1942 he joined a secret seminary run, in hiding from the Nazis, by the Lithuanian prince who was the heroic archbishop of Cracow, Cardinal Sapieha. Writing, acting and studying for the priesthood were all capital offences in Nazi Poland, where Hans Frank had proclaimed: "Every vestige of Polish culture is to be eliminated. . . . There will never again be a Poland." [148] In 1944, Wojtyła's closest friend among the hidden seminarians was arrested and shot; four months later, in a Gestapo roundup after the Warsaw uprising, he himself very narrowly escaped capture, which would have meant death. After the war, Stalinist power strengthened in Poland. In 1946 he was ordained priest and spent the next two years in Rome, studying theology and confirming his childhood sense that the Church, of and for the whole world, might support but was never to be confused with Polish nationalism. On his return, he discovered at a school reunion in Wadowice in 1948 how many of his classmates had perished in and after the war, as soldiers and in concentration camps, or had been deported to Russia or Kazakhstan. "I was spared", he wrote years later, "much of the immense and horrible drama of the Second World War. I could have been arrested any day, at home, in the stone quarry, in the factory, and taken away to a concentration camp. . . . Why not me?" [149] He had also been lucky to escape death when he was run over by a German truck in Cracow and badly injured. Like Miłosz, he felt that he was preserved for a reason and for a responsibility not to be avoided. Also like Miłosz, he learned from the slaughter in Poland, "the great sacrifice of countless men and women of my generation" on "the great altar of history",[150] a permanent distrust of "history" used, abused, to justify slaughter and oppression.

Wojtyła was a trained philosopher. In Rome and then at home in Cracow, where in 1949 he became a parish priest and university chaplain, writing poems and plays that were published under pseudonyms and directing student and parish theatre, he completed two doctorates, in mystical theology and in ethics. In the Jagellion and later in the University of Lublin, where he became a lecturer in 1954 and professor of ethics in 1956, he set himself to take on the intellectual challenge of Marxism, the imposed orthodoxy of Stalinist Poland that was crushing the "captive minds" of his contemporaries and students. Under fierce censorship and constant government bullying, one serious Catholic paper, the *Universal Weekly*, published in Cracow, just survived in Poland and managed to publish essays by de Lubac, Yves Congar and Karl Rahner, to the horror of the more conservative Polish bishops. Wojtyła wrote for the paper. At Lublin, the only Catholic university in any Communist country—isolated and harassed by the government "like a Hasidic ghetto",[151] as one of its professors said—Wojtyła sustained, in a course of lectures on the being and obligations of the human person, a thoroughly grounded academic onslaught on the ethics of both Marxism and relativism. This work was eventually developed and published in 1969 as *The Acting Person*, a book that seeks to move, in the spirit of Plato and Augustine as well as Aquinas, the basis of philosophical ethics from Descartes's *cogito ergo sum* (I think, therefore I am) to *cognosco ergo sum* (I understand, therefore I am)—from, therefore, the intransitive to the transitive, from man alone to man in relation to God. At the core of the book is the identification of the utilitarian perspective that Marxism and relativism share: in both, a person is valued, or dispensed with, according to his utilitarian yield to the other, to society, or to "the Spirit of History"—in other words, to the will to power. In 1968 Wojtyła wrote to Henri de Lubac:

> I devote my very rare free moments to a work that is close to my heart and devoted to the metaphysical sense and mystery of the PERSON. It seems to me that the debate today is being played on that level. The evil of our times consists in the first place in a kind of degradation, indeed in a pulverization, of the fundamental uniqueness of each human person. This evil is even much more of the metaphysical order than of the moral order. To this disintegration, planned at times by atheistic ideologies, we must oppose, rather than sterile polemics, a kind of "recapitulation" of the inviolable mystery of the person.[152]

The philosophical impulse here is very close to the impulse of Miłosz's poems: "I would like everyone to know they are the king's children."

In 1958 Wojtyła, at thirty-eight, became an auxiliary bishop in the archdiocese of Cracow. In the following year, Pope John XXIII announced, to the astonishment of the Catholic world, the summoning of the Second Vatican Council. When, in that same year, all bishops were asked to submit suggestions for the Council's agenda, Wojtyła sent to Rome a remarkable essay pleading for the Church to respond, through her discussions at the Council, to the desperate need of the modern world for true answers to the questions, What is man? What sets him free? Where is meaning? to which false answers, "scientific, positivist, dialectical", promising illusory freedom and meaning, led only to emptiness of soul. The essay, in sum, said:

> The crisis of humanism at the midpoint of a century that prides itself on its humanism should be the organizing framework for the Council's deliberations. The Church does not exist for itself. The Church exists for the salvation of a world in which the promise of the world's humanization through material means has led, time and again, to dehumanization and degradation.[153]

Wojtyła was a very junior bishop at the start of the Council, though before it ended he had been appointed archbishop of Cracow. But he met and made a deep impression on some senior figures whose work he had admired for years. These were scholars of "the new theology". They had revived study of the Greek and Latin Fathers of the early Church to restore theological depth and wholeness to the neo-Scholasticism nervously taught since Vatican I. The work of these scholars had been condemned by the reactionary Vatican of Pius XII. Now they were summoned by John XXIII and Paul VI as expert advisers to the Council, and it was their thought that made possible the scope of its documents. In meetings early in 1965 for the drafting of *Gaudium et spes*, the longest and most wide-ranging of the Council's constitutions, Wojtyła met Henri de Lubac. They became friends. Yves Congar, the great Dominican theologian of the Church, wrote in his diary of Wojtyła at one of these meetings, wanting, in the spirit of his original submission, to broaden the scope of the draft document so that it would recognise and counter "the answers that the contemporary world is offering". "Wojtyła made a remarkable impression."[154] On 28 September that year, in the full Council debate on *Gaudium et spes*, Wojtyła spoke forcefully of what should be, and what became, the scope of the document. That God entered the created world to redeem it has "fixed once and for all the Christian meaning of the world." The telling of this truth is the Church's duty to God and to the world; there must be a "dialogue with everyone". True freedom is freedom of the soul in God, "interior liberty", the very opposite of the illusory freedom of the rejection of God that delivers only loneliness and the false promises of "the collective".[155] Thirteen years to the day after delivering this speech, Wojtyła, by now a cardinal, celebrated the twentieth anniversary of his consecration as a bishop. That night Pope John Paul I died. Seventeen days later Wojtyła was elected Pope on the second day of voting at the conclave and at once broke with precedent: instead of blessing in Latin the huge crowd outside Saint Peter's, he addressed the people in resonant, confident Italian. In due course he made cardinals of the venerable theologians de Lubac and Congar, and also of Balthasar, who was not at the Council but who was later known to be Pope John Paul II's favourite theologian. Balthasar died two days before he was to receive his red hat.

The young actor and poet, risking his life writing, performing and studying for the priesthood under Nazi terror because he knew, as Miłosz knew, "that truth is a proof of freedom and that the sign of slavery is a lie",[156] became the old Pope writing encyclicals that stress again and again "the fundamental dependence of freedom upon truth, a dependence which has found its clearest and most authoritative expression in the words of Christ: 'You will know the truth, and the truth will set you free.'"[157] These words are at the heart of *Veritatis splendor* (The splendour of the truth). The dangerous alternative is the false freedom promised by teaching that "would grant to individuals or social groups the right *to determine what is good or evil*. Human freedom would thus be able to 'create values' and would enjoy a primacy over truth, to the point that truth itself would be considered a creation of freedom"[158]—as Nietzsche perfectly understood. *Fides et ratio* (Faith and reason) is a lengthier exposition of the same alternative and an appeal to philosophers but also to every thinking person to understand it and the scale of its implications. The whole encyclical rests on the faith, expressed exactly by Simone Weil, that to turn aside from Christ toward the truth will lead the human mind, sooner or later, to Christ. Into the human world of sin, suffering and death, Christ comes, "from outside", the truth in him "utterly gratuitous, moving from God to men and women, in order to bring them to salvation."[159] There is objective truth in God, or there is no objective truth. If there is no objective truth, it is "possible to erase from the countenance of man and woman the marks of their likeness to God" and to lead them "either to a destructive will to power or to a solitude without hope. Once the truth is denied to human beings, it is pure illusion to try to set them free. Truth and freedom either go together hand in hand or together they perish in misery."[160]

Fides et ratio acknowledges the chaos of information and explanation with which the modern mind—"the soul, poor bird, not knowing which way to fly"[161]—has to contend. "In the maelstrom of data and facts in which we live and which seem to comprise the very fabric of life, many people wonder whether it still makes sense to ask about meaning."[162] It also acknowledges the positivist consensus that "consigns all that has to do with the question of the meaning of life to the realm of the irrational or imaginary".[163] But it is as far as can be from conceding that the life of faith and the use of reason must therefore be separated. On the contrary, while philosophy cannot, on account of "the inherent weakness of human reason" be self-sufficient, the life of faith and the use of reason can be as one: "The human being—the one who seeks the truth—is also *the one who lives by belief*."[164] And the chapter insisting that neither theology nor philosophy can prosper without the other is summed up in two quotations from Augustine: "To believe is nothing other than to think with assent.... If faith does not think, it is nothing." On the other hand: "If there is no assent, there is no faith."[165] Reasoning (like other creative uses of the mind and imagination) will always be fallible, frail in relation to God, who is *semper maior*, always greater. But reasoning has a glorious history—the encyclical reminds its readers of the death of Socrates, Augustine and Anselm as well as of Aquinas, Pascal, Newman and Soloviev—and there is in every human being "the capacity to know the transcendent and metaphysical dimension in a way that is true and certain, albeit imperfect and analogical", because "reality and truth do transcend the factual and the empirical".[166] What is more (here the encyclical quotes *Gaudium et spes*), it is possible to speak of this dimension so as to be understood by those of other faiths and by those of none: "The desire for such dialogue excludes no one, neither those who cultivate the values of the human spirit while not yet acknowledging their Source, nor those who are hostile to the Church and persecute her in various ways."[167]

In a poem for the eightieth birthday, in 2000, of Pope John Paul II, Miłosz wrote:

> Foreigners could not guess from whence came the hidden strength
> Of a novice from Wadowice. The prayers and prophecies
> Of poets, whom money and progress scorned,
> Even though they were the equals of kings, waited for you.[168]

One of them was Adam Mickiewicz: John Paul II reinforced the contrition for Christian anti-Semitism of the Council's constitution *Nostra aetate* and always worked "to promote respect, appreciation, and indeed love for one and the other

[Jews and Catholics], as they are both in the unfathomable design of God, who 'does not reject his people'."[169] Another was Cyprian Norwid, whose "attention", in Miłosz's words, "constantly turned to early Christianity because he was convinced that Christ had led man out of the realm of fatality and into the realm of freedom."[170] The fidelity of their exiled poets; the fate of their friends, and of the Jews they knew and the millions they did not know; the crucible of horror that was twentieth-century Poland—formed Miłosz the poet and Wojtyła the Pope. The birthday poem, a tribute from one to the other, has a bearing on them both:

> Then, suddenly, like the clear sound of the bell for matins,
> Your sign of dissent, which is like a miracle.[171]

1. Czesław Miłosz, *To Begin Where I Am: Selected Essays*, ed. Bogdana Carpenter and Madeline G. Levine (New York, 2001), p. 329. Miłosz's poems and much of his later prose were translated by himself with a number of different collaborators, acknowledged in each book. Where a whole book has one named translator, the translator will be given here.
2. Ibid., pp. 329–30.
3. Czesław Miłosz, *The Witness of Poetry* (Cambridge, Mass., 1983), p. 4.
4. Miłosz, *To Begin Where I Am*, p. 20.
5. Czesław Miłosz, *Native Realm*, trans. Catherine S. Leach (1968; London and Manchester, 1981), p. 30.
6. Geoffrey Chaucer, "Prologue", line 54, in *The Canterbury Tales*.
7. Czesław Miłosz, *The Issa Valley*, trans. Louis Iribarne (1978; London and Manchester, 1981), p. 4.
8. Miłosz, *To Begin Where I Am*, p. 24.
9. Czesław Miłosz, *New and Collected Poems 1931–2001* (New York and London, 2001), p. 657.
10. Czesław Miłosz, *The Captive Mind*, trans. Jane Zielonko (New York, 1981), p. 65.
11. Ibid., p. 66.
12. Miłosz, *Native Realm*, p. 79.
13. Ibid., p. 76.
14. Ibid., p. 77.
15. Ibid., pp. 86, 79.
16. Ibid., p. 81.
17. Ibid., p. 85.
18. Miłosz, *New and Collected Poems*, p. 745.
19. Ibid., p. 157.
20. Miłosz, *Native Realm*, p. 56.
21. Ibid., p. 98.
22. Ibid., p. 83.
23. Ibid.
24. Ibid., p. 95.
25. Miłosz in conversation; quoted in Abraham Brumberg, *Times Literary Supplement*, 2 March 2001.
26. Quoted in Czesław Miłosz, *The History of Polish Literature* (London, 1969), pp. 230–31.
27. Ibid., p. 232.
28. Miłosz, *Native Realm*, pp. 117, 119.

29. Ibid., p. 182.
30. Ibid., p. 214.
31. Ibid., pp. 211–12.
32. Miłosz, *New and Collected Poems*, p. 344.
33. Miłosz, *Native Realm*, p. 230.
34. Ibid., p. 237.
35. Miłosz, *To Begin Where I Am*, p. 193.
36. Miłosz, *History of Polish Literature*, p. 458.
37. Miłosz, *New and Collected Poems*, p. 59.
38. Ibid., p. 63.
39. Miłosz, *History of Polish Literature*, p. 459.
40. Miłosz, *New and Collected Poems*, p. 45.
41. Ibid., p. 50.
42. Miłosz, *To Begin Where I Am*, pp. 199–201.
43. Czesław Miłosz, *The Seizure of Power*, trans. Celina Wieniewska (London, 1985), p. 5. Previously published as *The Usurpers* (London, 1955).
44. Ibid., p. 191.
45. Ibid., pp. 112–13.
46. Ibid., p. 217.
47. Ibid., p. 218.
48. Ibid., p. 223.
49. Czesław Miłosz, *Visions from San Francisco Bay*, trans. Richard Lourie (New York and Manchester, 1982), p. 54.
50. Miłosz, *Native Realm*, pp. 263–64.
51. Ibid., p. 261.
52. Ibid., p. 290.
53. Czesław Miłosz, *Emperor of the Earth* (1977; London, 1981), pp. 1–14. This piece was translated by Lillian Vallee.
54. Miłosz, *Native Realm*, p. 291.
55. Ibid., p. 292.
56. Ibid.
57. Ibid., p. 294.
58. Miłosz, *New and Collected Poems*, p. 109.
59. Miłosz, *Captive Mind*, p. 216.
60. Miłosz, *New and Collected Poems*, p. 113.
61. Ibid., p. 117.
62. Miłosz, *Issa Valley*, p. 140.
63. Ibid., p. 81.
64. Miłosz, *New and Collected Poems*, p. 124.
65. Ibid., p. 125.
66. Ibid., pp. 128–30.
67. Ibid., p. 133.
68. Ibid., p. 139.
69. Ibid., p. 147.
70. Ibid., p. 142.
71. Ibid., p. 147.
72. Miłosz, *Native Realm*, p. 283.
73. Miłosz, *New and Collected Poems*, p. 151.
74. Miłosz, *Native Realm*, p. 248.
75. Miłosz, *Visions from San Francisco Bay*, p. 11.
76. Ibid., p. 25.
77. Ibid., p. 75.
78. Ibid., p. 198.

79. Quoted in Miłosz, *History of Polish Literature*, p. 273.
80. Miłosz, *Visions from San Francisco Bay*, pp. 180–81.
81. Ibid., p. 220.
82. Ibid., pp. 81–83.
83. Ibid., p. 183.
84. Miłosz, *New and Collected Poems*, pp. 240–41.
85. Ibid., p. 275.
86. Miłosz, *Emperor of the Earth*, p. viii.
87. Ibid., p. vii.
88. Ibid., p. 97.
89. Ibid., p. 70.
90. Ibid., p. 80.
91. Ibid., p. 252.
92. Ibid., p. 29.
93. Ibid., p. 25.
94. Ibid., p. 23.
95. Ibid., pp. 31, 27, 31.
96. Quoted in *The Daily Telegraph*, 16 June 2003.
97. Miłosz, *Emperor of the Earth*, p. 29.
98. Czesław Miłosz, *The Land of Ulro*, trans. Louis Iribarne (New York and Manchester, 1985), pp. v–vi.
99. Ibid., p. 229.
100. Ibid., pp. 46–47.
101. Ibid., p. 187.
102. Miłosz, *To Begin Where I Am*, p. 182.
103. Miłosz, *Land of Ulro*, p. 51.
104. Ibid., p. 127.
105. Ibid., p. 229.
106. Ibid., pp. 240–42.
107. Miłosz, *Captive Mind*, p. 201.
108. Miłosz, *Land of Ulro*, p. 245.
109. Ibid., pp. 246–47.
110. Ibid., pp. 251–52.
111. Ibid., p. 253.
112. Ibid., p. 275.
113. Ibid., pp. 262–63.
114. Miłosz, *Witness of Poetry*, pp. 73–74.
115. S. T. Coleridge, *The Friend*, ed. Barbara E. Rooke (Princeton and London, 1969), 1:514; S. T. Coleridge, *Aids to Reflection*, ed. John Beer (Princeton and London, 1993), pp. 404–5.
116. Miłosz, *Witness of Poetry*, p. 49.
117. Ibid., p. 37.
118. Ibid., p. 115.
119. Quoted in ibid., p. 45.
120. Miłosz, *To Begin Where I Am*, p. 185.
121. Miłosz, *New and Collected Poems*, p. 738.
122. Miłosz, *To Begin Where I Am*, p. 56.
123. Miłosz, *New and Collected Poems*, p. 383.
124. Ibid., p. 331.
125. Ibid., p. 353.
126. Ibid., p. 498.
127. Ibid., p. 537.
128. Ibid., p. 609.
129. Ibid., p. 443.

130. Ibid., p. 733.

131. Miłosz, *To Begin Where I Am*, p. 21.

132. Miłosz, *New and Collected Poems*, p. 606.

133. Wallace Stevens, *Letters*, ed. Holly Stevens (London, 1967), pp. 649–50.

134. Wallace Stevens, *Collected Poems* (London, 1955), p. 496.

135. Miłosz, *Witness of Poetry*, p. 57.

136. Miłosz, *To Begin Where I Am*, pp. 314–28.

137. Augustine, *Confessions* 4.15.25, trans. Henry Chadwick (Oxford, 1991).

138. Miłosz, *Land of Ulro*, p. 183.

139. Miłosz, *To Begin Where I Am*, p. 326.

140. Miłosz, *New and Collected Poems*, p. 742.

141. Miłosz, *Issa Valley*, p. 57.

142. Miłosz, *New and Collected Poems*, p. 747.

143. Quoted in George Weigel, *Witness to Hope: The Biography of Pope John Paul II* (New York and London, 1999), p. 87.

144. Martin Gilbert, *The Righteous* (London, 2002), pp. 217–18.

145. Pope John Paul II, *Gift and Mystery* (New York and London, 1997), p. 7.

146. Ibid.

147. Ibid., p. 8.

148. Quoted in Weigel, *Witness to Hope*, p. 51.

149. Pope John Paul II, *Gift and Mystery*, p. 36.

150. Ibid., p. 39.

151. Quoted in Weigel, *Witness to Hope*, p. 131.

152. Henri de Lubac, *At the Service of the Church*, trans. Anne Elizabeth Englund (San Francisco, 1993), pp. 171–72.

153. Weigel, *Witness to Hope*, p. 159.

154. Quoted in ibid., p. 168.

155. Ibid., pp. 168–69.

156. Miłosz, *New and Collected Poems*, p. 711.

157. John Paul II, encyclical *Veritatis Splendor*, no. 34 (London, 1993), p. 56.

158. Ibid., no. 35, p. 57.

159. John Paul II, encyclical *Faith and Reason*, no. 7 (London, 1998), p. 14.

160. Ibid., no. 90, pp. 131–32.

161. Saul Bellow, *Mr. Sammler's Planet* (London, 1972), pp. 3–4.

162. John Paul II, *Faith and Reason*, no. 81, p. 119.

163. Ibid., no. 88, p. 130.

164. Ibid., no. 31, p. 47.

165. Quoted in ibid., no. 79, p. 116.

166. Ibid., no. 83, p. 122.

167. Quoted in ibid., no. 104, p. 149.

168. Miłosz, *New and Collected Poems*, p. 709.

169. Quoted in Weigel, *Witness to Hope*, p. 492.

170. Miłosz, *History of Polish Literature*, p. 273.

171. Miłosz, *New and Collected Poems*, p. 709.

EPILOGUE

The time that has passed from the fifth century B.C. to the start of the twenty-first century A.D., the time of the civilisation to which every text explored in this book belongs, is no more than an instant in the galactic time of the universe. But it is the time to which I, and you, reading this, belong, our transient home as the time between the birth and the death of each of us is our brief chance to learn, to understand, to love. In this time many other civilisations, each entangled in the mixture of good and evil that binds all human life, have flourished and subsided on the earth. In many regions of the earth, other religions prevail. But as the civilisation of the West, because of its science and technology translated into wealth and power (and vice versa), affects the lives of more and more of the earth's people, it has become urgent to recall, against many assertions to the contrary, that this civilisation and Christianity are not the same thing. They are no more the same thing than were Christianity and the Roman Empire, from the time of Constantine to the imperial collapse, or than Christianity and any state or empire have, ever since, been the same thing. Augustine understood this as no one else in his time understood it. This is one reason for exploring the writing of those who, in the sixteen centuries since, have shared his understanding, have pinned their faith and their hope on the *civitas Dei*, which is neither of this world nor of history, though only in the world and from history, where we live in the *civitas terrena*, are we given the possibility of anchoring in it our faith, our hope and our love.

The other, not unconnected, reason has to do with beauty, with its unity with truth and goodness in the unity of God, and with its appeal to human beings one by one who, for all the changes of the world and history, have not themselves changed, at least in the time in which writing, above all, has left us much that we can learn about the soul in relation to God. Every writer whose work has been explored in this book knew or suspected or feared that it is meaningless to talk about the soul except in relation to God and that to deny the existence of one is to deny the existence of the other. That both were illusions that we

620

should abandon to the disregarded past is now the ordinary intellectual view in the post-Christian West. If nothing beyond the factual and the empirical is thought to be true, there is an empty space in the soul, but only if there is a soul. In 1951 Miłosz wrote in *The Captive Mind*: "Today man believes there is *nothing* in him, so he accepts *anything*, even if he knows it to be bad, in order to find himself at one with others, in order not to be alone." [1] "Even if he knows it to be bad": it is a core Christian belief that there is an instinct for the good, for God, a trace of his image in which we were made, in everyone. In the last chapter, we saw Pope John Paul II insisting in *Fides et ratio* that in every human being there is "the capacity to know the transcendent and metaphysical dimension in a way that is true and certain, albeit imperfect and analogical.... Reality and truth do transcend the factual and the empirical." [2]

If this is the case, it is also the case that every human being, consciously or not, is "a stranger on the earth", a pilgrim passing through "the region of unlikeness", but not to nowhere. It is *sub specie aeternitatis* that we recognise all beauty— most readily, perhaps, the beauty of human lives. In God's eternity the goodness, the nobility, of countless people lost to history, lost to memory, are not lost. "Known to God", says the inspired inscription on the tomb of the Unknown Soldier in Westminster Abbey. Often nobility achieves nothing in the world. Miłosz, writing about the savagery of the nineteenth-century frontier in America, thinks of the "heroism of nameless people" that "remains the irreducible secret of their personal fate, just as it would later on for some behind the barbed wire of European prisons".[3] Nobility, "irreducible", is something everyone knows about; in the most ordinary, as in the most dreadful, circumstances, it shines with a light not its own. "In a morally debilitated age," Aidan Nichols, the Dominican theologian, has written in a recent book, "a Christian philosophy has to put nobility—the natural analogue of sanctity—before people with all the persuasiveness it can command." [4]

The same capacity that enables people to perceive in others "nobility, the analogue of sanctity" enables them to perceive in great writing the truth that lies beyond the character, the speech, the image or the argument, presented in the always "imperfect and analogical" arrangement of words. This is why, alongside the academic consensus that the value of the major texts of the Western tradition has evaporated beyond rational recovery, there is widespread resistance, however incoherent its justification, to abandoning these texts to the scrapheap of meaninglessness. People read the books, remember the poems, go to the plays and are anxious that children and students should not be educated in ignorance of them. People value this writing because, for reasons about which they are likely to be far from clear, it helps them to live their lives—it gives them adequate words, beyond their capacity to speak for themselves, for what they think and feel. For many, the writing of the Christian tradition, or its painting, architecture or music, is what has brought them as close as they have yet got to Christian truth and also to the recognition of a hunger in themselves that longs for sustenance; of a flaw, an inevitability of failure; of harm done to others and disappointment in mistaken ends that needs forgiveness and healing. The space in the soul that can be completely, adequately, filled by nothing other than God's disclosure of himself in Christ—because it is in God's image that we are made—is what Augustine called "the restlessness of the heart until it rests in God"[5] and Pascal called *misère de l'homme sans Dieu*. Aidan Nichols says:

> The revelation of man's supernatural vocation in Christ brings home to us with special force the radical insufficiency or neediness which afflicts the very substance of our being. An Augustine, a Pascal, is needed to evoke that unquiet heart, the sense we have that our spirit is not fully at home here, that all is not well with us (even under the canopy of the sacred cosmos), that what we are is so much less than what we might be.[6]

Henri de Lubac wrote: "All men know God 'naturally,' but they do not always recognize him.... Thus, when I see Peter coming towards me—the comparison is St. Thomas's—it is certainly Peter whom I see in that being coming towards me, but I do not yet know that it is he."[7]

"In Augustine's vision," Balthasar wrote, "which has remained determinative until the present day ... , the history of the world is a dialogue between creation and covenant, the kingdom of the world and the Kingdom of God."[8] "Our conversation", Saint Paul wrote, "is in heaven, and it is from there that we are waiting for a saviour, our Lord Jesus Christ."[9] "We are waiting", as Vladimir and Estragon wait—"And if he comes?" "We'll be saved"[10]—in a conversation that can be like the *conversatio morum*, the sustained turning to God, of the Benedictine monk. In reading all the writing discussed in this book, we are overhearing passages of beauty and truth in the dialogue, the conversation, between human beings and God. But nothing said or written from the "region of unlikeness" in which we live is perfected, concluded, finished. Balthasar, we may recall, said, "*Art*, great art, has a special, reserved place among human endeavors.... Ultimately, however, it is all a writing in the sand."[11] Three months before his death, Thomas Aquinas (the Saint Thomas referred to above by de Lubac), who had laboured for years to produce the greatest of all attempts to settle and define the perfected understanding of God, had a mysterious experience while saying Mass. Though the *Summa* was not finished, he wrote not a word more, saying: "All that I have written now seems like straw." [12] This story has always cheered those brought up to believe that the *Summa* is a complete, closed account of Christian truth. Miłosz in 1985 wrote of it in a rueful poem of mixed verse and prose that reflects on the multiplicity of "transient, fleeting forms" that we are too frail to be allowed to renounce "in the name of an absolute desire.... No, we cannot look straight at the sun."

> Thomas Aquinas ... said before his death: "Everything I wrote seems to me straw." Which should be understood as renouncing a gigantic edifice laboriously erected with syllogisms because it was too human and thus is no more than mist, nothing when we look at it backward, facing the last thing, almost before the highest throne. [13]

We have to live, almost all the time, in the mists, among "things visible" in Plato's cave, itself an image, a metaphor, of miraculous premonition, where the only man who can "look straight at the sun" is killed.

But because Christ, himself "the unclouded light of unchangeable Truth", did come into the world, into mortality and history, as "the visibility of the invisible God", [14] our reasoning, our images and our fictions, imperfect and analogical though, being human, they inevitably are, can stand closer to that truth than even Plato's could. No text discussed in this book has the closeness or the authority of the Bible, the record of God's dealings with the people of Israel and their response in prayer and praise, obedience and disobedience, and the record of the life, death and Resurrection of Christ and the first developments of their meaning. Those who wrote (down) the books of the Bible were human beings, and even in their work, even in the Gospels, a gap is occasionally evident between the words, the story-telling, the purposes of men, and the truth. It is nevertheless only in the Bible that we can read the promise of the Incarnation in the Old Testament and the reality of the Incarnation in the New, so long as we read both "in the light of that event, and both together by Christ's Spirit", and, a Catholic, wary of the dangers described by Coleridge in *Confessions of an Inquiring Spirit*, will add, with the help and support of the teaching tradition of the Church and in openness to Christ's presence in the sacraments. [15]

The gap between the truth that is in God and words, our human words, disappears in Christ, the Word of God. But elsewhere and always, in the words we continue to speak and write, the gap remains open. To shut the truth inside

one definitive, completed version we have chosen is one kind of fundamentalism; to shut truth outside all our speculations and ideas is another. Christian
fundamentalism requires us to abandon our intelligence. By this time, it should
not surprise a reader of this book to find Miłosz, in the open space between
them, addressing these lines to Pope John Paul II:

> You are with us and will be with us henceforth.
> When the forces of chaos raise their voice
> And the owners of truth lock themselves in churches
> And only the doubters remain faithful.[16]

Among intellectuals, however, the doubt-free, Nietzschean denial of the trace of
God can become a fundamentalism, belonging to human "owners of truth" and
closed to critical scrutiny, as crude and excluding as any religious fundamentalism—
and as unintelligent. In 2002 an otherwise-appreciative review in the *Times Literary Supplement* of Miłosz's *New and Collected Poems* and *To Begin Where I Am*
dismissed as "a gesture" the resilient Catholic loyalty of decades and said, with
an automatic wave of the correct intellectual banner: "Miłosz's humane post-
modernism seems to be sanctioned only by a brittle Victorian faith, and cries
out for a course of Nietzschean intellectual hygiene." [17]

The contempt of relativist fundamentalists for what are dismissed as "truth-
claims", is, as we have seen many times in this book, not as new as postmodernists
like to think. Augustine understood that it is the clue in every soul to the truth,
different from a fact, of the story, different from a lie, of the Fall:

> It is a perverse kind of exaltation to abandon the basis on which the
> mind should be firmly fixed, and to become, as it were, based on one-
> self, and so remain.... This then is the original evil: man regards him-
> self as his own light, and turns away from that light which would make
> man himself a light if he would set his heart on it.[18]

And outside either kind of fundamentalism there are still those, intimately familiar
to Augustine—who once belonged among them—whose minds remain shut to the
apparently preposterous assertions of Christianity but who understand that, in
de Lubac's words:

> If the mind did not affirm God—if it were not the affirmation of God—it
> could affirm nothing whatsoever. It would be without laws; like a world

deprived of its sun. It could no longer exercise any rational activity, and could only sink back into the dark limbo of obscure psychical subjectivism. It could no longer judge.[19]

They are likely always to want to return, as did, if not consciously, the Wordsworth of the *Immortality Ode*, to Plato. Iris Murdoch is a contemporary example. In the words of another Dominican, Fergus Kerr, summarising Murdoch's nostalgia: "We have to go back to Plato and the sovereignty of the form of the good to save ourselves, morally, ethically—indeed to save Western civilization from anarchy."[20] In Murdoch's own words: "We need a theology which can continue without God."[21]

Not that we do not have one. In the last volume of *The Glory of the Lord*, Balthasar wrote in 1969:

> Theology is the unique science across the methods of which the decision of faith cuts, and divides it into two halves that cannot be united to each other: a genuine theology, which presupposes faith and does its thinking within the nexus of Christ and the Church; and a false theology, which rejects faith as methodologically dubious and irresponsible, and subsumes the truth of the phenomenon which discloses itself, under an anthropological truth (however this may be understood).[22]

Anthropology is a science; it deals, therefore, with "the factual and the empirical". Balthasar made the same point more simply eleven years later: "Behind the front lines of the 'scientific' arguments [of theologians], with their endless skirmishing, we can discern the two fundamental attitudes of faith and unbelief.... These ... are irreducible: one sees the form, the other is blind to it." The first is "the faith of the first community and of the Church in all ages, the faith of the simple."[23] That Christ is "the form of the good", of whom Plato could not know, is this faith. It is in this same passage that Balthasar says: "The more *relative* many forms of expression are shown to be, the more clearly we discern the 'primal word' that they approximate and the appropriate 'primal answer' that this word elicits."[24]

It has been the purpose of this book to explore and illustrate what is said in the above sentence. What gives to the great texts of the Christian tradition their value, lasting and powerful though also relative and "in the sand", is both their quality and, distinguishable but connected, their closeness to the context that validates them: their truthfulness and goodness, that is to say, as well as their beauty. The book has suggested that these texts can best be understood from within the Catholic, Augustinian structure of belief to which they belong, or to which, in the case of some Orthodox or Protestant writing, they are close. The suggestion is likely to seem to some readers not only old-fashioned but narrowing, excluding. The reverse is the intention. The beauty of great writing, which is one among many imperfect reflections of the beauty of God, is for anyone to love; it does not belong to academics or specialists any more than the truth of God belongs to theologians. It is there to be shared. We should approach these texts in the spirit in which they were written. "Poetic discipline", Miłosz wrote, "is impossible without piety and admiration, without faith in the infinite layers of being that are hidden within an apple, a man, or a tree." [25] Or in a great writer's work. Piety and admiration are responses to the beauty and goodness of the truth, which is for everyone. Pope John XXIII opened the Second Vatican Council in a spirit of penitence and hope for the Church, which should be "a light for all people", "no longer labouring under the delusion that her structures are coextensive with the Kingdom of God or that she possesses the truth in the way that one possesses an object." [26] Of the beauty of wisdom, Augustine wrote: "We have that which we can all enjoy equally and in common.... What you take remains unharmed for me to take also." [27]

There is an analogy, implicit everywhere in this book, between reading with a mind open to the truth, which is in God, and living in the same spirit. None of the writers whose work has been examined here, including those who wrote before Christ's coming and those who were or are afraid that the time of God has passed, would have turned away in disagreement from the account of Augustine's view of a life in God given by the present archbishop of Canterbury in his book *The Wound of Knowledge*:

> The emphasis must be not upon achievement but upon attitude. What holds a life together is simply the trust—or faith—that the eyes and the heart are turned towards truth, and that God accepts such a life without condition, looking on the will rather than *merely* the deed. God asks not for heroes but for lovers. [28]

God asks for our response to his gift to us of himself, in his Son, his grace, his truth, his creation and his Church, and the responses given back to him in words by the writers of the Christian tradition can but help us with our own. Miłosz wrote a poem for his own eighty-eighth birthday. It ends with the hope that, "despite his gray head and the afflictions of age", he is, perhaps, "saved by his amazement, eternal and divine." [29] It remains as true for us as it was for Balthasar—and for Augustine, whose words these are—that "our entire task in this life consists in healing the eyes of the heart so that they may be able to see God." [30]

1. Czesław Miłosz, *The Captive Mind* (1951), trans. Jane Zielonko (New York, 1981), p. 81.
2. Pope John Paul II, encyclical *Faith and Reason*, no. 83 (London, 1988), p. 122.
3. Czesław Miłosz, *Visions from San Francisco Bay*, trans. Richard Lourie (New York and Manchester, 1982), p. 61.
4. Aidan Nichols, *Christendom Awake* (Edinburgh, 1999), p. 67.
5. Augustine, *Confessions* 1.1.1, trans. Henry Chadwick (Oxford, 1991).
6. Nichols, *Christendom Awake*, p. 46.
7. Henri de Lubac, *The Discovery of God*, trans. Alexander Dru (Edinburgh, 1996), p. 75.
8. Hans Urs von Balthasar, *My Work in Retrospect*, trans. Brian McNeil et al. (San Francisco, 1993), p. 37.
9. Phil 3:20.
10. Samuel Beckett, *Waiting for Godot* (London, 1965), p. 94.
11. Hans Urs von Balthasar, *Theo-Drama*, trans. Graham Harrison, vol. 4 (San Francisco, 1994), p. 109.
12. Anthony Kenny, *Aquinas* (Oxford, 1980), p. 26.
13. Czesław Miłosz, *New and Collected Poems 1931–2001* (New York and London, 2001), pp. 488.
14. John O'Donnell, S.J., in *Hans Urs von Balthasar: His Life and Work*, ed. David L. Schindler (San Francisco, 1991), p. 209.
15. Aidan Nichols, *No Bloodless Myth: A Guide through Balthasar's Dramatics* (Edinburgh, 2000), p. 57.
16. Miłosz, *New and Collected Poems*, p. 710.
17. Adam Kirsch, in *Times Literary Supplement*, 15 February 2002.
18. Augustine, *City of God* 14.13, trans. Henry Bettenson (London, 1972).
19. De Lubac, *Discovery of God*, p. 41.
20. Fergus Kerr, *Immortal Longings* (London, 1997), p. 68.
21. Quoted in ibid., p. 73.
22. Hans Urs von Balthasar, *The Glory of the Lord*, vol. 7, trans. Brian McNeil (Edinburgh, 1989), p. 115n.
23. Balthasar, *Theo-Drama* 4:461.
24. Ibid., p. 462.
25. Czesław Miłosz, *Native Realm*, trans. Catherine S. Leach (Manchester and London, 1981), p. 280.
26. Alberto Melloni, "A Speech that Lit the Flame", *The Tablet*, 2 November 2002.
27. Augustine, *On Free Will* 2.14, in *Augustine: Earlier Writings*, trans. J. H. S. Burleigh (Philadephia, 1953), p. 158.
28. Rowan Williams, *The Wound of Knowledge* (London, 1979), p. 86.
29. Miłosz, *New and Collected Poems*, p. 680.
30. Augustine, sermon 88.6.

ACKNOWLEDGEMENTS

The author and publisher gratefully acknowledge permission to include the following copyright material:

Abelard: extracts from *The Letters of Abelard and Heloise*, translated by Betty Radice (Penguin, 1974), © 1974 by Betty Radice, used by permisssion of Penguin Books Ltd.

Aelred of Rievaulx: extracts from *Spiritual Friendship*, translated by Mary Eugenia Laker S.S.N.D. (Cistercian Publications, 1977), © 1974 by Cistercian Publications Inc., and from *Treatises and Pastoral Prayer* (Cistercian Publications, 1971), © 1971 by Cistercian Publications Inc., used by permission of Cistercian Publications, Kalamazoo.

Aeschylus: extracts from *Prometheus Bound and Other Plays* by Aeschylus, translated by Philip Vellacott (Penguin Classics, 1961), © 1961 by Philip Vellacott, used by permission of Penguin Books Ltd. Extracts from "Agamemnon" by Aeschylus, "The Eumenides" by Aeschylus and "The Serpent and the Eagle" by Robert Fagles and W. B. Stanford, from *The Oresteia* by Aeschylus, translated by Robert Fagles (Viking Penguin Inc., 1975; Penguin Classics, 1977), © 1966, 1967, 1975, 1977 by Robert Fagles, used by permission of Sheil Land Associates and of Viking Penguin, a division of Penguin Group (USA) Inc.

Saint Anselm: extracts from *The Prayers and Meditations of Saint Anselm with the Proslogion*, translated by Benedicta Ward (Penguin Classics, 1973), © 1973 by Benedicta Ward, used by permission of Penguin Books Ltd.

Aristotle: extract from *On the Art of Poetry* in *Classical Literary Criticism*, translated by T. S. Dorsch (Penguin Classics, 1965), © 1965 by T. S. Dorsch, used by permission of Penguin Books Ltd.

Saint Augustine: extracts from *City of God*, translated by Henry Bettenson (Pelican Books, 1972), © 1972 by Henry Bettenson, used by permission of Penguin Books Ltd. Extracts from *Confessions*, translated by Henry Chadwick (World's Classics, 1992), © 1991 by Henry Chadwick, and from *On Christian Teaching*, translated by R. P. H. Green (World's Classics, 1997), © 1997 by R. P. H. Green, used by permission of Oxford University Press. Extracts from *Augustine: Earlier Writings*, edited by J. H. S. Burleigh, Library of Christian Classics, vol. VI (S.C.M. Press Ltd., London, and The Westminster Press, Philadephia, 1953), and from *Augustine: Later Writings*, edited by John Burnaby, Library of Christian Classics, vol. VIII (S.C.M. Press Ltd., London, and The Westminster Press, Philadelphia, 1955), used by permission of the Canterbury Press and of Westminster John Knox Press.

Hans Urs von Balthasar: extracts from *The Glory of the Lord: A Theological Aesthetics* (Ignatius Press and T. & T. Clark, 1982–1991), volume 1, translated by Erasmo Leiva-Merikakis, © 1982 by Ignatius Press, San Francisco; volume 2, translated by Andrew Louth et al., © 1984 by Ignatius Press, San Francisco; volume 3, translated by Andrew Louth et al., © 1986 by Ignatius Press, San Francisco; volume 4, translated by Brian McNeil, C.R.V. et al., © 1989 by Ignatius Press, San Francisco; volume 5, translated by Oliver Davies et al., © 1991 by Ignatius Press, San Francisco; volume 7, translated by Brian McNeil, C.R.V., © 1989 by Ignatius Press, San Francisco; used by permission of Ignatius Press and T. and T. Clark International. Extracts from *Theo-Drama* (Ignatius Press, 1988–1998), volumes 1, 2, 3 and 4, translated by Graham Harrison, © 1988, 1990, 1992, 1994 by Ignatius Press, San Francisco; used by permission of Ignatius Press. Extracts from *Theo-Logic* volume 1, translated by Adrian J. Walker (Ignatius Press, 2000), © 2000 by Ignatius Press, San Francisco, used by permission of Ignatius Press. Extracts from *The Word Made Flesh: Explorations in Theology* 1, translated by A. V. Littledale and by Alexander Dru (Ignatius Press, 1989), and from *Creator Spirit: Explorations in Theology* 3, translated by Brian McNeil, C.R.V. (Ignatius Press, 1993), © 1989, 1993 by Ignatius Press, San Francisco, used by permission of Ignatius Press. Extracts from *My Work in Retrospect*, translated Brian McNeil, C.R.V. et al. (Ignatius Press, 1983), © 1983 by Ignatius Press, San Francisco, used by permission of Ignatius Press. Extract from *The Moment of Christian Witness*, translated by Richard Beckley (Ignatius Press, 1994), © 1994 by Ignatius Press, San Francisco, used by permission of Ignatius Press. Extracts from *Mysterium Paschale*, translated by Aidan Nichols, O.P. (T. and T. Clark, 1990; Ignatius Press, 2000, 2005), © T. and T. Clark 1990, used by permission of T. and T. Clark International.

Samuel Beckett: extracts from *Waiting for Godot* (Faber and Faber Ltd., 1956; 1965 edition), © 1955 by Samuel Beckett, and from *Krapp's Last Tape* in Samuel Beckett: *The Complete Dramatic Works* (Faber and Faber Ltd., 1986), © 1958 and 1986 by Samuel Beckett, used by permission of the publishers, Faber and Faber Ltd.

Kathleen Coburn: extracts from *The Self-Conscious Imagination* (Oxford University Press, 1974), used by kind permission of the University of Newcastle upon Tyne.

Samuel Taylor Coleridge: extracts from Volumes 1, 2, 3 and 5 of *Collected Letters of Samuel Taylor Coleridge*, edited by Earl Leslie Griggs (Oxford University Press, 1956–1971), used by permission of Oxford University Press.

Anthony Cronin: extracts from *Samuel Beckett: The Last Modernist* (HarperCollins, 1996), © 1996 by Anthony Cronin, used by permission of HarperCollins Publishers Ltd.

Emily Dickinson: extracts from *The Poems of Emily Dickinson*, Thomas H. Johnson Ed., Cambridge, Mass.: The Belknap Press of Harvard University Press, © 1951, 1955, 1979, 1983 by the President and Fellows of Harvard College, by permission of the publishers and the Trustees of Amherst College.

Fyodor Dostoyevsky: extracts from *Memoirs from the House of the Dead*, translated by Jessie Coulson (Oxford University Press, 1965), © 1965 by Oxford University Press, used by permission of Oxford University Press. Extracts from *Crime and Punishment*, translated by David Magarshack (Penguin Classics, 1951, reprinted 1966), © 1966 by David Magarshack; from *The Devils* (*The Possessed*), translated by David Magarshack (Penguin Classics, 1953), this translation copyright 1953 by David Magarshack; from *The Idiot*, translated by David Magarshack (Penguin Classics, 1955), © 1955 by David Magarshack; from *The Brothers Karamazov*, translated by David Magarshack (Penguin Classics, 1958), © 1958 by David Magarshack; from *Notes from Underground/The Double*, translated by Jessie Coulson (Penguin Classics, 1972, 1989), © 1972, 1989 by Jessie Coulson; all used by permission of Penguin Books Ltd.

T. S. Eliot: extracts from *Collected Poems 1909–1962* (Faber and Faber Ltd., 1963), © 1963 by T. S. Eliot; from *Selected Essays* (Faber and Faber Ltd., 1932, revised edition 1934); from *Notes towards the Definition of Culture* (Faber and Faber Ltd., 1948); and from *The Use of Poetry and the Use of Criticism* (Faber and Faber Ltd., 1933, new edition 1964), used by permission of the publishers Faber and Faber Ltd. and of Harcourt Inc.

Pope John Paul II: extracts from *Veritatis Splendor* (Catholic Truth Society, 1993), © 1993 by The Incorporated Catholic Truth Society; from *Gift and Mystery* (Doubleday and the Catholic Truth Society, 1997), © 1996 by Libreria Editrice Vaticana; from *Faith and Reason* (Catholic Truth Society, 1998), © 1998 by The Incorporated Catholic Truth Society; used by permission of the Catholic Truth Society.

Harvard University Press; from *The Issa Valley*, translated by Louis Iribarne (Farrar, Straus and Giroux, 1981), translation © 1981 by Farrar, Straus and Giroux Inc., reprinted by permission of Farrar, Straus and Giroux LLC; from *The Land of Ulro*, translated by Louis Iribarne (Farrar, Straus and Giroux, 1981; Carcanet, 1985), translation © 1984 by Farrar, Straus and Giroux Inc., reprinted by permission of Farrar, Straus and Giroux LLC and Carcanet Press Ltd.; from *Visions from San Francisco Bay*, translated by Richard Lourie (Farrar, Straus and Giroux, 1982), translation © 1975, 1982 by Farrar, Straus and Giroux Inc., reprinted by permission of Farrar, Straus and Giroux LLC; from *The Seizure of Power*, translated by Celina Wieniewska (Farrar, Straus and Giroux, 1982), translation © 1982 by Farrar, Straus and Giroux Inc., reprinted by permission of Sterling Lord Literistic; from *Emperor of the Earth: Modes of Eccentric Vision* (University of California Press, 1977), © 1977 by the Regents of the University of California, used by permission of the Regents of the University of California and the University of California Press; from *Native Realm*, translated by Catherine S. Leach (Doubleday, 1968), © 1968 by Doubleday, a division of Random House Inc., used by permission of Doubleday, a division of Random House Inc., and the Wylie Agency; from *To Begin Where I Am*, edited by Bogdana Carpenter and Madeline G. Levine (Farrar, Straus and Giroux, 2001), © 2000 by Czesław Miłosz, reprinted by permission of Farrar, Straus and Giroux, LLC, and the Wylie Agency; from *The History of Polish Literature* (Macmillan, 1969), © 1969 by Czesław Miłosz, by permission of the Wylie Agency.

Aidan Nichols O. P.: extracts from *Christendom Awake* (T. and T. Clark, 1999), © 1999 by T. and T. Clark Ltd., used by permission of T. and T. Clark International.

Friedrich Nietzsche: extracts from *Twilight of the Idols / The Anti-Christ*, translated by R. J. Hollingdale (Penguin Classics, 1968), translation © 1968 by R. J. Hollingdale, used by permission of Penguin Books Ltd; extracts from *A Nietzsche Reader*, translated by R. J. Hollingdale (Penguin Classics, 1977), © 1977 by R. J. Hollingdale, used by permission of Penguin Books Ltd.

Boris Pasternak: extracts from *Doctor Zhivago*, translated by Max Hayward and Manya Harari (Harvill Press, 1958), © 1958 by Giangiacomo Feltrinelli Editore, Milan, Italy, and in the English translation 1958 by William Collins Sons and Co. Ltd., London, reprinted by permission of Giangiacomo Feltrinelli Editore S.r.l. and of the Random House Group Ltd. Extracts from *People and Propositions*, translated by Ann Pasternak Slater (Polygon, 1990), used by permission of Birlinn Ltd.

Plato: extracts from *The Symposium*, translated by Walter Hamilton (Penguin Classics, 1951), © 1951 by Walter Hamilton; from *The Republic*, translated by Desmond

Lee (Penguin Classics, 1955), © 1953 by H. D. P. Lee; from *The Last Days of Socrates*, translated by Hugh Tredennick (Penguin Classics, 1954), © 1954 by Hugh Tredennick; from *Phaedrus and the Seventh and Eighth Letters*, translated by Walter Hamilton (Penguin Classics, 1973), © 1973 by Walter Hamilton, used by permission of Penguin Books Ltd.

Adrian Poole: extracts from *Tragedy: Shakespeare and the Greek Example* (Blackwell, 1987), used by permission of Blackwell Publishing Ltd.

Christopher Ricks: extracts from *T. S. Eliot and Prejudice* (Faber and Faber Ltd., 1988 and 1994), © 1994 by Christopher Ricks, used by permission of the publishers Faber and Faber Ltd.

George Santayana: extracts from *Selected Critical Writings of George Santayana*, edited by Norman Henfrey (Cambridge University Press, 1968), © 1968 by Cambridge University Press, used by permission of Constable and Robinson Ltd.

Michael Scammell: extracts from *Solzhenitsyn* (Hutchinson, 1985), © 1984 by Michael Scammell, used by permission of A. P. Watt Ltd. on behalf of Michael Scammell and International Creative Management Inc.

David L. Schindler (editor): extract from *Hans Urs von Balthasar: His Life and Work* (Ignatius Press, 1991), © 1991 by Ignatius Press, San Francisco, used by permission of Ignatius Press.

Hugh Seton-Watson: extracts from *The Russian Empire 1801–1917* (Oxford University Press, 1967), © 1967 by Oxford University Press, used by permission of Oxford University Press.

Alexander Solzhenitsyn: extracts from *Cancer Ward* translated by Nicholas Bethell and David Burg (Bodley Head, 1968), © 1968, 1969 by The Bodley Head Ltd., reprinted by permission of the Random House Group Ltd.; extracts from *Stories and Prose Poems* translated by Michael Glenny (Bodley Head, 1971), © 1971 by Michael Glenny, reprinted by permission of the Random House Group Ltd. Extracts from Solzhenitsyn's Nobel Prize Lecture, translated by Nicholas Bethell (Stenvalley Press, 1973), © 1973 by Nicholas Bethell.

Sophocles: extracts from *Antigone*, from *Three Theban Plays*, translated by Robert Fagles (Viking Press, 1982; Penguin Classics, 1984), © 1982 by Robert Fagles, used by permission of Sheil Land Associates, and of Viking Penguin, a division of Penguin Group (USA) Inc.

R. W. Southern: extracts from *Saint Anselm: A Portrait in a Landscape* (Cambridge University Press, 1990), © 1990 by Cambridge University Press, used by permission of Cambridge University Press.

George Steiner: extracts from *Tolstoy or Dostoevsky* (Faber and Faber Ltd., 1960), © 1959 by George Steiner; from *The Death of Tragedy* (Faber and Faber Ltd.,

1961), © 1961 by George Steiner; from *Real Presences* (Faber and Faber Ltd., 1989), © 1989 by George Steiner; from *No Passion Spent* (Faber and Faber Ltd., 1996), © 1996 by George Steiner; and from *Grammars of Creation* (Faber and Faber Ltd., 2001), © 2001 by George Steiner, all used by permission of the author and the publishers, Faber and Faber Ltd. Extracts from *Antigones* (Oxford University Press, 1984), © 1984 by George Steiner, used by permission of the author and Oxford University Press. Extracts from *Errata* (Weidenfeld & Nicholson, 1997), © 1997 by George Steiner, used by permission of the author and Weidenfeld and Nicholson, a division of The Orion Publishing Group.

Wallace Stevens: extracts from *The Collected Poems of Wallace Stevens* (Alfred A. Knopf, 1954; Faber and Faber Ltd., 1955), © 1954 by Wallace Stevens; from *The Necessary Angel* (Alfred A. Knopf, 1951; Faber and Faber Ltd., 1960), © 1951 by Wallace Stevens; from *Opus Posthumous* (Alfred A. Knopf, 1957; Faber and Faber Ltd., 1959), © 1957 by Elsie Stevens and Holly Stevens; from *Letters of Wallace Stevens*, edited by Holly Stevens (Alfred A. Knopf, 1966; Faber and Faber Ltd., 1967), © 1966 by Holly Stevens, used by permission of the publishers, Faber and Faber Ltd.

Leo Tolstoy: extracts from *War and Peace*, translated by Louise and Aylmer Maude (Oxford University Press, The World's Classics, 1933 etc.), used by permission of Oxford University Press; extracts from *Anna Karenin*, translated by Rosemary Edmonds (Penguin Books, 1954), © 1954 by Rosemary Edmonds, used by permission of Penguin Books Ltd.; extracts from *Resurrection*, translated by Rosemary Edmonds (Penguin Classics, 1966), © 1966 by Rosemary Edmonds, used by permission of Penguin Books Ltd.; extracts from *A Confession and Other Religious Writings*, translated by Jane Kentish (Penguin Classics, 1987), © 1987 by Jane Kentish, used by permission of Penguin Books Ltd.

Ivan Turgenev: extracts from *Fathers and Sons*, translated by Rosemary Edmonds (Penguin Classics, 1965), © 1965 by Rosemary Edmonds; and from *Home of the Gentry*, translated by Richard Freeborn (Penguin Classics, 1970), © 1970 by Richard Freeborn; used by permission of Penguin Books Ltd.

David Vital: extract from *A People Apart: The Jews in Europe 1789–1939* (Oxford University Press, 1999), © 1999 by David Vital, used by permission of Oxford University Press.

George Weigel: extracts from *Witness to Hope* (HarperCollins, 1999), © 1999 by George Weigel, used by permission of HarperCollins Publishers Inc. and HarperCollins Publishers Ltd.

Simone Weil: extracts from *Waiting on God*, translated by Emma Craufurd (Routledge and Kegan Paul Ltd., 1951); from *The Need for Roots*, translated

INDEX

References in **bold** indicate the main entry.

References in parentheses indicate appearances in Dante's *Divine Comedy*.